FROM CHARPY TO PRESENT IMPACT TESTING

Other titles in the ESIS Series

For information on how to order titles 1-21, please contact MEP Ltd, Northgate Avenue,
Bury St Edmonds, Suffolk, IP32 6BW, UK. Titles 22-29 can be ordered from Elsevier Science
(http://www.elsevier.com).

FROM CHARPY TO PRESENT IMPACT TESTING

Editors: D. François and A. Pineau

ESIS Publication 30

This volume contains 52 peer-reviewed papers selected from those presented
at the Charpy Centenary Conference held in Poitiers, France, 2-5 October 2001.

2002

Elsevier

Amsterdam – Boston – London – New York – Oxford – Paris
San Diego – San Francisco – Singapore – Sydney – Tokyo

ELSEVIER SCIENCE Ltd.
The Boulevard, Langford Lane
Kidlington, Oxford OX5 IGB, UK

First edition 2002

Library of Congress Cataloging in Publication Data.
A catalog record from the Library of Congress has been applied for.

British Library Cataloguing in Publication Data.
A catalogue record from the British Library has been applied for.

ISBN : 0 08 043970 5
ISSN : 1566-1369

⊚ The paper used in this publication meets the requirements of ANSI/NISO Z39.48-1992 (Permanence of Paper).
Printed in The Netherlands.

The papers presented in these proceedings have been reproduced directly from the authors' 'camera ready' manuscripts. As such, the presentation and reproduction quality may vary from paper to paper.

CONFERENCE COMMITTEES

Elsevier Science Internet Homepage - http://www.elsevier.com

Consult the Elsevier homepage for full catalogue information on all books, journals and electronic products and services.

Elsevier Titles of Related Interest

CARPINTERI
Minimum Reinforcement in Concrete Members.
ISBN: 008-043022-8

FUENTES *ET AL.*
Fracture Mechanics: Applications and Challenges.
ISBN: 008-043699-4

JONES
Failure Analysis Case Studies II.
ISBN: 008-043959-4

MACHA *ET AL.*
Multiaxial Fatigue and Fracture.
ISBN: 008-043336-7

MARQUIS & SOLIN
Fatigue Design of Components.
ISBN: 008-043318-9

MARQUIS & SOLIN
Fatigue Design and Reliability.
ISBN: 008-043329-4

MOORE *ET AL.*
Fracture Mechanics Testing Methods for Polymers, Adhesives
and Composites.
ISBN: 008-043689-7

MURAKAMI
Metal Fatigue Effects of Small Defects and Nonmetallic
Inclusions
ISBN: 008-044064-9

RAVICHANDRAN *ET AL.*
Small Fatigue Cracks: Mechanics, Mechanisms & Applications.
ISBN: 008-043011-2

RÉMY and PETIT
Temperature-Fatigue Interaction.
ISBN: 008-043982-9

TANAKA & DULIKRAVICH
Inverse Problems in Engineering Mechanics II.
ISBN: 008-043693-5

UOMOTO
Non-Destructive Testing in Civil Engineering.
ISBN: 008-043717-6

VOYIADJIS *ET AL.*
Damage Mechanics in Engineering Materials.
ISBN: 008-043322-7

VOYIADJIS & KATTAN
Advances in Damage Mechanics: Metals and Metal Matrix
Composites.
ISBN: 008-043601-3

WILLIAMS & PAVAN
Fracture of Polymers, Composites and Adhesives.
ISBN: 008-043710-9

Related Journals

Free specimen copy gladly sent on request. Elsevier Science Ltd, The Boulevard, Langford Lane, Kidlington, Oxford, OX5 1GB, UK

Acta Metallurgica et Materialia
Cement and Concrete Research
Composite Structures
Computers and Structures
Corrosion Science
Engineering Failure Analysis
Engineering Fracture Mechanics
European Journal of Mechanics A & B
International Journal of Fatigue
International Journal of Impact Engineering
International Journal of Mechanical Sciences
International Journal of Non-Linear Mechanics
International Journal of Plasticity

International Journal of Pressure Vessels & Piping
International Journal of Solids and Structures
Journal of Applied Mathematics and Mechanics
Journal of Construction Steel Research
Journal of the Mechanics and Physics of Solids
Materials Research Bulletin
Mechanics of Materials
Mechanics Research Communications
NDT&E International
Scripta Metallurgica et Materialia
Theoretical and Applied Fracture Mechanics
Tribology International
Wear

To Contact the Publisher

Elsevier Science welcomes enquiries concerning publishing proposals: books, journal special issues, conference proceedings, etc. All formats and media can be considered. Should you have a publishing proposal you wish to discuss, please contact, without obligation, the publisher responsible for Elsevier's mechanics and structural integrity publishing programme:

Dean Eastbury
Senior Publishing Editor, Materials Science & Engineering
Elsevier Science Ltd
The Boulevard, Langford Lane
Kidlington, Oxford
OX5 1GB, UK

Phone:	+44 1865 843580
Fax:	+44 1865 843920
E.mail:	d.eastbury@elsevier.com

General enquiries, including placing orders, should be directed to Elsevier's Regional Sales Offices – please access the Elsevier homepage for full contact details (homepage details at the top of this page).

CONTENTS

Polymers

Test Procedures

Applications

PREFACE

Georges Charpy was born in 1865. He was 20 when he succeeded in the competitive examination to enter "École Polytechnique", the most prestigious engineering school in France. After graduating, instead of starting a career in high administration, the normal route for "polytechniciens", he prepared a Ph.D. thesis in chemistry on the properties of saline solutions. In 1892 he joined the Naval Central Laboratory where he began his career as a metallurgist. He was a pioneer in the use of ternary diagrams; and also developed sleeve bearing alloys.

In 1898 he moved into industry as a research engineer at the Châtillon-Commentry factory in Montluçon where he became director in 1916. Later he moved to Paris to join the "Marine et Homecourt" company as deputy director. In 1922 he was elected as a member of the Academy of Sciences and was chosen as professor at the School of Mines of Paris showing that, in spite of his industrial responsibilities, he had not abandoned scientific research. He also became professor of chemistry at École Polytechnique, a partial return to his first endeavour. He remained very active until his death in 1945 at the age of 80.

A boss in industry and an academic, Georges Charpy had many talents. The emphasis of this book will be on his scientific achievements. However, it must be mentioned that he was very interested by the scientific organisation of labour and that he was one of the proponents of Taylorism in French industry.

An important, although little known, contribution of Georges Charpy concerns the development of silicon steel sheets for magnetic applications. He studied these steels to improve their characteristics in relation to the grain size. A balance needed to be found to obtain good magnetic properties and rolling capacities at the same time; Georges Charpy found the convenient compositions to produce this balance.

However, the name of Charpy remains associated with impact testing on notched specimens. At a time when many steam engines exploded, engineers were preoccupied with studying the resistance of steels to impact loading. Drop weight tests only gave qualitative indications but in the U.S., S.B. Russel may have been the first to invent a test using a pendulum. It allowed the measurement of the energy spent in breaking a specimen, by calculating the difference between the height of the striker before and after the shock. It had also been realised, by Considère and by André Le Chatelier in particular, that notched specimens were needed to increase the sensibility of the tests. However, Georges Charpy thoroughly investigated the various parameters of the test so as to obtain reproducible results. As an example, he realised that the machining of the notch was of crucial importance. In order to locate the machining grooves parallel to the length of the specimen to avoid their additional notch effect, he invented the key-hole notch. He published his results in 1901 at a congress in Budapest, as well as in the Société des Ingénieurs Civils de France. Later he was extremely active in international workshops and standardisation commissions. It is thus well justified that in laboratories all over the world the daily testing of the resilience of steels bears the name of Georges Charpy.

The Charpy test has provided invaluable indications on the impact properties of materials. It revealed the brittle ductile transition of ferritic steels. Did the engineers who built the Titanic know that the steel sheets they used had a brittle ductile transition temperature above 0°C, explaining the catastrophe which took place when she hit the iceberg? The lesson was certainly unknown to the builders of the Liberty Ships, so many of which failed during World War II. The Charpy test is able to provide more quantitative results by instrumenting the striker, which allows the evolution of the applied load during the impact to be determined. The Charpy test is of great importance to evaluate the embrittlement of steels by irradiation in nuclear reactors. Progress in computer programming has allowed for a computer model of the test to be developed; a difficult task in view of its dynamic, three dimensional, adiabatic nature. Together with precise observations of the processes of fracture, this opens the possibility of transferring quantitatively the results of Charpy tests to real components. This test has also been extended to materials other than steels, and is also frequently used to test polymeric materials.

Thus the Charpy test is a tool of great importance and is still at the root of a number of investigations; this is the reason why it was felt that the centenary of the Charpy test had to be celebrated. The Société Française de Métallurgie et de Matériaux decided to organise an international conference which was put under the auspices of the European Society for the Integrity of Structures (ESIS).

This Charpy Centenary Conference (CCC 2001) was held in Poitiers, at Futuroscope, a scientific park, from October 2 to 5, 2001. More than 150 participants from 17 countries took part in the discussions and about one hundred presentations were given. An exhibition of equipment showed, not only present day testing machines, but also one of the first Charpy pendulums, brought all the way from Imperial College in London.

The present book puts together a number of significant contributions. They are classified into 6 headings:

- Keynote lectures,
- Micromechanisms,
- Polymers,
- Testing procedures,
- Applications,
- Modelling.

A number of papers might not fall precisely into the above classifications. We hope that this will not be too troublesome.

We believe that this book will be useful to students, scientists and engineers and that it will still be read in 2101!

Keynote Lectures

From Charpy to Present Impact Testing
D. François and A. Pineau (Eds.)

3

HISTORICAL BACKGROUND AND DEVELOPMENT OF THE CHARPY TEST

L.Tóth*, H.-P. Rossmanith**, and T.A. Siewert***

* Bay Zoltán Applied Research Foundation, Institute for Logistics and Production Systems,
Miskolc, Hungary
** Vienna University of Technology, Institute of Mechanics, Vienna, Austria
*** National Institute for Standards and Technology, Boulder, Colorado, USA

ABSTRACT

The impact test method based on a pendulum, generally called the Charpy test, is one of the more cost-effective material testing procedures, both with respect to acceptance of products and to surveillance. This contribution attempts to present a brief historical review about the general development of material testing, starting at the beginning of the intense industrialisation in the second half of the 19th century, and tries to point out the role and the position of impact testing during this period. Several periods in the evolution of impact testing based on a pendulum are discussed in detail.

KEYWORDS

Charpy impact testing, history of material testing, instrumented impact testing, pendulum impact testing

INTRODUCTION

It has been said (Harvey, 1984) that "No man is civilised or mentally adult until he realises that the past, the present, and the future are indivisible." This statement applies equally to all fields of science and technology, including material testing.

This contribution focuses on the development of material testing using the Charpy test method, which is based on the use of a pendulum to apply an impact force to a specimen. Some of the milestones in the development of this technique have been outlined in a recent conference on *Fracture Mechanics in Design and Service - Living with Defects* by the Royal Society in 1979, where the important role of the impact pendulum test machine was highlighted. The present history-oriented contribution illuminates the development of impact testing from a material toughness characterisation point of view.

Historically, the impact-pendulum test method and associated apparatus were suggested (in nearly their current forms) by S. B. Russell in 1898 (Russell, 1898) and G. Charpy in 1901 (Charpy, 1901a, b). A. G. A. Charpy (Fig.1) presented his fundamental idea in France in the June issue of the Journal of the Soc. Ing. Civ. de Francais and in the Proceedings of the Congress of the International Association for Testing of Materials, which was held in Budapest in September 1901 (see Fig.2.) The impact-test procedure seems to have become known as the Charpy test in the first half of the

1900's, through the combination of Charpy's technical contributions and his leadership in developing the procedures to where they became a robust, engineering tool.

The consideration of material behaviour in the design of different types of construction that operate at very different conditions is as old as the material test procedures themselves, because the science

Figure 1
Augustin Georges Albert Charpy
Born 1 September 1865 in Ouillis, Rhone
Died 25 November, 1945 in Paris

Figure 2
Title page of Charpy's paper
at the VIIth Congress of the
International Assoc. For Testing of
Materials in Budapest, 8-13
September 1901

and technology of failure prevention is intimately associated with failures and accidents. From this, it follows that the development of new material-testing procedures occurred in close connection with the history of engineering science. It is unfortunate that many engineers still derive a large body of their knowledge from accidents, although *learning from failures and accidents* is regarded as the most costly way to improve one's skills and technologies.

The early development of material testing was driven by the rapid expansion of the railway network between about 1830 and 1900. Figures 3 and 4 compare the development of the railway network in Germany and in the whole world. The world's first public railway was opened in northern England

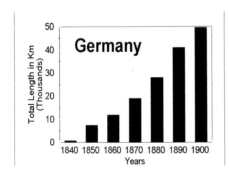

Figure 3. The growth of
railway network in Germany

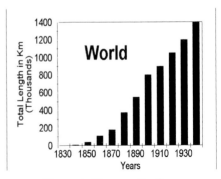

Figure 4. The growth of
railway network in the world

between Stockton and Darlington on 27 September 1825, whereas the first public railway in Germany was operated on June 12 in 1835 between the city of Nuremberg and the neighbouring city of Fürth. The first railroad in the U.S., the Baltimore and Ohio, began in 1828 serving Baltimore and points west, and by 1835, Boston was the first railroad hub in the U.S., serving as the terminus of three railroads. In the territory of present Hungary, the first railway line (39 km) was installed on July 15, 1846 connecting the cities of Budapest and Vác. The situation was similar in most other countries, and by 1900 there was an extensive railway network serving most of Europe. By 1900, the total length of railway network in the world was in excess of 800.000 km, with an annual increase of more than 10.000 km (a quarter of the circumference of the globe).

The development of all aspects of engineering science during this time was strongly motivated and promoted by the rapid expansion of the global railway network, through the enormous demand for rails, locomotives, cars, tunnels, bridges, dams, railway stations and other mechanical and civil engineering structures. In the field of material testing and behaviour, a basic understanding was developed of the load-carrying capacity of a component and its critical fracture stress.

The characterisation of brittle and ductile behaviour of materials, as well as the clarification of the ductile-brittle transition behaviour of metals, was driven by the large number of failures of rails and axles that began to catch people's attention during the 19th century in all industrialised countries. As early as 1836 or 1838, Stendhal, a French writer, mentioned a serious problem related to fatigue damage in his novel "Mémoires d'un touriste". Unexpected and unexplained breakages continued to increase between 1840 and 1860. Most of these failures caused catastrophic accidents without any warning because they were brittle failures, i.e., the fractures were not preceded by noticeable plastic deformation to serve as a warning of incipient fracture.

The situation because still more serious when it was found that machine components could also fail at stress levels well below the critical fracture stress. All that was necessary for this type of failure to occur was the presence of cyclic load fluctuations, either random or periodic. It was observed (although the reason was not understood until later) that a fracture would originate and initiate at certain locations and slowly, then more rapidly, propagate into the material and finally rupture the component, most often in a brittle fashion. Thus, a new type of failure, *fatigue*, was identified. Once it was recognized that fatigue damage propagated by the growth of a sharp crack through a component, a variety of notch configurations were added to specimens to evaluate how their performance was degraded by such damage. A contributing factor to the rapid rise in unexpected failures was the increase in the use of metals, instead of the construction materials (wood, brick, stone, etc.) previously used, for which design guidelines, service history, and maintenance procedures were well known. The relative use of metals for construction changed from approximately 20 % at the beginning of the industrial revolution to about 80 % at the turn of the last century.

Material testing procedures were developed to collect information about the behaviour of various materials, predominantly metals, operating at different external conditions. This information was then processed to characterise these materials for engineering purposes.
This, in turn served as the driving force for:

- the general development of engineering science, especially the disciplines of mechanics and strength of materials;
- the construction and manufacture of large engineering structures (such as bridges, ships, steam engines, railway stations, towers.);
- the development, in materials science, of new types of materials, metals, steel-producing technologies, etc.;

- the appearance of new disciplines (metallography, description of the different types of metallurgical processes, micro-structures, etc.);
- the appearance of new material testing methods, procedures, equipment, etc.

During the second industrial revolution in the 19th century, England and Germany played dominant roles. A major part of the research efforts in these two countries was focused on developing an understanding of unexpected fracture failures. Top priority was devoted to avoiding, or at least limiting and controlling these unexpected failures (Braithwaite 1853; Mann 1970; Rankie 1843; Rolt 1970; Schütz 1970; Wöhler 1858). Ever since, there has been a steady stream of results, experiences, new developments and inventions in the field of fatigue in the leading technical journals (Bauschinger 1896; Kirkaldy 1862; Paris 1982; Rossmanith 1997; Sedov et al 1972; Timoshenko 1953). The importance of the subject can best be appreciated by the rapid increase of technical papers associated with fatigue failures, as shown in Fig 5.

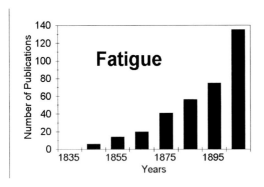

Figure 5. Total number of publications related to fatigue failures in the 19th century

In spite of the huge efforts being applied towards eliminating the failures that take place under conditions of general yielding, there was no generally accepted and agreed-upon method of testing for the characterisation of ductile and brittle material behaviour of metals over a range of working conditions. Unexpected and unexplainable failures of rails, axles, etc. were observed all around the world. As a result of this, a new type of material – steel – was developed around the middle of the 19th century, new testing equipment was created, and new, independent (private) testing laboratories emerged. In 1858, D. Kirkaldy was the first to open a private public material testing laboratory in Southwark in London and developed a quality seal for his test documents, to differentiate his measurements from those developed with older procedures. Kirkaldy also suggested the introduction of the *true stress at the moment of fracture* and *percentage reduction of area* as quantities most useful for the characterisation of metals subjected to tensile loading. The results of various test methods performed in the Kirkaldy testing works were summarised in an excellent book (Kirkaldy, 1862) and his conclusive remarks were fully supported by the experiments. Todhunter and Pearson (1886), in their three-volume treatise on the development of elasticity and materials testing, frequently refer to Kirkaldy's work, but do not mention the behaviour of materials under dynamic loading conditions.

Within the development of materials testing, the following important milestones can be identified:

- the development of fatigue testing techniques,
- the founding of research institutes and testing laboratories,
- the observation and clarification of the nature of metal fatigue,

- the determination of material properties that can be used for elimination (decrease of risk) of fatigue of railway axles,
- the development of new steel-making technologies,
- the founding of the first private material-testing laboratory,
- the development of tensile test methods for the characterisation of material behaviour.

Table 1 in Appendix A features a partial sequence of selected important events in the historical development of materials testing.

EVOLUTION OF THE MATERIAL TESTING COMMUNITY

While metals were gaining increasing importance in engineering, two needs became apparent:
- mechanical engineers wanted to determine the behaviour of metals with respect to a variety of external working conditions, and
- a strong demand was developing for unifying the various proposed material characterisation procedures, as a way of accurately defining shipping and acceptance conditions.

Both needs served as excellent bases for the organisation of specialist meetings. Johann Bauschinger in Munich was the first to clearly recognise this opportunity and organised the first of a series of (so-called *Bauschinger) Conferences* in Munich in 1884 with a participation of 79 specialists from all over the world. The second *Bauschinger Conference* was organised in Dresden in 1886, the third one in Berlin in 1890, and the last one, the fourth in Vienna in 1893, just before his death. The translation of the proceedings of the *Bauschinger Conferences* into English and publication by the U.S. Government Printing Office in Washington D.C. reflect the importance of these conferences. A group of material testing experts, derived from the attendees at the Bauschinger Conferences, participated at the World Exhibition in Paris in 1889. This team was a technical committee of the "Applied Mechanics Section" and was led by Johann Bauschinger. The need for international co-operation and organisation in the field of material testing became immediately clear. In reality, the *Bauschinger Conferences* had already enjoyed an international character, a fact that was noticed in the *Resolutions of the Conventions* held at Munich, Dresden, Berlin and Vienna (Bauschinger 1896):

> *"Not only has there been an increase in the number of delegates from countries already represented (Germany, Austria-Hungary, Switzerland, Russia), but delegates have come from other countries (France, America, Norway, Holland, Italy, Spain), so conventions have assumed a truly international character".*

The sudden death of Bauschinger in 1893 left the job of founding a new international association to Ludwig von Tetmajer (born 14 July 1850 in Krompah, Austrian-Hungarian Empire, died 31 January 1905 in Vienna) who had previously founded the Eidgenössische Materialprüfungs-Anstalt (EMPA) in Zurich and was serving as director at the time. He took over the responsibility of continuing the *Bauschinger Conferences* and, during the conference that he organised in Zurich during the period 9 to 11 September 1895, founded the *International Association for Testing of Materials* (IATM). This conference is regarded the "first" international conference on material testing. If the previous Bauschinger Conferences are included, the Zurich Conference is the 5th *Bauschinger Conference*. The international conferences of the *International Association for Testing of Materials* were held periodically: 1897 in Stockholm, 1901 in Budapest, 1906 in Brussels, 1909 in Copenhagen, 1912 in New York, 1915 in St. Petersburg, and 1927 in Amsterdam. After World War I, the association lost its technical focus and became much more political. Mirko Ross, who served as director of the EMPA, re-established the society now named *New International Association for the Testing of Materials = Neuer Internationaler Verband für Materialprüfungen =*

Nouvelle Association Internationale pour l'Essai des Matériaux. The new organisation held its first conference during 11 to 16 September 1931 in Zurich; the proceedings of this meeting, however, were published one year earlier (!) in 1930 (Rosenhain 1930).

EVOLUTION OF IMPACT TESTING

The evolution of impact testing may be divided into the following four periods:

- Early developments: up to the time of standardisation of testing procedures,
- The stage of brittle fracture: period up to the beginning of the 1950s including the brittle-fracture story and the transition-temperature concepts (Liberty ships),
- The development of fracture mechanics: up to the early 1980s including the correlation between the absorbed energy measured with CVN and other fracture-mechanics parameters, (covered in other papers in this publication)
- The current stage: including instrumented impact testing, testing on sub-size specimens, etc. (covered in another keynote lecture)

Early Developments in Impact Testing

The question "How can the results of static and dynamic material tests be correlated?" was not addressed in the first edition of the book by Kirkaldy in 1862. Questions of this kind were first raised only later in the 19th century. In his 1901 paper, Charpy noted that the lack of correlation between the static and dynamic testing results may have been addressed for the first time by Mr. Lebasteur in his book *Les métaux á L'exposition de 1878*. Impact testing of rails using the drop-weight test method had become an unofficially accepted standard method in Germany. This is noted in the *Resolutions of the Conventions held at Munich, Dresden, Berlin and Vienna* (see paragraph 10 of the General Provisions: 13-16).

The status of impact-testing technology was summarised in the International Association for Testing of Materials *Steering Committee Report for the period of 1879-1901* by L. Tetmajer. In the following years, the characteristic features of the impact-testing procedure continued to be developed by specialists in IATM, and their reports were discussed at the conferences held following 1901. The development of consistent impact procedures was recognized to be of such importance by about 1905 that the impact testing activities were taken out of Committee 22 (on uniform methods of testing materials), and used as the basis for a new committee, Committee 26 (with impact testing as its only focus). The meetings brought a truly international group of experts to a single location, facilitated the exchange of ideas, and allowed the formulation of research plans for reports at the next meeting. Also, by 1905, Charpy had proposed a machine design that is remarkably similar to present designs, and the literature contained the first references to "the Charpy test" and "the Charpy method".

A.G.A. Charpy became the chair of the impact-testing activity after the 1906 IATM Congress in Brussels, and presided over some very lively discussions on whether impact-testing procedures would ever be sufficiently reproducible to serve as a standard test method. The activities within IATM at this time are covered in more detail in the following paragraphs because this is the period in which the Charpy test developed substantially into its present form, under the able leadership of A. G. A. Charpy. The discussions centred around the importance of the geometry of the notch (depth, root radius), impact velocity, specimen size, and the possibilities of practical application of the impact testing (i.e., transferability of results to machine parts, life predictions, etc.). Highlights of these meetings included:

a) *Report by A.G.A. Charpy at the Brussels Conference in 1906:*
   - The pendulum impact test method was being used by the National Marine for testing of armour plate,
   - Boiler steels tested and the testing results published by Yarrow et al. in the *Journal of Engineering* on 18 April 1902; the main conclusion of the paper was that the Charpy test method could be employed to categorise the notch toughness (or conversely, the brittleness) of boiler steels.
   - Two types of pendulum impact machines have been accepted:
       Machine type 1 was characterised by the impact velocity of 7,8 m/s and the impact energy level of 200 kg-m (approximately 2000 J);
       Machine type 2 was characterised by the impact velocity of 5,28 m/s and the impact energy level of 30 kg-m (approximately 300 J).
   - Two types of notches were in use: sharp notches and rounded ones.
   - The effect of impact velocity was investigated by dropping the striker from various heights: 3.3 m, 2.3 m and 1.1 m. The dynamic drop test results were compared with those of quasistatic bending tests. It was found, that the effect of impact velocity on the absorbed energy was much higher in the case of sharply notched specimens.
   - A Technical Committee was established for analysing the results of Charpy tests. The members included Martens, Stibek, Lasche, and Ehrensberg.

b) *Report by A.G.A. Charpy at the Copenhagen Conference in 1909:*
   - the discussion of the Report of the Technical Committee mentioned above (published by E. Ehrensberger) during the meeting of the German Material Testing Association on 5 October, 1907 (republished in Stahl und Eisen, 50 and 51, 1907, (Blumenauer)).
   - The current state of practical use of impact testing was reviewed, discussed and reported in different countries. The report by Simonot (1907) was discussed at the common meeting of the French and Belgian members of ISTM on 1 June 1907. Breuill (1908) published a paper on material testing procedures in the Revue de Mechanique. In England, Stanton and Baristow (1908) reported in the Institution of Mechanical Engineers on impact testing of metals and Harbord (1908) reported on impact testing methods using notched specimens.
   - The experiences of Hatt published by ASTM in 1904 were analysed.
   - An intense discussion developed about the topic of ductile-brittle phenomena.
   - The effect of strain rate on the behaviour of metals was discussed.
   - Requirements for impact testing machines were defined.
   - The information content of impact testing was analysed.
   - Different kinds of practical applications were reported (naval applications, metallurgical plants, engineering works, etc.).

c) *Report by A.G.A. Charpy at the New York Conference in 1912:*
   - A Technical Committee was formed in 1910, composed of international experts
   - Two types of specimens were suggested:
       ⇒ 30x30x160 mm³ with a notch depth of 15 mm, notch root radius of 2 mm and span length of 120 mm;
       ⇒ 10x10x53 mm³ with a notch depth of 5 mm, a notch root radius of 0,6 mm and a span length of 40 mm.

- Experiments conducted by Charpy, Ehrensberger and Bartel showed a size effect: the specific absorbed energy (kgm/m^2) was larger for smaller specimens.
- The law of similarity for the behaviour of different specimen sizes was accepted. It was published in the following journals: Memorial de l'Artillerie Navale Francaise, 10, 11, and 12/1910 and Revue d'Artillerie Francaise, 7/1911. (It is interesting to note that, later in 1921, Stanton and Batson conducted tests featuring the breakdown of the law of similarity in notched-bar impact tests! (Stanton et al. 1921)).
- The requirements of the impact-testing equipment and machines to assure comparability of the testing results were discussed. The Commission proposed establishing a standard impact procedure that would assure that the results produced by two separate machines are comparable. Some of the procedural details that they proposed to control included:
  ⇒ the depth and radius of the notch,
  ⇒ limits on the velocity of the striker,
  ⇒ a minimum ratio of anvil mass to the mounting base (to reduce vibrational losses),
  ⇒ recognition of the need to limit frictional losses, and
  ⇒ recognition of the artificial increase in energy as ductile specimens deform around the edges of a wide striker.
- The Technical Committee recommended that the following topics be discussed at the next IATM conference:
  ⇒ comparability of the testing results
  ⇒ establishment of a database with respect to technical parameters of the existing impact testing machines
  ⇒ definition of possible fields of application for impact testing.

Charpy's drive toward standardization and practical application of the impact test procedure are revealed in some of his comments in the later IATM reports, such as (A.G.A. Charpy , 1912). Near the beginning of this report to the IATM leadership and to the other Committees, he reiterates the main goals of Committee 26 as to "fix the conditions to be fulfilled by two distinct tests in order that the results may be comparable and to correlate these numerically definite results to the qualities determining the practical values of a material for different uses". Toward the end of the report, Charpy made his view of the situation even more clear.

> *"Consequently, ...the investigation of the conditions which the impact testing machines should fulfill in order that they may furnish comparable results, should commence with the establishment of a method of standardization and verification..."*

While Charpy continued to guide the work in IATM, until at least 1914, much was happening within individual countries and at machine manufacturers. A number of machine designs and procedures were under consideration at this time, and in 1907 the German Association for Testing Materials adopted one developed by Ehrensberger (1907). Because the pendulum machine had not yet achieved dominance, designers and manufacturers of impact machines offered three major types; Drop Weight (Fremont, Hatt-Turner, and Olsen), Pendulum Impact (Amsler, Charpy, Dow, Izod, Olsen, and Russell), and Flywheel (Guillery). By 1909, there was broad recognition of a difference between static and dynamic loading, but little understanding of how to measure it, or even what to call it (fragility? resilience?).

Meanwhile, national chapters of the IATM were being formed in countries or countries were organizing separate standardization societies, apparently because the international Congresses met too infrequently to bring about the desired progress on the development of procedures to meet pressing national needs. A national standardisation institution was founded in Germany in 1896. In

1898, the national chapter of IATM in the U.S. became the nucleus for the American Society for Testing and Materials (ASTM). These organizations worked in parallel with IATM and other national organizations to standardise the Charpy impact test procedure. Unfortunately, the different groups chose some slightly different approaches to meeting the standardization needs. As a result of many such choices by the different standards organizations over the years, we now find some remaining variation in impact test procedures around the world. Certainly, world-wide comparison of test data would be simplified if the procedures could be further harmonized between countries and between the various standards.

The rapid development of impact testing around the turn of the last century is documented in a bibliography on impact tests and impact testing machines by Hatt and Marburg published in the 1902 Volume of the Proceedings of ASTM. This bibliography listed more than 100 contemporary papers on impact testing published in the U.S., France, and Germany. Supporters of some of the different machine and specimen designs participated in the different standardization groups, leading to the variations between the standards mentioned above.

Meanwhile in Germany, the extensive report by E. Heyn (1901) concerning the presentation by A.G.A. Charpy at the Budapest Congress on Materials Testing in 1901, led to the establishment of a comprehensive program by the *Deutscher Verband für Materialprüfungen der Technik* to evaluate the facilities for notch impact bending testing (1901). A detailed review of the activities on the new Charpy method during the first three decades of the 20th century was prepared by F. Fettweis (1919). The difficulty in harmonising the different procedures is clearly reflected in the German Encyclopaedia on Material Testing edited and published in 1961, where 27 types of impact specimens are still mentioned.

However, even while the procedural details were under discussion, the Charpy impact test was demonstrating its value in reducing the risks of service failures in components. In 1912, Derihon reported that factories in Liege and Jeumont were performing 10,000 impact tests each month. They were able to correlate the components that gave brittle results to various attributes of the steel: the composition (especially high levels of phosphorus and sulphur), casting defects (especially piping), and heat treatments. After revising their production procedures and acceptance criteria, they were able to reduce the amount of material rejected due to brittleness in the impact tests from as much as 40 % to only 0.3 %.

Serious work on standardising the procedures resumed after World War I. ASTM Committee E-1 on Methods for Testing sponsored a Symposium in 1922 on Impact Testing of Materials as a part of the 25th Annual Meeting of the Society, in Atlantic City, New Jersey. The Preface of the Symposium lists the goals as *"study the impact testing of materials more definitely and intensely...considering not only the details of methods...and possible standardization of methods, but inquiring into the true significance of the impact test...and the applicability of the data obtained to problems of engineering design and construction."* The Symposium included a history of the developments in this area, a review of work done by the British Engineering Standards Association, and several technical presentations.

Also at this symposium, Warwick presented the results of a survey sent to 64 U.S. testing laboratories. Twenty-three respondents to the survey offered detailed information on topics such as the types of machines in use, the specimen dimensions, and procedures. In addition, many responded positively to a question about their willingness to develop an ASTM standard for impact testing.

The group interested in developing an ASTM Standard Procedure finally published a tentative procedure, E 23-33T, in 1933. As experience was developed with the tentative procedure, the group continued to make revisions. The minutes of the 1939 and 1940 meetings for the Impact Subcommittee of E-1 state that the striker radius was discussed, and a survey was made of the geometries used in the United Kingdom and in France. Those countries were found to be using radii of 0.57 mm and 2 mm, respectively. For reasons that were not recorded, the members of the Subcommittee agreed to a radius of 8 mm at the 1940 meeting and ASTM E 23 was revised and reissued as E 23-41T. Two other changes that occurred with this revision were that metric units became the preferred units, and keyhole and U notches were added for Charpy test specimens.

Similar discussions were occurring in standardisation bodies around the world in the 1930s and 1940s, although the exact dates of certain changes to the impact testing procedures in the some countries could not be located. The discussions included the types of specimens (Charpy U, Charpy keyhole, Izod, etc.), the testing method (Charpy or Izod) and the geometry of the striking edge (i.e. the geometry of the striker or *tup*). Although many contradictory opinions were put forward at these discussions, standardised testing procedures were established.

Evolution of the Impact Testing up to the Beginning of the 1950s

Impact testing seems to have been adopted for internal use by some organisations around the world, but was not a common requirement in purchase specifications and construction standards until the recognition of its ability to detect the ductile-to-brittle transition in steel. Probably the greatest single impetus toward implementation of impact testing in fabrication standards and material specifications came as a result of the large number of failures in Liberty ships (a U.S. design) that occurred during World War II. These fractures occurred without any remarkable plastic deformation. Understanding the circumstances and elimination of these failures became a national effort during the war and a large research project was launched where impact testing was found to reveal a brittle-ductile transition behaviour of steels. These problems were so severe that the Secretary of the U.S. Navy convened a Board of Investigation to determine the causes and to make recommendations to correct them. The final report of this Board stated that of 4694 welded-steel merchant ships studied from February 1942 to March 1946, 970 (over 20 %) suffered some fractures that required repairs (Anon 1947). The magnitudes of the fractures ranged from minor fractures that could be repaired during the next stop in port, to 8 fractures that were sufficiently severe to force abandonment of these ships at sea. Remedies included changes to the design, changes in the fabrication procedures and retrofits, as well as impact requirements on the materials of construction. The time pressures of the war effort did not permit thorough documentation of the effect of these remedies in technical reports at that time; however, assurance that these remedies were successful is documented by the record of ship fractures that showed a consistent reduction in fracture events from over 130 per month in March 1944 to fewer than 5 per month in March 1946, even though the total number of these ships in the fleet increased from 2600 to 4400 during this same period (Anon 1947).

After the war, the U.S. National Bureau of Standards released its report on an investigation of fractured plates removed from some of the ships that exhibited these structural failures and so provided the documentation of the importance of impact testing (Williams et al. 1948). The NBS study included chemical analysis, tensile tests, microscopic examination, Charpy impact tests, and reduction in thickness along the actual fracture plane in the ship plates. A notable conclusion of the report was that the plates in which the fracture arrested had consistently higher impact energies and lower transition temperatures than those in which the fractures originated. This was particularly important because there was no similar correlation with chemical composition, static tensile properties (all steels met the ABS strength requirements), or microstructure. In addition, the report first established 15 ft-lb (often rounded to 20 J for metric requirements) as a minimum toughness requirement, and recommended that "some criterion of notch sensitivity should be included in the specification requirements for the procurement of steels for use where structural notches, restraint, low temperatures, or shock loading might be involved", leading to a much wider inclusion of Charpy requirements in structural standards.

This characterisation of the ductile-brittle behaviour of steels led to the inclusion of impact requirements in codes and standards, and then to a more detailed understanding of the fracture phenomena. Consequently, the relevance of the parameters on the *transition temperature* determined by Charpy tests was systematically investigated.

By 1948, many users of the ASTM Standard on impact testing thought that the scatter in the test results between individual machines could be reduced further, so additional work was started to more carefully specify the test method and the primary test parameters. Much of the work that showed that impact tests did not have inherently high scatter, and could be used for acceptance testing, was done (Driscoll 1955) at the Watertown Arsenal. Driscoll's study set the limits of 1 ft-lb (1.4 J) and ± 5 % for individual machines. Driscoll's work showed the materials testing community that not all machines in service could perform well enough to meet the indirect verification requirements, but that most impact machines could meet the proposed requirements if the test was conducted carefully and the machine was in good working condition. With the adoption of verification testing, it could no longer be convincingly argued that the impact test had too much inherent scatter to be used as an acceptance test.

Early results of verification testing showed that 44 % of the machines tested for the first time failed to meet the prescribed limits, and it was thought that as many as 50 % of all the machines in use might fail. However, the early testing also showed that the failure rate for impact machines would drop quickly as machines with good designs were repaired, machines with bad designs were retired, and more attention was paid to testing procedures. It was estimated that approximately 90 % of the machines in use could meet the prescribed limits of ± 1 ft-lb (1.4 J) or ± 5 %.

By 1964, when the ASTM E 23 standard was revised to require indirect verification testing, the primary variables responsible for scatter in the test were well known. In a 1961 paper, Fahey summarised the most significant causes of erroneous impact values as follows: (1) improper installation of the machine, (2) incorrect dimensions of the anvil supports and striking edge, (3) excessive friction in moving parts, (4) looseness of mating parts, (5) insufficient clearance between the ends of the test specimen and the side supports, (6) poorly machined test specimens, and (7) improper cooling and testing techniques. While the machine tolerances and test techniques in ASTM E 23 addressed these variables, it was becoming apparent that the only sure method of determining the performance of a Charpy impact machine was to test it with standardised specimens (verification specimens).

Meanwhile, in the 1950s, it was recognised that a more accurate understanding of the dynamic fracture process could be achieved only by instrumenting the pendulum machine and, thus, determine force vs. deflection / time records. The product between the rate of deceleration and the mass of the hammer resulted in values for the impact force. In the world's first commercial instrumented impact testing machine (called PSWO) manufactured by Werkstoffprüfmaschinen Leipzig in Germany (Siebel 1958), the impact load was measured by a piezoelectric sensor attached behind the striker. An oscillograph that was triggered by a photocell recorded the output signal from the sensor and a flag fixed to the pendulum. The same kind of instrumentation was also used for a rotating impact machine (RSO), which allowed test velocities up to 100 m/s.

During the following years, various committees were busily engaged with the determination of experimental requirements and procedures for valid evaluation of test data. The results were documented in two specifications (Anon. 1986; Anon 1987) that formed the basis for the ISO standard 14556 *Charpy V-notch pendulum impact test - instrumented test method* (German version DIN EN ISO 14556). Using these specifications, a DVM-Group on *Instrumented impact testing* performed a round robin test series with about 400 instrumented Charpy tests to compare the accuracy of the measurements (Böhme & Klemm 1993). The instrumented Charpy test on pre-cracked (and partly side-grooved) specimens (PICHT) opened the way to evaluate fracture mechanics parameters relevant to initiation and growth of cracks at higher loading rates. The influence of dynamic effects was analyzed by J. F. Kalthoff (1985) who developed the concept of *impact response curves* for measuring the impact fracture toughness K_{Id}. This concept extends the conventional quasi-static evaluation procedure into the low time-to-fracture range. The PICHT has been widely used to characterize the toughness of metallic and nonmetallic materials in research as well as in the industrial quality management. An essential step towards the applicability for accurate analysis of component safety has been reached by numerical simulation in combination with micro-mechanical material models.

Today the procedure of fracture-mechanics-based instrumented Charpy testing using pre-cracked specimens is accepted in the majority of textbooks on materials testing and fracture mechanics for education in engineering disciplines. Honoring 100 Years of Charpy testing, a special issue of the *Journal Materialwissenschaft und Werkstofftechnik* was published (Blumenauer 2001).

ACKNOWLEDGEMENT

The authors acknowledge numerous interesting technical and historical comments provided by their many colleagues in various countries. In particular, Prof. H. Blumenauer provided details on the development of impact standards in Germany, and Tim Holt and Karl Schmieder provided their collections of documents from the early years of ASTM Committee E28.

The authors also apologise for not mentioning the many other researchers around the world who made important contributions in the past 100 years. The limitations on article length forced this summary to be condensed several times. The bibliography lists sources of further details.

BIBLIOGRAPHY

Anon. (1922). "Preface to Symposium on Impact Testing of Materials," In: Proceedings ASTM, 22, Part 2, p. 5.

Anon. (1947). *The Design and Methods of Construction of Welded Steel Merchant Vessels: Final Report of a (U.S. Navy) Board of Investigation*, Welding Journal, 26, 7, July 1947, p. 569.

Anon. (1986). *Meßtechnische Anforderungen beim instrumentierten Kerbschlagbiege-versuch.* DVM-Merkblatt 001/1986.

Anon. (1987). *Kerbschlagbiegeversuch mit Ermittlung von Kraft und Weg, Empfehlungen zur Durchführung und Auswertung.* VDEh, Stahl-Eisen-Prüfblatt (SEP) 1315.

Bauschinger, J. (1896). *Resolutions of the Conventions at Munich, Dresden, Berlin and Vienna.* Washington, Government Printing Office.

Blumenauer, H. (2000). *Some Remarks on the History of the Charpy Test in Germany.*

Blumenauer, H. (Ed.) (2001). 100 Jahre Charpy Versuch (100 Years of Charpy Testing). Special issue of the Journal *Materialwissenschaft und Werkstofftechnik*, 32, No. 6.

Böhme, W. & W. Klemm (1993). Ergebnisse des Ringtests „Kerbform" der DVM-Arbeitsgruppe „Instrumentierter Kerbschlagbiegeversuch", *IWM-Bericht* W7/93, Freiburg. und *Berichtsband 26. Tagung DVM-AK Bruchvorgänge*, Magdeburg, Februar 1994, 1- 45.

Braithwaite, F. (1853). On the Fatigue and Consequent Fracture of Metals. *Min. Proc. Inst. Civ. Engineers* 13: 463-475.

Breuill, P. (1908). Revue de Méchanique, April issue.

Charpy, A.G.A. (1901a). *Essay on the Metals Impact Bend Test of Notched Bars*. (translated from the original French by E Lucon), reprinted in: *The Pendulum Impact Testing: A Century of Progress*, 2000 (Eds: T.A. Siewert and S. Manahan), ASTM STP 1380, West Conshohoken.

Charpy A.G.A. (1901b). *Note sur L'essai des métaux á la flexion par choc de barreaux entaillés. Association internationale pour l'essai des matériaux.* Congrés de Budapest. 1901. (This paper was also published in Soc. Ing. Civ. de Francis, June 1901. pp. 848-877.)

Charpy, A.G.A. (1912). "Report on Impact Tests and the Work of Committee 26," *Proceedings of the Sixth Congress of the International Association for Testing Materials*, IV1, New York. p. 1-10.

Derihon, M. (1912). "Notes on the Brittleness Test," In: *Proceedings of the Sixth Congress of the International Association for Testing Materials*, IV3, New York. p. 1-5.

Driscoll, D.E. (1955). *Reproducibility of Impact Test.* Impact Testing. ASTM STP 176.

Ehrensberger, E.(1907). Die Kerbschlagprobe im Materialprüfungswesen. *Deutscher Verband für die Materialprüfung der Technik* 1907, Nr. 35, 1- 32; *Stahl und Eisen* 27, 1797 – 1809.

Fahey, N. H. (1961). "Effect of Variables in Charpy Impact Testing," *Materials Research Standards.* Vol.1, No 11, Nov. 1961.

Fahey, N. H. (1970). *The Charpy Impact Test – Its Accuracy and Factors Affecting Test Results.* Impact Testing of Metals, ASTM STP 466.

Fettweis, F. (1919). Die Kerbschlagprobe. Entwicklung und Kritik. *Arch. Eisenhüttenwesen* 2: 625 – 672.

Harbord (1908). Impact Testing Methods on Notched Specimens. Institution of Mechanical Engineers, 20 November.

Harvey F.G. (1984). *A Historical Appraisal of Mechanics.* International Textbook Company. Scranton, Pennsylvania.

Hatt, W.K., and Marburg, E. (1902). *Proceedings ASTM*, 2, p. 283.

Heyn, E. (1901). Internationaler Verband für die Materialprüfungen der Technik (Bericht über die 3. Wanderversammlung), *Stahl und Eisen* 1197 – 1201.

Kalthoff, J. F. (1985). On the measurement of dynamic fracture toughness-review of recent work. *Int. J. Fracture* 27: 277 – 298.

Kirkaldy, D. (1862). *Results of an Experimental Inquiry the Tensile Strength and Other Properties of Various Kinds of Wrought-Iron and Steel.* Glasgow.

Mann, J.Y. (1970). *Bibliography on the Fatigue of Materials, Components and Structures 1838-1950.* Pergamon Press, Oxford.

Paris, P. C. (1982). Twenty Years of Reflection on Questions Involving Fatigue Crack Growth. in *Fatigue Thresholds - Fundamentals and Applications* 3-10 (Eds: Bäcklund J. et al), EMAS.

Rankie, W.J.M. (1843). On the causes of the unexpected breakage of the journals of railway axles; and on the means of preventing such accidents by observing the law of continuity in their construction. *Min. Proc. Inst. Civ. Engineers* 2:105-108,

Rolt, L.T.C. (1970). *Victorian Engineering.* Penguin Books.

Rosenhain, W. (1930). First Communications of the New International Association for the Testing of Materials. *Group A, Metals.* NIATM. Zurich.

Rossmanith, H.P. (Ed.) (1997). *Fracture Research in Retrospect. An Anniversary Volume in Honor of George R. Irwin's 90th Birthday.* A.A. Balkema, 1997.

Russell S.B. (1898). *Experiments with a New Machine for Testing Materials by Impact.* American Society of Civil Engineers, Vol. 39. No 826, pp.237-250. (reprinted in: *The Pendulum Impact Testing: A Century of Progress,* (Eds: T.A. Siewert and S. Manahan). 2000: 17-45, ASTM STP 1380., West Conshohoken, Pennsylvania.

Schütz, W. (1970). To the history of fatigue resistance (in German). *Mat.-Wiss. u. Werkstofftechnik* 24: 203-232.

Sedov, L. et al. (Eds) (1972). *Mechanics during the last 50 years in Soviet Union* (1972) (in Russian) Nauka, Moscow.

Siebel, E. (Hrsg.) (1958). *Handbuch der Werkstoffprüfung (Handbook of Materials Testing),* Vol. 1:145 – 148, Springer Verlag.

Simonot (1907). *Réflexions au sujet des méthodes d'essai de piéces métalliques du Congrés de Bruxelles de 1906.* Societé de l'Industrie minérela.

Stanton, T.E. and Baristow (1908). *Impact Testing of Metals.* Institution of Mechanical Engineers, 20 November, 1908.

Stanton, T.E. & Batson, R.G.C. (1921). On the characteristics of notched-bar impact tests. *Minutes of Proc. Inst. Civil Eng.* 211:67-100.

Timoshenko, S. P. (1953). *History of Strength of Materials.* Mc.Graw-Hill.

Todhunter, I. & Pearson, K. (1886). *History of the Theory of Elasticity and of the Strength of Materials.* Cambridge University Press, UK.

Warwick, C. L. (1922). In: *Proceedings of ASTM, 22*, Part 2, 1922, p. 78.

Williams, M. L. and Ellinger, G. A., (1948). *Investigation of Fractured Steel Plates Removed from Welded Ships*, National Bureau of Standards Report, December 9, 1948.

Wöhler A. (1858). Report on tests of the Königl. Niederschlesisch-Märkische Eisenbahn made with apparatus for the measurement of the bending and torsion of railway axles in service (in German). *Zeitschrift für das Bauwesen* 8 642-651.

Appendix A

Table 1. Milestones in material testing

Year	Event
1495	tensile testing of wires (Leonardo da Vinci)
1638	testing of beams loaded in bending (Galileo Galilei)
1675	testing of elongation of springs (Robert E. Hooke)
1680	elastic deformation of beams (Emde Mariotte)
1696	definition of virtual deformation (John Bernoulli)
1744	description of the shape of elastically deformed beams (Leonard Euler)
1773	determination of the load capacity of beams loaded in bending (Augustin Columb)
1775	registration of the load-deflection diagram of woods beams (Francois Buffon)
1781	patent of the steam engine (James Watt)
1788	systematic mechanical testing of 906 materials (Franz Carl Achard)
1807	definition of the elastic modulus (Thomas Young)
1807	first steam ship (7 October 1807) (Ressel, Fulton)
1822	definition of mechanical stress (Augustin Cauchy)
1825	opening of the first public railway (27 September 1825)
1829	definition of the transverse strain (Denis Poisson)
1837	first publication on fatigue of driving rope
1836	fatigue damage first mentioned in a novel "Mémoires d'un touriste", by Stendhal
1842	railway accident in Versailles with extensive loss of life
1843	first paper on fatigue tests of railway axles (York, Rankie)
1852	first 100 tonne tensile machine constructed by Werder
1855	new steel making technology (Henry Bessemer)
1856	electric resistance of wires and their lengths (Lord Kelvin)
1858	opening the first material testing laboratory (D. Kirkaldy)
1858	first paper by Wöhler
1864	first metallographical investigation (Henry Clifton Sorby)
1870	Wöhler`s material selection and design system against fatigue of railway axles
1871	foundation of the Laboratory for Mechanical Technology in Munich (J. Bauschinger)
1873	foundation of the Laboratory for Mechanical Technology in Vienna (K. von Jenny)
1874	foundation of the Laboratory for Mechanical Technology in Budapest
1879	Material Testing Laboratory (MPA) in Zurich (L. v. Tetmajer)
1880	optical microscope by Martens with magnification of 200x (A. Martens)
≈1881	Bauschinger-effect $\Rightarrow$ low cycle fatigue
1884	1st Bauschinger Conference on Material Testing in Munich
1886	2nd Bauschinger Conference on Material Testing in Dresden
1890	3rd Bauschinger Conference on Material Testing in Berlin
1891	foundation of the Commission des méthodes d'essai des matériaux de construction (by decree of the French President)
1893	4th Bauschinger Conference on Material Testing in Vienna
1895	1st Congress of the International Society for Testing of Material (ISTM) (L. Tetmajer, Zurich, 9-11 September) (5th Congress)
1895	discovery of X-rays by W. C. Röntgen
1896	foundation of the German Society for Material Testing (President: A. Martens)
1896	demonstration of X-ray testing in New York at the National Electrochemical Exhib.
1898	establishment of the American Society for Testing of Materials (ASTM)
1900	hardness testing method by Brinell
1904	observation of the upper and lower yield stress (Carl v. Bach)
1906	4th Congress of the ISTM in Brussels (8th Congress)
1907	stress distribution at the vicinity of sharp notches and cracks (K. Wieghardt)
1908	Rockwell hardness testing method
1910	analytical description of stress versus life-time curve (Basquin)
1912	production of stainless steel by the Krupp company
1912	X-ray testing of crystalline structures (Max v. Laue)

1912	new testing machine for alternating load tests, (B.P. Haigh)
1913	stress distribution at the vicinity of sharp notches, crack (C.E. Inglis)
1917	foundation of the German Standards Association (DIN)
1919	first creep test (P. Chevenard)
1920	energy balance concept for cracks (A.A. Griffith)
1924	concept on fatigue damage at different stress level (Palmgren)
1929	patent of ultrasonic testing for detection of flaws in metals (S.J. Sokolov)
1930	creep test at biaxial loading conditions (R.W. Bailey)
1930	stress concentration and fatigue strength (R.E. Peterson)
1931	determination of the residual stresses by etching of layers (N.N. Davidenkov)
1932	load spectrum measurements for agricultural machines (Kloth, Stoppel)
1934	magnetic testing (W. Gerhard)
1935	introduction of "shape-strength" phenomena (Gestaltfestigkeit) (A. Thum)
1935	notch factor definition in fatigue β_k (A. Thum)
1936	first crack-propagation law (A. V. de Forest)
1937	automatic crack detection equipment (F. Förster)
1937	concept on notch theory (Neuber)
1937	damage accumulation from stress cycles of varying amplitude (B.E. Langer)
1932-38	load spectrum measurements and publication for aircraft (H.W. Kaul)
≈ 1939	introduction of "working-strength" phenomena (Betriebsfestigkeit - Gaßner)
1939	introduction of strain-gauge technology in strain measurements
1939	statistical nature of fatigue (W. Weibull)
1939	introduction of cracks solutions for elastic bodies (Westergaard)
1943	residual stress influence on fatigue (O.J. Horger)
1945	concept in cumulative damage in fatigue (Miner)
1945	thickness measurement with ultrasound (Ewin)
1946	crack solutions for elastic body for different loading conditions (I.N. Sneddon)
1951	foundation of International Committee on Aeronautical Fatigue
1953	low-cycle-fatigue at NACA/NASA (S.S. Manson)
1953	random fatigue (A.M. Freudenthal, E.J. Gumbel)
1954	low-cycle-fatigue at General Electric (L.F. Coffin)
1954	de Havilland Comet airplane accidents (Elba on 10/01 and near Naples on 8/04)
1956	non-linear Corten-Dolan approach on cumulative fatigue damage
1956	concept of crack extension force at NRL (G.R. Irwin)
1959	introduction of the DGS diagram (J. Krautkrämer)
1959-62	Crack-tip cohesive model (G.I. Barenblatt, Panasyuk, Dugdale)
1959	determination of the size of flaws using ultrasonic testing (J. Krautkrämer)
1960	Electro-hydraulic closed-loop testing machine
1961	Fracture-mechanics-based crack growth law (P.C. Paris, Gomez, Anderson)
≈ 1964	Computer-aided (analogue) material testing system (P. Mast)
1968	introduction of ΔK_{eff}, crack-growth model (W. Elber)
1968	conservation integrals (J. Rice, Cherepanov)
1970	first standard for fracture-mechanics testing (ASTM E 399-70)
1983	first standard for testing of fatigue crack growth (ASTM E 647-83)
1986	application of RS232/V24 to ultrasonic testing equipment
1994	digital ultrasonic testing equipment with built-in DGS diagrams

From Charpy to Present Impact Testing
D. François and A. Pineau (Eds.)

MICROMECHANISMS AND THE CHARPY TRANSITION CURVE

D. François
École Centrale de Paris, F92295 Chatenay-Malabry Cedex

ABSTRACT

Fracture mechanisms which play a role in the ductile brittle transition temperature (DBTT) as determined by Charpy tests are reviewed. Cleavage is triggered by heterogeneous plastic deformation which initiates cracks in carbides and in inclusions. It is then propagation controlled, in most cases at the interface of initiation sites or else at grain boundaries. The role of inclusions is often to raise the stress locally, thus allowing initiation in nearby small particles. It is usually considered that the DBTT, as the cleavage stress and the yield strength do, follows a relation with the inverse of the square root of the grain size ; this is questioned. Fast cooling rates lower the DBTT owing to finer microstructures in martensite as well as in bainite ; they produce also smaller carbides after tempering. The presence of delta ferrite raises the DBTT. The shape of inclusions has an important influence on the initiation as well as on the further propagation of cleavage cracks. Solutes atoms modify the yield strength as well as the fracture energy ; nickel has a solution softening effect and raises the fracture energy ; silicon lowers it. Intergranular fracture due to temper embrittlement is another mechanism which has an effect on the DBTT. It competes with cleavage mechanisms explaining the associated role of carbides.

KEY WORDS Micromechanisms, Cleavage, Ductile-Brittle Transition Temperature, Ferritic Steels, Grain Size, Intergranular Fracture, Inclusions, Carbides

INTRODUCTION

The influence of microstructure on resilience as determined by the Charpy test has been studied by a great number of scientists and the number of papers devoted to this subject is extremely large. In 1980 Kotilainen [1] cited more than 400 references already. Comprehensive reviews were published which remain quite topical[2,3]. I will then attempt to give information about more recent studies as well as views about the deficiencies of our present knowledge. This implies nevertheless that I should remind of accepted assumptions and facts. My task is made easier as the number of studies about microstructural effects peaked some thirty years ago but has decreased more recently.

Apparently recent active research in this area has been motivated mostly by the nuclear industry. While research continues on A533B and A508 steels used for the walls of nuclear vessels, stainless ferritic steels devoid of elements which are activated are experimented. Thus attempts have been made to replace molybdenum in chromium steels by tungsten. It is then important to understand the metallurgical factors affecting the impact behaviour of such steels in the irradiated and unirradiated condition. Quite a few papers can be found concerning ferritic chromium steels in the last fifteen years [4-14].

One of the main concerns remains the Ductile Brittle Transition Temperature (DBTT). As it is determined by cleavage mechanisms triggered by some plastic deformation, I will devote the largest part of this review to these aspects. Next to the sizes of grains and of carbides that are obvious influencing parameters, it appears that inclusions play a major role in most cases. For more than twenty years now stochastic aspects have been considered to be of major importance in the case of cleavage fracture. Intergranular fracture must not be disregarded and some aspects will also be reviewed. Ductile fracture by voids coalescence determines the upper shelf of the resilience. Although they control the ductile tearing which precedes cleavage in the transition range, since they do not play the most important role close to the lower shelf, they will not be considered in this review. I will limit myself to the case of steels.

THE DUCTILE-BRITTLE TRANSITION

The well-known elementary sketch of Davidenkov (Fig.1) points out the main features of the ductile-brittle transition. Below the nil ductility temperature (NDTT) the yield strength must be reached for plastic deformation to nucleate cleavage cracks; their propagation then follows immediately ; the elongation is zero. Above this transition temperature, strain hardening is needed in order to reach the level of stress required for the propagation of cleavage cracks. Above the Fracture Appearance Transition Temperature (FATT) the cleavage cracks are blunted and voids growth and coalescence takes over. (The acronyms DBTT and FATT designate in practice conventional temperatures : TK28 for instance, temperature for which the resilience is equal to 28J. For simplicity I use these same acronyms for the well marked critical temperatures on the Davidenkov diagram which is an oversimplification of reality). In cases of grain boundaries embrittlement cleavage is replaced by intergranular fracture.

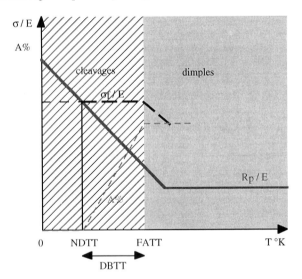

Fig.1 Davidenkov schematic diagram explaining the ductile-brittle transition temperature. The stresses divided by the Young's modulus, to eliminate the effect of temperature on this parameter, are plotted as a function of the absolute temperature.

This diagram shows that the elements of microstructure which are important for the DBTT are the ones which affect the yield strength on the one hand, and the cleavage critical stress (or the intergranular failure stress) on the other. For the yield strength can be listed: the grain size, the elements in solid solution, the shape and size of carbides, the amount and morphologies of pearlite, of bainite, of martensite, of acicular ferrite, the shape and size of inclusions, the defects due to irradiation [15,16]. For the cleavage stress, the same features are to be considered to which might be added the texture, as this might have a greater influence on cleavage than on the yield strength. It must be stressed that in the case of cleavage fracture the distributions of sizes of carbides and inclusions and of their distances play quite an important role. In the case of intergranular fracture, the degree of segregation of impurities to the grain boundaries, plus again the grain size itself are parameters to be considered.

It must not be forgotten that strain rate and constraint are important factors that control the level of the yield strength. Hence they modify the DBTT, but can also affect the active micromechanisms.

CLEAVAGE MECHANISMS

Cleavage Cracks Initiation

Rice and Thomson [17] studied the condition for a cleavage crack to be blunted by the nucleation of dislocation loops at its tip. An essential parameter in their model is the cleavage surface energy γ_c. The early models of Zener [18] and Stroh [19] for the nucleation of cleavage cracks due to dislocation pile-ups against grain boundaries are not applicable to steels: this results from the fact that the fracture energy γ_c for the propagation of a non moving microcrack in ferrite has a very low transition temperature; it is estimated to be around -200°C [2], by comparison with that of iron silicon (Fe3Si) which was measured to be about –100°C [20]. The same consideration applies to the model of Cottrell of nucleation at the impingement of two slip lines. On the contrary dislocation pile-ups can nucleate cleavage cracks in cementite according to the model of Smith [21] because γ_c in that case has a transition temperature around 300°C [22]. Twins can concentrate stress in the same way as dislocation pile-ups. It has been observed that cleavage cracks indeed nucleate on carbide particles [23]. If the yield strength follows the Hall-Petch law, the model of Smith yields for the cleavage fracture stress σ_f:

$$\sigma_f^2 = \frac{4\gamma_c\mu}{\pi(1-v)c_0} - \frac{k_y^2}{c_0}\left(1 + \frac{4\sqrt{c_0}\,\tau_i}{\pi k_y}\right) \qquad (1)$$

In this expression μ is the shear modulus and v the Poisson ratio, τ_i is the friction stress on the dislocations, k_y the Hall-Petch coefficient and c_0 the size of the carbide. The first term on the right hand side represents the stress needed to propagate a long crack of width c_0 ; the second one represents the influence of the pile-ups of dislocations which produce stress concentrations. To give an order of magnitude, for $c_0 = 1$ micron, $\tau_i = 100$ MPa, $k_y = 0.33$ MPa√m, this term is equal to (400 MPa)^2, while the first one is equal to (400 γ_c MPa)^2, γ_c being expressed in J/m^2.

Now γ_c for cementite is very low, of the order of 1 to 2 J/m^2, yielding very low values for the fracture stress corresponding to the initiation of a crack in a platelet.

Smith made the remark that for twinning the friction stress on the dislocations is very low, so that, in that case, the second term in the equation can be neglected.

This mechanism as envisaged for the initiation of cracks on carbides particles can operate as well for inclusions. For instance, this was observed in low-carbon weld metal from silicates or from oxides [24], from manganese sulphides [25], again from oxides and MnS [26], from titanium nitrides [27, 28]. Initiation of cleavage cracks in A533 steel has been carefully studied showing the role of MnS and of oxide inclusions [29, 30].

Cleavage Crack Propagation

However the crack, once initiated in a carbide particle, must cross the cementite-ferrite interface. The corresponding fracture energy was estimated by Curry and Knott [31] to be 14 J/m^2. Thus cleavage is propagation controlled. 14 J/m^2 is a value lower than the static fracture toughness of ferrite as we deal with a fast propagating crack [2]. Under those conditions it turns out that the influence of the dislocations pile-ups in the equation of Smith can be neglected. The fracture stress for a one micron carbide particle is equal to 1400 MPa. The only microstructural parameters which now come into play are the size of the carbides and the fracture energy γ_c. As it was underlined by Knott [3], the grain size d disappears when the model of Smith is applied. He reconciled this with the experimental observation [32] that the cleavage stress varies as $d^{-1/2}$ by noting that there was a correlation between the size of the carbides and the size of the grains [31]. A convenient representation of the relation between the critical size of cleavage cracks and the fracture stress is shown on figure 2 due to Hahn [2]. It derives from the Griffith relation which is written as :

$$\sigma_f = \alpha K_{Ia}^B s^{-1/2} \tag{2}$$

where α is equal to $\sqrt{2/\pi}$ for a long crack of width s, or to $\sqrt{\pi/2}$ for a penny shaped crack of diameter s. s will be either d, the grain size, or c_0, the size of the inclusion, accordingly. On this figure the data points should fall on a straight line through the origin, the slope of which gives the representative fracture toughness K_{Ia}^B, thus designated by Hahn because it represents an arrest value at a boundary. It can be seen that indeed the results of Curry and Knott [31] whether for cementite platelets or for round carbides correspond to a fracture toughness of 2.5 MPa√m, that is to say 14 J/m². However Tsann Lin, Evans and Ritchie [33] quoted a somewhat higher value : 30 to 50 J/m². Martin-Meizoso et al. [34] determined a fracture toughness equal to 17 J/m² for the crossing of carbide boundaries in SA533B bainitic steel.

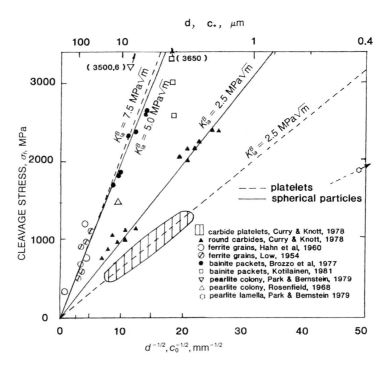

Fig. 2 Brittle fracture stress-particle dimension measurements for different microstrucrures [2]. (with the permission of Metallurgical Transactions A)

In the case of propagation from inclusions, it is their size, or in some cases the size of clusters of inclusions, which is the essential parameter. In A533B steel three types of initiation sites were observed [29, 30] : type I corresponds to isolated MnS inclusions, Type II to MnS clusters of inclusions which produced a coalesced cavity, type III to other non metallic inclusions. The relation between the size of the initiation sites (0.25 to 0.38 mm for the largest) and the cleavage stress (between 1400 and 2200 MPa) allows to calculate a fracture toughness which is statistically distributed around 1600 J/m^2. This very high value, plus the dispersion demonstrate that the clusters of inclusions act really as local stress raisers and that the true initiation sites are smaller features close to these clusters [30].

So far only the case of a ferritic matrix has been considered. In the case of pearlite the cleavage cracks initiate in the cementite lamellae in linear arrays and propagate in the ferrite. It seems that it is the size of the pearlite colony rather than the thickness of the cementite platelets which is the controlling parameter [2, 35]. In the case of bainite and martensite, the size of the packets of lath appears to be the controlling parameter [36, 37]. In that case the influence of the prior austenite grain size is simply an effect of the correlation between this size and that of the packets. The size of the so called covariant packets [38], sub-packets of a similar variant of the Kurdjumov-Sachs relation, does not seem to have an influence. A crack which has been nucleated in a carbide or in an inclusion and which propagates in the surrounding matrix, can still be stopped at an high angle boundary [33]. In that case the controlling parameter, following the Griffith equation, is the grain or the packet size. This again is shown on figure 2. It is the obstacle which needs the highest stress to be overcome which is controlling. Martin-Meizoso et al. [34] for the crossing of ferrite-ferrite boundaries in SA533B bainitic steel determined a fracture toughness equal to 39 J/m^2 (7 MPa$\sqrt{m}$), a higher value than the one which is reported on figure 2.

Owing to difficulties of observations, the truly efficient barriers to the propagation of a cleavage crack were not easy to identify. Electron Back-Scatter Diffraction (EBSD) allows now much more precise determination of the orientation of microstructural elements. In this way Lambert et al. [39] were able to show that cleavage cracks in bainites were stopped at high angle boundaries which can include several packets of lath.

INFLUENCE OF MICROSTRUCTURAL FEATURES ON THE DBTT

Influence of the Size of the Grains or of the Packets of Laths

The DBTT being the temperature at which the yield strength is equal to the cleavage stress, is influenced by the size of grains or of packets which modifies both these properties. As shown in the preceding section, the size of the dislocation pile-ups, which is connected to the size d of the grains or of the packets of lath in bainite and in martensite, is important for the nucleation of cracks in carbides and in inclusions. However this is not the critical step. For the propagation past the boundary of a carbide or of an inclusion it is their size c_0 which is the controlling factor.

Nevertheless a relation of the DBTT with $d^{-1/2}$ would be expected if the size c_0 of the carbides was correlated with d [3] and because in some cases it is the propagation across high angle boundaries which is the critical step. However Gerberich et al. [40] putting together the results of Low [41], of Almond, Timbres and Embury [42] and their own arrived at the conclusion that the cleavage stress was proportional to $d^{-1/4}$. This size d is correlated with the prior austenite grain size.

The yield strength itself follows the Hall-Petch relation. The following relation was proposed for bainitic steels :

$$DBTT = T_0 - Bd^{-1/2} \qquad (3)$$

in which B has an average value of 17°Cmm$^{1/2}$ for packets [37,43,44], going from 10 to 19°C$\sqrt{mm}$.

For a 12% chromium steel Gooch and Ginn [8] give the following relation :

$$DBTT(^\circ C) = 140 + 0.58(\%martensite) - 27d^{-1/2}(mm^{-1/2}) \qquad (4)$$

Again, Gerberich et al. [40], from a number of results on the influence of grain size on the DBTT, questioned this type of dependency ; they stated that in reality it is quite low.

Nevertheless, reducing the grain size cannot do any harm to lower the DBTT. It can be achieved by austenizing at low temperatures to keep the grain size of the austenite as small as possible, and by rolling or forging in a controlled manner, again at low temperatures. TiN is efficient to pin the grain boundaries of austenite and thus to reduce its grain size. Ni and FCC alloying elements which lower the eutectoid temperature help to keep down the temperature of the processing. However the well known strong beneficial effect of nickel is mostly due to other factors than the influence on the grain size and they will be examined later.

Influence of the Constituents of Steel

Martensite. Martensite which has limited slip possibilities and a high yield strength ought to be brittle. However the small size of the packets, as seen in a previous section, has a beneficial effect on the cleavage stress. Hence it is not systematically detrimental, except for twin martensite. Fast cooling rate are to be preferred to produce lath martensite. There exists an optimum cooling rate allowing, before reaching Ms, to produce a certain amount of bainite (10 to 20%) [45-47]. Intergranular martensite inhibiting slip propagation from one grain to the next has a beneficial effect in 12% Cr steel [8].

Bainite. Carbide free acicular bainite obtained by fast cooling rates has better properties than carbide free granular bainite [14]. This is to be related to the size of the laths.

Retained Austenite. Retained austenite does not always have a beneficial effect [48-53]. In upper bainite are found MA (martensite-austenite) constituents which have a strong embrittling effect [54]. Thin films of interlath retained austenite in martensitic as quenched steels improve the fracture toughness. This is probably due to the instability of this austenite upon deformation.

Delta-Ferrite. The amount of delta-ferrite, which is an increasing function of the amount of chromium, increases the DBTT in martensitic Cr Mo or Cr W steels [7]. The effect is stronger after ageing. The increase of the DBTT over the volume fraction of delta-ferrite reaches 190°C under those conditions. It amounts to 160°C after tempering. This detrimental effect is due to the cleavage of the delta-ferrite across micro-twins [55].

Cementite and carbides. The location of the cementite precipitation has a strong effect on the DBTT. Lower bainite in which the precipitates of cementite are within the laths have a lower DBTT than upper bainite in which they are on the lath boundaries [56-58]. According to Irvine and Pickering [57] the fine cementite precipitates in lower bainite could act as crack arresters and could deviate cracks. This effect might even be stronger in tempered martensite because of the multi directional nature of the precipitation. The fast cooling rate minimises the diffusion of carbon and hence carbide segregation. Then the formation of large carbides during tempering is prevented and this results in low DBTT [14]. The same goal could be achieved by increased hardenability. As an example better properties were obtained by adding tungsten and vanadium to 3% chromium steel.
The nature of the carbides seems also to play a role after tempering : in 5Cr3WV steel most of the carbides are M_7C_3 which precipitate during slow cooling and which grow easily during tempering ; this increases the DBTT. In 9Cr3WV and in 12Cr3WV steels the primary precipitation produces $M_{23}C_6$ carbides which do not grow so much ; hence the properties are improved. The nature and the size of the carbides have also an influence on irradiation embrittlement. While the increase of the yield strength due to irradiation would suffice to explain the increase of the DBTT, and the fact that irradiating at higher temperatures lowers the shift of the DBTT, the growth of carbides increases the embrittlement. As an example, M_7C_3 in 5Cr3WV steel produce an inverse effect of the irradiation temperature [14].
But considering the role of cementite particles in the nucleation of cleavage crack reducing the carbon content always brings an improvement.

Influence of Inclusions

As already noted the size of the inclusions is the key parameter. However the effect of their shape should also be considered. The stress concentration in the inclusions can be evaluated from the theory of Eshelby [59]. This was extended to plastic deformation of the matrix by Berveiller and Zaoui [60]. The stress σ in the inclusion is given, in the case of an axisymmetric loading, by :

$$\sigma = \Sigma_m + \frac{2}{3}\Sigma_{eq} + kE_pE_{eq}^p$$

(5)

where Σ_m is the remote hydrostatic applied stress, Σ_{eq} the remote equivalent applied stress, k a stress concentration factor which depends on the shape of the inclusion and which is given in table I, E_p the slope of the hardening curve and E_{eq}^p the remote equivalent plastic strain.

Table I. Values of the shape factor k for different eccentricities s of inclusions (A,B,C and D refer to Fig.3)

case	k	k
Prolate inclusion (s>1)		s = 7
direction : longitudinal (A)	$\frac{2}{3}\left[\frac{1}{3}\frac{1+2s^2}{2\log(2s-1)-1}-1\right]$	4.66
transverse (B)	$\frac{1}{2}\left[\frac{1}{9}\frac{1+2s^2}{2\log(2s-1)-1}+1\right]$	1.83
Spherical inclusion	1	
Oblate inclusion (s<1)		s = 1/7
direction : face (C)	$\frac{2}{3}\left(\frac{4}{3\pi s}-1\right)$	1.31
side (D)	$\frac{2}{3}\left(\frac{10}{3\pi s}-1\right)$	1.83

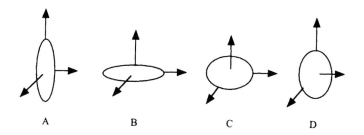

A   B   C   D

Fig.3 Expression of the shape parameter k for the stress concentration in rigid ellipsoidal inclusions for various values of their excentricity expressed as the ratio s of the axial to the radial dimension. Cases A and B, s>1 ; cases C and D, s<1. The loading is axisymmetric

This table I shows that prolate inclusions loaded in the longitudinal direction (case A) and oblate inclusions loaded on their side (case D) are the ones for which the stress concentration factor is the largest. They are the ones which will cleave more easily.

This theory neglects the interaction between inclusions. Within clusters the stress concentration could be even higher.

Once the crack has been initiated in the inclusion it propagates in the stress field which exists at its vicinity. Thus the use of the Griffith equation (2) which disregards this stress concentration strictly speaking is not valid, so that the energy of propagation γ_c deduced from it is only an apparent one.

It can be calculated that, in uniaxial tension σ, for a penny shaped crack growing from an inclusion, the evolution of the stress intensity factor is given by the equation :

$$\sqrt{\frac{c_0}{2a}}\,\frac{K_I}{K_I(a=2c_0)} = N_\sigma^I + \left(1 - \sqrt{\frac{c_0}{2a}}\right)^{1/2}\left\{1 - N_\sigma^I + \frac{1}{6}\left[2(7-5v)Q + 1 - K_\sigma^I\right]\left(\frac{c_0}{2a}\right)^2 + 3Q\left(\frac{c_0}{2a}\right)4\right\} (6)$$

where c_0 is the radius of the spherical inclusion, a the radius of the penny shaped crack, K_I the stress intensity factor. Its value when $a = 2c_0$ is :

$$K_I(a = c_0/2) = \sigma\sqrt{\frac{2c_0}{\pi}} \qquad (7)$$

The ratio of the shear modulus of the inclusion to the shear modulus of the matrix is designated by m.

The stress concentration factor in the inclusion for an hydrostatic remote stress field is :

$$K_\sigma^I = \frac{3(1-v)k^I}{2(1-2v)k + (1+v)k^I}$$

$$(8)$$

where k is the bulk modulus of the matrix, v the Poisson's ratio of the matrix and k^I the bulk modulus of the inclusion.

In a pure shear remote loading the stress concentration factor in the inclusion is :

$$M_\sigma^I = \frac{15(1-v)m}{(7-5v) + 2(4-5v)}$$

$$(9)$$

Hence for a remote uniaxial stress it is :

$$N_\sigma^I = 2M_\sigma^I + K_\sigma^I$$

$$(10)$$

The factor Q is given by :

$$Q = \frac{1-m}{(7-5v) + 2(4-5v)m} \qquad (11)$$

Fig.4 shows the evolution of the ratio K_I / K_{I0} assuming that the Poisson's ratios of the inclusion and of the matrix are the same, in which case :

$$m = \frac{\mu^I}{\mu} = \frac{k^I}{k} = \frac{E^I}{E} \qquad (12)$$

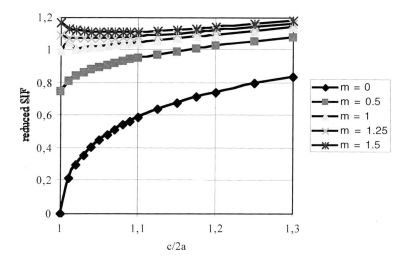

Fig.4 Evolution of the stress intensity factor for a penny shaped crack emanating from a spherical inclusion as a function of the ratio of its radius, c, to the radius of the inclusion, a. m is the ratio of the elastic modulus of the inclusion to the elastic modulus of the matrix, the Poisson's ratios being equal.

This figure shows that hard inclusions (m > 1) raise the stress intensity factor needed for crack propagation, which is the minimum on the curves. Hence using Griffith formula under-evaluates the fracture energy. It is the contrary for soft inclusions. Furthermore, owing to the difference between the expansion coefficients of the inclusion and of the ferrite, there exists also a residual stress field around the inclusion introduced during cooling which would modify the stress intensity factor.

However, except in the case where dislocations pile ups initiate cracks in the inclusions, more or less extended plasticity erase the residual stress field. Lastly linear elastic fracture mechanics is only relevant if there is no plastic deformation so that the above formula (6) for the stress intensity factor is to be taken with care.

The shape factor of the inclusion influences also the propagation of the cleavage crack in the ferritic matrix because it determines the stress in the inclusion and in the immediate vicinity. Furthermore, as discussed in a preceding section, inclusions in many cases act as local stress raisers, triggering cleavage initiation for instance from nearby small carbides [30].

The nature of the initiation sites seems to change as the temperature is raised [29, 61]. It is not known whether this is due to a modification of the conditions for the initiation of cracks in the inclusions or for the propagation across the interface, or to the modification of the stress field in their vicinity. It seems that when the temperature is increased, the decrease of the flow stress smooth out the stress concentration so that the inclusions are less efficient stress raisers [30]. That is to say enough knowledge about γ_c corresponding to the cleavage of inclusions or to the fracture of their interfaces, or for the further dynamic propagation to the surrounding matrix, is still lacking. The bonding between inclusions and matrix is also not too well known.

Better knowledge could explain for instance the various interplays between (TiV)(CN), Al_2O_3 and MnS inclusions and ferrite as studied by Stanwood, Balart and Davis [62] in a vanadium microalloyed medium carbon steel. They found that in a Ti treated steel initiation of cleavage took place on 35 micron (TiV)(CN) inclusions; in Ti free steel on 3 to 9 micron (TiV)(CN) inclusions, while in thicker sections of this Ti free steel it was the pearlite which initiated cleavage; in the first two cases the Al_2O_3 and MnS inclusions did not crack, while in the last one they decohered.

Another important effect is the influence of temperature on the efficiency of various kinds of inclusions to initiate cleavage. When the number of initiating inclusions decreases as the temperature is raised, the reference volume in a statistical analysis increases. This has of course consequences on the evaluation of the failure probability.

Influence of Solutes

Elements in solid solution modify the flow strength of the ferrite, and other constituents, and they also have an effect on the energy of cleavage. The problem was treated by Chen et al. in two companion papers [63,40]. The first effect is a modification of the Peierls stress, which, according to the model of Dorn and Rajnak is a decreasing linear function of the concentration of solute. Furthermore the solute also decreases the activation energy for the nucleation of double kinks, while the energy of migration increases; a minimum results for the activation energy as a function of the solute concentration. This is reflected on the evolution of the yield strength with the temperature.
The second effect is the pinning of dislocations by solute atoms. Knott [3] stressed that this was needed for cleavage cracks not to blunt at the interface of cementite and ferrite. Raising the yield strength, this pinning increases the DBTT.
Klueh and Alexander [14] found that adding Ta in solid solution to 9Cr3WV steel decreased the DBTT. This was attributed to a possible increase of the fracture stress.

Effect of Nickel. It is well known that nickel is an element which has a strong effect to lower the DBTT. It can be attributed to the above mentioned modification of the Peierls stress and of the activation energy resulting in solid solution softening [40]. It can also be connected to an increase in the ease of cross slip, resulting in more difficult crack initiation by slip and by twinning [64]. Lastly, nickel additions also increase the surface energy of iron [65,66]. The cleavage energy was measured by Gerberich et al. [40], who showed an increase from 25 up to 30 J/m^2 by the addition of 4 atom % of nickel.

Effect of Silicon. Addition of silicon reduces the surface energy for cleavage. It was shown to drop from 25 down to 15 J/m^2 for 4 atom% [40]. In that case the solid solution softening is sufficient to decrease the DBTT for low concentrations only. Over 2 atom% it increases.

INTERGRANULAR FRACTURE

Intergranular fracture results from the segregation of impurities to grain boundaries [67]. The ones which are harmful are metalloidic impurities : Si, P, S, Ge, As, Se, Sn, Sb, Te, Bi. Sulphur and phosphorus are the more common ones. Diffusion at high temperature is responsible for temper embrittlement. The presence of transition elements Cr, Mn, Ni is needed to enhance the segregation. Irradiation can also induce segregation in high alloy steels [68]. It has been shown, by molecular dynamics calculations, that P weakens the bonds between Fe atoms [69,70]. As in the case of cleavage, local stress concentrations are needed to reach the bond strength even when they are weakened. Dislocation pile-ups against the grain boundaries can produce the necessary stress enhancement. In that case the grain size is a controlling parameter and a $d^{-1/2}$ relation is expected. Often after grain boundary initiation, the propagation occurs by cleavage. Guttmann proposed a formula to predict the DBTT shift :
$$\Delta DBTT = -120 + 4.8P + 2(H - 20) + 0.15(7 - G)P + 0.23(H - 20)P + 0.036(7 - G)(H- 20)P$$
$$(13)$$
where P designate the P composition, H the hardness and G the grain size.
In PWR pressure vessel steels, the segregation of P to austenitic grain boundaries can occur either in coarse grain structures in heat affected zones, or in impurities enriched zones [61,69]. These ghost lines are the result of primary segregation in the centre of ingots. Temper embrittlement is greater in these zones than elsewhere. One obvious reason is that the concentration of impurities is larger there. Another one is that quenching produces martensite in

the ghost lines, whereas outside of these it is the bainitic transformation which takes place. Now, as already evoked, the fine carbides produced in the tempering of martensite are too small to trigger cleavage, so that intergranular cracking predominates. On the contrary, in upper bainite, the carbides which are bigger initiate cleavage, the more so owing to the larger segregation of impurities at their interface instead of at the grain boundaries.

CONCLUSION

Micromechanisms of fracture which determine the Charpy transition curve are known. Below the DBTT cleavage fracture is propagation controlled in most cases by the crossing of the boundaries of cementite or of inclusions. In other cases the critical boundaries are the grain boundaries. Above the FATT the fracture depends on the nucleation, growth and coalescence of cavities which are initiated on inclusions.

In any case the role of inclusions, of their nature, of their size, of their distribution is essential. Detailed studies on these parameters are still needed. More experimental research should also be performed on the exact local stresses at the initiation sites of cleavage. Detailed knowledge about the mechanical properties of the matrix must be acquired at the same time. This should allow to gain a better knowledge about the fracture energy and, thus, to better understand the influence of various parameters: composition of the steels, thermal treatments, test temperature, dose of irradiation.

REFERENCES

1- Kotilainen, H. (1980). *PhD. Dissertation,* Helsinki University of Technology, Otaniemi, Finland.
2- Hahn, G.T. (1984) *Met. Trans A* **15A**, 947.
3- Knott, J.F. (1992). In : *ECF9 Reliability and Structural Integrity of Advanced Materials*, pp. 1375-1400, Sedmak, S., Sedmak, A. and Ruzic, D. (Eds). EMAS, Warley.
4- Veistinen, M.K. and Lindroos, V.K. (1985). *J. Heat Treatments* **4**, 56-68.
5- Veistinen, M.K. and Lindroos, V.K. (1985). In *New Developments in Stainless Steel Technology*, pp. 29-43, American Soc. Metals, Metals Park.
6- Knudsen, R.D. and Hutchings, R. (1988) *Mater. Sci. Tech.* **4**, 127-135.
7- Abe, F., Araki, H., Noda, T. and Okada, M. (1988) *J. Nuclear Mat.* **155-157B**, 656-661
8- Gooch, T.G. and Ginn, B.J. (1990) *Welding J.* **69**, 431s-440s.
9- Miyahara, K., Kobayashi, Y; and Hosoi, Y. (1991) *J. Nuclear Mat.* **179-181**, 667-670.
10- Washko, S.D. and Grubb, J.F. (1991). In : *Stainless Steels '91*, Iron and Steel Inst. Japan, Tokyo.
11- Abe, F., Araki, H. and Noda, T. (1992) *Mater. Sci. Tech.* **8**, 767-773.
12- Orava, U.H., Karjalainen, L.P. and Kyrolainen, A.J. (1993). In : *1st European Stainless Steel Conf.*, Associazione Italiana di Metallurgia, Milano.
13- Kuzuku, V., Aksoy, M. and Korkut, M.H. (1998) *J. Mater. Process. Tech.* **82**, 165-171.
14- Klueh, R.L. and Alexander, D.J. (1999) *J. Nuclear Mater.* **265**, 262-272
15- François, D., Pineau, A. and Zaoui, A. (1998). *Mechanical Behaviour of Materials.* Kluwer Acad. Pub., Dordrecht.
16- Pisarenko, G.S. and Krasowsky, A.J. (1978) *2nd. Inter. Conf. Mechanical Behaviour of Materials, Spec. Vol.* pp348, Am. Soc. for Metals.
17- Rice, J.R. and Thomson, R. (1974) *Phil. Mag.* **29**, 73.
18- Zener, C. (1948). *Fracturing of Metals*, ASM, Cleveland.
19- Stroh, A.N. (1957) *Advances in Physics* **6**, 418.
20- Pilkington, R. and Hull, D. (1968). *Cont. On FractureToughness*, Iron and Steel Inst., **20**, 5.
21- Smith, E. (1966). In : *Proc. Conf. Physical Basis of Yield and Fracture*, Inst. Physics and Physical Soc., Oxford.
22- Inoue, A., Ogura, T. and Masumoto, T. (1977) *Metal. Trans. A* **8A**, 1689
23- McMahon, C.J. and Cohen, M. (1965) *Acta. Met.* **13**, 59.
24- Tweed, J.H. and Knott, J.F. (1987) *Acta. Met.* **35**, 1401
25- Baker, T.J., Kavishe, F.P.L. and Wilson, J. (1986) *Mater. Science Tech.* **2**, 576-582.

26- Brooksbank, D. and Andrews, K.W. (1972) *JISI* **210**, 246-255.
27- Linaza, M.A., Romero, J.M., Rodrigez-Ibabe, J.M. and Urcola, J.J. (1995) *Scripta Met.* **32**, 395-400.
28- Linaza, M.A., Romero, J.M., Rodrigez-Ibabe, J.M. and Urcola, J.J. (1997) *Fatigue Fract. Engngn. Mater. Struct.* **20**, 619-632.
29- Rossoll, A. (1998) *Thèse,* École Centrale de Paris.
30- Carassou, S. (2000) *Thèse* École Supérieure des Mines de Paris, CEA-R-5856.
31- Curry, D.A. and Knott, J.F. (1978) *Metal Science* **12**, 511.
32- Low, J.R. (1956). In *Deformation and Flow of Solids.* pp 50. Springer Verlag, Berlin.
33- Tsann Lin, Evans, A.G. and Ritchie, R.O. (1987) *Met. Trans.* **18A**, 641.
34- Martin-Meizoso, A., Ocana-Arizcorreta, I., Gil-Sevillano, J. and Fuentes-Pérez, M. (1994) *Acta Metall. Mater.* **42**, 2057.
35- Rosenfield, A.R., Votava, E. and Hahn, G.T. (1968) *Trans. ASM* **61**, 807.
36- Ohtani, H., Tersaki, F. and Kunitake, T. (1972) *Trans. I. S. I. Japan* **12**, 118.
36- Brozzo, P., Buzzichelli, G., Mascanzoni, A. and Mirabile, M. (1977) *Metal Science* **11**, 123.
38- Inoue, T., Matsuda, S., Okamura, Y. and Aoki, K. (1970) *Trans. Jap. Inst. Metals* **11**, 36
39- Lambert, A., Garat, X., Sturel, T., Gourgues, A.F. and Gingell, A., (2000) *Scripta Mater.* **43**, 161.
40- Gerberich, W.W., Chen, Y.T., Atteridge, D.G. and Johnson, T. (1981) *Acta Met.*, **29**, 1187
41- Low, J.R. Jr. (1963) *Iron and its Dilute Solid Solutions*, pp.255, Wiley.
42- Almond, J.A., Timbres, D.H. and Embury, J.D. (1969) In *Fracture 1969*, pp.253, Pratt, P.L., Chapman & Hall.
43- Matsuda,S., Inoue, T., Mimura, H. and Okamura, Y. (1972) *Trans. I. S. I. Jap.* **12**, 325.
44- Lonsdale, D. and Flewitt, P.E.J. (1978) *Met. Trans.* **9A**, 1619.
45- Desalos, Y. and Laurent, R. (1979) *Mem. Scien. Rev. Met.* **76**, 73.
46- Kunitake, T., Terasaki, F., Ohmori, Y. and Ohtani, H. (1972) *Iron and Steel* **45**, 647.
47- Edwards, D.P. (1979) *J.I.S.I.* **207**, 1494.
48- Thomas, G. (1973) *Iron and Steel Int.* **46**, 451.
49- Jin, S., Hwang, D. and Morris, J.W. (1976) *Met. Trans.* **7A**, 637.
50- Pampillo, C.A. and Paxton, H.W. (1972) *Met. Trans.* **3A**, 2895.
51- Thomas, G. (1978) *Met. Trans.* **9A**, 439.
52- Horn, R.M. and Ritchie, R.O. (1978) *Met. Trans.* **9A**, 1039.
53- Parker, E.R. and Zackay, V.F. (1975) *Eng. Fract. Mech.* **7**, 371.
54- Lambert, A;, Drillet, J., Gourgues, A.F., Sturel, T. and Pineau, A., (2000), *Science Tech. of Welding and Joining,* **5**, 168.
55- Broek, D. (1974) *Int. Met. Rev.* **19**, 136.
56- Irvine, K.J., Pickering, F.B. and Garstone, J. (1960) *J.I.S.I.* **196**, 66.
57- Irvine, K.J. and Pickering, F.B. (1963) *J.I.S.I.* **201**, 518.
58- Der-Hung Huang and Thomas, G. (1971) *Met. Trans.* **2A**, 1587.
59- Eshelby, J.D. (1957) *Proc. Royal Soc. London*, **A241**, 376.
60- Berveiller, M. and Zaoui, A. (1979) *J. Mech. Phys. Solids*, **26**, 325
61- Marini, B. (2001) to be published in ICF10 Conference.
62- Srangwood, M., Balart, M.J. and Davis, C.L. (2000) *Mater. Scien. Engn. A.*, **284**, 1.
63- Chen, Y.T., Atteridge, D.G. and Gerberich, W.W. (1981) *Acta Met.*, **29**, 1171.
64- Floreen, S., Hayden, H.W. and Devine, T.M. (1975) *Met. Trans.* **2A**, 1403.
65- Loria, E.A. (1965) *Trans. A.S.M.*, **58**, 221
66- Leslie, W.C., Sober, R.J., Babcock, S.G. and Green, S.J. (1965) *Trans. A.S.M.*, **62**, 690.
67- Guttmann, M. (1980) *The Donald McLean Symposium*, 59.
68- Grandjean, Y., Bellon, P. and Martin, G. (1994) *Phys. Rev.*, B50, 4228.
69- Raoul, S. (1999) *Thèse* École Supérieure des Mines de Paris, CEA-R-5874
70- Messmer, R.P. and Briant, C.L. (1982) *Acta Met.*, **30**, 457.

From Charpy to Present Impact Testing
D. François and A. Pineau (Eds.)
© 2002 Elsevier Science Ltd. and ESIS. All rights reserved

Finding G_C for Plastics using Modified Charpy Tests

J. G. WILLIAMS*and A. RAGER‡

Abstract

The modification of the basic Charpy test to determine G_c is described. Sharp cracks of various lengths are used and the energy absorbed at fracture plotted versus a function of normalized crack length $bW\Phi(a/W)$ to give a straight line of slope G_c. Kinetic energy effects are important in this plot and they can be best understood using a spring - mass model including a contact stiffness. A more refined beam model is also described which includes higher frequency effects which become important at short times. For these short times, which are attained at high velocities, a displacement method has to be used and some data are given for such a test.

Keywords: Charpy tests; Strain energy release rate; Impact; Three point bend test.

*Corresponding author. Department of Mechanical Engineering, Imperial College, University of London, London SW7 2BX, United Kingdom.
Phone: ++44 594 7200,
Fax: ++44 207 594 7017,
e-mail: g.williams@ic.ac.uk.
‡Department of Mechanical Engineering, Imperial College, University of London, London SW7 2BX, United Kingdom.

1   Introduction

The Charpy test configuration has long been recognized as a convenient and effective way of characterizing the impact toughness of plastics. There are standard test methods which are essentially modifications of the metals versions which define toughness in terms of the energy absorbed.

The fracture of polymers has been a fruitful area for the use of Fracture Mechanics [1, 2] and most interest has centered on the determination of G_c, the energy per unit area or the critical energy release rate at crack initiation. The Charpy scheme has been adapted to measure G_c by using sharp notches and measuring energies or displacements to fracture at both low and high rates. This paper outlines the development of these tests and suggests how they may be improved.

2   Energy Methods

The most common method of determining G_c is via the fracture load, P, and the specimen compliance $C(a)$ via,

$$G_c = \frac{P^2}{2b} \frac{dC(a)}{da} \qquad (1)$$

where b is the thickness and a the crack length. However, if elastic behaviour is assumed, the load is related to the energy at fracture U via,

$$U = \frac{P^2}{2} C \qquad (2)$$

and hence G_c may be found from U,

$$G_c = \frac{U}{bC} \frac{dC}{da} = \frac{U}{bW\Phi} \qquad (3)$$

where

$$\Phi(a/W) = \frac{C}{\frac{dC}{d(a/W)}}$$

a calibration function for energies which may be deduced from C(a/W) and is evaluated for the Charpy three point bend configuration [1]. For an S/W ratio of four, where S is the span as shown in Figure 1, which is the most

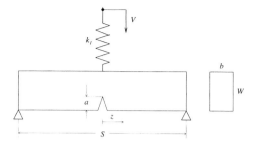

Figure 1: The Charpy three point bend test

Table 1:

a/W	0.1	0.2	0.3	0.4	0.5
Φ	0.782	0.469	0.354	0.287	0.234

commonly used, Φ has the values shown in Table 1. The usual test procedure is to make a series of specimens of different a/W values and then determine the energy to fracture them, U. The energy in equation (3) is the elastic energy in the specimen and for static tests it is assumed that this is the same as the impact energy. A graph of U versus $bW\Phi$ is then plotted giving a straight line with a slope of G_c.

The same procedure has been adopted for impact tests with speeds, V, up to about 3 m/s. Here it was recognized, as it was 100 years ago, that the measured energy included the kinetic energy imparted to the specimen, i.e. the "toss factor". For the rigid body impact of a large body moving at a velocity V (the striker) onto a stationary small body (the specimen) a velocity of 2V is imparted and hence a kinetic energy U_k,

$$U_k = 2mV^2 \qquad (4)$$

where m is the specimen mass, ρbWS and ρ is the density. One strategy is to impact unsupported specimens and measure U_k (the toss factor) and then subtract it from the input energy, U_1, before plotting it against $bW\Phi$. The most usual practice, however, is to plot U_1, versus $bW\Phi$ and have a positive intercept, U_k.

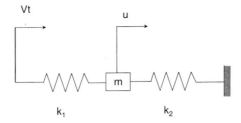

Figure 2: The Spring-Mass Model

This procedure is quite satisfactory for high G_c values and modest speeds (≈ 1 m/s) but is inaccurate when the U_k is a significant fraction of U_1. In these cases the static definition of G, equations (1) and (3), is not correct and G_c cannot be found easily. This problem is greatly clarified by considering a spring-mass model of the test.

3   The Spring-Mass Model

The model is shown in Fig. 2 and the spring of stiffness k_2 is the specimen stiffness given by C^{-1}. m is the effective mass of the specimen and for this loading is $1/2\rho bWS$. k_1 is the contact stiffness between the striker and the specimen and plays a vital role in controlling the dynamic behaviour of the specimen. The contact point moves at Vt imparting a displacement u to the specimen which is at rest at $t = 0$ and $u = \dot{u} = 0$. The equation of motion is,

$$m\ddot{u} + (k_1 + k_2)u = k_1 Vt \tag{5}$$

for which the solution is

$$u = \frac{\alpha Vt}{1 + \alpha}\left(1 - \frac{sin(\omega t)}{\omega t}\right) \tag{6}$$

where $\alpha = k_1/k_2$ and ω is the natural frequency of the system given by,

$$\omega^2 = \frac{k_2}{m}(1 + \alpha) = 8(1 + \alpha)\left(\frac{CW}{S^2}\right)^2 \tag{7}$$

where $C = \sqrt{E/\rho}$ is the elastic wave speed.

k_1 has an effect on the static energies which can be seen by considering the quasi-static deformations i.e.

$$u_{QS} = \frac{\alpha}{1 + \alpha} Vt$$

The energy input is;

$$U_1 = \int_0^t k_1 (Vt - u_{QS}) V dt = \frac{1}{2} \left(\frac{\alpha}{1 + \alpha} \right) k_2 (Vt)^2 \qquad (8)$$

and the energy in the specimen is

$$U_2 = \frac{1}{2} k_2 u_{QS}^2 = \frac{k_2}{2} \left(\frac{\alpha}{1 + \alpha} \right)^2 (Vt)^2 \qquad (9)$$

There is a factor of $\alpha/(1 + \alpha)$ difference which represents the energy stored in the contact stiffness k_1 and the G_c value taken from the slope of the U versus $bW\Phi$ graph should be corrected by the factor $\alpha/(1 + \alpha)$ to give the true value.

For the dynamic case the energies are,

$$\frac{U_1}{mV^2} = \frac{1}{2} \frac{\alpha}{(1 + \alpha)^2} \left(x^2 + 2\alpha (1 - \cos(x)) \right)$$

$$\frac{U_2}{mV^2} = \frac{1}{2} \frac{\alpha^2}{(1 + \alpha)^3} (x - \sin(x))^2$$

and the kinetic energy

$$\frac{U_3}{mV^2} = \frac{1}{2} \left(\frac{\alpha}{1 + \alpha} \right)^2 (1 - \cos(x))^2 \qquad (10)$$

where $x = \omega t$. Using the static definition of G_c, $U_2 = bW\Phi G_c$ and the equivalent of the U_1, versus $bW\Phi$ plot is U_1/mV^2. versus $bW\Phi G_c/mV^2 = U_2/mV^2$ which are shown in Fig. 3 for $\alpha = 2$ and 10. An upper bound for U_1, is given for $\cos(x) = -1$, $\sin(x) = 0$ for which

$$\frac{U_1}{mV^2} = \left(\frac{1 + \alpha}{\alpha} \right) \frac{bW\Phi G_c}{mV^2} + 2 \left(\frac{\alpha}{1 + \alpha} \right)^2$$

and this is also shown in Fig. 3.

A more precise definition of G is obtained from,

$$bG = \frac{dU_1}{da} - \frac{d}{da} (U_2 + U_3) \qquad (11)$$

$$\text{and} \qquad \frac{dU_1}{da} = k_1 (Vt - u) \frac{du}{da}.$$

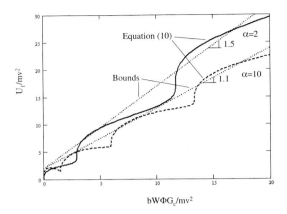

Figure 3: Input energy U_1 versus specimen energy U_2, static definition of G, from Equation (10)

It should be noted that both α and ω vary with a via dk_2/da and after considerable manipulation,

$$\frac{bW\Phi G_c}{mV^2} = \frac{1}{2}\frac{\alpha^2}{(1+\alpha)^3}\left(x^2 + x\sin(x) - 4\left(1 - \cos(x)\right)\right) \tag{12}$$

The relationships for U_1/mV^2 versus $bW\Phi G_c/mV^2$ for this, more precise, solution is shown in Fig. 4 together with the upper bound

$$\frac{U_1}{mV^2} = \left(\frac{1+\alpha}{\alpha}\right)\frac{bW\Phi G_c}{mV^2} + \frac{2\alpha\left(2+\alpha\right)}{\left(1+\alpha\right)^2} \tag{13}$$

The form is very similar to that of the energy plot in Fig. 3. Figure 5 shows an experimental plot taken from [1] showing both a positive intercept and the oscillatory form. A similar procedure is now part of an ISO standard [3] in which the contact energies are determined separately and then subtracted from that measured. Figure 6 shows two such sets of data taken from [3] where U_Q is the original data and $U_{Q,corr}$ that with the contact energy removed. The form is linear, as expected, and the slopes suggest an α value of about 2. The data in Fig. 6 are also an example of how the contact stiffness can be manipulated in that a thin layer of plasticine is used to reduce k_1 and hence the inertial effects. In general polymer specimens give $\alpha = 10$ so that the plasticine reduced the value to 2.

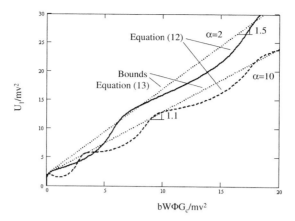

Figure 4: Input energy U_1 versus $bW\Phi G_c/mV^2$ using the dynamic definition of G from Equation (12)

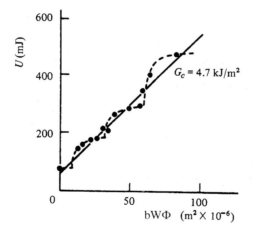

Figure 5: Impact data for HDPE at 20^oC ($S = 72$ mm, $b = W = 6$ mm), Charpy test [1]

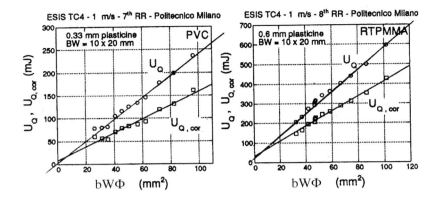

Figure 6: Examples of G_C determination. Material: (left) PVC, (right) RTPMMA [3]

4   High Frequency Effects

A refinement of the simple, single frequency, spring-mass model is to use Timoshenkos dynamic beam theory to deduce the frequency response in more detail [4,5]. The equation of motion used is,

$$\frac{\partial^4 u}{\partial z^4} + \frac{12}{C^2 W^2} \frac{\partial^2 u}{\partial t^2} = 0 \tag{14}$$

where z is the distance from the beam centre (see Fig. 1). A variable separable form of solution is used for the transient part which has the form,

$$u = \chi(\zeta)\sin(\omega_n t) \quad , \quad \zeta = 2z/S$$

giving a characteristic equation of,

$$\frac{d^4\chi}{d\zeta^4} - Z_n^4\chi = 0$$

where $Z_n^4 = \dfrac{3}{4}\dfrac{S^4\omega_n^2}{C^2W^2}$.

Roots of this equation are both real and imaginary giving hyperbolic and harmonic terms. Using the appropriate boundary conditions gives an eigen equation for Z_n

$$\alpha = \frac{2}{3}\frac{Z_n^3}{\tanh(Z_n) - \tan(Z_n)} \tag{15}$$

At the beam centre the displacement becomes,

$$u_0 = \left(\frac{\alpha V t}{1 + \alpha} \right) \left(1 - \sum_{i=1}^{n} \frac{A_n \sin(\omega_n t)}{\omega_n t} \right) \tag{16}$$

which may be compared to equation (6). For $\alpha = 10$ the values of Z_n and A_n are shown in Table 2.

Table 2:

n	1	2	3
Z_n	2.76	4.84	7.89
A_n	0.84	0.14	0.02

It should be noted that 84% of the displacement is contributed by the lowest frequency. The mass-spring model can be used with Equation (7) to find this value and it may be written as,

$$Z_n^4 = 6 \left(1 + \alpha \right) \tag{17}$$

and hence $Z_n = 2.85$, i.e. 3% difference. A rather complex exercise using MATHCAD [5] enables the same functions as in Fig. 3 and 4 to be plotted and these are shown in Fig. 7. The effects of the high frequencies can be seen around the points of rapid change but there is no significant effect in this form of analysis.

5 The Displacement Method

The limitation of the energy method is that as the velocity increases the failure moves to lower values on the curves as in Fig. 5. Eventually all the experimental points are in regions dominated by kinetic effects. If G_c values are required at these higher speeds then one must rely on the details of the dynamic analysis and compute G_c directly from the failure time. This may be measured by instrumenting the specimen with a strain gauge near the crack tip which will give a strain signal which will rise and then give a sharp drop when fracture initiates so that the fracture time may be found [5]. A limitation is that a modulus of elasticity must be found by some other high

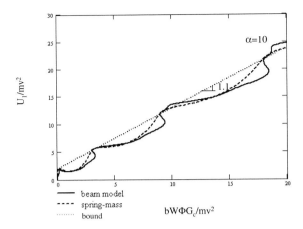

Figure 7: Input energy versus $bW\Phi G_c/mV^2$ for the beam model compared with the mass spring model, $\alpha = 10$

rate test. For the spring-mass model Equation (12) may be used and is usually written in terms of the parameter

$$G_c = g_d \cdot G_s$$

where

$$G_s = \frac{2}{\Phi}\left(\frac{W}{S}\right)^3\left(\frac{\alpha V t}{1+\alpha}\right)^2\frac{E}{W} \tag{18}$$

This relationship is derived from equation (1) but uses the displacement form by replacing the load with,

$$P = \frac{u_Q S}{C}. \tag{19}$$

The correction factor g_d for the spring-mass model is,

$$g_d = 1 + \frac{\sin(x)}{x} - \frac{4}{x^2}\left(1 - \cos(x)\right) \tag{20}$$

$$\text{and} \quad x^2 = (\omega t)^2 = 8\left(1+\alpha\right)\left(\frac{CWt}{S^2}\right)^2.$$

The function is shown as g_d versus x in Fig. 8 and can be seen to rise very slowly at first since for small values,

$$g_d \approx \frac{x^4}{360} \tag{21}$$

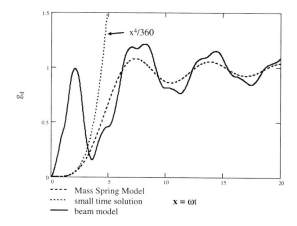

Figure 8: Displacement method correction function, $\alpha = 10$

which reflects the fact that initially the energy goes into the mass and not the spring. The function passes through unity at $x = 2\pi$ and then oscillates slightly about this value. The effects of high frequency terms are very marked in this form of analysis and g_d for $\alpha = 10$ computed using the beam analysis is also shown in Fig. 8. Here g_d is plotted versus $\omega_1 t$ which is very close to the spring mass value ωt. For $x < \pi$ there is a very large effect of the high frequencies with g_d rising to unity at $x \approx 2$. For $x > \pi$ the solution converges onto the simple form. Some experimental results are given in Table 3 for an epoxy resin tested at up to 28 m/s giving failure times down to 8.3 μs [5]. The x values are down to 0.7 for the first frequency here of $8.2 \cdot 10^4$ rad/s so that the simple model would give very small values of g_d. However, the high frequency effects lead to larger values as shown. The G_s values rise with speed but after correction G_c is essentially constant.

6   Conclusions

The traditional energy measuring scheme for characterising toughness can be modified to determine G_c. Due consideration must be given to kinetic effects and the spring-mass model describes the important influence of contact

Table 3:

$V(m/s)$	1	4.85	10	20	28
$t(\mu s$	134	21.4	14.7	11.8	8.3
x	11.0	1.75	1.2	0.91	0.68
g_d	0.78	0.93	0.51	0.38	0.27
$G_s(J/m^2)$	164	98	197	450	493
$G_c(J/m^2)$	128	91	100	173	131

stiffness in determining the frequency of the response. Such energy methods are useful only up to moderate speeds (3 m/s) after which the fracture must be timed and G_c determined from displacement and a dynamic correction factor. This factor is very sensitive to high frequency effects. Overall the Charpy test has proved to be very robust and reflects the sound science on which it is based.

References

[1] Williams, J.G. (1984). *Fracture Mechanics of Polymers*. Ellis Horwood, Chichester.

[2] Moore, D. R., Pavan, A. and Williams, J.G. (2001). *Fracture Mechanics testing Methods for Polymers, Adhesives and Composites*, ESIS Publication 28. Elsevier Science, Oxford.

[3] Pavan, A. and Williams, J.G. (2000). In: *Limitations of Test Methods for Plastics ASTM STP 1369*, J.S. Peraro (Ed). ASTM, Philadelphia.

[4] Timoshenko, S., Young, D.H. and Weaver, W. Jr. (1974). *Vibration problems in Engineering*. 4th Ed. John Wiley and Sons, New York.

[5] Williams, J. G., Tropsa, V., MacGillivray, H. and Rager, A. (2001) *Int. J. Fracture* **107**, 259.

From Charpy to Present Impact Testing
D. François and A. Pineau (Eds.)

MODELLING OF THE CHARPY TEST AS A BASIS FOR TOUGHNESS EVALUATION

W. Schmitt, I. Varfolomeyev, W. Böhme

Fraunhofer-Institut für Werkstoffmechanik, Freiburg, Germany

ABSTRACT

Micro-mechanical material models are applied for the evaluation of fracture toughness properties from results of instrumented Charpy tests. In the first example the ductile fracture resistance of a weld material from the irradiation surveillance of a nuclear pressure vessel is determined. The initiation values were converted into pseudo plane strain fracture toughness values and used to adjust the ASME reference fracture toughness curve.

The second example summarises modelling efforts towards the description of the cleavage-to-ductile transition region of a ferritic steel. Here, the Beremin model revealed substantial deficiencies concerning the transferability of the results between different specimen types and temperatures. Modifications of the failure models considering the failure mechanisms observed seem to improve the situation.

In order to give some additional insight into stress and strain fields in Charpy and fracture mechanics specimens, preliminary results of a study with irradiated weld material will be presented. This study aims at the assessment of upper shelf toughness curves, however the existing numerical models are also applicable for the determination of the stress and strain fields in Charpy specimens tested in the transition temperature regime.

KEYWORDS

Charpy V-Notch specimen, instrumented Charpy test, numerical simulation, GTN model, cleavage fracture, ductile fracture

INTRODUCTION

Ferritic steels show cleavage fracture with low fracture toughness at low temperatures and ductile tearing with higher toughness values at higher temperatures. In the transition temperature region both failure modes co-exist and compete. The transition temperature is characteristic for the material, but it depends strongly on the testing conditions.

For about a century the Charpy impact test [1] has been used as an acceptance criterion to determine the transition temperature of different materials. In its original and later standardised form the basic result of the test is the consumed energy. In a pendulum test equipment this energy is easily evaluated from the difference of the pendulum angles before and after impact. Testing specimens at different temperatures and plotting the consumed energy versus temperature yields a KV(T)-curve from which the transition temperature can be determined.

For materials relevant for nuclear installations a fracture toughness curve $K_{Ic}(T - RT_{NDT})$ was introduced as a lower bound of many valid fracture mechanics tests. The curve has a unique shape. The position of the curve with respect to the temperature axis is defined by the nil-ductility reference temperature RT_{NDT}, which is determined from drop weight (Pellini) and Charpy tests. The shift of the reference temperature, ΔRT_{NDT}, due to embrittlement, e.g. by irradiation, is monitored by the respective shift in the Charpy energy vs. temperature curve, KV(T), taken at a certain level of energy.

Although fundamental differences exist between the Charpy impact test and fracture mechanics tests many efforts have been undertaken to correlate Charpy energy or the KV(T)-curve with the fracture toughness K_{Ic} (e.g., [2,3,4]). These empirical co-relations require large efforts in comparative testing and have, in principle, only limited applicability for a small group of materials. The most frequent application of the Charpy test for the assessment of pressure vessels is that the Charpy transition temperature is used to adjust the fracture toughness reference curve $K_{IR}(T)$.

By applying calibrated strain gauges onto the impacting tub it has later become possible to measure force vs. time curves, thus providing more quantitative information about the test. Now it became not only possible to estimate the dynamic yield stress [5]. Under certain conditions it was also possible to estimate the fracture stress [5,6,7,8] analytically. Above all, results of instrumented Charpy tests provide an excellent basis for numerical simulations. Those numerical simulations started with Norris [9] as early as 1979 and have since become more and more elaborate.

EVALUATION OF UPPER SHELF TOUGHNESS VALUES

The material under investigation in this study [10] was a weld material out of the irradiation surveillance. The goal of the study was the assessment of a ductile J-resistance curve through the application of the Gurson-Tvergaard-Needleman (GTN) model [11,12,13,14]. From the surveillance programme the load vs. time records of a series of Charpy tests were available. The Charpy energies of these tests are plotted versus temperature in Fig. 1. One test at 100°C (see circle mark) was selected for the evaluation.

To complement the data base a sub-sized smooth tensile specimen (diameter 2.6 mm) and four side-grooved SE(B)-specimens (4.9x4.9x24.5 mm³) were fabricated from broken halves of Charpy specimens and tested at 100°C in the DAP accredited testing laboratory Hot Cell Erlangen of SIEMENS. Figure 2 shows the comparison of experiment and simulation of the tensile test. From the analysis the static stress-strain curve and the GTN parameters are determined. These parameters were now used to simulate the Charpy test. To describe the strain rate dependency of the flow stress, $\sigma_d(\dot{\varepsilon}_p)$, the following equation was used

$$\frac{\sigma_d}{\sigma_0} = \left(\frac{\dot{\varepsilon}_p}{\dot{\varepsilon}_0}\right)^m \tag{1}$$

Here σ_0 is the flow stress measured at the reference strain rate $\dot{\varepsilon}_0$. The strain rate sensitivity factor, $m = 0.013$, was determined by simulating the Charpy test with a combined plane-strain/plane-stress model and adjusting the strain rate exponent until a satisfactory agreement between simulated and calculated load levels is achieved (Fig. 3).

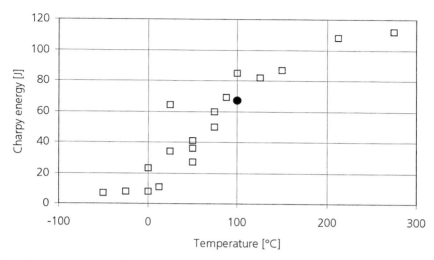

Fig. 1.   Charpy energy as a function of temperature for irradiated weld material.

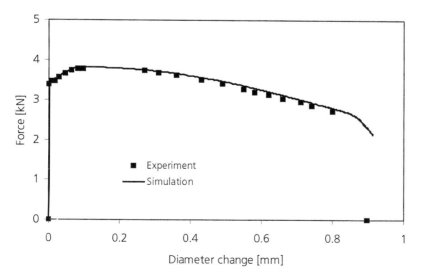

Fig. 2.   Measured and calculated force versus diameter change curves of the tensile specimen
(irradiated weld material).

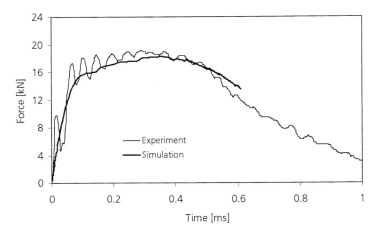

Fig. 3.   Measured and calculated force versus time curves of the (irradiated) Charpy specimen.

The characteristic length parameter, l_c, was determined from the simulation of an impact test with one of the SE(B)-specimens. With this now complete set of deformation and damage parameters the SE(B)-test was once more simulated, and a (dynamic) J-resistance curve was determined (Fig. 4). To confirm the consistency of the result, three additional tests with the remaining SE(B)-specimens were performed with different impact energies resulting in different amounts of ductile crack extension between 0.2 and 2 mm. These tests define an experimental J-resistance curve also shown in Fig. 4. Especially the first two data points are in excellent agreement with the calculated curve. Finally, the so validated set of parameters was used to simulate a fictitious static experiment with a compact C(T)20 specimen. The resulting J-resistance curve is also shown in Fig. 4.

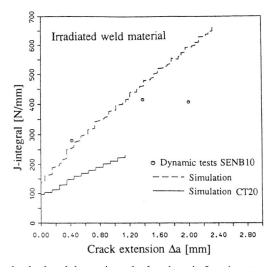

Fig. 4.   Measured and calculated dynamic, calculated static J-resistance curves.

Here it was demonstrated that the application of numerical simulation employing micromechanical material models describing ductile tearing in combination with advanced experimental techniques is a powerful tool for the assessment of transferable toughness properties even if only small quantities of the material are available and if the testing has to be done under difficult (hot cell) conditions.

MODELLING OF CLEAVAGE FRACTURE

The dominant brittle failure mechanism of ferritic steels is trans-crystalline cleavage. Three stages of the cleavage fracture process have been identified:

- A "hard" particle (e.g., carbide) breaks, thus forming a micro-crack. This requires a certain amount of plastic deformation.

- The micro-crack overcomes the boundary between particle and ferrite. This is dependent on the particle size, the specific energy for forming new surfaces, and the opening stress.

- The micro-crack overcomes the adjacent ferrite-ferrite grain boundary. This is dependent on the ferrite grain size, the specific energy for forming new surfaces, and the opening stress.

For a given material, the relative importance of these stages varies with temperature and, according to some authors, also with stress tri-axiality.

In contrast to ductile fracture by void nucleation and growth, cleavage fracture is essentially stress controlled. For the assessment of cleavage fracture Ritchie, Knott and Rice [15] suggested that the local stress ahead of a crack tip must exceed a critical fracture stress σ_f over a characteristic distance X_0 (RKR-model). The fracture stress σ_f can be determined from notched specimens.

The statistical nature of cleavage fracture has led to the development of the "Local Approach to Cleavage Fracture", or the Beremin model, [16,17]. The failure probability of a structure with or without a crack is given by

$$P_r = 1 - \exp\left[-\left(\frac{\sigma_w}{\sigma_u}\right)^m\right]$$

with the loading parameter "Weibull stress"

$$\sigma_w^m = \sum_i \left(\sigma_i^i\right)^m \frac{V^i}{V_0}$$

which is defined via the sum of the maximum principal stress over all elements within the plastic zone. The scaling or material parameter, σ_U, is determined from the statistical evaluation of a sufficiently large number of experiments. The Weibull exponent m characterises the scatter of the material properties, the characteristic volume V_0 is related to the characteristic distance X_0 in the RKR-model.

Bernauer *et al.* [18,19] examined a ferritic pressure vessel steel, German designation 22 NiMoCr 3 7, in the transition temperature regime. They analysed a great number of tests with laboratory specimens tested under a variety of conditions: different temperatures, static and dynamic loading, tensile and bending configurations, notched and pre-cracked specimens. The stress distributions in all specimens were calculated using a visco-plastic GTN-model which allows for the interaction between the elastic-plastic stress and strain fields and the softening effects due to ductile damage and crack growth.

The investigations showed that a straightforward transfer of the Beremin model parameters from one test situation to another was not possible. Since no unique trends in the dependencies of the model parameters were found, simple corrections like the introduction of temperature dependent parameters were not successful. Therefore, modifications of the model taking into account micro-structural processes were introduced and examined.

Among those modifications, the void modified Beremin model which couples the process of cleavage fracture initiation with ductile void formation produced an improvement with respect to transferability of the model parameters between different test series. It is based on the assumption that voids are also formed around carbide particles which are as a consequence no longer available for cleavage initiation. Together with modifications of the parameter evaluation procedure this model predicted a realistic temperature dependence of cleavage fracture toughness. Nevertheless, many questions remained still to be answered.

Maybe in view of the forthcoming centenary of the Charpy test and certainly fostered by the nuclear industry new research efforts have been undertaken towards a better understanding of the Charpy test, employing state-of-the-art simulation techniques and investigations into the failure mechanisms [20,21,22,23].

A project currently under way at Fraunhofer IWM aiming at the assessment of upper shelf toughness of an irradiated weld material gives us the chance to use the available numerical models and to a certain extent also the experimental data base. With this, we want to contribute to the clarification of some aspects of the test.

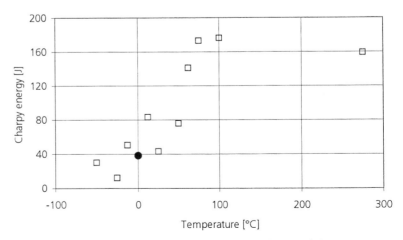

Fig. 5.   Charpy energy versus temperature for irradiated weld material.

The experimental basis includes force vs. time records of instrumented Charpy impact tests (the resulting Charpy energies versus temperature are plotted in Fig. 5) and one tensile test at an upper shelf temperature (150°C) in which the cross section of the specimens was monitored during necking. All tests were performed by SIEMENS in their hot cell facilities. The parameters of the modified Gurson model (except the characteristic length, l_c) were determined from the simulation of the tensile test.

In the subsequent analysis of a Charpy V-notch specimen test, a three-dimensional finite-element model was used with a notch root element size of 0.2 mm. The results obtained using this model and the optimised material parameters representative for an upper shelf temperature are found to be in good agreement with the experimental measurements (Fig. 6). The complete set of the GTN parameters is to be applied in a future study to simulate a fictitious test with a compact C(T)25 specimen and, hence, to calculate the J-resistance curve. In the material description the strain rate dependency of the yield stress is taken into account.

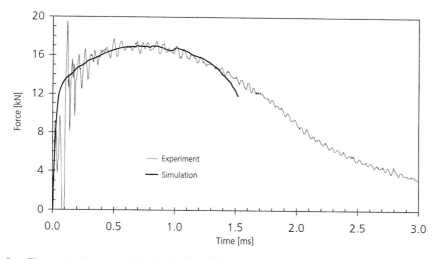

Fig. 6.   Charpy test, measured and calculated force versus time curves (upper shelf).

The three-dimensional model of the Charpy specimen was also used to simulate tests at lower temperatures. The force versus time records for seven specimens tested in the temperature range between –50°C and 50°C are given in Fig. 7, together with the numerically calculated curve with material parameters representative for a temperature of 0°C.

In view of the fact that all specimens considered here showed brittle fracture, an analysis of the maximum principal stress and its development with time (i.e. with crack extension) is of particular interest. This maximum stress can be then correlated to individual tests. Figure 8 shows the stress profiles ahead of the notch (crack) tip in the middle cross-section of the specimen at different times. One can see that the maximum principal stress (i.e. the opening stress at the notch root) slightly increases with time, and hence with ductile crack growth.

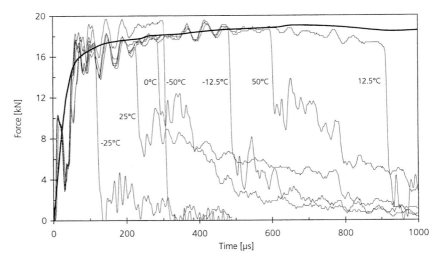

Fig. 7.   Force versus time records of Charpy tests at different temperatures (-50°C to 50°C), and results of numerical simulation (solid line).

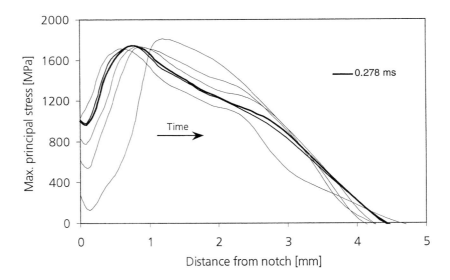

Fig. 8.   Development of the maximum principal stress with time.

In order to estimate the fracture toughness K_{Ic} at 0°C, a three-dimensional analysis of a (fictitious) compact tension specimen C(T)25 is performed using the same set of material parameters as was used for the Charpy specimen. For every load increment the stress intensity factor, K_I, is calculated and the distribution of maximum principal stress ahead of the crack tip is evaluated. As can be seen from Fig. 7 the calculated force versus time curve is in good agreement with the experimental curve for 0°C, especially at the onset of cleavage. Hence, the real stress distribution in the Charpy specimen at the time of failure is equal to the calculated stress distribution at this time. Figure 9 shows the corresponding distributions of the maximum principal stress for the Charpy specimen at the onset of cleavage (after 278 μs), and for the compact specimen at two load levels with stress maxima slightly below and above the maximum in the Charpy curve corresponding to stress intensity factors K_I of 71.3 and 88.8 MPa·m$^{1/2}$. Interpolation with respect to the maximum stress in the Charpy specimen yields K_I = 81.7 MPa·m$^{1/2}$. Under the assumption that cleavage failure in both the Charpy and the compact specimen occurs at the same local stress level one may regard this value as a reasonable estimate for the cleavage fracture toughness K_{Ic}.

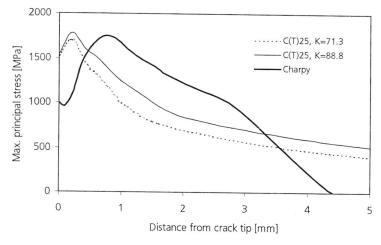

Fig. 9.   Maximum principal stress ahead of the crack tip and notch root, C(T)25 and Charpy specimens.

There are no real fracture mechanics tests available for this material condition, only a reference temperature RT_{NDT} has been determined. Figure 10 shows the fracture toughness reference curve according to ASME together with the "synthetic toughness" obtained from the simulation of the Charpy specimen. One can state that this value is in a reasonable relation with the reference curve.

Effects of stress tri-axiality, characteristic volumes etc. have been neglected in this study. The stress tri-axiality plays an important role in the transferability of results between different specimen types. An impression of the three-dimensional distribution of the tri-axiality (defined as ratio of the hydrostatic stress to the equivalent von Mises stress, σ_h/σ_e) in the Charpy specimen can be gained from Fig. 11. Here, the deformed model of a quarter of the specimen (due to symmetry) is presented. The maximum of the tri-axiality factor, h, is observed some distance ahead of the notch correlating with the position of the maximum principal stress.

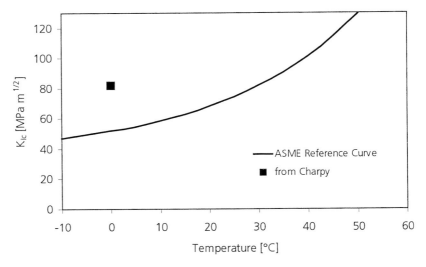

Fig. 10. Toughness estimate from Charpy and ASME reference curve.

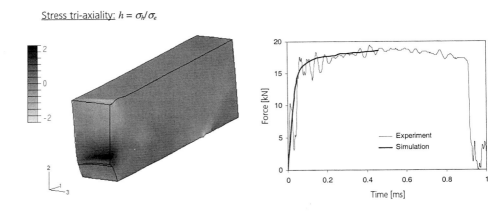

Fig. 11. Contour plot of the stress tri-axiality factor for a Charpy specimen.

Also of interest is the development of the strains in the notch root. The calculated opening strain at several integration points of elements next to the notch root is shown as a function of time in Fig. 12. One can conclude from this plot that the local strain rates are of the order of 1000/s - 1500/s. This means that the strain rate sensitivity of the material data must be properly modelled, as has been the case in this analysis.

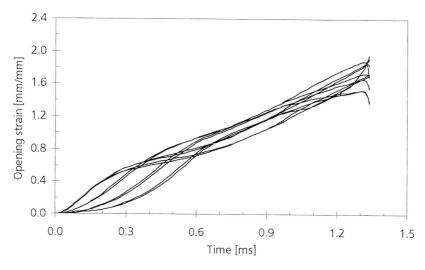

Fig. 12.   Strain history in the notch root (different curves correspond to different integration points of the finite-element model).

CONCLUSIONS

For about a century, the Charpy test has successfully been used as an acceptance test characterising the brittle-to-ductile transition temperature. Attempts to correlate Charpy energy and transition temperature with fracture toughness were moderately successful within certain classes of steel utilised in nuclear installations.

The appearance of numerical techniques like the finite element method and, in particular local approach concepts, together with the rapid increase in computer power have opened new possibilities for the evaluation of the test. However, while the treatment of ductile failure has brought quite promising results from the beginning, modelling of cleavage fracture still poses some difficulties to be resolved in future research.

This concerns not only the understanding of all relevant failure mechanisms, and their variation with temperature, loading rate and more, but also the interaction of ductile and cleavage failure, and the appropriate modelling of these effects. For example, state-of-the-art finite element techniques in combination with local approach concepts yield mesh dependent results. This intrinsically negative aspect offers so far the only viable chance to include characteristic distances in the models.

Unfortunately, the characteristic distance for ductile failure (assumed to correlate with the average spacing of large inclusions) is in general different from that for cleavage (assumed to correlate with grain size in many cases). Thus, the combined treatment of ductile and cleavage failure in one finite element model will always be a compromise, until new concepts to overcome this mesh dependency will be available.

Nevertheless, significant progress has been made in the last two decades, and, in this study it had even been possible to establish a reasonable estimation of the material fracture toughness. The positive interplay of experimental and numerical techniques will certainly help to resolve most of the open questions of today. Modelling and simulation may be seen as instruments to look into the specimen and disclose essential quantities, maybe not all of them at the same time, though.

ACKNOWLEGEMENT

The authors are grateful to EON Kernkraft for supporting part of this work.

REFERENCES

1. Charpy, G. (1901) *Mémoires et Comptes Rendus de la Société des Ingénieurs Civils de France,* 848-877.
2. Barsom, J. and Rolfe, S. (1970). In: *Impact Testing of Metals, ASTM STP 466,* American Society for Testing and Materials, Philadelphia, USA, 281-302.
3. Sailors, R. and Corton, H. (1972). In: *Fracture Toughness, Proceedings of the 1971 National Symposium on Fracture Mechanics, Part II, ASTM STP 514,* American Society for Testing and Materials, Philadelphia, USA, 164-191.
4. Marandet, B. and Sanz, G. (1977). In: *Flaw Growth and Fracture, ASTM STP 631,* American Society for Testing and Materials, Philadelphia, USA, 72-95.
5. Fearnehough, G. and Hoy, C. (1964) *Journal of the Iron and Steel Institute,* 912-920.
6. Wilshaw, T. and Pratt, P. (1966) *Journal of the Mechanics and Physics of Solids* **14**, 7-21.
7. Knott, J. (1967) *Journal of the Mechanics and Physics of Solids* **15**, 97-103.
8. Wullaert, R. (1970). In: *Impact Testing of Metals, ASTM STP 466,* American Society for Testing and Materials, Philadelphia, USA, 148-164.
9. Norris, D. M., Jr. (1979) *Engineering Fracture Mechanics* **11**, 261-274.
10. Schmitt, W., Sun, D.-Z., Böhme, W. and Nagel, G. (1994) *International Journal of Pressure Vessels and Piping* **59**, 21-29.
11. Gurson, A. (1977) *Journal of Engineering Materials and Technology,* 2-15.
12. Tvergaard, V. (1981) *International Journal of Fracture* **17**, 381-388.
13. Tvergaard, V. (1982) *International Journal of Fracture* **18**, 237-252.
14. Tvergaard, V. and Needleman, A. (1984) *International Journal of Fracture* **32**, 157-169.
15. Ritchie, R.O., Knott, J.F. and Rice, J.R. (1973) *Journal of the Mechanics and Physics of Solids* **21**, 395-410.
16. Beremin, F.M (1983) *Metallurgical Transactions* **14A**, 2277-2287.
17. Mudry, F. (1987) *Nucl. Engng. & Design* **105**, 65-76.
18. Bernauer, G., Brocks, W. and Schmitt, W. (1999) *Engineering Fracture Mechanics* **64**, 305-325.
19. Böhme, W., Bernauer, G. and Schmitt, W. (1999) *Nucl. Engng. & Design* **188**, 149-154.
20. Rossol, A. (1998). *Ph. D. Thesis,* Ecole Centrale des Arts et Manufactures, Chatenay-Malabry, France.
21. Rossol, A. (2001), private communication.
22. Tanguy, B. (2001). *Ph. D. Thesis,* Ecole des Mines de Paris, France.
23. Tanguy, B., Besson, J., Piques, R. and Pineau, A. (2001). In: *Charpy Centenary Conference CCC2001* (to be published).

From Charpy to Present Impact Testing
D. François and A. Pineau (Eds.)
© 2002 Elsevier Science Ltd. and ESIS. All rights reserved

EVOLUTION OF THE CHARPY-V TEST FROM A QUALITY CONTROL TEST TO A MATERIALS EVALUATION TOOL FOR STRUCTURAL INTEGRITY ASSESSMENT

KIM WALLIN, PEKKA NEVASMAA, TAPIO PLANMAN, MATTI VALO
VTT Manufacturing Technology
P.O. Box 1704, FIN-02044 VTT, Finland

ABSTRACT

Originally, the Charpy-V test was used mainly as a quality control test. However, after World War II, with the development of the transition temperature philosophy, the Charpy-V test evolved into a tool for material selection and toughness evaluation. With the development of fracture mechanics, further evolution of the interpretation of the Charpy-V test has made it a quantitative materials evaluation tool for fracture mechanics based structural integrity assessment. This presentation will give an outline of the evolution of the Charpy-V test, focussing on the latest developments regarding its use in structural integrity assessment.

KEYWORDS

Charpy-V, fracture toughness, brittle fracture, ductile fracture, correlations, material selection.

HISTORICAL PERSPECTIVE

Originally, the Charpy-V test was used mainly as a quality control test. However, after World War II, the analysis of the failures in welded merchant ships changed the nature of the Charpy-V test more to a design tool. Out of 4694 ships made during the war, 1289 experienced serious or potentially serious fractures. The ship plates where the crack had initiated showed generally a lower impact energy (KV) at the failure temperature, than the plates where the fracture had arrested. This led to the introduction of the transition temperature concept. It was found that generally, the plates with initiation had an impact energy below 10 ft-lb (13.6 J) and the ones where fracture ended had more than 20 ft-lb (27.1 J) [1,2]. A statistical analysis of the "initiation" plates gave as a result a 95 % upper bound value of 15 ft-lb (20.3 J). These investigations led to the even presently used transition criteria of 20/21 J and 27/28 J. In further studies, it was found that the 15 ft-lb transition temperature for the ship steels in question also correlated with the ESSO wide plate transition temperature [3]. The 10 ft-lb transition temperature, on the other hand was correlated to the explosion bulge test transition temperature which corresponds to NDT [4]. However, when more modern fully killed fine grained steels were examined, it was found that the correlations were not the same [3,4]. The Charpy-V energy absorption at the ESSO transition temperature or

NDT was higher for fully killed steels. In terms of the ESSO transition temperature, specifically the 30 ft-lb (40.6 J) energy level was found appropriate [3] (Fig. 1).

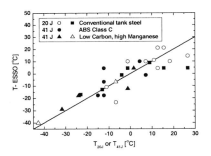

Fig. 1 Comparison of ESSO test transition temperature and Charpy-V transition temperatures for conventional and modern steels [3].

With continuing research, it was found that also the materials strength level required different transition criterion to be used. The idea was that irrespective of strength level, each material should have the same deformability. The parameter correlating with deformation, in the Charpy-V test is the lateral expansion (LE). Thus, a constant LE (15 mil = 0.381 mm) was considered as a good transition criteria [5]. In terms of energy, this lead to an increased impact energy demand for higher strength steels. Since LE is a result of plastic deformation, it depends on the strength properties of the material. Specifically, the relation between impact energy and LE is controlled by the materials ultimate strength, σ_U, (Fig. 2 [6,7]). For some reason, this relation has not become widely recognised. The energy requirement has been connected to the materials yield strength instead. This penalises unduly higher strength steels where the yield/ultimate ratio is larger.

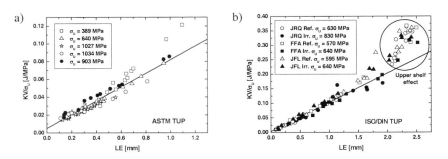

Fig. 2 Relation between Charpy-V impact energy and lateral expansion for a) ASTM tup [6] and b) ISO/DIN tup [7].

Another parameter that became popular for determining a transition temperature is the fracture appearance describing the percentage of ductile fracture (SA). A typical criterion is 50 % ductile fracture (FATT$_{50\%}$). The philosophy with this criterion is that at 50 % ductile fracture appearance, the crack arrest properties in the material are assumed to be sufficient to safeguard against fracture propagation in the structure. Also this parameter was correlated against the NDT [5]. Instead of fracture appearance, proportional impact energy could be used as well. Figure 3a shows the proportional correlation between impact energy and SA. The parameters are linearly related, but with an offset of approximately 5 %, since energy is absorbed, even when there is no ductile fracture. Because of the parameters close relation, also the correlation between the two transition temperatures is well defined (Fig. 3b). The small offset, causes the $TK_{50\%US}$.(50 % of upper shelf energy) to be about 8°C lower than $FATT_{50\%}$.

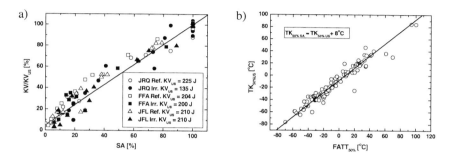

Fig. 3 Relation between a) Charpy-V impact energy and fracture appearance [7] and b) $TK_{50\%US}$.and $FATT_{50\%}$ [8].

The classical transition temperature criteria, were mostly concerned with determining a material condition which would make brittle fracture propagation difficult, regardless of structural details. Thus the transition criteria had to be fulfilled at the lowest service temperature of the structure. i.e. if the service temperature is -20°C, the selected transition criteria had to be fulfilled at -20°C. New problems arouse when the effect of plate thickness was added to the transition criteria. It was found, e.g. with drop weight tear tests (DWTT), that the transition temperature was also a function of plate thickness [9] (Fig. 4). This thickness effect led to an additional temperature correction to the transition criteria, i.e. the original idea of having a specific transition criterion for the lowest service temperature became muddled. First, the materials yield strength affects the transition criterion to be used and second, the plate thickness leads to an additional temperature adjustment to where the transition criteria must be fulfilled. Presently most workmanship standards, pressure vessel and ship codes are based on such a simple, yet obscure, methodology.

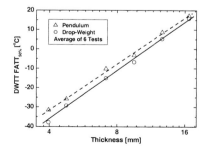

Fig. 4 Effect of specimen (plate) thickness on DWTT $FATT_{50\%}$ [9].

FRACTURE MECHANICAL PERSPECTIVE

The design criteria took a large step forward with the introduction of fracture mechanics. Useful parameters for the assessment of critical steel (metal) structures based on fracture mechanics are parameters, which are capable of describing a component's resistance against flaws. Such parameters are e.g. the fracture toughness K_{Ic} (K_{Jc}) , the ductile initiation toughness J_{Ic}, the ductile tearing resistance, J-R, and the crack arrest toughness, K_{Ia}. In case of steels K_{Ic} usually describes the materials resistance against brittle cleavage type fracture, but for e.g. aluminium alloys and some extra high strength steels it may also correspond to ductile initiation toughness.

Since the Charpy-V test does not provide a direct measurement of fracture toughness some kind of correlation must be used. Numerous different empirical correlations relating impact energy to fracture toughness have been determined for a variety of materials, over the past years [10-15]. Finding an empirical correlation that would be universally applicable has proven to be quite difficult. Even though both tests describe the materials fracture behaviour, they have many important differences. Due to the differences in the tests, empirical correlations are usually very case dependent. It is also difficult to decide which correlation to use in a given case.

The British pressure vessel standard, BS5500 App. D, introduced in 1976, was still quite crude. It is not based on a real fracture mechanical model. Instead, it is based on empirical correlations between Charpy-V impact tests and wide plate tests [16].

A major development was made when Sanz [17] developed the new fracture mechanics based brittle fracture Charpy-V transition criterion for the AFNOR standard [18]. Sanz found that the fracture toughness temperature dependence was quite material insensitive and thus enabled a general correlation between the K_{IC} 100 MPa$\sqrt{m}$ and TK_{28J} transition temperatures. The method applies linear elastic fracture mechanics and uses an empirical plate thickness correction which implicitly contains also the assumed flaw size information. Additionally, the model also includes a loading rate correction in the form of a strain rate related temperature shift. The Sanz model was subsequently modified by Sandström [19]. The two models use different CVN-K_{Ic} correlations and treat the empirical section thickness correction differently, but use the same temperature and strain rate dependence for the fracture toughness and treat all stresses as tensile stresses. Sandström furthermore, limits himself to a quarter thickness deep surface crack with an undefined width. The biggest difference in the models, lies in the treatment of the empirical thickness correction. Sandström connects the degree of thickness correction to the stress level, so that the lower the stress level, the smaller the thickness correction. Sandström's definition of crack size leads to that the thickness correction should be applied only at stress levels $\sigma/\sigma_y > 0.71$. The Sandström model forms the basis of the present Swedish Pressure Vessel Code. Subsequently, Wallin [8,20] re-assessed the Sanz Charpy-V - fracture toughness correlation using the new Master Curve method [21], which accounts for the intrinsic statistical size effects in fracture toughness (description given in state of the art section). This new correlation, and size adjustment, forms the basis of the new EUROCODE 3, annex C brittle fracture assessment. It is also included in the new BS 7910 fracture assessment standard and forms the default level of fracture toughness estimation in the European SINTAP fracture assessment procedure [22]. All of these new more sophisticated methods apply elastic plastic fracture mechanics and enable an assessment with respect to fracture initiation, contrary to the simple methods which only provide assessment against fracture propagation.

STATE OF THE ART

The SINTAP method represents the present state of the art in structural integrity assessment. An imperative part of the method is the determination of the materials fracture toughness. It is clear that one cannot simply correlate the impact energy directly with the fracture toughness. One must first clarify which parameters are realistic to correlate. In order to do this the basic features of each test must be examined separately to see which features correspond to the same physical event. This way it is possible to derive comparatively simple, adequately accurate, general correlations between parameters determined from the Charpy-V impact test and brittle fracture initiation, ductile fracture initiation, tearing resistance and even crack arrest toughness (from instrumented Charpy-V test). Examples of this are presented next.

Brittle Fracture Initiation

The Master Curve method enables a complete characterisation of a materials brittle fracture toughness based on only a few small size specimens. The method is based on a more than 15-year research at VTT Manufacturing Technology and has led, e.g., to the ASTM standard E1921, the first standard that accounts for the statistical specimen size effect and variability in brittle fracture toughness. The Master Curve method has been shown to be applicable for practically all steels with a body-centred cubic lattice structure, generally identified as ferritic steels. The method combines a theoretical description of the scatter, a statistical size effect and an empirically found temperature dependence of fracture toughness (Fig. 5). The fracture toughness in the brittle fracture regime is thus described with only one parameter, the transition temperature T_0.

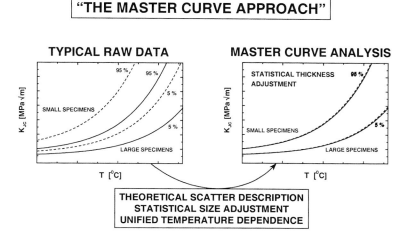

Fig. 5 Basic principle of the Master Curve fracture toughness description.

The T_0 transition temperature has successfully been correlated to the Charpy-V 28 J transition temperature [8, 20]. The correlation is shown in Fig. 6 a-d. Besides showing the correlation, Fig. 6 also indirectly verifies some of the assumptions of the Master Curve method. It verifies the size adjustment since the correlation is unaffected by specimen size (Fig. 6 a and b) and it verifies the validity of the elastic plastic fracture toughness since the correlation is unaffected by parameter type (Fig. 6 a and c). As mentioned earlier, the correlation has been implemented into all major fracture mechanics based assessment methods.

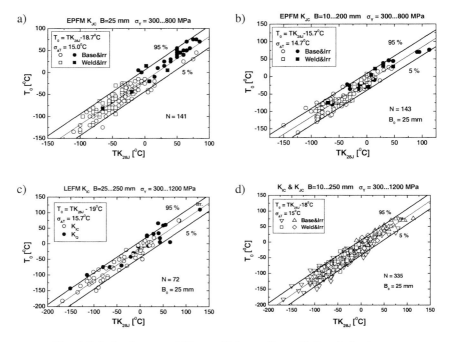

Fig. 6 Relation between TK_{28J} and Master Curve T_0 for a) elastic plastic fracture toughness from 25 mm thick specimens, b) elastic plastic fracture toughness from other than 25 mm thick specimens, c) linear elastic fracture toughness and d) combination of all results. (Irr. stands for irradiated.)

The TK_{28J} - T_0 correlation does have a few restrictions. Since it is based upon cleavage fracture, the correlation should not be used for steels with upper shelf energies below 70 J, where the 28 J energy level contain more than 20 % ductile fracture appearance, or where the brittle fracture mode is something else than cleavage fracture (eg. grain boundary fracture, low energy tear etc.). The correlation should neither be used for strongly inhomogeneous materials which may show a so called pop-in behavior in the fracture toughness test [8]. In such cases it is impossible to determine the fracture toughness from the Charpy-V test and therefore actual fracture toughness testing is required. Normally these restrictions are not an obstacle for the use of the correlation to determine the lowest allowable service temperature.

Figure 7 [23] gives an example of the application of the correlation for extra high strength steels. The test geometries consisted of ⊔- and ☐-profiles tested in bending. The ⊔-profiles contained two edge cracks, one on each flange, and the ☐-profiles contained an elliptic surface flaw on the upper web, or a through thickness crack. In Figs. 7 b-d the estimated temperatures T_{calc} (based upon the fracture load), for all tests showing brittle fracture, are compared with the actual test temperatures T_{meas}. A total of 68 tests showed brittle fracture. Fig. 7 b is a "best" estimate corresponding to 50 % failure probability and the mean Charpy-V - K_{IC} correlation (50 % confidence level). Figs. 7 c and 7 d correspond to a 85 % confidence level with respect to the correlation and failure probabilities of 20 % and 5 % respectively.

For the best estimate, 41 % of the results are non-conservative. The corresponding percentages are, for the other cases, 9 % and 3 %. Based upon a Monte Carlo simulation the theoretical expectation limits for non-conservative estimates were calculated, assuming all parts of the methodology to be valid. For the best estimate the percentage of non-conservative results should be, with a 50 % probability between 47 % to 56 %. The corresponding percentages are for the other cases 9 % to 15 % and 1 % to 4 %. The percentages of non-conservative estimates comply very well with the theoretical expectation values. Overall, the predictions are accurate or conservative

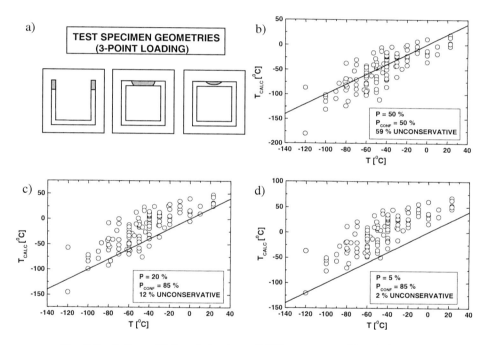

Fig. 7 Prediction of failure behaviour of different test profiles a), for best estimate b), estimate for non-critical case c) and estimate for critical case, compared to test results for extra high strength steels [23].

Crack Arrest

The mechanism of brittle crack arrest differs from that of initiation. Thus the scatter and size effects are not the same as those found for brittle fracture initiation. Mechanistically, arrest occurs when the local crack driving force at the crack tip decreases below the local arrest toughness over a sufficiently large portion of the crack front. A single local arrest is not sufficient to arrest the whole crack front, i.e. the scatter is more a function of the mean properties of the matrix (and not the local). Therefore the scatter is less than for initiation and there are no statistical size effects in the case of crack arrest. It has been shown that the temperature dependence of crack arrest toughness is the same as for brittle initiation toughness [24]. The main difference is a material dependent temperature shift between the two properties [25]. This similarity to the initiation behaviour, in principle enables a correlation between crack arrest toughness and the Charpy-V test. However, the parameters normally determined from the test produce rather poor correlations with K_{Ia}. Depending on which parameter is chosen, different trends are seen. E.g. in the case of TK_{41J}, yield strength does not affect the correlation, but a low upper shelf energy does (Fig. 8). For LE, also the yield strength will affect the correlation. In the case of FATT, the upper shelf energy has less effect, but the yield strength has an effect.

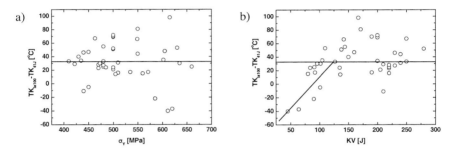

Fig. 8 Effect of yield strength a) and upper shelf energy b) on the relation between TK_{Ia100} and TK_{41J} [24].

The best information regarding crack arrest can be obtained from the instrumented Charpy-V impact test in terms of the 4 kN crack arrest load temperature (Fig. 9 [25]). This is a parameter that physically corresponds to an actual crack arrest event and provides therefore a true measure of the materials crack arrest properties. The conventional parameters are reacting to several other factors than crack arrest and therefore, they can never be accurately correlated to crack arrest on a general basis.

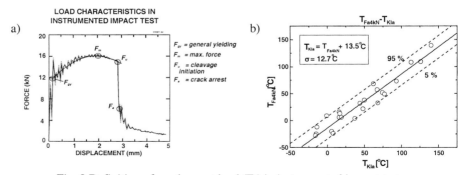

Fig. 9 Definition of crack arrest load (F_a) in instrumented impact test a) and correlation between 4 kN arrest load temperature and TK_{Ia100} b) [25].

Ductile Fracture

The Charpy-V notch test provides information about the energy needed to fracture a small specimen in half. On the upper shelf this energy relates to ductile fracture resistance and it is possible to correlate it to the J-R -curve. Recently, 112 multi-specimen J-R -curves from a wide variety of materials were analyzed and a simple power law based description of the J-R -curves was correlated to the CVN_{US} energy (Fig. 10 [26]). This new correlation corresponds essentially to a 5 % lower bound and conforms well with the earlier correlations, regardless of the definition of the ductile fracture toughness parameter. The correlation gives a conservative tearing resistance estimate in terms of the J-integral as follows:

$$J = J_{1mm} \cdot \Delta a^{m} \dots \left[kJ/m^{2}, mm\right] \tag{1}$$

where

$$J_{1mm} = 0.53 \cdot CVN_{US}^{1.28} \cdot \exp\left(-\frac{T-20}{400}\right) \dots \left[kJ/m^{2}, J, °C\right] \tag{2}$$

and

$$m = 0.133 \cdot CVN_{US}^{0.256} \cdot \exp\left(-\frac{T-20}{2000}\right) - \frac{\sigma_{Y}}{4664} + 0.03 \dots \left[J, °C, MPa\right] \tag{3}$$

With the above expressions, practically all previous ductile fracture CVN-"K_{IC}" correlations can be explained [26]. The expressions can be used either to estimate J_{IC} from equation (4) or to estimate the J-integral at any amount of ductile tearing between 0...6 mm for temperatures lower than 300°C.

$$\frac{J_{IC}}{2 \cdot \sigma_{f}} + 0.2\,mm - \left(\frac{J_{IC}}{J_{1mm}}\right)^{1/m} = 0 \tag{4}$$

where the flow stress can be approximated by:

$$\sigma_{f} \approx \sigma_{Y} \cdot \left(1 + \left[\frac{150\,MPa}{\sigma_{Y}}\right]^{2}\right) \tag{5}$$

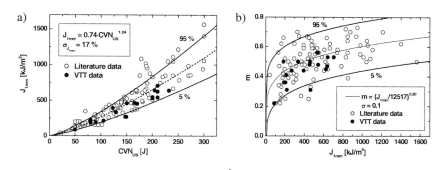

Fig. 10 Relation between CVN_{US} and the J-integral value at 1 mm crack growth a) and relation between J-R curve shape (described by power m) and the J-integral value at 1 mm crack growth b) [26].

Treatment of Sub-size Specimens

When the plate thickness is less than 10 mm, testing with standard sized Charpy-V notch specimens is impossible. In such cases the testing must be based on subsized specimens. The difficulty lies in extrapolating the result from the subsized specimen to correspond to the result from a standard sized specimen. Basically two different methodologies can be used. The extrapolation can be based either directly upon the measured parameter, e.g. impact energy KV or on some transition temperature criterion.

The presently used simple codes apply the direct extrapolation of the impact energy. Specifically, for a 5x10 mm^2 specimen, normally the energy is multiplied by 1.5 to make it correspond to a full size specimen. The problem with the direct extrapolation lies in the fact that the specimen thickness yields different effects in different regions of the transition (Fig. 11 [8]). On the lower shelf subsized specimens yield proportionally higher impact energies as compared to standard size specimens. They may even produce higher absolute energies than a full size specimen. On the upper shelf the behavior is reversed so that subsized specimens yield either proportionally equal or even lower impact energies than standard sized specimens [27-29]. The reason for this is that the different fracture micromechanisms yield different specimens thickness effects. In the transition region there is a competition between ductile and brittle fracture micromechanisms thus yielding a very complex combined thickness effect. This effectively invalidates the method of direct extrapolation which is used today. A much more reliable extrapolation of the brittle fracture behaviour is obtained by using a transition temperature criterion (Fig. 12 a [30]). For the upper shelf energy a separate correction, which accounts for the transition to shear fracture with decreasing specimen thickness, has also recently been developed (Fig. 12 b [30]). Thus sub-sized specimens can be used both to estimate brittle fracture initiation as well as ductile tearing.

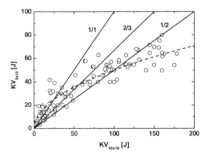

Fig. 11 Dependence between impact energies measured from full- and sub-size CVN specimens.

BEYOND STATE OF THE ART

Even though the correlations presented here take into consideration the physical aspects of the fracture parameters being correlated, they are still empirical in nature. The next generation of CVN correlations will undoubtedly take the step forward to a fully theoretical interpretation of the Charpy-V test. Already, efforts are undergoing to model the Charpy-V impact energy with the help of the French local approach [31] and other similar micromechanism based models. Eventually, also fracture assessment may change so that conventional fracture mechanical parameters like K_{IC} and J may become obsolete and only material parameters used in the micromechanical models are needed. Then, the Charpy-V test may become a true materials evaluation tool.

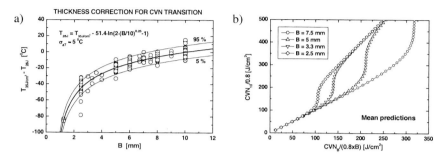

Fig. 12 The effect of specimen thickness on CVN 35 J/cm^2 transition temperature a) and upper shelf energy b) [30].

SUMMARY AND CONCLUSIONS

Originally, the Charpy-V test was used mainly as a quality control test. However, after World War II, the analysis of the failures in welded merchant ships changed the nature of the Charpy-V test more to a design tool. The ship plates where the crack had initiated showed generally a lower impact energy (KV) at the failure temperature, than the plates where the fracture had arrested. This led to the introduction of the transition temperature concept. The classical transition temperature criteria, were mostly concerned with determining a material condition which would make brittle fracture propagation difficult, regardless of structural details. Thus the transition criteria had to be fulfilled at the lowest service temperature of the structure. Problems arouse when the effect of plate thickness was added to the transition criteria. This led to an additional temperature correction to the transition criteria, i.e. the original idea of having a specific transition criterion for the lowest service temperature became muddled. First, the materials yield strength affects the transition criterion to be used and second, the plate thickness leads to an additional temperature adjustment to where the transition criteria must be fulfilled. Presently most workmanship standards, pressure vessel and ship codes are based on such a simple, yet obscure, methodology.

The SINTAP method represents the present state of the art in structural integrity assessment. An imperative part of the method is the determination of the materials fracture toughness. By analysing the Charpy-V test on a physical basis, it has been possible to derive comparatively simple, adequately accurate, general correlations between parameters determined from the Charpy-V impact test and brittle fracture initiation, ductile fracture initiation, tearing resistance and even crack arrest toughness (from instrumented Charpy-V test). Examples of this have been presented.

The next generation of CVN correlations will undoubtedly take the step forward to a fully theoretical interpretation of the Charpy-V test. Then, the Charpy-V test may become a true materials evaluation tool.

ACKNOWLEDGEMENTS

This work is a part of the Structural Integrity Project (STIN), belonging to the Finnish Research Programme on Nuclear Power Plant Safety (FINNUS), performed at VTT Manufacturing Technology and financed by the Ministry of Trade and Industry in Finland, the Technical Research Centre of Finland (VTT) and the Radiation and Nuclear Safety Authority (STUK).

REFERENCES

1. Williams, M.L. and Ellinger, G.A. (1953). *Welding Journal Research Supplement* **32**, 498-s.
2. Williams, M.L. (1954). *ASTM STP 158*, pp. 11-44.
3. Feely, F.J., Northup, M.S., and Kleppe, M.G. (1955). *Welding Journal Research Supplement* **34**, 596-s.
4. Puzak, P.P., Eschbacher, E.W. and Pellini, W.S. (1952). *Welding Journal Research Supplement* **31**, 561-s.
5. Gross, J.H. (1960). *Welding Journal Research Supplement* **39**, 59-s.
6. Gross, J.H. and Stout, R.D. (1958) *Welding Journal Research Supplement* **37**, 151-s.
7. Wallin, K., Valo, M. (1993). Unpublished data.
8. Wallin, K. (1986). *VTT Research Reports 428*. (In Finnish).
9. Norris, E.B. and Wylie, R.D. (1970). *ASTM STP 466*, pp. 192-223.
10. Roberts, R. and Newton, C. (1981). *Welding Research Council Bulletin 265*.
11. Barsom, J.M. and Rolfe, S.T. (1979). *ASTM STP 466*, pp. 281-302.
12. Sovak, J.F. (1982). *JTEVA*, **10**, 102.
13. Thorby, P.N. and Ferguson, W.G. (1976). *Mat. Sci. Eng.* **22**, 177.
14. Sailors, R.H. and Corten, H.T. (1972). *ASTM STP 514*, pp. 164-191.
15. Marandet, B. and Sanz, G. (1977). *ASTM STP 631*, pp. 72-95.
16. Dawes, M.G. and Denys, R. (1984). *Int. J. Pres. Ves. & Piping* **15**, 161.
17. Sanz, G. (1980). *Revue de Métallurgie* **77**, 621. (In French)
18. AFNOR NF A 36-010, May 1980.
19. Sandström, R. (1987). *Scand. J. Metallurgy,* **16**, 242.
20. Wallin, K. (1989). In: *Innovative Approaches to Irradiation Damage and Fracture Analysis*, pp.93-100, Marriott, D.L., Mager, T.R. and Bamford, W.H. (Eds). PVP-Vol.170, The American Society of Mechanical Engineers.
21. Wallin, K. (1999). *Int. J. Materials & Product Technology,* **14**, 432.
22. SINTAP - Structural Integrity Assessment Procedures for European Industry - Final Procedure. (1999). Contract No BRPR-CT95-0024, Project No. BE95-1426.
23. Wallin, K. (1994). *Jernkontorets Forskning,* Serie D 735.
24. Wallin, K. (2001). *ASTM STP 1406*. In press.
25. Wallin, K., Rintamaa, R. and Nagel, G. (2201). *Nuclear Engng and Design,* **206**, 185.
26. Wallin, K. (2001). *FFEMS*. In press.
27. Towers, O.L. (1986). *Metal Construction,* **18**, 171R.
28. Towers, O.L. (1986). *Metal Construction,* **18**, 254R.
29. Towers, O.L. (1986). *Metal Construction,* **18**, 319R.
30. Wallin, K. *IJPVP*. To be published.
31. Rossoll, A. (1998). Détermination de la Ténacité d'un Acier Faiblement Allié á Partir de L'essai Charpy Instrumenté. Thése, École Centrale Paris, 98-43.

Micromechanisms

From Charpy to Present Impact Testing
D. François and A. Pineau (Eds.)

DETERMINATION OF DUCTILE CRACK INITIATION BY MAGNETIC EMISSION AND POTENTIAL DROP TECHNIQUES USING PRE-CRACKED CHARPY SPECIMENS

Z. RADAKOVIĆ, A. SEDMAK, Faculty of Mechanical Engineering, Belgrade
Gy. B. LENKEY, Bay Zoltán Institute for Logistics and Production Systems, Miskolc
V. GRABULOV, Military Technical Institute, Belgrade

ABSTRACT

Magnetic emission (ME) and potential drop (PD) techniques were used for instrumented Charpy impact testing in order to determine critical crack initiation properties of standard pre-cracked three-point bending specimens at room temperature. Results for high strength low-alloyed steel specimens, with ductile properties, were compared for determination of critical fracture mechanics parameters upon the onset of ductile crack growth.

In the case of ductile, or mixed ductile/cleavage fracture at temperatures well above nil-ductile, or at lower impact energies, it is sometimes difficult to distinguish crack initiation from ME signal, while the integrated magnetic emission signal (MF) sometimes has a slower changing rate. Results were also obtained by applying the potential drop technique with single specimen HSLA steels and by evaluating the R-curve. Initiation of stable crack growth may also be depicted from local minimum (or maximum) of potential drop value and it may not give clear local extreme values when conditions of fracture change from brittle to ductile. Alternatively, if the change of slope in the PD-t diagram can be used to evaluate critical crack behaviour, compared to similar changes of slope in the MF-t diagram, it may provide a better understanding of both.

Keywords: fracture mechanics, impact testing, ductile crack growth, magnetic emission, potential drop, dynamic resistance curve.

INTRODUCTION

In an urge to develop appropriate material compositions that would at least prevent steel structures from undergoing cleavage fracture, particularly at lower temperatures, it is not unusual to deal with HSLA steels having high ductile properties, even when moderately increasing the strength level. Dynamic loading is more critical for a structure than static, and determination of dynamic fracture mechanics properties of materials is necessary. Various type of fracture is evident from force-time records of instrumented impact tests. The HSLA steel behaviour is tested by applying dynamic loads at room temperature, and impact rates by using initial energy levels in the range E_o=26; 30; 40; 45; 50; 60; 70 J, enabling impact loading rates v_o=1.69; 1.79; 1.82; 2.09; 2;22; 2.33; 2.56; 2.75 m/s. The introduced fatigue cracks produced on standard three-point bending specimens that also influence the fracture toughness are within the range: a/W=0.47÷0.57.

One of the most widely used techniques for this purpose is instrumented impact testing. In this case the instrumentation includes combined magnetic emission (ME) technique and potential drop technique. The ME technique is used to determine initiation of crack propagation and is applied for instrumented impact testing of certain types of steels [1].

The potential drop method (PD) has been successfully applied for the same purpose by recording the change in electrical resistance measured by DC or AC –drop in electric potential (ΔE) near the crack tip [2]. Results were also obtained by applying this technique on a single specimen with a method for evaluating the dynamic R-curve on instrumented Charpy pendulum with HSLA steels [3]. Stable crack initiation in this case is also depicted from the local minimum (or maximum) of the potential drop value and, as in the case with the ME technique, this may not give clear local extreme values when fracture is ductile.

Therefore, these two techniques were implemented in a Charpy instrumentation that gave independent and simultaneous recordings of ME and PD signals and the results were analyzed in order to check their validity.

EXPERIMENT AND RESULTS

Micro-alloyed steels have a wide range of use in metal structures in general. The tested ferrite-pearlite steel is micro-alloyed with Nb and Ti and is obtained by controlled rolling and accelerated cooling. The yield stress is 411 MPa, and the material is very ductile at lower temperatures, with a wide brittle-to-ductile transition range. The as-received chemical composition (in wt. %) is shown in Table 1.

Table 1. Chemical composition in weight percent

C	Si	Mn	P	S	Al	Cu	Cr	Ni	Mo	Nb	Ti
0.08	0.20	1.12	0.027	0.011	0.033	0.065	0.027	0.019	0.010	0.026	0.017

Upper shelf values for ductile fracture at room temperature are evident from load-time or load-displacement data. All tests are performed at room temperature. The standard V-notched Charpy specimens were cut from a 12 mm plate perpendicular to rolling direction, and pre-cracked by high frequency fatigue in programmed sequence in order to avoid large-scale plastic deformation. Owing to experience, specimens were then prepared in the manner for applying the potential drop technique [4]. In Fig. 1, the required instrumentation is shown connected to the specimen, positioned on the anvil of the Charpy machine. Thin steel-wire, Ni-wire, or Ni-Cr-wire connections for PD signal output were either resistance-spot-welded, or soldered to the specimen at positions in the vicinity of notch opening (locations A, Fig. 1). Massive input Cu-wires from the DC power source were connected to the specimens by bolts (position III on Fig. 1). The power source input DC electric current of 30 A was selected as nominal for producing output PD values that could be distinguished, ranging from several to at least 10 mV. In order to produce stronger output signals, some specimens required input signals as high as 40 A, even 50 A, being the limit, since higher values produce electrically induced heat. Locally induced, this heat might affect pronounced ductility behaviour by additional softening of the material, predominantly within the fracture-processing zone ahead of the crack, since electric currents must close the circuit, passing through the ligament. Other limiting effects contribute from massive wire connections, e.g. inertial characteristics of specimens are influenced, and this problem is yet to be solved. As a consequence, 'interrupted' fracture occurs at higher strain rates. During impact, this is caused by mutual contact and/or collision of wire-connections with inclined anvil wall surfaces, appearing much later after stable crack initiation, even after the maximal force (F_m), and so these unwanted effects are not taken into consideration. These effects are evident from the load–time, and MF–time or PD–time diagrams, Fig. 2, and in the shown example appear at approximately 3.5 ms.

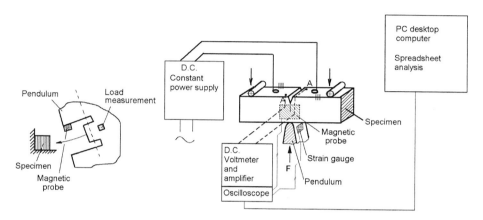

Fig 1. The Charpy instrumentation

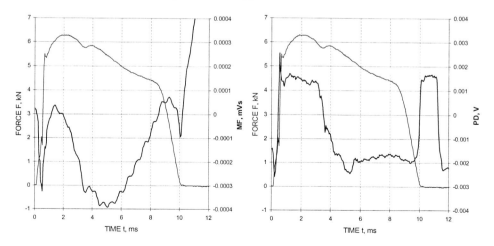

Fig. 2. F(t) diagrams with MF and PD signals for specimen C12
(Applied energy E_o=50 J; a_o/W=0.48; PD input 50 A; insulated specimen)

Changes in the external magnetic field are recorded in the vicinity of the propagating crack, through the magnetic emission probe, Fig. 1. The TEKTRONIX TDS 420A data acquisition equipment is connected to a DC amplifier and voltage supply. The HP transient recorder with an interior circuit amplifier is tied to the remaining channel on the oscilloscope. Both magnetic and electric potential drop signals are monitored and recorded in real sampling time intervals of 2, 4, 10 and 40 µs. All data is handled by spreadsheet procedures, including the evaluation of absorbed energy (U) and the fracture resistance critical dynamic J-integral.

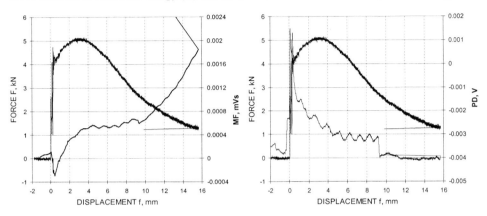

Fig. 3. F(t) diagrams with MF and PD signals for specimen A6
(Applied energy E_o=60 J; a_o/W=0.54; PD input 50 A; grounding, tape insulation inside of anvil; soldered thin NiCr-wire contacts; coupling impedance 50 Ω)

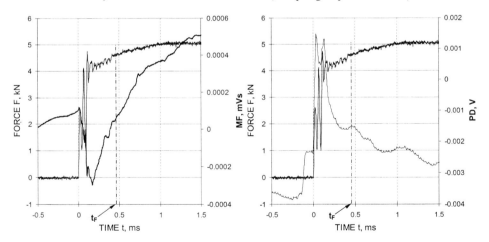

Fig. 4. F(t) diagrams with MF and PD signals for specimen A6, shown time-to-fracture (t_F), (measured and calculated data: pre-crack length a_o=5.38 mm; crack extension Δa=3.99 mm; impact load rate v_o=2.56 ms^{-1}; maximum impact load F_{max}=5.14 kN; stable crack initiation times (time-to-fracture), and released energies, determined from ME and PD tests, in respect: $t_{i(ME)}$=460 µs, $t_{i(PD)}$=458 µs, $U_{(ME)}$=4.39 J, $U_{(PD)}$=4.36 J; dynamic J-integral values calculated from ME and PD tests: J_{cm}^{d}=190.1 kJm^{-2}, J_{cpd}^{d}=189.1 kJm^{-2})

Fracture resistance is determined from the J-integral at the initiation of stable crack growth under dynamic conditions (J_I^d), and is determined from the most appropriate formula, for single or multiple specimen testing:

$$J_I^d = \frac{\eta U}{B_n(W - a_o)},$$

(1)

where $\eta=2$ for single edge notch bend specimens, and $B_n=B$ is the non-sidegrooved specimen thickness. The released energy U, in the upper formula, is the area under the load–displacement curve F(t)-f(t) and is integrated according to:

$$U_i = \int_0^{f_c} F(f)df$$

(2)

The displacement at stable crack growth initiation $f_c(t=t_i)$ is determined at a time-to-stable crack initiation interval (t_i) or by the time-to-fracture interval (t_F), whose determination mostly draws the attention of many researchers. It is very difficult to assess the point of crack initiation, especially in the case of complete ductile fracture, when recorded diagrams, ME(t) and PD(t), do not always show clear discontinuity. In these circumstances, it is necessary to analyze and compare all other diagrams as well: F(t), integrated-ME(t), or MF(t), or several multi-point linear or polynomial PD(t)-trendlines. Some authors have successfully used other methods, [6], i.e. the Double Displacement Ratio (DDR)–the ratio of crack opening displacement vs. specimen displacement, to indicate the onset of ductile crack initiation and growth, and evaluate critical J_i^d-values.

Results of the tests performed here are shown in Figs. 5 and 6 with a high level of similarity between ME and PD signals, and indicate a satisfying agreement on the evaluation of ductile crack initiation for this type of ductile steel.

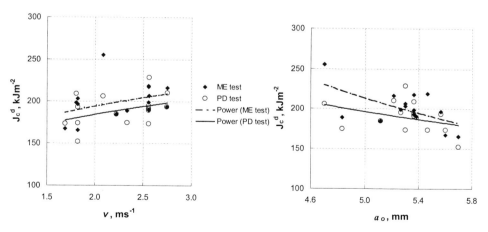

Fig. 5. J_c^d–v dependence   Fig. 6. J_c^d–a_o dependence

Preliminary stretch zone measurements indicate that for some specimens, not totally cracked, the stretch zone width (SZW) values measured at three locations, with three local measurements, give a critical mean value of $SWZ_i=120$ µm, and according to the DVM

Merkblätter procedure 002 (1987), and by assuming plane strain conditions, the characteristic equation for the critical J-integral can be described in the form:

$$J_i^d = 1692 \cdot SZW_i \ (kJm^{-2}),$$ (3)

where the value SZW_i is given in (mm).

According to this, the fracture resistance J-integral at the onset of stable crack growth is $J_i^d = 203$ kJm^{-2}, and this value agrees very well upon critical dynamic J-integral values calculated from ME and PD tests, in respect: $J_{cme}^d = 190.1$ kJm^{-2}, $J_{cpd}^d = 189.1$ kJm^{-2}, as for specimen A6 (specimen data are given in the Fig. 4 caption). But even though this result may seem in very good agreement with data calculated by means of ME and PD experiments, it should be accepted with reserve, since it is only a preliminary result, and presumably large scatter is sure to be expected.

The R-curve is constructed and shown in Fig. 7, together with fracture resistance data. The figure also shows the corrected fracture resistance J-integral allowing for crack growth, as would be calculated according to test procedures [8,9], and the equations describing the fitted curves, from the offset power law.

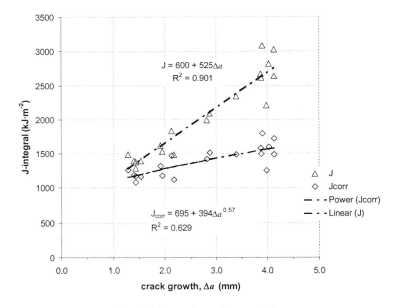

Fig. 7. J-integral–crack growth Δa.

DISCUSSION

Analysis of the fractured surface shows portions of 'slant' and 'square' type surfaces, indicating a fracture profile typical of the both plane stress and plane strain modes. This is regularly noticed when using non-side grooved specimens for this type of steel.

It is noticed that by fitting the dynamic R-curve (Fig. 7) by the equation of the general form: $J = A + C \cdot \Delta a^D$, where A, C and D are constants, results in a linear behaviour.

It is interesting to notice that if the fracture resistance determined from J-integral calculation allowing for crack growth is corrected according to certain test procedures [8,9] given for quasi-static conditions, using the formula:

$$J = J_o \left\{ 1 - \frac{(0.75\eta - 1)\Delta a}{(W - a_o)} \right\},$$ (4)

where errors in the J-values should be negligible only for crack growth less than $0.1(W\text{-}a_o)$, the corrected J-integral values become sufficiently lower, from 14.9% to 43.7% lower than if calculated from Eq.(1). All the crack growth values are within the range $\Delta a = 2.28 \div 4.13$ mm, and relative differences between J and J_o, below 40%, are in 12 of the total 19 specimens. In these cases the initial impact energies were below 60 J, and it is only for these cases that the fractured surface did not extend over the entire net surface area. However, in the performed dynamic tests, all fractured surfaces were generally ductile, where the ratio of elastic/plastic energy was very small ($J_{el} < 0.03 \cdot J_{pl}$).

The dynamic fracture toughness of the material is affected by strain rate, and for ductile materials, the fracture mechanism is controlled by the strain field. This may increase or decrease, depending on the loading rate [4,5]. The presence of the corresponding ductile fracture model here is particularly sensitive to the absolute size and spacing of the various populations of microstructural particles. For this type of ductile steel, it is possible that the volume-fraction of carbide particles is much less than that of oxides, and a larger degree of crack-tip deformation is required to increase crack-tip radii and enclose a sufficient number of the oxide particles, within the logarithmic spiral field of large plastic-strain and high mean-normal stress, to form the fracture surface [7]. Preliminary SEM fractographic analyses show that stretch zone widths have values that range from as low as 20 μm to as high as 130 μm.

CONCLUSIONS

Results shown in Figs. 5 and 6 indicate an increasing tendency of the fracture resistance dynamic J-integral (J_c^d) with impact load rate (v), and a decreasing tendency for larger initial cracks (a_o). Fitted power curves $J = f(v^x)$, $J = f(a_o^x)$, are very close, indicating good agreement between ME and PD techniques on evaluation of ductile crack growth initiation.

The ME power curve is constantly above the PD power curve indicating slightly higher J-integral. This is true in the average, since PD evaluated time-to-fracture (t_i) is usually shorter than its ME equivalent. The released energies $U(t)$ are thus smaller, and also the dynamic J-integral values, Eqs. (1) and (2). Multiple peaks in $F(t)$-ME(t) and $F(t)$-PD(t) are related to the complex development of crack initiation and propagation. In most of the tested cases, ME peaks follow PD peaks by a small delay, and both peaks usually precede $F(t)$ peaks. The delay is probably related to specimen–strain gauge, or specimen–probe interaction, or hysteresis effects in the electric and magnetic properties of the tested material. For impact energy $E_o = 60$ J or higher, the crack extension value (Δa) reaches the maximum ($a/W \geq 0.9$). Crack extension is very large, and the applied formula (Eq. 1) may be considered as an approximation, since the shift from plane stress state to plane strain becomes pronounced. If the criterion for fracture resistance J, allowing extensive crack growth, is corrected (Eq. 4) and used for approximations in dynamic loading conditions, the corrected J-integral values are reduced by 30% and even less.

According to regression analysis, the characteristic fracture resistance dynamic R-curve is linear for this type of HSLA steel, having a high R square value of 0.901. Ductile material behaviour is maintained by strain-rate hardening.

ACKNOWLEDGEMENTS

The authors gratefully acknowledge the support of the OTKA T 030057 project.

REFERENCES

1. Gy.B.-Lenkey, S.R. Winkler (1997), On the Applicability of the Magnetic Emission Technique for the Determination of Ductile Crack Initiation in Impact Tests, Fatigue and Fracture of Engineering Materials and Structures, Vol 20, No 2, p.143-150.
2. MacGillivray, H.J. and Turner, C.E. (1989) A Comparison of Dynamic R-Curve Methods. Fourth International Conference on the Mechanical Properties of Materials at High Rates of Strain, Oxford.
3. Grabulov, V., MacGillivray, H.J., Tomić, D. and Jovanić, P. (1992) Evaluation of Static and Dynamic R Curve Using DC Potential Drop Single Specimen Method. ECF9 - Reliability and structural integrity of advanced materials (Ed. S. Sedmak, A. Sedmak and D. Ružić), EMAS, Warley West Midlands, 315-320.
4. Grabulov, V. (1995). PhD Thesis, University of Belgrade, Department of Technology and Metallurgy, Yugoslavia.
5. Yoon, J.H., Lee, B.S., Oh, Y.J. and Hong, J.H. (1999). International Journal of Pressure Vessels and Piping 76, 663.
6. Rintamaa, R., (1993) PhD Thesis, Helsinki University of Technology, Espoo, Finland.
7. Thomas, P.F. (1990). *Ductile Fracture of Metals*. Pergamon Press, Oxford.
8. ESIS P2-92 (1992).
9. GKSS: EFAM GTP 94 (1994).

From Charpy to Present Impact Testing
D. François and A. Pineau (Eds.)
© 2002 Elsevier Science Ltd. and ESIS. All rights reserved

INFLUENCE OF DUCTILE TEARING ON CLEAVAGE TRIGGERING IN DUCTILE-TO-BRITTLE TRANSITION OF A508 STEEL

P. HAUŠILD[1,2], P. BOMPARD[1], C. BERDIN[1], C. PRIOUL[1], M. KARLÍK[2]

1) Ecole Centrale Paris, Lab. MSS-Mat, Grande Voie des Vignes, 92 295 Châtenay-Malabry Cedex, France

2) CTU, Faculty of Nucl. Sci. & Phys. Engng, Dept. of Materials, Trojanova 13, 120 00 Praha 2, Czech Republic

ABSTRACT

A large quantitative fractographic study was carried out on an A508 Cl.3 pressure vessel steel in the temperature range corresponding to the ductile-to-brittle transition. Fractographic analyses of fractured Charpy V-notch (CVN) and compact tension (CT) specimens revealed a certain proportion of ductile fracture preceding cleavage, even if the specimens were tested at temperatures below the DBTT. The influence of the ductile tearing on cleavage triggering was studied. In particular, the stress concentrations in CT and/or CVN specimens induced by the presence of an ellipsoidal defect representing the cluster of debonded MnS inclusions were calculated by finite element method and related to the fracture probability given by Beremin model.

Keywords: Ductile-to-brittle transition temperature (DBTT), ductile fracture, cleavage, fracture toughness, local approach, fractography

INTRODUCTION

In the ductile-to-brittle transition temperature range of low alloyed steels, two fracture mechanisms are in competition – ductile fracture characteristic for high temperatures, and transgranular cleavage characteristic for low temperatures.

Ductile fracture by dimpled rupture occurs in low alloyed steels by three steps: microvoid nucleation on cracked or debonded second phase particles, microvoid growth, and coalescence of the microvoids forming the final fracture surface. Void growth occurs by plastic deformation of surrounding matrix, which is controlled by the triaxial stress state. Therefore the stress triaxiality controls in turn the void growth. Several models of the damage process have been proposed, the most known are [1], [2], and [3].

Cleavage fracture can be characterized as a sequential stochastic process of crack nucleation and crack propagation by a local re-initiation of cleavage facets. The growth stage can further be divided into initial growth of microcracks and consequent growth of a macrocrack as the first obstacles are encountered. It is generally recognized that the development of cleavage can be described by the *Griffith's criterion*, in which the critical stress, σ_f, is inversely proportional to the square root of the length of the microcrack [4].

In low alloy mild steels, the critical fracture event is commonly assumed to be a propagation of carbide microcracks into the surrounding ferrite matrix [5]. A model relating the fracture toughness of mild and/or low alloy steels to its yield and fracture stresses through a microstructurally determined characteristic distance has been proposed by *Ritchie, Knott and Rice* [6]. The fracture criterion is given by the condition that the stress must exceed the critical stress over some critical distance, X_o, ahead of the crack tip.

The probability of failure induced by cleavage can be predicted using the statistical local approach to fracture proposed by *Beremin* [7]. With this approach, the increasing scatter of K_{Ic} data can be described in lower shelf and fracture toughness was successfully predicted by *Rossoll* [8] from instrumented Charpy tests.

Nevertheless, none from the above mentioned models can still explain the sharp upturn in the ductile-to-brittle transition. On the one hand, the stresses ahead of the crack tip are lowered for temperatures near DBTT, and on the other hand, the ductile crack occurs. The effect of the size of volume sampled by the ductile crack propagation has to be introduced. The growing ductile crack is consequently sampling the volume ahead of the crack tip and searching for the pre-existing weak points, which results in a high degree of correlation between the ductile area and the fracture toughness (K_{Jc}) for tests conducted at DBTT [9]. Cleavage fracture is then controlled by the occurrence of the critical defect in the process zone. Since stresses are lower, the size of critical defect must be larger. The probability of finding of the critical defect is commonly assumed to be decreasing with increasing size of defect (e.g. [7]).

Besides carbide particles of relatively small size ($< 1 \mu m$), big non-metallic inclusions (mainly composed of MnS) are present in killed steels. These inclusions are elongated in the rolling direction and they are often situated in clusters. Although the influence of the size and the morphology of the MnS inclusions on ductile fracture is well known, their role on the triggering of cleavage remains unclear.

A direct role of MnS inclusions as micro defects initiating cleavage has been reported in [10], [11], but in most cases cleavage is thought to be initiated by dislocation pile-up or carbide microcracking. The presence of clusters of debonded elongated MnS inclusions in the vicinity of cleavage initiation site was found in the 16MND5 pressure vessel steel [8], [12-14]. A probabilistic model based on the spatial distribution of MnS inclusions has been proposed in [13] and used for the prediction of fracture toughness from notched tensile specimens [13], [14]. Nevertheless, this model cannot explain several cases in which the cleavage initiation is not associated with presence of MnS inclusions.

In the present work the influence of MnS inclusions as the stress concentrators is studied. An extensive metallographic study of the statistical distribution of size and geometry of MnS inclusions was therefore undertaken. 3-D reconstruction of the fracture surface containing clusters of MnS was created. Obtained information served for finite element computations of the stress concentration effect of these inclusions.

EXPERIMENTAL

A tempered bainitic pressure vessel steel was studied. The chemical composition of the French steel 16MND5 considered as an equivalent of the American standard A508 Cl.3 is given in Table 1. The microstructure corresponds to upper bainite. The primary austenite grain size is about 30 μm, the mean size of bainitic packets is about 10 μm. The lath width varies between 1 and 2 μm. Inside the bainitic lathes, transmission electron microscopy (TEM) revealed a typical recovered structure – low-angle subgrain boundaries with the dislocation networks inside the subgrains as shown in Fig. 1. The submicron carbide particles are localized more or less uniformly on the lath boundaries.

Table 1 - Chemical composition of 16MND5 (A508 Cl.3) steel (mass %).

C	S	P	Mn	Si	Ni	Cr	Mo	Cu	Al
0.159	0.008	0.005	1.37	0.24	0.70	0.17	0.50	0.06	0.023

The mechanical tests were carried out in the temperature range from –196 °C to room temperature (RT). The results of fracture toughness tests on the standard CT 25 specimens and impact tests on CVN specimens sampled in the T-S (long transverse-short transverse) orientation are presented in the contribution of *Rossoll et al.* [15]. The ductile-to-brittle transition temperature is about –20 °C for impact tests on CVN specimens, whereas for CT specimens the transition temperature is shifted up to 0 °C.

Three tests of CT 25 specimens at -60 °C were interrupted at different load levels and fatigue loaded to fracture (details reported in [8]).

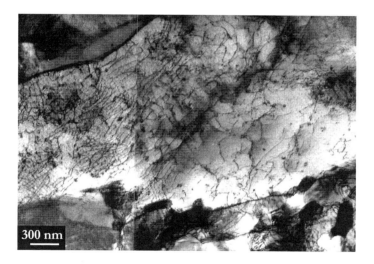

Fig. 1 - Typical dislocation structure inside the bainitic lath of A508 steel (TEM).

FRACTOGRAPHY

The fracture surfaces of all examined specimens exhibit transgranular cleavage facets. The characteristic size of cleavage facets corresponds to the size of bainitic packets. The cleavage crack initiates mostly on grain boundary. In some cases, a carbide or small MnS inclusion can be found in the center of the initiating cleavage facet. At low temperature, multiple initiation occurs in both types of specimens. The number of initiation sites decreases with increasing temperature.

In CT specimens tested at –90 °C, the main initiation sites were in most cases situated at a distance less than 100 μm from fatigue pre-crack. In all the CT specimens tested at 0 °C, only one initiation site was found but the distance from the actual ductile crack tip was about 1 mm. The total distance between the initiation site and the fatigue pre-crack is then given by the sum of the ductile crack length and the distance from actual ductile crack tip. With increasing temperature, the clusters of large, elongated inclusions (mainly composed of manganese sulfides) occur on the background of dominant cleavage fracture.

In Charpy specimens, even at low temperatures (below the DBTT), cleavage initiated mostly at the tip of the ductile crack developed from the notch. The total distance of initiation sites from the notch increases with increasing temperature. In Charpy specimens tested at –30 °C, the values of the total distance of the initiation sites from the notch are much more dispersed than at lower temperatures. The source of this dispersion is the dispersion in the ductile crack length characteristic for the DBTT. Moreover, the presence of MnS clusters in the vicinity of cleavage initiation sites, characteristic for CT specimens, was not observed in CVN specimens.

So two major differences can be underlined comparing two type of specimens – the distance of cleavage initiation points from crack and/or notch, and the occurrence of clusters of MnS inclusions in the vicinity of cleavage initiation sites.

The different positions of cleavage initiation sites in CT 25 and CVN specimens can be explained by different stress distributions given by the different geometry of the specimens.

The finite element analysis using the Gurson model has shown that the ductile crack initiation in CT 25 specimen does not introduce a significant increase in the stress level (height of the stress peak) ahead of the crack tip, but only changes the width of the stress peak [16]. For a lower temperature (-90 °C), the stress ahead of the crack tip is sufficiently high and the cleavage fracture is triggered when a critical stress is exceeded over some critical distance [6], which is about 50 μm (estimated from fracture surfaces). For higher temperature (~ DBTT), the stresses are lowered and the effect of the size of sampled volume has to be introduced. The fracture is then controlled by the occurrence of the critical defect in the process zone, which is now enlarged (to about 1 mm ahead of the ductile crack tip).

On the other hand, in CVN specimens the ductile crack initiation increases significantly the stress level ahead of the notch tip transformed into the ductile crack. The width of stress peak is also considerably lower than in the case of CT 25 specimen. In Charpy specimens, the fractographic observations confirmed that the cleavage initiated mostly at the tip of the ductile crack (Fig. 2). The ductile crack then plays two roles – the role of stress concentrator required for the triggering of cleavage at lower temperatures, and the role of volume sampler at temperatures near DBTT.

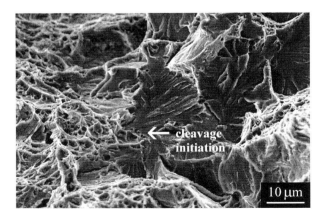

Fig. 2 – Cleavage initiation on the ductile crack tip in the CVN
specimen broken at -30 °C.

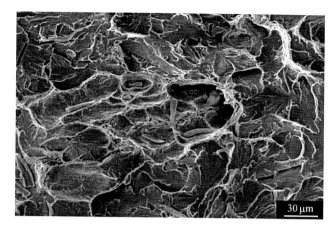

Fig. 3 – Cluster of debonded MnS inclusions on the background of
dominant cleavage fracture (CT 25 specimen broken at 0 °C).

However, the ductile crack growth analysis did not allow to explain the lack of presence of
MnS clusters on fracture surfaces of the CVN specimens. To explain this difference, one
cluster of typical elliptical shape, situated near the cleavage initiation site in CT 25 specimen
broken at 0 °C, was more detailed analyzed (Fig. 3). The three-dimensional (3-D)
reconstruction of fracture surface was realized in order to trace the profiles along *x* and *y* axis.
The cluster was idealized by ellipsoidal defect of measured dimensions and the stress
concentration effect was computed using the finite element method.

INFLUENCE OF MNS CLUSTERS - CELL COMPUTATION

The cluster of MnS inclusions characterized in the previous paragraph (Fig. 3) was
numerically modeled in order to compute the local stress-strain fields surrounding the defect.
The cluster of dimples is assumed to be an ellipsoid. Two axes can be measured on the
fracture plane (which is approximately the principal plane of the defect considering the
fabrication process). The last one is more difficult to obtain, so the ellipsoid was often
considered with an axial symmetry. 3-D reconstruction of fracture surface allowed to define
the ellipsoidal void by three lengths: $a=100$ μm, $b=50$ μm measured in the fracture plane, and
$c=10$ μm (corresponding to the measured depth), which is oriented in the direction of the
largest principal strain.
The stress-strain fields around such a defect located in front of the ductile crack tip of a CT
specimen is computed using the finite element method (ABAQUS *ver.* 5.8 software package).
The macroscopic loading is given by the stress level and the constraints computed in the CT
specimen. The loading is assumed to be shear free (which is the case on the macroscopic
crack plane) and the principal macroscopic stresses are defined as follows: the stress
triaxiality is chosen to be 2.5 (corresponding to the stress triaxiality at the crack tip) and plane
strain conditions are assumed in the direction of the longest axis of the ellipsoid. These
conditions allow a complete definition of the macroscopic loading of the defect assuming that
the load is proportional, which is certainly the most critical assumption. The different

macroscopic stresses (pressures) applied to the cell faces are therefore related with:

Along the smallest axis (c) : Σ_I

Along the middle axis (b) : $\Sigma_{III} = \dfrac{2.5\sqrt{3}-1}{2.5\sqrt{3}+1}\Sigma_I$ (1)

Along the longest axis (a) : $\Sigma_{II} = 1/2\ (\Sigma_I + \Sigma_{III})$

Since neither the defect geometry nor the loading has an axial symmetry, a 3-D modeling is performed. Considering the plane symmetry, only one eighth of the ellipsoid is taken into account. The mesh presents 4 000 of 8-node elements representing the volume of 1 mm³. The mechanical behavior of the matrix is taken as the elastic-plastic part of the mechanical behavior defined for this material [8]. A large displacement formulation is used.

Figure 4 shows the largest principal stress, σ_I, around the ellipsoidal void, when the plasticity is generalized into the cell. It should be noted that the maximum value of the microscopic largest principal stress occurs at the end of the a axis, whereas in pure elasticity, the maximum occurs at the end of the b axis (the smaller axis perpendicular to the maximal load direction). The maximum value of σ_I exceeds 15 % of the applied macroscopic stress (Σ_I=1 500 MPa), which corresponds to a limited stress amplification. A large volume above the ellipsoidal void is unloaded due to the free surface of the void.

In order to assess the stress concentration effect of the ellipsoidal cavity on cleavage triggering, the probability of fracture of the cell is computed and compared to the failure probability of the uniform cell of the same volume without cavity. The failure probability P_F, is estimated using the Beremin model. In this model based on weakest link assumption, the number of microcracks in the reference volume, V_o, is assumed to be a power law function of the microcrack length. Fracture probability is then given by a two-parameter Weibull's distribution as:

$$P_r = 1 - exp\left[-\left(\frac{\sigma_w}{\sigma_u}\right)^m\right]$$ (2)

where m and $\sigma_u V_0^m$ are the parameters, and the so called Weibull stress, σ_w, is defined as an integral of the positive maximum principal stress, σ_1, over the plastic zone volume, V_{pl}:

$$\sigma_w = \sqrt[m]{\int_{Vpl} \sigma_1^m \frac{dV}{V_o}}$$ (3)

Computations are made using a post-treatment of the finite element results for the cell with cavity and can be processed analytically for the uniform cell. The parameters m=20, σ_u=2 500 MPa, and V_o=(100 μm)³ were employed. The plastic zone is defined above 10^{-4} of equivalent plastic strain.

The evolution of the Weibull stress versus the macroscopic loading for both cases is shown at the figure 4. In the beginning of loading, the Weibull stress is higher in the defect containing cell than in the uniform cell because of the earlier occurrence of plasticity due to the stress concentration effect of the void. However, since the plasticity is present in the entire cell, the trend in Weibull stress is reversed, so that the fracture probability of the void containing cell is slightly lower than the fracture probability of the uniform cell. This is due to the effective volume which is smaller in the cell containing a void because of the unloaded zone above the cavity. In the case studied here, the unloading effect is greater than the stress concentration effect of the cavity. This result is in contradiction with the computations presented in [14]. Considering the well known results of the stress concentration caused by an ellipsoidal cavity

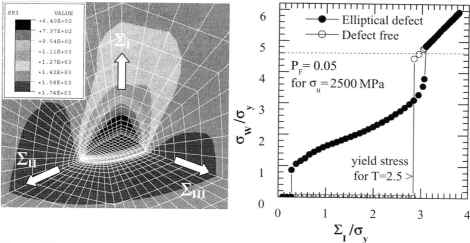

Fig. 4 – Cell computation results. Stress concentration due to the presence of an elliptical defect at the macroscopic stress level $\Sigma_I = 1,500$ MPa (left), normalized Weibull stress for the uniform cell and the cell containing the elliptical defect (right).

in pure elasticity [17], it can be shown that the most critical case is the one studied in [14], i.e. the oblate cavity ($a=b>c$) loaded in the opening direction. Furthermore, the stress concentration factor increases with the ratio a/c of the cavity, with a limit case which is the "penny-shaped" crack.

In this study, the geometry of the cavity seen on the fracture surface, near the initiation site of cleavage was described as realistically as possible. In this case, it is very difficult to conclude whether this defect triggered cleavage by a stress concentration effect or not.

Another question arises from the result of an interrupted test, after that a cluster of cleavage facets was found on fracture surface between the stretch zone and debonded MnS inclusions (Fig. 5). In this case, the role of MnS clusters could be completely opposite, i.e. the dislocation emitted during the void growth preceding the local cleavage initiation has arrested crack propagation.

CONCLUDING REMARKS

Recent studies [12-14] have emphasized the role of MnS clusters on the initiation of cleavage in ductile-to-brittle transition regime. This role has been carefully investigated in the present study taking into account the quantitative fractographic analysis of fracture surfaces of CT and CVN specimens fractured in this temperature regime, and the stress and strain modifications around debonded MnS cluster computed by the finite element method. The results can be summarized as follows:

In the presence of such a defect, the fracture probability is enhanced at the beginning of loading, when the matrix remains globally elastic, but as plasticity develops in the matrix, and cavity growth takes place, an unloaded region extends above the free surface of the cavity, and the fracture probability can even be reduced.

The presence of MnS clusters on the fracture surfaces could therefore be more probably related to an unloading effect of the associated cavities, attracting the propagating crack.

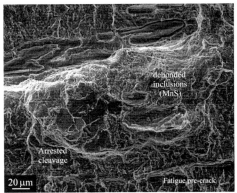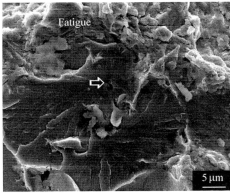

Fig. 5 – Interrupted test of CT 25 specimen. Arrested cleavage facets between the debonded inclusions and the fatigue pre-crack (left), detail of arrested cleavage origin on a second phase particle marked by the arrow (right).

This result can also explain the lack of MnS clusters in the vicinity of cleavage initiation sites in CVN specimens. Therefore, the stress concentration of MnS clusters should not be responsible for the sharp upturn of fracture toughness in the DBTT regime. The sharp upturn is probably more closely related to the effect of temperature on the physical micromechanisms which are responsible for cleavage initiation on the one hand, and cleavage propagation through microstructural barriers on the other hand.

Acknowledgement: *The authors wish to thank to French and Czech governments for the financial support in the frame of BARRANDE Project No. 2001-05-1 as well as EDF/EMA Renardières.*

REFERENCES

[1] McClintock, F.A. (1968). *J. Appl. Mech.*, 363.
[2] Rice, J.R. and Tracey, D.M. (1969). *J. Mech. Phys. Solids* **17**, 201.
[3] Gurson, L.A. (1977). *J. Eng. Mat. Tech.* 2.
[4] Griffith, A.A. (1920). *Phil. Trans. R. Soc.* **A221**, 163.
[5] Curry, D.A. (1980). *Met. Sci.* **14**, 319.
[6] Ritchie, R.O., Knott, J.F. and Rice, J.R. (1973). *J. Mech. Phys. Solids* **21**, 395.
[7] Beremin, F.M. (1983). *Metall. Trans.* **A14**, 2277.
[8] Rossoll, A. (1998). PhD. thesis, Ecole Centrale Paris. France.
[9] Nedbal, I. Siegl, J. and Kunz, J. (1998) In: *WORKSHOP '98*, Prague, Czech Republic, p. 453.
[10] Rosenfield, A.R. and Shetty, D.K. (1981). *Engng. Frac. Mech.* **14**, 833.
[11] Baker, T.J., Kavishe, F.P.L. and Wilson, J. (1986). *Mat. Sci. Tech.* **2**, 576.
[12] Mäntylä, M., Rossoll, A., Nedbal, I., Prioul, C. and Marini B. (1999). *J. Nuc. Mat.* **264**, 257.
[13] Renevey, S. (1998). PhD. thesis, Université de Paris-Sud, France.
[14] Carassou, S. (2000). PhD. thesis, Ecole Nationale Supérieure des Mines de Paris, France.
[15] Rossoll, A., Berdin, C. and Prioul, C. (2002) In: *From Charpy to Present Impact Testing; Proceedings of CCC 2001*, Elsevier Science.
[16] Haušild, P., Bompard, P., Berdin, C. and Prioul, C. (2001). In: *MECAMAT, Multi-Approche en Mécanique des Matériaux*, Aussois, France, pp. 203-206.
[17] Mura, T. (1987). *Micromechanics of defects in solids*. Kluwer Academic Press

From Charpy to Present Impact Testing
D. François and A. Pineau (Eds.)

CORRELATION BETWEEN IMPACT RESISTANCE AND FRACTURE TOUGHNESS IN AGED DUPLEX STAINLESS STEELS

L. SÁNCHEZ & F. GUTIÉRREZ-SOLANA

Departamento de Ciencia e Ingeniería del Terreno y de los Materiales
E.T.S. Ingenieros de Caminos, Canales y Puertos,
University of Cantabria, 39005 Santander, Spain.

ABSTRACT

As a part of a more extensive study [1] of aging embrittlement at low temperature (280-400°C) of cast duplex stainless steels, a close characterization of the evolution of toughness of three duplex steels with different ferrite content (12, 18 and 22%) has been performed.

Fracture toughness characterization was based on the determination of J_R curves, in accordance with the European Recommendations ESIS P1-92 and following the unloading compliance single specimen method. Impact toughness was determined with an instrumented Charpy pendulum, which permits the load-deflection and energy deflection curves to be obtained.

From the obtained results, a phenomenological model based on the presence of brittle ferrite in the fracture path has been developed. This model enables the impact toughness and the fracture toughness to be determined as a function of aging time and aging temperature for a duplex steel, and therefore to predict fracture toughness values from Charpy results. Finally, a comparison has been made between energy predicted from impact and experimentally obtained fracture toughness for the three steels.

KEYWORDS

Cast duplex stainless steels, aging embrittlement, microhardness, instrumented pendulum, impact resistance, toughness.

INTRODUCTION

For many years duplex stainless steels have been widely used in the chemical and petrochemical industries as well as being employed in risk elements in power plants. These steels have a biphasic microstructure composed of a discontinuous ferrite network distributed throughout the austenitic matrix. The presence of ferrite in the duplex structure increases the mechanical resistance and the resistance to stress corrosion cracking, improves the weldability, and makes castings more resistant to hot cracking during solidification. However, it has been known since the 80's that these steels are susceptible to thermal aging processes when they are used in service conditions at temperatures of around 280°C. This leads to material embrittlement [1-5].

Many studies [1, 4] have shown that the aging processes, taking place in the 280-400°C range, are principally due to the spinodal decomposition of the ferrite and its G phase precipitation. The presence of $M_{23}C_6$ carbides and Cr_2N nitrides may contribute to these embrittlement processes.

Austenoferritic stainless steel embrittlement, which depends on ferrite aging may be observed at two different levels: the local embrittlement of the ferrite itself and the consequent bulk material embrittlement. This bulk material embrittlement depends on the percentage and distribution of the ferrite as well as the evolution in the relative participation of the aged ferrite and its interfaces in the fracture mechanisms [1]. These mechanisms are those which determine the limits of the overall mechanical behaviour of the material.

An extensive research program was carried out in order to analyse the effect of aging at low temperatures on the mechanical behaviour of three duplex stainless steels with different chemical composition and ferrite content. Some of the results were presented in previous publications [1,6-10]. This work summarizes the correlation between fracture toughness and impact energy.

MATERIAL

Table 1 shows the chemical composition and ferrite content of the three steels analysed, named 12F, 18F and 22F after their ferrite content. 12F is a commercial CF8M duplex stainless steel taken from a valve aged in service for 10 years at ~280°C. 18F and 22F are similar duplex steels obtained from experimental casts.

TABLE 1- Chemical composition and ferrite content of the studied CF8M steels.

STEEL	C	Mn	Si	Cr	Ni	Mo	%Ferrite
12F	0.035	0.70	1.10	18.6	10.4	2.00	12.2
18F	0.076	0.83	1.25	19.4	9.6	2.29	17.8
22F	0.045	0.82	1.23	18.4	8.9	2.36	21.6

The overaging treatments performed on the 12F steel at 280, 350 and 400°C, reached up to 18000, 14000 and 14800 hours, respectively. For the 18F steel and 22F different aging treatments at the three temperatures have also been performed, up to a maximum value around 10000 hours.

EXPERIMENTAL

To analyse the effect of aging on these steels a mechanical characterization has been performed including fracture toughness tests, instrumented impact tests and a fractographic analysis.

Fracture toughness evolution

Fracture toughness at room temperature was determined by J-integral R-curve, following European Recommendations ESIS P1-92 [11], and the unloading compliance single specimen method. CT specimens, 20 mm wide, were used, with 2 mm deep sidegrooves machined after fatigue precracking. Figure 1 shows the J_R curves for the 12F steel aged at 400°C. Figure 2 shows the same for the 22F steel at different temperatures. These figures demonstrate the important influence of aging on toughness such that fracture toughness clearly decreases with longer aging times at any temperature between 280 and 400°C.

From de J_R curves fitted by means of the power function

$$J_R = A \cdot \Delta a^D \qquad (1)$$

the crack initiation parameters $J_{0.2/BL}$ were obtained.

Instrumented Charpy impact tests

In order to obtain the brittle-ductile transition curves standardized Charpy impact tests were carried out at -196°C, -80°C, 20°C, and 280°C. Figure 3 shows the evolution of the most representative transition temperature (TT) curves with aging for the 18F steel. From this figure we can conclude that the upper and lower shelf energies decrease and the transition temperature increases with aging.

Figure 4 shows the load-deflection curves (P-Δ) for the 18F steel for different aging times at 400°C. The results show that thermal aging leads to a reduction of impact energy and an increase of the strain-hardening rate of the material. The strain-hardening rate increases after aging for a relatively short time and does not change significantly with further aging, in the same way as hardness evolves with aging time [1, 10] reaching a final plateau.

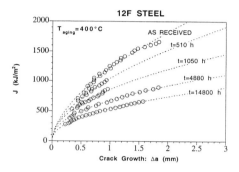

Figure 1. Evolution of J_R curves. 12F steel.

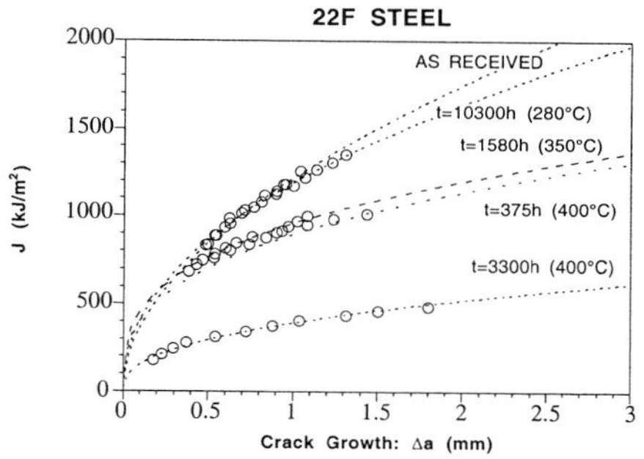

Figure 2. Evolution of J_R curves. 22F steel.

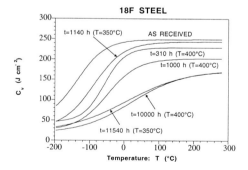

Figure 3. Evolution of C_v curves. 18F steel.

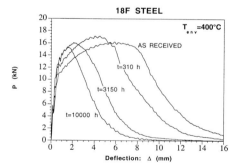

Figure 4. Evolution of P-Δ curves. 18F steel.

Fractographic analysis

A fractographic study was made using scanning electron microscopy (SEM) to quantify ferrite presence on the fracture surface. Figure 5 shows a fractography of the unaged 12F steel near stretch zone in a CT sample. The fracture type was very ductile caused by microvoid coalescence in austenite and no presence of ferrite was found. Generally, the percentage of ferrite in the fracture path increases with aging. Figure 6 shows an example obtained from a broken Charpy specimen. The embrittled islands of ferrite break by cleavage and the corresponding facets nucleate voids. The damage material finally breaks.

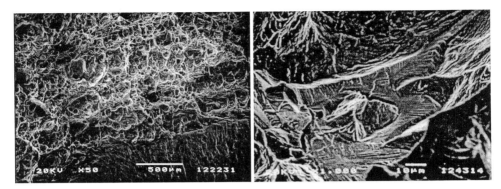

Figure 5. Fractography of 12F steel as received.   Figure 6. Fractography of 12F steel aged for 14800 hours at 400°C.

PHENOMENOLOGICAL MODEL

Using the exhaustive fractographic study a phenomenological fracture model was developed [1]. The crack initiation parameter $J_{0.2/BL}$, as well as tearing modulus, and impact resistance at room temperature were related to the percentage of broken ferrite on the crack surface by using the following equations

$$J_{0.2/BL} = J_{0.2/BL}^{\gamma} \cdot X_{\gamma}^{J_R} \left(1 - \mu_J \cdot X_{\alpha}^{J_R} \right) \tag{2}$$

$$C_v = C_v^{\gamma} \cdot X_{\gamma}^{C_v} \left(1 - \mu_C \cdot X_{\alpha}^{C_v} \right) \tag{3}$$

where X_{γ} and X_{α} were, respectively, the unitary fractions of austenite and ferrite on the crack surface and $J_{0.2/BL}^{\gamma}$ and C_v^{γ} are values associated with pure austenite which coincide with the as-received values of each steel because the fracture process occurs only through austenite in the unaged materials. The parameters μ_J and μ_C are related to the effect of the broken ferrite surface on the toughness, measured by $J_{0.2/BL}$ or C_v respectively. These parameters, as a function of X_{α}, come from the preliminary following, experimentally obtained, equations

$$\mu_J = 2.1 + 9.5 \cdot exp\left(-9.9 \cdot X_{\alpha}^{J_R} \right) \tag{4}$$

$$\mu_C = 2.1 + 7.1 \cdot exp\left(-19.2 \cdot X_{\alpha}^{C_v} \right) \tag{5}$$

The unitary fractions of ferrite in the fracture surfaces, both in toughness and impact tests, have been determined as a function of ferrite aging measured by microhardness increment ΔHV and the ferrite content by the equations

$$X_{\alpha}^{J_R}(\%) = \left(-4.20 + 0.65 \cdot \%\alpha \right) 0.01 \cdot \Delta HV \tag{6}$$

$$X_{\alpha}^{C_v}(\%) = \left(-9.12 + 1.02 \cdot \%\alpha \right) 0.01 \cdot \Delta HV \tag{7}$$

IMPACT RESISTANCE AND FRACTURE TOUGHNESS CORRELATION

Experimental

From the results of the instrumented impact tests it is possible to obtain the load-deflection (P-Δ) and energy deflection (E-Δ) curves. Figure 7 shows the characteristic curves obtained for the 12F steel. In the P-Δ curve there are three singular points: the limit of the elastic zone, the maximum load point and the point were the fracture was initiated.

Using the values of the P-Δ curve a new compliance parameter Δ/P was introduced. This parameter represents the inverse of the slope of the secant line, stiffness, which joins the origin with any point in the P(Δ) curve. The new curve Δ-Δ/P makes it possible to determine the point at which the propagation starts, looking at the maximum change of the slope [6, 8, 12]. Using this point it is possible to obtain the initiation energy, E_i.

The total energy absorbed in the Charpy test, E_t, can by separated into initiation energy and a propagation energy:

$$E_t = E_i + E_p \qquad (8)$$

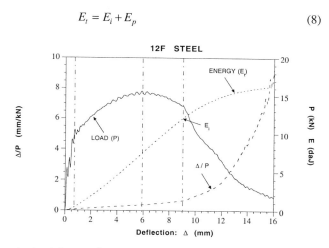

Figure 7. Curves obtained from an instrumented impact test.

Figures 8 and 9 show the good correlation that exists between E_i and E_t for the 12F and 18F steels. A good correlation can be observed between both variables, which even seems to be independent of the steel considered. Plotting together the obtained results for both materials, a general relation can be obtained as follows

$$E_i = -26.9 + 0.86 \cdot E_t \qquad (9)$$

with a correlation coefficient R=0.97.

Taking into account that E_i is the energy necessary to initiate the propagation in an impact test, the possibility of establishing a correlation between E_i and the initiating parameter $J_{0.2/BL}$ obtained from the J_R curves was studied. Despite the fact that the correlation between E_i and E_t is good, the direct correlation between the resilience C_v and the $J_{0.2/BL}$ parameter it is more useful. This is because most of impact toughness results from conventional pendulum are not instrumented. Figures 10, 11 and 12 show the obtained results for the 12F, 18F and 22F, respectively. Figure 10, representing 12F steel, offers a good correlation between both parameters for a wide range of values. In the case of the 18F and 22F steels the number of data is smaller (Figures 11 and 12), and although it is possible to consider a linear correlation, this was only made for the 22F steel because results for the 18F steel are clustered mainly in two zones low aging and high aging conditions. For the 12F and 22F steels the linear correlation found shows a parallel behaviour, with greater value of toughness for a given resilience in the 22F steel. Finally, Figure 13 shows the correlation between resilience C_v and $J_{0.2/BL}$ fracture toughness parameter for the 12F and 22F steels. Correlation curves are very similar when analysing the data separately or together. The difference between both steels is the shift to higher toughness values for a given impact resistance C_v, with the increase in ferrite content.

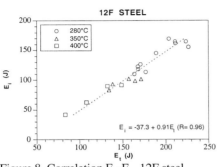

Figure 8. Correlation E_i-E_t. 12F steel.

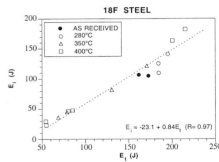

Figure 9. Correlation E_i-E_t. 18F steel.

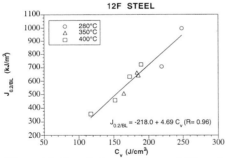

Figure 10. Correlation C_v - $J_{0.2/BL}$. 12F steel.

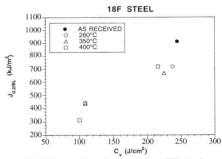

Figure 11. Correlation C_v - $J_{0.2/BL}$. 18F steel.

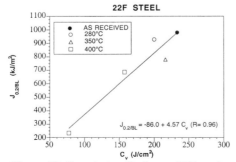

Figure 12. Correlation C_v-$J_{0.2/BL}$. 22F steel.

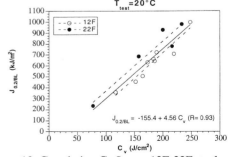

Figure 13. Correlation C_v-$J_{0.2/BL}$. 12F-22F steel.

From modelling

With the phenomenological model described before it is possible to establish, for each tested steel (12F, 18F and 22F) or a new one, pairs of C_v - $J_{0.2/BL}$ values obtained for increasing HV values, simulating the aging process. Figure 14 shows the obtained values using this method, correlating C_v and $J_{0.2/BL}$ for the three steels. On it two linear zones, A and B, can be distinguished. Zone A is the same for the three steels and defines the correlation zone for highly embrittled conditions. A linear correlation has been established for zone B independently for each steel, as a function of ferrite level. A similar slope has been obtained for all steels according to the experimental correlations.

In order to simplify, for the three steels zone B correlation lines, a single slope has been chosen from the mean value of all of them: 6.3. Also in zone A the lowest line with the best fit has been chosen in order to ensure safety conditions in the correlation. Taking this into account the following equations define the final correlation between C_v and $J_{0.2/BL}$ obtained from the model of aging embrittlement behaviour. For zone A:

$$J_{0.2/BL} = 86.1 + 1.7 \cdot C_v \tag{10}$$

For zone B:

- if 12F steel

$$J_{0.2/BL} = -623.2 + 6.3 \cdot C_v \tag{11}$$

- if 18F steel

$$J_{0.2/BL} = -531.6 + 6.3 \cdot C_v \tag{12}$$

- if 22F steel

$$J_{0.2/BL} = -438.5 + 6.3 \cdot C_v \tag{13}$$

Figure 15 show the correlation equations together with the obtained experimental data for the 12F and 22F steels. It can be seen that the 12F steel fits well with the model, and is generally on the safe side. The 22F steel is also accurate but with greater dispersion. However, it never deviates more than 20% away from the experimental values.

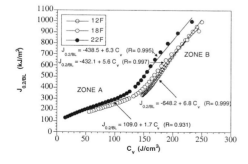

Figure 14. Correlation C_v - $J_{0.2/BL}$.

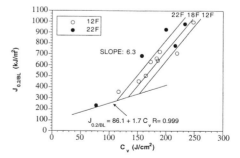

Figure 15. Correlation C_v - $J_{0.2/BL}$.

CONCLUSIONS

In duplex stainless steels the effect of aging leads to a reduction in both impact resistance at any temperature and fracture toughness. The effect is greater for longer exposure at elevated temperatures and for increasing ferrite content.

The transition curves for impact toughness show a decrease in the upper and lower shelf energies, and a shift of the transition temperature towards higher temperatures with increasing aging levels. Also J_R curves show the effect of aging on both fracture toughness and tearing modulus.

The fractographic analysis performed at both static and dynamic testing procedures show that austenite produces ductile fracture by coalescence of microvoids regardless of the aging level, while ferrite suffers brittle fracture at elevated aging levels. The tendency of the fracture path to follow the ferrite phase, previously broken, increases with aging.

A linear correlation was established between the fracture behaviour and the impact resistance for these steels, with the same slope independently of ferrite content. A phenomenological model based on the fracture micromechanisms observed was used to predict the values of $J_{0.2/BL}$ and C_v determined at each aging condition. Therefore a new correlation can be obtained between both toughness parameters that differentiates two zones of behaviour: the zone for highly embrittled conditions with a single correlation and the rest where the correlation depends on ferrite content, maintaining the same slope. Good agreement with the experimental results have been shown, always within the range of 20% of scattering which is comparable with the level of experimental scattering due to non-uniform material behaviour and experimental variation effects.

REFERENCES

1. Sánchez, L. (1996). PhD Thesis, University of Cantabria, Spain.

2. Trautwein, A. and Gysel, W. (1982). *Stainless Steel Casting*, ASTM STP 756, pp. 165-189, Behal, V.G. and Melilli, A.S. (Eds). ASTM, Philadelphia, PA.

3. Slama, G., Petrequin, P. and Mager, T.R. (1983). In: *SMIRT Post-Conference Seminar*, Monterey, CA.

4. Chung H.M. (1992). *Int. J. Pres. Ves. & Piping*, **50**, pp. 179-213.

5. Massoud, J.P., Bethmont, M. and Champredonde, J. (1991). In: *Duplex Stainless Steels'91*, Beaune, pp. 93-100.

6. Sánchez, L., Gutiérrez-Solana, F., Fordeyn, J. and Verstraeten, S. (1994). *Anales de Mecánica de la Fractura* **11**, pp. 236-242.

7. Sánchez, L., Gutiérrez-Solana, F., Gorrochategui, I. and González, J. (1994). In: *Tenth European Conference on Fracture*. Berlin, pp. 823-828.

8. Sánchez, L., Gutiérrez-Solana, and González, J. (1995). In: *Materials Ageing and Components Life Extension*. Milan, pp. 519-528.

9. Sánchez, L., Gutiérrez-Solana, and González, J. (1996). In: *Eleventh European Conference on Fracture*. Poitiers, pp. 571-576.

10. González, J.J., Gutiérrez-Solana, F., Sánchez, L. and Setién, J. (1997). *J. Testing Eval.*, **251 (2)**, pp. 154-162.

11. ESIS P1-92 (1992). "ESIS Recommendations for Determining the Fracture Resistence of Ductile Materials". European Structural Integrity Society.

12. Kobayashi, T., Yamamoto, I. and Niinomi, M. (1993). *J. Testing Eval.*, **21 (3)**, pp. 145-153.

From Charpy to Present Impact Testing
D. François and A. Pineau (Eds.)

INSTRUMENTED TESTING OF SIMULATED CHARPY SPECIMENS MADE OF MICROALLOYED Mn-Ni-V STEEL

SVETO CVETKOVSKI,
Faculty of Technology and Metallurgy, University of Skopje, Macedonia
TODOR ADZIEV, GORGI ADZIEV,
Faculty of Mechanical Engineering, University of Skopje, Macedonia
ALEKSANDAR SEDMAK,
Faculty of Mechanical Engineering, University of Belgrade, Yugoslavia

ABSTRACT

Standard Charpy specimens were thermally treated using "SMITHWELD" device to simulate different areas of HAZ in the base metal and in the weld metal. The base metal was microalloyed Mn-Ni-V steel of StE 460 class, welded by submerged arc process with S2 Ni welding wire and OP 121 TT welding flux. Simulation of HAZ in base metal was carried out under different regimes, including re-heating. Specimens for simulation of different areas of HAZ in weld metal were cut from welded joints transverse to the welding direction and also simulated under different regimes. Testing of simulated specimens from base metal was performed at +20, -20 and -60^0C, whereas simulated specimens from weld metal were tested at -60^0C. Using Charpy instrumented pendulum with oscilloscope the total energy (A_t) was separated into the energy for crack initiation (A_i) and the energy for crack propagation (A_p). Using these investigations a region with the lowest impact toughness in the HAZ in base and weld metal was determined. The microstructure was also examined in order to explain the values of toughness obtained by Charpy instrumented pendulum.

KEYWORDS:

Instrumented Charpy Testing, High-Strength-Low-Alloyed Steel, Heat-Affected-Zone

INTRODUCTION

Heat-affected-zone (HAZ) is normally formed in base metal during arc welding and in the weld metal during multipass welding. Both zones consist of few different areas (coarse grained, fine grained and intercritical) with specific mechanical and microstructural properties. Some of these areas could be very harmful to the quality of welded joints due to low toughness. Investigation of their properties on a real specimens is very difficult task, because of their small size and irregular geometry. Using welding simulators, wider areas with homogeneous and reproductive microstructure can be formed, enabling more reliable evaluation of their properties. Therefore, this method has been used, mainly for the determination of the area having the lowest mechanical properties in HAZ, which is the aim of this paper /1-3/.

EXPERIMENTAL PROCEDURE

The base metal was microalloyed Mn-Ni-V steel of StE 460 class, welded by the submerged arc process with S2 Ni welding wire and OP 121 TT welding flux. The thickness of the plates was 25 mm. The symmetrical X welding groove was prepared as shown in Fig. 1 and filled in six runs, three from each sides. Heat input was 2 kJ/mm.

For the simulation of different areas of HAZ in the base metal, samples from the microalloyed Mn-Ni-V steel (StE 460 class) have been used. To simulate areas of HAZ in weld metal, samples from the real welded joint, with primary/dendritic microstructure, were cut transverse to the welding direction, Fig. 2.

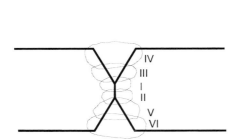

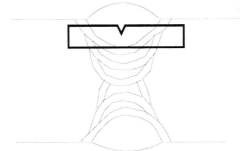

Figure 1. Groove preparation   Figure 2. Position of specimens in the weld metal

Samples, with dimensions 11x11x60 mm, were cut from both base metal and weld metal, and heat treated using "SMITHWELD" device. Thermocouples Pt-RhPt were connected to the samples to control the maximum temperature, Fig. 3. After simulation the samples were machined to obtain standard Charpy specimens. Simulation of HAZ in base metal was carried out with different maximum temperatures (T_{max}) and different cooling times in the critical region from 800 to 500 °C ($\Delta t_{8/5}$), showed in Tab. 1, while only the maximum temperature was varied for the weld metal, showed in Tab. 2. As shown in Tab. 1, two sets of samples underwent double simulation treatment, with 1350 ^{0}C as the maximum temperature in both cases, but with different maximum temperature in the second cycle, 750 and 600 ^{0}C.

Table 1. Regimes for the base metal simulation

T_{max}, ^{0}C	1350	1350	1350	1150	950	850	1350/750	1350/600
$\Delta t_{8/5}$, s	15	5	25	15	15	15	15	15

Table 2. Regimes for the weld metal simulation

T_{max},^{0}C	1350	1150	950	850
$\Delta t_{8/5}$, s	15	15	15	15

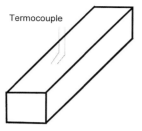

Termocouple

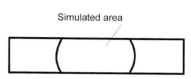

Simulated area

Figure 3. a) Connection of thermocouple to the specimen   b) Specimen after simulation

For comparison with simulated specimens, 'classical' Charpy specimens with a notch in HAZ were prepared, as shown in Fig. 4.

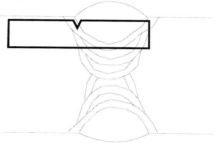

Figure 4. 'Classical' Charpy specimen taken from coarse grained HAZ

RESULTS OF CHARPY IMPACT TESTING

Charpy instrumented pendulum was used for the impact toughness testing. Three specimens have been tested in each condition. The Charpy pendulum was connected with oscilloscope from which two diagrams were obtained, force-time and energy-time, Fig. 5a. These diagrams were used to separate the total impact toughness energy (A_t) into the energy for crack initiation (A_i) and the energy of crack propagation (A_p), according to maximum force value, as indicated in Fig. 5b.

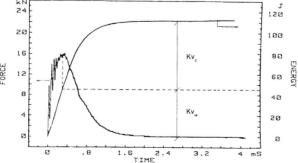

Figure 5a. Diagrams force-time and energy-time

The results of weld metal impact toughness testing at -60 °C are shown in Tab. 3. It can be seen that the lowest values of total impact toughness energy is obtained for the simulation at peak temperature of 1350 °C. It can be seen too that in all cases, the energy for crack initiation (A_i) is significantly higher than the energy for crack propagation (A_p).

Table 3. Impact toughness of specimens from weld metal

T_{sim}, °C	$\Delta t_{8/5}$	Impact toughness, -60 °C		
		A_t (J)	A_i (J)	A_p (J)
1350	15	32	26	6
1150	15	61	31	30
950	15	63	52	11
850	15	51	37	14

The results of impact toughness testing of simulated specimens from base metal at +20, -20 and -60 °C are shown in Tab. 4. It can be seen that at +20 °C, there is no significant difference between the crack initiation and crack propagation energy. Anyhow, at the lower testing temperatures (-20 and -60 °C) the crack initiation energy is higher then the crack propagation energy, i.e. the latter one is more temperature dependent, as shown in Fig. 6 for the specimens tested at 1350 °C for $\Delta t_{8/5}$=5 s. Such a behaviour can be explained by the fact that the energy for crack initiation mainly depend on stress conditions at the crack tip.

Table 4. Impact toughness of specimens from base metal

T_{sim}, °C	$\Delta t_{8/5}$	Impact toughness (J)								
		+20 °C			-20, °C			-60, °C		
		A_t	A_i	A_p	A_t	A_i	A_p	A_t	A_i	A_p
1350	25	26	15	11	20	15	5	10	6	4
1350	5	51	25	26	39	24	15	20	14	6
1350	15	36	17	19	27	15	12	16	9	7
1150	15	69	39	30	38	29	9	16	12	14
1050	15	69	36	33	43	36	7	27	22	5
950	15	66	35	31	40	32	8	24	18	6
850	15	63	32	31	32	25	7	23	19	4
1350/750	15	87	39	48	35	16	19	22	9	13
1350/600	15	84	26	58	45	29	16	23	14	9

The lowest values of Charpy energy correspond to the specimens simulated at 1350 °C. In this case it is also clear that the influence of cooling rate is very important. For example, highest values of impact toughness energy are obtained for the lowest heat input ($\Delta t_{8/5}$ = 5s), and vice verse. The basic reason for such behaviour is the size of primary austenitic grains and microstructure. It practically means that better result can be expected in the coarse grained regions of HAZ if welding is performed with lower heat input.

If the impact toughness values, obtained on specimens simulated to the peak temperature of 1350 °C (coarse grained), are compared with the values obtained by testing real Charpy specimens with a notch in a coarse grained region (Fig. 4), it can be seen that much higher values (172 J at 20 °C and 90 J at -60 °C) are obtained in the latter case. To explain this, one should keep in mind that the real HAZ microstructure is very complex and heterogeneous, consisting of narrow regions with different constituents, while the simulated microstructure is homogeneous, consisting only of coarse grained microstructure and thus representing the 'worst-case property'. The same explanation can be offered for significantly higher impact toughness values obtained for the simulated specimens from weld metal (Tab. 3), as compared to simulated specimens from the base metal at -60 °C (Tab. 4).

As can be seen from the Tab. 4, the best results for all testing temperatures are obtained in regions of simulation between 950 and 1050 ^{0}C. On should also notice that the results for double simulation specimens (1350/750 ^{0}C and 1350/600 ^{0}C) indicate relatively high toughness, although some authors treated these areas as critical regions in HAZ, because of formation of MA constituent /4-5/.

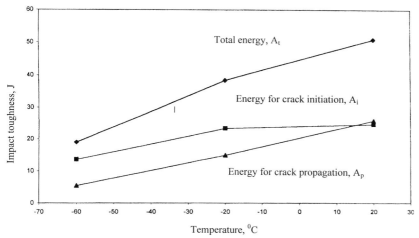

Figure 5b. Impact toughness energy dependence on temperature (specimens simulated at 1350 ^{0}C, $\Delta t_{8/5}$=5 s)

METALLOGRAPHY

Figures 6-8 represent the microstructure obtained by simulating the base metal at 1350°C with different cooling rates, $\Delta t_{8/5}$=5 s, 15 s and 25 s, respectively. General conclusion is that although each figure shows typical needle-like microstructure, there is significant difference among them. For example, the microstructure in Fig. 6 consists mainly of lath martensite (hardness 311 HV10), while the microstructure in Fig. 8 is mainly upper bainite (hardness 280 HV10), with a very coarse primary austenitic grains.

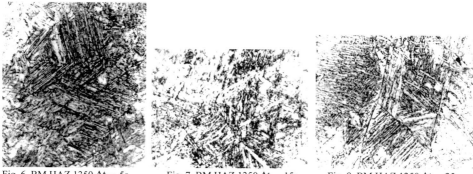

Fig. 6. BM HAZ 1350 $\Delta t_{8/5}$=5s   Fig. 7. BM HAZ 1350 $\Delta t_{8/5}$=15s   Fig. 8. BM HAZ 1350 $\Delta t_{8/5}$=25s

Comparing the results of impact toughness and microstructure, one can conclude that upper bainite and coarse primary austenitic grains, formed as results of highest heat input ($\Delta t_{8/5}$=25 s), is more harmful for the impact toughness than lath martensite. This conclusion is in agreement with references /6-7/.

Fractographic analysis, Fig. 9 and 10, confirmed that specimen with the microstructure of upper bainite shows typical brittle fracture (Fig. 10), while the specimen with the microstructure of lath martensite shows mainly quasi-crystal fracture (Fig. 9). This is yet another proof that microalloyed steels should be welded with lowest possible energy input.

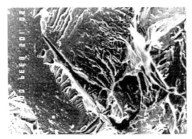

Fig. 9 Fracture surface BM HAZ 1350°C/5s

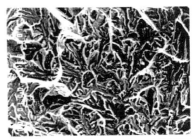

Fig. 10. Fracture surface BM HAZ 1350°C/25s

The specimen simulated at 1150°C, Fig. 11, indicates needle-like microstructure of upper bainite, as in Figs. 6-8, but with significantly smaller needles. By further decrease of the simulation temperature, needles disappear and acicular bainitic ferritic microstructure is formed at 1050°C, Fig. 12. Finally, the microstructure obtained by simulation at 850°C (Fig. 13) consist of polygonal grains of bainitic ferrite. Presented microstructures are in agreement with the impact toughness energies, shown in Tab. 4.

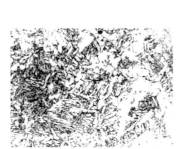
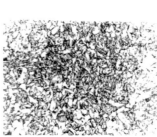
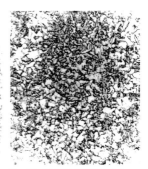

Fig. 11. BM HAZ 1150°C/15s   Fig. 12. BM HAZ 1050°C/15s   Fig. 13. BM HAZ 850°C/15s

Dendritic microstructure, typical for weld metal, is shown in Fig. 14, indicating the primary microstructure which was then simulated at 850, 950, 1150 and 1350 °C, to obtain the secondary microstructure in the weld metal. Figure 15 shows the microstructure, obtained by simulation in two-phase region at 850 °C, whereas Fig. 16 shows the microstructure, corresponding to 950°C, consisting of bainitic-ferritic grains. The microstructures, corresponding to 1150°C and 1350°C, shown in Figs. 17-18, respectively, consist of equiaxial grains with proeutectoid ferrite at the boundaries and acicular ferrite inside the grains. All of these microstructures are in agreement with relatively high impact toughness energies, as shown in Tab. 3.

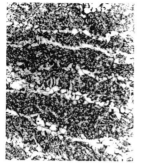

Fig. 14. Weld Metal (WM)

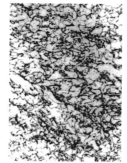

Fig. 15. WM HAZ 850°C/15s

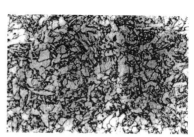

Fig. 16. WM HAZ 950°C/15s

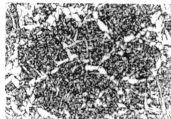

Fig. 17. WM HAZ 1150°C/15s

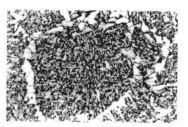

Fig. 18. WM HAZ 1350°C/15s

CONCLUSIONS

Based on the results obtained by Charpy impact testing and metallographical investigations following conclusions can be drawn:

- The lowest impact toughness energy for the weld metal has been obtained for specimen simulated at 1350°C due to the unfavourable microstructure containing proeutectoid ferrite at the grains boundaries;
- The lowest impact toughness energy for the base metal has been also obtained for the specimen simulated at a temperature of 1350°C. In this case it was also shown that the lower cooling rates i.e. higher input energy produce lower impact toughness, due to upper bainite microstructure, with a very coarse primary austenitic grains.
- Double simulation 1350/700 and 1350/600°C has not worsened impact properties.
- Almost in all cases the energy for crack initiation is higher than the energy for crack propagation and less temperature dependent at the same time.

REFERENCES

1. M.Kilpatrick (1972): THE APLICATION OF THERMAL SIMULATION TECHNIQUES TO THE ASSESSMENT OF MECHANICAL AND METALLURGICAL PROPERTIES OF HAZ IN HIGH YELD STEELS, A Research application Seminar, London, April 1972
2. A. Imamovic, V. Semjan (1991): Simulacija zavarivackih termickih ciklusa kao metoda za ocenjivanje zavarljivosti, Zavarivanje Vol. 36, No. 1/2 21-28
3. R.E. Dolby, M.A. Widgery (1972): THE SIMULATION OF HAZ, MICROSTUCTURES, A Research application Seminar, London, April 1972

4. O.M. Akselsen, O. Grong, J.K. Solberg (1987): Structure-Properties Relationship in Inter-critical Heat Affected Zone of Low-carbon Microalloyed Steels, Materials Science and Technology, August 1987, Vol. 3649

5. J.H. Chen, T. D. Xia, C. Yan (1993), Study of impact toughness of C-Mn Multilayer weld metal at −60 ^{0}C, IIW Doc II-A-882-93

6. Yan Cheng, Chen Jianhong (1994): Microstructure and toughness of local brittle zone of HSLA steel multipass weld metals, IIW Doc II-A-912-94

7. D.P. Fairchild: Local Brittle Zones in Structural Steels, Exxon Production Research Company, Houston, Texas 77001

From Charpy to Present Impact Testing
D. François and A. Pineau (Eds.)
© 2002 Elsevier Science Ltd. and ESIS. All rights reserved

ON THE UTILIZATION OF THE INSTRUMENTED CHARPY IMPACT TEST FOR CHARACTERIZING THE FLOW AND FRACTURE BEHAVIOR OF REACTOR PRESSURE VESSEL STEELS

R. Chaouadi and A. Fabry
SCK•CEN, Boeretang 200, 2400 Mol, Belgium.

ABSTRACT

The Charpy impact test is extensively used in the surveillance programs to monitor nuclear reactor pressure vessel degradation induced by neutron irradiation. The energy absorbed during the test is the main parameter used for engineering characterization of the materials. At SCK•CEN, a large effort was put into taking advantage of the test instrumentation allowing for load versus time recording during the whole test.

Analysis of the load – time trace allows to determine a number of key parameters, in particular, the flow properties, the microcleavage fracture stress, the crack arrest performance and the characteristic transition temperatures which are more physically grounded than conventional indexing to fixed absorbed energy or lateral expansion levels.

Combination of static tensile tests with instrumented Charpy impact tests allows for establishing the so-called stress diagram. This can be used as input to micromechanical modeling of the static as well as dynamic initiation fracture toughness trends. Furthermore, the Charpy arrest load correlates well to the nil ductility temperature as determined from the Pellini drop weight test and allows concurrent application of a crack arrest safety approach.

As it will be illustrated by relevant examples, a significant advantage of the above considerations is that they allow to incorporate a physically grounded understanding of irradiation effects into the evaluation of reactor vessel integrity.

KEYWORDS

Slow bend test, Charpy specimen, load diagram, microcleavage fracture stress, flow properties, crack arrest, shear fracture appearance, tensile properties, static testing, dynamic testing, transition temperature, radiation embrittlement, reactor pressure vessel steels.

INTRODUCTION

The Charpy impact test is widely used in the industry mainly as a quality control means. After world war II, this test was also adopted by the nuclear industry to monitor the reactor pressure vessel embrittlement induced by irradiation [1,2]. With the development of fracture toughness methods, a number of investigators have proposed correlations allowing prediction of fracture toughness from Charpy impact data. However, these correlations remain empirical and therefore questionable as they are solely based on experimental data.

In the early 60's, the Charpy impact test gained interest with the instrumentation of the tup. Indeed, the instrumented test provides a load-time record which gives more insight on the fracture history of the Charpy sample.

In the nuclear industry, the Charpy impact test plays a key role in the evaluation of reactor pressure vessel lifetime. Indeed, the radiation-induced shift of the Charpy impact transition curve is used as an index to fracture toughness behavior. The level at which the temperature shift is evaluated is empirically chosen, varying from one regulation to another. However, it is known and it will be shown in this paper that this procedure is inadequate not only because of lack of physical background, but also because it may lead to an unnecessary large conservatism.

This paper provides a detailed analysis of the Charpy impact trace to show the valuable information that can be obtained from the Charpy impact test beside the usual data related to energy, in particular:
- the flow properties;
- the microcleavage fracture stress;
- the crack arrest performance;
- the characteristic transition temperatures, which are more physically grounded than conventional indexing to, fixed absorbed energy or lateral expansion levels.

BACKGROUND

During the Charpy impact test, the specimen goes through a number of distinct phases [3-5]. This is illustrated in Fig. 1, which shows a typical load-time test record. The characteristic loads that are used throughout this paper are also indicated.
- load at general yield (P_{gy}) : corresponds to the point where the plastic zone is such that it has reached the opposite surface of the specimen cross-section below the notch;
- maximum load (P_m);
- load at unstable fracture (P_u) : load at which brittle unstable fracture occurs;
- arrest load (P_a) : load at which fracture arrest occurs resulting in a transition from cleavage to ductile fracture.

In Fig. 2, the load-time test record is expressed in terms of the various stages of fracture that can be observed on the fracture surface. First, the energy is spent for the formation of a ductile crack front which is assumed to occur after general yielding, at a point midway between the latter and the maximum load. This was experimentally verified using a magnetic emission detector [6]. This crack front will extend in a stable manner until unstable cleavage fracture occurs followed immediately by an arrest of the propagating crack. Finally, the energy is spend in shear lips formation. Of course, depending on test temperature, the different mechanisms can be dominating or vanishing. For example, when fracture occurs at general yield, the crack is usually not arrested. On the other side at upper shelf temperature, the fracture process is stable leading to fully ductile fracture.

So, the load-time trace correlates very well to the fracture appearance. As it will be seen later, the percentage of shear fracture appearance is a potential transition temperature index.

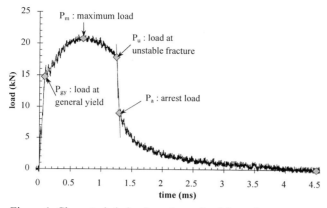

Figure 1. Characteristic loads as determined from the test record.

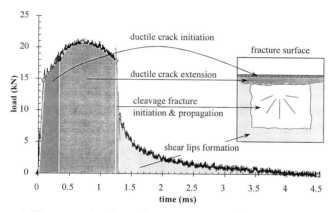

Figure 2. Energy partitioning and correspondence with the fracture surface.

It is known that the monitoring of reactor pressure vessel degradation relies worldwide on the Charpy impact test. All regulatory procedures use the concept in which the shift of the fracture toughness lower bound is indexed by the shift of the Charpy impact transition curve. Only a small difference is found in the energy level at which the transition temperature is determined, i.e., 41J for the American, 47J for the Russian and 56J in French regulation. The inadequacy of the transition temperature based on an energy fix is known for a long time [5]. In particular, this procedure is known to be too conservative in many cases.

For illustration, a comparison of the load-time record of two samples that ruptured with an absorbed energy of about 41J is shown in Fig. 3 for WWER-440 weld, in the unirradiated and irradiated condition. The shift of the transition curve and consequently of the fracture toughness lower bound curve is about 125°C. In Fig. 3, the unirradiated and irradiated specimens are compared in terms of test temperature, absorbed energy, shear fracture appearance (SFA) and lateral expansion. As it can be seen, the main difference except test temperature is the SFA. Having in mind Fig. 2, the ductile crack extension ahead of the notch was measured for each specimen. Figure 4 shows the correlation between the SFA and the ductile crack growth measured ahead of the notch. As the brittle surface is usually centered with respect to the specimen ligament, the maximum crack extension at 100%-SFA is 4 mm. Within the experimental and statistical uncertainties, there is a unique trend curve although various data corresponding to different conditions were used. This correlation was also verified on many other steels [7]. Considering now Fig. 5 where the SFA is plotted against the absorbed energy for both conditions and Fig. 4 for the correlation between SFA and ductile crack extension, the ductile crack extension below the notch is only 0.3 mm in the unirradiated material while it is about 1 mm for the irradiated sample. On the other hand, the crack arrests for the irradiated material at a load twice higher than for the unirradiated one. Without the latter compensation, the transition temperature shift would be much larger. Finally, note that for this material, the SFA-shift is only 100°C, in comparison to 120°C of the 41J-energy shift. This situation is not singular but was found in many other cases.

This clearly shows the inadequacy of such an energy-based temperature index mainly because the underlying mechanisms of crack formation, propagation and arrest are ignored. In the following, other parameters will be considered in order to remedy the lack of physically-based concept, in particular by associating the various parameters to the micromechanisms occurring during the whole deformation and fracture process.

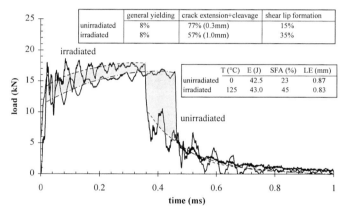

Figure 3. Effect of irradiation on the load-time trace at the 41J energy level. (WWER-440 weld).

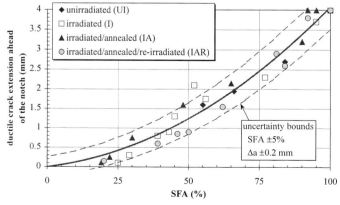

Figure 4. Correlation between ductile crack extension and % of shear fracture appearance (SFA) for WWER-440 weld at various conditions .

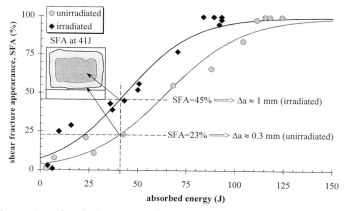

Figure 5. At constant absorbed energy level, ductile crack propagation is larger in irradiated material than in the initial condition (WWER-440 Weld).

MATERIALS AND TESTING

Two A533B-type RPV steels were selected for this investigation. The 20MnMoNi55 forging was thoroughly investigated at GKSS in Germany by J. Heerens and coworkers [8]. This steel has properties which are very similar to many steels used in RPV technology. A broken 4T compact tension specimen was provided by GKSS to SCK•CEN for further investigation.

The second steel is an A533B Cl.1 steel which was provided by the Japan Steel Works through K. Onizawa from JAERI and used in a Japanese round robin organized by the Japan Society for the Promotion of Science (JSPS) [9]. The main interest in this steel is that it was deliberately embrittled by increasing the S and P concentration (see Table 1). As a result, the upper shelf energy in very low (USE $\approx$ 70 J) and the transition temperature is above the ambient temperature ($T_{50\%}$=43°C). This steel is representative of an irradiated steel subjected to a very high neutron exposure.

Table 1. Chemical composition.

steel	origin	C	Si	P	S	Cr	Mn	Ni	Cu	Mo
20MnMoNi55	GKSS	0.19	0.20	0.007	0.008	0.12	1.29	0.80	0.11	0.53
A533B Cl.1	JSPS	0.24	0.41	0.028	0.023	0.08	1.52	0.43	0.19	0.49

Table 2. Mechanical properties.

steel	origin	yield stress (MPa)	tensile strength (MPa)	elongation (%)	reduction of area (%)	USE (J)	FATT (°C)
20MnMoNi55	GKSS	430	576	22	73	181	-24
A533B Cl.1	JSPS	461	640	18	59	72	43

As it can be seen from Table 2, the Charpy upper shelf energy (USE) of the A533B steel is 60% lower than the 20MnMoNi55 and the transition temperature measured with the fracture appearance transition temperature, FATT, is 67°C higher than the 20MnMoNi55.

Different tests were performed:
- Static (or quasi-static) tensile: strain rate = 1.33×10^{-4} s^{-1}

- Dynamic tensile: strain rate = 10 s^{-1}
- Charpy specimens in slow 3-point bending : loading velocity = 4.16 mm/min
- Charpy impact tests : loading velocity = 5.42 m/s
- Griffiths–Owen type specimens [10] in slow 4-point bending: loading velocity = 0.5 mm/min.

The Charpy impact tests were performed on the 300 J Toni Mfl impact machine with an ISO tup. The static Charpy tests were carried out using the same loading geometry as for the impact tests. The loading system for the dynamic tests is such that the crosshead velocity is quasi-constant throughout the whole test. Finally, all tests, instrumented with the appropriate devices, were performed according to prevailing standards.

LOAD DIAGRAM

The Charpy impact load diagram has received a large attention for many years [3-5,11]. However, the concept was successfully integrated in an engineering approach to study radiation effects of RPV steels by Fabry and coworkers [6] only in the last decade. This approach rationalizes the instrumented Charpy impact and static tensile data into a unique description of the material including the strain rate effects on the flow properties, the fracture at general yield and the crack arrest behavior. In the following, the load diagram approach is briefly recalled. Very much detailed analysis of the load diagram is given in [6].

The characteristic loads can be determined from the instrumented Charpy impact test record according to Fig. 1. In order to uniquely describe static as well as dynamic flow properties, these loads should be expressed in terms of stress. The associated stresses can easily be derived using the following relation [6,12]:

$$\sigma = \frac{\beta \, S \, P}{2 \, C_f \, (W - a)^2 \, B}$$

where σ is the stress, S is the span (=40 mm), P is the load, W is the specimen width (=10 mm), B is the specimen thickness (=10 mm), a is the notch depth (=2 mm);
C_f is the constraint factor which depends on the tup configuration: C_f=1.274 for ISO tup and C_f=1.363 for ASTM tup [6];
β is a constant depending on the yielding criterion: β=2 for Tresca and β=$\sqrt{3}$ for von Mises criterion.
At SCK•CEN, as also found by Fearnehough [13], an intermediate criterion between Tresca and von Mises ($\beta_{average}$=1.866) gives the best agreement. Figure 6 compares yield strength values obtained with uniaxial tensile tests to stress values obtained with static Charpy tests using the above-mentioned equation with β=1.866.

Application of these values leads to the following conversion formula for an ISO tup:

$$\sigma \, (\text{MPa}) = 45.8 \times P \, (\text{kN})$$

Once the stresses are calculated, a diagram can be constructed which combines the static tensile and the Charpy impact characteristic stresses of the material under consideration. The static and dynamic yield strength data can be fitted with physically grounded equations while other stress components corresponding to maximum and arrest loads are empirically fitted.

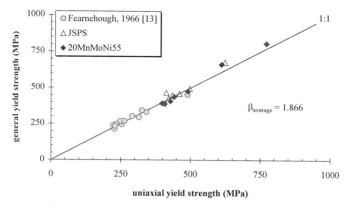

Figure 6. An average criterion between von Mises and Tresca gives the best agreement for general yield.

Flow properties

Details on the representation of the flow behavior of solids can be found in the literature. Basically, the yield strength can be represented by the sum of two components:

1. the athermal stress, σ_{ath}, which is not thermally activated, accounting for the interaction between dislocations with long range obstacles (precipitates, grain boundaries, ...);
2. the thermally activated stress, σ_P, which accounts for short range obstacles (<10 atom diameters) to dislocation motion. These short-range barriers include the Peierls-Nabarro stresses and dislocation forests. σ_P is also called effective Peierls stress.

The equation used to describe the yield strength as a function of strain rate and temperature is [6,14]:

$$\sigma(\dot{\varepsilon}, T) = \sigma_P \left(1 - \alpha T\right) \left[1 - \left(\frac{k\, T\, \mathrm{Ln}\left(\dot{\varepsilon}_0 / \dot{\varepsilon}\right)}{H_c} \right)^{1/m'} \right]^m + \sigma_{ath}\left(1 - \alpha T\right)$$

where H_c is the activation energy (enthalpy) of a given barrier, T is the temperature, $\dot{\varepsilon}_0$ is the intrinsic strain rate sensitivity of the material, m and m' are constants that describe the lattice energy barrier [6,14] and k is the Boltzmann constant (k=8.62 10^{-5} eV/K).

Note that the flow stress is corrected to take into account the decrease of elastic modulus with increasing temperature, $(1-\alpha T)$, where α is the coefficient of temperature dependence of the Young modulus.

While the strain rate can easily be determined in a uniaxial tensile test, this is not the case for the Charpy-type bend geometry. It is known, for instance, that the strain rate at the tip of the notch is around 3000 s^{-1}. However, one should consider an effective strain rate which takes into account the whole geometry and not the notch tip only. This effective strain rate is the one that gives the same yield strength as in the uniaxial test. Hence, it is found that $\dot{\varepsilon}=10\ s^{-1}$ for the standard Charpy impact test. Typical examples of application are given in Figures 7 and 8 for both steels under consideration in this paper. Solid lines are obtained with the yield strength equation given above. A statistical and experimental deviation of about ±6% is usually found on these curves.

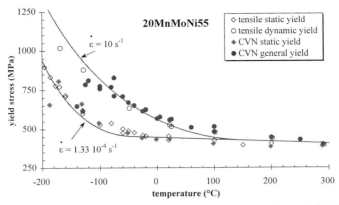

Figure 7. Temperature and strain rate effects on the flow behavior of 20MnMoNi55.

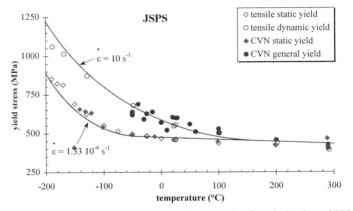

Figure 8. Temperature and strain rate effects on the flow behavior of JSPS.

Stress at maximum load

The stress corresponding to maximum load is not a material intrinsic property, but a geometry-dependent quantity. It is therefore empirically modeled by adding to the yield strength a quantity fitted on the experimental Charpy impact data, i.e.:

$$\sigma_m\big|_{model} = \sigma_{gy}\big|_{model} + \left(\sigma_m - \sigma_{gy}\right)_{fit}$$

where σ_{gy} is the general yield strength and σ_m is the stress at maximum load.

Crack arrest

Licensing rules related to safety against brittle fracture of reactor pressure vessel steels are based on the nil ductility transition temperature. The latter is based on the Pellini drop-weight test. The reference temperature, RT_{NDT}, is determined using nil ductility transition temperature and Charpy impact data. However, in the irradiated condition, only Charpy data are available for surveillance purposes. Therefore, the shift of the RT_{NDT} is indexed to the shift of the Charpy impact transition curve measured at a fixed energy level, for example, 41J according to the American regulation. This shift is known to be very conservative.

The use of crack arrest load to correlate the nil ductility temperature was first proposed at GKSS [15,16]. More recently, Wallin [17], Iskander [18] and Fabry [19] have used this characteristic load to better describe the crack arrest behavior of RPV steels.

In [19], a crack arrest master curve-type formulation was adopted using the following equations [6,7] for the temperature dependence of the arrest load, $P_a(T)$ or arrest stress, $\sigma_a(T)$:

$$P_a(T) = 3\exp(\lambda T - NDT)$$

$$\sigma_a(T) = \kappa\exp(\lambda T - NDT)$$

where is λ is a constant (λ=0.020 for T<NDT and λ=0.026 for T>NDT), κ=137 MPa/°C for an ISO tup, P_a and σ_a are expressed in kN and MPa, respectively. The nil-ductility temperature, NDT, corresponds to a median CVN arrest load indexing level of 3 kN. More information on this characteristic temperature can be found in [19]. Figure 9 shows the agreement between experimental data and the proposed equation with its 95% confidence bounds.

It should be noted that alternative crack arrest load levels were used with success to determine the NDT but the best load level and NDT-accuracy should be validated on large experimental databanks (see Table 3).

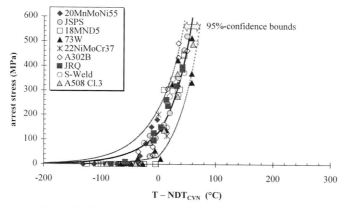

Figure 9. Rationalization of the crack arrest behavior.

Table 3. Various load levels used for NDT determination.

load level P_a (kN)	number of materials N	deviation from NDT$_{Pellini}$ ΔT (°C)	reference
4.0	7	±10	[17]
2.45	8	±11	[18]
3.0	26	±15	[19]

In Fig. 10, a comparison is made between NDT as determined form standardized Pellini drop weight tests and Charpy impact data, which clearly shows a reasonable agreement.

Stress diagram and consistency with SFA

A consistent stress diagram can then be constructed from which some characteristic temperatures can be determined (see Figures 11 and 12):

- T_I : temperature at which fracture occurs at general yielding;

- T_N : temperature above which cleavage fracture occurs after the maximum load was reached. Below T_N, unstable fracture occurs at maximum load;
- T_O : temperature corresponding to the onset of upper shelf (100% fibrous fracture).

As it will be seen later, the stress at T_I, σ_{T_I}, correlates well with the microcleavage fracture stress.

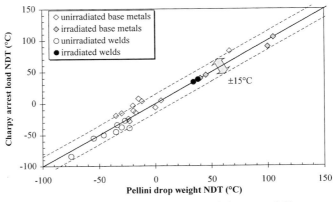

Figure 10. NDT correlation between Pellini drop weight test and Charpy arrest load.

As it can be expected from Fig. 2, there should be a direct correlation between these characteristic parameters and the shear fracture appearance. This was shown in [6,14] where the SFA can be estimated from the characteristic loads through the following equation:

$$\mathrm{SFA}(\%) = 100 \left[1 - \frac{(P_u - P_a)}{P_m + k(P_m - P_{gy})} \right]$$

where k=0 for T< T_N and k=0.5 for T>T_N. Note that the constant k=0.5 corresponds to ductile fracture initiation occurring between the general yield and the maximum load. Of course, SFA=0% for T<T_I and SFA=100% for T≥T_O. Figure 13 shows the application of such an equation to 20MnMoNi55 and JSPS together with the experimental data. As it can be seen, there is a consistency between the stress diagram (Figures 11 and 12) and the corresponding shear fracture appearance (Fig. 13).

For both steels, slow bend tests at 25°C and 290°C were interrupted at a load midway between the general yield and maximum loads. After heat tinting and fracture at liquid nitrogen temperature, examination under optical microscope of the fracture surface revealed a ductile crack front of about 40 to 50μm-thick. This clearly supports the value of k=0.5 for determining the shear fracture appearance from the loads.

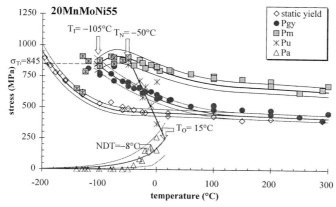

Figure 11. Stress diagram of 20MnMoNi55.

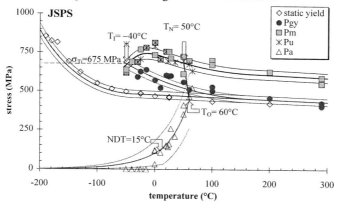

Figure 12. Stress diagram of JSPS.

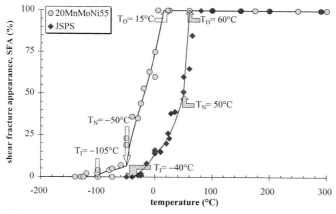

Figure 13. The characteristic parameters allow to describe the SFA as a function of test temperature.

Microcleavage fracture stress

It is known that cleavage fracture is the dominant fracture mechanism of RPV steels in the region below upper shelf regime. Fracture is associated with reaching a critical stress, the so-called microcleavage fracture stress, over a microstructurally significant length [20]. The microcleavage fracture stress was successfully measured using the single-edge specimen loaded in 4-point bending, called also the Griffiths-Owen type specimen [10]. Fracture initiation sites were determined using scanning electron microscopy examination and the corresponding maximum principal stress is determined using the Griffiths and Owen [10] finite element results.

The microcleavage fracture stress can also be determined from the Charpy impact data by multiplying the stress at general yielding by the plastic stress concentration factor, $K_{\sigma p}$, which is equal to 2.52 or 2.18, depending on the selected yield criterion, von Mises or Tresca, respectively. In our case, in consistence with stresses calculated from Charpy specimen, an intermediate criterion is selected which gives $K_{\sigma p}$, =2.35.
The 4-point bend tests using Griffiths-Owen type specimens were investigated with a scanning electron microscopy to determine the crack initiation sites. Using the Griffiths and Owen finite element calculation [10], the local cleavage fracture stress was calculated for each sample. For both materials, a very good agreement is obtained between the various specimen geometries and strain rates (see Table 4). These microcleavage fracture stresses derived from the Charpy specimen compared to experimental values determined locally at the fracture initiation sites also show a good agreement (see Fig. 14). Some of the 4-point bend (tested at −196°C) and all CT test results on 20MnMoNi55 are taken from [8].

Table 4. Specimen geometry and strain rate effects on the stress at general yield.

specimen	strain rate	20MnMoNi55			JSPS		
		T_I (°C)	σ_{T_I} (MPa)	σ_c^* (MPa)	T_I (°C)	σ_{T_I} (MPa)	σ_c^* (MPa)
CVN	static	-170	810	1900	-140	670	1572
CVN	impact	-105	845	1982	-40	675	1584
4-point bend	static	-170	804	1886	-130	610	1430

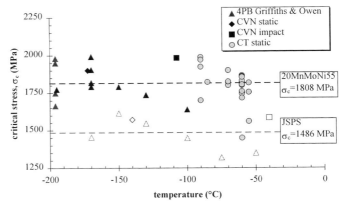

Figure 14. Temperature and strain rate effects on the microcleavage fracture stress of 20MnMoNi55 (full symbols) and JSPS (open symbols).

Discussion

It is interesting at this point to examine how such a load diagram approach can be used for engineering problems. A comprehensive and well-described example of application can be found in [14]. Here, we have gathered a number of data in Fig. 15 for radiation-induced shifts as measured with T_I and NDT (for initiation and arrest) and compared to the 41J-energy fix that is used in US regulation. As it can be seen, the latter is mostly higher than the former transition temperatures. The $T_{50\%}$ and the static fracture toughness transition temperature, T_0, are also shown for comparison. Within the experimental and statistical uncertainties, it is clear that the energy-fix is inadequate for fracture toughness indexation, for both initiation and arrest toughness. Alternatively, the $T_{50\%}$ provides a better estimate of the transition temperature shift than T_{41J}. Finally, it is important to emphasize here that 15°C margin on the transition temperature shift corresponds to about 3 to 10 years of operation of a nuclear power station, depending on the material radiation-sensitivity. This clearly shows the importance of reducing unnecessary conservatism introduced by engineering parameters such as T_{41J}. Finally, the load diagram can be used as an input to micromechanical modeling of the static as well as dynamic initiation fracture toughness trends [21,22].

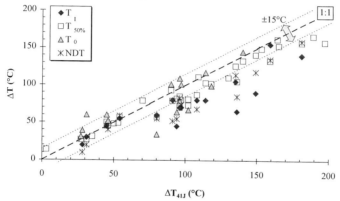

Figure 15. Over-conservatism of the 41J-energy level for evaluating radiation-induced transition temperature shift.

CONCLUSIONS

Thanks to tup instrumentation, the Charpy impact test contains much more information than it is usually done. Indeed, not only the global quantities, i.e., absorbed energy, lateral expansion and shear fracture appearance, can be derived, but also valuable information on the flow properties, strain rate effects and crack arrest performance can be obtained. For comparative studies, as in irradiation effects, the transition temperature shift is used to measure the irradiation sensitivity of reactor pressure vessel steels. It is shown that global quantities are inadequate to index fracture toughness transition curves. Better temperature indexes, like T_I, the temperature at which fracture occurs at general yielding, is more physically-grounded than any energy-fix which is biased by the multiple processes that occur during the Charpy impact test. These processes include ductile crack initiation and propagation, unstable fracture followed by crack arrest and finally shear lip formation. These processes are not equally affected by irradiation and therefore, the use of global parameters like energy to measure the effect of irradiation is biased.

An important capacity of the Charpy impact test is also that it allows to determine the NDT, the nil ductility temperature, which is usually measured with Pellini drop weight tests requiring large samples and a careful weld bead preparation. This is very important as the ASME lower bound fracture toughness curve, K_{IR}, is based on such a concept.

The consistency of the load diagram approach was verified from different points of view. The effective strain rate during a Charpy test is comparable to dynamic tensile tests with cylindrical specimens at a strain rate of $\dot{\varepsilon} = 10 \text{ s}^{-1}$. Slow bend Charpy tests have been used to qualify the procedure allowing to determine the yield stress from the load at general yield. The shear fracture appearance, experimentally measured, is also consistent with the load diagram. Finally, the microcleavage fracture stress can be reliably determined from Charpy impact data. The values found for the steels investigated here are in good agreement with local values determined with Griffiths-Owen type as well as with fracture toughness specimens. The microcleavage fracture stress can then be used in a micromechanical model to predict fracture toughness trend curve.

ACKNOWLEDGEMENTS

This work was performed within the frame of SCK•CEN – Electrabel convention. The authors gratefully acknowledge the support and interest of R. Gérard from Tractebel Energy Engineering. Many thanks to the LHMA technical assistance for the experimental work, in particular, R. Mertens and R. Sneyers for specimen fabrication, A. Pellettieri, J.L Puzzolante and L. Van Houdt for testing and A. Leenaers for SEM analysis. Special thanks to J. Heerens (GKSS) and K. Onizawa (JAERI) for providing the steels investigated here.

REFERENCES

1. U.S. Nuclear Regulatory Commission, Regulatory Guide 1.99 Revision 2, Office of Nuclear Regulatory Research, 1988.
2. Federal Register, Vol. 56, No. 94, Rules and Regulations, May 15, 1991 and Code of Federal Regulation, Title 10, Part 50, Article 61, July 1991.
3. Nichols, R.W. and Harries, D.R. (1963). In: *Radiation Effects on Metals and Neutron Dosimetry*, **ASTM STP 341**, pp. 162-198. American Society for Testing and Materials, Philadelphia.
4. Fearnehough, G.D. and Hoy, C.J. (1964). *J. Iron Steel Inst.*, November, pp. 912-920.
5. Wullaert, R.A., Ireland, D.R. and Tetelman, A.S. (1970). In: *Irradiation Effects on Structural Alloys and Nuclear Reactor Applications*, **ASTM STP 484**, pp. 20-41. American Society for Testing and Materials, Philadelphia.
6. Fabry A., van Walle E., Chaouadi R., Wannijn J.P., Verstrepen A., Puzzolante J.L., Van Ransbeeck T. and Van de Velde J. (1993). In: *IAEA/OECD Specialists Meeting on Irradiation Embrittlement and Optimization of Annealing*, Paris, and SCK•CEN Report BLG-649.
7. Chaouadi, R. et al., to be published.
8. Heerens, J., Read, D.T., Cornec, A. and Schwalbe, K.H. (1991). In: *Defects Assessment in Components – Fundamentals and Applications*, pp. 659-678, Blauel, J.G. and Schwalbe, K.H. (Eds). Mechanical Engineering Publications, London.
9. "Standard Test Method for Fracture Toughness within Ductile-Brittle Transition Range," Standard of the 129th Committee, Japan Society for the Promotion of Science, 1995, (in Japanese).
10. Griffiths, J.R. and Owen, D.R. (1971) *J. Mech. Phys. Solids*, **19**, 419-431.

11. Wullaert, R.A. (1976). In: Proceedings of the IAEA meeting on Reactor Pressure Vessel Surveillance, Vienna, 1977, pp. 173-192.
12. Server, W.S. (1978), *J. Eng. Mat. Techn.*, **100**, 183-188.
13. Fearnehough, G.D. (1966), In: *Physical Basis of Yield and Fracture*, pp. 88-99, Institute of Physics and Physical Society, Oxford.
14. Fabry A., Van de Velde J., Biemiller E.C., Carter R.G., Petrova T. (1996). In: *Effects of Irradiation on Materials*, **ASTM STP 1270**, pp. 138-187, Gelles, D.S., Nanstad, R.K., Kumar A.S. and Little, E.A. (Eds). American Society for Testing and Materials, Philadelphia.
15. Ahlf, J, Bellmann, D., Föhl, J., Hebenbrock, H.D., Schmitt, F.J. and Spalthoff, W. (1986). In: *Radiation Embrittlement of Nuclear Reactor Pressure Vessel Steels*, **ASTM STP 909**, pp. 34-51, L.E. Steele (Ed). American Society for Testing and Materials, Philadelphia.
16. Schmitt, F.J. (1990). In: *Effects of Radiation on Materials*, **ASTM STP 1046** (Vol. II), pp. 373-384, Packan N.H., Stoller, R.E. and Kumar, A.S. (Eds). American Society for Testing and Materials, Philadelphia.
17. Wallin K. (1996). In: *Evaluating Material Properties by Dynamic Testing*, pp. 165-176, ESIS 20, E. van Walle (Ed). Mechanical Engineering Publications, London.
18. Iskander, S.K., Nanstad, R.K., Sokolov, M.A., McCabe, D.E., Hutton, J.T. and Thomas, D.L. (1999). In: *Effects of Radiation on Materials*, **ASTM STP 1325**, pp. 204-222, Nanstad, R.K., Hamilton, M.L., Garner, F.A. and Kumar, A.S. (Eds). American Society for Testing and Materials, West Conshohocken.
19. Fabry A., (1997), SCK•CEN Report BLG-750.
20. Ritchie R.O., Knott J.F. and Rice J.R. (1973) *J. Mech. Phys. Solids*, **21**, 395-410.
21. Ritchie R.O., Server W.L. and Wullaert R.A. (1979) *Met. Trans.*, **10A**, 1557-1570.
22. Fabry A. (1998). In: *Small Specimen Test Techniques*, **ASTM STP 1329**, pp. 274-297, Corwin, W.R., Rosinski, S.T. and van Walle, E. (Eds). American Society for Testing and Materials, 1998, West Conshohocken.

From Charpy to Present Impact Testing
D. François and A. Pineau (Eds.)
© 2002 Elsevier Science Ltd. and ESIS. All rights reserved

DUCTILE-BRITTLE TRANSITION EVALUATION OF JAPANESE SWORD AND WELD METALS USING MINIATURIZED IMPACT SPECIMENS

TOSHIHEI MISAWA and SHIN-ICHI KOMAZAKI

Department of Materials Science and Engineering,

Muroran Institute of Technology,

27-1 Mizumoto-cho, Muroran,

050-8585 JAPAN

Abstract: A small specimen impact test using miniaturized specimens with 1.5, 1.0 and 0.7 mm square and 20 mm length has been demonstrated for evaluating the strength-toughness balance along a cross section of Japanese sword and the ductile-brittle transition properties of three different kinds of weld metals. The traditional empirical processing of Japanese sword gave the excellent gradated balance of strength-toughness. The edge side consisting of the hard structure of martensite showed low absorbed impact energies. On the other hand, the back side of the ferrite/pearlite coexisting structure exhibited higher values. In the case of weld metals, the statistically reliable ductile-brittle transition curves and the values of DBTT and FATT were obtained by using the miniaturized specimens sampled from the different weld metals. They were correlated to those of the conventional Charpy-V specimens. Consequently, the laser welded steel metal composed of an extremely fine acicular ferritic structure has a superior toughness and was estimated to exhibit a DBTT as large as 168 K when converted to the value estimated for standard size specimen.

Key words: small specimen testing technique, small specimen impact test, ductile-brittle transition, Japanese sword, weld metal, laser weld steel, DBTT, FATT

INTRODUCTION

Small punch (SP) testing method using miniaturized specimens, which is a kind of small specimen testing technique (SSTT), has been developed for two decades for the purpose of estimating the ductile-brittle transition temperature (DBTT) [1, 2] and the fracture toughness [3] for advanced nuclear energy structural steels. In recent years, the small specimen impact test has been carried out in our laboratory [4-6] to evaluate the strength-toughness balance of the traditional Japanese sword, and to obtain the ductile-brittle transition temperature (DBTT) and the fracture appearance transition temperature (FATT) correlated to conventional standard Charpy-V impact specimens in welded steel metals.

The present paper aims to demonstrate a possible extension of the small specimen impact test to ductile-brittle transition evaluation using miniaturized specimens extracted from the various microstructure parts in forged Japanese sword and in different welded steel metals. Indeed it would have been difficult to appreciate directly the fracture toughness and the mechanical properties from conventional full size specimens due to a limited shape of sword and a fracture path deviation from weld metal to base metal.

EXPERIMENTAL PROCEDURE

Materials

The following two kinds of steel samples were cut into miniaturized impact specimens.

(1) The as-received Japanese sword [5] made by means of TSUKURIKOMI process, which combines four kinds of edge, core, back and side steels with different carbon contents. By this process, edge (HASAKI) side becomes high carbon steel and back (MUNE) side is made of low carbon steel. The cooling velocity in quenching of the Japanese sword is controlled by a process, which coats the sword with clay, thinner in the edge side and thicker in the back side. The edge side is quickly cooled and the back side is slowly cooled. The microstructure in the edge side shows martensite while the back side shows a mixed structure of ferrite and pearlite. Figure 1 shows the cutting procedure of miniaturized V-notched impact specimens with 1.0 and 0.7 mm square and 20 mm length (Fig. 2) from a Japanese sword made by Mr. Tanetada Horii, Japanese sword smith of JSW, Muroran.

(2) Three kinds of miniaturized V-notched impact specimens with 1.5, 1.0 and 0.7 mm square and 20 mm length, as shown in Fig. 2, were employed to evaluate the toughness of different weld metal steels. Three kinds of weld metals with quite the same composition of low carbon steel (API grade X60) [6] were prepared as shown in Fig. 3: submerged arc weld metal (type S), CO_2 laser weld metal welded on the submerged arc weld metal (type L), and the submerged arc weld metal subjected to a thermal cycle with water quenching after welding (type T). The microstructures of type S, L and T were homogeneous acicular ferrite, fine acicular ferrite and martensite, respectively.

Small Specimen Impact Tests

Figure 4 is a schematic drawing of the developed three-point bending type impact testing apparatus for small specimens over a range from liquid nitrogen temperature to 500 K [4, 6]

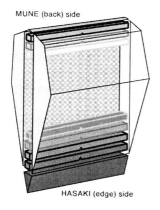

Fig. 1 Cutting of miniaturized V-notched impact specimens from a Japanese sword.

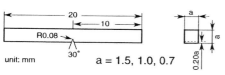

Fig. 2 Shape and dimension of impact specimen.

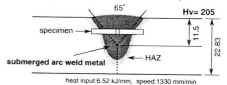

(a) Type S (submerged arc weld metal)

heat input:6.52 kJ/mm, speed:1330 mm/min

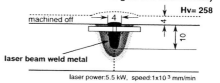

(b) Type L (CO$_2$ laser weld metal welded on submerged arc weld metal)

laser power:5.5 kW, speed:1x10^3 mm/min

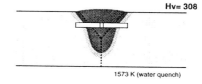

(c) Type T (submerged arc weld metal subjected to thermal cycle)

1573 K (water quench)

Fig. 3 Three kinds of weld metal steels used.

Impact speed of 1 m/s was adopted for Japanese sword and welded metal specimen tested in this report. In all cases the load-displacement curves were recorded and the values of fracture energy were calculated from the full area under the curves, for the evaluation of ductile-brittle transition behavior.

RESULTS AND DISCUSSION

Strength-Toughness Balance Evaluation along a Cross Section of Japanese Sword [5]

Figure 5 shows the distribution of micro-Vickers hardness on a cross section of the Japanese sword from edge to back sides. The microstructures corresponding to symbols I , III ∼IV, II in Fig. 5 are martensite in quenched region, mixture of proeutectoid ferrite/fine pearlite in the range of slowly cooled region and martensite matrix with nodular pearlite in the boundary area of intermediate cooling rate, respectively. The edge side has a very high value of 800 Hv-1kgf for cutting function. In contrast to the edge side, the back side takes part in high toughness of lower hardness, through the gradated intermediate region.

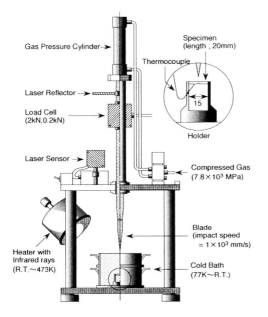

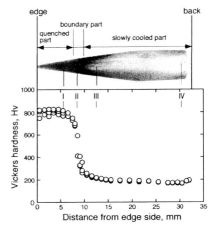

Fig. 5 Distribution of micro-Vickers hardness
on a cross section of the Japanese sword.

Fig. 4 Schematic illustration of the developed three-point
bending type impact testing machine.

Figure 6 shows a sequence of changes in the load-displacement curves of the impact test
on the position I $\sim$ IV for the 1.0 and 0.7 mm square specimens. It can be seen that the present
measurement of a load using a strain gauge succeeds in preventing large oscillations [5]. The
absorbed impact energy necessary for fracture was calculated from the area under the load-
displacement curve obtained. The absorbed impact energy and normalized impact value by
initial cross-sectional area from V-notch bottom were plotted against the distance from edge side
in Figs. 7 (a) and (b), respectively. The ductile-brittle transition behaviors can be clearly seen in
both of the 1.0 and 0.7 mm square specimens and large scattering results are not observed in the
present measurements. There is almost no variation in the lower shelf energy between both of
the specimens though the energies are quite low. It seems that the energies in the lower shelf
region could be precisely measured, as well as the other regions, because of relatively good
reproducibility of results, even though the energies are quite low. In contrast to the lower shelf
energy, the upper shelf energy obtained from 0.7 mm square specimen lies below that of 1.0 mm
square specimen with larger cross-section. However, normalizing by initial cross-section results
in the same absorbed energy per square cm, namely, the same impact value. The changes in
absorbed impact energy and impact value on a cross-section show the inverse dependence on the
micro-hardness. The width of the gradated transition region of ductile-brittle extends due to
cyclic folding forging [5], when compared with the narrow hardness distribution in Fig. 5. Thus,

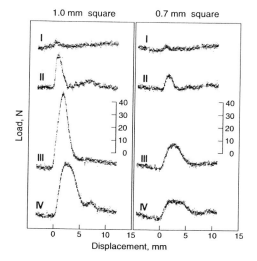

Fig. 6 Examples of load-displacement curves measured.

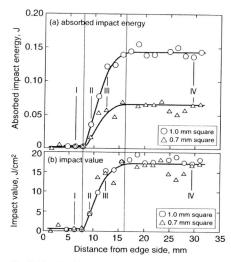

Fig. 7 Absorbed impact energy and impact value plotted against distance from edge side.

it was found that the traditional empirical process of Japanese sword gave the excellent gradated balance of strength-toughness consisting of edge side of the martensite structure showing a lower value and back side of the ferrite-pearlite coexisting structure showing a higher value in the absorbed impact fracture energies across a section.

Ductile-Brittle Transition Evaluation of Different Weld Metal Steels [6]

Figure 8 shows the ductile-brittle transition curves and DBTTs obtained from the three kinds of small impact specimens with three varieties of weld metals. Each of solid and dotted lines in Figs. 8 (a), (b) and (c) shows the statistically reliable curves determined on the basis of the Weibull distribution parameters and the data partitioning method, described in the previous papers [1, 2, 6, 7]. The type L laser weld metal carried out by impact specimen with 1.5 and 1.0 mm square demonstrates higher upper shelf energy and lower DBTT than those of type S and T weld metal specimens. In addition, the small size of the specimens used for type L weld metal (< 0.7 mm square) leads to a lowering in DBTT below the test temperature of liquid nitrogen.

Since it was possible to determine DBTTs of type S and T by use of conventional full and sub size Charpy-V specimens with 10 x 10 x 55 mm and 5 x 10 x 55 mm, DBTTs of the miniaturized impact specimens versus those of standard impact specimen for type S and T weld metals are plotted in Fig. 9. It will be noted that the type L laser weld metal which failed to obtain the value of DBTT by employing the standard size specimen should lie on a linear relationship together with different weld metals for each same size specimen and the standard

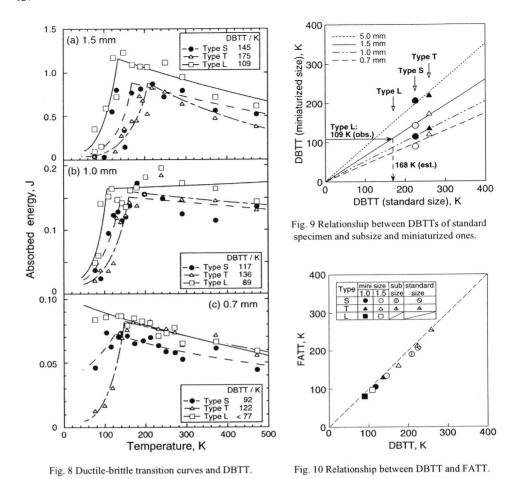

Fig. 8 Ductile-brittle transition curves and DBTT.

Fig. 9 Relationship between DBTTs of standard specimen and subsize and miniaturized ones.

Fig. 10 Relationship between DBTT and FATT.

size DBTT value of laser weld metal can be estimated from the DBTT obtained by the use of miniaturized specimens, as can be seen from Fig. 9. The standard size DBTT of laser weld metal was estimated to be 168 K from the observed 109 K DBTT of 1.5 mm square specimen and 167 K from the observed 89 K DBTT of 1.0 mm square specimen from the corresponding each straight line, respectively. The CO_2 laser welding was found to be superior to conventional submerged arc welding in the fracture toughness degradation owing to ductile-brittle transition in ferritic structural steels.

The fracture appearance transition curves and temperatures (FATT) of the 1.5 and 1.0 mm square impact specimens were examined and the linear correlations between the FATTs of the standard impact specimen and subsize and miniaturized impact specimens were also recognized [6], as well as DBTTs in Fig. 9. Therefore, all of the DBTTs were plotted against the FATTs for different size specimens in this investigation, as shown in Fig. 10. A good linear relationship was found between DBTT and FATT against all varieties in both impact specimen size and weld metal. This linear correlation between DBTT and FATT, independent of varieties of specimen size and weld metal suggests unequivocal evidence concerning the direct evaluation of ductile-brittle transition properties for a narrow region of welded or jointed metals, sheet steels and small samples extracted from long-term operating plant steels by the present miniaturized specimen impact testing technique.

CONCLUSIONS

(1) It was proved that the traditional empirical processing of Japanese sword gave an excellent gradated balance of strength-toughness consisting of edge side of the hard microstructure of martensite showing a lower value and back side of the ferrite/pearlite mixed microstructure showing a higher value in the absorbed impact energies across a section.

(2) The statistically reliable ductile-to-brittle transition curves and the values of DBTT and FATT were obtained by using the miniaturized specimens of different weld metals keeping the same correlations as those used for conventional Charpy-V specimens. The laser welded steel metal composed of an extremely fine acicular ferritic structure was estimated to exhibit a DBTT as large as 168 K when converted to the value estimated for standard size specimens.

(3) The miniaturized specimen impact testing has been demonstrated as a useful method to evaluate the fracture toughness in a small and local region.

REFERENCES

1. Misawa, T., Adachi, T., Saito, M. and Hamaguchi, Y. (1987) *J. Nucl. Mater.* **150**, 194.
2. Misawa, T., Suzuki, K., Saito, M. and Hamaguchi, Y. (1991) *J. Nucl. Mater.* **178-181**, 421.
3. Misawa, T., Nagata, S., Aoki, N., Ishizaka, J. and Hamaguchi, Y.(1989) *J. Nucl. Mater.* **169**, 225.
4. Kimura, A., Koya, A., Morimura, T. and Misawa, T. (1994) *Mater. Sci. and Eng.* **A176**, 425.
5. Sasaki, N., Horii, T., Fujiwara, M., Saitoh, H., and Misawa, T. (2000) *Tetsu-to-Hagane* (ISIJ) **86**, 45.
6. Misawa, T., Takasa, S., Nakano, Y and Yasuda, K (1996) *Tetsu-to-Hagane* (ISIJ) **82**, 707.
7. Manahan, M. P., Quayle, S., Rosenfield, A. R. and Shetty, D. K., (1986). In: *Fatigue, Corrosion Cracking, Fracture Mechanics and Failure Analysis,* pp.495-500, Goel, V.S. (Ed). ASM, Ohio.

Polymers

From Charpy to Present Impact Testing
D. François and A. Pineau (Eds.)
© 2002 Elsevier Science Ltd. and ESIS. All rights reserved

APPLICATION OF ELECTRIC EMISSION TECHNIQUE FOR DETERMINING THE DYNAMIC FRACTURE TOUGHNESS OF POLYMERS

GY. B. LENKEY[*], Z. MAJOR[**]

* Bay Z. Institute for Logistics and Production Systems, Hungary
** Institute of Polymer Technology, JOANNEUM RESEARCH Forschungsges.m.b.H,
Leoben, Austria

ABSTRACT

The polymers have much stronger strain rate sensitivity than the metallic materials. Instrumented impact testing is widely used for determining dynamic fracture toughness characteristic of polymers. Above 1 m/s impact velocity the traditional force-based analyses cannot be applied. In this case the measurement of time-to-fracture value is usually necessary for dynamic analyses. The electric emission technique has the potential ability to detect the initiation of brittle fracture of polymers. In the present work the applicability and the accuracy of this technique have been investigated. The dynamic fracture toughness of different polymeric materials has been determined using different measurement techniques and data reduction methods. Moreover, the effect of local loading rate (dK/dt) was also studied.

KEYWORDS

Instrumented impact testing, electric emission measurement, dynamic fracture toughness, polymers, loading rate sensitivity

INTRODUCTION

The plastic materials usually show a significant strain rate sensitivity in the case of loading rate of most engineering applications. While impact properties of plastics are usually characterised in terms of notched and un-notched impact fracture energies, there has been an increasing tendency to apply fracture mechanics techniques over the last decades. The instrumented impact testing technique is widely used for determining dynamic fracture toughness properties of engineering polymers. However, due to dynamic effects several special problems are encountered in high rate fracture testing. Therefore the application of conventional force based analyses to polymer fracture is limited up to approximately 1 m/s loading rate. Over this range the dynamic effects very often overshadow the true material response and additional measurement techniques must be applied to determine dynamic fracture toughness.

The electric emission technique (EE) has potential ability for detecting the crack initiation, therefore the real time-to-fracture can be determined for dynamic analyses [1]. The principle of the electric emission technique is shown in Fig.1. The sensor of an electric transducer is a capacitor. Any variation of the electric field at the location of the capacitor gives rise for a voltage signal which is named *electric emission (EE)*. The physical phenomena which can cause variations of the electric field may be different from material to material. Molecule deformations or charge separations during a fracture process are examples.

The aim of our work was to investigate the applicability of EE technique in dynamic fracture mechanics testing of different engineering polymers.

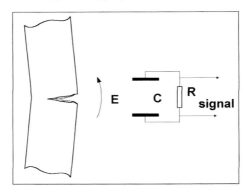

Fig. 1. The principle of the electric emission measurement technique

EXPERIMENTS AND RESULTS

To characterise the dynamic fracture behaviour of the investigated polymers, instrumented impact tests have been performed on a CEAST Resil 15/25 (CEAST S.p.A., Pianezza, I) instrumented impact pendulum (at the Dept. of Mechanical Engineering, University of Miskolc). Beside the traditional force measurement (instrumented tup with strain gauges) the impact pendulum has been additionally instrumented with a small electric emission probe. The instrumentation of the hammer can be seen in Fig. 2.

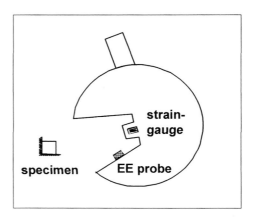

Fig. 2. Instrumentation of the hammer

Various polymeric materials of different structure and properties have been selected for investigation: PE (PE-MD and PE-HD), POM, PVC, PMMA, ABS. All materials were supplied as extruded sheets with a nominal thickness of 12 mm and 10 mm (PVC). Charpy-type specimens (10x10x55 mm) were machined from the sheets and subsequently notched and razor blade pre-cracked parallel to the extrusion direction. The normalised crack length, a_0/W (a_0 is the initial crack length and W is the specimen width), ranged from 0.3 to 0.35. In order to check and prove the ability of the EE technique for detecting the crack initiation, some specimens were instrumented using crack tip strain gauges (MM CEA-06-032UW-120, Measurements Group, Raleigh, NC, USA), located 2.5-3 mm far from the crack tip in horizontal position. In order to study the loading rate effect of the investigated plastic materials, different impact velocities were applied: 1, 2, 3 and 3.7 m/s.

All materials broke brittle or quasi.brittle at each loading rate. In most cases the EE signal showed a sudden change at brittle fracture initiation, except of one PE-HD material. Examples of the experimental curves are shown in Fig. 3. and Fig. 4. for PVC. The time-to-fracture values were determined on the basis of the strain gauge signals (t_{fsg}) and the EE signals (t_{fEE}). When the brittle fracture was detected by EE measurement, the change in the EE signal coincides well with the crack tip strain gauge signal (some examples of the time-to-fracture values are shown in Table 1.)

Table 1. Time-to-fracture, t_f, values determined with different methods.

Material	v_0, m/s	t_{fsg}, μs	t_{fEE}, μs	Difference, %
POM	1	708	706	0.28
	3.7	203	201	0.01
PVC	1	524	512	2.29
	3.7	136	136	0
ABS	1	1344	1364	1.49
	3.7	320	332	3.75

For the lower rate tests ($v_0 = 1$ m/s) the traditional quasistatic, force based analyses could be applied [3], and the fracture toughness, K_{Ic} was determined as:

$$K_{Ic} = \frac{Y\left(a_0/W\right) \cdot F_{max}}{B\sqrt{W}}, \qquad (1)$$

where
F_{max}	-	maximum force, N
a_0	-	initial crack length, mm
W	-	specimen width, mm
B	-	specimen thickness, mm
$Y(a_0/W)$	-	geometry function for SENB specimen:

$$Y\left(a_0/W\right) = 6\sqrt{\frac{a_0}{W}} \frac{\left[1.99 - \frac{a_0}{W}\left(1 - \frac{a_0}{W}\right)\left(2.15 - 3.93\frac{a_0}{W} + 2.7\left(\frac{a_0}{W}\right)^2\right)\right]}{\left(1 + 2\frac{a_0}{W}\right)\left(1 - \frac{a_0}{W}\right)^{3/2}} \qquad (2)$$

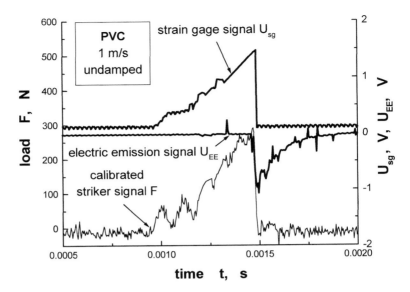

Fig. 3. Calibrated striker (load), F, strain gauge, U$_{sg}$, and electric emission, U$_{EE}$, signals of PVC at a testing rate of 1 m/s.

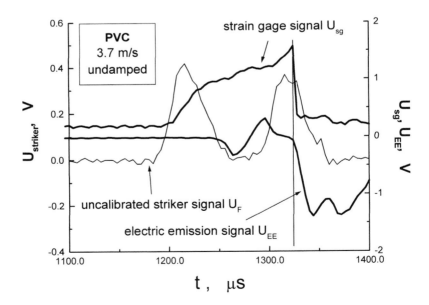

Fig. 4. Uncalibrated striker, U$_{striker}$, strain gauge, U$_{sg}$, and electric emission, U$_{EE}$, signals of PVC at a testing rate of 3.7 m/s.

For loading rates higher than 1 m/s due to the strong oscillation in the load signals the quasistatic force based evaluation cannot be applied. For these cases on the basis of the measured time-to-fracture, t_f, values dynamic fracture toughness, K_{Id}, values have been determined using the dynamic key-curve (DKC) method invented by Böhme [3, 4].

$$K_{Id} = \frac{E \cdot Y\left(\frac{a_0}{W}\right)}{\sqrt{W} C_s^* \left(1 + \frac{C_m}{C_s}\right)} v_0 t_F k^{dyn} \quad (t = t_F)$$ (3)

where $E(t)$ -   specimen's Young modulus (time dependent), MPa
            C_s -   specimen compliance, m/N
            C_m -   machine compliance, m/N
            $C_s^* = EBC_s$-   dimensionless specimen compliance:

$$C_s^*\left(\frac{a_0}{W}\right) = 20.1 + 135\left(\frac{a_0}{W}\right)^2 \left\{ \begin{array}{l} 1 - 2.11\left(\frac{a_0}{W}\right) + 8.76\left(\frac{a_0}{W}\right)^2 - 19.9\left(\frac{a_0}{W}\right)^3 + 41.4\left(\frac{a_0}{W}\right)^4 \\ -67.7\left(\frac{a_0}{W}\right)^5 + 92.1\left(\frac{a_0}{W}\right)^6 - 76.7\left(\frac{a_0}{W}\right)^7 + 35.6\left(\frac{a_0}{W}\right)^8 \end{array} \right\}$$ (4)

where v_0 -   impact velocity, m/s
            $k^{dyn}(t_f)$ -   dynamic key curve
            t_f -   time-to-fracture, s.

According to the DKC method, the value of $k_{dyn}=1$ if $t_f > 9.2W/c_1$, where c_1 is the longitudinal wave propagation velocity for plane strain:

$$c_1 = \sqrt{\frac{E}{\rho(1-\nu^2)}} \cdot$$ (5)

This condition was fulfilled for all the experiments. C_m was determined with low-blow experiments on un-notched specimens as described in [3], and was $C_m = 0.33$ mm/MN. In the analyses the time dependent material parameters (E, ν) were used which were determined from the experiments performed in a frequency range from 0.01 up to 300 Hz on a high speed servohydraulic test system (MTS 831 Polymer test System, MTS Systems Co. MN, USA) in Leoben at the Institute of Materials Science and Testing of Plastics, at the University of Leoben (see Fig. 5. and Fig. 6.).

The results of the evaluations for POM and PVC are shown in Fig. 7. and Fig. 8. together with the K_{Ic} and K_{Id} values determined from the experiments performed on a high rate servohydraulic testing machine with different loading rates. As it can be seen from these figures, both materials show a significant strain rate dependent behaviour, and the K_{Id} values determined with different experimental and evaluation methods are in a good agreement.

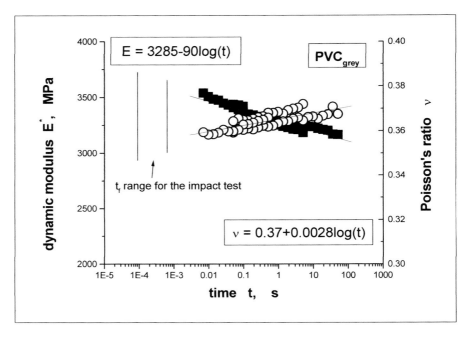

Fig. 5. Time dependence of the dynamic modulus and the Poisson's ratio values for PVC.

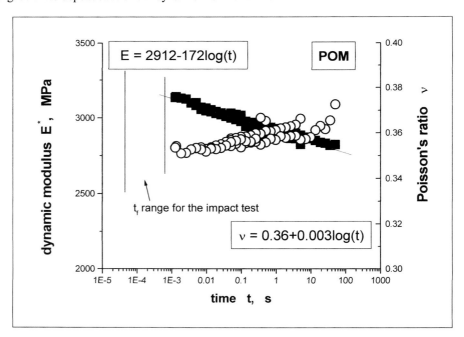

Fig. 6. Time dependence of the dynamic modulus and the Poisson's ratio values for POM.

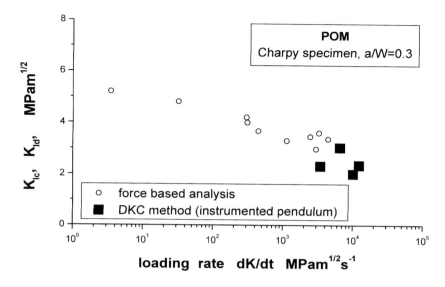

Fig 7. Loading rate dependence of fracture toughness of POM.

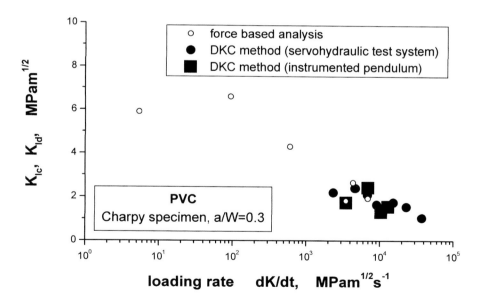

Fig. 8. Loading rate dependence of fracture toughness of PVC.

SUMMARY AND CONCLUSIONS

On the basis of the obtained results the following can be concluded:

1. The electric emission measurement indicated the crack initiation during impact test in the case of most of the investigated materials, except of PE-HD.
2. The strain gauge signals and the EE signals gave practically same time-to-fracture (t_f) values. The differences were within 5-12 microsec for the investigated materials.
3. Good agreement was found between the fracture toughness values determined with different testing and evaluation methods, (i.e., servohydraulic testing using quasi-static force based analysis, instrumented impact testing using the dynamic key-curve method).
4. Large data scatter of K_{Id} values were obtained, but the global time dependent fracture behaviour can be characterised by the low rate and the high rate dynamic signals.

ACKNOWLEDGEMENT

The support of OTKA T 030057 project is acknowledged.

REFERENCES

1. Lenkey, Gy. B., Winkler, S., Major, Z. and Lévay, I. (1996) *11th European Conference on Fracture*, Poitiers, 3-6. September 1996., Vol. III. pp. 1989-1994.
2. ASTM D 5045-93 (1993) *Standard Test Methods for Plane-Strain Fracture Toughness and Strain Energy Release Rate of Plastic Materials*, ASTM
3. Böhme, W. (1990) *Fracture Mechanics: Twenty-First Symposium, ASTM STP 1074*, Gudas, J. P. and Hackett, E. M. (Eds.), American Society for Testing and Materials, Philadelphia, pp. 144-156.
4. Böhme, W. (1992) *Application of the Method of Dynamic Key Curves to the Determination of the Impact Fracture Toughness K_{Id}*, ESIS TC4 document, Draft 1.

From Charpy to Present Impact Testing
D. François and A. Pineau (Eds.)
© 2002 Elsevier Science Ltd. and ESIS. All rights reserved

DETERMINATION OF RATE DEPENDENT FRACTURE TOUGHNESS OF PLASTICS USING PRECRACKED CHARPY SPECIMENS

Z. MAJOR, R.W. LANG
Institute of Polymer Technology, JOANNEUM RESEARCH Forschungsges.m.b.H
Institute of Materials Science and Testing of Plastics, University of Leoben,
A-8700 Leoben, Austria

ABSTRACT

To characterize the rate dependent fracture behavior of various engineering polymers, instrumented impact tests were performed with bending and tensile type specimens in the testing rate range of 10^{-5} m/s up to 8 m/s. Load-time signals were recorded using an instrumented striker and a fixture equipped with a piezoelectric load cell and strain gages, respectively. Furthermore, the time-to-fracture was detected with different strain gage types applied to the specimen side surfaces in the vicinity of the crack tip. The data reduction to determine rate dependent fracture toughness values was carried out according to different procedures (conventional force based analysis and "dynamic key curve" method) taking specific local crack tip loading rates into account. In the quasi-brittle failure regime, good agreement was found between the fracture toughness values determined by force based and dynamic data reduction schemes.

KEYWORDS

Fracture toughness, rate dependence, bending and tensile type specimens, force-based analysis and dynamic data reduction, engineering polymers.

INTRODUCTION

For many engineering applications, impact fracture behavior is of prime practical importance. While impact properties of plastics are usually characterized in terms of notched or un-notched impact fracture energies, there has been an increasing tendency to also apply fracture mechanics techniques over the last decade [1-3]. For quasi-brittle fracture, a linear elastic fracture mechanics (LEFM) approach with a force based analysis (FBA) is frequently applied to determine fracture toughness values at moderate loading rates. However, in high rate fracture testing, several special problems are encountered due to dynamic effects (inertia effects, wave propagation, etc.) which may completely overshadow the true mechanical response of the material to be characterized. While, the control of dynamic effects for plastics at impact rates up to 1 m/s frequently makes use of mechanical damping in the load transmission by placing a soft pad between the striker and the specimen, for intermediate impact rates above 1 m/s to 10 m/s, a dynamic technique referred to as dynamic key curve method (DKC) has been proposed.

The objectives of this paper are (1) to compare force based and dynamic tests methods and data reduction schemes for both bending and tensile type fracture specimens, (2) to define the requirements and limitations for the applicability of FBA and DKC methods, and (3) to determine fracture toughness values of several engineering polymers over a wide range of loading rates (up to 7 decades).

EXPERIMENTAL

Materials
For this study two amorphous engineering polymers, commercial grade poly(carbonate) (PC) (LEXAN 9030, GE Plastics, NL) and commercial grade poly(vinylchloride) (PVC) (SICODEX (grey), EVC, I), and two semi-crystalline engineering polymers, commercial grade poly(oxymethylene) (POM) (Hostafrom C2552, Hoechst AG, D) and β-nucleated poly(propylene) homopolymer (β⁺-PP(H)) (Borealis AG, former PCD Polymere Ges.m.b.H, A) were used. The materials PC, PVC and POM were supplied as extruded sheets with a nominal thickness of 10 mm, β⁺-PP(H) was compression molded to plaques with a thickness of 10 and 15 mm, respectively.

Specimen configurations and Test Procedures
Charpy-type specimens with dimensions of 10x10x55/40 (in mm) were machined from the sheets and plaques and were subsequently notched and razor blade pre-cracked to a relative crack length, a/W (crack length, a, specimen width, W), of 0.3-0.35 (in case of the extruded sheets the notch and crack direction was parallel to the extrusion direction). In addition, to study the effects of specimen geometry and configuration on the dynamic specimen response and fracture toughness, plane-sided (ps) and side-grooved (sg) single edge notched bending (SENB) specimens (W=2B, a/W=0.5; specimen thickness, B), compact type (C(T)) specimens (W=40 mm, B=10-15 mm, a/W=0.5) and cracked round-bar (CRB) specimens (diameter, D=12 mm, a/W=0.5) were machined and also razor blade precracked.

Instrumented impact tests were performed using a high-rate servohydraulic testing machine (MTS 831.59 Polymer Test System, MTS Systems Corp., MN, USA). The striker for the bending type specimens and the fixtures for the tensile type specimens were equipped with transducer type strain gages (WK-05-125AD-350, MM, USA) and a piezoelectric load washer (Kistler 9041A, Kistler AG, CH). The load-point displacement associated with the striker movement was determined from an LVDT signal of the piston. For impact rates above 1 m/s some specimens were also instrumented. In several test series, strain gages (CEA-06-32UW-120, same supplier as before) were applied in the vicinity of the crack tip.

Data Reduction
Quasi-static fracture toughness values, K_c were calculated according to equation (1):

$$K_c = \frac{F_p}{BW^{1/2}} Y\left(a/W\right)$$

(1)

where W is the specimen width, Y(a/W) is the LEFM geometry factor and F_p is the peak force value obtained in the force-time curves (reasons for choosing the peak force, F_p, instead of F_Q are described elsewhere [3, 4]). The geometry factors for SENB and C(T) specimens were taken from [5] and for the CRB specimen from [6].

The dynamic fracture toughness, K_d, was calculated according to the simplified equation (2) proposed in [8]:

$$K_d = \frac{ESY}{4W^{3/2}C_s^*\left(1+\dfrac{C_m}{C_s}\right)} v_0 t_f k^{dyn}\left(t=t_f\right) \qquad (2)$$

where E is the elastic modulus of the specimen, S the span length, C_s^* is the dimensionless compliance, C_s is the specimen compliance, C_m is the machine compliance, v_0 the effective testing rate, t_f the time-to-fracture and $k^{dyn}(c_1 t/W)$ is the "dynamic key curve" (with c_1 the wave propagation velocity and t the time). The essential parameters for the calculation of K_d are the time-to-fracture, t_f, and the material modulus, E. Values for t_f were determined via crack tip strain gage signals according to a procedure described in [7, 8]. Adequate values for the rate dependent modulus E (as well as for the rate dependent Poisson's ratio which enters into the proper definition of c_1) of the various engineering polymers used in this study, were determined experimentally [4].

RESULTS AND DISCUSSION

Typical examples of load-time traces of pre-cracked Charpy specimens at impact rates from 0.5 up to 3.3 m/s are shown in Fig. 1 for PVC and β^+-PP(H). While the recorded non-damped signal up to about 0.5 m/s is of sufficient quality to directly determine the fracture force, F_p, significant force oscillations are visible on the signals for higher loading rates. The control of dynamic effects at impact rates up to 1 m/s (in some instances somewhat higher) frequently makes use of mechanical damping in the load transmission by placing a soft pad (elastomer or grease) between the striker tup and the specimen [9,10]. Above about 1 m/s inertia effects overshadow the true mechanical response of the specimen. Due to such dynamic effects, the applicability of FBA is limited to loading rates up to about 2 m/s for bending type fracture specimens.

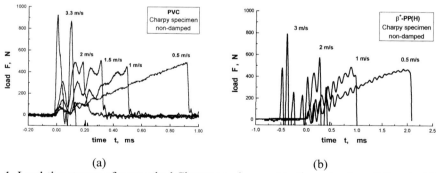

(a)   (b)

Fig. 1. Load-time traces of precracked Charpy specimens at testing rates from 0.5 up to 3.3 m/s for; (a) PVC, (b) β^+-PP(H).

Typical traces of striker signals ($U_{striker}$) and specimen strain gage signals (U_{sg}) also for PVC Charpy specimens but for a higher loading rate (3.7 m/s) are shown in Fig 2. Detailed experiments with numerous materials and measurement techniques have shown that crack tip strain gage signals may be used to determine accurate time-to-fracture values, t_f. Based on the results for t_f, k^{dyn} values were determined to be equal to 1 for most tests performed up to 8 m/s, except for PVC at test rates above 5 m/s, and for PC and for POM at test rates of 8 m/s, in which cases k^{dyn} was calculated according to the definition in [8].

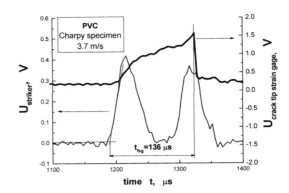

Fig. 2. Uncalibrated striker, ($U_{striker}$) and crack tip strain gage, (U_{sg}) signal traces at a testing rate of 3.7 m/s for PVC.

Examples of force/load-point displacement curves for the tensile loading mode specimens of the C(T) and CRB type are shown in Fig. 3 for β^+-PP(H) for testing rates of 10^{-5} m/s up to 6 m/s. In contrast to the results with the Charpy bending type specimens in Fig.1, the load-displacement results of the tensile load specimens in Fig. 3 apparently are of sufficient quality to determine fracture force values even at loading speeds above 1 m/s. As described before [11], the improved signal quality of the tensile mode C(T) and CRB specimens over bending type specimens is a result of the higher specimen and lower contact stiffness associated with the former specimen configurations as well as the more effective damping situation in the loading unit.

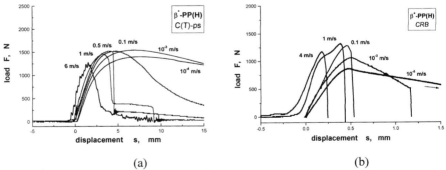

(a)   (b)

Fig. 3. Load-displacement curves for β^+-PP(H) with various testing rates (a) C(T)-ps specimens, (b) CRB specimens.

On the other hand, the load-displacement traces for β^+-PP(H) in Fig. 3 at low loading rates (below 0.5 m/s) indicate a transition from quasi-brittle to ductile fracture behavior, so that an LEFM data analysis based on the stress intensity factor K may no longer be applicable. Similar effects with regard to this brittle-ductile transition with reduced loading rates are shown in Fig. 4 for Charpy type bending specimens of β^+-PP(H).

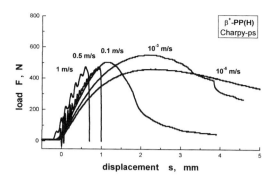

Fig. 4: Load-displacement curves for Charpy specimens of β^{+}-PP(H) at various testing rates.

Loading rate dependent fracture toughness values for the four materials investigated are shown in Figs. 5 to 8. Each of these figures includes fracture data generated with various specimen configurations using the appropriate force based and dynamic data reduction method, respectively. The local loading rate, dK/dt, used in these diagrams as proper rate parameter was determined as K_c/t_f. In all diagrams the onset of ranges for quasi-brittle failure (based on load-displacement traces) and for valid K_{Ic} determination according to relevant standards [6] using the appropriate rate dependent yield stress values is indicated.

In the loading rate regime of quasi-brittle fracture, good to excellent agreement of the fracture toughness values can be seen for all materials. That is, for a given material grade bending and tensile type specimens yield equivalent K_c values. Moreover, in the high loading rate regime, good correspondence was found between K_c (FBA method) and K_d (DKC method) values, thus corroborating the applicability of the DKC method for engineering polymers if appropriate rate dependent material properties (elastic modulus, Poisson's ratio) are used.

As expected, in the ductile failure regime and in the ductile-brittle transition regime of the loading rate scale, where LEFM methods are no longer applicable, large differences in "apparent" fracture toughness values were obtained for various specimen configurations, as is shown in Fig. 8 for β^{+}-PP(H). Nevertheless, in this case too, the apparent K_c values of the different specimen types converge at in the quasi-brittle fracture regime at high loading rates.

CONCLUSIONS

Based on the investigations performed covering 7 decades of loading rates, the following conclusions may be drawn with regard to the determination of rate dependent fracture toughness values of engineering polymers in the quasi-brittle failure regime:

— LEFM methods are applicable to characterize the rate dependent fracture behavior of engineering polymers in the regime of quasi-brittle failure, yielding material specific fracture toughness values independent of specimen configuration.

— Up to 0.1 m/s, non-damped force-time signals are of sufficient quality to directly determine the fracture force, F_c, for applying an FBA methodology.

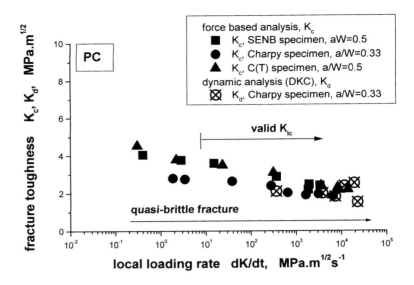

Fig. 5. Effect of local loading rate on fracture toughness for PC using various specimen configurations and data reduction schemes.

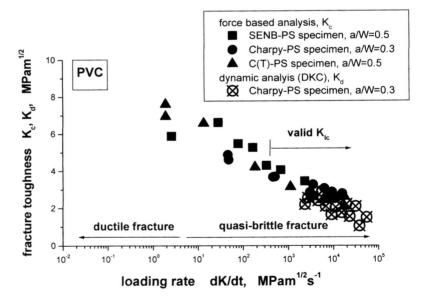

Fig. 6. Effect of local loading rate on fracture toughness for PVC using various specimen configurations and data reduction schemes.

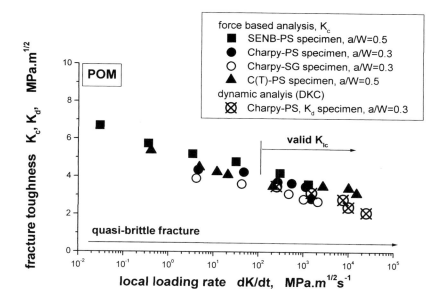

Fig. 7. Effect of local loading rate on fracture toughness for POM using various specimen configurations and data reduction schemes.

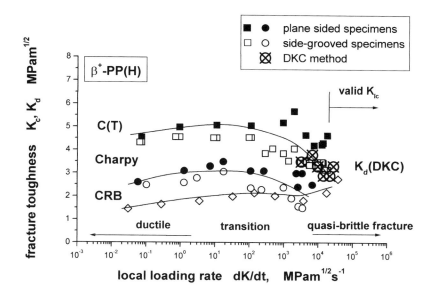

Fig. 8. Effect of local loading rate on fracture toughness for β^+-PP(H) using various specimen configurations and data reduction schemes.

- When applying an appropriate damping procedure, FBA methods can be effectively used up to 2 m/s for bending type and up to 8 m/s for tensile type fracture specimens.

- At even higher loading rates, for which no valid force-time signal for applying an FBA data reduction scheme can be recorded, the DKC-method may be used to determine dynamic fracture toughness values, K_d. This requires an adequate technique to measure the time-to-fracture (e.g., specimens instrumented with crack tip strain gages) and the characterization of proper rate dependent values for modulus and Poisson's ratio.

- Over equivalent local loading rate ranges, experiments with tensile type specimens using an FBA data reduction and experiments with bending type specimens using the DKC data analysis method yield equivalent fracture toughness values.

- In the regime of quasi-brittle failure, there is a clear tendency for a decrease in fracture toughness with increasing impact rate for all materials investigated. However, the rate sensitivity of fracture toughness values strongly depends on the specific polymer type.

REFERENCES

1. Williams, J.G. (1984). Fracture Mechanics of Polymers, Ellis Horwood Series in Engineering Science, Chichester.

2. Leevers, P.S. and Douglas, M. (1999). In: Limitations of Test Methods for Plastics, ASTM STP 1369, J.S. Pesaro, (Ed.) ASTM, West Conshohocken, PA.

3. Béguelin, Ph. and Kausch, H.H. (1995). In: ESIS 19 Impact and Dynamic Fracture of Polymers and Composites, J.G. Williams and A. Pavan (Eds.) Mechanical Engineering Publ., London, pp. 93-102.

4. Major, Z. (2002). PhD Thesis, University of Leoben.

5. ESIS TC4 (1990). A Linear Elastic Fracture Mechanics Standard for Determining K_c and G_c for Plastics, Testing Protocol – March.

6. Scibetta, M., Chaouadi, R. and Van Walle, E. (2000) Int. J. of Fracture 104: 145-168.

7. Böhme, W. (1998). Application of Dynamic Key Curves (DKC) on the determination of the Impact Fracture Toughness, K_{Id} of Plastics at High Rates of Loading „> 1 m/s", FI-IWM, Freiburg.

8. Böhme, W. (1995). In ESIS 19 Impact and Dynamic Fracture of Polymers and Composites, J.G. Williams and A. Pavan (Eds.) Mechanical Engineering Publications, London, pp. 93-102.

9. ESIS TC4, (1997). A Linear Elastic Fracture Mechanics Standard for Determining K_c and G_c for Plastics, Appendix 3 – High Rate Testing (draft 9).

10. Pavan A. (1998). In Fracture from Defects, pp. 1363-1368., Brown. M.W., de los Rios, E.R. and Miller, K.J., (Eds)., EMAS, ECF 12, Sheffield.

11. Major, Z., Lang, R.W. (1997) J. Phys IV France 7, C3-1005.

From Charpy to Present Impact Testing
D. François and A. Pineau (Eds.)
© 2002 Elsevier Science Ltd. and ESIS. All rights reserved

DETERMINATION OF GEOMETRY-INDEPENDENT FRACTURE MECHANICS VALUES OF POLYMERS

W. GRELLMANN[1], R. LACH[1] AND S. SEIDLER[2]

[1] Martin-Luther-University Halle-Wittenberg, Institute of Materials Science, D-06099 Halle, Germany
[2] Vienna University of Technology, Institute of Materials Science and Testing, A-1040 Vienna, Austria

ABSTRACT

Specific requirements on the specimen geometry necessary for the determination of fracture mechanics parameters for polymers by using the instrumented Charpy impact test are summarized. As examples, the influences of the specimen thickness and a/W ratio are considered. For characterizing the geometry independence of fracture mechanics parameters, geometrical factors are used, which make possible an estimation of the requirements on the specimen geometry without any further experiments. For polymers, the experimentally determined geometrical factors vary in a wide range; this means that the use of constant geometrical factors must cause a pronounced under- or overevaluation of the requirements on the specimens. The relationships between geometrical factors and fracture mechanics parameters, which were found to be generally valid for polymers, are independent of the kind of loading (static, impact-like) and the crack propagation behaviour (stable, unstable).

KEYWORDS

Polymers, fracture mechanics, geometrical criteria, specimen thickness, a/W ratio

INTRODUCTION

For testing the fracture behaviour of polymers under practice-relevant, impact-like loading conditions, the instrumented Charpy impact test is state of the art. Further information on the parameter evaluation is given in Refs. [1–5]. The determination of toughness parameters by using the Charpy test is closely connected with the technological application of resins in aeroplane industry. Since 1924, unnotched specimens had been used for the determination of toughness parameters. By introduction of the standard 'Kerbzähigkeit (Schlagbiegefestigkeit an gekerbten Stäben)' in 1937, the experimental basis of the determination of toughness parameters was substantially extended.

However, from investigations of pressed resins partly filled with wood flour, Kuntze and Nitsche [6] early recognized discrepancies between these conventionally measured values and the real material behaviour. As a consequence, they deduced that the impact strength is not really a measure of toughness. The solution of this problem has been started with the electronic recording of the load-deflection behaviour [7–9].

As one of the fundamental advantages of the instrumented Charpy impact test with its high test speed, in comparison with a quasi-static fracture mechanics test, the requirements on the specimen geometry for the determination of geometry-independent fracture mechanics parameters are significantly reduced [10]. Thus, an extension of the usual in-firm quality control becomes possible by the determination of fracture mechanics toughness parameters on the basis of three-point bending specimens with the dimensions length $L = 80$ mm, thickness $B = 4$ mm and width $W = 10$ mm [1]. A detailed description of experimental procedures for the determination of fracture mechanics parameters of polymeric materials is given by Grellmann and Seidler in Ref. [5].

BASIC REMARKS

The geometry dependence of fracture mechanics parameters in terms of B, a and $(W–a)$ is characterized independently of the fracture mechanics concept (LEFM, J-integral or CTOD concept) by a transition from geometry-dependent (K_Q, J_Q and δ_Q) to geometry-independent values in terms of a universal brittle-to-tough transition (BTT). The BTT is connected with a change from a predominant plane stress state to a predominant plane strain state. The values of B, a and $(W–a)$, for which K_Q, J_Q and δ_Q are constant for the first time, are the minimum specimen thickness, minimum crack length and minimum ligament length (B_{min}, a_{min} and $(W–a)_{min}$). For polymers, B_{min}, a_{min} and $(W–a)_{min}$ range typically in the order of a few millimetres. Furthermore, because of the low heat conductance of polymers in comparison with metallic materials, the change from isothermal to adiabatic behaviour is important, especially for such polymers which are strongly plastically deformed under load.

For a generally valid description of the geometry dependence of fracture mechanics parameters, geometrical criteria with the factors ε, β and ξ were introduced. These factors make possible an estimation of the minimum requirements on the specimen geometry without any experimental determination of the influence of the geometry on fracture mechanics parameters, this means that no further check of validity is required. The estimation of minimum requirements on specimen size and crack length is performed according to:

$$B, a, (W - a) \geq \varepsilon \cdot \frac{J}{\sigma_y} \tag{1}$$

in the case of the J-integral concept with the geometrical factor ε,

$$B, a, (W - a) \geq \xi \cdot \delta \tag{2}$$

in the case of the CTOD concept with the geometrical factor ξ and

$$B, a, (W - a) \geq \beta \cdot \left(\frac{K}{\sigma_y}\right)^2 \tag{3}$$

in the case of LEFM with the geometrical factor β, where σ_y is the yield stress.

For metallic materials, the geometrical factors are fixed to $\varepsilon = 25$ [11], $\xi = 50$ [10] or 35 [11] and $\beta = 2.5$ [11,12]. These values are also often used for polymers or are taken into account in standard drafts [13]. However, also for metals, these values are not universally valid. For example, experimental values of ε in the range from 25 to 200 [14,15] are known.

This fact and the fundamental differences between the mechanical behaviour of metals and polymers result in the conclusion that the requirements on minimum specimen size defined above can not be transferred self-evident to polymers as it should be shown in the following sections.

INFLUENCE OF SPECIMEN GEOMETRY ON FRACTURE MECHANICS PARAMETERS

The influence of the geometry on fracture mechanics parameters related to both resistance against stable and unstable crack propagation can be characterized experimentally by variation of the specimen configuration (compact tension (CT), single-edge-notched bending (SENB), single-edge-notched tension (SENT) specimens etc.) and the specimen size, especially the thickness B and the crack length a (a/W ratio), as well as the notch radius. Exemplary in this study, the influences of specimen thickness and a/W ratio are considered. More detailed information can be found in Ref. [16].

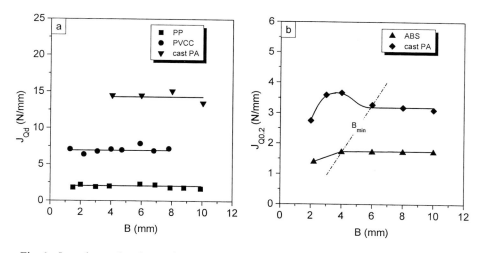

Fig. 1. J_{Qd} values related to resistance against unstable crack initiation (a) and $J_{Q0.2}$ values related to resistance against stable crack initiation (b) as a function of the specimen thickness and the material

Fracture Mechanics Parameters as a Function of Specimen Thickness for Various Polymers

The determination of the influence of specimen thickness on the material parameters is one of the most relevant fields in fracture mechanics material characterization, because the independence of the thickness is an important criterion for the transferability of parameters determined using specimens to components. Many results of fracture mechanics examinations of the influence of thickness on the material parameters are available. In Fig. 1, various J values are summarized obtained from instrumented Charpy impact tests at room temperature. Figure 1a shows the dependence of J values on specimen thickness $J_{Qd} = f(B)$ in the case of unstable crack propagation (PP, PVCC and cast PA). In Fig. 1b, the influence of the specimen thickness on the technical crack initiation value $J_{Q0.2} = f(B)$ is illustrated for ABS and cast PA showing stable crack propagation. In any case, values of B_{min} can be determined experimentally.

Influence of Temperature on the Requirements on Specimen Dimensions

Figure 2 shows the influence of the temperature on J_{Qd} in dependence on thickness for PC under impact loading conditions. With increasing temperature, the minimum specimen thickness increases from $B_{min} = 1.5$ mm at 0 °C and $B_{min} = 2$ mm at 20 °C to $B_{min} = 3$ mm at 40 °C [17]. This change in requirements on specimen thickness in a relatively small temperature range ($\Delta T = 40$ °C), which approximately corresponds to the temperature range of application of PC, is a polymer-specific phenomenon that can be clarified by the assumption of a generalized brittle-to-tough transition (BTT). It is assumed that the BTT's corresponding to the loading conditions (temperature, speed etc.), the material behaviour (mechanism of deformation, concentration, particle size and distance etc.) and the geometry (specimen thickness, notch radius etc.) are interdependent due to the polymer-specific viscoelastic–viscoplastic behaviour. As a consequence, a variation of the loading conditions leads to a change in the BTT, as it is shown in Fig. 2 using the variation of the temperature as an example. Here, the change of the BTT is due to a change of the deformation mechanisms. Thus, the minimum specimen thickness increases. Therefore, if limits of application should be fixed and the transferability of parameters to components should be evaluated, these changes must be taken into account.

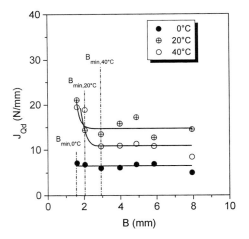

Fig. 2. Influence of the temperature and the specimen thickness on the J_{Qd} values for polycarbonate

Fracture Mechanics Parameters as a Function of the a/W Ratio

For predominantly unstable crack propagation, a variation of the a/W ratio, i.e. the initial crack length in the case of a constant specimen geometry, leads to relationships that are qualitatively comparable to that from a variation of specimen thickness (Fig. 3a).

In the case of unstable crack propagation, the influence of the a/W ratio can be described easily using specimens with different a/W ratios. However, if stable crack propagation occurs, for example during R-curve measurements, continuous changes of the a/W ratio during the fracture process are observed, which are caused by the increasing amount of stable crack growth. On the one hand, because the J-integral is – strictly speaking – only defined for a stationary crack, the amount of stable crack growth must be limited by definition of a maximum valid amount of stable crack growth Δa_{max} ensuring J-controlled crack propagation (Fig. 3b). Guidelines for it were formulated for example in the standard draft of ESIS TC4 [13]. On the other hand, as it was shown in Ref. [18], no limiting of the amount of stable crack growth is necessary, if J values are corrected regarding the finite stable crack growth Δa and the influence of the instationary stress field ahead of the crack tip. J values calculated using an iterative procedure and J values determined using an approximative method for R-curve determination suggested by Seidler, including a correction of the crack growth, are in very good agreement [18,19].

Nevertheless, the influence of specimen geometry on J and CTOD values remains. With increasing amount of stable crack growth, the external energy cannot be dissipated any longer into a large region of the specimen by an increasing plastic-zone size because of interactions between the plastic zone and the specimen boundary. Furthermore, the crack propagates into the pressure zone of the specimen. This leads to an increase of the energy density and the local deformation in the spatially finite plastic zone. As a result, a strong increase of the crack resistance at a certain amount of stable crack growth, the maximum valid amount of stable crack growth Δa_{max}, occurs, which corresponds to the transition from a plane strain to a plane stress state (Fig. 3b). Thus, valid J values can only be determined if $\Delta a \leq \Delta a_{max}$.

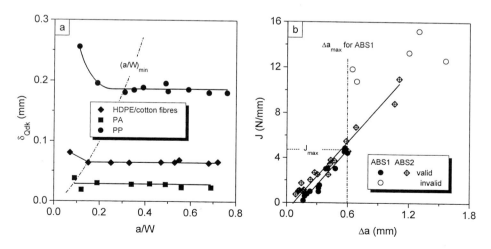

Fig. 3. Critical crack-tip-opening displacement values δ_{Qdk} as a function of the a/W ratio (a) using HDPE, PA and PP as examples; experimental determination of the maximum valid amount of stable crack growth under impact loading using ABS (b) as an example

REQUIREMENTS ON SPECIMEN GEOMETRY FOR POLYMERS

In order to consider the influence of the material on the geometrical criterions [equations (1–3)], the experimental determination of the geometrical factors on the basis of the dependence of thickness or a/W ratio (Figs. 1–3) was found to be suitable. From such measuring data, correlations of the geometrical factors ε, β and ξ, and the related fracture mechanics parameters can be determined (Figs. 4–6) which are generally valid for polymers, because of their independence of the kind of loading (quasi-static/impact-like) and the material behaviour (stable/unstable). The data points in the $\varepsilon(J)$, $\xi(\delta)$ and $\beta(K)$ plots were calculated from B_{min} (Figs. 1 and 2), $(W–a)_{min}$ (Fig. 3a) und $[W-(a+\Delta a_{max})]$ (Fig. 3b) for example and the 'critical' fracture mechanics values (J_{Ic}, J_{Id}, $J_{0.2c}$, $J_{0.2d}$ and J_{max}; δ_{Id} and $\delta_{0.2c}$; K_{Ic} and K_{Id}) using equations (1–3) (equal signs). The indices 'Ic' and 'Id' point out measurement of the resistance against unstable crack propagation under quasi-static ('c') and impact-like ('d') loading conditions respectively. The indices '0.2c', '0.2d' (resistance against stable crack initiation, quasi-static and impact-like loading conditions) and 'max' mark values resulting from the determination of crack resistance curves.

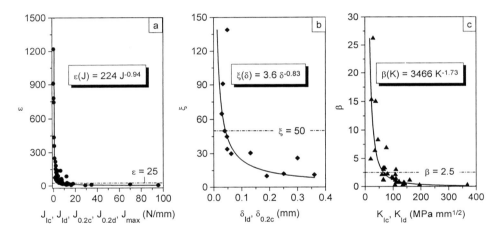

Fig. 4. Geometrical factors as functions of 'critical' fracture mechanics values

From the linear and double-logarithmic plot of the geometrical factor ε versus the 'critical' J values (J_{Ic}, J_{Id}, $J_{0.2c}$, $J_{0.2d}$ and J_{max}) in Figs. 4a and 5, a general empirical connection can be derived:

$$\varepsilon = A_1 \cdot J^{A_2} \tag{4}$$

Analogously, for ξ as a function of the 'critical' δ values (δ_{Id} and $\delta_{0.2c}$) and for β as a function of 'critical' K values (K_{Ic} and K_{Id}) (Figs. 4b, 4c and 6), following equations result:

$$\xi = B_1 \cdot \delta^{B_2}, \tag{5}$$

$$\beta = C_1 \cdot K^{C_2} \tag{6}$$

By fitting of A_1, B_1 and C_1, and A_2, B_2 and C_2, the following empirical connections can be derived:

$$\varepsilon = 224 \cdot J^{-0.94} \quad (J \text{ in Nmm}^{-1}), \tag{7}$$

$$\xi = 3.6 \cdot \delta^{-0.83} \quad (\delta \text{ in mm}) \text{ and} \tag{8}$$

$$\beta = 3466 \cdot K^{-1.73} \quad (K \text{ in MPamm}^{1/2}). \tag{9}$$

These equations represent the essential basis for the estimation of the minimum specimen size. Owing to the wide range of experimentally determined geometrical factors ($\varepsilon = 5.2$–1220, $\xi = 10$–139 and $\beta = 0.24$–26), the assumption of constant values of $\varepsilon = 25$ [11], $\xi = 50$ [10] or 35 [11] and $\beta = 2.5$ [11,12] would lead to a pronounced under- or overevaluation of the requirements on the specimen geometry. The use of these constant values is too restrictive for tough polymers (such as UHMWPE) and non-conservative for brittle polymers (such as epoxy resins). In principle, equations (7–9) combined with equations (1–3) make possible a material-specific estimation of the requirements on specimen geometry within the complete toughness range ranging from linear elastic behaviour with unstable crack propagation to elastic-plastic behaviour with stable crack propagation.

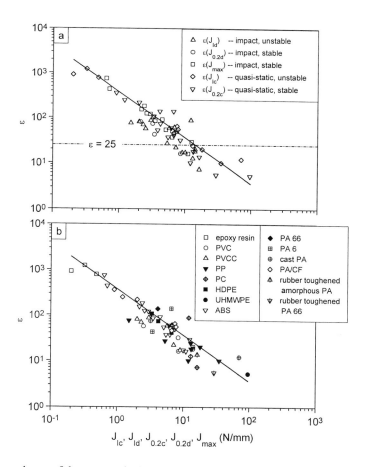

Fig. 5. Dependence of the geometrical factor ε on the J values for different loading conditions and different crack propagation behaviour (a), and for various materials (b)

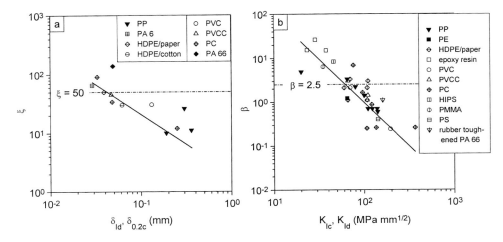

Fig. 6. Geometrical factor ξ as a function of the crack-opening displacement values $\delta_{Id}\square$, $\delta_{0.2c}$ (a) and geometrical factor β as a function of the stress intensity factor K_{Ic}, K_{Id} (b) for polymers

Strictly speaking, the use of such empirical relationships is limited to the range of values considered. Therefore, a noticeable generalization is necessary. Assuming that A_1 and A_2 are independent on J and B_1 and B_2 are independent on δ, i.e. $A_2 = -1$ and $B_2 = -1$, it follows:

$$\varepsilon = 370\,\mathrm{Nmm}^{-1} \cdot J^{-1} \tag{10}$$

and

$$\xi = 2.2\ \mathrm{mm}^{-1} \cdot \delta^{-1}. \tag{11}$$

A motivation of this assumption is that the values empirically determined for A_2 and B_2, $A_2 = -0.94$ and $B_2 = -0.83$, are relatively closed to -1. But, essentially, the small differences of these empirical values and -1 indicate that weak dependencies of A_2 and B_2 on the fracture mechanics values J und δ exist. In support of a practice-oriented simplification of equations (7) and (8), however, these discrepancies should be neglected here.

By replacing the initial with the effective crack length $a_{\mathrm{eff}} = a + \Delta a$ and using equations (1), (2), (10) and (11), following requirements on the maximum valid amount of stable crack growth for J–R and δ–R curves can be derived:

$$\Delta a \le (W - a) - \frac{370\,\mathrm{Nmm}^{-1}}{\sigma_y} \tag{12}$$

and

$$\Delta a \le (W - a) - 2.2\,\mathrm{mm}. \tag{13}$$

In equation (12) that is more restrictive then equation (13), the influence of the plastic zone size on maximum valid stable crack growth is carried by the yield stress σ_y.

Thus, the basis of a material-specific criterion of valuation for fixing the maximum valid amount of crack growth values is established.

SUMMARY

The influence of the geometry on the fracture mechanics parameters related to both resistance against stable and unstable crack propagation can be characterized experimentally by variation of specimen size and configuration, and the crack length. Besides the initial crack length, the amount of stable crack growth must be considered, if non-negligible stable crack propagation is observed.

The connection between fracture mechanics parameters and minimum requirements on the specimen geometry can be formulated independently of the fracture mechanics concept, the kind of crack propagation, the test speed and temperature, and the material. The transition from geometry-dependent values to geometry-independent parameters can be understood in terms of a generalized brittle-to-tough transition by the change of a predominant plane stress to a predominant plane strain state. For polymers, the brittle-to-tough transitions corresponding to loading conditions, the material behaviour and the geometry are interdependent because of the viscoelastic–viscoplastic behaviour. This means that different geometrical requirements resulting from varying loading condition and/or materials exist, which are to take into account for the definition of limits of application. In addition, the geometry dependence of fracture mechanics parameters of polymers is influenced by the transition from isothermal to adiabatic behaviour.

The fixed values of the constants $\varepsilon = 25$ (*J*-integral concept), $\xi = 50$ or 35 (CTOD concept) and $\beta = 2.5$ (LEFM) are not suitable. From the analysis of various experimental results of measurements regarding the influence of thickness and a/W ratio, it was found that ε ranges from 5.2 to 1220, ξ ranges from 10 to 139 and β ranges from 0.24 to 26. These strong differences point out that the use of constant values of the geometrical factors for the verification of the geometry independence would lead to a pronounced under- or overevaluation of the requirements on the specimens according to the material and the conditions. Thus, substantial consequences for the transferability of parameters measured using specimens are expected.

For a qualitative evaluation of the minimum specimen dimensions for polymers, the universal functions $\varepsilon = f(J)$, $\xi = f(\delta)$ und $\beta = f(K)$ are proposed, which are independent of the loading conditions, the crack propagation behaviour and the material. This makes possible a material-specific estimation of the requirements on specimen geometry within the complete toughness range ranging from linear elastic behaviour with unstable crack propagation to elastic–plastic behaviour with stable crack propagation.

REFERENCES

1. DIN EN ISO 179 (2000) *Plastics – Determination of Charpy Impact Properties, Part 1: Non-Instrumented Test, Part 2: Instrumented Impact Test.*
2. Ramsteiner, F., Schuster, W. and Forster, S. (2001). In: *Deformation and Fracture Behaviour of Polymers*, p. 27, Grellmann, W. and Seidler, S. (Eds.). Springer, Berlin Heidelberg.
3. ISO/DIS 13586.2 (2000) *Plastics – Determination of Fracture Toughness (G_C and K_C) – Linear Elastic Fracture Mechanics (LEFM) Approach.*
4. Akay, M. (1999). In: *Handbook of Polymer Testing*, p. 533, Brown, R. (Ed.). Marcel Dekker Inc., New York.

5.   Grellmann W. and Seidler, S. (Eds.) (2001) *Deformation and Fracture Behaviour of Polymers*. Springer, Berlin Heidelberg.

6.   Kuntze, W. and Nitsche, R. (1938) *Kunststoffe* **28**, 180.

7.   Richard, K., Diedrich, G. and Gaube, E. (1959) *Kunststoffe* **49**, 671.

8.   Grimminger, H. (1960) *Kunststoffe* **50**, 618.

9.   Borgwardt, A. (1959) *Plaste Kautschuk* **6**, 68.

10.   Blumenauer, H. and Pusch G. (1993) *Technische Bruchmechanik*. Deutscher Verlag für Grundstoffindustrie, Leipzig Stuttgart.

11.   ASTM E 1820 (2001) *Standard Test Method for Measurement of Fracture Toughness*.

12.   ASTM E 399 (1997) *Standard Test Method for Plane-Strain Fracture Toughness of Metallic Materials*.

13.   Standard Draft ESIS TC4 (1995) *A Testing Protocol for Conducting J-Crack Growth Resistance Curve Tests on Plastics*.

14.   Landes, J.D. and Begley, J.A. (1974) *ASTM STP* **560**, 170.

15.   Marandet, B., Phelippeau, G. and Roussellier, G. (1981). In: *Advance in Fracture Research (Fracture 1981: 5th International Conference on Fracture, Cannes 29.3. – 3.4.1981)*, vol. 2, p. 871.

16.   Grellmann, W., Che, M. (1997) *J. Appl. Polymer Science* **66**, 1237.

17.   Lach, R. (1998) *VDI-Fortschritt-Berichte, VDI-Reihe 18, Nr. 223*. VDI-Verlag, Düsseldorf.

18.   Seidler, S. (1998) *VDI-Fortschritt-Berichte, VDI-Reihe 18, Nr. 231*. VDI-Verlag, Düsseldorf.

19.   Grellmann, W. and Seidler, S. (1999). In: *Material Mechanics – Fracture Mechanics – Micro Mechanics*, p. 336, Winkler, T. and Schubert A. (Eds.). DDP Goldenbogen, Dresden.

TERMINOLOGY

ABS	acrylonitrile butadiene styrene copolymer
HDPE	high-density polyethylene
HIPS	high-impact polystyrene
PA	polyamide
PA/CF	carbon fibre reinforced polyamide
PC	polycarbonate
PE	polyethylene
PMMA	poly(methyl methacrylate)
PP	polypropylene
PVC	poly(vinyl chloride)
PVCC	chlorinated poly(vinyl chloride)
UHMWPE	ultra-high-molecular-weight polyethylene

From Charpy to Present Impact Testing
D. François and A. Pineau (Eds.)

INSTRUMENTED IMPACT TESTING OF POLYMERS

SHIGEKI MORITA, KAZUO HOSOI and TOSHIRO KOBAYASHI

Department of Production Systems Engineering, Toyohashi University of Technology,
Toyohashi, 441-8580, Japan

ABSTRACT

The vibrational wave superimposed on the load-deflection curve recorded by the instrumented Charpy impact test was analyzed and the effect of specimen dimension on the vibrational wave was investigated. Moreover, the change in fracture toughness values with changing loading rate was studied. Furthermore, the validity of the use of shock-absorbing material, which can suppress the generation of the vibrational wave at impact, was examined. Lastly, the time history of the stress intensity factor evaluated by the one-point bend test was compared with the one in the impact response curve in the instrumented impact test, and the differences in fracture toughness values between the one-point bend test and the Charpy impact test were discussed. The results of present study are summarized as follows. (1) The vibrational wave can be prevented by the use of a smaller specimen which shortens the period of the vibrational wave. (2) The load value is lowered by the use of shock-absorbing material. (3) The differences in the impact response curves and the fracture times evaluated from the instrumented Charpy impact test and the one-point bend test are rather large at the lower impact velocity of 3.10 m/s; however, the obtained K_{Id} values are nearly coincident.

KEYWORDS

instrumented Charpy impact test, vibrational wave, stress intensity factor, dynamic fracture toughness, one-point bend test.

INTRODUCTION

Since polymers are very light and have a good formability, they are used in various capacities from industrial components to daily necessities. Polymers, for which the specific strength is competitive with that of light metals, have been developed recently. These polymers are expected to be increasingly used as structural materials. In order to increase the use of polymers in this role, it is very important to be able to assure safety against fracture and to establish a method of evaluation for dynamic fracture toughness.

In general, many polymers are used below the glass transition temperature and their fracture behaviors are brittle. In the case of the dynamic loading test for brittle materials, a vibrational wave is superimposed on a load-deflection curve due to the inertial effect and a stress wave is generated at impact. Therefore, it is very difficult to measure the exact load-deflection curve

and to evaluate the exact fracture toughness under the dynamic loading conditions.
In the present study, the vibrational wave superimposed on the load-deflection curve recorded
by the instrumented Charpy impact test was analyzed and the effect of specimen dimension
on the vibrational wave was investigated for four kinds of polymers. Moreover, the change in
fracture toughness values with changing loading rate was studied. Furthermore, the validity of
the use of shock-absorbing material, which can suppress the generation of the vibrational
wave at impact, was examined. Lastly, the time history of the stress intensity factor measured
by the one-point bend test [1,2] was compared with the impact response curve measured by
the instrumented Charpy impact test [3], and the differences in fracture behavior and fracture
toughness values between the one-point bend test and the Charpy impact test were discussed.

EXPERIMENTAL PROCEDURES

Materials and Specimen Dimensions

In the present study, four kinds of polymers, PMMA, polyamide, nylon and silica-filled epoxy
resin, and seven kinds of specimens were used. The dimensions of the specimens are
summarized in Table 1. All specimens were machined from the plate in the direction of the
edge-width. Of these specimens, (A), (B), (C), (D) and (E) were used to clarify the effect of
specimen dimension on the vibrational wave superimposed on the load-deflection curve. In
contrast, (F) and (G) were used to assess the fracture toughness values for the various loading
rates. In addition, they were used to clarify the effect of shock-absorbing material and the
difference in fracture behaviors between the one-point bend test and the Charpy impact test.
Therefore, they were precracked to a crack length of $a_0/W=0.5$ (a_0 is the initial crack length
and W is the specimen width) using the "dead-load" method, which applies a constant load to
the specimen until a pop-in crack appears.

Table 1   Specimen dimensions

Specimen	Thickness(mm)	Width(mm)	Span(mm)	Length(mm)	Notch geometry
(A)	15	15	60	90	U
(B)	10	10	40	55	U
(C)	4	6	40	50	Slit
(D)	4	10	60	80	V
(E)	10	10	40	55	V
(F)	15	15	60	90	Crack
(G)	10	10	40	55	Crack

Dynamic and Static Three-point Bending Tests

In the dynamic bending test, the 14.7J capacity instrumented Charpy impact testing machine
was used for all materials. The instrumented Charpy impact test was conducted in atmosphere
and the specimen was loaded under the recommended conditions of $E_0>3E_t$ (E_0 is the applied
energy and E_t is the total absorbed energy) [4]. Incidentally, in the dynamic bending test, a
shock-absorbing material was used in order to suppress the vibrational wave generated at
impact and its effectiveness was examined. The shock-absorbing material (GELNACN-30
(thickness:2mm), Japan Automation Co.) was applied to both impact points of the specimen
and anvil portions of the 14.7J capacity instrumented Charpy impact testing machine.
The static bending test was carried out using an Instron-type universal testing machine.

Evaluation Method of Dynamic Fracture Toughness and Static Fracture Toughness

Dynamic fracture toughness was evaluated by the impact response curve method presented by Kalthoff [5] using the 14.7J capacity instrumented Charpy impact testing machine. Fracture time (t_f) is obtained from the change in strain gauge output attached to the specimen [5]. That is, the rapid unloading point of the strain gauge output is defined as the crack initiation point in this study. Moreover, the one-point bend test was conducted by modifying the anvil portion of the 14.7J capacity instrumented Charpy impact testing machine. In the one-point bend test, the time history of the stress intensity factor and the fracture time were measured in the same way as that used in the impact response curve method. The static fracture toughness was evaluated according to the ASTM E399 method.

RESULTS AND DISCUSSION

Effect of Specimen Dimensions on the Vibrational Wave Superimposed on the Load-Deflection Curve

Figure 1 shows the typical load-deflection curves recorded by the instrumented Charpy impact test for specimen (G). It is found that all load-deflection curves are of the elastic-brittle fracture type and the vibrational waves are superimposed on the load-deflection curves. Incidentally, the Charpy impact test may be modeled as in the vibrational system shown in Fig.2 (a) [6, 7]. In this system and when brittle fracture is considered, the superimposed vibrational wave can be thought to converge with linearly increasing load with time [6, 7]. Then, when the initial amplitude (a_1/P_f) and the logarithmic decrement (δ) in the vibrational wave are defined as in Fig.2 (b), the relationships between initial amplitude or logarithmic decrement and time period of the vibrational wave (τ) for the load-time curve satisfying the recommended condition of $t_f>3\tau$ [8] were investigated. The results are shown in Fig.3. It is found that smaller size specimens shortened the time period of the vibrational wave, producing a small initial amplitude and large logarithmic decrement. That is, the vibtational wave superimposed on the load-deflection curve can be suppressed by means of the specimen

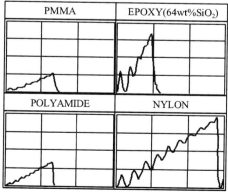

PMMA	EPOXY(64wt%SiO$_2$)
POLYAMIDE	NYLON

Vertical axis ; Load(100N/div.)
Horizontal axis ; Deflection(0.2mm/div.)

Fig.1. Typical load-deflection curves obtained by instrumented Charpy impact test. (Specimen(G))

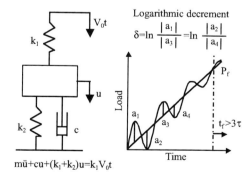

Logarithmic decrement

$$\delta=\ln\frac{|a_1|}{|a_3|}=\ln\frac{|a_2|}{|a_4|}$$

$$m\ddot{u}+c\dot{u}+(k_1+k_2)u=k_1V_0t$$

Fig.2. Vibrational mode in Charpy impact test and quantification of vibrational wave superimposed on load-deflection curve.
(a) Vibrational mode in Charpy impact test
(b) Quantification of vibrational wave superimposed on load-deflection curve

geometry which shortens the time period of the vibrational wave.
Server experimentally presented the time period of the vibrational wave as Eq. (1) [8].

$$\tau = 1.68(SWEBC_S)^{1/2}/C_0 \tag{1}$$

where B is the specimen thickness, E is Young's modulus, C_s is elastic compliance of the
specimen and C_0 is sound speed in the specimen. Equation (1) shows that the time period of
the vibrational wave is proportional to the specimen dimensions; therefore, the time period of
the vibrational wave can be shortened by the use of a small-size specimen.
It has already been confirmed for used materials that τ calculated from Eq. (1) shows good
agreement with that obtained from the load-time curve measured by the instrumented Charpy
impact test. Therefore, Eq. (1) can be applied for calculating the time period of the vibrational
wave. Accordingly, it is clear from the results of Fig.3 (a) and Eq. (1) that the small-size
specimen produces small initial amplitude and large logarithmic decrement. That is, it can be
considered in the specimen geometry which shortens the time period of the vibrational wave
that the inertial effect is reduced and the load-deflection curve reflects the deformation and
fracture behaviors of the specimen itself. Such a specimen is considered to be suitable for a
dynamic loading test such as the instrumented Charpy impact test. However, the variation in
toughness may be caused by the use of a small-size specimen. Therefore, from this viewpoint
the specimen size must be further investigated.

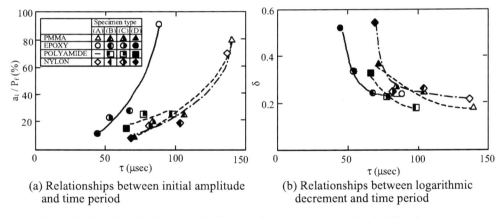

(a) Relationships between initial amplitude   (b) Relationships between logarithmic
    and time period   decrement and time period

Fig. 3. Evaluation of behaviors of vibrational superimposed on load-deflection curve.

Effect of Loading Rate on Fracture Toughness of Silica-filled Epoxy Resin

Figure 4 shows the change in fracture toughness of a silica-filled epoxy resin with stress
intensity rate, which is defined as the stress intensity factor (K_1) divided by fracture time (t_f)
[8]. In Fig. 4, at a low stress intensity rate, an Instron-type universal testing machine was used
and the stress intensity rate was controlled by changing the cross-head speed. On the other
hand, at a high stress intensity rate, the 14.7J capacity instrumented Charpy impact testing
machine was used and the test was carried out at 10°, 30°, 50°, 70°, 90°, 110° and 140°
impact angles of the hammer. As mentioned previously, the static fracture toughness was
evaluated according to the ASTM E399 method and the dynamic fracture toughness was
evaluated by the impact response curve method. In these tests, specimens (F) and (G) were

used because specimen (F) most easily generates the vibrational wave and specimen (G) was same dimensions as the standard Charpy specimen for metallic materials. From the results of the test, the fracture toughness values of both specimens (F) and (G) showed a loading rate dependency. Also, the fracture toughness values changed in three phases with the loading rate [9]. That is, the fracture toughness increases monotonously (A area), then decreases rapidly (B area), and increases again (C area). These behaviors were not dependent on the specimen dimensions.

Figure 5 shows the schematic explanation of the change in crack propagation mode near the precrack tip with changing stress intensity rate. In the A area, where the stress intensity rate is low, crack propagation behaviors can be assumed to occur as follows: (a) the crack propagates in the matrix deflecting at the large-size silica particles, and when the stress intensity rate increases, (b) the crack propagates with fracturing of the large-size silica particles. In the B area, the crack propagates mostly with fracturing of the large-size silica particles, however, (c) debonding of the interface between silica particles and the matrix can also be observed. In the C area, the crack propagates in the matrix deflecting at the large-size silica particles or debonding at the interface between silica particles and the matrix. It is found from these observations that the fracture toughness changes in silica-filled epoxy resin with changing stress intensity rate are strongly affected by the existence of coarse silica particles [9].

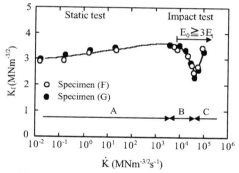

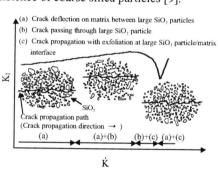

Fig.4. Change in fracture toughness values of silica-filled epoxy resin with stress intensity rate.

Fig.5. Change in fracture surface of silica-filled epoxy resin with stress intensity rate.

Effect of Shock-absorbing Material

Figure 6 shows the typical load-deflection curves which were tested statically using an Instron-type universal testing machine (cross-head speed: 0.5mm/min). Figure 6(a) is the load-deflection curve with shock-absorbing material and Fig.6 (b) is without shock-absorbing material. In the case of brittle materials, measurement of the exact maximum load is very important because the crack propagates unstably from the maximum load. Hence, the values of maximum load and maximum load deflection were measured under the static loading conditions in order to examine the effect of shock-absorbing material. Table 2 shows the comparisons of the maximum load and maximum load deflection with and without shock-absorbing materials. It is found that the use of shock-absorbing material produces both small maximum load and large maximum load deflection. That is, the maximum load with shock-absorbing material is 10% smaller than that without shock-absorbing material and the maximum load deflection with shock-absorbing material is about 7 times larger than that without shock-absorbing material. As an aside, one of the functions of the shock-absorbing

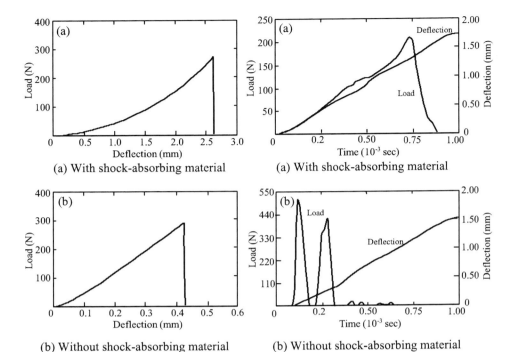

(a) With shock-absorbing material

(a) With shock-absorbing material

(b) Without shock-absorbing material

(b) Without shock-absorbing material

Fig. 6. Load-deflection curves of PMMA measured by static tree-point bending test. (specimen (F))

Fig. 7. Curves of load-time and deflection-time of PMMA measured by instrumented Charpy impact test. (specimen (F))

material is to decrease both load and deformation generated at impact. However, the shock-absorbing material cannot decrease both load and deformation simultaneously under constant impact energy; therefore, the structure of shock-absorbing material is generally designed to decrease the load at the expense of deformation [10]. Accordingly, the results of Table 2 are explained.

Table 2   Maximum load and maximum load deflection measured by static bending test (comparisons of tests with and without shock-absorbing material)

Test number	With shock-absorbing material		Without shock-absorbing material	
	Maximum load (N)	Maximum load deflection (mm)	Maximum load (N)	Maximum load deflection (mm)
1	264.8	2.62	279.5	0.422
2	264.8	2.82	289.3	0.410
3	250.1	2.82	287.3	0.388
Average	259.9	2.75	285.4	0.407

As specimen (F) is the most vibratory according to the previous results, it was used to clarify the effect of shock-absorbing material under the dynamic loading conditions. Figure 7 shows the typical curves of load-time and deflection-time of PMMA recorded by the instrumented Charpy impact test (impact velocity: 1.98m/s). Figure 7 (a) shows the load-time and deflection-time curves with shock-absorbing material, and Fig.7 (b) shows those without shock-absorbing material. It is observed that the shape of the load-time curve is changed drastically and the vibrational wave superimposed on the load-time curve disappears completely by the use of the shock-absorbing material. On the other hand, it can be found from the shape of the load-time curve shown in Fig.7 (b) that the specimen without shock-absorbing material is fractured by the inertial load. Therefore, the maximum load is not a substantial fracture load and the difference in maximum load or maximum load deflection between the tests with and without shock-absorbing material cannot be clarified quantitatively as the static bending test. However, it is presumed from the results of the static bending test that the maximum load may be decreased by the use of the shock-absorbing material. However, it is very effective to use the shock-absorbing material for decreasing the initial oscillations in the impact test of brittle materials. Therefore, it is necessary to study carefully the usefulness of the shock-absorbing material from various viewpoints hereafter.

Result of One-point Bend Test

Figure 8 shows the impact response curve, the crack initiation point measured by the instrumented Charpy impact (3-point bend) test, the time history of the stress intensity factor and the crack initiation point measured by the one-point bend test for specimen (G) of PMMA. Figure 9 shows those for specimen (G) of silica-filled epoxy resin. It can be observed from Figs.8 (a) and (b) that the vibrational wave is superimposed on the impact response curve of Charpy test at an impact speed of 3.10m/s. However, in the case of a test at the impact speed of 4.28m/s, the vibrational behavior cannot be observed in the impact response curve, and moreover, the shape of the impact response curve agrees with that of the time history of the stress intensity factor in the one-point bend test for both materials. In addition, in both materials, the difference in fracture time between the one-point bend test and the Charpy impact test increases with decreasing impact velocity. That is, the fracture time obtained using the instrumented Charpy impact test is longer than that of the one-point bend test. The reason for this can be explained as follows. (1) The specimen tested at the impact velocity of 3.10m/s does not fracture within the natural frequency of the specimen. (2) In such case, the fracture time is affected by the loading mode of the specimen. (3) Moreover, the loading mode in the one-point bend test is only by inertia and different from that in the Charpy impact test. However, it can be clarified that K_{Id} measured by the one-point bend test is almost the same as

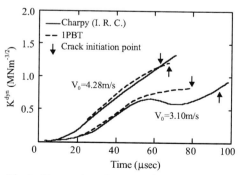

Fig.8. Comparison between impact response curve measured by instrumented Charpy impact test and time history of stress intensity factor measured by one-point bend test. (PMMA, specimen (G))

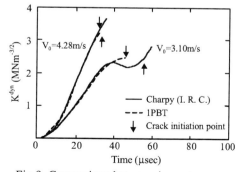

Fig.9. Comparison between impact response curve measured by instrumented Charpy impact test and time history of stress intensity factor measured by one-point bend test. (Silica-filled epoxy resin, specimen (G))

that obtained by the instrumented Charpy impact test.

CONCLUSIONS

The test method for dynamic fracture toughness of brittle polymers was studied from various viewpoints. The results of this study can be summarized as follows.

(1) The vibrational wave generated at impact in the load-deflection curve can be suppressed by using a specimen geometry which shortens the time period of the vibrational wave.

(2) The fracture toughness values of silica-filled epoxy resin are dependent on the loading rate and are affected strongly by the existence of coarse silica particles.

(3) In the static bending test, the maximum load with shock-absorbing material appears to be 10% smaller than that without shock-absorbing material and the maximum load deflection with shock-absorbing material is about 7 times larger than that without shock-absorbing material. In the dynamic bending test, the maximum load may also be reduced by the use of shock-absorbing material.

(4) In PMMA and silica-filled epoxy resin, the vibrational behavior can be observed by means of the impact response curve measured at the impact speed of 3.10m/s using the instrumented Charpy impact test. However, at the impact speed of 4.28m/s, the vibrational behavior cannot be observed. Moreover, the fracture time in the instrumented Charpy impact test is longer than that in the one-point bend test. It is possible that the fracture time is affected by the loading mode in the specimen. However, K_{Id} measured by the one-point bend test is nearly coincident with that obtained by the instrumented Charpy impact test.

REFERENCES

1. Giovanola, J. H., Investigation and Application of the One-point-bend Impact Test, ASTM STP 905 (1986), p.307

2. Sakata, M., Aoki, S. and Kishimoto, K., Measurement of Dynamic Fracture Toughness of Ceramics Materials at Elevated Temperature by One-point Bend Impact Test, Adv. Frac. Res. (ICF7), Vol.1 (1989), p.827

3. Kobayashi, T., Matsunuma, K., Ikawa, H. and Motoyoshi, K., Evaluation of Static and Dynamic Fracture Toughness in Ceramics, Eng. Frac. Mech., Vol.31, No.5 (1988), p.873

4. Kobayashi, T., Yamamoto, I. and Niinomi, M., On the Accuracy of Measurement of Dynamic Elastic-Plastic Fracture Toughness Parameters by the Instrumented Charpy Test, Eng. Frac. Mech., Vol.26, No.1 (1987), p.83

5. Kalthoff, J.F., On the Measurement of Dynamic Fracture Toughness – A Review of Recent Work, Int. J. Frac., Vol.27 (1985), p.277

6. Williams, J.G. and Adams, G.C., The Analysis of Instrumented Impact Test using a Mass-Spring Model. Int. J. Frac., Vol.33 (1987), p.209

7. Williams, J.G. and Badi, M.N.M., The Effect of Damping on the Spring-Mass Dynamic Fracture Model, Int. J. Frac., Vol.39 (1989), p.147

8. Sever, W.L., Impact Three-point Bend Testing for Notched and Precracked Specimens, J. Testing and Eval., Vol.6, No.1 (1987), p.29

9. Niinomi, M., Uwai, K., Kobayashi, T. and Okahara, A., Impact Fatigue Properties of Epoxy Resin Filled with SiO_2 Particles, Eng. Frac. Mech., Vol.38, No.6 (1991), p.439

10. Chatani, A., Impact Strength Design, Kikai-no-kenkyu (in Japanese), Vol.41, No.5 (1989), p.613

Test Procedures

From Charpy to Present Impact Testing
D. François and A. Pineau (Eds.)

DEVELOPMENT IN THE INSTRUMENTED IMPACT TEST
- COMPUTER AIDED INSTRUMENTED IMPACT TESTING SYSTEM -

TOSHIRO KOBAYASHI
Department of Production Systems Engineering,
Toyohashi University of Technology, Tempaku-cho, Toyohashi, 441-8580 Japan

ABSTRACT

To determine the toughness of materials, Charpy V notch test has been widely utilized over the world. This method is easy to conduct, but obtained values are very qualitative. Instrumented test has also a long history and gives us a loading history during impact. However this method is also still remaining in a range of screening test.

Using a precracked specimen, it is possible to estimate dynamic fracture toughness K_d, but there are many problems accompanying with measurements. Oscillations and size effect are most troublesome ones.

The author has successfully developed CAI (Computer Aided Instrumented Impact Testing) System for the evaluation of dynamic fracture toughness. In this CAI system, dynamic fracture toughness parameters such as K_d, J_d, T_{mat} and various absorbed energies can be obtained from regarding the load-deflection curve of a single precracked specimen for both ductile and brittle materials. The details and validity of this procedures are shown and discussed.

KEYWORDS

CAI System, Absorbed Energies, Dynamic Fracture Toughness, Material Tearing Modulus, Specimen Size Requirement

INTRODUCTION

Charpy impact test has been widely used as a simple method for semi-empirically evaluating impact toughness of various materials. Consistent development and modification which was firstly invented by Charpy M. G. [1] made it enabled to be standardized and then documented by famous international standard organization such as ASTM Standard Method E23 [2] and ASTM STP 1072 [3]. Nevertheless of many advantages, for example, small size of specimens, ease of testing, high strain rate, correlations with service experiences and other fracture tests, economy and large sampling capacity etc. [4-6], the absence of a measure directly applicable to design has restricted the applicability of the Charpy V-Notched (CVN) impact test results. Instrumenting the striker of the impact machine was found to provide valuable data in terms of the load-time history experienced by the specimen during impact loading. After the instrumentation of the striker presented by R. Yamada in 1928 [7] in Japan, extensive development and quantitative interpretation of the results in conjunction with the development of fracture mechanics and use of precracked CVN specimens enabled derivation of dynamic strength and fracture toughness parameters by T. Kobayashi in 1980's [8].

In Japan, "Research on the standardization of instrumented impact machine" by the federation of Japanese machine industries and the federation of Japanese testing machine manufacturers was conducted for 2 years from 1990. Based on the report, standard draft 1, "Impact testing machines for metallic materials-Instrumentation" was submitted. Japanese Industrial Standard (JIS) committee on the instrumented impact testing was inaugurated for the establishment of the standards. As a result, JIS standards named "Impact testing machines for metallic materials-Instrumentation (JIS B. 7755)" and "Impact testing machines for plastics materials-Instrumentation (JIS B. 7756)" were established in 1993.

On the other hand, T. Kobayashi has already developed the CAI (Computer Aided instrumented Impact Testing) system, where dynamic fracture toughness parameters are obtained from the analysis of the load-deflection curve of a single precracked specimen [8]. He has applied fracture mechanics approach to instrumented Charpy impact test and has successfully developed a new dynamic fracture toughness parameters evaluation system called CAI system [9, 10]. Using the CAI system, the evaluation of fracture mechanics parameters such as K, J, T_{mat} and various absorbed energy analyses can be carried out easily.

Recently, the instrumented Charpy impact test is used for the evaluation of toughness of many kinds of materials such as steel [11], aluminum alloys [12], polymer and an alloy for dentistry [13] and with miniaturized specimens [11, 14].

HISTORICAL VIEW ON ANALYSIS OF THE SIGNAL FROM INSTRUMENTED CHARPY V TEST

G. Charpy invented Charpy type impact test at the beginning of the last century. This test method became widespread in the world for the evaluation of toughness of materials. However, only information on an absorbed energy can be obtained.

Owing to the technological development of instrumentation, Körber [15] firstly developed instrumented impact tester in 1926. More information on load-deflection or load-time relationship experienced by the specimen during impact loading became possible to be obtained. Interpretation of the recorded load history of the specimen gives us a useful knowledge to understand elastic-plastic behavior of a material under dynamic loading conditions.

According to the results obtained by Raring [16] in the static bend test or by Hartbower [17] and Otani [18] in the double blow test, the crack initiation and propagation stages in the Charpy test are explained as follows. At first, a ductile crack is formed at the center of the notch root after general yielding and spreads laterally, acquiring full specimen width at the maximum load. Then the crack propagates into the width direction in tensile tear fracture mode even in the case of ductile fracture. As these fracture stages are believed to be applicable to general impact testing. It is defined that the nominal crack initiation and propagation stages correspond to the pre-maximum and post-maximum load regions, respectively. Expressing the energies absorbed in the initiation and propagation stages as E_i and E_p, respectively, the total energy E can be given by Eq.(1):

$$E = E_i + E_p = E_i + E_c + E_f + E_s \approx E_i + E_f + E_s \qquad (1)$$

where E_c is energy absorbed in the cleavage fracture portion, E_f is energy absorbed in the flat fibrous fracture portion and E_s is energy absorbed in the shear lip(slant fracture) portion.

In the brittle boundary layer specimens such as carburized or pressed notch ones [19], it can be shown from the analysis of the load-time curve that $E_i \approx 0$. Therefore brittle crack initiates directly from the notch root, and $E \approx E_p = E_c + E_f$; this energy is important because it represents the plane strain fracture toughness for conditions of no shear lip formation.

CONFIGURATION OF THE CAI SYSTEM

Figure 1 shows the configuration of the developed CAI system. The CAI system consists of the instrumented Charpy impact testing machine aided with a personal computer containing CAI software. In this system, load is measured by semi-conductor strain gage attached to the striker and deflection is measured by a potentiometer located at the rotating axis of the hammer for testing ductile materials or measured by a magnetic sensor attached to the base of testing machine for testing brittle materials. Load and deflection data are amplified by a high-frequency type amplifier and stored in a digital storage oscilloscope, then transferred from the digital storage oscilloscope to the personal computer by a GBIP interface.

There are two kinds of the CAI software, one for ductile materials and the other for brittle materials. Both softwares mainly consist of five functions; (1) data acquisition, (2) smoothing of the load-time and deflection-time curves, (3) data analysis, (4) display and (5) data store.

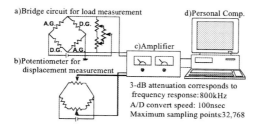

Fig.1. Configuration of the CAI system.

EVALUATION OF THE DYNAMIC FRACTURE TOUGHNESS IN DUCTILE MATERIALS [8-10]

In the CAI system, fracture mechanics parameters such as the J integral value(J_1), the stress intensity factor(K_1) and the material tearing modulus(T_{mat}) and also various absorbed energies such as the energy absorbed in a specimen or testing machine can be obtained under the dynamic loading conditions from analyzing the load-deflection curve of a single precracked specimen.

Detection of Crack Initiation Point and Evaluation of J_d Value

According to elastic-plastic fracture mechanics, a crack initiation point must be detected to evaluate the fracture toughness. In the dynamic properties analysis software for ductile materials, this point is detected by the compliance changing rate method. The compliance changing rate is defined as

$$\Delta C/C = (C - C_{el}) / C_{el} \tag{2}$$

where $\Delta C/C$ is compliance changing rate, C is an apparent elastic compliance, and C_{el} is an elastic compliance.

When $\Delta C/C$ is plotted against the deflection, a sudden transition point of the gradient will appear as schematically shown in Fig.2.

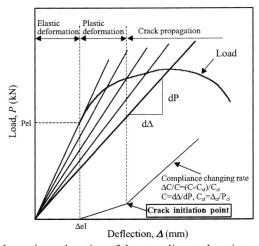

Fig.2. Schematic explanation of the compliance changing rate method.

It has been ascertained from the result of the stop block method [8] for various metallic materials such as steel, aluminum alloy, ductile cast iron and titanium alloy that the sudden transition point of the $\Delta C/C$ curves correspond to the deflection where the critical stretched zone width is formed [20].

In the dynamic properties analysis software for ductile materials, this point is defined as the crack initiation point and the energy absorbed up to this point is calculated from the area of the load-deflection curve in order to evaluate the dynamic elastic-plastic fracture toughness, J_d.

In the dynamic properties analysis software for ductile materials, the dynamic elastic-plastic fracture toughness value J_d is calculated using Rice's equation [21].

$$J_d = 2E_i / B(W - a_0) \tag{3}$$

where B is specimen thickness, W is specimen width and a_0 is initial precrack length.

Prediction of Crack Growth and Evaluation of the Material Tearing Modulus

Crack extension is estimated by the key curve method. In the dynamic properties analysis software for ductile materials, the key curve function is given by Eq.(4) [22].

$$PW / b_0^2 = k(\Delta_{pl} / W)^n \qquad (4)$$

where P is a load, b_0 is an initial ligament width (= W - a_0), Δ_{pl} is the deflection due to the plastic deformation, and n and k are constants determined by fitting the load-deflection curve using Eq.(4).

The key curve method is based on the assumption that the load-deflection curve with crack growth will intersect the one without crack growth at the same a/W ratio, as schematically shown in Fig.3. Eq.(4) can be rearranged like Eq.(5).

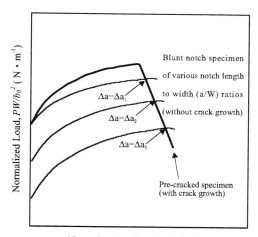

Fig.3. Schematic explanation of the key curve method (Δa shows the crack extension).

$$b_0 = \{(PW^{n+1}) / (k(\Delta_{pl}^n) \}^{1/2} \qquad (5)$$

When the crack extends by the amount Δa, the remaining ligament width can be calculated by Eq.(6).

$$b = b_0 - \Delta a = W - (a_0 + \Delta a) \qquad (6)$$

where b is remaining ligament width and Δa is crack extension length. Therefore, by inserting Eq.(6) into Eq.(5) instead of b_0, crack extension can be calculated as:

$$\Delta a = W - ((PW^{n+1} / k(\Delta_{pl}^{n})^{1/2} + a_0)) \tag{7}$$

The validity of Eq.(5) has been ascertained by the comparison with the results of stop block method for various materials. Fig.4 shows the crack extension versus deflection plot for the standard size Charpy precracked specimen of A533B steel obtained from the key curve method and the stop block method. It is found that the crack extension versus deflection plot obtained by the key curve method agrees with the one obtained by the stop block method until a crack extension of 2 mm[8]. Furthermore the crack propagation resistance curve, that is, J-R curve can be obtained by calculating Eqs.(3) and (7) for the load-deflection curve of a single precracked specimen. The material tearing modulus, T_{mat}, is defined by Eq.(8) [23].

$$T_{mat} = (E / \sigma_0^2) / (dJ / da) \tag{8}$$

where σ_0 is flow stress, which is the averaged value of ultimate tensile stress and yielding stress, and dJ / da is a slope of the J-R curve.

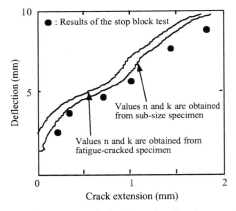

Fig.4. Crack extension versus deflection plot for the standard size Charpy specimen (A533B steel).

SPECIMEN SIZE REQUIREMENT FOR VALID DYNAMIC FRACTURE TOUGHNESS

It has been considered in fracture mechanics that fracture toughness is a material constant reflecting the resistance against fracture when the specimen dimensions satisfy the valid criterion of ASTM E 813, Test Method for J_{Ic}, a Measure of Fracture Toughness, defined in Eq.(9).

$$B, a_0, (W - a_0) > 25(J / \sigma_0) \tag{9}$$

However, there is now no such valid criterion for a specimen under dynamic loading and it is doubtful whether the criterion of Eq.(9) can be applied to dynamic loading. Therefore, effects of specimen thickness on J_d and a valid criterion for specimen thickness were investigated for

A533B steel under dynamic loading using the CAI system. The results are shown in Fig.5. In Fig.5, the dotted line shows the limit line for satisfying Eq(9). The dependency of J_d on specimen thickness can be observed even in this region. From Fig.5, it is understood that J_d is dependent upon the specimen thickness even if the constant in Eq(9) is larger than 25. Also the constant in Eq.(9) needs to be larger than about 75 in order to obtain a valid J_{Id} which is not dependent upon specimen thickness. However, it has been found in the case of a U-type side-grooved standard size Charpy specimen with the groove depth of 1 mm that the constant in Eq.(9) can be reduced up to 50.

However, experimental procedures are largely included in the method and it will take some time to adapt this analysis into the CAI software. However, the CAI system has been already put into practical use in Japan. It is expected to become a worldwide test procedure. On the validity of specimen size requirement on obtained fracture toughness values by this procedure has been reported [11, 24]. Moreover, on the accuracy of load measurement in the instrumented impact testing has been also reported recently by the present author [25].

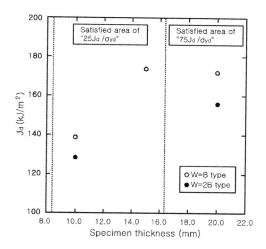

Fig.5. Effect of specimen thickness on J_d under dynamic loading condition of A533B steel.

SUMMARY

Hundred years have passed since Charpy impact test has been proposed. The idea to measure a resilience (one parameter of the toughness) of materials using pendulum type machine was unique at that time. This paper summarized and reviewed on the progress and development of the Charpy test and the instrumented Charpy test mainly based on the studies of T. Kobayashi. Instrumented impact test has started since 1920's. ISO or JIS standard on this method has appeared in 1990's. It is becoming possible to obtain dynamic fracture toughness simply from this method. Standardization on this subject will become next important problem.

REFERENCES

1. Charpy G.: Soc. Ing. Civ. de Français, June 1901; reprinted in ASTM STP 1380(2000), p.46.
2. ASTM Standard Method E 23-88, 1990 Annual Book of ASTM Standards, Vol. 03. 01 (1990), p.197.
3. Holt J. M.: Charpy Impact Test: Factors and Variables, ASTM STP 1072, ASTM (1990).
4. Pellini W. S.: Welding J., 50 (1971), p.91-s.
5. Wullaert R. A.: in Impact Testing of Metals, ASTM STP 466, American Society for Testing and Materials, Philadelpia (1970), p.148.
6. Wullaert R. A. et al: in Fracture Prevention and Control, (ed) Hoeppner, D. W, ASM Materials /Metal Working Technology Series No. 3 (1974), p.255.
7. Yamada R.: J. Japan Soc. of Mechanical Engineers, 31 (1928), p.420.
8. Kobayashi T.: Eng. Frac. Mech., 24(1986), p.773.
9. Kobayashi T. and Niinomi M.: Nucl. Eng. and Design, 111(1989), p.27.
10. Kobayashi T., Yamamoto I. and Niinomi M.: Journal of Testing and Evaluation, May (1993), p.145.
11. Sugiura N., Isobe E., Yamamoto I. and Kobayashi T.: ISIJ International, 35 (1995), p.419.
12. Hafiz M. F. and Kobayashi T.: Z. Metalkd, 89 (1998), p.445.
13. Takahashi S., Niinomi M., Hukui H., T. Kobayashi and J. Hasegawa: The Journal of the Japanese Society for Dental Materials and Devices, 15 (1996), p.577.
14. Yamashita M., Viswanathan U. K., Yamamoto I. and Kobayashi T., ISIJ International, 37(1997), p.1133.
15. Körber F. and Strop A. A.: K-W-I. Eisenf, 8 (1926), p.8.
16. Raring R., Proc. Amer. Soc. Test. Mat., 52(1952), p.1034.
17. Hartbower C. E., Welding J., 36(1957), p.494.
18. Otani M.: J. Japan Welding Soc., 23(1954), p.250.
19. Kobayashi T., Takai K. and Maniwa H.: Trans. ISIJ, 7(1967), p.115.
20. Kobayashi T., Kajino T., Kamimura M. and Ikawa H.: Adv. Frac. Res., ICF7 (1989), p.651.
21. Rice J. R., Paris P. C. and Merkle J. G.: ASTM STP 536 (1973), p.231.
22. Ernst H. and Paris P. C.: ASTM STP 677(1979), p.581.
23. Paris P. C., Tada H., Zahoor A. and Ernst H.: ASTM STP 668(1979), p.5.
24. Kobayashi T., Morita S. and Toda H.: Mat. Trans., 42, No.1, (2001), pp.52-57.
25. Kobayashi T., Inoue I., Morita S. and Toda H.: ASTM STP 1380(2000), p.198.

From Charpy to Present Impact Testing
D. François and A. Pineau (Eds.)

ANALYSIS OF TEST DATA OBTAINED FROM CHARPY V AND IMPACT TENSILE TEST

TOSHIRO KOBAYASHI*, HIROYUKI TODA* and TOMOKAZU MASUDA**

*Department of Production Systems Engineering, Toyohashi University of Technology,
**Graduate School of Toyohashi University of Technology, Toyohashi University of Technology,
1-1, Hibarigaoka, Tempaku-cho, Toyohashi-shi, Aichi, 441-8580, Japan

ABSTRACT

The standard Charpy V-notch specimen has received a great deal of attention as small, inexpensive and convenient material test specimen which provides deep insights of inherent fracture toughness problems. In this study, Charpy impact tests are performed utilizing the Computer-Aided Instrumented Charpy impact test (CAI) method which has been developed by one of the present authors (TK) for nearly 40 years. The well-known Server's equation is used to estimate tensile properties directly from the Charpy tests. Agreement between the prediction and experiments are checked for major practical aluminum alloys heat-treated to respective standard heat treatment states. Discrepancy between them is almost negligible in the case of age-hardening alloys, while it amounts sometimes several ten % in the solution hardening alloys. Especially in the case of age-hardening alloys, which is considered important as primary structural materials, feasibility of utilizing the Charpy tests to obtain tensile properties over a wide strain range is clarified by being based on the thermally activated deformation process of the aluminum alloys.

KEYWORDS

Instrumented Charpy impact test, Commercial aluminum alloys, Impact tensile test, three point bend test, Server's equation

INTRODUCTION

It is a pressing need that properties of light metals should be measured and evaluated under dynamic loading conditions, because they have began to be used widely for the civil engineering and constructions and transportations. The three point bend properties under the moderate dynamic loading condition have been extensively measured by the Charpy impact testing machine. Due to its simple and convenient nature, the Charpy impact test method [1,2] has been used widely for screening of materials. Recently, the instrumented Charpy impact test machine has been established by Japanese Industrial Standards committee (JIS) [3] and therefore the usefulness of the instrumented Charpy impact test is being recognized more and more even in Japan. On the other hand, since various impact test machines such the split-Hopkinson bar apparatus, the servo hydraulic impact testing machine and etc. have been developed owing to the above-mentioned social demands, dynamic mechanical properties became to be measured at high strain rate in well-equipped laboratories. However, those test machines are large, more expensive than Charpy impact test machines and also needs special skills and knowledge to obtain accurate values.

More than 20 years ago, W. L. Server [4] proposed the simple equation which correlated yield stress values of a nuclear pressure vessel steel obtained in the Charpy V-notch three point bend tests with those from conventional tensile test data on the basis of the slip-line fields solution for general yielding. Thereafter, one of the present authors (TK) revealed the possibility of such correlation between the Charpy V-notch tests and the tensile tests even in some practical aluminum cast alloy [5]. In this study, the tensile stresses and the three point bend loads on five kinds of commercial aluminum alloys are measured under impact loading conditions in order to clarify relationships between the tensile and three point bend properties.

MATERIALS AND EXPERIMENTS

The materials used for this study are four widely used wrought aluminum alloys and a cast aluminum alloy which were heat-treated to respective ordinary heat treatment conditions. Chemical compositions of used samples are shown in Table 1. Geometry and nominal dimensions of specimens are given in Fig.1 [5]. Specimens both for Charpy V-notch and impact tensile tests are sampled in longitudinal orientation.

Table 1   Chemical compositions of samples used. (mass%)

	Si	Fe	Cu	Mn	Mg	Cr	Zn	Ti	Li	Zr	Al
A2091-T8	0.03	0.06	2.00	-	1.50	-	-	-	2.10	0.12	bal.
A5083-H112	0.14	0.20	0.03	0.65	4.64	0.11	-	0.02	-	-	bal.
A6061-T6	0.73	0.20	0.25	0.11	1.00	0.05	0.06	0.02	-	-	bal.
A7075-T6	0.12	0.20	1.60	0.06	2.40	0.19	5.80	0.02	-	-	bal.
AC4CH-T6	6.76	0.07	-	-	0.36	-	-	0.13	-	-	bal.

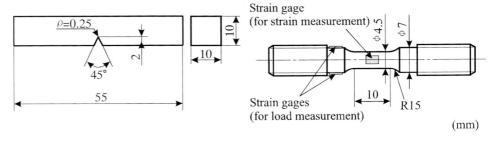

(a) Three point bend specimen   (b) Tensile specimen

Fig.1.   Geometry of specimens used.

The instrumented Charpy impact test was performed on a pendulum Charpy impact machine having a capacity of 490 J at room temperature. Fig. 2 shows a diagram of the CAI (Computer Aided Instrumented Charpy impact testing) system used in this study. The initial loading velocity was 5m/s. Load was picked up from semi-conductor strain gages attached on a hammer tap. Origin, development, calibration and accuracy of the system are reported somewhere else in this volume [6,7].

The impact tensile tests were conducted using a servo-hydraulic impact test machine with a capacity of 49kN. Fig. 3 shows the schematic diagram of the impact tensile test system. In

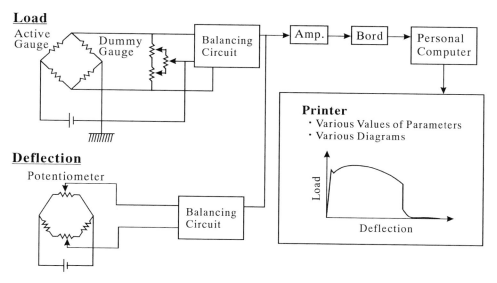

Fig.2.   Schematic diagram of the CAI testing system.

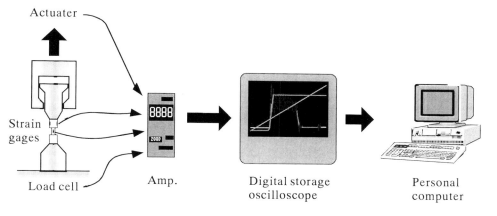

Fig.3.   Schematic diagram of the instrumented impact tensile test system.

order to record the true load-time and strain-time history avoiding the effects of oscillation accompanying with inertial impact loading, two strain gages were attached onto specimen surface of the parallel body shown in Fig. 1(b) to measure load directly. The loading velocity was varied from 0.01 to 12m/s. These data obtained from a load-deflection curve and stress-strain curve were compared as a function of strain rate.

The instrumented Charpy impact specimen and impact tensile specimen are different in their shape and fracture mode. However, Server, W. L. [4] proposed that impact tensile properties can be correlated through a simple equation by applying a slip line fields solution for general yielding.

$$\dot{\varepsilon} = \frac{6K_\sigma W}{24.4(W-a)^2}\dot{d} \tag{1}$$

where $\dot{\varepsilon}$ is strain rate, K_σ is elastic stress concentration factor, W is specimen width, a is V-notch depth and $\dot{d}$ is deflection rate. In this case, $K_\sigma = 4.28$ [8].   Later, Green, A. P. and Hundy, B. B. [9] performed the analysis of plane strain bending of V-notched specimens. Assuming a Tresca yield criterion, the relationship between three point bending moments, PW, at general yield is given by:

$$\sigma = \frac{\alpha PW}{B(W-a)^2} \tag{2}$$

where B is specimen breadth and $\alpha = 2.99$ [4]. P is load value obtained the instrumented Charpy impact test.

RESULTS AND DISCUSSION

Figure 4 shows stress-strain curves of four popular wrought aluminum alloys and a cast aluminum alloy at two different strain rates. In all of the cases, Young's modulus is almost constant at all strain rates. 0.2% proof stress slightly increases with increasing strain rate, but this dependence is not similar, because negative strain rate dependency is reported in solution hardening aluminum alloys [10]. All of the stress-strain curves at various strain rates are replotted as 0.2% proof stress vs. logarithm of the strain rate as shown in Fig. 5. As for the 0.2% proof stress, the strain rate sensitivity appears to increase at higher strain rates. However, there is no considerable rate sensitivity up to the intermediate strain rate of $10^2\,s^{-1}$.

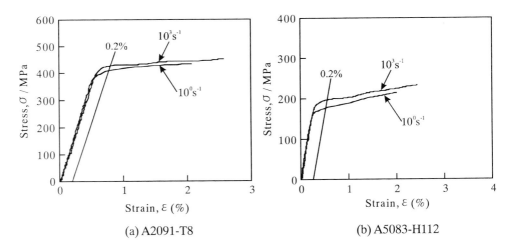

(a) A2091-T8   (b) A5083-H112

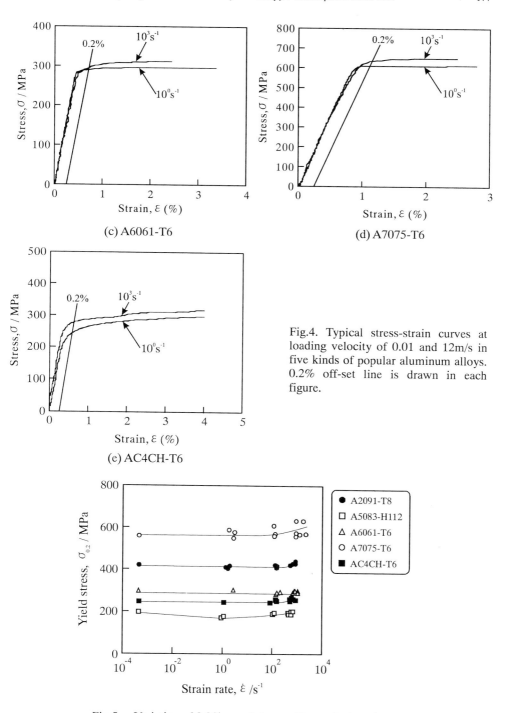

(c) A6061-T6

(d) A7075-T6

(e) AC4CH-T6

Fig.4. Typical stress-strain curves at loading velocity of 0.01 and 12m/s in five kinds of popular aluminum alloys. 0.2% off-set line is drawn in each figure.

Fig.5. Variation of 0.2% proof stress with nominal strain rate.

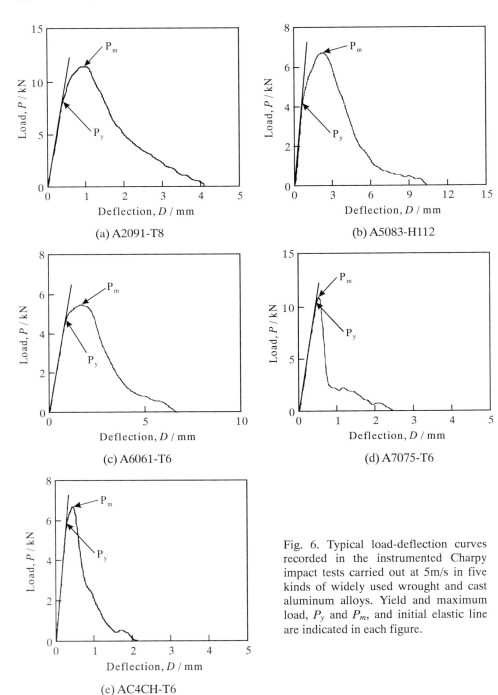

(a) A2091-T8

(b) A5083-H112

(c) A6061-T6

(d) A7075-T6

(e) AC4CH-T6

Fig. 6. Typical load-deflection curves recorded in the instrumented Charpy impact tests carried out at 5m/s in five kinds of widely used wrought and cast aluminum alloys. Yield and maximum load, P_y and P_m, and initial elastic line are indicated in each figure.

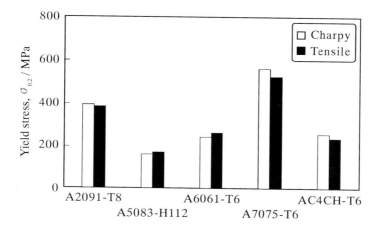

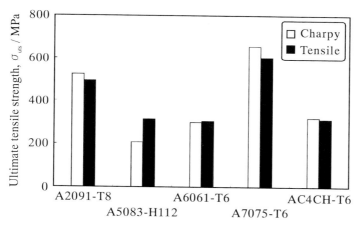

Fig.7. Comparisons of strength obtained by impact tensile tests and 3-point bend tests.

Figure 6 shows typical load-deflection curves in the instrumented Charpy impact tests, where P_y is defined as a point from which a stress-strain curve deviates from the initial linear line. Fig. 7 shows comparisons of yield stresses and ultimate tensile strengths calculated by equation (2). Yield stress, $s_{0.2}$, and ultimate tensile strength, s_{uts}, shown in Fig. 6 were calculated by equation (2) from P_y and P_m, respectively. Strain rates of three point bend tests calculated by equation (1) were between 600 and 700 s^{-1},which are relatively close to those of the impact tensile tests when the tensile loading velocity was 7m/s. The data obtained provided the evidence that Charpy V-notch yield stresses could be used to determine dynamic tensile yield stress values for the widely used aluminum alloys. In an age hardening aluminum alloys having low solute atoms concentration such as A6061 and AC4CH-T6, the agreement seems to be fairly good, while difference in the solution hardening aluminum alloys reached more than 30% especially for ultimate tensile strengths. Since the work hardening coefficient of the materials is not taken into consideration in the Server's equation, the strength calculated from the three point bend load was relatively underestimated for the solution hardening aluminum alloy. In addition, once its agreement is confirmed by such a comparison, strain rate dependency of each material like Fig. 5 can be utilized to estimate tensile properties at various strain rates from quasi-static to impact such as strain rate of about $10^3 s^{-1}$. This is because strain rate sensitivity of widely used aluminum alloys is relatively moderate and it can be evaluated by analyzing thermally activated deformation process. This is especially true for the age-hardening aluminum alloys like A6061-T6 in which the agreement in Fig. 7 was fairly good.

CONCLUSIONS

Computer-aided instrumented Charpy impact testing system, which has been developed and accuracy of which has been pursued by one of the authors (TK), was utilized to obtain yield and maximum loads in the V-notch Charpy bend tests. Also servo-hydraulic impact testing system was used to obtain tensile stress-strain relationships over a wide strain rate range with special care on accurate load measurement. Strain rates estimated for the Charpy V-notch specimen tested at 5m/s almost corresponded to those for the impact tensile tests at 7m/s. Relatively good agreement between the prediction by the Server's equation and experiment was obtained especially for age-hardening alloys, while solution hardening alloy showed discrepancy up to 30% in the later stage of strain hardening such as ultimate tensile strength. Since the agreement was fairly good, it is possible to estimate the tensile properties over a wide strain rate range up to $10^3 s^{-1}$ by performing ordinary Charpy V-notch impact test together with the analysis of the thermal activation process of the practical aluminum alloys.

REFERENCES

[1] T. Kobayashi, I. Yamamoto, J. Jpn. Inst. Met. 32 (1993) 151-159.
[2] T. Kobayashi, J. Jpn. Inst. Met. 12 (1973) 546-556.
[3] Japanese Industrial Standards Committee. (1993) JIS B 7755-1993
[4] W. L. Server, J. Eng. Mat. Tech. 100 (1978) 183-188.
[5] N. Sugiura, T. Kobayashi, I. Yamamoto, S. Nishido, K. Hayashi, J. Jpn. Inst. Light Met. 45 (1995) 638-642.
[6] T. Kobayashi, Proc. CCC2001 (2001) in press.
[7] S. Morita, M. Otani, T. Kobayashi, Proc. CCC2001 (2001) in press.
[8] Rau, C. A., Jr. PhD Thesis, Stanford University, U. S. A. 1967.
[9] A. P. Green, B. B. Hundy, J. Mech. Phys. Solids. 4 (1956) 128-144.
[10] T. Mukai, K. Higashi, S. Tanimura, Met. Sci. Eng. A176 (1994) 181-189.

rom Charpy to Present Impact Testing
. François and A. Pineau (Eds.)
2002 Elsevier Science Ltd. and ESIS. All rights reserved

The Validation of the Draft Standard for Instrumented Impact Testing (IIT) of Metallic Materials Version 10:1994

Ravi K. Varma and **Malcolm S. Loveday**

NPL Materials Centre
National Physical Laboratory
Teddington, Middlesex
United Kingdom, TW11 0LW

BSTRACT

iis paper summarises the findings of a Standards Measurement & Testing (SMT)
uropean collaborative project to validate the draft standard for Instrumented Impact
:sting (IIT) of metallic materials. Thirteen laboratories from different European States
ere selected on the basis of proficiency testing, to participate in a comprehensive test
·ogramme.

ie validation of IIT software was carried out by an Inter-comparison Exercise in which the
ita from a Reference Charpy Impact test was supplied in ASCII format and compared by
even laboratories. Subsequently an IIT inter-comparison exercise was carried out by the
irticipants to compare the repeatability and reproducibility data. Good agreement was
und between the various laboratories using different software and different makes of
achines conforming to the specifications in Document ISO/TC 164/SC4 N191 (Rev 3)
tandard method for the instrumented Charpy V-notch impact test on metallic materials,
·aft 10:1994".

ie results from this research investigation demonstrated the validity of the approach
commended in the draft standard for establishing the test method for Instrumented Impact
:sting. The proposed draft ESIS Instrumented Charpy V-notch Impact Test method was
blished in May 2000 as EN ISO 14556: 2000 ' *Steel- Charpy V-notch pendulum impact*
;t- Instrumented test method.'

EYWORDS

iarpy , Intrumented Impact Testing, Standards, Reference Materials, Validation.

NTRODUCTION

the time when the work started, no European or International standards existed for
strumented Impact Testing (IIT) Charpy V-notch impact test. In spite of this, the IIT technique
is used in many situations for quality control in the manufacture and fabrication of industrial
mponents from both steel and non-ferrous materials.

veral countries including Germany, Italy, France, UK, Austria, Ireland, Netherlands, Japan,
A, Sweden and Finland have adopted the Instrumented Impact Testing technique to obtain

impact toughness data in the manufacturing, automotive and power generation industries. Sor
of these instrumented systems have been developed "in-house", others are marketed by machi
manufacturers, but at the time none conformed to an agreed international code of practice
standard. Despite this, the Instrumented Impact Test provides a wealth of information on impa
toughness. In some cases the test is used to provide the fracture toughness data, and can provide
cheaper and quicker alternative to the conventional fracture toughness test. The procedure h
been widely adopted by the nuclear power generation establishments worldwide to assess t
fracture toughness values of the irradiated pressure vessels.

The draft "Standard method for the instrumented Charpy V-notch impact test on metal
materials" was issued by ESIS TC5 sub-committee for intermediate strain rates as a committ
document, which established the requirements for carrying out and evaluating instrument
impact tests performed on metallic Charpy V-notch specimens of metallic materials. The dra
was based on experience gained during testing of steels from the German Association f
Materials Testing, using data from several laboratories in an early German Standards DVM 0
(1986)[1] and SEP 1315 (1987)[2] provides further information of the fracture behaviour of t
tested materials. Minimum requirements were given for measurement and recording equipme
so that similar sensitivity and comparable measurements could be achieved.

The objectives of the work carried out in this inter-comparison programme were to validate t
draft standard and to establish the repeatability and reproducibility of the instrumented systems
the participants using BCR Reference V-notch Charpy testpieces at two energy levels.

The organisations participating in the work were:

1	Belgium: CEN/SCK, Mol	2	Germany: BAM, Berlin
3	Germany: IWM, Freiburg	4	Germany: MPA, Stuttgart
5	Germany: Roell Amsler	6	Hungary: Miskolc University
7	Italy: CISE, Milan	8	Spain: Madrid University
9	UK: AEA Technology, Harwell	10	UK: Instron, High Wycombe
11	UK: Manchester Metropolitan University		
12	UK: National Physical Laboratory, Teddington		
13	UK: Royal Military College of Science, Swindon		

EXPERIMENTAL

The tests were performed, following EN10045-Part 1*, using the standard BCR (Bureau
Community of Reference) Charpy V-notch reference specimens obtained from IRMM (Ge
Belgium) with nominal energy levels of 60 and 80 Joules (CRM014 & CRM015), s
Marchandise, Perez-Sainz & Collinet [3] and Marchandise [4].
10 mm square V-notch reference Charpy specimens from batches CRM014 and CRM015 we
used in this exercise, in accordance with the specification in EN10045-Part 2, **.
Typical results of ductile specimens are included in this report to demonstrate the repeatability
the instrumented tests on the BCR reference Charpy specimens. The results generally she
acceptable agreement between the mechanical energy (dial energy) and the calculated energy fr
the typical traces
* 'Charpy Impact test on metallic materials', BS EN 10045-1:1990 - Part 1.Test Method.
** 'Charpy Impact test on metallic materials', BS EN 10045-1:1990 - Part 2.Method for the
   verification of impact testing machines. [Table B1: Dimensions of Reference Testpieces].

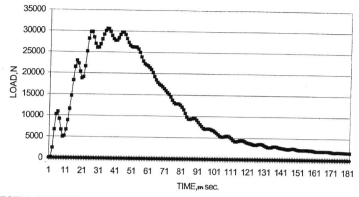

TOTAL ABSORBED ENERGY = 55.4 J, Fmax. = 29.23 kN , Fgy =25.5kN

Figure 1. Typical Charpy Instrumented Impact curve , CRM14

The first task was to assess the IIT software used by the participants. It was agreed to carry out a software evaluation of each of the participant's system, by using Instrumented Impact Data from a test carried out on a selected sample of the BCR Reference Material, CRM14. The data was acquired in ASCII format, and was supplied to all the participants, in order to evaluate their software - which was either developed "in house" or was propriety software. A typical plot of load versus time is shown in Figure 1.

Labs	Total Absorbed Impact Energy Value from Participant's Software, J	Force kN			Displacement mm		Software Correction Factor: (Total Absorbed Energy minus CRM Value), J
		F_{max}	F_{gy}	F_{iu}	S_{max}	S_{gy}	
1	54.9	29.02	25.13	0.168	0.74	0.40	- 1.4
2	55.6	29.10	25.5	0.16	0.93	0.522	- 0.7
3	56.1	31.7	26.8	0.19	0.91	0.59	- 0.2
4	55.9	31.4	26.6	0.195	0.843	0.54	- 0.4
5	55.4	29.2	25.5	0.170	0.79	0.51	- 0.9
6	56.2	29.23	25.69	0.145	0.87	0.412	- 0.1
7	55.6	30.54	26.12	0.172	0.76	0.56	- 0.7
8	57.7	28.65	26.5	0.180	0.765	0.40	+ 1.4
9	56.4	29.40	25.4	0.176	0.84	0.46	+ 0.1
10	55.8	29.23	25.69	0.192	0.795	0.49	- 0.5
11	55.6	28.2	25.2	-			- 0.7

TABLE I: Results of the software evaluation of a tested BCR V-notch Charpy specimen: batch 46b, EP370 .Data was supplied in ASCII format for analyse by the participants Test Temperature = 20 ± 2 °C; Certified Value = 56.3 J

The results computed from all the laboratories are shown in Table I and Figs 2 and 3.

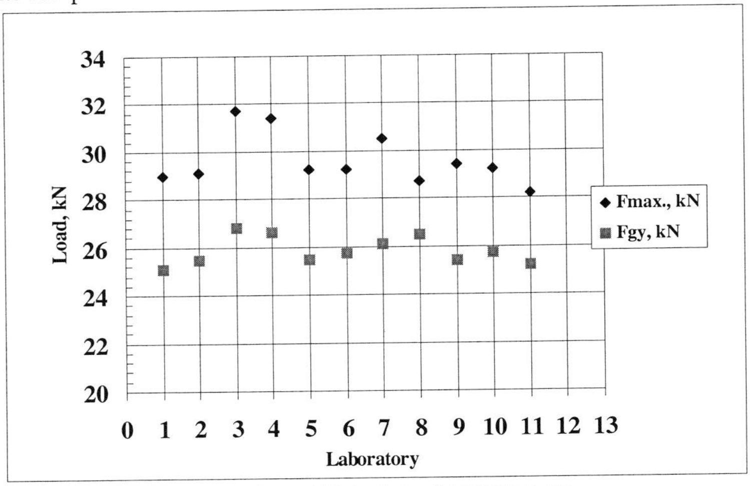

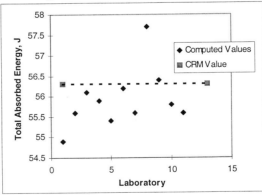

Figure 2. Charpy IIT Analysis of ASCII Data File,
Variation of Fmax & Fgy

The total absorbed energy, which is normally obtained from the dial reading on a conventional Charpy impact testing machine, is indicated by how far the pendulum swings upwards after striking the testpiece. In the case of Charpy IIT, the total absorbed energy is derived by software which calculates the total area under the load-time trace recorded by the sensors (strain-gauges) attached to the tup. The difference between the certified value of a specimen from batch 46B of CRM014 of 56.3 J and the total absorbed energy calculated by the software is given in Table I.

Figure 3. Total absorbed energy calculated from ASCII Data file by various laboratories

It can be seen in Figure 3 that, in general, the software computed value of the total absorbed energy level is slightly lower than the mean certified value of the CRM. However, it should be appreciated that the ASCII data set was obtained from one reference Charpy testpiece which may well have had a slightly lower value than the certified CRM value, but is of course, still within its associated tolerance limits, and this may account for the distribution of results shown in Figure 3. It should be noted, however, that the result from Laboratory 8 appears anomalously high. With the exception of Laboratories 1 and 8, there was good agreement between the various software analysis packages, with all the results lying within a scatter band of ±0.5J, ie within ~±1%, as can be seen in Table I . These two laboratories reported results indicating differences of 1.4J (ie ~ 2.4%). Given that the uncertainty of the CRM is quoted as ± 1.8J for the 60J material, a systematic error of 1.4J in the software would leave very little margin of error on the repeat measurements of a batch of five samples. Thus it was suggested that the two laboratories indicating significant discrepancies would be well advised to investigate the reasons for the apparent discrepancy. The difference between the CRM value and the software indicated value could be used as a Correction Factor to compensate for the systematic error. It should be noted, however, that in this present investigation only one ASCII data set was analysed for the nominal ~60J energy level, and in the absence of any other information, it has been assumed that the same correction factor is applicable to the higher, ~80J energy level. It may be prudent in future to repeat this part of the investigation using an ASCII data file recorded from a test undertaken with CRM 015, i.e. the 80 J material.

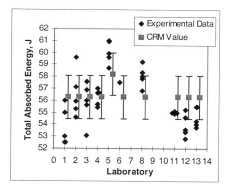

Figure 4. 60 J Experimental IIT Data.
(without Software Correction factors)

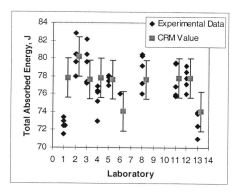

Figure5. 80 J Experimental IIT Data
(Without Software Correction)

The next part of the validation programme comprised an inter-comparison exercise, using BCR V-notch reference testpieces from CRM014 and CRM015 batches, ie a nominal energy level of 60 and 80 joules respectively. The major common factors were that a) all the machines were calibrated to EN10045 Pt 2 and b) the tests were carried out complying with the draft standard for IIT of metallic materials. The results are summarised in Table II whilst the results from the various laboratories from the IIT Software at the nominally 60J and 80J energy levels are shown in Figs 4 & 5. The same laboratory numbering has been retained throughout the analysis to facilitate ease of comparison of the data, although the order of the laboratories is different to that listed above in order to preserve anonymity. Not all the laboratories that undertook the software analysis participated in the subsequent experimental testing programme, whilst two laboratories 12 and 13 did not participate in the software analysis exercise and hence no information is available concerning their Software Correction Factors. One laboratory, Number 6, only supplied mean values for the experimental testing programme. It can be seen in Figures 4 & 5 that in all cases for each laboratory there is an overlap between some of the individual readings and the tolerance band for the CRM.

Lab No.	CRM 014 Set No	CRM 014 value for CEN TUP, J	Mean, for CEN TUP J	CRM 015 Set No	CRM 015 value J	Mean, CRM 015, J	Data supplied
1	49B	56.3 ± 1.8	53.8	60C	77.8 ± 2.1	72.6	Full
2	60B	56.3 ± 1.8	56.5	80G	80.2 ± 2.3	80.2	Full
3	47B	56.3 ± 1.8	55.8	75B	77.6 ± 2.3	79.3	Full
4	45B	56.3 ± 1.8	56.3	64C	77.8 ± 2.1	77.5	Full
5	24A	58.2 ± 1.8	60.0	64B	77.6 ± 2.3	77.7	Full
6	48B	56.3 ± 1.8	57.5	71A	74.1 ± 2.2	76.0	Mean values only
7	-	-	-	-	-	-	Software evaluation only
8	50B	56.3 ± 1.8	58.0	41B	77.6 ± 2.3	78.6	Full
9	-	-	-	-	-	-	Software evaluation only
10	-	-	-	-	-	-	Software evaluation only
11	46B	56.3 ± 1.8	55.0	68C	77.8 ± 2.1	77.5	Full
12	44B	56.3 ± 1.8	53.9	67C	77.8 ± 2.1	77.7	Full (No software evaluation)
13	56B	56.3 ± 1.8	54.6	46C	74.1 ± 2.1	73.0	Full (No software evaluation)

TABLE II. Instrumented impact results using BCR V-notch Charpy Reference
Testpieces at nominal energies of 60 J(CRM 014) and 80 J (CRM 015) at 22 ± 2°C.

Lab No.	CRM 014			CRM 015	
	Software correction factor, J	(Measured mean minus CRM value), J	Corrected differences, J	(Measured mean - CRM values), J	Corrected values, J
1	- 1.4	- 2.5	- 1.1	- 5.2	- 3.8
2	- 0.7	0.2	0.9	0	0.7
3	- 0.2	- 0.5	- 0.3	1.7	1.9
4	- 0.4	0	+ 0.4	- 0.3	0.1
5	- 0.9	+ 1.8	2.7	+ 0.1	1.0
6	- 0.1	1.2	1.3	1.9	2.0
7	- 0.7	-	-	-	-
8	+ 1.4	1.7	0.3	1.0	- 0.4
9	+ 0.1	-	-	-	-
10	- 0.5	-	-	-	-
11	- 0.7	- 1.3	- 0.6	- 0.3	0.4
12	-	- 2.4	-	- 0.5	-
13	-	- 1.7	-	- 1.1	-
	Tolerance band ± 1.8 J			Max tolerance ± 2.3 J	

TABLE III. COMPARISON OF MEASURED MEAN VALUES AGAINST
CRM VALUES USING CRM 014 (~60J) AND CRM 015 (~80J)

The difference between the mean value of the five measurements undertaken by each laboratory and the mean value of the CRM are summarised in Table III.

An allowance should be made for the systematic error due to the different software packages used to compute the total absorbed energy, so the "Software Correction Factor" shown in Figure 6 has been applied to give the corrected differences between the mean values of the five measurements and the Certified value, as shown in Figure 7. No data is shown for laboratories 12 and 13 in Figure 7, since they did not participate in the software evaluation exercise. Of the eight complete data sets available for analysis, seven lie with ±1.3J and half of the results are better than ±0.5J indicating very good agreement between the IIT Charpy data and the mean of the certified values of the reference material which were determined using conventional Charpy impact machines. It should be noted that in five of the eight data sets at the ~60J level, applying the Software Correction Factor significantly reduced the discrepancy between the IIT measured energy level and the CRM mean value, however, in the case of one Laboratory, number 5, the discrepancy was significantly worse.

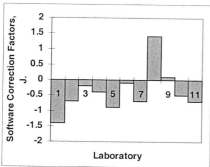

Figure 6. Software Correction Factors obtained from analysis of single ASCII data file.

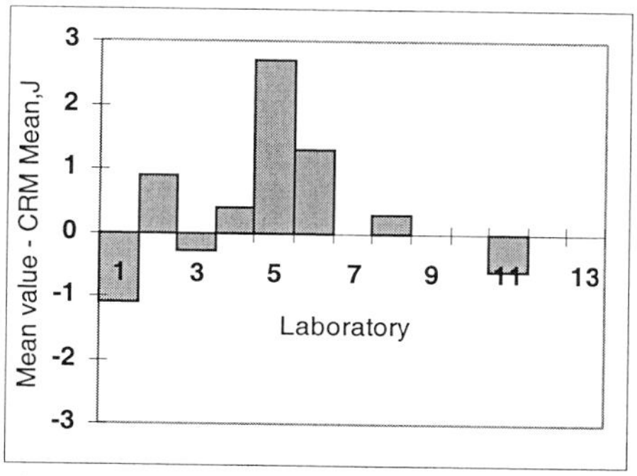

Figure 7. Difference between measured mean of five tests and the Certified Reference Value using CRM 014 testpieces after applying Software Correction Factors.(60J)

A similar analysis has been undertaken for the data obtained using the ~80J CRM015; the difference between the mean of the experimental readings from the individual laboratory and the mean of the CRM values are given in Table III.. Of the eight sets of readings, five are within ±1 J (ie better than ±1.3%).

Even when an allowance is made for the systematic error by applying the Software Correction Factor, it is clear that the data for Laboratory 1 appears to be an outlier. A possible explanation may be that the value used for the CRM mean value is incorrect, since because of the lack of availability of new batches of the CRMs at the time of testing, old batches of the CRM were used for which certified values were taken from the original BCR Certification reports, since formal certificates were not available. Thus, in general, there is good agreement between the CRM values and the measured Charpy IIT values for both the 60 J and 80 J energy levels, provided an allowance is made for systematic error in the software analysis package, and that the testing is carried out following the Draft Guidelines.

CONCLUSIONS

1. An inter-comparison of the various software analysis packages using an ASCII data set recorded from a single IIT Charpy test on a sample of the ~60 J CRM014, showed that the majority of the software packages gave good agreement with ~±1% (~±0.5 J) for the total absorbed Charpy impact energies.

2. The majority of the results from the IIT Charpy testing programme gave results within ~±1 J of the CRM values obtained using uninstrumented Charpy Impact Testing Machines at both the 60 J and 80 J energy levels, provided an allowance was made for systematic differences in the various software analysis packages.

3. The intercomparison exercise validated the concepts outlined in the Instrumented Impact Testing Draft Standard (Version 10:1994).

RECOMMENDATIONS

1. It was recommended that the Draft Standard for "Instrumented Impact Testing of Metallic Materials" (Version 10:1994) be progressed through the European Standards Committee, ECISS TC1, with a view to being adopted as a joint ISO/CEN standard.

2. It was also recommended that a further investigation be undertaken to compare the various IIT recording and analysis software packages at the 30, 80, 120 and 160J energy levels using an ASCII data set acquired from an IIT using a sample of the Certified Reference Materials at each of those energy levels, to determine the appropriate "Software Correction Factors" at each of the energy levels.

3. It was also suggested that consideration be given to incorporating an Annex to the standard indicating the method of using an appropriate ASCII data file to verify the IIT Analysis Software at the various energy levels, as part of the regular calibration of the testing machine.

ACKNOWLEDGEMENT

This report has been complied at NPL as part of a collaborative project funded by the European Commission and UK Department of Trade and Industry. The work was financed by CEC DGXII through the contract no: MAT1-CT-940053. Additional financing was provided through the Materials Measurement Programme via the DTI Engineering Industries Directorate.
This report was prepared with the co-operation of all the participants within the European Community to whom the authors extend their gratitude.

REFERENCES

1. DVM-Merkblatt 001(1986) Messtechnische Anforderungen beim instrumentierten Kerbschlagbiegeversuch, Deutscher Verband für Materialforschung und –prüfung, Berlin.
2. SEP1315 (1987) Kerbschlagbiegeversuch mit Ermittlung von Kraft und Weg, Stahl-Eisen-Prüfblatt des Vereins Deutscher Eisenhüttenleute (VDEh), Düsseldorf.
3. Marchandise, H, Perez-Sainz, A and Collmet, E (1990). *Certification of the impact toughness of V-notch Charpy specimens* Euro Report EUR 12598 EN.
4. Marchandise, H. (1992) *Standardisation of the Impact Toughness Test*, Chapter 5. In *Harmonisation of testing practice for high temperature materials.* Edited by M S Loveday & T B Gibbons. Pub: Elsevier applied Science.

From Charpy to Present Impact Testing
D. François and A. Pineau (Eds.)
© 2002 Elsevier Science Ltd. and ESIS. All rights reserved

RESULTS OF A DVM ROUND ROBIN ON INSTRUMENTED CHARPY TESTING

Wolfgang Böhme

Fraunhofer-Institut für Werkstoffmechanik (IWM), Wöhlerstr. 11, D-79108 Freiburg, Germany

ABSTRACT

The DVM-group on "Instrumented Impact Testing" (DVM = Deutscher Verband für Material-forschung und -prüfung, i.e. German Society of Materials Research and Testing) was running a round robin exercise in 1992, in order to support the development of an international standard on instrumented Charpy testing. Seventeen international participants from research institutes and industry performed about 400 instrumented Charpy-tests using a German pressure vessel steel at four different temperatures. The specimens were prepared with standardized V-notches, spark-eroded crack-similar slits or fatigued cracks. The tests were based on existing standards and specifications and on a draft standard for instrumented Charpy-tests. Standardized material data like the Charpy-energy, lateral expansion, and percentage of shear fracture were measured. In addition, characteristic forces and partial energies were determined and fracture mechanical quantities were evaluated. One interesting observation was a "cleavage-gap", i.e. a region of crack extension, where transition to cleavage was not observed with pre-cracked specimens but with notched specimens. The results of the participants showed an excellent agreement and a very good accuracy of the force measurements was observed. Therefore, these results supported international activities to standardize the instrumented Charpy test as ISO 14 556 (2000).

KEYWORDS

Charpy-Test, Instrumented Impact Test, Round Robin, Impact Energy, Force-Measurement, Ductile-Brittle Transition, Crack Resistance, Dynamic Fracture Toughness

1. INTRODUCTION

Based on the specifications DVM 001 [1] and SEP 1315 [2], the German DVM-group on "Instrumented Impact Testing" prepared in the nineties, in cooperation with ESIS, a draft standard on instrumented Charpy tests [3] which was recently accepted as ISO 14 556 [4]. In order to support this standardisation, a round robin exercise on instrumented Charpy-tests has been carried out by the DVM-group in 1992 with seventeen participants (see Tab. 1). The results are published in detail in [5,6].

In addition to this standardisation the DVM round robin was motivated by additional questions concerning the differences between results of V-notched and pre-cracked Charpy-specimens, on the correlations between the Charpy-energy, KV, the lateral expansion, LEX, or the percentage of shear fracture, PSF. Furthermore, the accuracy of measured forces, F, and of advanced evaluation-procedures, like fracture mechanics evaluations to determine J-Integral-values or crack resistance curves were of special interest. The investigations were based on standards for Charpy-V tests like DIN EN 10 045 [7] and DIN 50 115 [8]. All tests were performed with pendulums, which were instrumented to measure the force-time trace according to [1-4].

The material under investigation was a reactor pressure vessel steel 22 NiMoCr 3 7 (comparable to ASTM 508 Cl.2), which was provided by SIEMENS-KWU/Erlangen. The same material was investigated within the European round robin "Local Approach" [9]. A technological characterisation of this material is given in [10]. A total of 384 Charpy-specimens with the dimensions 55 mm x 10 mm x 10 mm were machined in S-L orientation and distributed to the participants.

Three different types of initial notches/cracks with a depth of $a_0 = 2.0 \pm 0.1$ mm were prepared and identified by the initials V, E and R:

V = standardized V-notch, machined by broaching: notch-root radius ≈ 0.25 mm
E = crack-similar slit, prepared by spark-erosion with wires: notch-root radius ≈ 0.02 mm
R = fatigued crack, prepared with $K_{f,max} < 12$ MPam$^{1/2}$:   crack-tip radius ≈ 0.00 mm

The impact tests were performed at different temperatures to investigate different levels of toughness: lower shelf, respectively lower transition region at -40 °C, transition region at 0 °C, upper transition region at +20 °C, and upper shelf region at +100 °C.

One complete set consists out of 24 specimens, one-third being V-, E- and R-specimens, respectively. Every participant had to test two specimens of the same type at each of the four temperatures. The available impact energies of the different pendulums were about 300 Joule and the impact velocities between 5.0 m/s and 5.5 m/s.

About 20 characteristic values were extracted from the results of each instrumented test. A data-set of about 8000 data was finally available at Fraunhofer-IWM for the concluding evaluation presented here, respectively in more detail in [5,6].

Table 1: List of Participants of the DVM round robin; the sequence is not corresponding to participant-number as used later on

Organisation	City	Participant
AMSLER OTTO WOLPERT-WERKE	LUDWIGSHAFEN	F.A. SPIES
BUNDESANSTALT FÜR MATERIALFORSCHUNG UND -PRÜFUNG (BAM)	BERLIN	K. WOBST, P. WOSSIDLO
EIDGENÖSSISCHE MATERIALPRÜFANSTALT (EMPA)	DÜBENDORF (SWITZERLAND)	R. HUWILER, H.-J. SCHINDLER
FACHHOCHSCHULE OSNABRÜCK	OSNABRÜCK	K. REIFF
FRAUNHOFER-INSTITUT FÜR WERKSTOFFMECHANIK (IWM)	FREIBURG	W. BÖHME, M. HUG, W. KLEMM
GKSS-FORSCHUNGSZENTRUM	GEESTHACHT	J. MÜLLER-ROOS
INST. FÜR MATERIALFORSCHUNG UND ANWENDUNGSTECHNIK (IMA)	DRESDEN	G. MÜLLER
KERNFORSCHUNGSZENTRUM (KFK)	KARLSRUHE	L. SCHÄFER
MATERIALPRÜFUNGSANSTALT (MPA)	STUTTGART	W. STOPPLER
MAX-PLANCK INSTITUT (MPI)	DÜSSELDORF	K. E. HAGEDORN, CH. MICHELS
INST. F. EISENHÜTTENKUNDE (IEHK), RWTH	AACHEN	W. DAHL, J. FALK
SIEMENS AG - UB KWU	ERLANGEN	E. KLAUSNITZER
THYSSEN-STAHL AG	DUISBURG	H.-J. KAISER, B. MÜSGEN
TECHN. UNIVERSITÄT "OTTO VON GUERICKE"	MAGDEBURG	H. BLUMENAUER, R. ORTMANN, B. EICHLER
TECHNISCHE VERSUCHS- UND FORSCHUNGSANSTALT (TVFA)	WIEN (AUSTRIA)	T. VARGA, F. LOIBNEGGER
TECHNICAL RESEARCH CENTRE (VTT)	ESPOO (FINLAND)	R. RINTAMAA
FORSCHUNGSZENTRUM ROSSENDORF (FZR)	DRESDEN	H.-W. VIEHRIG

2. CONVENTIONAL CHARPY-DATA

The mean values and individual data points of the determined Charpy impact energies, KV, are given versus temperature in Fig. 1a,b. As expected, there is no significant difference at 100 °C between the mean values of the Charpy-energies for the different notch-types due to the very ductile behaviour. The results at 100 °C have been used to determine the scatter of the material and the accuracy of the impact-devices according to [7]. The homogeneity of the material is indicated by a small scatter of the KV-data in the upper shelf region: the standard deviation of ± 4.6% of the V-specimens at 100 °C practically meets the requirement for reference-specimens according to DIN EN 10 045, which allows for a standard deviation of ± 5%. In addition, practically all pendulums meet the requirements of DIN EN 10 045 for classifying them as "faultless" pendulums, some even meet requirements for reference-pendulums (for details see [5,6]).

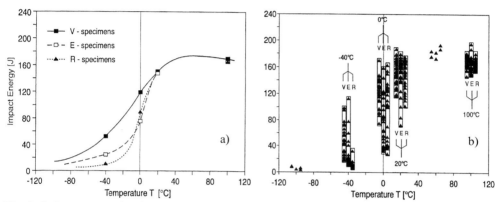

Fig. 1a,b: Impact energies for three notch-types versus temperature: a) each data point represents the average value of 30-34 experiments, and b) individual data points

As discussed in detail in [5,6], the bandwidth of scatter is large in general in the transition-range at 0 °C (see Fig. 1b). It is larger for R- and E-specimens with individual values between 30 J and 160 J than for V-specimens with values between 80 J and 160 J. This scatter cannot be explained by experimental difficulties but must be considered as a physical reality in the transition-range as explained in [5,6].

In the lower shelf region at - 40 °C the results of the three notch-types clearly separate with the meaningful trend of the lowest values for the highest notch-acuity: KV(V) > KV(E) > KV(R). As a result the transition region of the pre-cracked specimens is shifted roughly by + 20 °C to higher temperatures in comparison with V-notched specimens.

An excellent correlation between the impact energy KV and the lateral expansion LEX was observed [5,6]. Neither the shape of the notch nor the temperature was of significant influence to this linear correlation. However, a significant scatter was observed for the correlation between KV and the percentage of shear fracture PSF [5,6].

3. RESULTS OF INSTRUMENTED CHARPY-TESTS

The instrumentation of the striker [1-4] leads to additional information like the force-time signal during a Charpy test. By integration a force-displacement diagram with characteristic forces can be obtained (Fig. 2), and another integration finally results in the absorbed energy. These data enable additional evaluations including the determination of fracture mechanics properties [5,6].

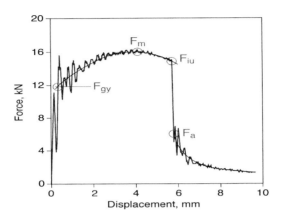

Fig. 2: Definition of the characteristic forces according to SEP 1315 [2] and ISO 14 556 [4]

3.1 The force F_m at maximum and accuracy of force measurements

Fig. 3 shows the maximum forces, Fm, of the tests at +100 °C as measured by the participants. The standard-deviation of F_m is about ± 3.5 %. Taking into account all possible errors like the scatter of the material, and errors due to the individual instrumentation, calibration and handling then this scatter is remarkably small.

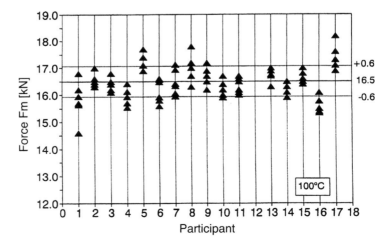

Fig. 3: Forces at maximum, F_m, of the different participants at +100 °C

3.2 The force at general yield F_{gy}

The force at general yield, F_{gy}, was determined according to [4]. An approximate estimate on the dynamic general yield strength is given by [11]:

$$\sigma_{gy,d} \approx 3 F_{gy} \frac{S}{4 B (W-a)^2} \tag{1}$$

where S = support distance, B = thickness and W-a = initial ligament length. The obtained data with a bandwidth of scatter of about ± 4,5 % according to [5] are given in Fig. 4. The $\sigma_{gy,d}$ - values at strain-rates corresponding to Charpy-tests of about 100/s are for this material about 30 % above the corresponding static yield strength data [10], as can be seen from Fig. 4.

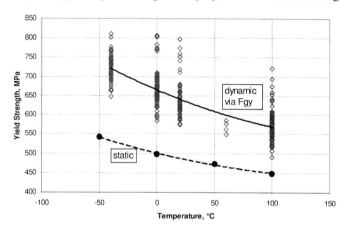

Fig. 4: Temperature dependent dynamic general yield strength data obtained via F_{gy}

3.3 The force F_a at arrest of unstable crack extension

The forces F_a at the end of unstable crack extension are presented in Fig. 5 for V-specimens. The scatter of the F_a-values is with about ± 30 % significantly larger than the scatter of the F_m- or F_{gy}-values. This is due to the pronounced force-oscillations at arrest. According to Wallin [12], the temperature $T_{4kN} \approx -2$ °C was determined, resulting in $T_{KIa=100MPam^0.5} \approx +10$ °C. (For pre-cracked R-specimens a ten centigrade lower temperature was evaluated.)

3.4 Percentage of shear fracture PSF determined by the instrumentation

Instrumented Charpy-tests enable an automatic calculation of the percentage of shear fracture, PSF, via an evaluation of measured characteristic force-values. In the annex of ISO 14 556 [4] four different equations are given, which were applied to the round robin data . The most accurate 1:1-correlation with a bandwidth of scatter of ± 10% between the measured and calculated PSF was obtained with the following equation (see [5,6]):

$$PSF = \{1 - \frac{F_{iu} - F_a}{F_m + 0.5(F_m - F_{gy})}\} \times 100\% \tag{2}$$

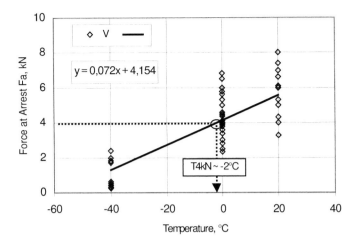

Fig. 5: $F_a(T)$ for V- specimens and determination of T_{4kN}

3.5 "Cleavage Gap"

During this round robin an attempt has been made to evaluate a crack-extension curve via a multi-specimen technique: for all specimens tested in the transition range the ductile crack extension up to the onset of cleavage fracture, Δa, was measured simply by averaging the apparent crack fronts "by eye" to an accuracy of about ± 0.2 mm, which hardly can be improved by multiple-point measurements for Charpy-specimens.

The Δa-data are shown for V- and R-specimens in Fig. 6a,b versus the corresponding displacement, s_{iu}, at the onset of unstable crack propagation. All measured Δa-values follow with little scatter the same line, the crack-extension curve, $\Delta a(s_{iu})$. The scatter is remarkably small, if one considers, that Fig. 6 includes results of seventeen different laboratories, of different notch acuity, and results of experiments in the temperature-range between -40 °C and +20 °C. The resulting crack-extension curve, $\Delta a(s_{iu})$, is practically independent of these parameters. This independency is meaningful for ductile crack extension, because - due to blunting - the initial notch-acuity is less important in a narrow range of temperatures.

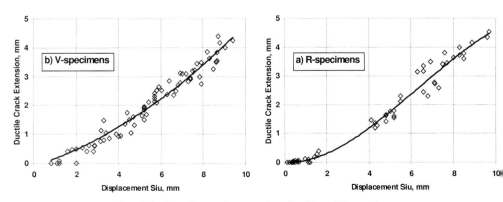

Fig. 6a,b: Ductile crack extension for V- and R-specimens

However, the distribution of the data is different for V-notched or pre-cracked specimens. Despite many experiments with pre-cracked R-specimens, no transition to cleavage was observed in any of the laboratories in the displacement-range of 1.6 mm < s_{iu} < 4.1 mm (Fig. 6b). The pre-cracked R-specimens obviously experience either an early transition to cleavage fracture immediately after blunting, or a late transition behind the force-maximum after more than 1.0 mm ductile crack extension. There is obviously a gap in the transition to cleavage fracture, a "cleavage-gap," in the range of crack-lengths of 0.3 mm < Δa < 1.2 mm and the corresponding range of displacements of 1.6 mm < s_{iu} < 4.1 mm.

A similar cleavage-gap is not visible from the homogeneously distributed results of V-specimens (Fig 6a), whereas E-specimens seem to show a narrow cleavage-gap in the displacement-range of 1.5 mm < s_{iu} < 2.2 mm [5,6]. This implies, that a more pronounced separation between brittle fracture behaviour and ductile-brittle transition behaviour can be achieved by the high "notch"-acuity of natural cracks (R) or spark-eroded slits (E), whereas V-notches (V) smooth such effects, possibly due to the lower constraint ahead of the notch. It is still unknown, if other materials show a similar behaviour. Fractographic analyses as well as numerical investigations could be helpful to understand, why such a cleavage-gap occurs with higher probability for fatigued, natural cracks (R), than for V-notches (V).

Based on the evaluated crack-extension data and partial energies up to the onset of cleavage fracture also dynamic crack resistance curves have been determined and discussed in [5,6].

4. CONCLUSIONS

The DVM round robin enabled a detailed comparison of results of seventeen different laboratories and resulted in an excellent agreement of the obtained data like the characteristic forces, the energies, and of additionally evaluated data like, e.g., the general yield strength. The expected influence of the notch acuity was confirmed and quantified. One interesting observation was a "cleavage gap", i.e. a region of crack extension, where transition to cleavage fracture was not observed with pre-cracked specimens but with V-notched specimens.

The results qualify the documents DVM 001 [1] and SEP 1315 [2] as well as the thereon based standard ISO 14 556 [4] as useful tools to perform unified instrumented Charpy-tests. Compared to conventional Charpy tests the instrumented Charpy tests enable additional possibilities to characterize materials, including the application of single specimen methods to determine fracture mechanics properties [13,14]. However, due to the small size of Charpy-specimens the transferability of the results is limited. Then numerical calculations with damage models can be applied to extend the range of applicability [15-17].

ACKNOWLEDGEMENTS

The author is indebted to all participants of this round robin for putting their results into his hands to enable these comprehensive evaluations to be completed. Their engagement and the care during performing and evaluating of all the experiments is gratefully acknowledged.

REFERENCES

[1]   DVM-Merkblatt 001 (1986) Messtechnische Anforderungen beim instrumentierten
       Kerbschlagbiegeversuch, Deutscher Verband für Materialforschung und -prüfung, Berlin
[2]   SEP 1315 (1987) Kerbschlagbiegeversuch mit Ermittlung von Kraft und Weg, Stahl-
       Eisen-Prüfblatt des Vereins Deutscher Eisenhüttenleute (VDEh), Düsseldorf
[3]   Proposed Standard for Instrumented Charpy-V Tests, Draft 7 (1993) European Structural
       Integrity Society (ESIS), TC5 Sub-Committee on Dynamic Testing at Intermediate
       Strain Rates
[4]   ISO EN DIN 14 556 (2000) Instrumented Impact Test, Beuth Verlag, Berlin
[5]   W. Böhme, W. Klemm (1993) Scientific report W 7/93, Fraunhofer-Institut für Werk-
       stoffmechanik, Freiburg, and (1994) 26. DVM-Arbeitkreis Bruchvorgänge, Magdeburg
[6]   W. Böhme (1996). In: *Evaluating Material Properties by Dynamic Testing, ESIS 20,*
       pp.1-23, E. van Walle (Ed.), Mech. Engng. Publ. (MEP), London.
[7]   DIN EN 10 045, Kerbschlagbiegeversuch nach Charpy, Teil 1 (1991): Prüfverfahren,
       Teil 2 (1993): Prüfung der Prüfmaschine (Pendelschlagwerk)
[8]   DIN 50 115 (1991) Kerbschlagbiegeversuch, besondere Probenformen und Auswertever-
       fahren
[9]   F. Mudry, DiFant (1993) Round Robin on the Measurement of Local Criteria, IRSID-
       Report RE 93.319
[10]   E. Klausnitzer (1992) Siemens-KWU report KWU/S51/92/04, Erlangen
[11]   W. L. Server (1978) *J. Engng. Mat. Technol., Trans. ASME*, **100**, pp. 183-188
[12]   K. Wallin (1996) In: *Evaluating Material Properties by Dynamic Testing, ESIS 20,*
       pp.165-176, E. van Walle (Ed.), Mech. Engng. Publ. (MEP), London
[13]   H.J. Schindler, W. Böhme, D. Stark-Seuken, H. Blumenauer, K. Wobst (1996) DVM-
       Arbeitskreis Bruchvorgänge, Bremen, DVM-Tagungsband, Berlin, S. 67-76
[14]   W. Böhme and H.-J. Schindler (2000) In: *Pendulum Impact Testing: A Century of Pro-
       gress, ASTM STP 1380,* T.A. Siewert and M. P. Manahan (Eds.), pp. 327-336
[15]   W. Schmitt, D.-Z. Sun, W. Böhme, G. Nagel (1994) *Int. J. of Pressure Vessels and Pi-
       ping,* **59**, pp. 21-29
[16]   D.-Z. Sun, A. Hönig, W. Böhme, W. Schmitt (1994) In: *Fracture Mechanics, 25th Vol.,
       ASTM STP 1220,* F. Erdogan and R.J. Hartranft (Eds.), Philadelphia
[17]   W. Böhme, G. Bernauer, W. Schmitt (1999) *Nuclear Engng. and Design,* **188**, pp. 149-
       154

From Charpy to Present Impact Testing
D. François and A. Pineau (Eds.)
© 2002 Elsevier Science Ltd. and ESIS. All rights reserved

SOME HISTORICAL ASPECTS AND THE DEVELOPMENT OF THE CHARPY TEST IN RUSSIA

N.A. MAKHUTOV[1], E.M. MOROZOV[2] and Yu. G. MATVIENKO[1]

[1]Mechanical Engineering Research Institute of the Russian Academy of Sciences,
4 M. Kharitonievsky Per., 101990 Moscow, Russia, e-mail: matvienko7@yahoo.com
[2] Moscow State Engineering Physics Institute – Technical University,
Kashirskoe Shosse 31, 115409 Moscow, Russia.

ABSTRACT

Historical background, development and possible application of the impact test in Russia are presented. Special attention is paid to loading conditions, notch and specimen configuration and sizes, impact test machines and test facilities, elastic energy accumulated in the system "test machine – specimen", test methodology and interpretation of the results on the Charpy impact energy, the brittle-to-ductile transition temperature and fracture surface. Possible application of the Charpy test based on the shift of the brittle-to-ductile transition temperature due to damage has been presented for the evaluation of mechanical properties degradation and structural integrity assessment. The procedure is illustrated for nuclear pressurised water reactor.

KEYWORDS

Charpy test, notch and specimen configuration, transition temperature, cracks, degradation of materials, "trepan" program, structural integrity.

INTRODUCTION AND HISTORICAL BACKGROUND

Historical background and an evolution of the impact test and theory of dynamic fracture mechanics in Russia have been discussed in the Russian books (e.g., [1-10]) and recent review was presented by Makhutov, Morozov and Matvienko [11]. The present paper deals with principal aspects of the development of the Charpy test in Russia.

Systematic investigation on the brittleness of metals using impact test procedure was started by Dragomirov and Davidenkov in early part of the last century. In 1939 Vitman and Stepanov have shown that there is quantitative correlation between the strain rate and the brittle-to-ductile transition temperature because physical nature of the rate and temperature effect is the same and related with temperature fluctuation of atoms. The correlation can be expressed in the form $\lg \dot{\varepsilon} = A - B/T_{tr}$, where $\dot{\varepsilon}$ is the strain rate, T_{tr} is the brittle-to-ductile transition temperature, A and B are experimental material constants. In 1946 Drozdovsky has discussed the problem of dividing the absorbed energy on the energy of plastic deformation, failure initiation and crack propagation.

The Charpy test provides also the opportunity to investigate the change in the fracture mechanisms using the fracture surfaces and makes it possible to estimate the transition temperature. This procedure has been proposed by Shevandin in 1947 and used in USA from 1949. Historical and update aspects of experimental estimation of the difference between total absorbed energy and energy required for the crack propagation, criteria for determination of the brittle-to-ductile transition temperature and the fracture mechanisms analysis in the transition region have been also discussed.

SPECIMEN AND NOTCH CONFIGURATIONS

The analysis of welded joints, thin sheets and damaged structural components demanded further development of the test methodology to estimate the impact energy and the transition temperature. As a result new configurations of impact specimens (Fig. 1), impact test machines and statistical treatment of the impact energy data were worked out in the first half of the last

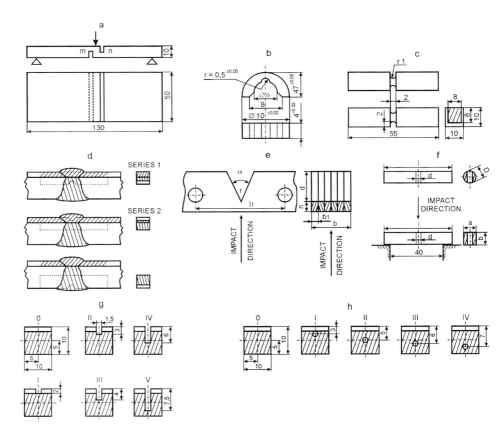

Fig. 1. Some non-standard specimen, notch and defect configurations for the impact test.

century. Some results of the effect of specimen and notch configurations are in the following. The impact energy and the transition temperature are most sensitive to defects and thickness of steel structures. A decrease in the thickness of the impact specimen shifts the transition temperature to the side of lower temperatures. An increase in specimen size and crack length can lead to considerable increase in the transition temperature of structural elements.

The sensitivity of cast iron and low-alloy steels to brittleness by varying the sharpness of the notch was investigated by In'shakov. The10x10x55-mm impact specimens had a 2-mm deep notch with a tip radius of 1, 0.5, 00.1 mm. The temperature at which the impact energy is less than 200 kJ/m^2 was adopted as the transition temperature. The transition temperature increased in the case of very sharp notches.

The effect of the number of layers in composite specimens has been also considered for determination of the impact energy and the transition temperature. For steels with a mixed type of fracture the use of composite specimens normally results in a shift of the transition temperature towards lower temperatures. The use of composite specimens was recommended for assessing the level of the impact energy of the base metal of laminated tubes and multilayer materials in the manufacture of gas and oil pipeline.

The anisotropy of the impact energy was investigated by Fridman and Miklyaev using the specimen with an initial crack. The characteristics of the sensitivity to initial cracks depend on the direction in which the specimens are cut out and also on the orientation of the crack relative to the plane of deformation (rolling, pressing, etc.).

Development of the testing procedure for determination of the impact energy and the transition temperature has led to the Russian Standard (GOST 9454-78) for instrumented impact test of metals. Three principal types of the impact specimen are shown in Fig. 2.

METHODOLOGY OF THE IMPACT TEST

Impact test machines, test facilities and test methodology were developed for clear understanding the nature of the impact fracture. The effect of elastic energy accumulated in the system "test machine – specimen" has been investigated by Pogodin-Alekseev [3]. Special attention was paid to the problem of dividing the absorbed energy on the energy of failure initiation a_i and crack propagation a_p. The last problem was considered by Gulyaev, Rakhmanov, Livshitz, Drozdovsky, Fridman et. al.

The important problem is to obtain a considerable amount of information in one test. This was done by the method of testing with recording. One can notice that load-time oscillograms ($P - \tau$), obtained with the assistance of the rod dynamometer of the hammer during impact fracture of the Charpy test specimen with a crack, consist of the total signal from several factors: the resistance of the specimen to deformation and fracture, inertial loading, and the longitudinal vibrations of the pendulum beam. To determine the "dynamic fracture" toughness it is necessary to separate from the recording multicomponent process only that load which causes the Charpy specimen to bend and to establish its critical load P_c when the crack initiates. Oscillograms of synchronous recording of $P - \tau$ (curve 1) and deflection-time $f - \tau$ (curve 2) (see Fig. 3) allow to establish the time at which deflection of the specimen begins.

At the initial stage (time bc on curve 1) the effect of inertial loading is rapidly reduced, but the resistance to bending of the specimen increases. Since the subsequent section cd shows a practically linear increase in the load and deflection , then, knowing the time at which the deformation of the specimen begins (point 0) it is possible to correct the load sustained by it in the initial deformation stage. The corrected portion of the $P - \tau$ curve is shown dashed line in

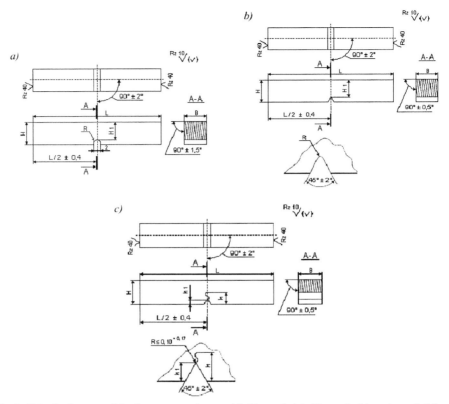

Fig. 2. Principal types of the impact specimen with U-notch (a), V-notch (b) and crack (c) according to Russian Standard: H=10 mm, H$_1$=8 mm, B=10 mm, L=55 mm, h=3mm, h$_1$=1.5 mm, R=1 mm (for U-notch) and R=0.25 mm (for V-notch).

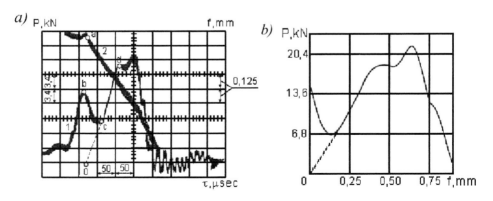

Fig. 3. Oscillograms of synchronous recording of $P - \tau$, $f - \tau$ (a) and $P - f$ (b) plotted from the experimental data [12].

Fig. 3 *a*. In Fig. 3 *b* the $P - \tau$ and $f - \tau$ oscillograms are replotted as a load-deflection curve $P - f$ which enables the load P_Q (from the 5% secant) to be determined by the Charpy test and the dynamic crack growth resistance to be computed.

In the second half of 80-s in the Soviet Union the works of direct study of the reactor pressure vessel materials properties after reactor decommissioning have been begun. It is the most informative (also extremely laborious) procedure to estimate the effect of service conditions on the material properties. To the present time there were executed four local programs of trepan (trough wall specimens). The specimens were cut from pressure vessels of power and propulsion reactors, that were in operation for long time (20 years of the first unit of Novovoronezh nuclear power plant (NPP) in 1987, 30 years of stand-prototype 27/BM in 1992, 20 years of the second unit of Novovoronezh NPP in 1993, 19 years of nuclear icebreaker pressure vessel «Lenin» in 1998). The greater part of unique scientific data was obtained at testing of the Charpy specimens ($10 \times 10 \times 55$ mm) and also subsize ($5 \times 5 \times 27.5$ mm) impact test specimens. Lets discus some results of this research program [13,14].

The standard (66 specimens) and subsize (128 specimens) Charpy type specimens were cut from reactor pressure vessel trepan for study of the brittle-to-ductile transition temperature distribution in the pressure vessel. Test equipment for evaluation of irradiation effect on the transition temperature shift has been changed from elementary pendulum testing machines to computerised and instrumented ones, that allows to record oscillograms of the process of specimen impact fracture with high resolution. Testing with recording gives an information to estimate not only the impact energy, but also records dependence "load-time" or "load-displacement".

Typical correlation between the transition temperatures T_{tr} of the Charpy and subsize Charpy specimens for different criteria of T_{tr} determination (a and b) is shown in Fig. 4.

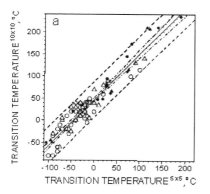 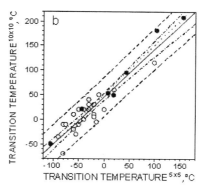

Fig. 4. Typical transition temperature correlations for the Charpy and subsize Charpy specimens.

As it was already noted, surveillance programs provided the Charpy impact specimen sets for irradiation embrittlement estimation. However, available quantity of specimens is often insufficient for getting correct temperature dependencies and additional research works are needed (for example, validation of recovery annealing conditions of reactor pressure vessel). In this case there are developed, and used, methods of specimen reconstitution from broken halves of tested specimens by welding and their subsequent machining up to standard sizes (Fig. 5).

The Charpy test of irradiated specimens allows the estimation of the transition temperature shift ΔT_Φ due to irradiation damage of reactor vessel materials. For WWPR (water-moderated water-cooled power reactor) vessels the shift ΔT_Φ induced by irradiation may in the general case be presented as $\Delta T_\Phi = A_\Phi(\Phi)^n$, where A_Φ is the irradiation embrittlement factor, $^\circ C$; Φ is the fast-neutron fluence, in units of 10^{18} cm^{-2}; n is power index. The shift ΔT_Φ as a function of the fast-neutron fluence for 15Cr2MoVA steel (1) and its weld metal (2) exposed at $270\,^\circ C$ in a WWPR-440-type reactor are shown in Fig. 6. As it is seen, this relation is approximated sufficiently well by the power law up to the neutron fluence of 5×10^{20} cm^{-2}, and the ΔT_Φ curves reveal no evidence of saturation.

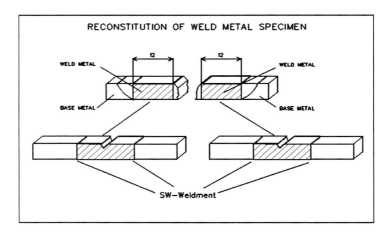

Fig.5. Reconstitution scheme of two Charpy specimens from broken halves of tested specimens of reactor pressure vessel weld metal.

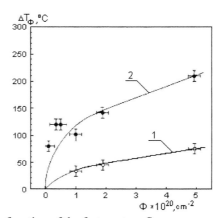

Fig. 6. The shift ΔT_Φ as a function of the fast-neutron fluence.

If the temperature dependence of the fracture toughness K_{Ic} is known and the transition temperature and the shift ΔT_Φ are determined for a reactor vessel material, it is possible to find the value of K_{Ic} for current irradiation damage. In this case, structural integrity can be analysed by means of fracture mechanics approaches.

Thus, during 50 years of impact testing the Charpy test remains the competitive method of irradiation effect analysis for serviceability of nuclear reactor pressure vessels. Introduction of the reconstitution methods increases efficiency of research work, decreases circulation of radioactive materials in many times and confirms the significance of the Charpy test in radiation materials science.

CRITERIA FOR DETERMINATION OF THE TRANSITION TEMPERATURE

The variety of criteria for determination of the brittle-to-ductile transition temperature T_{tr} was pointed out by many scientists. At the same time such a variety should not be viewed as a shortcoming because under different conditions of service of materials and structures, different criteria should also be applied. An interesting feature of many Russian publications is that they deal with the type of the fracture surfaces (in the form of percentage of the ductile component) while proposing different criteria with each other. One cannot help by feeling that the authors unintentionally use this criterion as some point of departure, as the basis for comparisons, and as a standard of a convincing argument for all other criteria.

For example, it was suggested to determine the transition temperature directly from the condition of the validation of the fracture toughness or from the condition of initiation of slow subcritical crack propagation. Another important parameter within the temperature range of brittle-ductile transition is the critical length l_c of the ductile crack [15]. A functional relationship was established between the impact energy and critical crack length (Fig. 7).

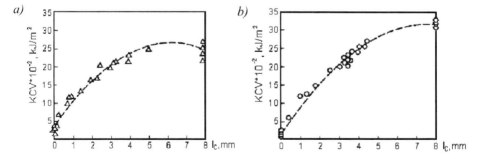

Fig. 7. The impact energy as a function of critical ductile crack (a – steel 1, b – steel 2).

These criteria certainly have an obvious physical meaning, mechanical substantiation and an obvious interpretation. However, it is quite possible that the transition temperature obtained by these criteria for low strength steels will turn out to be too low, and that brittle fracture may also occur at higher temperatures in operation.

It seems therefore relevant to assume that the available variety of criteria can be divided according to their eventual purpose into the following two basic groups: for research and for structural integrity analysis. The criteria for research purposes are used to work out new alloys and technology, to compare different alloys and also to establish the effectiveness of scientific developments in creation of new fracture criteria and new characteristics of materials. The criteria for purposes of structural integrity analysis and design can be used for choosing steel and heat treatment including the establishment of a temperature reserve factor. There may be many criteria in the first group, but in our opinion there must be only one criterion for structural integrity analysis. This important criterion should be the energy of crack propagation that follows from fundamentals of the brittle fracture mechanics. This actual value has to be established, either on the basis of experience in the operation of the structure or by special experiments simulating the loading conditions in service.

CONCLUSIONS

Historical background and an evolution of the Charpy test in Russia have been presented. The impact energy and the brittle-to-ductile transition temperature are sensitive to loading conditions, notch and specimen configurations, crack orientation and size, thickness of structural elements. Oscillograms of synchronous recording of load-time and deflection-time allow to determine the dynamic crack growth resistance. It was illustrated that the Charpy test is very useful for the evaluation of mechanical property degradation and the service life analysis of nuclear power plants. Criteria for determination of the transition temperature can be divided according to their eventual purpose into the following two basic groups: for research and structural integrity assessment.

REFERENCES

1.   Davidenkov, N.N. (1936). *Dynamic Testing of Metals*. ONTI. Moscow (in Russian).
2.   Davidenkov, N.N. (1938). *Problems of Impact in Metal Science*. AN USSR. Moscow-Leningrad (in Russian).
3.   Pogodin-Alekseev, G.I. (1953). *The properties of Metals under Impact Loads*. Metallurgizdat. Moscow (in Russian).
4.   Potak, Ya.M. (1955). *Brittle Fracture of Steel and Steel Elements*. Oboronizdat. Moscow (in Russian).
5.   Drozdovsky, B.A. and Fridman, Ya.B. (1960). *The Effect of Cracks on the Mechanical Properties of Structural Steels*. Metallurgizdat. Moscow (in Russian).
6.   Shevandin, E.M. and Razov, I.A. (1965). *Coldbrittleness and Limit Plasticity of Metals in Shipbuilding*. Sudostroenie. Leningrad (in Russian).
7.   Cherepanov, G.P. (1974). *Brittle Fracture Mechanics*. Nauka. Moscow (in Russian).
8.   Makhutov, N.A. (1981). *Deformation Criteria of Fracture and Strength Calculation of Structural Elements*. Mashinostroenie. Moscow (in Russian).
9.   Slepian, L.I. (1981). *Mechanics of Cracks*. Sudostroenie. Leningrad (in Russian).
10.   Parton, V.Z. and Boriskovski, V.G. (1988). *Dynamic of Brittle Fracture*. Mashinostroenie. Moscow (in Russian).
11.   Makhutov, N.A., Morozov, E.M. and Matvienko, Yu.G. (2001). *Zavodskaya Laboratoria*[*] **67** (N 7), pp. 42-49.
12.   Bondarovich, L.A., Zlochevsky, A.B. and Makhutov, N.A. (1980). *Zavodskaya Laboratoria* **46** (N7), pp. 1036-1041.
13.   Amaev, A.D., Korolev, Yu.N., Krasikov, E.A. and Shtrombakh, Ya.I. (2000). *Industrial Laboratory. Diagnostics of Materials*. **66** (N7). pp. 462-471.
14.   Amaev, A.D., Korolev, Yu.N., Krasikov, E.A., Nikolaev, Ya.A., Platonov, P.A. and Shtrombakh, Ya.I. (2001). *Zavodskaya Laboratoria* **67** (N 8), pp. 47-51.
15.   Zotov, A.D. and Il'insky, K.L. (1982). *Zavodskaya Laboratoria* **48** (N6), pp. 65-69.

[*] Journal *Zavodskaya Laboratoria* is translated in English by Plenum Publishing Corporation in USA from 1955 under the title: *Journal Industrial Laboratory*.

From Charpy to Present Impact Testing
D. François and A. Pineau (Eds.)
© 2002 Elsevier Science Ltd. and ESIS. All rights reserved

INSTRUMENTED CHARPY TEST REVIEW AND APPLICATION TO STRUCTURAL INTEGRITY

WILLIAM L. SERVER
ATI Consulting
P.O. Box 5769
Pinehurst, NC 28374 USA

ABSTRACT

The Charpy V-notch test has been used for a century now as an indirect, inexpensive method of assessing fracture toughness properties for ferritic steels. This dynamic test of a blunt notched specimen has been widely used to correlate material toughness behavior for quality control and material acceptance criteria for many industries. Some applications have gone beyond the intended use for low strength steels to higher strength steels and even non-ferritic materials. The ability to instrument the Charpy striker, or tup, has led to the ability to better measure the material response in terms of general yielding and potential fast fracture response. The actual loading of the Charpy specimen can be observed as a function of time and, more recently, as a function of direct specimen deflection for the three-point bend test. The evaluation of instrumented behavior at different test temperatures can provide a better understanding of the ductile-to brittle transition response than merely meeting either Charpy energy or other related ductility criteria. This paper reviews the historical development of the instrumented Charpy test and discusses load-energy-time parameters that can be determined to assess material strength and fracture toughness initiation, propagation, and arrest behavior.

KEY WORDS

Charpy V-notch specimen, instrumented Charpy test, fracture toughness, general yielding, structural integrity

BACKGROUND

In the standard Charpy V-notch impact test, a small 10 mm square cross section specimen with a V-notch notch 20% through the specimen width, is broken in three-point bending by a falling weight attached to a pendulum arm. The energy absorbed in breaking the specimen is determined from a dial indication of the change in the height of the pendulum before the impact and after breaking the specimen. This change in potential energy is carefully calibrated to assure reliable readings through testing of calibrated standard specimens [1]. Other methods of validating Charpy fracture energy have been performed utilizing changes in kinetic energy [2] from measurements of velocity both before and after fracture of the test specimen. The results have been shown to be equivalent for both pendulum impact machines and vertical drop weight machines [3]. The determination of the fracture energy from an instrumented impact measurement of the load-time record also has been shown to be a reliable and reproducible method of measuring fracture energy for both pendulum and vertical drop weight machines [2,3]. In addition, the instrumented Charpy tests allows measurement of other key parameters such as the general yield load, maximum load (either ductile or fast fracture), fracture arrest load, and energy partitioning between pre- and post-maximum load energies, including shear lip formation energy. These various parameters have been discussed in terms of physical significance by Fearnehough and Hoy [4] and are presented idealized in Fig. 1 as a post-general yield fracture load-displacement diagram; note that the time during fracture can be converted to displacement by using the initial impact velocity and correcting for the reduction in tup velocity during the fracture event. Evaluation of these parameters has most recently been utilized by Fabry et al. to assess differences in ferritic steel behavior [5].

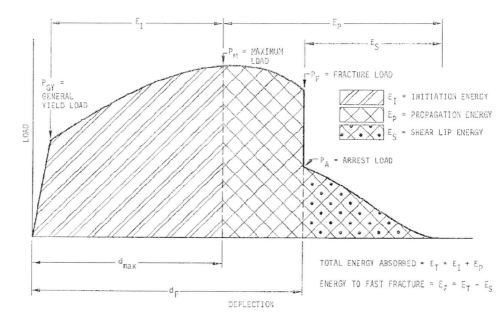

Fig. 1. Schematic illustration of load-displacement for a post-general yield fracture.

Watanabe measured load-time response as early as 1929 [6] by applying stain gages on the anvils of the Charpy machine. The striker, or tup, has been more commonly instrumented based on techniques initially presented by Fearnehough [7]. The first measures of the actual load-time records required high speed oscilloscopes and camera systems expertly triggered to record the dynamic signal. Oscilloscopes with special storage screens in the mid-1970s allowed easier and more efficient recording of the signals. In the early 1980s, digital oscilloscopes that could record the dynamic signal at rates of 0.5-2.0 μs became available and made the recording and evaluation of the signals more efficient and precise, since the stored signals could be sent to computers for later analysis. Current digital amplifiers and data acquisition equipment provide direct transfer of data to computers and almost instantaneous analysis of the dynamic load-time response. Another major achievement has been the direct measurement of specimen crack-opening-displacement [8] and conversion to load-line displacement.

The direct measurement of specimen displacement eliminates the need for correcting for machine compliance when evaluating J-integral fracture toughness measures using the precracked Charpy specimen. The Charpy V-notch specimen can be converted to an accepted small fracture toughness specimen by fatigue precracking from the V-notch or by modifying the notched area to closely match fracture toughness specimen requirements and then fatigue cracking following ASTM or ISO Standards. Early work in evaluating linear elastic type fracture toughness for a reactor pressure vessel steel [9] showed excellent agreement when compared to other measures of dynamic fracture toughness using more conventional and larger (up to 250 mm thick) test specimens. The early work was valid only when the notch plus precracked depth was somewhat shallow (less than 35% of the width of the specimen); this need was due to the full impact velocity of about 5 m/s being used and the associated inertial impact loads which can complicate the evaluation of brittle, linear elastic measures of fast fracture loads. For typical blunt notch Charpy tests with the notch depth of only 20% of the width, inertial effects are minimal except in the most brittle materials. The other approach, which is more in keeping with having a deeper crack between 45-55% of the width for fracture toughness testing (see for example ASTM E 399 [10]), requires a reduction in the impact velocity. Often this reduction requires an impact velocity of only 1-2 m/s to obtain acceptable load-time measurements [11].

Procedures for obtaining reliable load-time signals were developed in the late 1970s and considered inertial load effects [12], signal condition monitoring [13], load cell calibration [13, 14], and data reduction methods [15]. These procedures were used for a large reactor pressure vessel steel characterization program and evaluated independently using a round robin test program [16]. Further development of instrumented impact methods has been underway in Europe since the 1980s [5, 8, 17].

APPLICATION TO STRUCTURAL INTEGRITY

There are several ways that the instrumented Charpy test, or some modification of it, has been used for structural reliability and assurance. First, the original intended use was as a quality control test to assure that adequate material toughness was met for the intended design. This application generally relied upon the total impact energy or some other generalized gross ductility parameter (e.g., lateral expansion). There are examples where the instrumented load-time signal has been applied to better assess the quality of varied structural materials for their design applications (see for example ASTM STP 563 [18]). The second application was to assess metallurgical/ material parameters that were sensitive to degradation during service. The neutron radiation embrittlement of reactor pressure vessel ferritic steel is a unique example, since the need to assure safety is crucial to protect the safety of the public. Many of the parameters that can be deduced from the load-time and load-displacement have unique relationships relative to the radiation embrittlement process. As shown in Fig. 2, which was developed from slow bend testing of a high nitrogen steel that allowed sectioning and etching to reveal plastic deformation [19], the behavior of ferritic steels during bending reveals significant information about the development of plastic zones which eventually encompass the entire width of the specimen at general yielding, and later hinge as predicted from slip line field solutions [20].

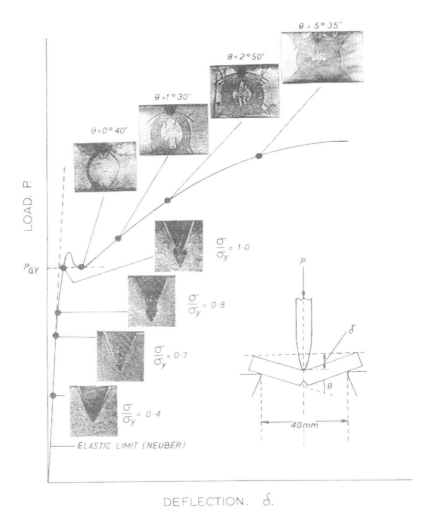

Fig. 2. Plastic zone development for bending of Charpy bars (Wilshaw and Pratt [19]).

The general yield load (P_{GY}) in Fig. 2 can be related to the yield strength for materials under dynamic loading. The conversion to yield strength was initially established based on slip-line field solutions, which matched the experimental results generated for the high nitrogen steel. The conversion requires the use of a constraint factor, geometry, and the choice of either a Tresca or a Von Mises yield criterion. The size of the tup is also a factor since the constraint factor is dependent on the tup indenter width; the ASTM tup has a higher constraint factor than the ISO tup. The material assumed is also not totally realistic since it is assumed to be rigid-plastic with no strain hardening capacity. Given these assumptions, good agreement has been shown when comparing dynamic tensile data with measurements of general yield load converted to dynamic yield strength [21]; these studies also included evaluations using precracked Charpy specimens where the constraint value was adjusted slightly to accommodate the near straight-sided crack area.

Evaluation of micro-cleavage fracture can be studied by generating load-temperature diagrams from the instrumented Charpy data. The effects of irradiation exposure on reactor pressure vessel steels can be observed through increases in the general yield load and measurement of the other brittle fracture and arrest loads as a function of temperature [22]. Neutron embrittlement mechanisms can often be identified through these diagrams, and estimates of shifts in initiation and arrest fracture toughness values are possible [5, 23]. The knowledge of these parameters is also important when characterizing and assessing correlations between measured fracture toughness and indirect Charpy parameter estimates of toughness [24].

The direct measurement of dynamic initiation fracture toughness using precracked Charpy specimens is a third method for providing key data for assessing structural integrity. This approach became widely assessed in the 1970s [9, 14, 16] and measurements of dynamic fracture toughness are still being made following the procedures developed during that time period (see the application papers in ASTM STP 1380 [25]). The key issue for measuring dynamic fracture toughness of brittle materials is to avoid the effects of inertial impact loading, as discussed earlier. Using an ASTM allowable fracture toughness specimen (i.e., the precracked Charpy), with a crack depth halfway through the width, requires judicious selection of the impact velocity. The key is to get a time to fracture that is at least three times longer than the inverse of the natural bending frequency of the three-point bend specimen. Reduction in the impact velocity from the full drop height is the easiest solution. For brittle cleavage fracture, the fast fracture load is easily definable on the load-time record. In near linear elastic fractures, the fast fracture load can be used almost directly to determine the initiation fracture toughness. In elastic-plastic fractures, the energy to reach the fast fracture load has to be determined by integrating the load-displacement response, adjusting for the machine compliance contributions if the displacement is not measured directly, and determining the J-integral toughness. Slow bend testing of precracked Charpy specimens is now common practice for directly measuring fracture toughness (linear elastic or elastic-plastic) for ferritic steels and applying the Master Curve (see ASTM E 1921 [26]).

When assessing the upper shelf ductile initiation fracture toughness, it is necessary to determine the initiation of ductile tearing. Under dynamic loading, this determination is difficult unless some sort of initiation detector (for example, acoustic emission [27] or a justified criterion for initiation (such as half way between general yield and maximum load [5]). Multi-specimen techniques also have been utilized, such as stop blocks to limit the amount of specimen deflection [28]. Figure 3 shows static and dynamic ductile initiation results obtained for pressure vessel base metals and welds. The high rate dynamic results were developed using multi-specimen testing of 25.4 mm thick bend bars using the stop block deflection method. The dynamic ductile initiation toughness results are higher than the static results. This difference can be attributed to the higher yield strength of the material under dynamic loading which affects the microvoid coalescence process leading to initiation of a ductile crack. The results are also consistent with upper shelf energy correlations, as shown in Fig. 3, that include the material yield strength as a parameter.

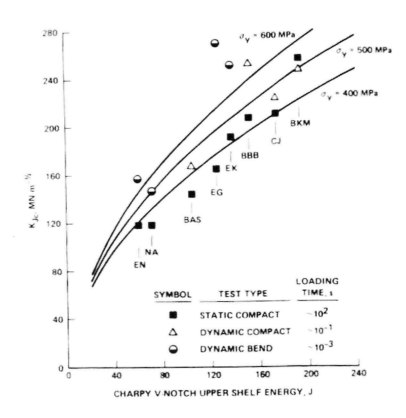

Fig. 3. Initiation toughness results measured on the upper shelf at 177°C [28].

CONCLUSIONS

The instrumented Charpy V-notch test and test specimen modifications (i.e., fatigue cracking) to directly measure parameters related to fracture toughness have been explored for seventy years. Major strides were made in the early 1970s, as high-speed digital data acquisition equipment emerged, as well as the development of computers dedicated to evaluate the digital data. In that same time period, analytical and experimental development of elastic-plastic fracture mechanics also led to the use of small Charpy test specimens to directly measure initiation fracture toughness.

The need to measure dynamic fracture toughness is an issue that is relevant in many industries. Structures that see dynamic loads must consider changes in the properties that can result from the type and duration of loading. In particular, ferritic steels in the transition temperature region are very sensitive to dynamic loading. However, the degree of dynamic loading needs to be assessed for the entire structure. When the structure is large and complex, some of the localized dynamic effects can be dissipated depending upon the size and stiffness response of the structure.

The Charpy V-notch test has stood the test of time as a good quality control measurement. Advances in instrumentation and techniques, understanding the nature of the test, and relating parameters from the instrumented results to actual material fracture toughness have been made. Assuring continued structural integrity will still rely on Charpy V-notch testing in many industries.

REFERENCES

1. McCowan, C.N., Pauwels, J., Revise, G., and Nakano, H. (2000), In: *Pendulum Impact Testing: A Century of Progress, ASTM STP 1380*, American Society for Testing and Materials, West Conshohocken, Pennsylvania, pp. 73-89.
2. Henderson, G.R. and Server (1979), W.L., *ISA Transactions*, **18**, 3, pp. 35-39.
3. Server, W. L. and Henderson, G.R. (1981), *J. of Testing and Evaluation*, **9**, 3, pp. 210-213.
4. Fearnehough, G.D. and Hoy, C.J. (1964), *J. Iron & Steel Institute*, **202**, pp. 912-920.
5. Fabry, A. et al. (1996), In *Evaluating Material Properties by Dynamic Testing, ESIS Publication 20*, Mechanical Engineering Publication Limited, London, pp.59-78.
6. Watanabe, S. (1929), *Scientific Papers of the Institute of Physical and Chemical Research*, **12**, 213, pp. 99-120.
7. Fearnehough, G.D. (1966), MSc Thesis in Materials Technology, University of Manchester, England.
8. Rintamaa, R. (1993), *Single Specimen Fracture Toughness Determination Procedure Using Instrument Impact Test, VTT Publication 140*, Technical Research Center of Finland, Espoo.
9. Server, W.L. and Tetelman, A.S. (1972), *Engineering Fracture Mechanics*, **4**, pp. 367-375.
10. ASTM Standard E 399 (1990), In: *Annual Book of ASTM Standards*, American Society for Testing and Materials, Philadelphia, Pennsylvania.
11. Server, W. L. (1985), In: *Metals Handbook, Ninth Edition, Vol. 8, Mechanical Testing*, American Society for Metals, Metals Park, pp. 261-268.
12. Saxton, H.J., Ireland, D.R. and Server, W.L. (1974), In *Instrumented Impact Testing, ASTM STP 563*, American Society for Testing and Materials, Philadelphia, Pennsylvania, pp. 50-73.
13. Ireland, D.R. (1974), In *Instrumented Impact Testing, ASTM STP 563*, American Society for Testing and Materials, Philadelphia, Pennsylvania, pp. 3-29.
14. Server, W.L., Wullaert, R.A. and Sheckherd, J.W. (1977), In: *Flaw Growth and Fracture, ASTM STP 631*, American Society for Testing and Materials, Philadelphia, Pennsylvania, pp. 446-461.
15. Server, W.L. (1978), *J. Testing and Evaluation*, 6, 1, pp. 29-34.
16. Oldfield, W., Server, W., and Wullaert, R. (1975), *Fracture Toughness Data for Ferritic Nuclear Pressure Vessel Materials; Task A – Program Office, Control Material Round Robin Program*, Effects Technology, Inc.TR75-34R, Santa Barbara. California.

17. Lucon, E. et al. (2000), In: *Pendulum Impact Testing: A Century of Progress, ASTM STP 1380*, American Society for Testing and Materials, West Conshohocken, Pennsylvania, pp. 146-163.

18. *Instrumented Impact Testing, ASTM STP 563*, American Society for Testing and Materials, Philadelphia, Pennsylvania.

19. Wilshaw, T.R. and Pratt, P.L. (1966), *J. of Mechanics and Physics of Solids*, **14**, pp. 7-19.

20. Green, A.P. and Hundy, B.B. (1956), *J. of Mechanics and Physics of Solids*, **4**, pp. 128-144.

21. Server, W.L. (1978), *J. of Engineering Materials and Technology*, **100**, pp.183-188.

22. Wullaert, R.A. (1970), In: *Impact Testing of Metals, ASTM STP 466*, American Society for Testing and Materials, Philadelphia, Pennsylvania, pp. 148-164.

23. Sokolov, M.A. and Merkle, J.G. (2000), In: *Pendulum Impact Testing: A Century of Progress, ASTM STP 1380*, American Society for Testing and Materials, West Conshohocken, Pennsylvania, pp. 382-393.

24. Norris, D.M., Reaugh, J.E., and Server, W.L. (1981), In: *Fracture Mechanics: Thirteenth Conference*, American Society for Testing and Materials, Philadelphia, Pennsylvania, pp. 207-217.

25. *Pendulum Impact Testing: A Century of Progress, ASTM STP 1380*, American Society for Testing and Materials, West Conshohocken, Pennsylvania.

26. ASTM Standard E 1921 (1997), In: *Annual Book of ASTM Standards*, American Society for Testing and Materials, West Conshohocken, Pennsylvania.

27. Viehrig, H. et al. (2000), In: *Pendulum Impact Testing: A Century of Progress, ASTM STP 1380*, American Society for Testing and Materials, West Conshohocken, Pennsylvania, pp. 354-365.

28. Server, W.L. (1979), In: *Elastic-Plastic Fracture, ASTM STP 668*, American Society for Testing and Materials, Philadelphia, Pennsylvania, pp. 493-514.

From Charpy to Present Impact Testing
D. François and A. Pineau (Eds.)

PROBLEMS RELATED TO THE MEASUREMENT OF LOAD SIGNAL IN THE INSTRUMENTED CHARPY IMPACT TEST

SHIGEKI MORITA, MASAHIRO OTANI and TOSHIRO KOBAYASHI

Department of Production Systems Engineering, Toyohashi University of Technology, Toyohashi, 441-8580, Japan

ABSTRACT

The load calibration in instrumented Charpy impact testing was performed to develop an accurate measurement method of impact load. A decrease in specimen thickness results in a slight decrease of the calibration factors. This was attributed to strain localization near the region in which strain gages were attached. The results strongly suggested that the system must be calibrated for the different thicknesses of specimens to know the accurate impact load. The accurate impact load was not measured from the gage around the end of the slit which was introduced to release the constraining effect of deformation of the gage position from surrounding hammer; the effect of the vibration of the hammer appeared strongly around this position. However, it was possible to prevent the effect of such vibration by attaching the gage away from such position.

KEYWORDS

instrumented Charpy impact test, load calibration, instrumented striker, strain gage position, FEM.

INTRODUCTION

One of the authors has already developed the CAI (Computer Aided Instrumented Impact Testing) System, where dynamic fracture toughness parameters are obtained simply from the analysis of the load-deflection curve of a single precracked specimen [1]. In the test, therefore, it is important to record an accurate impact load. Generally one can obtain the impact load by multiplying the strain signal from attached strain gages on the instrumented striker with a load calibration factor assuming a linear relationship between the strain gage signal and applied load.

Recently, the instrumented Charpy impact test has been used for the evaluation of toughness of many kinds of materials and miniaturized specimens. In those cases, a significant variation in the calibration factor has been reported because the Charpy specimen was changed from the standard steel specimen to another material or geometry [2-4]. Though a lot of methods of load calibration are proposed [5, 6], no report considers the effect of change of material or geometry of the specimen. The elucidation of the mechanism that the load calibration factor changes by material or geometry of the specimen is important to measure accurate impact load and to enact the standard of load calibration method.

Although both JIS and ISO standards describe about the instrumented striker, amplifier, data processing parameter and etc., however precise and detailed load measurement method has not been described in any standard. In the current ASTM and ISO standards, there is no specific regulation regarding the accurate strain gage position (sometimes 11-15 mm from the tip is recommended).

In order to take into account the change in the material and geometry of the specimen, the load calibration test was performed in the present study. Finite element method based simulation of strain distributions in the instrumented striker was carried out to explain the mechanism of change in load calibration factor. Moreover, to investigate the effect of gage position on actual impact load, instrumented Charpy impact tests were performed with strain gages attached on the instrumented striker. The changes in strain with respect to the time were simulated by finite element analysis to explain the effect of the vibration of hammer on the measured load for the specified strain gage positions.

EXPERIMENTAL AND ANALYTICAL PROCEDURES

Load Calibration Test

An instrumented Charpy impact test machine with 98 J capacity was used for the load calibration. The semi-conductor strain gages were attached on both sides of instrumented striker. The attached gages were 16 mm apart from the tip of instrumented striker. The instrumented striker was loaded with the compressive load P through the specimen under the static condition. There is a linear relationship between P and the output voltage V from the bridge circuit and load calibration factor C can be calculated as

$$C = \Delta P / \Delta V \tag{1}.$$

In this calibration, the maximum compressive load of 6 kN and 3 kN were applied for the specimen thicknesses of 10 to 3 mm and 1.5 mm, respectively.

Instrumented Charpy Impact Test

An instrumented Charpy impact test machine with a capacity of 100 J was used. Two different

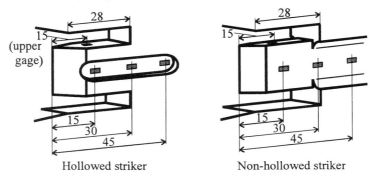

Hollowed striker   Non-hollowed striker

Fig. 1. Schematic illustration of instrumented striker for instrumented Charpy impact test (mm).

types of instrumented strikers as shown in Fig. 1 were employed. The hollowed striker is of conventional type. On the other hand, Non- hollowed striker was designed to prevent the strain localization [2]. The semi-conductor strain gages were attached at 15, 30 and 45 mm from the tip of instrumented striker on its both sides. The loading velocity was 4.5 m/s.

Finite Element Analysis

A non-linear analysis, based on a commercial available FEM code i.e. ANSYS, was conducted to calculate the strain fields in the instrumented striker. Whole finite element models of the instrumented Charpy hammers with specimens are shown in Fig. 2. The hammer arm was not considered in the model. The model was three-dimensional and eight-node brick elements was employed. Due to the symmetry, only 1/4th of the model was considered to save the computational time. The contact elements were formed at contact points between surface of the instrumented striker and the specimen to calculate contact forces. Full-Newton-Raphson method was used as a convergence criteria. The elastic moduli of the instrumented striker, steel and aluminum specimens were takes as 210 GPa, 210 GPa and 70 GPa, respectively.

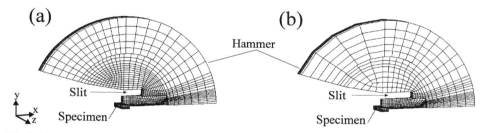

Fig.2.(a) Finite element model of Charpy hammer with specimen for low blow instrumented Charpy test. (b) Finite element model by introducing deep cutting slit.

RESULTS AND DISCUSSION

Effects of Materials and Sizes of the Specimen on Load Calibration Factor

Figure 3 shows the relationships between the load calibration factor C and specimen thickness B for A508 steel and 6061 aluminum alloy specimens. It is clear from Fig. 3 that C linearly decreases with thickness of the specimen in both the materials. These results suggest that a change in strain field around the strain gage position takes place due to complex contact mechanism of the instrumented striker with the specimen.

Generally, various types of specimens with different materials and sizes then those of the standard specimens have been used in the instrumented Charpy impact test to evaluate the dynamic properties such as the aging degradation of the structural materials and neutron radiation embrittlement of the nuclear reactor. In those tests, the calibration of the measured impact load is based on assumption that C does not change with the material or size of the specimen. However, Fig. 3 shows that material and specimen size does affect load calibration factor. Keeping in view this fact, it has been recommended that the instrumented striker must be calibrated for the different materials and sizes to ensure accurate impact load data [2].

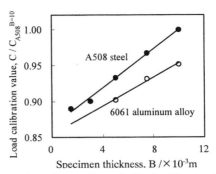

Fig.3. Effect of the thickness of specimens, B, on the load calibration factor, C, of A508 and 6061 Al. C is normalized with a load calibration factor of a specimen thickness of 10 mm and made of A508 steel, $C_{A508}^{B=10}$.

Effects of Specimen Sizes on Strain Distribution in the Instrumented Striker

Figure 4 shows contour maps of predicted strain in the x direction, ε_x, in the instrumented striker. Here, only the instrumented striker part of the hammer has been shown with the decrease in the thickness, complex changes in strain distributions take place. The strain is localized in the center of the instrumented striker with the decrease in the thickness from $B=10$ mm to $B=3$ mm. It can be seen that the strain is concentrated that region of the instrumented striker which is correspond to the thickness of the specimen and comes in direct contact with the specimen. The maximum compressive strain ε_x^m with $B=3$ mm is 2.7 times higher than that of $B=10$ mm. In the upper part of the instrumented striker, the tensile strain is developed with the decrease in the specimen thickness.

The situation of the instrumented striker is different from that of the standard load cell, when output is always same regardless of changes in material and geometry of specimen. The experimental and analytical results clearly indicate that the material and geometry of specimen influence strain fields in the instrumented striker, loading to a change in the load

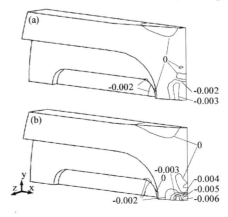

Fig. 4. Contour maps of the strain in x direction ε_x, within the instrumented striker. Specimen thickness, B, is (a) 10 mm and (b) 3 mm. Applied load, P, is 6 kN.

calibration factor. When this phenomenon is not take into account, the consequence is an error in the measured load. Thus it can be said that sensitivity of the instrumented striker depends not only on the change in specimen material and size but also on the design of the instrumented striker itself.

Effect of the Strain Gage Position on the Measured Impact Load

Figure 5 shows the typical load-deflection curves recorded with two types of the instrumented strikers on 6061-T6 aluminum alloy. The load-deflection curve recorded with gage position 15 mm is smooth. On the other hand, in the other strain gage positions, it can be clearly seen that after the maximum load the load-deflection curves are wavy, thus indicating the presence of vibrations. There are no differences between two types of striker geometries excepting the hollowing. The absorbed energies were estimated from the load-deflection curves of all the strain gage positions. The absorbed energy estimated from load-deflection curve of the gage position of 15 mm is approximately similar to the dial energy. Hence, the strain gage position of 15 mm recorded the accurate impact load history.

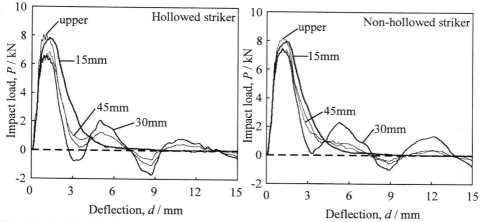

Fig.5. Typical load-deflection curves recorded from specified strain gage positions in hollowed and non-hollowed strikers for the V-notched 6061-T6 Al alloy Charpy specimen.

Figure 6 shows the prediction of the change in compressive strain along (x) and orthogonal to (y, z) direction of blow calculated by finite element analysis for specified strain gage positions. The strain in x direction shows a symmetric pattern with respects to the time shown in Fig.6(a). However, in Fig.6(b), the vibrations can be observed in the strain in y direction recorded with the gage positions of 30 and 45 mm. This effect can be attributed to the vibration of the hammer as shown in Fig.7.

As far as the effect of time on vibration is concerned, same pattern of 30 and 45 mm as shown in Fig.6(b). It has been reported in the previous work [7] that hammer deforms elastically and then vibrates periodically. Therefore, it was concluded that the both ends of hammer are deformed conversely and edge portion of hammer (near the end of slit), where the strain gage

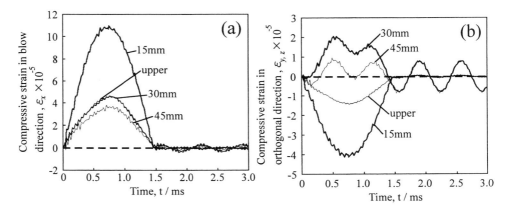

Fig.6. Changes in compressive strain with respect to time for specified strain gage positions in FEM analysis. (a)Compressive strains along the direction of blow (x-direction). (b)Compressive strains, orthogonal to the direction of blow for 15, 30, 45mm and upper positions, respectively, in y and z-directions.

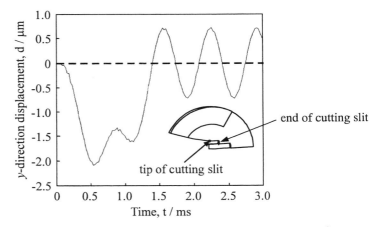

Fig.7. Variation of y-direction displacement at the tip of cutting slit with respect to time upon impact.

is attached, is bent by the natural vibration of hammer. Keeping in view this fact, it can be recommended that the strain gage should be attached near the tip of striker.

Effect of the Slit Depth of Striker on the Measured Impact Load

Figure 8 depicts the changes in compressive strain based on the predictions of the model shown in Fig.2(b) but with a deeper depth of slit. The constraining of deformation of the gage position of 30 mm from surrounding hammer was released by the slit. In Fig.8(a), the strain in x direction is symmetric with respects to time and it is similar to the behavior previously shown in Fig.6(a). However, the strain-time curve with the gage position of 45 mm still shows vibrations in the strain y direction. The accurate impact load could not be measured around the end of slit which had been introduced to release the constraining effect of deformation of the gage position from surrounding hammer; the effect of the vibration of the hammer appeared strongly around this position. However, the effect of such vibration could be eliminated by attaching the gage away from such a position.

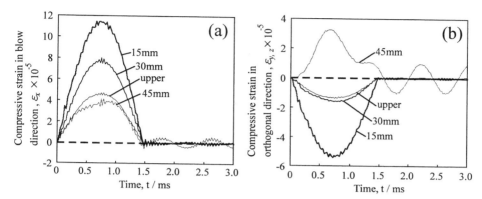

Fig.8. Changes in compressive strain with respect to time for specified strain gage positions in FEM analysis. (a) Compressive strains along the direction of blow (x-direction). (b) Compressive strains, orthogonal to the direction of blow for 15, 30, 45mm and upper positions, respectively, in y and z-directions.

CONCLUSIONS

(1) In the calibration tests, the load calibration factor linearly decreases with the thickness of specimen. It means that the measured load gives an overestimate of the total absorbed energy and impact load when the material and the size effects on load calibration factor are not take into account.

(2) Finite element analyses indicate that even for the same applied load, a compressive strain in the center of the instrumented striker is localized with the decrease in specimen thickness. Doe to this the load calibration factor decreases as well.

(3) The changes in the material and the size of specimens influence the strain fields in the instrumented striker and thus load to change in the load calibration factor. Moreover, large change take place in compressive strain in the instrumented striker near the point where it touches the specimen. These results strongly suggest that the need for system calibration to obtain accurate impact load, for the different materials and sizes of specimens.

(4) Due to the strong effect of the vibrations of the hammer, the accurate impact load could not be measured around the end of slit which had been introduced to release the constraining effect of deformation of the gage position from surrounding hammer.

REFERENCES

1.   Kobayashi, T., Yamamoto, I. and Niinomi, M. (1993) *J. Test. Eval.* 21, 145.
2.   Kobayashi, T., Morita, S., Inoue, N. and Toda, H. (2000). In: *Pendulum Impact Testing: A Century of Progress, STP 1380*, pp.198-209, Siewert, T. A. and Manahan, M. P. Sr. (Eds). ASTM, West Conshohocken, PA.
3.   Marur, P. R., Shimha, K. R. Y. and Nari, P. S. (1995) *J. Test. Eval.* 23, 267.
4.   Kalthoff, J. F., Walle, E. van and Wilde, G. (1996). In: *Evaluating Material Properties by Dynamic Testing, ESIS20*, pp.25-35, Walle, E. van (Ed). Mechanical Engineering Publications, London.
5.   Winkler, S. and Boβ, B. (1996). In: *Evaluating Material Properties by Dynamic Testing, ESIS20*, pp.37-44. Walle, E. van (Ed). Mechanical Engineering Publications, London.
6.   Wilde, G., Covic, M. and Gregor, M. (1996). In: *Evaluating Material Properties by Dynamic Testing, ESIS20*, pp.89-96, Walle, E. van (Ed). Mechanical Engineering Publications, London.
7.   Yamamoto, I. and Kobayashi, T. (1993) *Int. J. Pressure Vessels & Piping*, 55, 295.

From Charpy to Present Impact Testing
D. François and A. Pineau (Eds.)

STUDIES TOWARD OPTIMUM INSTRUMENTED STRIKER DESIGNS

M. P. Manahan, Sr.[1] and R. B. Stonesifer[2]

[1] President MPM Technologies, Inc., 2161 Sandy Drive, State College, PA 16803
[2] President Computational Mechanics, Inc., 1430 Steele Hollow Road, Julian, PA 16844

ABSTRACT

Experimental and numerical studies have shown that the accuracy of indicated loads from instrumented Charpy impact test strikers may be adversely affected by inertial forces in the striker and by variations in the contact force distribution between the striker and the specimen. This study identifies the factors that affect contact force distribution on the striker and discusses how they can adversely affect the load cell's calibration and use during dynamic testing. Results of numerical simulations are presented which show that inertial errors increase significantly as strain gages are moved farther from the contact surface and that significant errors for high frequency components of the load signal may be experienced for some designs. Numerical and experimental studies show that load cell designs can be made significantly less sensitive to the load distribution variations that occur in a Charpy V-notch test by optimizing the strain gage locations. Experimental data are provided which demonstrate that proper design and calibration can adequately address inertial and load distribution effects and result in acceptable errors in the dynamic loads.

KEYWORDS: Charpy, instrumented impact test, absorbed energy, encoder, calibration.

INTRODUCTION

Charpy impact testing has been in use for over 100 years and remains a key means for fracture toughness testing due to its low cost and reliability. Through continued refinements in testing and certification standards, the Charpy test has evolved with the requirements of the engineering community. Due to its low cost and convenience, there is a growing interest in using the test to obtain more sophisticated fracture mechanics related material information (e.g., K_{Ic}, K_{Ia}). Accurate determination of load versus displacement behavior during the test is essential to obtaining such information. The most common way for determining the transient load history during a Charpy test is to place strain gages on the striker so that the striker becomes a load cell. Displacements are typically obtained by integrating the acceleration versus time record twice with respect to time. It can be seen that the accurate determination of any material fracture properties from these load measurements will depend very significantly on the accuracy of the striker load cell.

FORCE DISTRIBUTION EFFECTS

Building a load cell into the striker of a dynamic test machine requires solution to two fundamental problems. The first is that the measured loads must be accurate for very high rates of loading since the rapidly changing loads (initial loading, brittle fracture unloading) being measured are typically applied and removed over a microsecond time scale. At these rates of loading, the striker material's inertial forces are not entirely negligible in comparison to the contact forces between the specimen and the striker. The other problem is that the striker geometry is not inherently ideal for use as a precision load cell. The principal problem is that the measured strains for a given load magnitude are dependent on the manner in which the load is distributed over the specimen/striker contact region. Some results of finite element simulations related to load distribution effects on striker accuracy were reported in a previous study [1]. Additional finite element simulations and experimentation toward minimizing inertial and contact force distribution effects on load cell accuracy are presented here.

For a standard Charpy V-notch test, there are numerous reasons why the contact force distribution can vary from specimen-to-specimen or during a test on a single specimen. The most significant reasons (in no particular order) are listed below:
1. elastic deformations of the striker and pendulum
2. rotations of the striker due to pendulum rigid body rotation
3. initial specimen machining tolerance on squareness (10 minutes)
4. wear of the striker, anvils, or supports
5. plasticity in the specimen leading to force redistribution
6. wrapping of the specimen around an 8 mm striker with plowing of the specimen surface and associated pinching of the striker nose
7. specimens of different material elastic and plastic behavior
8. specimen height
9. nonsymmetry in crack growth behavior

The effects of force distributions on the striker can be grouped according to whether the distribution is defined with respect to a vertical coordinate (i.e., parallel to the specimen's notch root when placed in the testing machine), or a horizontal coordinate (perpendicular to the intended fracture plane of the specimen). In our previous work, simulations of bounding horizontal load distribution variations on an 8 mm striker (nominal 4 mm wide contact surface with an 8 mm radius) striker showed a maximum load cell error of 1.2%. The considered contact force distributions were a) uniform pressure, b) vertical line of force at the centerline of the striker, and c) two vertical lines of force at the corners of the 4 mm wide contact surface. The simulated strain gage placement was 7.4 mm from the contact surface. Recent simulations with a 7.9 mm gage placement predicted a 1.0% maximum load cell error for these same distributions.

Kalthoff et al [2] experimented with load distribution effects on 2 mm and 8 mm strikers. Their study focused on horizontal load distribution effects by considering the effect that wrapping around the striker at large specimen deformation levels could have on load cell accuracy. They found load cell errors as large as 10%, with titanium strikers being more prone to error than steel, and the 8 mm design being more prone to error than the 2 mm design. The 8 mm striker results of the current horizontal load distributions study are consistent with the Reference [2] experimental results of ±1 to 2% error (steel striker with strain gages on the sides of the striker).

Simulations of vertical load distribution variations on an 8 mm striker showed a much larger potential for load cell error than variations in horizontal distributions. Bounding distributions (which are never realized in actual tests) where all load was concentrated at either the top or the bottom specimen edge led to large load cell differences when the load cell output is compared with a uniform contact pressure. Although the range of realistic contact distributions are not known, this earlier study suggested that errors on the order of 8% might be expected. This level of error is consistent with those reported by Kobayashi et al [3]. They discuss the effect of specimen thickness and specimen elastic modulus on a 2 mm radius striker load cell calibration. Their finite element simulations show that load errors on the order of 10% can be expected if a test is done on an aluminum specimen after calibration using a steel specimen. They also found that calibrating with a 10 mm thick specimen and then testing a 2 mm thick specimen could lead to load errors on the order of 10%. Although they do not clearly state that the load cell errors are due to changes in load distribution on the striker, this is clearly the explanation for their observations. They reasonably conclude that an instrumented striker system must be calibrated for any new specimen material or specimen size. They do not broach the subject of changing contact force distributions that can occur within a single test due to plasticity or striker rotation. Winkler and Voβ [4] report experiments that show a maximum 5% error in an 8 mm style striker due to variations in load distribution. The variations they considered were those due to wear or small permanent deformations in the calibration specimen and/or striker that led to different contact force distributions and different calibration factors with subsequent calibrations and with different calibration force levels.

The Manahan and Stonesifer study [1] on striker load cell sensitivity to load distribution showed that the elastic contact surface rotation for an 8 mm striker on a U-hammer machine is similar in magnitude to the allowable 10 minute squareness requirement of the ASTM E23 standard, thus making the 10 minute squareness tolerance seem reasonable. Very high energy Charpy specimens can be in contact with the striker while the pendulum rotates as much as 1 to 2 degrees. At the 2 degree angle of rotation, a typical 400 J machine will have displaced the bottom edge of the specimen by about 0.35 mm more than the top edge. This top-to-bottom nonsymmetry provides significant opportunity for a larger portion of the applied load being applied to the bottom half of the specimen during a significant portion of the test duration. It seems likely that the nonsymmetry would be greatest after peak load since the increasing loads and associated plasticity prior to peak load would be more effective at preserving top-to-bottom symmetry in the contact force distribution.

Finite element simulation showed that the contact forces between an 8 mm striker (U-hammer) and a Charpy specimen under linear elastic conditions are not uniformly distributed. The distribution will have peaks at the top and bottom edges of the contact region with the top peak being larger in magnitude than the bottom peak. The peaks are due to the corners of the specimen pressing into the striker surface. The top-to-bottom asymmetry results from the striker being connected to the hammer only at its top edge and is made even more significant by the specimen contact region being relatively close to the free bottom edge of the striker. The tendency for larger contact forces at the specimen's top edge is significant. The ratio of the top and bottom edge node forces was 1.21. A statically equivalent linear pressure distribution has a top-to-bottom ratio of 1.25. Examination of broken Charpy V-notch specimens that have undergone significant plasticity prior to fracture shows clear signs of the contact forces tending to concentrate near the middle of the specimen's contacting surface. The mid region concentration is due to a tendency for the mid region to bulge relative to the top and bottom edges during large fully plastic bending deformations at the notched plane. The initial elastic distribution for a specimen is probably a good approximation to the distribution during calibration if the calibration specimen is not worn from previous calibrations [4]. However, the distribution of force during later stages of deformation of a ductile specimen will probably never be reasonably approximated by calibration on a typical calibration specimen. If the load cell is to accurately measure the load for both distributions, it must either be generally insensitive to changes in load distribution or it must be designed to be accurate for at least the specific load distributions that occur during calibration and testing.

The described numerical and experimental studies clearly show that significant errors in the indicated load from a striker load cell can occur if the load during the test is not distributed on the striker surface in a manner similar to that experienced during calibration. This sensitivity to contact force distribution is an illustration of Saint-Venant's principle. Basically, application of this principle leads to the conclusion that if one hopes to measure strains that are insensitive to load distribution, the strain gages must be relatively far from the loaded surface relative to the dimensions of the contact region. Unfortunately, it is not feasible to design a striker load cell that makes use of this principle to minimize load distribution sensitivity. Even if the striker was large enough to accommodate such distances, the sensitivity of the load cell to the magnitude of the load would suffer significantly. However, an even more limiting factor is the effect of this distance on the load cell's dynamic response.

INERTIA EFFECTS

Consideration of inertial effects is important because the accuracy of loads measured during high frequency events (e.g. brittle fracture events) can be significantly affected for inferior striker designs. The inertia of the material between the contact surface and the strain gage affects the ability of a statically calibrated load cell to faithfully reproduce the shape and magnitude of load versus time impulses applied at the contact surface. As the strain gages are moved closer to the contact surface, the inertial effects become smaller due to the reduced intervening mass. Comparing the results for the two simulated strain gage positions (3.3 mm and 7.4 mm from the contact surface), it can be seen that the closer gages follow the applied force versus time curve more faithfully than the farther gages. It has also been verified by comparing results for 25 and 50 kHz inputs that the "inertial errors" (i.e., difference from the applied force behavior) increase as the duration of the pulse is decreased (i.e., higher frequency). The non-zero indicated forces after the applied force is zero are associated with audible "ringing" of the striker (from stress waves that continue to bounce from surface to surface within the striker). For an impulse duration of 100 microseconds (5 kHz case), the peak load error is less than 1% for both simulated gage locations and the maximum inertial errors are 3.6% and 5.5% for the 3.3 and 7.4 mm position, respectively. This pulse duration is similar to the duration of A533B Class 1 steel tested on the lower shelf and therefore it might be expected to be representative of typical inertia related load cell errors for such a test. However, the load oscillations that typically occur until damped by specimen plasticity have a frequency of around 20 kHz. If the amplitude of this oscillatory load is say 20% of the peak load then, the larger inertial errors associated with this 20 kHz component can effectively about double the magnitude of the indicated load error suggested by the 5 kHz input case.

The importance of the errors at these higher frequencies depends on the high frequency content of the load signals of interest. One could do a Fourier analysis of typical load signals and then estimate errors based on the amplitudes of the various frequencies. However, a more direct and probably more reliable approach is to input actual force versus time records from a variety of Charpy tests and compare the input and indicated loads. Finite element simulations of an actual lower shelf 4340 steel test specimen record using a simulated load cell with gages 7.9 mm from the contact surface led to load errors near peak load of 2 to 4% and load errors near the crack arrest load of 5 to 14%. This simulation confirmed the importance of the higher frequency load components in the overall accuracy of the indicated load. Simulations of an upper transition region specimen led to load errors near peak load of 0.5% to 2% and load errors near the arrest load (arrest load being ~2/3 peak load) of 1 to 3%. The smaller errors near peak load were due to damping of high frequency oscillations by specimen plasticity and were expected. The smaller errors near the rapid crack extension event (compared to the low energy simulation) were not expected.

OPTIMUM STRIKER LOAD CELL DESIGN

The striker load cell FEM simulations led to the conclusion that while the 3.3 mm gage location was better in terms of reducing inertial effects, it was too sensitive to load distribution effects. Based on the significant inertial errors (primarily for crack arrest load measurement) for 25 kHz and higher frequencies at the 7.4 mm gage location, it was concluded that placing gages significantly farther than 7.4 mm from the contact surface would make the load cell too sensitive to inertial effects. Having established that gages that are about 7.4 mm from the loaded surface seem to provide a reasonable balance between load distribution related errors and inertia related errors, an experimental study was conducted to refine the gage placement in an attempt to minimize sensitivity to load distribution effects. Since the distance from the contact surface was being confined to values close to 7.4 mm, the only other geometric parameter to be determined was the vertical position of the gage relative to the center of the nominal striker contact region. In preparation for the optimization process, strain distributions and simulated load cell outputs were computed for a variety of assumed vertical distributions of contact force. A very significant finding was that for a selected pair of contact force distributions, a vertical gage position could be identified for which the simulated load cell outputs would exactly reproduce the input force magnitudes for both selected load distributions. It was also found that some vertical gage locations tended to give smaller indicated load errors for a range of assumed distributions. By assuming which contact distributions were of key importance, the finite element results could provide the associated optimum gage position.

Table 1   Example of measured load variation at or near peak load for four strain gage locations.

Material	Striker Strain Gage Location			
	FEM Calculation (below optimal location)	Strain Gage Position 2 (above optimal location)	Strain Gage Position 3 Near Optimum Location	Optimum Location
4340 Steel	-4.28 %	5.45 %	-1.06 %	0.09 %
17-4-H1150	-5.28 %	8.54 %	-1.70 %	-0.15 %
A36 Steel	-3.95 %	3.07 %	-1.75 %	-0.13 %
6061 Aluminum	-5.34 %	-3.63 %	-1.66 %	-0.06 %
17-4 PH condition A	-5.17 %	7.92 %	-0.78 %	-0.20 %

NOTE: Calculation of the variation was performed at peak load for cases where the deflection was less than 2.5 mm or at 2.5 mm of deflection.

In order to test the candidate strain gage locations, static load deflection measurements on standard Charpy specimens were made using the Charpy test machine striker and a NIST traceable calibrated load cell. The striker load cell was calibrated using a hardened, reusable calibration specimen. After calibration, slow bend tests were performed using conventional Charpy V-notch specimens fabricated from a variety of steels and aluminum. The results of the experimental gage placement optimization are summarized in Table 1 for peak load measurements. The load application fixture was not designed for deflections in excess of about

2.5 mm. Therefore, the loads in Table 1 are at peak load for cases where the deflection was less than 2.5 mm or at 2.5 mm of deflection. It was found that the FEM calculated optimum gage position (based on assumed key load distributions) resulted in the striker's indicated load being about 5% lower than the applied load. A second bounding location was chosen for the gages which yielded striker indicated loads that were generally above the applied load. These data suggested that a better gage position existed and that it was between the first two locations. Using these data, a new estimate of the optimum gage location was made and further experimentation was performed to verify it. As shown in Table 1, this third gage location gave peak loads accurate to within 2% of the applied load for the variety of steels and aluminum. Again using the existing data a fourth gage location was identified and tested. For this fourth location, the peak load errors were all 0.2% or less and therefore this position was declared the optimum gage location.

The experimental vertical position refinement resulted in about a 46% change to the initial finite element based vertical gage offset. This suggested that the force distributions used in the numerical optimization step were not the best choices. The experimental refinement of the numerical optimum location provided sufficient information to determine how the selected load distributions would need to be modified to bring the analysis and experimental results into agreement. To have the numerical optimization match the experimental optimum gage location required more load to be applied on the bottom half of the specimen than on the top half for the second of the two assumed load distributions. This is the opposite gradient from the initial contact distribution.

DESIGN OPTIMIZATION VERIFICATION

An experiment was designed to verify the accuracy of the optimized striker design. After construction of the striker, a static striker calibration was performed using a stiff, hardened, reusable calibrator specimen. After this calibration, the same calibration fixture was used to perform static load-deflection experiments using conventional Charpy specimens. These tests allowed the effects of changes in specimen stiffness, specimen material, and large specimen deflections on contact load distribution and load cell response to be studied. Fig. 1 shows the static load calibration results for several materials with widely differing properties and load-deflection responses. It can be seen that the striker's indicated loads are in excellent agreement with the applied loads. Therefore, it has been concluded that the striker design is not significantly affected by the type of load distribution changes that are experienced in going from a calibration specimen to a real Charpy specimen or the changes that can occur during testing of Charpy specimens.

As discussed earlier, load cell inertial effects on the crack arrest load measurement is a concern. Fig. 2 shows a load-time plot for a pressure vessel steel tested in the transition region. In cases where the brittle pop occurs after peak load, the specimen plasticity has damped the load oscillations and the brittle initiation load is expected to have no significant inertial effects. However, the brittle fracture and arrest events occur on a microsecond time scale and therefore load cell inertial effects on the indicated loads near the time of crack arrest are probably significant. As shown in Fig. 2, backward extrapolation of a fit to the post-brittle fracture load data appears to provide a reasonably well defined crack arrest load that should be relatively insensitive to load cell inertial effects. Since it seems likely that actual specimen load oscillations during this time may never be accurately separated from load cell inertial effects, it may be more meaningful and reliable for fracture mechanics analyses involving the crack arrest load to use the quasi-static fitting procedure to define the crack arrest load.

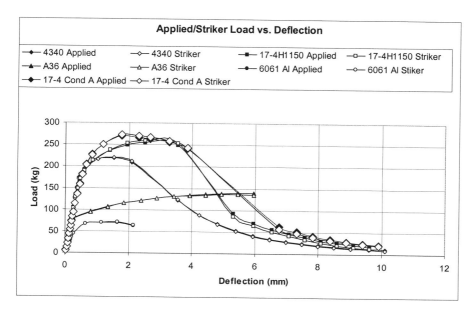

Fig. 1   Static load calibration results for five materials with various load-deflection responses. The load application device was designed to provide accurate data up to deflections of about 2.5 mm. Therefore, data at deflections above 2.5 mm should be viewed as approximate.

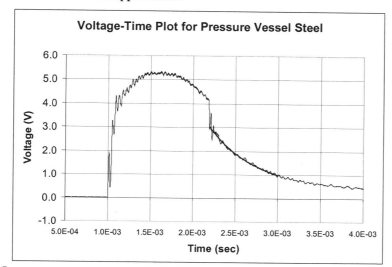

Fig. 2   Instrumented striker signal showing rapid unloading due to brittle crack propagation. Fitting of quasi-static post-brittle fracture data shows that the measured crack arrest load is well represented by the quasi-static load.

SUMMARY AND CONCLUSION

It has become apparent through a variety of experimental and numerical studies that the accuracy of indicated loads from instrumented Charpy impact test strikers are adversely affected by inertial forces in the striker and by variations in the contact force distribution between the striker and the specimen. Numerical and experimental evidence shows that the vertical distribution of striker contact force changes significantly during a typical Charpy test.

Inertial force effects on the load cell can be reduced by moving the load cell strain gages closer to the contact surface. Contact force distribution effects can be reduced by moving the load cell strain gages farther from the contact surface. A distance of 7 to 8 mm was found to provide a reasonable compromise between inertial and load distribution effects. It was shown that sensitivity of the load cell to variations in the contact force distribution (between calibration and testing and during a given test) is significantly improved by optimizing the vertical location of the load cell strain gages relative to the contact surface.

REFERENCES

1.   Manahan, M. P., Sr., and Stonesifer, R. B., **"The Difference Between Total Absorbed Energy Measured Using An Instrumented Striker and That Obtained Using an Optical Encoder,"** *Pendulum Impact Testing: A Century of Progress, STP 1380*, T. A. Siewert and M. P. Manahan, Sr., Eds., American Society for Testing and Materials, West Conshohocken, PA.

2.   Kalthoff, J. F., van Walle, E., and Wilde, G., **Variations of the sensitivity of instrumented ISO/DIN and ASTM tups and their influence on the determination of impact energies in tests with ductile steels**, *Evaluating Material Properties by Dynamic Testing*, ESIS 20 (Edited by E. van Walle), 1996, Mechanical Engineering Publications, London, pp. 25-35.

3.   Kobayashi, T., Inoue, N., Morita, S., and Toda, H., **"On the Accuracy of Measurement and Calibration of Load Signal in the Instrumented Charpy Impact Test,"** *Pendulum Impact Testing: A Century of Progress, STP 1380*, T. A. Siewert and M. P. Manahan, Sr., Eds., American Society for Testing and Materials, West Conshohocken, PA.

4.   Winkler, S. and Voß, B., **Static force calibration of Charpy impactors**, *Evaluating Material Properties by Dynamic Testing*, ESIS 20 (Edited by E. van Walle), 1996, Mechanical Engineering Publications, London, pp. 37-44.

From Charpy to Present Impact Testing
D. François and A. Pineau (Eds.)

OBSERVATIONS ON DIFFERENCES BETWEEN THE ENERGY DETERMINED USING AN INSTRUMENTED STRIKER AND DIAL/ENCODER ENERGY

M. P. Manahan, Sr. [1], R. B. Stonesifer[2], T. A. Siewert[3], C. N. McCowan[3], and D. P. Vigliotti[3]
[1] MPM Technologies, Inc., 2161 Sandy Drive, State College, PA 16803 USA
[2] Computational Mechanics, Inc., 1430 Steele Hollow Road, Julian, PA 16844 USA
[3] National Institute for Standards and Technology, 325 Broadway, Boulder, CO 80303 USA

ABSTRACT

Instrumented striker systems, dial indicators, and optical encoders are widely used for measurement of absorbed energy in both conventional and miniature Charpy tests. It has been observed that the total absorbed energy measured using these technologies, while generally in good agreement, sometimes differs by a significant amount. This paper presents experimental evidence from high speed photography of Charpy tests that the differences between dial/encoder energies and instrumented striker energies (measured with U-hammers) can largely be explained by post-fracture collisions with the striker. Further, experimental and numerical studies show that dynamic elastic deformations of the pendulum and striker, as well as load cell errors due to contact load distribution and inertial effects, can also significantly contribute to the energy differences for some test machine designs.

Experimental evidence from the literature that was originally expected to show the significance of residual vibrational energy in the test machine may actually show that low energy Charpy specimen behavior can be significantly affected by the design of the test machine. A simple dynamic model of a specimen and test machine system shows that a 20% increase in the stiffness of the striker and hammer assembly can lead to a 9% decrease in the energy required to fracture a low energy Charpy specimen.

KEYWORDS: Charpy, instrumented impact test, absorbed energy, encoder, vibration.

PENDULUM RESIDUAL VIBRATION ENERGY

Although dynamic test machine pendulums and their support structures are designed to be as close to rigid as practical, they can never be perfectly rigid. This means that an impulse load applied to the pendulum will result in elastic deformations in the machine components. These elastic deformations involve both strain and kinetic energy (vibrational energy). The ultimate source of the pendulum's vibrational energy is the initial potential energy of the pendulum and therefore the energy that is indicated by the machine's energy dial, or inferred from an optical encoder, includes any pendulum vibrational energy. Energies computed by integration of striker load cell forces do not include vibrational energy left in the pendulum since the integration of the force-deflection data provides the work done on the specimen over the few milliseconds required for the specimen to undergo fracture.

Finite element simulations of a previous study calculated how much energy is left in the pendulum of a 400 J U-hammer Charpy test machine in the form of residual vibrational energy [1]. Simulated strike positions included the nominal center of percussion (CP), 1% above the

CP, and 0.57% below the CP. Calculated residual vibrational energies in the pendulum were in the range of 0.07 to 2.9 J. It was concluded that pendulum residual vibrational energy is a significant factor in observed dial/encoder versus striker energy differences. In the present study, the finite element vibrational energy magnitudes were confirmed experimentally for strikes very near the center of percussion. The approach was to mount accelerometers at various locations on the pendulum and hammer. Accelerations were recorded during tests on National Institute of Standards & Technology (NIST) verification specimens (low energy specimens ~16 J, high energy specimens ~101 J, and super high energy specimens ~217 J). Converting the acceleration data into vibrational energy involved calculating the fundamental vibration modes of the pendulum and developing analytical models relating accelerations, strain energy, and kinetic energy for each mode. The accelerometer data was subjected to a Fourier analysis so accelerations could be associated with each fundamental mode of vibration. The vibrational energy was then calculated for each mode and summed to get the total vibrational energy. The results of the vibrational energy experiments are summarized in Table 1. Estimated vibrational energies based on the tube lateral vibration model ranged from 0.16 J to 0.47 J. The higher energy Charpy tests resulted in larger vibrational energy. Computed vibrational energy was between 0.2% and 0.7% of the measured Charpy energy with the larger percentages of vibrational energy being for the lower energy specimens. Vibrational energy estimates based on the U-hammer angular vibrations were nearly identical to those from the lateral vibration model for the lowest energy Charpy specimen. For the higher energy specimens, the energy estimates were somewhat higher than from the lateral vibration model (0.95 and 2.20 J). For the U-hammer machine of this study, it appears that vibrational energies approach, but do not exceed, 1% of the Charpy energy. The vibrational energy for the high and super high energy specimens was primarily contained in the lowest frequency fundamental vibration mode (136 Hz). The low energy specimen contained the most energy in the third or fourth fundamental mode (1224 or 2175 Hz).

Table 1   **Summary of pendulum vibrational energy estimates from analysis of pendulum acceleration data.**

Specimen Type	Charpy Energy (J)	Vibrational Energy (J)	Vibrational Energy (%)	Peak Energy Frequency (cps)
Tube Lateral Vibration Model				
Super high energy	227.7	0.47	0.2	136
high energy	131.9	0.35	0.3	136
low energy	23.0	0.16	0.7	1224
Hammer Angular Vibration Model				
Super high energy	211.8	2.02	1.0	136
high energy	131.0	0.95	0.7	136
low energy	22.3	0.15	0.7	2175

ENERGY ASSOCIATED WITH POST-FRACTURE IMPACTS

Instrumented striker measurements were made on a U-hammer test machine at NIST with simultaneous high speed photography. The high speed photographs of the impact event and subsequent interaction with the striker were made at 3000 frames per second. The camera was positioned both in front, and behind, the test machine so that the specimen/striker interaction could be viewed from both perspectives. Standard Reference Materials (SRMs)

2092 (low energy range of 12 – 20 J), 2096 (high energy range of 88 – 115 J), and 2098 (super high energy range of 210 – 224 J) were tested. The focus of this investigation was on characterizing the post-fracture interaction between the specimen and the striker so that the energy associated with post-fracture impact of the specimen halves with the striker could be quantified.

Over 50 high speed films were generated with simultaneous instrumented signal/optical encoder data acquisition. Depending on the test temperature and alloy, specimens either exited the back of the test machine (opposite the striker direction) or the front (direction of striker motion). Five categories of post-impact behavior were observed depending on the material and test temperature:

1. Specimen halves initially propagate normal to the crack plane away from the striker and exit the rear of the test machine without striker interaction.
2. Specimen halves undergo rotation, impact the anvils and exit the rear of the test machine without striker interaction.
3. Specimen halves undergo rotation, hit the rear of the striker, and either exit the rear or fall down on the support pedestal.
4. Connected or unconnected specimen halves exit the front of the test machine having one or more post-fracture impacts with the striker.
5. Connected or unconnected specimen halves exit the front of the test machine without interaction with the striker.

During the first round of tests, a qualitative correlation between the number of post-fracture hits and the energy difference between the encoder and instrumented striker energies was observed. In all of the low energy range tests, the instrumented striker energy was less than the dial energy and this difference was observed to be larger in cases where there were multiple post-fracture impacts with the striker. The best energy agreement (typically within about 1%) was obtained for the higher energy tests where the specimen exits the front of the test machine still connected and without any striker interaction. Good agreement was also obtained for low energy specimens for which the broken halves exit the rear of the test machine without contacting the striker. The largest differences occurred when the broken test specimens rebounded off the anvils and/or the test machine exit channel (characteristic of U-hammer test machines) and hit the striker. There were many cases where the test specimen rebounded several times off the exit channel and striker. It is interesting to note that the exit channel, which is typically constructed from low strength carbon steel, has indentation marks from specimen interaction. The accumulation of these indentations can be detrimental because they can facilitate exit channel/striker interactions.

Two more sets of tests were performed to quantify the magnitude of the energy difference. The first set of tests was conducted at 20 C using an alloy which is capable of complete fracture and which produces both front and rear test specimen exits. The tests conducted at 20 C strongly favored the front exit. The few specimens exiting the rear either had no interaction with the striker or at most had one minor glancing type contact where a rebound from the striker was not apparent. All of the specimens exiting the front had numerous rebounding type impacts with the striker. These data show that the post-fracture impacts with the striker associated with front exiting specimens add an average of 2.9 J to the dial energy (2.3 J standard deviation). Additional tests were then conducted with the same material at –40 C to obtain a higher percentage of rear exiting specimens and the results are shown in Table 2. These experiments gave a slightly higher post-fracture striker interaction energy of 4.6 J (3.3 J standard deviation). Overall, these experiments show that post-fracture specimen-striker interactions can account for a large share of the energy difference between the dial and the instrumented striker energies.

Table 2   **Optical encoder energy results for impact tests conducted with simultaneous high speed photography. Tests conducted at -40 C.**

Specimen Exited Rear of Test Machine			Specimen Exited Front of Test Machine		
ID LL1-	Energy (J)	Striker Contact	ID LL1-	Energy (J)	Striker Contact
250	16.2	No	73	19.7	Yes
252	15.5	No	126	18.2	Yes
182	17.2	No	15	21.3	Yes
242	18.9	1 hit	240	23.3	Yes
63	18.2	No	222	27.0	Yes
-	-	-	119	18.5	Yes
-	-	-	39	24.6	Yes
Average	17.2	-	Average	21.8	-
Std. Dev.	1.4	-	Std. Dev.	3.3	-

EXPERIMENTAL STUDIES FROM THE LITERATURE

ASTM Instrumented/Miniaturized Round Robin Test Program

Results from a round robin test program to compare Charpy energy test results obtained by different laboratories were compiled and reported by Manahan et. al. [2]. Standard Charpy V-notch (CVN) and miniature (half scale) Charpy V-notch specimens (MCVN) were included in the study. Instrumented strikers were used to obtain load vs. time records and key loads were reported along with striker based energies as well as dial/encoder energies. The round robin used material from a previously characterized A533B Class 1 plate and two varieties of 4340 steel prepared by NIST using methods similar to those used to prepare specimens for certifying Charpy test machines. The results of this ASTM round robin were examined as part of the current study to see if there was a statistically significant difference between the reported instrumented striker energies and the dial/encoder energies. As described above, differences could be due to residual vibrational energy in the pendulum, load errors due to contact force distributions being different in the test from those during calibration, or due perhaps to other unknown causes.

Comparing the dial/encoder energies to the instrumented striker energies it was found that, for CVN tests above 40 J, the energy agreement was within ±5%. For CVNs with energy below 40 J, the agreement was within ±18%. The MCVNs all had energies below 40 J and were in agreement to within ±12%. Since there were six duplicate tests for each material/temperature/lab combination, it was possible to get a sense of how much of the difference between the two measures of energy was due to random effects. Comparing the differences of the averaged values (6 tests) only tightened the above three levels of agreement to 3%, 15%, and 10%. This suggests that the differences in the reported energies are systematic rather than random.

A paired t test was used to determine the statistical significance of the observed differences between encoder/dial and instrumented striker energies. Each data point is based on the average differences from six duplicate tests by the same laboratory. For 9 out of 19 material/temperature/lab CVN data sets, the average energy difference was large enough compared to the standard deviation of the differences to conclude with 99% confidence that there is a systematic difference between the average measured dial energy and the average striker based energy. Lowering the confidence level to 95% results in 15 of the 19 CVN data sets being consistent with there being systematic differences. For 14 out of the 16 MCVN data sets, it can be concluded with 99% confidence that there is a systematic difference between the measured dial energy and the striker force based energy.

It is very clear from this comparison of dial/encoder and instrumented striker energies that there are significant systematic differences. There appears to be some bias in the less than 40 J range towards the instrumented striker energy being less than the dial/encoder energy. This is consistent with there being some residual vibrational energy included in the dial/encoder energies or that additional energy is removed from the pendulum by post fracture interactions between the specimen and the striker. The significantly larger differences for the MCVN tests could perhaps be the result of their being tested on the lower energy capacity machines. These machines could possibly be more prone to residual vibrational energy effects than larger capacity machines. Assuming that the load cell strain gages for MCVN testing were placed on the striker similarly to those in the CVN testing, it would be expected that the load distribution effects would be smaller in the MCVN tests due to the smaller contact region (half). Striker load cell inertial effects would not be expected to be the cause of the large energy differences due to the upper shelf behavior (much plasticity) making the specimen behavior largely quasi-static. However, test machine inertial/dynamic effects on the displacement histories computed from the striker load histories could be greater for the lower capacity and perhaps relatively less stiff MCVN test machines.

International Comparison of Impact Verification Programs

The keys to achieving reproducible test machine and laboratory independent dynamic test results have been adequate attention to testing machine design and maintenance and strict adherence to standard test procedures. The means for ensuring that various Charpy test laboratories can generate laboratory independent test results are the four international Charpy machine certification programs (described by McCowan et. al. [3]). The Reference [3] study is a round robin conducted by the four Charpy certification laboratories. Our original interest in studying these data was rooted in examining the striker encoder/instrumented energy differences. However, as will be discussed, a very interesting finding was made as a result of this study.

Each of the four participants provided three energy levels of calibration specimens for the study so that there were 12 different specimen groups. Each participant received 25 specimens from each specimen group. Each participant tested 15 of each group using a 2 mm striker and the remaining 10 with an 8 mm striker. The certified energy levels ranged from 16.5 J to 258 J. Participant 4 did not provide certified values for their specimens due to there being too few specimens to apply their standard certification procedure and still provide specimens to the round robin. It was not explicitly stated by McCowan et. al. in their conclusions, but each participant was able to pass the certification standards for each specimen and striker combination for which certified values were determined. In drawing this conclusion, the ISO 148-3 requirements were applied to the specimens of participants 1 and 2, and ASTM requirements were applied to the specimens of participant 3. Since participant 4's specimens did not have certified values, their specimens were not considered in making this conclusion. If participant 4's average round robin test values for its own specimen groups were treated as the certified values, the conclusion would still be that all passed. Interestingly, if the tighter ASTM tolerances at low energies (±1.4 J or 1 ft-lb) were substituted for the ISO requirements (±2 J), two participants would have failed to match the certified values to within required limits on some low energy specimen groups. With the ASTM limits, participant 4's energies would have been too low on all three certified specimen/striker combinations of the low energy specimen groups 1 and 2 (-1.5 to -1.8 J vs. ±1.4 J limit). Participant 3's energy would have been too high (1.5 J vs. ±1.4 J limit) on the low energy specimen group 1.

NIST records on certification failures show that the low energy specimens are statistically the most likely to result in test machine certification failure. The results for all data-years combined shows a failure rate of 12.0 % for the low energy test, 8.6 % for the high energy test, and 9.7 % for the super high energy test. It is interesting to note that the low energy test shows the largest difference between C-hammer and U-hammer test machines, with the U-hammer test machines recording higher energies on average. However, the difference between the medians is only about 0.2 J. This value is lower than expected because C-hammer test machines experience less post-fracture test specimen/striker interaction. It is believed that the small difference in the medians is due to the fact that the majority of low energy test specimens exit the rear of the test machine which would tend to result in closer agreement between C and U hammers. The NIST records also show that failures at the low energy level are more often due to measuring energies that are too high relative to the certified value.

Participant 4's tendency to obtain energies below the certified value is counter to this trend. The information provided by McCowan et. al. [3] shows that Participant 4 used a 500 J capacity test machine while the rest of the participants used 300 to 350 J machines. It was speculated that the use of the higher energy capacity machine was the root cause of the lower measured energies for the low energy specimens. The basis for this conjecture was the assumption that the higher capacity machine, due to its larger mass and stiffness, results in less residual vibrational energy in the machine than the lower capacity machines.

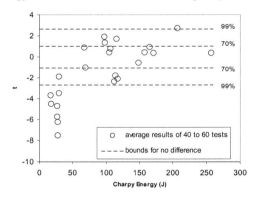

Fig. 1 Test statistic t for measured energy differences between the 500 J capacity machine and the average energies from the 300 to 350 J capacity machines.

The data from McCowan et. al. was subjected to a statistical analysis to determine the statistical significance of the above noted differences in energy measured by the 500 J machine of Participant 4 (relative to the 300/350 J machines of participants 1, 2, and 3). The large number of duplicate test specimens used in this study, combined with the small coefficient of variation of the specially manufactured calibration test specimens, makes the data from this study ideal for identifying and studying effects that are normally lost in the scatter due to small data sets and the inherent variability of Charpy test results. The fact that the data is obtained from perhaps the best maintained testing machines in the world should also not be overlooked. The average results from Participants 1, 2, and 3 were used as the basis for comparison with Participant 4's results. Means (E_{123}) and standard deviations (s_{123}) were computed for the combined data of participants 1, 2, and 3. Similarly, means (E_4) and standard deviations (s_4) were computed for Participant 4's test results. Then, for each test, the difference in the mean values ($E_4 - E_{123}$) and a pooled standard deviation (s_0) were computed. Fig. 1 shows test statistic t as a function of the energy level for the 24 data sets. Keep in mind that each point represents 60 Charpy tests with a 2 mm striker or 40 tests with an 8 mm striker, and the t test is applied to each of the 24 points (e.g., not to the mean trend of the combined 24 data sets). The statistical significance of the normalized energy differences (t) is determined by comparing to the expected statistical distribution of t if there was no effect of machine capacity on the measured energies (assumes normal distribution and random sampling). The horizontal dashed lines show the expected ranges of t for 70% and 99% of the t population if there is no energy difference. For Charpy energies above 40 J, it can be seen that the computed t values are reasonably consistent with the hypothesis that there is no machine capacity dependence. Below 40 J, the t values are significantly below the expected range and it is concluded that there is a very significant difference in the energies measured by the 500 J machine at low Charpy energy levels.

This statistical test has therefore shown that the -2% to -9% energy difference (average −6.2%) of the 500 J machine in the lower Charpy energy regime is not due to random effects. It was originally postulated that this systematic effect was due to residual vibrational energy. However, the accelerometer experiments described above and the numerical simulations of [1] could only explain differences of 1 to 2%. Calculations performed in this study using a simple two mass-two spring model of the specimen and striker system suggests that the energy difference can be explained in terms of a frequency shift in the applied load caused by a stiffer striker/hammer design in the 500 J machine. The frequency at which the specimen and striker vibrate during the initial elastic loading is affected by the specimen's stiffness (k_s) and mass (m_s) as well as the stiffness of the hammer assembly (k_h) according to $f = \left(1/2\pi\right)\sqrt{\left(k_s + k_h\right)/m_s}$. The mass of the hammer (m_h) is essentially infinite with respect to that of the specimen and therefore does not affect the frequency behavior of interest. As shown in Fig. 2, a 20% higher striker/hammer stiffness results in a 7% increase in the natural frequency of the specimen/striker/hammer system. The higher frequency results in the critical fracture load being reached at a smaller specimen displacement, which in turn, results in less absorbed energy to fracture the specimen. These findings not only suggest that the observed low energy measurements could be the result of the test machine design, but more importantly, that the test machine could be interacting with the specimen to materially affect the fracture behavior of the specimen.

SUMMARY

Numerical simulations and experimentation have demonstrated the potential for significant residual vibrational energy losses in Charpy test machines. For the 400 J U-hammer machine considered in this study, the estimated vibrational energy is on the order of 1% of the Charpy test energy. While the vibrational energy is significant, it is not sufficient to explain the differences in dial and instrumented energies observed when testing low energy specimens which exit the front of the test machine (on the order of 2% to 20%). These larger differences can be explained by the observed post-fracture striker/specimen interaction. Measurements performed during the current study showed that the post-fracture impacts with the striker add an average of 3 to 4.5 J to the dial energy. Thus, the post-fracture specimen-striker interactions can account for a large share of the observed energy differences between the dial and the instrumented striker energies. Other effects which add to the energy difference include: load cell load distribution effects; test machine inertial effects, striker inertial effects; and windage/friction correction of the dial.

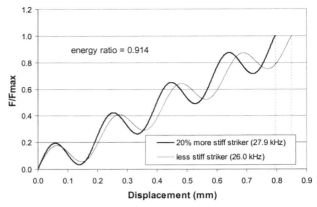

Fig. 2   **Results of two mass-two spring model calculations to determine the effect of stiffening the pendulum on the absorbed energy measurement.**

For the low energy specimens of the international round robin reported by McCowan et al. [3], the 500 J capacity machine gave energies that were 2 to 9% less than those measured using 300 to 350 J machines. It was originally postulated that this systematic effect was mostly due to residual vibrational energy n the test machine. However, experimental and numerical studies on test machine vibrational energy have been unable to explain more than a 1 to 2% difference. The simple two mass-two spring dynamic model of this study has shown that a 20% change in striker/hammer stiffness can lead to an absorbed energy difference of about 9% in low energy Charpy specimens. Therefore, it now appears that the observed 2 to 9% energy difference could be due to a stiffer striker/hammer design for the 500 J machine. The mechanism for this energy difference is that increasing the striker/hammer stiffness increases the frequency of the inertial peaks during the elastic portion of the specimen response. This higher frequency results in the critical fracture load being reached at a smaller displacement, which in turn, results in lower absorbed energy before fracture. These findings are potentially important because they suggest that the energy to fracture low energy specimens is significantly a function of the test machine design.

REFERENCES

1.   Manahan, M. P., Sr., and Stonesifer, R. B., **"The Difference Between Total Absorbed Energy Measured Using An Instrumented Striker and That Obtained Using an Optical Encoder,"** *Pendulum Impact Testing: A Century of Progress, STP 1380*, T. A. Siewert and M. P. Manahan, Sr., Eds., American Society for Testing and Materials, West Conshohocken, PA.

2.   Manahan, M. P., Sr., Martin, F. J., and Stonesifer, R. B., **"Results of the ASTM Instrumented/Miniaturized Round Robin Test Program,"** *Pendulum Impact Testing: A Century of Progress, STP 1380*, T. A. Siewert and M. P. Manahan, Sr. Eds., American Society for Testing and Materials, 2000.

3.   McCowan, C. N., Pauwels, J., Revise, G., and Nakano, H., **"International Comparison of Impact Verification Programs,"** *Pendulum Impact Testing: A Century of Progress, STP 1380*, T. A. Siewert and M. P. Manahan, Sr., Eds., American Society for Testing and Materials, West Conshohocken, PA, 2000.

From Charpy to Present Impact Testing
D. François and A. Pineau (Eds.)

DYNAMIC FRACTURE TOUGHNESS DETERMINATION USING PRECRACKED CHARPY SPECIMENS

D M Shuter

Health and Safety Laboratory, Broad Lane, Sheffield S3 7HQ, UK

ABSTRACT

The dynamic fracture behaviour of pre-cracked Charpy specimens and sub-size Charpy specimens, 5x10mm in cross-section, manufactured from a low alloy pressure vessel steel has been determined. Load-time data has been used to analyse the relationship between a piezoelectric force transducer mounted on the specimen striker and strain gauges mounted on the specimen surface near the crack tip over a range of impact velocities and temperatures.

At impact velocities below 2m/s, the load output from the piezoelectric force transducer compared favourably with those obtained from crack tip strain gauges. At higher velocities, the load-time curves (particularly the first load oscillation) obtained using the piezoelectric transducer were affected by the inertia of the specimen. An optimum cut off frequency was identified which was used to filter the load-time data. From the filtered data, fracture toughness (K_{ID}) values in good agreement with those based on the strain gauge data were determined.

Having developed a suitable test technique, impact tests on both specimen types were conducted at 3 different temperatures in the lower ductile to brittle transition temperature region and the results analysed in terms of a statistical cleavage fracture model. The results showed that the master curve approach was valid, in terms of the reference temperature (T_0), for both the 10 x10mm and 5x10mm specimens under dynamic test conditions.

KEYWORDS : Precracked Charpy, Small specimen test technique, Dynamic fracture toughness, Master curve, Reference Temperature

INTRODUCTION

An instrumented falling weight impact machine has been utilised to determine the dynamic fracture toughness (K_{ID}) of materials. It is capable of applying impact (dynamic) loads over a range of velocities (between 2 and 22 m/s) and energies up to 1kJ. Impact forces are measured using a piezoelectric force transducer (PFT) mounted in the load train.

The accuracy of the output from PFT is of paramount importance when determining the K_{ID} of a material - unfortunately, however, there are problems which complicate matters when using such a device. Firstly, it is positioned somewhat remotely from the specimen under test (particularly when conducting dynamic 3-point bend tests); and secondly, when conducting high velocity impact tests in excess of 1-2m/s, inertial effects can seriously affect the PFT output - particularly the first load oscillation, which is utilised to calculate the K_{ID}.

The objectives of the current work were twofold :

(i) To conduct impact tests on precracked Charpy specimens (at various impact velocities and temperatures) and determine the accuracy of the piezoelectric force transducer by comparing the transducer load outputs with those obtained from strain gauges mounted on the specimen in the vicinity of the crack tip; and

(ii) To determine whether current quasi-static small specimen 'Master Curve' test techniques (such as that outlined in the ASTM standard E-1921) [1], may be used to determine the effects of higher loading rates and specimen size on the reference temperature, T_0.

EXPERIMENTAL

Tests on Strain Gauged Specimens

A number of 10x10mm and 10x5mm (in cross-section) Charpy 'V' notch three-point bend specimens were manufactured from a 50mm thick ferritic steel plate to BS 1501. Specimens were fatigue pre-cracked to a depth of 5mm (a/W = 0.5) using a servo-hydraulic fatigue machine.

In order to determine the accuracy of the piezoelectric force transducer, tests were conducted on an instrumented falling weight impact machine under 3 point bend loading conditions with impact forces measured using two techniques:

(i) a PFT mounted just behind the striker mass. The load-displacement behaviour obtained could then be analysed, allowing the material characteristics under dynamic loading to be assessed. Since measuring the load-line displacement on a three point bend specimen is not a simple task, the displacement calculated from the acceleration was used as a close approximation; and

(ii) a strain gauge attached to the pre-cracked sample. Strain gauging was carried out in accordance with the draft proposed standard for testing pre-cracked Charpy specimens to determine K_{ID}, J_{ID} and CTOD [2]. Using this method, the strain gauge was mounted on the specimen in the vicinity of the crack tip, with the leading edge positioned ~1mm from the crack plane, using cyanoacrylate adhesive. Using a separate software-based high speed logging facility and a 500kHz amplifier (connected to the gauge via a quarter bridge configuration), it was possible to log the crack tip load-time behaviour at a speed of ~400kHz, i.e. 20000 points in 50 milliseconds [3].

Prior to testing the strain gauges were calibrated under quasi-static bending loading conditions (in the elastic regime) using a servohydraulic machine. Loads were applied up to the maximum pre-cracking load, allowing a calibration record of the strain gauge amplifier output against the applied load (or force) to be obtained for each specimen. The average of four loading-unloading calibrations was obtained for each specimen and then extrapolated to higher loads.

Impact tests were conducted at 1,2,5 and 10m/s, at 20°C and -40°C. The strain gauge application and calibration procedure has been shown to yield an accurate measurement of the load experienced by the specimen in the vicinity of the crack tip, even at higher velocities (>2m/s). [4,5,6]. It should be noted, however, that once the strain gauge exhibits any plastic strains, the calibration and therefore the test becomes invalid.

Determination of Reference Temperature, T_0

In order to determine the effects of higher loading rates and specimen size on the reference temperature, T_0, impact tests (using a velocity of ~1m/s to minimise inertial effects) were conducted on precracked 10x10mm and 10x5mm specimens, again using the instrumented falling weight impact machine. In all cases, the loads were measured using the PFT. Double integration of the load and drop mass data and thus the acceleration allowed the displacement to be obtained for each test. For comparison, 3 point bend tests were carried out on both types of specimen, under displacement-controlled quasi-static conditions in accordance with ASTM E1921-97 [1] (utilising a ramp rate of ~ 0.5mm/min).

Tests were performed at three temperatures in the lower ductile to brittle transition region, with load-time and load versus load-line displacement data being recorded for each test. Specimen temperature was controlled using an environmental chamber cooled by a liquid nitrogen spray and monitored in the vicinity of the crack tip, using a calibrated thermocouple. The test temperature was controlled within ±1°C. Upon completion of each test, specimens were broken open allowing the initial fatigue crack and any ductile crack extension to be measured. The critical (total) J integral at cleavage was then calculated based on the averaged crack length and the area under the load-displacement curve. Elastic-plastic fracture toughness, K_{JC}, values were then determined in accordance with the ASTM standard [1]. Each data set (corresponding to a specimen geometry, test temperature and loading rate) was then analysed, using the procedures outlined in ASTM E1921-97 [1] to give the reference temperature, T_0.

RESULTS AND DISCUSSION

K_{ID} Measurements - Strain Gauge and Piezoelectric Force Transducer Data

Load-time graphs were obtained from each test, examples of which are shown in Fig 1. From the load–time plots it was possible to determine the fracture force, F_{cd} or the force to cause yielding, F_y. Usually, in accordance with the ESIS proposed test method [2], if the drop in the force-time curve (F_{cd}) is not clear then J_{ID} or CTOD methods of analysis should be utilised. During the current study, as only a comparison of PFT and strain gauge data was required, F_{cd} was taken to be where the onset of plasticity occurred (see Fig 1), which enabled a measure of

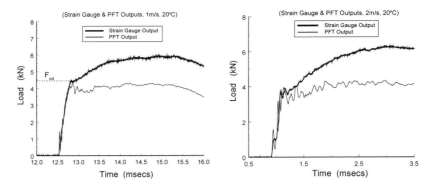

Fig 1 Examples of Load-Time Graphs Obtained at Impact Velocities of 1 and 2m/s

the toughness (K_{ID}) to be obtained using the equation :

$$K_{ID} = \frac{F_{cd} \cdot s}{B \cdot W^{1/2}} \cdot f(a/W) \qquad (1)$$

where F_{cd} = fracture load or force (kN)

                     s = span (= 4W)

                     B = specimen thickness (mm)

                     W = specimen width (mm)

                     a = pre-crack length (mm)

                     f(a/W) = compliance function for a 3 point bend sample

Following each test, the specimens were opened and the pre-crack length (a) measured using a nine-point average method to allow for crack tip bowing. This value was then used in determining f(a/W) in equation (1) above.

At higher impact velocities, the first load oscillation obtained from unfiltered PFT data depends primarily on the inertia of the specimen and not the toughness. It is clear from the current results (shown for example in Fig 1), however, that inertial effects do not significantly affect the load-displacement characteristics at impact velocities below ~2m/s. Above 2m/s, however, filtering of the data may be necessary in order to obtain a closer approximation of F_{cd} and therefore K_{ID}.

From the results of a spectral analysis of the transducer data, it was possible to determine a suitable cut off frequency which could then be used to filter the data - in the present case 5kHz. A low pass two pole Butterworth filter with a cut off frequency of 5kHz was applied to the transducer data obtained for a number of impact velocities [3] - an example of which is shown in Fig 2 (for a test conducted at 5m/s, at 20°C). It is evident from these results that suitable filtering of the data enables a better approximation of F_{cd} (and therefore K_{ID}).

Figure 3 shows a plot of K_{ID} (obtained from PFT, strain gauge and 5kHz filtered PFT data), against impact velocity at 20°C. It is evident that by utilising an appropriate level of filtering, a close approximation of K_{ID}, even for data obtained at higher velocities (>2m/s), may be

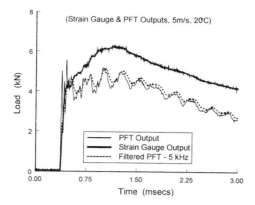

Fig 2 Effect of Filtering on Load-Time Behaviour

determined from the PFT data, eliminating the need for strain gauging at room temperature. At lower temperatures, however, toughness values derived from original PFT, strain gauge and filtered PFT data are all subject to a considerable amount of scatter, even at the lowest impact velocities - in contrast to the results obtained at 20°C. The variability in the amount of ductility exhibited in the load-time curve characteristics obtained at 1m/s and at -40°C seems to suggest that these low temperature tests were conducted in the transition region and not lower shelf.

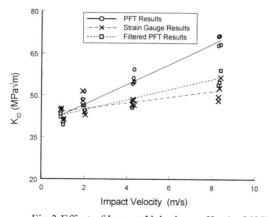

Fig 3 Effect of Impact Velocity on K_{ID} (at 20°C)

T_0 Determination and the Master Curve Technique

Table 1 summarises the T_0 and median K_{JC} values (corrected for 1T specimen equivalence) obtained for each of the different specimen geometry/loading rate/temperature data sets. Censored K_{JC} values, averaged T_0 values and associated static and dynamic master curves obtained from 10x10mm specimens are shown in Fig 4. Similar data are shown in Fig 5 for the 10x5mm single edge notch bend (SENB) specimens.

Table 1 . Summary of reference temperatures (T₀) and censored K_{JC} (median corrected for 1T equivalence) values obtained for the various specimen geometry/load rate/temperature data sets

Specimen Geometry	Loading Conds.	Test Temp. (°C)	Reference Temperature T_0 (°C)	Med. K_{JC} (1T) (MPa√m)	St. Dev. (Weibull Dist.)	Number of Valid Data Points
10x10	Quasi-Static	-120	-113.5	91.8	20.19	6/10
		-125	-123.1	97.5	21.78	6/11
		-135	-113.9	76.9	15.99	8/8
5x10	Quasi-Static	-125	-120.4	93.9	20.77	6/14
		-135	-120.5	85.5	18.45	6/9
		-145	-103.6	61.1	13.10	8/8
10x10	Dynamic	-35	9.4	60.0	11.23	12/12
		-40	-6.5	67.0	13.19	7/7
		-50	-1.4	56.0	10.19	10/10
5x10	Dynamic	-45	14.1	52.8	9.18	9/9
		-50	3.6	55.3	9.88	10/10
		-60	4.4	51.0	8.57	10/10

Note : M= 30 used for censoring K_{JC} data;
Standard deviation of the fitted Weibull distribution based on a Weibull slope, m = 4 and K_{min} = 20 MPa√m [1].

Effect of Loading Rate. It is evident that for 10x10mm and 5x10mm specimens, dynamic loading is responsible for a shift in the average reference temperature (T₀) of between 118 and 123°C, respectively (see Figs 4 and 5). The dynamic T₀ values obtained appear to be very consistent, over the range of temperatures considered here, with all data lying within the 95% confidence limits. However, it should be noted that some K_{JC} results obtained under quasi-static loading conditions lie outside the 5% tolerance bounds - possibly due to the fact that the test temperatures chosen here were very close to the lower shelf, which increases the uncertainty in determining T₀. In order to circumvent this problem, a larger number of tests would be necessary.

The effect of increasing constraint by testing precracked Charpy-type specimens using higher loading rates has been investigated by Joyce [7]. He conducted a number of tests using a range of loading rates and observed that for a rate of 380mm/s (~ 3 times slower than the current tests), a shift in T₀ of ~30°C could be achieved. Both the results of Joyce [7] and the current results suggest that the shift in the ductile-brittle transition temperature (DBTT) curve is strongly dependent on loading rate. It is concluded that the Master curve technique developed for data obtained under quasi-static loading conditions, may be applied to data obtained at higher loading rates.

Effect of Specimen Size. Again, from Figs 4 and 5, it is clear that the effect of specimen size on the determination of T₀ values is negligible, for this type of material. Under quasi-static loading conditions, the average T₀ values obtained for both 10x10mm and 5x10mm specimens are within 1°C. Even under dynamic loading conditions, the average T₀ values obtained for the two specimen sizes are within 6°C. Lee et al [8] suggest that for reactor pressure vessel steels, this does not appear to be the case for the material considered here. The applicability of the Master curve technique in determining T_0 values for smaller 5x5mm SENB specimens is currently under investigation.

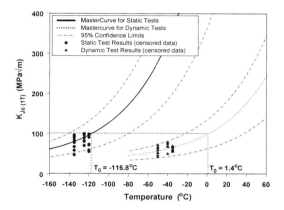

Fig 4 Effect of Loading Rate on T_0 and Master Curve (10x10mm specimens)

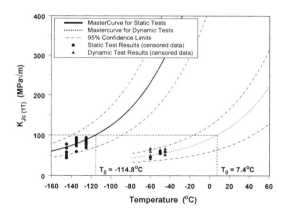

Fig 5 Effect of Loading Rate on T_0 and Master Curve (5x10mm specimens)

CONCLUSIONS

At room temperature, dynamic fracture toughness values (K_{ID}) derived from the piezoelectric force transducer and strain gauge data are similar at impact velocities less than 2m/s. At higher velocities K_{ID} values based on the transducer data are significantly affected by inertial effects (which affect the determination of F_{cd} from the first load oscillation).

In order to reduce inertial effects at higher impact velocities, the PFT data may be filtered using a suitable cut-off frequency, allowing a closer estimate of K_{ID} to be obtained without the use of strain gauges, particularly when working at higher temperatures. This would allow dynamic fracture toughness testing to be conducted quickly and cheaply over a range of impact velocities.

The current data seems to suggest that at -40°C, this material is operating in the transition region, which will ultimately cause large variations in the determination of K_{ID} values. However, on the upper shelf (at 20°C), the strain gauge and filtered PFT data collected at room temperature are very similar.

There appears to be little or no effect of specimen size/geometry on T_0 determination, under static or dynamic loading conditions, for this particular steel.

The shift in the DBTT curve is strongly dependent on loading rate for both 10x10 and 10x5 SENB specimens, but the Master curve technique developed for data obtained under quasi-static loading conditions, may be applied to data obtained at higher loading rates.

ACKNOWLEDGEMENTS

This work was funded by the UK Health and Safety Executive. Special thanks are due to Mr J T Dutton and Dr J W Hobbs for their help in the development of the master curves.

REFERENCES

1.   ASTM E-1921 (1997). Standard Test Method for Determination of Reference Temperature, T_0, for Ferritic Steels in the Transition Range. American Society for Testing and Materials, E-1921-97.

2.   ESIS Proposed Standard Methods for Instrumented Pre-cracked Charpy Impact Testing of Steels - Draft 7 (1997). Combined K_{IC}, J_{ID} and CTOD Tests Methods. ESIS Subcommittee on Testing at Intermediate Strain Rates (TC5).

3.   Shuter, D.M. (1999). Comparison of Load Measurement Techniques Used in Dynamic Fracture Toughness Tests. HSL Report MM/99/14.

4.   MacGillivray, H.J. and Cannon, D. F. (1990). ASTM Seminar on Rapid Load Fracture Testing, San Francisco.

5.   Giovanola, J.H.J. (1986). Metals Handbook. 9th Edition, 8, pp 271-275.

6.   Mall, S., Kobayashi, A.S. and Loss, F.J. (1980). ASTM STP 711, pp 70-85.

7.   Joyce, J.A. (1998). in : Small Specimen Test Techniques. ASTM STP 1329. pp 253-273.

8.   Lee, B. S., Hong, J.H., Yang,W.J., Huh, M.Y. and Chi, S.H. (2000). International Journal of Pressure Vessels and Piping, **77**, pp 599 - 604.

From Charpy to Present Impact Testing
D. François and A. Pineau (Eds.)

USE OF INSTRUMENTED CHARPY IMPACT TESTS FOR THE DETERMINATION OF FRACTURE TOUGHNESS VALUES

H.-W. Viehrig, J. Boehmert, J. Dzugan

Forschungszentrum Rossendorf e.V., Institute for Safety Research,
P.O. Box 51019, 01314 Dresden, Germany

ABSTRACT

The Master Curve concept (MC) allows to quantify the variation of fracture toughness with the temperature throughout the ductile-to-brittle transition region. Limit curves of fracture toughness for defined failure probabilities and a reference temperatures can be determined using this method. Thus, fracture mechanical values can be supplied for an integrity assessment of structural components.

The paper links MC concept and Charpy-V impact test to determine dynamic fracture mechanical parameters of ASTM A 533 B Cl. 1 nuclear pressure vessel steel. The MC based reference temperature, T_0^{dy}, is measured under impact loading using the instrumented impact test. The change in T_0^{dy} is determined as a function of the thickness position of a steel plate, and compared with the quasi-static reference temperature, T_0^{st}, and the Charpy-V transition temperature (TT). All three parameters simultaneously increase from the surface to the middle of the steel plate. However, in the middle section of the plate, T_0^{dy} is in average approximately 88 K higher than TT and 88 K higher than T_0^{st}. The results show that the MC concept is applicable for the fracture mechanical characterisation of material with different microstructure using Charpy size specimens.

KEYWORDS: instrumented impact testing, cleavage failure, fracture toughness, Master Curve, ductile-to-brittle transition, reference temperature, reactor pressure vessel steel

INTRODUCTION

The most essential progress in the Charpy-V impact test methodology was the pendulum instrumentation by force and displacement gauges. This allows more information to be obtained from the simple, quick and very efficient test. Above all, the instrumentation made it possible to use the impact pendulum for dynamic fracture mechanics testing and, thus to apply for the structural integrity assessment. In the range of lower shelf and the lower ductile-to-brittle transition (DBT) region, J-integral-based fracture toughness values, K_{Jc}, can be determined at the onset of cleavage crack initiation. The onset of cleavage fracture appears on the measured load versus time trace as a load drop. These K_{Jc} data have the drawback to be very restricted by the maximum K_{Jc} measuring capacity of the standard Charpy size specimen. The Master Curve (MC) concept developed by Wallin [1,2] enables the evaluation of K_{Jc} data determined with small Charpy size specimens. The MC quantifies the variation of fracture toughness with the temperature within the lower DBT region by providing a reference temperature, T_0, and limit curves of fracture toughness for defined failure probabilities. That directly relates the reference toughness curve to the measured K_{Jc} values.

The MC procedure was recently standardised in ASTM E 1921-97 "Standard Test Method for Determination of Reference Temperature, T_0, for Ferritic steels in the Transition Range". The standard is defined for quasi-static loading conditions. However, the use of the MC method for dynamic test is obvious. This paper presents such application using the instrumented Charpy impact test. The variation of the dynamic reference temperature, T_0^{dy}, through the thickness of a reactor pressure vessel (RPV) steel plate is determined. The results are compared with quasi-static reference temperatures, T_0^{st}, and Charpy-V transition temperatures, TT.

FRACTURE TOUGHNESS AND MASTER CURVE CONCEPT

The execution of tests and the calculation of dynamic toughness data of pre-cracked Charpy specimens have not yet ruled by any official standard of international liability. However, there are procedures and draft standards developed by the Electric Power Research Institute (EPRI [3,4] and ESIS TC5 Working Group [5], respectively. The J integral at the onset of cleavage fracture is determined in ASTM E 1921-97 in analogy to the standards ISO/DIS 12135 "Metallic Materials – Unified Method of Test for the Determination of Quasi-static Fracture Toughness" and ASTM E1820 "Standard Test Method for Measurement of Fracture Toughness". The absorbed impact energy is calculated from the area under the load-displacement curve up to the onset of cleavage fracture. This energy value contains some contributions which are not related to the fracture of the specimen. The true specimen energy at cleavage failure, E_W, is determined according to a procedure proposed by EPRI [3, 4]. If fracture occurs before general yielding E_W can be calculated from the measured maximum load P_{max} according to Eq. (1). Acceptable load values P_{max} are obtained when the inertia oscillations have been sufficiently dampened after 3-times of the free oscillation (3τ) [3-5].

$$E_W = \frac{C_{ND} \cdot (P_{max})^2}{2 \cdot E \cdot B_N} \qquad (1)$$

where

B_N: specimen net thickness
C_{ND}: non-dimensional specimen compliance for Charpy size SEN(B) specimens tabled in [3]
E: Young's modulus
P_{max}: maximum load in kN

For general yield fracture, the true specimen energy up to maximum load, E_W, is obtained by correcting the whole absorbed energy, W_M according to Eq. (2) [3].

$$E_W = W_M - \left[\frac{P_{max}^2}{2} \cdot (C_T - \frac{C_{ND}}{E \cdot B}) \right] \qquad (2)$$

where

W_M: energy absorbed up to the point of maximum load including contributions due to the test system
C_T: total specimen compliance, calculated at general yield and corrected for tup velocity decrease

$$C_T = \frac{V_0 \cdot t_{GY}}{P_{GY}} - \frac{V_0{}^2 \cdot t_{GY}{}^2}{8 \cdot E_0} \tag{3}$$

where

E_0:   initial impact energy of the pendulum
P_{GY}:   general yield load
t_{GY}:   time up to P_{GY}
V_0:   initial impact velocity

The measured J integral values at brittle failure, J_c, are transformed into elastic plastic stress intensity factors K_{Jc} using Eq. (4).

$$K_{Jc} = \sqrt{E \cdot J_c} \tag{4}$$

The MC approach describing the fracture of ferritic structural steels in the lower DBT region is based on deriving the cleavage fracture initiation as a statistical phenomenon. Cleavage fracture is modelled by a 3-parameter Weibull distribution. Cleavage fracture toughness values were used to evaluate the temperature dependence of the toughness within the lower DBT region. The temperature dependence of a median J integral-based cleavage fracture toughness, K_{Jc}, follows equation:

$$K_{Jc-1T} = 30 + 70 \cdot \exp \cdot \left[0.019 \left(T - T_0\right)\right] \tag{5}$$

where $K_{Jc-1T(med)}$ is the fracture toughness for a fracture probability of 50% adjusted to an equivalent value for a 1T (thickness 25,4 mm) specimen,
   T is the test temperature and
   T_0 is the reference temperature at which the $K_{JC-1T(med)}$ value is equal to $100 \ \text{MPa.m}^{1/2}$.

The concept considers size effect and statistical variability in a simple way. The ASTM standard E 1921-97 specifically describes the measurement of the elastic plastic parameters K_{Jc} and the   evaluation of the MC and its confidence intervals using these K_{Jc} values. The maximum K_{Jc} capacity of a specimen is given by:

$$K_{Jc(limit)} = \sqrt{\frac{E \cdot b_0 \cdot \sigma_{ys}}{30}} \tag{6}$$

where σ_{ys} is the material yield strength at the test temperature and
   b_0 is the initial specimen ligament.

The selection of the test temperature to obtain a sufficient number of valid K_{Jc} values is problematic. ASTM E 1921-97 recommends to measure K_{Jc} at temperature at which the median K_{Jc} value is close to $100 \ \text{MPa.m}^{1/2}$. This is only realisable in a iterative process by testing at different temperatures. As a consequence, the results of the preliminary tests for finding the appropriate test temperature are not taken into account. This drawback is avoided by a multi-temperature method that has been adopted in the reviewed ASTM E 1921 standard by the ASTM Committee E-28. The multi-temperature method considers the fact that T_0 should be relatively independent of the test temperature. K_{Jc} values spread over a restricted temperature range, namely $T_0 \pm 50$ K, can be used for the T_0 determination.

In ferritic steels the initiation of the cleavage fracture highly scatters due to the metallurgical heterogeneities. Thus, the risk exists to obtain K_{Jc} values above the validity criterion of Eq. (6) in particular when small Charpy size specimens are tested. Therefore the number of K_{Jc} values sufficient for the determination of a valid T_0 is fixed in reviewed ASTM E 1921 by the criterion given in Eq. (7)

$$\sum_{i=1}^{r} n_i \geq 1 \qquad\qquad (7)$$

where

n_i is the weight factor per specimen, as a function of $T_i - T_0$ it attains values 1/6 to 1/8

r is the number of valid K_{Jc} values

T_i is the test temperature of the specimen.

MATERIAL AND SPECIMENS

The investigated material is a rolled plate of the IAEA reference material JRQ (ASTM A533B Class 1 steel). Table 1 contains the chemical composition and the strength parameters.

The block with a thickness of 225 mm was cut into 20 layers over the thickness using an electroerosive cutting machine. Alltogether, specimen sets from the 20 different layers were tested. Each set consisted of up to 15 specimen providing sufficient number of K_{Jc} values for the valid MC according to standard requirements.

Table 1: Chemical composition (wt.%) and strength parameters of IAEA JRQ RPV steel

C	Si	Mn	Cr	Mo	Ni	P	Cu	S	Al
0.18	0.24	1.42	0.12	0.51	0.84	0.02	0.14	0.007	0.02

Tensile yield strength:	477 ± 10 MPa
Ultimate tensile strength:	630 ± 3 MPa

The microstructure of the plate varies through the thickness. At the surface there are both lower bainite and martensite. In the middle region heterogeneously composed upper bainite together with reticularly arranged martensite are visible. The reticularly arranged martensitic structure becomes more pronounced with the distance from the surface and could be explained by segregation.

Precracked and side grooved (20%) Charpy size specimens (TL orientation) were tested.

TEST METHODS

The impact tests were carried out on an instrumented 300 J impact-pendulum. The test conditions are presented in Table. 2.

Table 2: Test conditions

	Initial impact velocity V_0	Initial impact energy E_0
Charpy-V test	5,5 m/s	300 J
Fracture toughness test	2,8 m/s	78 J

The temperatures for the fracture toughness testing were selected corresponding to the Charpy-V based 28 J DBTT. The tests were performed at this temperatures. The further test temperatures were chosen corresponding to the feed-back from the first test results and so that a wide temperature range was covered. As main criteria the weight factor demanded by Eq. (7) has to be fulfilled. The measured J integral values at brittle failure were transformed into elastic

plastic stress intensities K_{Jc}. The K_{Jc} evaluation was performed according to multi-temperature procedure of the reviewed ASTM E 1921 standard as follows:
- Check of the measured K_{Jc} values whether they fulfil the validity criterion Eq. (6). K_{Jc} values above the validity criterion were censored on the validity limit.
- Adjustment of the measured K_{Jc} values to a specimen size 1T (25.4 mm). K_{Jc} values below 50 MPa.m$^{1/2}$ were not size adjusted.
- Calculation of T_0 according to the multi-temperature method including all valid and censored values.
- Calculation of the Master Curve and the tolerance bounds.

RESULTS AND DISCUSSION

The specimens were tested in the range from the lower shelf cleavage fracture, Fig. 1 a), up to ductile crack initiation followed by cleavage rupture, Fig. 1 b). Fig. 1a shows the time up to cleavage failure is lower than 3-times of the free specimen oscillation (3τ) and thus, the maximum load is influenced by inertial oscillations. In these cases the maximum load for true impact energy calculation according to Eq. (1) were corrected to half the value of the oscillation before failure. For the specimens failed after general yield (Fig. 1b) the true impact energy is calculated with Eq. (2).

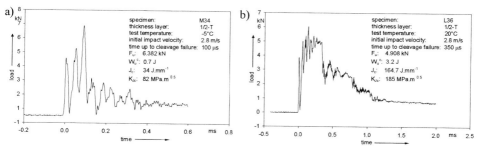

Fig. 1: Impact test records of specimens tested in the linear elastic (a) and elastic plastic (b) range

Fig. 2 shows the K_{Jc} values obtained from specimens from different thickness positions versus the difference of test temperature and T_0 evaluated for the respective test series (specimens from different thickness layers).

The scatter of the measured K_{Jc} values is large and is supposed to be connected with the reticularly arranged martensitic structure in the interior range of the plate. It is obvious that the dynamic K_{Jc} values do not strictly follow MC valid for quasi-static loading. The K_{Jc} values are remarkably higher than the MC for $(T-T_0) > 0$ and lower for $(T-T_0) < 0$. The deviation at lower temperatures can be caused by the application of the EPRI-procedure which, perhaps, the small amounts of the impact energy at cleavage failure of the specimen needed for the MC evaluation overcorrected. Really, the K_{Jc} values calculated with the uncorrected impact energy W_M follow the MC up to the validity limit of Eq. (6). Results from Finland measured with Charpy size SENB specimens of JRQ material show, that the non-corrected dynamic K_{Jc} values follow the course of the MC and lie within the 5 % and 95 % scatter bands [7]. A further difference to the results presented here probably comes from the fact that the K_{Jc} values were determined at higher temperatures. Thus, a large number of censored K_{Jc} values in [7] were included into the T_0 calculation. Recently published results [8] show that in this case lower T_0 are received.

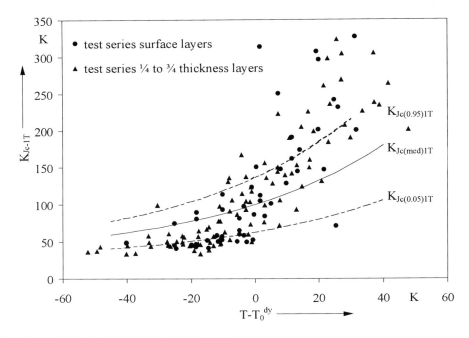

Fig. 2 Dynamic fracture toughness and MC

Further the Finnish results do not fulfil the weight factor of Eq. (7). Compared with the results presented here the difference between T_0^{dy} and T_0^{st} in [7] is substantially smaller ranking from 30 K to 40 K.

The influence of the loading rate on the T_0 value was also investigated using previously measured quasi-static data [6]. Fig. 3 shows the dependence of Charpy-V TT and reference temperatures, for quasi-static, T_0^{st}, and dynamic, T_0^{dy}, loading on the thickness of the plate. Obviously the trend curves have the same shape. The reference temperature increases between surface and ¼, respectively ¾, of the plate thickness and is almost constant in the middle section. The T_0^{dy} values are higher compared with the T_0^{st} values. For the middle section mean values of –70°C for T_0^{st}, of -21°C for TT_{41J} and of +18°C for T_0^{dy} were determined. Thus, there is a difference between quasi-static and dynamic reference temperature of 88°C. For the surface layers the differences between the DBTT's T_0^{st}, T_0^{dy} and TT_{41J}, are about 10 K lower compared with the middle section. Fig. 4 shows the correlation between the DBTT's (T_0^{dy} - T_0^{s} and T_0^{dy} - TT_{41J}). The difference in the DBTT's between surface and middle layers is one reason for the large scatter bands in the Fig. 4. The scatter of the Charpy-V TT is larger than the scatter of the fracture mechanical based reference temperatures. This fact is probably not caused by the difference in loading velocity, but rather by the fact, that the Charpy-V DBTT criteria is not clear defined by a fracture pattern. Basically correlations of this quality are not applicable in the safety assessment. However, the scatter bands are to be related to the heterogeneity of the material and cannot be generalised.

Moreover, the increase of the yield strength due to dynamic loading caused that the K_{Jc} measuring capacity of the Charpy size SENB specimen is about 30% higher in comparison with the quasi-static loading. The scatter of the measured K_{Jc} values led to the fact that the minimum number of 6 specimens, indicated in ASTM E 1921, was not sufficient for the determination of the valid T_0. A crucial point for the determination of valid K_{Jc} values is the

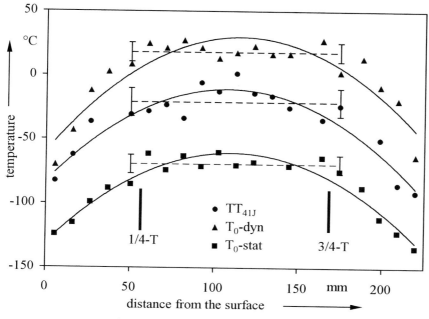

Fig. 3   DBTT's TT_{41J}, T_0^{dy} and T_0^{st} versus distance from the surface of the JRQ steel plate

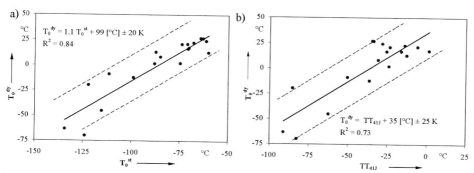

Fig. 4   Correlation between a) reference temperatures T_0^{dy} and T_0^{st} and b) reference temperatures T_0^{dy} and Charpy-V TT_{41J}

selection of the test temperature. As Fig. 4b shows an orientation on the Charpy-V TT's includes high inaccuracies. The application of the MC multi-temperature method has the advantage that wider range of the material transition behaviour can be covered and specimens tested at different temperatures are involved in the analysis.

CONCLUSION

Dynamic testing of various thickness layer across the plate thickness of the reactor pressure vessel steel provides information about the applicability of the Master Curve (MC) method.

The suitability of the MC to describe material behaviour in ductile-to-brittle transition region under dynamic loading conditions was proved.

The K_{Jc} values determined under dynamic loading do not follow the course of the MC designed for quasi-static conditions. On the basis of the test results a direct application of the quasi-static MC concept to dynamic conditions could not be verified. There is in evidence that an effect of the correction procedure for the determination of the true absorbed impact energy exists. The comparison with further quasi-static [6] and dynamic [7] K_{Jc} values obtained on the same material confirms the doubts against a simple, unmodified transfer to dynamic conditions. The results suggest further investigations with a broader spectrum of material. Further the influence of "censored" values should be investigated in more detail.

The dynamic tests confirmed the results of quasi-static tests related to relatively high material heterogeneity between the surface and the middle section caused by the production technology of the plate. The variation of the reference temperature T_0 across the plate thickness was the same for both loading conditions. The reference temperatures, T_0^{dy}, determined during impact loading are approximately 90 K higher than the temperatures corresponding to quasi-static loading.

REFERENCES

1.	Wallin, K. (1997). Small Specimen Fracture Toughness Characterisation - State of the Art and Beyond. In Proceedings Advances in Fracture Research, ICF 9, B.L. Karihaloo, Y.W. Mai, M.I. Ripley, R.O. Ritchie (Eds.), Amsterdam, pp. 2333-2344.

2.	Wallin, K. (1998). Master curve analysis of ductile to brittle transition region fracture toughness round robin data - The EURO fracture toughness curve. VTT Publications 367. VTT Espoo, Finland.

3.	McCornell, P., Server, W. L. (1980). EPRI Instrumented Impact Test Procedures. In Proceedings C.S.N.I. Specialists Meeting on Instrumented Precracked Charpy Testing EPRI NP-2102-LD, Prepared by Electric Power Research Institute, Ed. by R. A. Wullaert, Palo Alto, USA, pp. 1-1 to 1-22.

4.	Ireland, D. R. (1980). A Review of the Proposed Standard Method of Test for Impact Testing Precracked Charpy Specimen of Metallic Materials. In Proceedings C.S.N.I Specialists Meeting on Instrumented Precracked Charpy Testing. EPRI NP-2102-LD. Prepared by Electric Power Research Institute, Ed. by R. A. Wullaert, Palo Alto, USA, pp. 1-23 to 1-63.

5.	Draft International Standard: ESIS, European Structure Integrity Society: Proposed Standard Methods for Instrumented Pre-cracked Charpy Impact Testing of Steels - Combined K_{Id}, J_{Id} and CTOD Tests Methods.

6.	Viehrig, H.-W.; Boehmert, J. (1999). Some Issuses by Using the Master Curve Concept In Proceedings of the 15th International Conference on Structural Mechanics in Reactor Technology, SMiRT-15,(S.P. Chang, Ed.), Vol. V. Seoul, Korea, August 15-20 1999, pp V-383 to V-390.

7.	Wallin, K. (1995). Summary of the IAEA/CRP3 Fracture Mechanical Results Proceedings of a Specialists Meeting Organized by the International Atomic Energy Agency and held in Espoo., Finland 23-26 October 1999, IWG-LMNPP-95/5, Volume II IAEA, Vienna, Austria.

8.	Tregoning, R. L., Joyce, J. A. (2002). Investigation of Censoring Limits for Cleavage Fracture Determination. Fourth Symposium on Small Specimen Test Techniques, to be published in ASTM STP 1405, M. A. Sokolov, J. D. Landes, and G. E. Lucas, Eds. American Society for Testing and Materials, West Conshohocken, PA.

From Charpy to Present Impact Testing
D. François and A. Pineau (Eds.)

DISCUSSION OF TESTING PROCEDURES FOR THE DETERMINATION OF THE TOUGHNESS PROPERTIES OF LASER WELDED JOINTS

Dipl.-Ing. M. Nagel*; Dr.-Ing. P. Langenberg**; Dr.-Ing. F. Lüder***; Prof. Dr.-Ing. W. Bleck*; Prof. Dr.-Ing. U. Dilthey***

*Department of Ferrous Metallurgy (IEHK), Aachen University of Technology, Intzestraße 1, 52062 Aachen, Germany
**Ingenieurbuero fuer Werkstofftechnik (IWT), Dennewartstraße 25, 52068 Aachen, Germany
***ISF-Welding Institute, Aachen University of Technology, Pontstraße 49, 52062 Aachen, Germany

ABSTRACT

Laser welding of metallic materials offers a lot of advantages to potential users, e.g. in the automotive industry. The high and concentrated heat input causes a very narrow joint with a martensitic microstructure. The distortion is low so that dressing is minimised. The process can be automated easily so that there is also an economical benefit.

But these advantages also cause problems due to the characterisation of the weld itself. The high hardness of the laser weld leads to a deviation of the crack from the weld into the base material in the Charpy-V tests. For this, the resulting values represent a mixture of the toughness properties of the base material and of the laser weld. A characterisation of the laser weld itself is not possible with the standard test procedure.

Thus, alternative test methods which enable the characterisation of the toughness properties of laser welded joints were investigated. Four test methods were included: side grooves, oversized specimens, specimens with longitudinal welds and three weld specimens.

The results of these investigations are presented in the paper and a conclusion for the use of the Charpy test for the characterisation of the toughness level of laser weldments is given.

KEYWORDS

Laser beam welding, crack path deviation, Charpy test, transition curve, structural steels, Mismatch

INTRODUCTION AND AIM

Laser welding of metallic materials offers a lot of advantages to potential users, e.g. in the automotive industry for thin metal sheets and in ship building for thick plates. The high and concentrated heat input causes a very narrow joint with a martensitic microstructure. The distortion is low so that dressing is minimised. The process can be automated which offers an economical benefit.

On the other hand some problems arise from the typical characteristics of the laser weld. The higher strength resulting from the martensitic microstructure and at the same time the relatively low toughness of the laser weld lead to a critical fracture behaviour in the lower shelf and the transition region and to a deviation of the crack from the weld into the base material at upper shelf temperatures in the Charpy test. Following, the resulting values represent a mixture of the toughness properties of the base material and of the laser weld. A characterisation of the toughness level of the laser weld relative to the typically applied qualification criteria for conventional welds with the standardised test procedure of the Charpy test is not possible.

The task of the department of Ferrous Metallurgy within the research project LASER 2000, a German project with 28 project partners, was to develop a testing procedure which enables the characterisation of the toughness properties of laser welded joints. The aim was to use existing standard testing methods and to vary the specimen geometry. Standard Charpy-V specimens with the notch located in the centre of the welded joint and specimens with side grooves, which were milled in the region of the laser weld on both sides of the specimen to force the crack straight through the weld metal, were tested. Several depths of side grooves between 10 and 40% of the specimen thickness were investigated to find out whether there is a degree of side grooving for which the crack no longer deviates.

INVESTIGATED MATERIALS

With the use of high power CO_2-lasers it's possible to join plates in thicknesses up to about 15 mm in one pass without filler wire. At the moment, the industrial use of lasers is in general limited to the joining of plates up to thicknesses of 10 mm. Thus, several plate thicknesses in the range of 6 – 15 mm were investigated to enhance the potential use of lasers in this thickness range. The choice of the investigated materials was based on steels, which are used for ship building and steel structures. Four different fine grained structural steels with yield strengths between 460 and 890 MPa and the higher-temperature structural steel 10CrMo9-10 were investigated. The microstructure of the steels is ferritic pearlitic, except of the steel S890Q, which has a martensitic-bainitic microstructure. The weld metal of all laser welds has a martensitic microstructure with a higher strength compared to the base material. The Mismatch ratio lies between 1,5 and 2,6.

INVESTIGATED SPECIMEN GEOMETRIES

In general, the testing of laser welded materials causes a lot of problems. In the Charpy test, a crack, which initiated in the weld metal, deviates into the base material at upper shelf temperatures, even if the standard notch of the specimen was located in the centre of the weld metal. As a consequence, the determination of the toughness properties of the laser weld is not the same measure as for a base metal specimen. Nevertheless it's important to determine the toughness level of the laser weld for the qualification of laser welds with respect to brittle and ductile component behaviour. To find an alternative for such a qualification, the geometry of the Charpy specimens was varied. Beside the testing of standardised specimens, specimens with side grooves of several depths were tested, Fig. 1 a).

The side grooves were milled in the laser weld to enhance the stress triaxiality in that region of the specimen and so to force the crack to grow straight through the weld metal. This strategy is recommended in different works and guidelines at the moment to determine the Charpy toughness of laser welded materials [1-3]. The aim of the variation in crack depth from 10% -

40% of the specimen thickness was to find a minimum side groove depth where crack path deviation can be avoided.

Alternatively, specimens with a greater thickness than the standardised specimens were tested. The specimens were side grooved as well, so that the remaining ligament after side grooving had the same dimensions as the standard specimens, Fig. 1 b).

Longitudinal specimens were extracted from the plate, so that the direction of the weld metal was longitudinal to the specimen length. Thus, crack path deviation is impossible, Fig. 1 c).

In addition, specimens with three parallel welds were tested. For this, two additional welds were brought in the plate on both sides of the normal weld to widen the weld metal artificially. This should avoid crack path deviation, Fig. 1 d).

From the plates in the thickness range from 6 – 10 mm, sub sized specimens, which are also fixed in the standard [4], were extracted for the determination of the Charpy toughness (ISO-V7.5, ISO-V5.0).

All these steps aimed at getting information about the toughness properties of the laser weld itself, and thus to enhance the potential use of laser welding even in safety relevant applications.

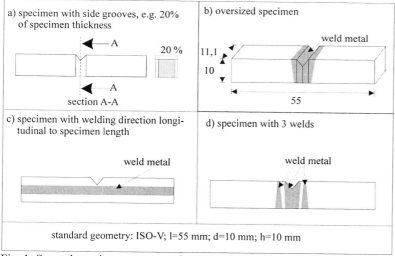

Fig. 1: Several specimen geometry for the Charpy test

RESULTS

The investigations on Charpy specimens, whose geometry was suited to the special requirements of the laser welded joint, showed that a characterisation of the laser weld is not possible even with an adjustment of the specimen geometry. The results of the testing of side grooved specimens showed that even a side grooving of the specimens of 40% of the specimen thickness does not help to avoid crack path deviation reliably, Fig. 2 a).

Moreover, by bringing in the side grooves, the distribution of the stresses in the cross section of the specimens is largely changed. The stress triaxiality is enhanced due to the notch and due to the smaller ligament, so that the test conditions cannot be compared with those of standard specimens.

For the specimens with the greater thickness compared to the standard specimens, crack path deviation at higher temperatures was observed as well, Fig. 2 b). The statements made for the sidegrooved standard ISO-V specimens are valid for these specimens as well.

For the longitudinal specimens, crack path deviation was avoided due to the fact, that the laser weld covers the whole specimen length. The disadvantage of this strategy is, that due to the very narrow laser weld (width in general 2 – 5 mm) the cross section of the Charpy specimen consists not only of weld metal but also of base material. Thus, the results are a mixture of the toughness properties of the laser weld and the base material properties, Fig. 2 c).

The results of the investigations on specimens with three welds show, that the toughness of the normal weld metal is influenced by the welding process of the other welds, the results scatter extremely, Fig. 2 d). Moreover, the process of bringing in two additional welds needs a lot of time, so that this strategy would not achieve any practical relevance.

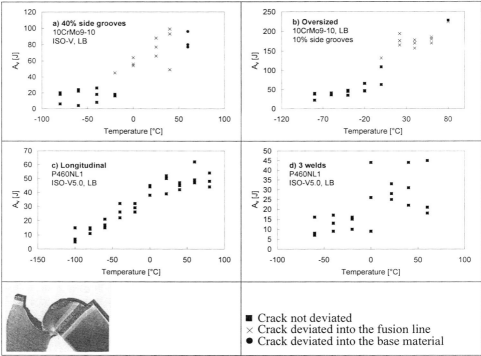

Fig. 2: A$_v$-T-curves for the different specimen geometries and ISO-V specimen with deviated crack

INTERPRETATION OF THE RESULTS

The results of the investigations show, that all strategies coupled with a change in specimen geometry of the ISO-V specimen are unsuitable for the characterisation of the weld metal. This allows the conclusion, that the Charpy test in its standardised form should still be used. The characterisation of the weld metal should then be done by a suitable interpretation of the transition curve with an explanation of the reasons for crack path deviation. For the interpretation of the curve it's necessary to explain what happens in the specimen during the test.

In the moment where the hammer peen hits the specimen, the specimen is loaded with a specified load. First the specimen behaves linear-elastic, it bends, and starting from the root of the notch elliptical fields of the same stresses are formed [5]. The stress grows until crack initiation, crack propagation and fracture of the specimen occurs.

Caused by the welding process the weld metal normally consists of a martensitic microstructure with a higher strength compared to the base material (Overmatch). Higher strength is in general equal to lower toughness of the weld metal. Crack initiation occurs, when the particular load exceeds the fracture-inducing stress. For the explanation of the crack deviation in the fusion line respectively in the base material in the Charpy test, the loading conditions and –stresses as well as the cleavage fracture stresses in the specimen are considered.

Locally, a Charpy specimen has two critical areas: the notch root, where cleavage fracture is expected, and the base material near to the weld metal, where plastic collapse can occur after exceeding the yield strength [6].

At low temperatures the Charpy specimens always fail brittle in the weld metal. This can be explained by regarding the temperature dependence of the yield strengths and the cleavage fracture stresses of the base material and the weld metal, Fig. 3. The temperature dependence of the yield strength is bigger than that of the cleavage fracture stress. The yield strength of the overmatched weld metal is higher than that of the base material, but the cleavage fracture stress of the weld metal is lower. Thus, the stresses resulting from the load applied by the hammer peen at low temperatures first exceed the cleavage fracture stress of the weld metal in the notch root, so that in this area the crack is initiated.

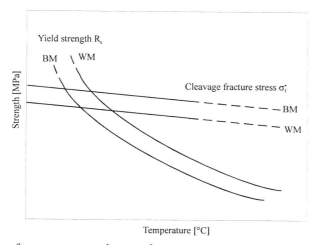

Fig. 3: Influence of temperature on cleavage fracture stress and yield strength

At higher temperatures, the yield strength of the base material can be exceeded due to its temperature dependence. The base material therefore already shows elastic-plastic behaviour while the weld metal still behaves linear elastic, Fig. 4.

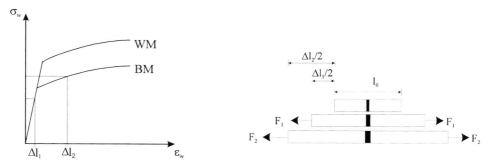

Fig. 4: Stress-strain curves of the weld metal and the base material

In this case, the failure of the specimen is determined by two conquering mechanisms: cleavage in the weld metal and plastic collapse in the base material [7-9].
The loading conditions in the fusion line are the most severe. Due to the vicinity to the centre of the specimen, this is the base material zone with the highest stresses. The constraint caused by the near weld metal is the highest, so that the triaxiality of the stress state is the highest as well. At the same time this part of the material has to compensate the low deformation of the weld metal, so that the strain also reaches a maximum. As a consequence, localised damage occurs in the microstructure near the fusion line. Consequently a crack initiating from the centre weld is likely to grow either in plane or into the pre-damaged base metal at the fusion line. This explains that both mechanisms occur in the transition region, Fig. 5.

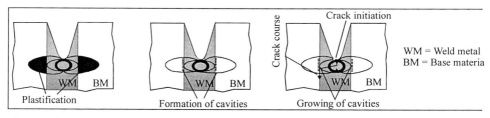

Fig. 5: Failure mechanisms at higher temperatures in the upper shelf

At higher test temperatures in the upper shelf, the yield strength of the base material decreases, Fig. 3. The plastic deformation rate of the base material increases accordingly and hence the material near to the fusion line is extremely pre-damaged. The crack initiating in the weld metal centre now grows directly into the base metal which explains the crack path deviation, Fig. 6.

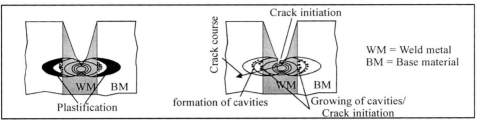

Fig. 6: Failure mechanism at very high temperatures

DISCUSSION AND CONCLUSION

Based on the considerations made in the previous chapter, the conclusion raises that the crack path deviation in the Charpy test must not be judged negative, but as a consequence of the specific mismatch-geometry combination of a laser weld. To use this observation for the qualification of laser welds a definition of additional transition temperatures describing the crack path deviation is proposed as follows.

The transition curves of the laser welds can be divided into three parts analogous to the base material (lower shelf, transition area and upper shelf), Fig. 7.

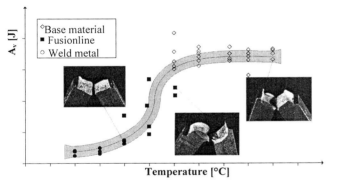

Fig. 7: Transition curve of laser weldments

In the lower shelf, the laser welded specimens all fail in a brittle manner in the weld metal due to the reasons explained in the previous chapter. The crack grows in plane. Only cleavage failure occurs with low energy values and a low scatter in the results. The transition area is characterised by a mixed fracture behaviour. At one temperature, specimens fail either in the weld metal, in the base material or in the fusion line. Consequently, the scatter in the results in the transition area is high. From a certain material-weldment dependent temperature crack path deviation is the typical fracture mechanism and such a limiting temperature $T_{CPD,100\%}$ above which CPD is 100% likely to occur is proposed as a typical measure for laser qualification procedures.

To define a measure for the brittle fracture avoidance it is recommended to select the T_{27J}-temperature. Fig. 8 shows results with a lower bound and a mean value curve. Assuming that the cracks initiating and running in plane always represent the lower toughness behaviour it is reasonable to define a minimum toughness level of 27 Joule at a required temperature for the qualification of laser welds to avoid brittle fracture.

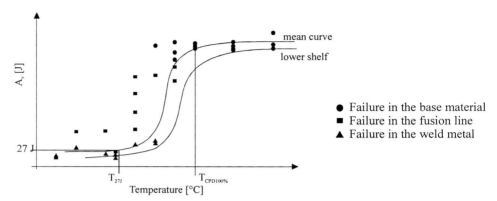

Fig. 8: Values for the characterisation of the transition area of Charpy curves

The newly defined criteria for upper-shelf behaviour and for lower shelf brittle fracture avoidance have yet to be linked to a fracture mechanics based concept and validated by large scale tests. An ongoing European research [10] is dedicated to this problem.

REFERENCES

[1]   N.N. (1995): *Prüfmethoden und Bewertungskriterien CO_2-laserstrahlgeschweißter Grobbleche aus Stahl*. VDI-Technologiezentrum (Publisher), VDI-Verlag, Düsseldorf

[2]   Devillers, L. and D. Kaplan (1986): *The electron beam welding of thick structural steel plates*. In: Int. Conf. on Trends in Welding Research (TWR '86) – Advances in Welding Sciences and Technology, Getlinburg, Tennessee/ USA

[3]   N.N. (1996): *Guidelines for the approval of CO_2-laser welding in ship hull construction.* Classification Societies unified

[4]   DIN EN 10 045-1 (1991): *Charpy impact test on metallic materials; test method*

[5]   Kristensen, J.K. and K. Borggreen (1996): *Evaluation of laser welds in structural steel*.In: J. of Materials 8, **2**, p. 48/54

[6]   Kocak, M. et al (1998): *Mechanical and fracture properties of laser beam welded joints*. IIW-Doc. XV-996-98

[7]   Kaplan, D. and L. Devillers (1988): *Interpretation d'essais de flexion entaillée sur soudures par faisceau d'électrons présentant une déviation de la rupture*.In: 4th Int. Colloquium on Welding and Melting by Electrons and Laser Beam (CISSFEL '88), Cannes/ Frankreich

[8]   Hall, B.E. et al: *Mechanisms of fracture path deviation in narrow fusion zone laser welds*. Proc. 2nd Int. Conference on Power Beam Technology, Stratford/ Großbritannien, p. 139/149

[9]   Goldak, J.A. and D.S. Nguyen (1977): *A fundamental difficulty in Charpy V notch testing narrow zones in welds*. Wdg. J. 56, **4**, p. 119-s/25-s

[10]   Kapoor, S.; Nagel, M.; Fersini, M.; Wegmann, H. (2000): *Fracture avoidance in laser welded thick structural steel plates with yield strength between 235 and 890 MPa*; Techn. Rep. No. 3, ECSC-Project No.: 7210.PR/181

From Charpy to Present Impact Testing
D. François and A. Pineau (Eds.)
© 2002 Elsevier Science Ltd. and ESIS. All rights reserved

USE OF CHARPY IMPACT TESTING TO EVALUATE
CRACK ARREST FRACTURE TOUGHNESS

KARSTEN MÜLLER

Department of Materials Engineering, Federal Institute for Materials Research and Testing,
BAM, Unter den Eichen 87, D-12205 Berlin, Germany

GERHARD PUSCH

Institute of Materials Engineering, Freiberg University of Mining and Technology,
Gustav-Zeuner-Str. 5, D-09599 Freiberg, Germany

ABSTRACT

Indirect measurements are commonly used for characterizing the crack arrest behaviour of ferritic structural steels instead of measuring the standard crack arrest fracture toughness.

In the present study, correlations are proposed for estimating the nil-ductility temperature (NDT) and the crack arrest fracture toughness (K_{Ia}) from transition temperatures, based on instrumented Charpy-V crack arrest load information.

Indirect experimental measures of the investigated pressure vessel steel show, that the transition temperature, $T(F_a = 0)$, at the arrest of the brittle crack is equivalent to the drop-weight nil-ductility transition temperature, T_{NDT}.

Furthermore, the transition criteria used are the 4kN crack arrest force from Charpy impact tests and the mean crack arrest fracture toughness of 100 MPa√m according to the master curve approach. Correlations between transition temperatures, $T(F_a=4kN)$, $T(K_{Ia})$, and T_{NDT}, which were proposed for various structural steels, work very well for the 18X2MFA material. The estimates of the correlation of the temperature for $F_a = 4kN$ with the temperature at 100 MPa√m level for a mean K_{Ia} "master" curve show that approximations of crack arrest fracture toughness values are possible.

KEYWORDS

Charpy-V, instrumented impact test, crack arrest fracture toughness, ferritic structural steel

INTRODUCTION

Modern structural integrity assessment relies upon fracture mechanics, thus utilizing fracture mechanical parameters describing the material fracture resistance against crack initiation and crack propagation as well as the material crack arrest behaviour.

According to ASTM E 1221 the crack arrest stress fracture toughness, K_{Ia}, is calculated from the measured crack length and load. Obtaining a standardized K_{Ia} value requires a comparatively large specimen. Therefore, indirect measurements are commonly used for describing the crack arrest behaviour of ferritic structural steels. As part of fracture mechanics investigations of the Cr-Mo-V steel 18X2MFA (Russian Reactor Pressure Vessel steel) in the ductile to brittle transition region reported in [1, 2], the present study deals with the question of how to estimate crack arrest toughness by means of transition criteria for different samples sizes like CVN, drop-weight, and CCA specimens.

TEST MATERIAL

The material under investigation was the 18X2MFA ferritic pressure vessel steel (comparable to 17 CrMoV 9). Static crack arrest toughness specimens (CCA) were first manufactured from the given metal sample, including both flange and cover material. After the K_{Ia} tests were conducted, smaller specimens were manufactured from the halves of the CCA-specimens. Mechanical properties of the cover material are presented in Table 1.

Table 1.   Mechanical properties of the investigated 18X2MFA steel at ambient temperature

18X2MFA (cover material)	T-direction			T-L-position			
	σ_{YS} [MPa]	σ_{UTS} [MPa]	A [%]	CV [J]	LE [mm]	T_{68J} [°C]	$T_{0,9mm}$ [°C]
wall thickness $1/3t \leq t \leq 2/3t$	634	732	20	156	1,66	16	25

nomenclature: σ_{YS} - yield stress, σ_{UTS} - ultimate tensile strength, A - elongation to failure, CV – Charpy-energy, LE - lateral expansion,

DROP-WEIGHT AND ARREST LOADS FROM INSTRUMENTED CHARPY TESTS

Charpy-V Fracture Arrest Parameter F_a

Various stages of the fracture process can be identified on the load versus displacement trace measured from instrumented Charpy impact test (see Fig. 1). Corresponding to the ductile-brittle transition region cleavage fracture has initiated at point F_{iu}. However, the CVN-specimen was not fractured completely, but the crack has arrested at point F_a.

The energy absorbed by the Charpy-V specimen is a measure of both fracture initiation and propagation process. Therefore, these properties are not directly compatible with crack arrest behaviour. However, the relationship between the force at arrest, F_a, and the test temperature, T, is examined to explore possible correlations with other experimental measures of crack arrest temperatures such as the drop-weight nil-ductility temperature (NDT), or a transition temperature for a given crack arrest fracture toughness, K_{Ia} (e. g. 100 MPa√m).

Estimation of Nil-Ductility Transition Temperature (T_{NDT})

The drop-weight test is a simple method to determine the nil-ductility transition temperature, T_{NDT}. According to ASTM E 208 the NDT is defined as the maximum test temperature at which the brittle crack initiated in a notched weld bead spreads completely across one or both of the tension surfaces on either side of the drop-weight test specimen. T_{NDT} is used in the definition of the reference nil-ductility transition temperature, RT_{NDT}, defined in the ASME pressure vessel and boiler Code.

The so-called 'P4' criterion was developed for those cases, when not enough material is available for drop-weight testing, or the definition of the RT_{NDT} is not appropriate because of insufficient upper shelf Charpy properties [3, 4]. The temperature is used at which the brittle crack extension in instrumented Charpy test caused the load at P_4 to drop to zero ($F_a = 0$, see Fig. 2) as the temperature which characterises crack arrest behaviour. For the 18X2MFA material $T(F_a=0)$ is equivalent to the nil-ductility transition temperature, $T(F_a=0) = T_{NDT} = 5°C$. This confirms investigations on other ferritic structural steels [4].

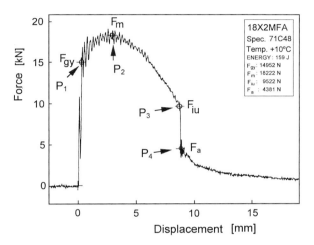

Fig. 1. Load-deflection curve from instrumented Charpy test of 18X2MFA steel (cover material) showing the points of brittle fracture initiation (F_{iu}, P_3) and arrest (F_a, P_4) acc. to DIN EN ISO 14556 and the P4-criterion [3], respectively.

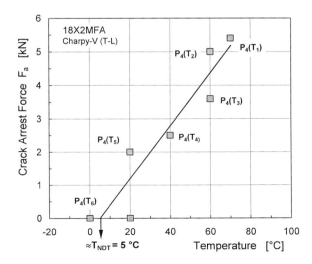

Fig. 2. NDT-temperature of 18X2MFA steel of 18X2MFA steel (flange material) determined from crack arrest forces, F_a, of instrumented Charpy-V tests.

Estimation of T(F_a=4kN)

In the transition region the crack arrest force has been found to increase with temperature significantly. In addition to the P4-criterion, an approach has been made by K. Wallin [5] to correlate the shift in crack arrest toughness transition temperature of a wide range of plate and weld materials. The mean temperature corresponding to a fixed arrest load, equal to 4 kN, was selected as transition criteria. The 4 kN arrest load is transferable approximately to a crack jump halfway through the ligament, $a_a \approx \frac{1}{2}$ (W-a), of the Charpy-V specimen and also to the rising part of the F_a-T-curve [6].

The CVN crack arrest load-temperature behaviour can almost be well represented by the exponential function [5]

$$F_a = 4e^{\{ (T - T(F_a = 4kN)) / A \}} \tag{1}$$

Crack arrest load vs. test temperature results are presented in Fig. 3. For the cover material of the 18X2MFA steel investigated here, the 4kN crack arrest force follows this power law function. The transition temperature, T(F_a=4kN), is 32°C and the material parameter A in Eq.1 comes to 17 °C.

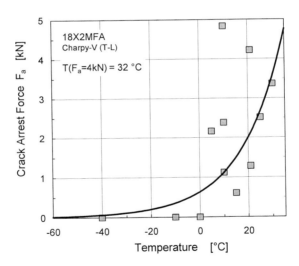

Fig. 3.   Measured crack arrest force vs. temperature with the mean curve of 18X2MFA ferritic steel.

The value of F_a is based on Charpy data and consequently reflects the scatter of Charpy impact testing in the ductile to brittle transition region. However, the scattering of the results is typical for CVN arrest load determination of Cr-Mo-V type steels and comparable to ferritic plate and weld materials in Fig. 4.

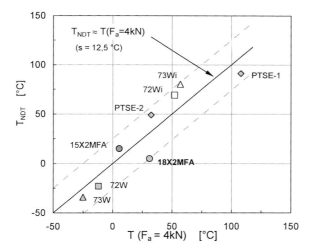

Fig. 4.   Comparison of transition temperatures, T_{NDT} and $T(F_a = 4$ kN$)$, of ferritic structural steels and welded joints with added data [5, 7]: PTSE-1 - A 508 Cl 2, PTSE-2 - 2 1/4Cr1Mo, 72W, 73W - welded joints (i = irrad.).

ANALYSIS OF CRACK ARREST TOUGHNESS K_{Ia}

K_{Ia} *vs. Temperature*

The crack arrest toughness data for cover and flange materials of 18X2MFA pressure vessel steel measured in this study together with the fitted transition curve are shown in Fig. 5.

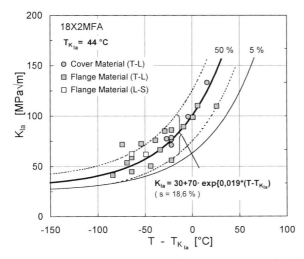

Fig. 5.   Temperature dependence of crack arrest fracture toughness for 18X2MFA steel using master curve function acc. to ASTM E 1921.

K_{Ia} results of 18X2MFA material were analysed assuming the same temperature dependance, that is used to describe the brittle fracture initiation toughness by means of the master curve function (ASTM E 1921)

$$K_{Ia} = 30 + 70 \cdot e^{\left[0,019 \left(T - T_{K_{Ia}}\right)\right]}$$

(2)

where K_{Ia} is the mean estimate for the crack arrest fracture toughness, and $T(K_{Ia})$ is the reference temperature corresponding to $K_{Ia} = 100$ MPa√m. This procedure is based on investigations on the temperature dependence and distribution of K_{Ia} for various ferritic steels [5, 6]. For the 18X2MFA pressure vessel steel the 100 MPa√m crack arrest toughness transition temperature, $T(K_{Ia})$, is 44°C.

Correlation Between Crack Arrest Parameters

Correlations between the crack arrest force transition temperature, $T(F_a=4kN)$, and the reference temperature, $T(K_{Ia})$, as well as the drop-weight nil-ductility temperature, NDT, are shown together with data points of some other steels in Figures 6 and 7.
The crack arrest behaviour can be reliable estimated from $T(F_a=4kN)$ with a standard deviation of about 9 K and 12 K, respectively. Correlations for various structural steels and welded joints [6] are confirmed by crack arrest parameters of the investigated 18X2MFA material according to the following equations

$$T_{K_{Ia}} = T_{F_{a4kN}} + 12 \,°C$$

(3)

$$T_{K_{Ia}} = T_{NDT} + 8,5 \,°C$$

(4)

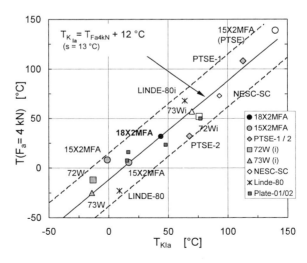

Fig. 6.   Correlation between transition temperatures, T_{KIa} and $T(F_a=4kN)$, for pressure vessel steels and welded joints, acc. to [2, 6].

The 4 kN arrest force transition temperature vs. $T(K_{Ia})$ as well as NDT show a moderate scatter especially for the pressure vessel cover material of the 18X2MFA steel (see Fig. 6 and 7).

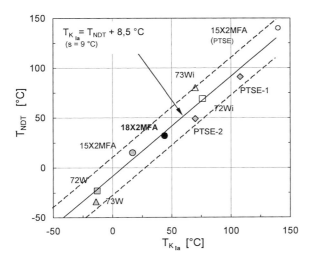

Fig. 7.   Correlation between transition temperatures, T_{KIa} and T_{NDT}, for pressure vessel steels and welded joints acc. to [2, 6]

SUMMARY AND CONCLUSIONS

Arrest force signals from instrumented Charpy test have been used as indirect experimental measures to describe the crack arrest behaviour. The estimates of the correlations show that prediction of values of crack arrest fracture toughness for various steel is possible. Scatter in the relations must be taken into consideration when applying the correlations to structural integrity assessments.

The transition temperature of the Charpy-V crack arrest force 4 kN seems to give a reliable estimation of $T(K_{Ia})$ as well as T_{NDT} for various ferritic structural steels.

For the steel 18X2MFA (comparable to 17CrMoV9) the nil-ductility temperature, T_{NDT}, can be estimated from $T(F_a=0)$, and T_{NDT} can been used to fix the fracture toughness reference curve, K_{IR}, according to ASME Boiler & Pressure Vessel Code. However, observed scatter suggest that varieties between Charpy-V and drop-weight testing like specimen sizes and energy effects must be considered in more detail.

REFERENCES

1. Müller, K., Pusch, G., Valo, M., Wallin, K., Nevalainen, M. and Planman, T. (1995), Fracture mechanics evaluation of the 18X2MFA steel. In: *Proc. of 21. MPA-Seminar*, Stuttgart, pp. 12.1-12.20.

2. Müller, K. (1999), *Doctorate Thesis*, Technische Universität Bergakademie Freiberg.

3. Berger, C., Ewald, J., Wiemann, W. and Wojaczyk, H.-H. (1979), Ermittlung von Spröd-bruch- und bruchmechanischen Kennwerten mittels Kerbschlagproben. In: *11. Sitzung, DVM-Arbeitskreis Bruchvorgänge*, Deutscher Verband für Materialforschung und – prüfung, Berlin, pp. 182-195.

4. Roos, E., Eisele, U., Beyer, H. and Gillot, R. (1986), Einordnung und Charakterisierung von Werkstoffen mittels bruchmechanischer Parameter. In: *Proc. of 12. MPA-Seminar*, Stuttgart, pp. 34.1-34.30.

5. Wallin, K. (1996), Descriptive characteristic of Charpy-V fracture arrest parameter with respect to crack arrest K_{Ia}. In: *Evaluating Material Properties by Dynamic Testing*, ESIS 20, E. van Walle (ed.), Mechanical Engineering Publications, London, pp. 165-176.

6. Wallin, K. and Rintamaa, R. (1998), Master Curve based correlation between static initiation toughness K_{IC} and crack arrest toughness K_{Ia}. In: *Proc. of 24. MPA-Seminar*, Stuttgart, pp.45.1 - 45.19.

7. Planman, T., Wallin, K. and Rintamaa, R. (1997), Evaluating crack arrest fracture toughness from Charpy impact testing. In: *Transactions of 14ᵗʰ Int. Conf. Structural Mechanics in Reactor Technology*, SMIRT-14, CEA Saclay, Livolant, Michel. Vol. 4. Division 6, pp. 415-422.

From Charpy to Present Impact Testing
D. François and A. Pineau (Eds.)

PREDICTING CRACK ARREST BEHAVIOUR OF STRUCTURAL STEELS USING SMALL-SCALE MATERIAL CHARACTERISATION TESTS

C. GALLO, J. A. ÁLVAREZ, F. GUTIÉRREZ-SOLANA, and J. A. POLANCO

Departamento de Ciencia e Ingeniería del Terreno y de los Materiales
E.T.S. de Ingenieros de Caminos, Canales y Puertos.
University of Cantabria. 39005, Santander. Spain.

ABSTRACT

The suitability of small-scale tests to characterise the crack arrest behaviour of structures is assessed in this work. Empirical correlations based on instrumented Charpy tests results have been used to obtain the main parameters that define the crack arrest properties, comparing the predicted values with those experimentally obtained. Furthermore, an energy approach has been applied to determine relationships, as a function of the test temperature, between the propagation energy and the crack arrest toughness. The experimental work has been performed on two different structural steels.

KEYWORDS

Crack Arrest, Structural Steels, Small-Scale Tests, Brittle Propagation Energy, Fracture Appearance, Large-Scale Tests.

INTRODUCTION

The safety of components and structures against fracture has usually been studied using two different approaches: (i) to ensure that the material is tough enough to prevent fracture initiation and (ii) to avoid the propagation of cracks in the component once these have been initiated in brittle areas. The latter is based on the crack arrest concept. In the first approach, safely designed components should only experience stress distributions below the critical condition for cracking to initiate. But with increasing size, the components present the possibility of having brittle zones, due to welded joints or other features, which could nucleate a crack able to propagate under the existing stress conditions. Accidental overloads also preclude that initiation can be prevented in any absolute sense. Crack arrest criteria can be applied in order to have some control over the behaviour of propagating cracks, avoiding the total failure of the structure. In different industries, such as naval, nuclear or oil gas, the construction of big components and uncertainty in loading justify the design using crack arrest criteria.

This paper reviews the testing procedures to characterize the crack arrest properties, mainly the crack arrest temperature (CAT) determined using large-scale tests, the crack arrest fracture toughness (K_{Ia}), and their correlation with instrumented Charpy testing results and other tests carried out using small size specimens. The experimental results obtained after the initial characterisation of two structural steels used in ship hull construction are analysed with the correlations obtained.

EXPERIMENTAL PROCEDURES

The existing crack arrest tests can be divided into three main groups [1]: Large-scale tests, tests based on the stress intensity factor at crack arrest and small-scale tests. Large-scale component testing provides the most realistic way of assessing real structures. A well-known example is the double tension test (DTT), which consists of provoking crack propagation from a defect generated in a brittle zone of the specimen. The objective of this test is to determine if an initiated crack will stop and, in that case, to obtain the lowest temperature at which the crack run stops. This temperature is known as crack arrest temperature (CAT).

The specimen configuration can be seen in Fig. 1 (a), [2]. It is submitted to the applied stress of interest normally a maximum tensile stress of 2/3 the yield stress of the material. A secondary tension load provokes the crack initiation in the specimen, which is submitted to a gradient temperature increasing from the crack initiation point. The CAT temperature is associated to the resulting crack length, and depends on the temperature gradient across the specimen and the stress applied. Large-scale tests provide accurate and realistic results, however, they are difficult and expensive to carry out. For this reason, the use of large-scale tests is restricted to obtaining criteria for selection.

Crack arrest fracture toughness tests produce crack initiation and determine the stress intensity factor at crack arrest. For this, the compact crack arrest (CCA) test (ASTM E1221/96) uses a wedge with a split-pin assembly to obtain a rapid run-arrest event in a side grooved crack line specimen under constant displacement conditions. The experimental set-up, which can be seen in Fig. 1 (b), ensures a decrease in the stress intensity factor when cracks propagate. For each test the obtained K_{Ia} factor depends on the local conditions at arrest. Therefore it can be used at the design or assessment level, but, as it is dependent on the temperature, many tests are required to determine the evolution of K_{Ia} with temperature for the CCA test.

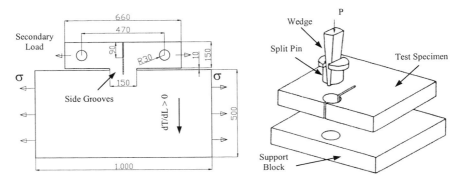

Fig. 1. - (a) Double tension test specimen. (b) Compact crack arrest test configuration [3].

Therefore, it is common to use small-scale tests to obtain information related to crack arrest conditions. Many comparisons exist between large-scale tests and small-scale tests, such as instrumented Charpy and the drop weight (Pellini) tests. Existing empirical correlations have been employed to obtain the crack arrest temperature (CAT) from instrumented Charpy and Pellini results. These are the starting point of this work when applied to the case of two structural steels.

APPLICATION: MATERIAL AND EXPERIMENTAL RESULTS

As mentioned above, the comparative analysis of crack arrest properties in this work is based on the behaviour characterisation of two structural steels used in the naval industry for the construction of ship hulls. The Grade A steel, which comes from 15 mm thick plate, is kept as rolled. The AH32 steel has been normalised and thermo-mechanically treated (TMCR) and comes from plate of 25 mm thickness. Table 1 and Table 2 contain respectively the chemical composition of the two steels and their mechanical properties [4].

Table 1. - Chemical composition.

Element	C	Si	Mn	P	S	Cr	Ni	Mo	Al	Nb	Cu	$C_{eq.}$
Grade A	0.13	0.24	0.66	0.015	0.016	<0.02	<0.02	<0.005	0.006	<0.005	<0.02	0.24
AH32	0.099	0.26	1.30	0.019	0.004	0.02	0.02	<0.005	0.034	0.012	<0.02	0.32

Table 2. - Mechanical properties.

Direction		LT	TL		LT	TL
Yield Stress (MPa)	Grade A	272.5	274.0	AH32	388.5	398.5
Tensile Strength (MPa)		450.0	455.2		504.0	455.2
Elongation (%)		16.3	17.2		15.7	17.2

Small-Scale Tests Characterisation Results

Instrumented Charpy tests and Pellini tests have been carried out on the two selected steels, using standard specimens. The curves representing the total energy and fracture appearance of the instrumented Charpy tests are shown in Fig. 2, showing the main parameters obtained.

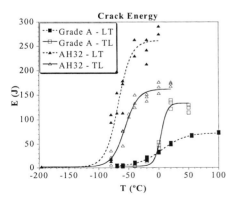
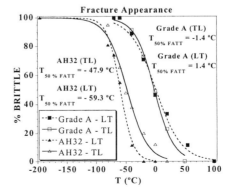

Fig. 2. - Instrumented Charpy test. Grade A and AH32 steels [4].

It is also possible to characterise the different steps in the processes taking place during fracture using the instrumented Charpy test. These are the elastic and plastic deformation before crack initiation, followed by the ductile and brittle crack propagation processes and the final ductile fracture [5]. One example from AH32 steel is given in Fig. 3 (a). Figure 3 (b) represents the corresponding energies of the different steps as a function of the test temperature. With these results, it is possible to associate the proportions of brittle and ductile fracture area with the respective energy spent in propagation. Table 3 contains the corresponding values for both steels in the transverse direction (TL).

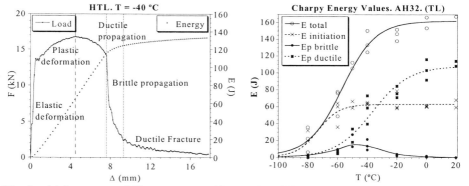

Fig. 3. - (a) Instrumented Charpy test graphic.   (b) Different energies of test vs. temperature.

Table 3. - Brittle and ductile behaviour characterization from the instrumented Charpy test.

	T (°C)	Total Energy (J)	Initiation Energy (J)	Brittle Propagation Energy (J)	Brittle Area (mm²)	E/A brittle (J/mm²)	Ductile Propagation Energy (J)	Ductile Area (mm²)	E/A ductile (J/mm²)
Grade A	-70	3.60	2.10	1.45	80.0	0.0181	0.05	---	---
	-60	5.75	3.75	1.75	80.0	0.0218	0.25	---	---
	-40	4.96	3.16	1.63	73.2	0.0222	0.17	6.8	0.025
	-20	21.87	13.50	2.23	58.4	0.0381	6.14	21.6	0.284
	0	46.91	24.58	2.73	39.2	0.0696	19.60	40.8	0.480
	20	121.65	52.80	2.54	18.4	0.1380	66.31	61.6	1.076
	50	129.43	49.94	---	---	---	79.49	80	0.993
AH32	-196	2.17	1.24	0.90	80.0	0.0112	0.03	0	---
	-80	22.34	19.61	2.52	76.0	0.0331	0.21	4.0	0.0525
	-60	48.89	36.04	5.55	52.4	0.1059	7.30	27.6	0.2645
	-50	105.39	58.68	12.79	38.4	0.3330	33.92	41.6	0.8153
	-40	150.39	63.61	13.59	30.4	0.4470	73.19	49.6	1.4756
	-20	151.86	78.62	2.19	16.0	0.1368	71.05	64.0	1.1101
	0	166.48	61.41	1.99	9.6	0.2073	103.08	70.4	1.4642
	20	173.45	59.29	0.14	---	---	114.02	80.0	1.4252

From the Pellini test, the NDTT values have been obtained. The results in the longitudinal direction (LT) have been: -15 and -55 °C for the Grade A steel and for the AH32, respectively.

All these results have been used to obtain, following the existing correlations, the CAT and to analyse the energy conditions for the different propagation mechanisms, to be compared with the arrest conditions at the CCA tests.

Large-Scale Test Characterisation Results

Some DTT have been carried out with the Grade A and AH32 steels, with the aim of evaluating the crack arrest properties, which became the reference for comparing the predicted values obtained after the other tests. Figure 4 presents the sections of the specimens tested indicating the code, the crack point initiation and the arrested length in mm for each one. The obtained CAT values have been included in Table 4.

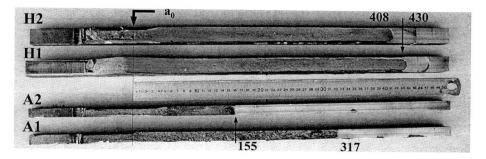

Fig. 4. - DTT specimens.

Table 4. - Double tension test results.

Material	Code	B (mm)	a_{arrest} (mm)	a_{arrest} / W	σ (MPa)	CAT (°C)
Grade A	A1	15	317	0.63	149	5
	A2	15	155	0.31	99	-30
AH32	H1	25	430	0.86	211	-8
	H2	25	408	0.82	164	-13

CCA Test Characterisation Results

CCA Tests have been carried out at some different temperatures to study the toughness at arrest conditions. Figures 5 (a) and (b) represent the fracture surface of one of the specimens tested on AH32 steel and the corresponding load-displacement graphic. Obtained K_{Ia} values are in Table 5.

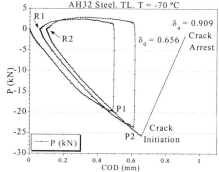

Fig. 5. - (a) CCA specimen.   (b) CCA test, load-displacement curve.

Table 5. - CCA test results

	T (°C)	K_{Ia} (MPa· m$^{1/2}$)	G_{Ia} (J/mm^2)
Grade A	20	*	---
	-20	65.61	0.0206
		61.03	0.0182
		*	---
	-70	*	---
		56.61	0.0153

	T (°C)	K_{Ia} (MPa· m$^{1/2}$)	G_{Ia} (J/mm^2)
AH32	-20	*	
	-50	*	---
		*	---
	-60	0	---
	-70	73.35	0.0262
		84.68	0.0350
		59.87	0.0175

(*) No crack propagation

ANALYSIS: PREDICTED VERSUS OBTAINED CAT VALUES

Numerous empirical correlations in order to predict CAT values from small-scale tests results have been proposed [8]. From the Charpy test results the CAT temperature is usually obtained as a function of the temperature for a percentage of fracture appearance (FATT). These correlations depend on the steel type, thickness and stress applied. Table 6, equations (1) to (3), contains the correlations that have been used with the selected steels. The Pellini test gives correlations with the NDTT value affected by the same parameters. Table 6, equations (4) and (5), contains the corresponding correlations for the selected steels.

Table 6. - CAT correlations from Charpy and Pellini tests [6-9].

Test	B (mm)	σ (MPa)	CAT Correlation (°C)	
Charpy	25	2/3· σ_Y	CAT = 50 % Shear FATT + 35 °C	(1)
	13	2/3· σ_Y	CAT = 50 % Shear FATT - 15 °C	(2)
	Any	Any	CAT = 1.35· (100% Brittle FATT) + 0.67· σ + 2.85· B - 129	(3)
Pellini	25	2/3· σ_Y	CAT = NDTT + 20 °C	(4)
	Any	Any	CAT = [NDTT + 10] + [0.13·σ - 16] + [5.3·(B - 12)$^{1/2}$ -19]	(5)

Table 7 contains the experimental data of the DT specimens shown in Fig. 4 (A1, A2, H1 and H2) as well as from some others obtained in the bibliography on the same steels (A3, A4, A5 and H3) [8]. Also it contains the predicted values from the multiple variables equations presented in Table 6. Figure 6 represents the CAT predictions obtained by equation (3) in comparison with the experimentally obtained values. To be safe, the predicted values of CAT should be higher than the real values. Predictions made by equation (3) on the samples tested in this work were in the unsafe region. In order to correct this situation a new correlation has been proposed substituting equation (3) as follows:

$$CAT = (50 \% \text{ Brittle FATT}) + 0.5 \cdot \sigma + 2.85 \cdot B - 129 \qquad (6)$$

This change permits more conservative predictions as can be seen in Fig. 6 once the values of Table 7, obtained by using equation (6), have been represented. At the same time, Fig. 6 compares the CAT predictions from equation (6) with the predicted values made by equation (5) from Pellini test, showing that equation (6) reduces the number and the level of non-conservative predictions even though all those normally have a difference with measured CAT lower than 15 °C [6, 9].

Table 7. - Obtained CAT results and predicted CAT values from small-scale tests.

Material	Grade A		AH32		Grade A			AH32
Code	A1	A2	H1	H2	A3	A4	A5	H3
B (mm)	15	15	25	25	12.7	20.1	25	20.3
a $_{arrest}$ (mm)	317	155	430	408	2x102	344	250	210
a $_{arrest}$ /W	0.63	0.31	0.86	0.82	0.2	0.69	0.5	0.42
CAT (°C)	5	-30	-8	-13	-38	12	5	-18
σ (MPa)	149	99	211	164	158	200	148	190
Predicted CAT - Pellini (5)	-11.4	-17.9	-33.4	-39.5	-30	1	-11.6	-37.5
Predicted CAT - Charpy (3)	-40.4	-73.9	-24.4	-55.9	-27.5	8.3	-12.6	-24.8
Predicted CAT - Charpy (6)	-10.3	-35.3	-11.5	-35.0	-28.8	33.2	8.7	-16.1

ANALYSIS: CCA AND INSTRUMENTED CHARPY TEST RESULTS CORRELATIONS

The obtained values of K_0 and K_{Ia}, stress intensity factor at the start and the arrest positions respectively at the crack run event on CCA tests, have been represented in Fig. 7 superimposed on the total energy instrumented Charpy test results, both as a function of the temperature. It can be seen that there is a threshold temperature above which the CCA specimens did not break. This temperature (between -60 and -50 °C for the AH32 steel, -20 and 20 °C for the Grade A steel) lies within the brittle-ductile transition temperature determined by the Charpy tests. Therefore the Charpy test results should help in the definition of temperature range of testing CCA samples, optimising the experimental effort.

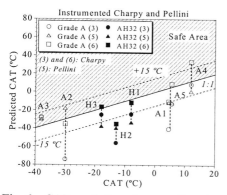

Fig. 6. - CAT predictions from small-scale tests vs. CAT results from DTT.

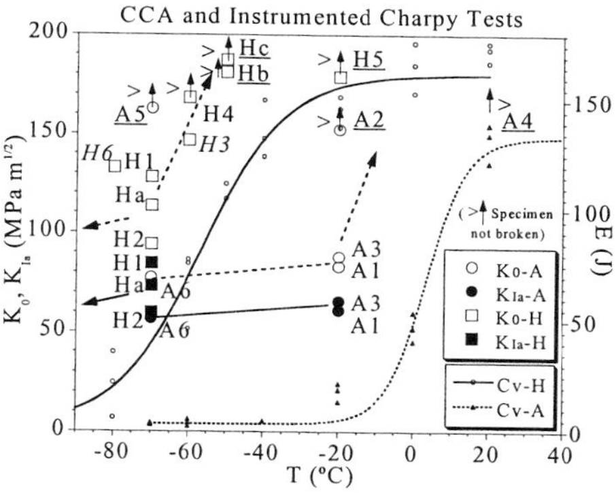

Fig. 7. - CCA and instrumented Charpy tests results.

Analysing the energy values per unit area for brittle propagation, it appears that the threshold temperature starts when these values are higher than the order of 0.02 J/mm², at about -60 °C for the AH32 steel and -20 °C for the Grade A steel, at which this energy increases sharply as can be seen in Table 3. This value is of the same order as the mean propagation energy per unit area obtained after completion of the CCA tests (Fig. 5) and the energy release rate, G_{Ia} value obtained from K_{Ia}, at arrest conditions, both varying between 0.015 and 0.03 J/mm² for the propagating samples in the two steels. Therefore, following an energy balance approach [10], comparing the internal energy with the energy needed for propagation, it may be possible to predict the conditions at crack arrest.

CONCLUSIONS

Two structural steels used in the naval industry, Grade A and AH32, have been studied to obtain the main parameters that define their crack arrest properties. Fracture and arrest behaviour has been characterised using instrumented Charpy tests and the total energy, the fracture appearance and the unitary energy for brittle propagation values related to the crack arrest parameters. CAT and K_{Ia}, have also been experimentally obtained. In all cases, it has been noted that the AH32 steel permits lower working temperatures than Grade A steel.

Existing correlations from instrumented Charpy and Pellini tests have been used to predict CAT values. Even though more research in this area is suggested, a new equation has been suggested to optimise the correlation between instrumented Charpy test results and CAT, keeping the predictions on the conservative side. This establishes an important advantage over the existing correlations from Pellini test results. In all cases, most predictions define a difference from the real values in the range of $\pm 15\ ^{\circ}C$.

An energy approach has been applied using the propagation energy values obtained by the instrumented Charpy tests. Charpy results can be directly used in order to define the temperature range for K_{Ia} ASTM experimental characterisation with CCA samples, after indirectly indicating the threshold temperature for running cracks.

Also the unitary energy for brittle propagation could define this threshold and could also be related to the energy release rate at arrest conditions, thus determining K_{Ia}. More work under energy balance considerations is in progress, based on all these testing procedures.

REFERENCES

1. Wiesner C. S. and Hayes B. (1999). "A review of crack arrest tests, models and applications", Crack arrest concepts for failure prevention and life extension. Abington publishing.
2. Lindley C., Bannister A. and Priest A. H. (1992). "Crack Arrest in modern structural steels - fundamentals, test development and significance to steel usage", British Steel Report.
3. "Standard Test Method for Determining Plane-Strain Crack-Arrest Fracture Toughness, K_{Ia} of Ferritic Steels" (1996). ASTM E 1221-96.
4. "An Energy Balance Approach For Crack Arrest" (2000). Technical Report No 2. ECSC Project. 7210/PR/182.
5. Barralis J., Maeder G. (1991). "Précis de Métallurgie. Élaboration, Structures-Propriétés et Normalisation". AFNOR, NATHAN.
6. Wiesner C. S. (1996). "Predicting structural crack arrest behaviour using small-scale material characterisation tests", Internal Journal Pressure Vessel & Piping 69, pp. 185-196.
7. Bala S. R., Malik L. and Graville B. A. (1992). "Short crack arrest capability of a structural steel for arctic ships", Proc. 11th OMAE Conf. Vol.III-B, pp.431-439, American Society of Mechanical Engineers.
8. "Steel selection criteria for fracture avoidance in welded ships" (1999). ECSC Project 7210/KA/824.
9. Smedley G. P. (1989). "Prediction and Specification of Crack Arrest Properties of Steel Plate", Internal Journal Pressure Vessel & Piping 40, pp. 279-302.
10. Priest A. H. (1998). "An energy balance in crack propagation and arrest", Engineering Fracture Mechanics, 61, pp. 231-251.

From Charpy to Present Impact Testing
D. François and A. Pineau (Eds.)

FRACTURE MECHANICS BASED SCALING CRITERIA FOR MINIATURE AND SUB-SIZE CHARPY-V SPECIMENS

KIM WALLIN, TAPIO PLANMAN, MATTI VALO
VTT Manufacturing Technology
P.O. Box 1704, FIN-02044 VTT, Finland

ABSTRACT

Besides the normal-size (ISO-V) Charpy specimen ($10*10*55$ mm^3), various types of sub-size specimens have been introduced. One standardised sub-size specimen is the so-called KLST specimen, which size is $3*4*27$ mm^3 and the center notch is 1 mm (DIN 50 115). However, the test data published for the KLST specimen, as well as sub-size specimens in general, is still very limited, though they can provide an overwhelmingly effective use of test material. The results from small specimen testing are typically used to evaluate the fracture behaviour of the ISO-V Charpy specimen. If there are no test results available for the correlation, as there usually is not, a general correlation has to be applied to evaluate the fracture behaviour of the ISO-V specimen. The applicability of a sub-size specimen depends therefore significantly on how reliably this relationship has been established. Here, the Charpy-V test is given a fracture mechanical interpretation and, based on this, new generally applicable scaling criteria are proposed both for miniature as well as sub-size Charpy-V specimens.

KEYWORDS

Charpy-V, Miniature specimens, Sub-sized specimens, brittle fracture, ductile fracture.

INTRODUCTION

A great deal of test data have been obtained on reactor pressure vessel steels using the standard Charpy-V test. Although more advanced test methods, based on elastic-plastic fracture mechanics, are both recommendable and already in use in the surveillance programmes of some nuclear power plants (NPPs), Charpy tests are still required, e.g., by regulatory guides.

Besides the normal-size (ISO-V) Charpy specimen ($10*10*55$ mm^3), various types of sub-size specimens have been introduced. One standardised sub-size specimen being in use is the so-called KLST specimen, the size of which is $3*4*27$ mm^3 with 1 mm central notch (DIN 50 115). So far the test data published for the KLST specimen, as well as sub-size specimens in general, is still limited.

The results from small specimen testing are typically used for evaluating the fracture behaviour of the ISO-V Charpy specimen and if there are no test results available for the correlation, as there usually is not, a general correlation has to be applied to evaluate the fracture behaviour of the ISO-V specimen. The availability of a sub-size specimen depends therefore significantly on how reliably this relationship has been established.

Impact test data measured with different specimens have been correlated using some appropriate criterion (or criteria) and since a total transition curve is normally measured, there are several ones available. The criterion can be a fixed energy or lateral expansion level describing the transition temperature or the level can be derived from the upper-shelf energy (USE). In general, the proposed criterion can be divided into two groups: those *derived from the dimensions* of the specimens and those *derived empirically* from experimental data. Test data measured with ISO-V and KLST -type Charpy specimens are discussed and the validity of two proposed, basically different transition temperature criteria and the resulting differences in the temperatures, that are inevitable because of the different size ligaments, studied. Specimens capability to describe consistently the transition temperature shift characteristic of ferritic steels due to irradiation and recovery annealing is discussed as well. The data consists of the test results published previously [1] and more recent test data measured at VTT with KLST-type specimens for non-irradiated and irradiated FFA, JFL and JRQ pressure vessel steels in an IAEA Co-ordinated research programme.

PROPOSED CORRELATIONS

One of the best established correlations for the KLST specimen, including over 30 transition curves, has been determined for absorbed energy (KV) and lateral expansion (LE) 1.9 J, 3.1 J and 0.3 mm (KLST specimen) and 41 J and 68 J and lateral expansion 0.9 mm (ISO-V specimen), respectively. The criteria have been derived using the mean ratio of USEs as a normalising factor. The resulting mean difference in the transition temperatures was found to be as follows [2]:

$$T_{KLST} = T_{ISO-V} - 65°C \quad \begin{array}{l} (KLST: 1.9\,J, 3.1\,J \text{ and } 0.3 \text{ mm lateral exp.}) \\ (ISO - V: 41\,J, 68\,J \text{ and } 0.9 \text{ mm lateral exp.}) \end{array} \tag{1}$$

The three proposed criteria are to be used together [2].

There has been presented also another way of correlating the transition temperatures [3]. The appropriate energy level for the KLST specimen (or the ratio of energies) was derived from the definition of the J-integral, according to which the J-integral, describing the elastic-plastic fracture toughness of a material, is inversely proportional to the ligament area of the specimen. When energy criterion 28 J is normalized in relation to the ligament area, the corresponding criterion for the KLST specimen is about 3.1 J (3.15 J), that is *35 J/cm²*. The 35 J/cm² transition temperature has, in a previous study, been determined for various types of steels as a function of specimen thickness (B) by dynamic tests [4]. In relation to the normal-size Charpy-V specimen, the transition temperature difference (ΔT) was found to depend on specimen thickness (B) as follows:

$$\Delta T = 51.4 \cdot \ln[2 \cdot (B/10)^{0.25} - 1] \quad (°C) \tag{2}$$

The standard deviation ($\sigma_{\Delta T}$)of the function was less than $5°C$ for specimens with $B \geq 3$ mm. The formula (2) is expected to be valid for various low-alloy steels having the yield strength within range 200 - 1000 MPa [4]. The measured data and the function fit are shown in Fig. 1.

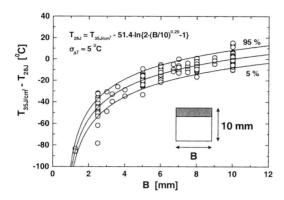

Fig. 1. Effect of specimen thickness on the 35 J/cm^2 transition temperature [4].

When the formula (2) is applied to the KLST specimen, ignoring the fact that the formula takes into account only the effect of specimen thickness, the correlation becomes as follows:

$$T_{KLST} = T_{ISO-V} - 38°C \qquad \begin{array}{l} (\text{KLST: 3.15 J and 0.3 mm lateral exp., e.g.}) \\ (\text{ISO} - \text{V: 28 J and 0.3 mm lateral exp., e.g.}) \end{array} \qquad (3)$$

On the basis of fracture mechanics the lateral expansion criterion should be equal for both specimens, independently of specimen size, for example 0.3 mm (Fig. 2 [3]).

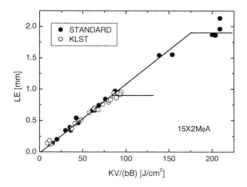

Fig. 2. Relationship between LE and normalized impact energy for standard and KLST CVN specimens.

The transition temperature(s) is typically the primary parameter to be determined by Charpy tests. The second one is the notch toughness at higher temperatures, i.e. the mean upper-shelf energy (USE) which can also be estimated from the sub-size specimen data. Such a procedure for evaluating the USE of the ISO-V specimen can be derived from fracture mechanics [3]. By combining the defining formula of the J-integral and power-law fit $J = (\Delta a)^m$ describing stable crack growth, the following relationship was derived between the USEs:

$$E_{ISO-V} = E_{B \cdot b} \cdot \frac{10}{B} \cdot \left(\frac{8}{b} \right)^{1+m} \tag{4}$$

where B is specimen thickness, b is ligament width and m is a material and geometry factor. The value of m depends on specimen size, dimensions of the notch and material. Factor m can be determined empirically from the USEs measured with different specimens. The value of m has been shown to depend primarily on the USE of the material [3].

MATERIALS AND TEST METHODS

The materials tested in this study were low-alloy quenched and tempered pressure vessel steels. Most data have been measured on 15X2MFA-type Cr-Mo-V steels with different irradiation conditions. The six examined material states consisted of two heats in either non-irradiated, irradiated or both irradiated and annealed condition. In addition, six states of the corresponding weld materials, with roughly the same contents of alloying elements but different main impurity contents, were tested. The IAEA CRP 3 steels, FFA, JFL and JRQ, were tested both in non-irradiated and irradiated conditions. The materials have been characterized in detail in an IAEA co-ordinated research programme (IAEA CRP 3 [5]). The Charpy ISO-V test data measured in this programme were in part used for this study. The irradiated sub-size specimens were fabricated from the halves of the corresponding tested ISO-V specimens. The other materials included in the study (three steels with different compositions) were non-irradiated and tested elsewhere.

The impact energy used for testing the KLST specimens was 15 J and the impact velocity 3.8 m/s. For the ISO-V specimens the corresponding values were 300 J and 5 m/s. A pneumatic mechanism was used to transfer the specimen from thermal bath to the proper striking position accurately and with minimum delay time. The transition temperatures were determined from a tanh-function fit obtained by minimizing the squared sum of temperature deviations in the transition region.

RESULTS

The transition temperatures based on the mean USE ratio of the ISO-V and KLST specimens [2] are compared in Fig. 3, which shows also the mean and 95% prediction bounds calculated for the measured data with slope 1:1. The difference between the transition temperatures given by the KLST specimens (at 1.9 J and 3.1 J) and the ISO-V specimens (at 41 J and 68 J) was approximately 63°C. The standard deviation (S.D.) of the correlation was 18°C. The result also shows (Fig. 3) that the temperatures hold the linear 1:1 relationship moderately up to about 70°C 68 J level but remain below the mean dependence at higher temperatures. The temperature difference (and the scatter with remarks) obtained here coincide with the result reported elsewhere (compare eq. 1) [2].

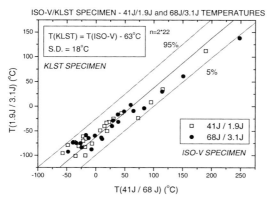

Fig. 3. Comparison of transition temperatures 41 J / 68 J and 1.9 J / 3.1 J measured with ISO-V and KLST-type impact specimens. The values of lateral expansion are excluded.

For comparison, the transition temperatures were determined also at the energy levels proportioned to the real (measured) USE value of each material instead of the average value. Neither the transition temperatures nor the mean dependence of them showed, however, any marked difference as compared with the results based on the mean USE ratio. Moreover, the standard deviations were very close to each other, suggesting that no improvement can be achieved by employing the USE ratio measured for each material rather than the mean value.

The transition temperatures based on the ratio of the ligament areas, i.e. the 3.15 J and 28 J criteria, are compared in Fig. 4.

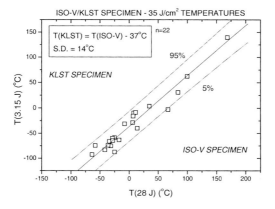

Fig. 4. Comparison of transition temperatures 28 J and 3.15 J measured with ISO-V and KLST-type impact specimens.

The difference between the transition temperatures given by the KLST specimens (at 3.15 J) and the ISO-V specimens (at 28 J) was in this case approximately 37°C. The standard deviation of the correlation was 14 C, i.e. somewhat lower than that given by the USE-based energy criteria (18°C). The result confirms that the thickness correction formula (2) [4] can be used for the KLST specimen (compare eq. 3) and also supports the validity of the formula (2) in general, i.e. the applicability of it for (notched) impact specimens with various dimensions. The dependence of the transition temperatures (Fig. 4) is also distinctly linear and follows the 1:1 slope.

The values of USE measured with the ISO-V and KLST specimens for the materials studied are shown together with the measurements published elsewhere for various steels [6] and for one 2 1/4Cr1Mo pressure vessel steel [7] in Fig. 5. These data were used for deriving the correlation between the USEs of the ISO-V and KLST specimens. An appropriate function [3] was fitted to the measured USE data so as to solve the unknown factor (m) in eq. (2) as follows:

$$m = \left(\frac{E_{ISO-V}}{A}\right)^{n} \tag{5}$$

where E_{ISO-V} is the USE of the ISO-V specimen, and A and n are fit parameters. The values estimated for these parameters were 188 J and 0.32, respectively. Using these values, the formulas (2) and (5) are now available for calculating, e.g. iteratively, the USE of the ISO-V specimen from the value measured with the KLST specimen.

The straight line in Fig. 5 shows the mean (constant) USE ratio, according to which energy criteria 1.9 J/3.1 J/0.3 mm vs. 41 J/68 J/0.9 mm have been determined [2]. The relationship used describes thus also the materials discussed in this study satisfactorily though it is not clear if the correlation actually is linear as it has been assumed.

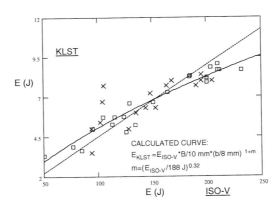

Fig. 5. Correlation of upper-shelf energies. The curve shows an estimate of given type and the straight line the relationship used for determining the proposed [2] transition criteria. Data from this work (o) and from ref. [6] (X) are included.

The USEs of the ISO-V specimens were also estimated from the USEs measured with the KLST specimens by using the derived relationship. It proved that the USE of the ISO-V specimen is predictable by this means with the accuracy of about ± 20%. Three measurements [6] diverged clearly outside this prediction.

The irradiated KLST and ISO-V specimens (15X2MFA-type steels) had been prepared so that the neutron fluences were equal, which made it possible to compare the transition temperature shifts of the base and weld materials exhibited by different specimens. The results indicate that the irradiation shift shown by the KLST specimen tends to be lower than the shift shown by the ISO-V specimen, with the same material condition. The largest difference was measured to be as big as 51°C, and in one case was the difference to the opposite direction, the shift shown by the KLST specimen being 5°C higher than the shift shown by the ISO-V specimen.

The neutron fluences of the KLST and ISO-V specimens fabricated from the irradiated FFA, JFL and JRQ steels were close to each other as well and thus the irradiation shifts of the transition temperatures measured with different specimens comparable. The shifts measured at different energy levels are compared in Fig. 6.

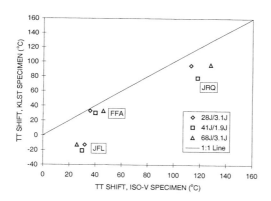

Fig. 6. Comparison of the irradiation shifts of transition temperatures measured with ISO-V and KLST-type impact specimens.

The degree of recovery was predicted quite accurately by the KLST specimen for those steels where the transition temperature shift in annealing was large, but failed to predict the shift for the ones where it was small. The best correlation was obtained at the 28 J/3.15 J energy levels and, which is important, the degree of recovery measured with the KLST specimen was in each case lower than or equal to that measured with the ISO-V specimen. In general, the degrees of recovery at 68 J and 3.1 J showed a large variation between the values measured with different specimens.

CONCLUSIONS

In total, 22 structural steels or steel conditions were included in the study. Steels with four basic compositions were studied in the irradiated condition. The discussion is limited to various energy criteria proposed for determining Charpy transition temperatures from sub-size specimen data, excluding the lateral expansions. With these remarks the following conclusions, regarding the studied materials, can be made from the results of this work.

1. The 3.1 J / 1.9 J / 0.3 mm transition temperatures of the KLST specimen are approximately 65°C lower than the 68 J / 41 J / 0.9 mm transition temperatures of the normal-size (ISO-V) Charpy specimen.
2. The 3.15 J transition temperature of the KLST specimen is approximately 38°C lower than the 28 J transition temperature of the ISO-V specimen, i.e. the difference is on the average equal to that measured with other types of impact specimens at the absorbed energy level normalized according to the ligament area, that is 35 J/cm^2.
3. The USE of the ISO-V specimen can be estimated from the USE measured with the KLST specimen by solving the formulas (4) and (5), where A and m have the values 188 J and 0.32, respectively. An iteration procedure can be used for solving E_{ISO-V}.
4. Transition temperatures should not be measured at energy/lateral expansion levels exceeding about 75% USE. The mean transition temperature shift (due to irradiation) measured with the KLST specimen may require to be raised by at least 30–40°C in evaluating the shift for the ISO-V specimen.

ACKNOWLEDGEMENTS

This work is a part of the Structural Integrity Project (STIN), belonging to the Finnish Research Programme on Nuclear Power Plant Safety (FINNUS), performed at VTT Manufacturing Technology and financed by the Ministry of Trade and Industry in Finland, the Technical Research Centre of Finland (VTT) and the Radiation and Nuclear Safety Authority (STUK).

REFERENCES

1.   Planman, T., Wallin, K., Valo, M., Ahlstrand, R. and Kohopää, J. (1995). Comparison of some impact test results on ISO-V and KLST type Charpy specimens. Espoo: VTT Manufacturing Technology. (Report VTT VALB93).
2.   Klausnitzer, E.N. (1991). *Materialprüfung*, **33**, 132.
3.   Wallin, K. (1992). Mini- ja normaalikokoisten Charpy-V-koesauvojen tulosten välinen korrelaatio. Espoo: Technical Research Centre of Finland, Metals Laboratory. (Report VTT-MET B-207). (In Finnish).
4.   Wallin, K. (1986). Fracture toughness correlations. Espoo: Technical Research Centre of Finland. (VTT Research Reports 428). (In Finnish).
5.   Valo, M., Wallin, K. and Planman, T. (1999). Fracture and impact toughness as measures of irradiation embrittlement based on small specimen data of some pressure vessel steels. Espoo: VTT Manufacturing Technology. (Report VTT VALB370).
5.   Amayev, A.D., Badanin, V.I., Kryukov, A.M., Nikolayev, V.A., Rogov, M.F. and Sokolov, M.A. (1993). *ASTM STP 1204*, 424.
6.   Bryan, R.H. et al. (1987). Pressurized-thermal-shock test of 6-in.-thick pressure vessels. PTSE-2: Investigation of Low Tearing Resistance and Warm Prestressing. NUREG/CR-4888, ORNL-6377.

Applications

From Charpy to Present Impact Testing
D. François and A. Pineau (Eds.)
© 2002 Elsevier Science Ltd. and ESIS. All rights reserved

CORRELATIONS BETWEEN CHARPY ENERGY AND CRACK INITIATION PARAMETERS OF THE J-INTEGRAL-CONCEPT

P. Hübner and G. Pusch

University of Mining, Institute of Materials Engineering, D 09596 Freiberg, Germany

ABSTRACT

For failure assessment procedures of components crack initiation parameters such as $J_{i/Bl}$ and $J_{0,2}$ are needed. Unfortunately in many cases these parameters are not available especially for welded joints. This paper is concerned with the evaluation of the fracture mechanics parameter of base metal and welded joints of high strength steels including the region of yield strength from 600 to 960 MPa. As shown the correlations of the Charpy energy and the crack initiation parameters agree well with theoretical predictions derived from the Schindler model.

KEYWORDS: High strength low alloy steel, Charpy energy, crack initiation, upper shelf

INTRODUCTION

High strength low alloy steels (HSLA) like S885 Q and S960 Q are used increasingly production of mobile cranes and vessels. The use of high strength behaviour demand the knowledge of the fracture behaviour. Newer structural integrity assessment procedures (like SINTAP) are used to assess the fitness for purpose of critical components and welded structures. For these procedures one needs in addition to the crack size and the stress in the component the yield strength and the fracture toughness crack initiation parameters. Thereby one has to take into consideration, that the fracture behaviour of ferritic steels depends on the temperature. For describing brittle fracture depending on temperature the Master curve approach is used [1] (fig. 1).

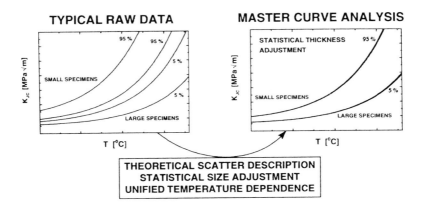

Fig. 1: Master curve approach for transition to brittle fracture [1]

In the Eurocode 3 a modified master curve approach for the selection of steels was suggested [2]. Because of the Master-curve only describing brittle fracture crack initiation values of the ductile fracture are necessary to describe the fracture behaviour in the upper shelf. For that the physical crack initiation values $J_{i/BL}$ and the technical crack initiation values e.g. $J_{0,2}$ are suitable. These values depend only little on the temperature and they limit the Master curve. In the following we want to examine whether the values of $J_{i/BL}$ and $J_{0,2}$ correlate with the Charpy energy in the upper shelf.

EXPERIMENTS AND RESULTS

For evaluation of the crack initiation and propagation in the regions of base metal (BM), heat affected zone (HAZ) and weld metal (WM) of S885 Q (25 mm plate) and S960 Q (10 mm plate) crack resistance curve in accordance with ESIS P2 in dependence of temperature were determined [3].

TABLE 1
RESULTS OF STATIC INVESTIGATIONS

	$R_{p0,2}$ [MPa]	R_m [MPa]	A_v [J]	$J_{i/BL}$ [kJ/m²]	$J_{0,2}$ [kJ/m²]	$T^J_{0,2-1}$ [kJ/m²/mm]
S885 BM	908	954	140	220	277	54
S885 HAZ	978	1032	125	178	222	24
S885 WM	1066	1168	43	59	99	7
S960 BM	1054	1060	83	110	152	14
S960 HAZ	787	1000	79	110	166	26
S960 WM	778	1142	48	58	93	9

The welded joints were produced as multi layer welding. Because of the different plate thickness cooling time between 800 and 500 °C ($t_{8/5}$) was 5sec in the case of S885 Q and 18 sec in the case of S 960 Q. In the HAZ of the S885 Q microstructure was martensitic and in the HAZ of the S960 Q it was bainitic. This can also be seen at the mechanical behaviour of the welding joint (figure 2).

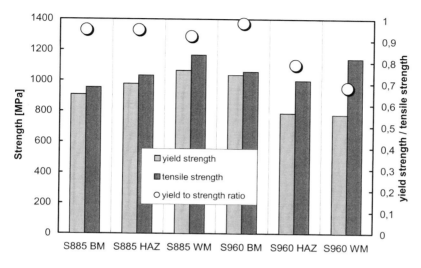

Fig. 2: Mechanical behaviour of the welding joint.

In the HAZ and the weld metal of S 960 Q the yield-to strength-relation was relatively low. This shows, that there is a higher content of bainite. In HAZ and WM of S 885 Q and BM of S 960 Q the yield to strength value over 0.9 point to a higher content in martensite.

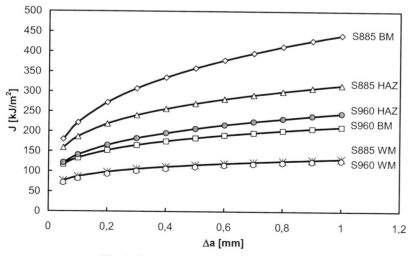

Fig. 3: R-curves of the investigated steels

The static fracture behaviour of the steels S 885 Q and S 960 Q is ductile in the BM, HAZ and WM. The WMs show the lowest toughness (fig. 3). With increasing crack initiation values also the crack resistance increases (see tearing modulus T^J in table 1).

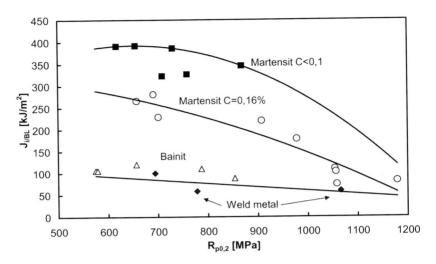

Fig. 4: Crack initiation parameter $J_{i/BL}$ in dependence on yield strength and microstructure

Figure 4 illustrates the influence of the yield strength ($R_{p0,2}$) and the microstructure on $J_{i/BL}$. The martensitic structure with lower carbon shows the highest values and the weld metal with bainitic structure shows the lowest values.

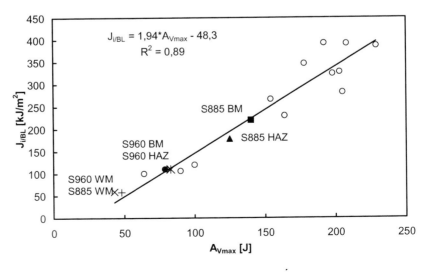

Fig. 5: Correlation between $J_{i/BL}$ and A_{Vmax}

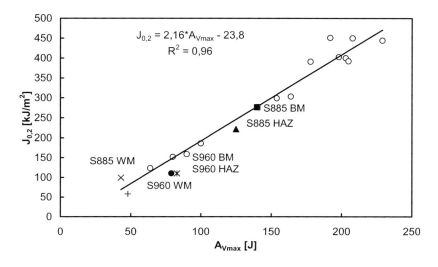

Fig. 6: Correlation between $J_{0,2}$ and A_{Vmax}

In the case of ductile fracture plastic deformation, crack initiation and propagation occur. Because of that we expect a correlation between crack initiation value $J_{i/BL}$ and $J_{0,2}$ and Charpy energy in the upper shelf. Figures 5 and 6 illustrate that this is really the case. All values of base metal, HAZ and WM can be included in this correlation, which was set up for HSLA steels in the yield strength region of 600-1066 MPa with quenched and tempered microstructure [4].

In a theoretical investigation Schindler [5] assumed, that the R-curve follows an power law:

$$J = C \cdot \Delta a^{2/3} \qquad (1)$$

The value C depends on strain hardening exponent n and on upper shelf energy A_{Vmax}.

$$J = 11.44 \cdot A_{V\,max} \cdot n^{1/3} \cdot \Delta a^{2/3} \qquad (2)$$

With the help of the assumption of $n = A_{gl}$ and using (2) with $\Delta a = 0{,}2$ mm follows a correlation between A_{Vmax} and $J_{0,2}$:

$$J_{0,2} = 3.92 \cdot A_{gl}^{1/3} \cdot A_{v\,max} \qquad (3)$$

A_{gl} is the elongation at tensile strength.

For A_{gl} there is an empirical correlation found by Dahl and Hesse [6]:

$$A_{gl} = 10^{-(\log(R_{p0,2})-\log(60))} \qquad (4)$$

An evaluation of (3) using (4) shows a very good correspondence between the experimental points and the model. At higher values of A_{Vmax} the prediction of the model is conservative.

A further statistical examination is necessary to find out whether this good prediction also applies for other steel groups (ferritic and ferritic-perlitic steels). The reason for this necessity is that Schindler assumed the crack propagation behaviour to be constant.

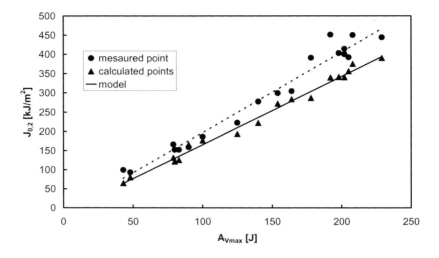

Fig. 7: Verification of the Schindler-model

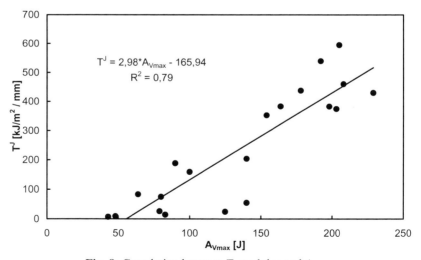

Fig. 8: Correlation between T-modulus and A_{Vmax}

For simplification Schindler assumed a constant exponent in the power law (1) of the R-curve. Figure 8 illustrates that this is not the case, because the tearing modulus depends on A_{Vmax}. Also the crack resistance curves in fig. 3 show different exponents. It follows that the good prediction could be limited if steels with very different crack resistance behaviour would be compared.

CONCLUSION

For failure assessment procedures of components, crack initiation parameters such as J_i and $J_{0,2}$ are needed. Unfortunately in many cases these parameters are not available especially for welded joints. Fracture mechanical tests and Charpy energy tests were realised in the BM and HAZ of S 885 Q and S 960 Q. As shown the correlations of the Charpy energy and the crack initiation parameters agree well with theoretical predictions of the Schindler model.

REFERENCES

1. Wallin, K. and R. Rintamaa (1998).
    In: 24. MPA-Seminar 8. und 9.10.1998 Stuttgart, Vortrag 45

2. Langenberg, P.; Kalinowski, B.; Dahl, W. and A. Mansfeld (1998)
    In: 24. MPA-Seminar 8. und 9.10.1998 Stuttgart, Vortrag 44

3. Hübner, P. (1996)
    Dissertation TU Bergakademie Freiberg, Germany

4. F. Fischer (1993)
    Dissertation TU Bergakademie Freiberg, Germany

5. H.-J. Schindler (1998)
    Proc. of the 12.European Conference on Fracture (ECF 12) Sheffield pp. 841-846

6. Dahl, W. and Hesse, W. (1986) Stahl u. Eisen **12,** 695

From Charpy to Present Impact Testing
D. François and A. Pineau (Eds.)
© 2002 Elsevier Science Ltd. and ESIS. All rights reserved

FRACTURE TOUGHNESS DETERMINATION IN THE DUCTILE -TO-BRITTLE TRANSITION REGIME- PRE-CRACKED CHARPY SPECIMENS COMPARED WITH STANDARD COMPACT SPECIMENS

J. Heerens, D. Hellmann
GKSS Research Centre, Geesthacht, Germany
R.A. Ainsworth
British Energy, United Kingdom

ABSTRACT

More than 400 pre-cracked Charpy specimens have been tested in the ductile-to-brittle transition regime. Their fracture behaviour was compared with that of standardised C(T) specimens of the Euro Fracture Toughness Dataset. It was found that for a wide range of temperatures the type of the specimen less affects the lower bound toughness. Toughness data above the lower bound were found to be specimen size and geometry dependent. The differences in fracture toughness between standardised C(T) specimen and pre-cracked Charpy specimens can not be verified in the conventional way by using statistical weakest link size effect predictions and specimen size criteria as proposed in test standards.

KEYWORDS

Fracture toughness, Ductile-to-brittle transition, Pre-cracked Charpy specimens, Lower bound toughness, Euro Fracture Toughness Dataset

INTRODUCTION

The application of pre-cracked Charpy specimens for material characterisation is of high interest for several reasons. Due to their small size Charpy specimens can be machined in cases where only a small amount of material is available. Furthermore, the use of smaller specimens reduces the testing costs. Pre-cracked Charpy bend specimens are of particular interest for the characterisation of irradiated steels within the framework of surveillance programs. The major concern regarding the application of pre-cracked Charpy specimens results from the observation that small specimens tend to have a lower crack tip constraint than conventional standardised specimens. A possible consequence could be that fracture toughness data obtained from pre-cracked Charpy specimen become non-conservative with respect to standard tests. Loss of constraint effects on cleavage fracture toughness were recently investigated by Ruggieri and Dodds in Ref. [1]. They applied the Beremin cleavage fracture model and found that loss of constraint in pre-cracked Charpy specimens can shift the ductile-to-brittle transition curve to lower temperatures, depending on the material's stress strain curve. In general cleavage fracture toughness has very large scatter and large experimental toughness data sets are required to validate theoretical and numerical predictions. Such experimental data sets are very rare. As far as the authors know there are no experimental data sets, which allow a comprehensive comparison of cleavage toughness data of pre-cracked Charpy specimens and large standardised specimens. In order to support the development of material characterisation methods the Euro Fracture Toughness Dataset (Euro-dataset) was generated [2]. It is a large data set which covers about 800 fracture toughness tests performed on standardised specimens with thickness ranging from 12.5 to 100 mm (Table 1). The specimens were made of a quenched and tempered pressure vessel steel. The dataset covers test temperatures ranging from lower shelf to upper shelf fracture. The Euro-dataset is an ideal reference data set to study possible differences between the fracture behaviour of pre-cracked Charpy specimens and standardised C(T) specimens.

The present paper compares the fracture behaviour of pre-cracked Charpy specimens and standardised compact specimens taken from the Euro-dataset. It was found that for a wide range of temperatures the lower bound toughness is less affected by the type of the specimen. Toughness data above the lower bound were found to be specimen size and geometry dependent with the possible effect that toughness data of pre-cracked Charpy specimens tend to become non-conservative compared to standardised compact specimens.

EXPERIMENTAL

The material of the Euro-dataset is a forged, quenched and tempered pressure vessel steel DIN 22NiMoCr37. It is widely used in nuclear power plants. To enable a direct comparison of test results, all Charpy specimens were machined from broken halves of 4T C(T) specimens tested for the Euro-dataset. A three-dimensional finite element analysis was performed to determine regions without plastic deformation in the broken 4T-specimens. From these regions, about 400 Charpy specimens were extracted. The specimen design is given in Figure 1

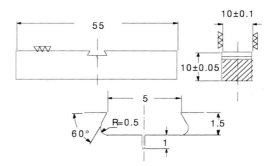

Fig. 1 Design of pre-cracked Charpy specimen

Pre-cracking of the specimens was performed at room temperature using a resonance testing machine. The pre-cracking frequency was between 80 to 100 Hz. The K_{min} / K_{max} ratio was 0.1 In order to sharpen the fatigue crack tip, the final 0.6 mm of the pre-cracking was done using the following K_{max}-values depending on the test temperature: $K_{max} \leq 12$ MPa√m for specimens to be tested at -154 °C, $K_{max} \leq 15$ MPa√m for specimens to be tested at - 91 °C and -110 °C, $K_{max} \leq 16$ MPa√m for all remaining test temperatures. All pre-cracking data are in agreement with the data used for C(T) specimens of the Euro-dataset.

For toughness testing, a three point bending device with a roller pin diameter of 5 mm and a roller pin distance of 40 mm was used. The alignment of the loading device was in accordance with the ESIS P2/92 test procedure [3]. Crack mouth opening displacement, CMOD, was measured via the integrated knife edges using a clip gauge, see Figure 1.

The bending device and the specimen were cooled in a temperature controlled environmental chamber, which was mounted between the loading rigs of the testing machine. The chamber was cooled by liquid nitrogen, sprayed into the chamber. A reference Charpy specimen was attached to the bending device close to the pre-cracked Charpy bend specimen. The test temperature was measured using a NiCr-Ni thermocouple inserted in a hole drilled into the reference specimen. Prior to start the test, the temperature was maintained constant within ±2 °C of the nominal test temperature for at least 30 minutes. This ensured a homogeneous temperature distribution inside the chamber and specimens. During the test, the temperature was also kept constant within ±2 °C. The temperature difference between the reference specimen and the actual specimen to be tested was found to be smaller than 0.3 °C at all test temperatures.

The tests were performed under displacement controlled conditions using a constant load line displacement rate of 0.5mm/min. Two types of load versus displacement characteristics were obtained:

Type A: For unstable fracture of the specimen, the recorded load and
              CMOD data are terminated by the instability point.
Type B: When unstable fracture did not occur , the load and the CMOD were
              continuously measured until the load dropped to 80% of the maximum load.
              The test was then interrupted and the specimen was unloaded.

Specimens, which did not exhibit unstable fracture *(Type B)* were broken in liquid nitrogen in order to mark the final crack front of stable crack extension. In cases where the specimen failed by unstable fracture no extra crack front marking can be performed. For those specimens possible stable crack extension is limited by a transition of fracture surface morphology from ductile tearing to cleavage facets. Stable crack extension and initial crack length were quantified using the nine point average method [3]. The J-integral was calculated at the onset of unstable fracture (record type A). In the case of fully ductile fracture behaviour (record type B), J-integral was calculated at the point where the test was stopped. The J-integral was determined according to Ref. [4] using the following equations:

$$J_0 = \frac{K^2(1-v^2)}{E} + \frac{\eta_{J-C}}{B \cdot (W-a_0)} A_{pl\ CMOD}$$

$$\eta_{J-C} = 3,785 - 3,101\frac{a_0}{W} + 2,018(\frac{a_0}{W})^2$$

$$K = \frac{F_{end} \cdot S}{B \cdot W^{1.5}} \cdot f(a_0/W)$$

$$f(a_0/W) = \frac{3 \cdot (a_0/W)^{0.5}\left[1,99 - (a_0/W) \cdot (1-a_0/W) \cdot (2,15 - 3,93 \cdot (a_0/W) + 2,7 \cdot (a_0/W)^2)\right]}{2 \cdot (1 + 2 \cdot (a_0/W)) \cdot (1-(a_0/W))^{1.5}}$$

(1)

where K is the linear elastic stress intensity factor, v is Poisson's ratio, E is Young's modulus, B is the thickness of the specimen, W is the specimen width, and a_0 is the pre-crack length determined according to ESIS P2/92. $A_{pl|CMOD}$ is the plastic part of the area under the load versus crack mouth opening displacement diagram, F_{end} is the load at the end of the test and S is the roller distance of the bending device which was 40 mm.

RESULTS AND DISCUSSION

The fracture surfaces of pre-cracked Charpy specimens exhibited either pure cleavage facets or a zone of ductile tearing located in front of the fatigue crack tip, which was followed by cleavage facets. In cases where specimens did not show unstable fracture, the fracture surfaces exhibited ductile tearing. This fracture surface morphology is typical of fracture of ferritic steels in the ductile-to-brittle transition regime. The same morphology was observed for the standardised C(T) specimens as reported in the Euro-dataset [1].

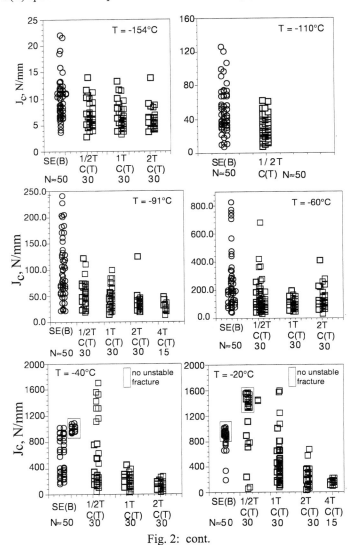

Fig. 2: cont.

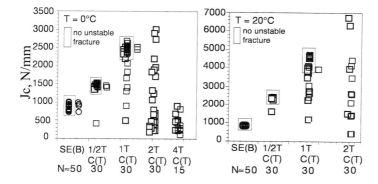

Fig. 2: Comparison of toughness scatter of C(T) and pre-cracked Charpy (SE(B)).

Figure 2 compares the fracture toughness scatter of pre-cracked Charpy specimens and C(T) specimens taken from the Euro-dataset. Note, at temperatures higher than -40 °C, -the scatter bands can not be simply compared. This is because the upper tails of toughness scatter become artificially terminated due to the fact that an increasing fraction of specimens of the data sets does not exhibit unstable fracture. In such cases the tests had to be stopped when the measurement capacity of the specimen was exhausted. By definition, this was the case when the load dropped to 80 percent of the maximum load. For such tests, the J-integral values are not related to cleavage initiation and do not represent cleavage fracture toughness values. In general, Figure 2 indicates that the toughness scatter of pre-cracked Charpy specimen is larger compared to that of C(T) specimens. This is mainly due to the fact that the upper part of the scatter band is stretched out whereas the lower bound of the scatter is less affected. This is most clearly seen for data sets obtained at test temperatures lower than -40 °C.

A statistically based analysis of size effects can be performed by comparing the cumulative failure probability curves of the toughness data sets. Compared to the toughness scatter shown in Figure 2, failure probability curves have the advantage of being independent of the number of data points. The curves are determined for the individual toughness data sets by ranking all toughness data and calculating the cumulative failure probability, P_{fi}, of the individual data points [5] by the following equation.:

$$P_{fi} = \frac{i - 0.3}{N + 0.4} \qquad (2)$$

where N is the total number of data points in the data set and *i* indexes the individual toughness data points in the ranked data set. In Figure 3 probability curves of pre-cracked Charpy specimens and 1/2T C(T) specimens are compared. The main trend of the curves in Fig. 3 is as follows: the probability curves of the C(T)- and Charpy specimens coincide in the low probability regime and split-off with increasing toughness. This behaviour was also observed for the 1T, 2T and 4T C(T) specimens [2].

Toughness data, which are related to a small failure probability are of particular interest in structural assessment. In general the data sets shown in Figure 2 contain 30 to 50 data points in total. It can be assessed from Eq.(2) that the lowest measured toughness value of such large data sets are related to a failure probability P_f smaller than 3 %. In order to investigate size effects in the low failure probability regime, the lowest measured toughness values of all individual data sets are compared in Figure 4. The figure demonstrates that below -60°C the lowest measured toughness value is similar for all C(T) specimen sizes and pre-cracked Charpy specimens. A drastic change is observed when test temperature is increased from -60°C to -40°C. At this temperature the lowest measured toughness of pre-cracked Charpy specimens becomes large compared to that of C(T) specimens.

In the regime above the lower bound where the failure probability is high, the cumulative failure probability curves demonstrate the presence of a specimen size effect. According to the literature [6-10] specimen size effects on cleavage fracture toughness can be due to a statistical size effect

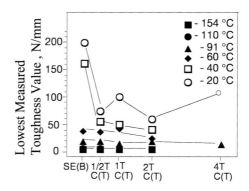

Fig.4:   Comparison of toughness lower bounds obtained at the various test temperatures using C(T) and pre-cracked Charpy specimens (SE(B)).

or due to a constraint induced size effect, or both. A statistical based size effect is caused by the weakest-link nature of cleavage initiation. According to the weakest-link model [7], statistical size effects on cleavage fracture toughness are supposed to be predictable by the following relationship:

$$J_{C,CT} = J_{C,Charpy} \left(\frac{B_{Charpy}}{B_{CT}} \right)^{0.5}$$

(3)

where B_{Charpy} and B_{CT} indicate the thickness of the C(T) and Charpy specimens. According to Eq. (3), the statistical size effect on the toughness data in Figure 3 is supposed to be $J_{C,1/2TCT}$= 0.89 $J_{C,Charpy}$. Clearly, the statistical size effect factor of 0.89 is too small to explain the differences between the probability curves seen in Figure 3.

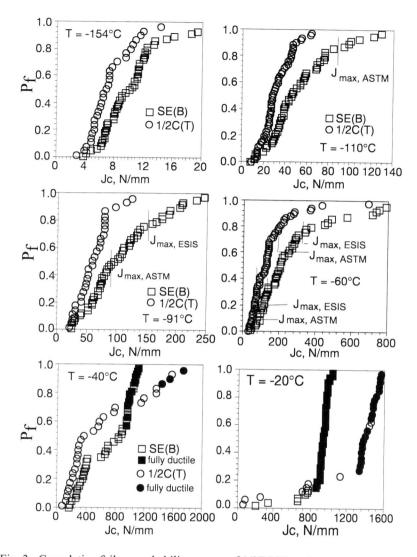

Fig. 3: Cumulative failure probability curves of 1/2TC(T) and pre-cracked Charpy specimens (SE(B)) at different temperatures.

One possible explanation for the behaviour of the curves is constraint induced size effects, as follows. A common way of treating constraint induced size effects on fracture toughness is the introduction of specimen size criteria. Specimen size criteria define upper limits for the application of the J-integral. It is assumed that constraint effects on fracture toughness vanish when J-Integral remains below the limit defined by these criteria. In test standards the limits of the J-integral are defined by the Equation:

$$J_{max} = \sigma_y \, (W-a_0)/\rho, \tag{4}$$

where σ_y is the yield strength of the material and the ρ-factor determines the stringency of the criterion. A range of ρ-factors have been proposed for cleavage fracture toughness data. It varies form $\rho = 30$ and $\rho = 20$ given in the ASTM-Standard [11] and ESIS [3] test procedure. In previous investigations much higher ρ-factors up to 200 were proposed for cleavage fracture toughness data [12]. In Figure 3 the J_{max} limits of ASTM and ESIS are indicated. In all cases a large difference of the curves is seen below the J_{max} limit. This means that the proposed specimen size criteria are not able to "remove" the size effects. Even a combination of the, statistical size effect prediction (Eq.3) and application of the specimen size criterion is not able to explain the behaviour of the probability curves in Figure 3.

Altogether, the difference in fracture toughness between pre-cracked Charpy and C(T) specimens can not be verified consistently by using the conventional statistical size effect prediction and specimen size criteria as proposed in the standards. Above the lower bound toughness regime where the cleavage failure probability P_f is high, the toughness data from pre-cracked Charpy specimens tend to be non-conservative with respect to standardised C(T) specimens. This should be taken into account when pre-cracked Charpy specimens are used to for material characterisation in the transition regime. Nevertheless, over a wide range of test temperatures pre-cracked Charpy specimens are capable of providing cleavage toughness lower bounds which are comparable with those obtained from much larger standard test C(T) specimens.

CONCLUSIONS

More than 400 pre-cracked Charpy specimens have been tested in the ductile-to-brittle transition regime. Their fracture behaviour was compared with that of standardised C(T) specimens of the Euro Fracture Toughness Dataset. Due to a high number of tests it was possible to investigate size effects on the cleavage fracture toughness over a wide range of failure probability and a wide range of temperature. The main results are highlighted as follows:

- At test temperatures lower than -40° C pre-cracked Charpy bend specimens and standardised C(T) specimens with a size range from 1/2T to 4T provide similar lower bound toughness data. With increasing temperature the lower bound toughness of pre-cracked Charpy bend specimens increases and becomes significantly larger than that of C(T) specimens.
- Above the lower bound toughness regime where the cleavage failure probability P_f is high, the toughness data from pre-cracked Charpy specimens tend to be non-conservative with respect to standardised C(T) specimens.
- The differences in fracture toughness between standardised C(T) specimen and pre-cracked Charpy specimens can not be verified in the conventional way by using statistical weakest link size effect predictions and specimen size criteria as proposed in test standards.

Acknowledgements:
Thanks are due to Olaf Kreienbring from GKSS and Michelle Dixon from British Energy for their technical support. The authors acknowledge the financial support from British Energy, which made it possible to perform this comprehensive experimental study.

able 1: Specimen sizes and specimen types investigated

ata source	specimen designation	width ,W, (mm)	thickness,B, (mm)	pre-crack ratio a_0/W
	1/2TC(T)	25	12.5	0.55
	1TC(T)	50	25	0.55
uro-dataset	2TC(T)	100	50	0.55
	4TC(T)	200	100	0.55
his project	SE(B) (Charpy)	10	10	0.55

EFERENCES

Ruggieri C, Dodds R. H., Wallin K. (1998) *Eng. Frac. Mech.* **60**, No. 1, pp.19-36.
Heerens J., Hellmann D. (2002) *Eng. Frac. Mech.* **69**,No.4.
ESIS P2-92 (1992) Procedure for Determining the Fracture Behaviour of Materials. European Structural Integrity Society.
Kirk M. T. and Dodds, R. H. (1993) *Journal of Testing and Evaluation* **21**, No. 4, pp. 228-238.
Kimball F., (1960) *Jour. Am. Stat. Ass.* **55**, pp. 546-560.
Curry D.A., Knott J.F. (1978) *Metal Scienc* **12**, pp. 511-514.
Landes J.D. and Shaffer G.H. (1980) *ASTM STP 700*, pp. 368-382.
Evens A. G. (1983) *Metallurgical Transactions* **14A**, pp. 1349-1355.
Heerens J., Read D.T., Cornec A. and Schwalbe K.H. (1991) *Defect Assessment in Components,* pp. 659-678, Blauel J.G., Schwalbe K.-H. (Eds.).Mech. Eng. Pub. London,.
). Wallin K. (1991) *ASTM STP 1171*, pp.264-288.
. ASTM E1921/97 (1997) Standard Test Method for Determination of Reference Temperature, T_0, for Ferritic Steels in the Transition Regime, American Society for Testing & Materials.
. Anderson T.L., Dodds R.H. JR. (1991) *Journal of Testing and Evaluation* **19**, No. 2, pp 123-134.

From Charpy to Present Impact Testing
D. François and A. Pineau (Eds.)

CORRELATING CHARPY AND J-FRACTURE TOUGHNESS PARAMETERS IN STRUCTURAL INTEGRITY ASSESSMENTS

J.R. Tarpani [1] and D. Spinelli [1]

[1] Engineering School of São Carlos, SMM-EESC-USP
13566-590, Brazil, *jrpan@sc.usp.br*

ABSTRACT

The Paris & Johnson's J_{50} criterion against ductile instability and the here proposed J-value for a 5 mm ductile crack growth (J_{5mm}) have been correlated to the Charpy impact energy of pre-cracked side-grooved testpieces, for a wide range of fracture toughness of a nuclear grade steel. The correlation has been performed in terms of lower bounds, which have been applied to the structural integrity assessment of internally pressurized flawed vessels. The results have shown that both the J_{50} and J_{5mm} criteria can be applied, through the Charpy impact testing, for periodic inspections and hydrotest evaluations of this class of structural components.

KEY WORDS

Charpy–fracture toughness correlation, J-R curve, RPV steel, Structural integrity, Tearing instability

INTRODUCTION

The J-integral is regularly applied in structural integrity assessment of nuclear fuel containment vessels, aiming to ensure safe operational conditions against fracture by ductile cracking mechanisms [1,2]. The most widely used J-criteria are the crack initiation value, J_i [3], and the Paris & Johnson's J_{50} against ductile tearing instability [4]. Inasmuch as J-integral testing of irradiated materials is complex, costly, hazardous and time consuming, there has been a natural interest in establishing trusty correlation between elastoplastic J-integral criteria and those derived from simpler, cheaper, safer and faster test methodologies, as the Charpy impact testing [5,6]. In this work, J_{50}–values resulting from miniaturized compact tensile testpieces, C[T], were tentatively correlated to Charpy impact energies of pre-cracked side-grooved testpieces machined from a nuclear grade steel presenting a broad range of fracture resistance. The same was performed for the here-proposed J_{5mm} criterion, i.e., J-value for a 5 mm ductile crack extension. Lower bound correlation results were then applied to the analytical structural integrity assessment of prototype and full-scale PWR vessels.

MATERIAL AND TESTPIECES

Miniaturized J-compact tensile specimens [7,8] were machined with a variety of plastic constraints from a thick forged plate (T/4 position, T-L orientation) of a nuclear grade steel (A508-3A, chemistry in Table 1), in the as-received and several thermally embrittled conditions. They were fatigue pre-cracked to 0.5 crack length to specimen width ratio (a/W), then side-grooved to 20% or 33% of reduction in their gross-thickness. Figure 1 shows the mini-specimens tested for this programme, compared to more massive standard compact tensile testpieces. Also, Charpy bend bar testpieces (10x10x55 mm^3) were extracted from the heat-treated plates at the same position and orientation, fatigue pre-cracked and side-grooved to identical conditions than J-compact specimens.

Table 1. Chemical composition determined for the A508-CL3A steel (wt%).

C	Si	Mn	Ni	Mo	P	S
0.19	0.24	1.30	0.72	0.51	0.007	0.009

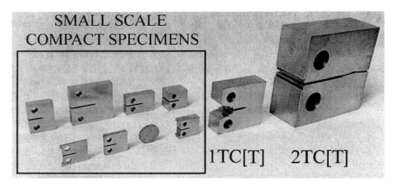

Fig. 1. Miniaturized testpieces for determining the J_{50} [4] and J_{5mm} [3] criteria.

EXPERIMENTAL AND ANALYTICAL PROCEDURES

J-Integral Testing

J-R curve testing was conducted at 300°C, via simultaneously the unloading elastic compliance [9] and the linear normalization [10] techniques. J-Δa (Δa is the crack growth) data points were fitted using power-law, logarithmic and linear fits within well-known limits of J-validity [3]. The J_{50}–values were determined on the J-T space (T is the tearing modulus), by means of a special graphical procedure described elsewhere [4]. The J_{5mm}–values were obtained straightforwardly from J-R curves upon considering a crack propagation level of that order.

Charpy Impact Testing

The bend bar specimens were tested under dynamic loading at 300°C in a Charpy instrumented testing machine using a 300 Joules hammer at an impact speed of 5.5 m/s. The absorbed net energy due to the impact fracture of the testpieces was digitally recorded. The use of pre-cracked Charpy testpieces has become a widespread procedure [11], although side-grooving these bend bar specimens is considered a non-usual practice [12]. This has been used here to equalize the lateral plastic flow restraining in both J-compact and Charpy specimens, thus favoring reliable correlation between toughness parameters obtained from static and dynamic loading conditions.

J–Charpy Energy Correlation

The Charpy energy was plotted against J_{50} and J_{5mm}, respectively, aiming to check out the existence of a well defined correlation between them. Inasmuch as a relatively high J data scatter was obtained in both cases, basically due to the wide variety of tested J-specimen size, geometry and side-grooving level (i.e., plastic constraint), the several utilized J-testing techniques and fitting methods for J-R curves, a lower bound approach was employed, following an exponential law for each J-criteria. As very often comparison is made among J-results derived from a multitude of experimental and data processing procedures, and also taking into account the inherent scatter of J-values due its statistical nature, it can be argued that the use of lower bounds constitute a realistic approach, adequately conservative, for dealing with structural integrity assessment in the nuclear industry.

Structural Integrity Analysis

J_{50} and J_{5mm}–Chapy lower bounds were applied to the analytical structural integrity assessment of prototype and full-scale PWR vessels. They are illustrated in Fig.2, with the principal dimensions supplied in Table 2. The vessels supposedly contain, in the beltline region, axial and circumferencial flaws, which are individually considered during the ever-increasing internal pressurization of the components at 300°C. The analytical procedures established in the ASME Code, concerning the J-T stability assessment diagrams methodology, were employed regarding small-scale yielding solutions [13]. The instability condition occurs [4] when the increase rate on the crack driving force due to the internal pressurization of the cracked vessel (T_{APP}) equals the decrease rate on the material cracking resistance as the ductile crack propagates in the structural component (T_{MAT}), where T is the tearing modulus, a dimensionless parameter.

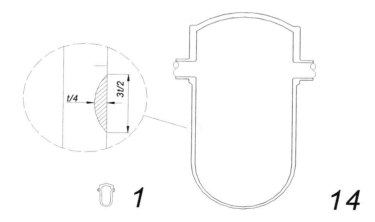

Fig. 2. Cylindrical pressure vessels (*V1* and *V14*) analytically assessed in this study (notice that the numbers' height corresponds to that of a medium size man).

Table 2. Pressure vessels dimensions in millimeters.

VESSEL	wall-thickness, t	inner diameter, ID	height, H
V1	150	690	2130
V14	300	7620	17700

RESULTS AND DISCUSSION

Figure 3 presents J_{50} and J_{5mm} scatter bands related to the Charpy impact energy, along with their respective lower bounds. It should be emphasized that data points correspond to the minimum value obtained for each testing conditions considering the three J-R curve fitting method employed, namely, power-law, linear and logarithmic fits. With a few exceptions, the logarithmic fit provided the minimum results for both J criteria. It can be noticed the slight conservatism of the J_{50} results as compared to J_{5mm}. As a consequence, crack growth at the ductile instability of the components, as predicted by J_{50}, would be expected to be slightly lower than 5 mm. Since J_{50} is a healthy conservative estimate of ductile instability, J_{5mm} may play this role as well.

It must be stated that the J_{5mm}–value has been proposed here on the basis of the original ligament length of the pre-cracked and side-grooved Charpy specimens, established as of order of 5 mm. It was deliberately introduced to improve correlation between the net absorbed energy during impact and the quasi-static J_{5mm}–value.

Simply for comparison, J_{50}–Charpy lower bound referring to experimental data available in literature [2,4-6], is also supplied in Fig.3. It can be observed that it is quite unduly conservative compared to lower bounds obtained in this study. It should be mentioned that literature data refers to standard compact tensile (1T C[T]) and conventional notched and flat-sides Charpy specimens only. Thus, as these conventional Charpy specimens have a significantly larger original ligament area than the pre-cracked and side-grooved ones (about 80 mm^2 against 40 mm^2, at most), the former obviously demand much higher energy levels than those tested for this research programme. This loosely overweighs the well-known conservatism typically exhibited by small-scale highly constrained J-specimens results [4,6,7,14,15].

Figure 3 still shows that both J_{50} and J_{5mm} scatter bands are relatively wide, due to the large scatter on data derived for the as-received and embrittled (quenched and tempered [16] and annealed [17]) microstructures of the A508-steel. However, their lower contours seem to be sufficiently well defined in the whole Charpy energy range, to allow one drawing lower bound correlation.

It should be emphasized that none of the microstructures presented fully brittle behavior either in quasi-static or dynamic conditions, though some very low energy absorption capacities exhibited mixed-mode fracto-features.

Figure 4 provides results on structural integrity assessment of the PWR vessels in terms of internal pressure, so an appraisal over the performance of both J_{50} and J_{5mm} criteria can be conducted related to operational parameters in this class of components. It is readily noticed that, as expected from Fig.3, J_{50} predictions are lower than J_{5mm} ones. As can be promptly noted as well, the prototype vessel (V1) withstands very superior pressure levels than the full-scale one, for identical loading conditions and flaw geometry and positioning. Thermal crack driving force, due to temperature transients typically developed during start-up and shutdown events (cooling rates ranging from 0 to 56 °C/hr), clearly reduces de load bearing ability of the components.

Typical operating in-service pressure (ISP) of 15.5 MPa is pointed out in Fig.4. It can be seen that axial cracks are quite harmful than circumferencial ones. As indicated in Fig.4, high toughness levels overshoot the maximum limit imposed by ASME Code related to the crack depth attained due to internal pressurization, established as half-wall-thickness (t/2). In the V14 case, this observation holds to the J_{5mm} only. For circumferencial flaws, high toughness levels are also associated to the plastic collapse of the V14 vessel-wall, which precedes the ductile instability of the component as predicted by either J_{50} or J_{5mm}. This occurrence therefore prevents these criteria from precisely inferring, if existent, any crack instability event.

The same analysis made regarding Fig.4, are reproduced in Fig.5, now upon considering the average hoop and axial strains through the wall vessel. The plots reveal that there is only a small vessel-scale effect on ductile instability (by means of J_{50}) or other failure criterion (e.g. J_{5mm}) if strain, or stress as preferred, is used as an operational parameter to quantify instability conditions in pressure vessels subjected to in-service or hydrotesting loading circumstances.

It can be also noted that, within ASME Code validity conditions, in this case Charpy energy up to 50 Joules, vessels instability is not accompanied of gross plastic yielding of the vessel wall, in full agreement with the application of small-scale yielding solutions throughout this analysis.

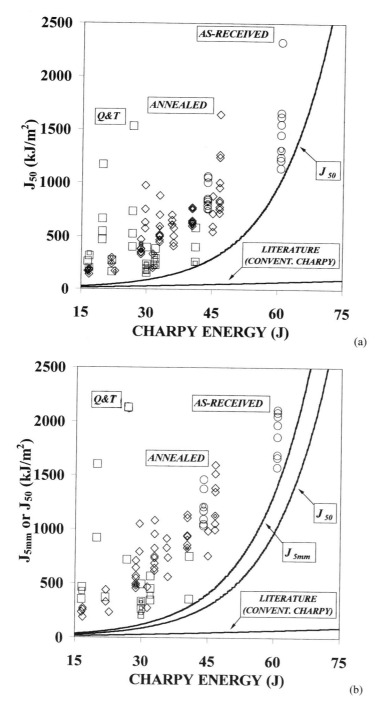

Fig. 3. Scatter bands of (a) J_{50} and (b) J_{5mm} data points versus Charpy energy.

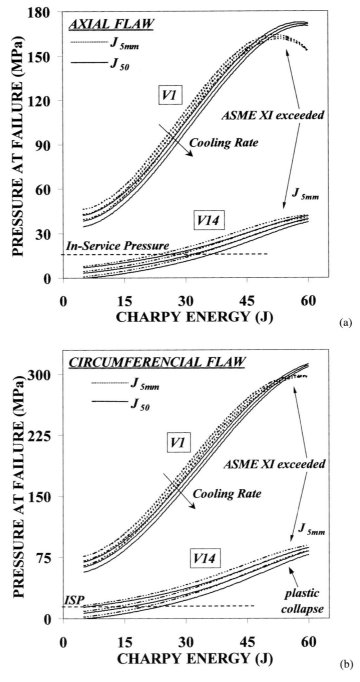

Fig. 4. Failure predictions in terms of internal pressure as
determined for (a) Axial and (b) Circumferencial flaws.

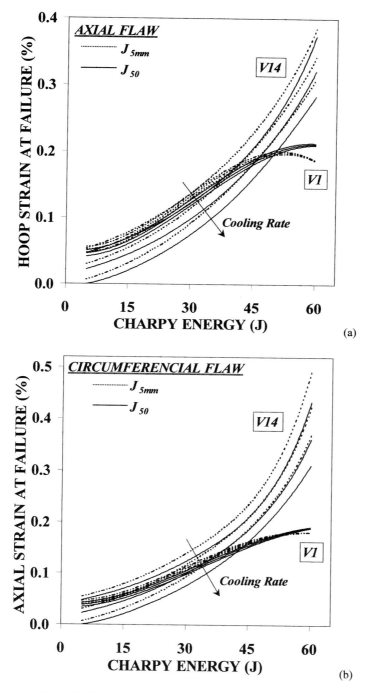

Fig. 5. Failure predictions in terms of average wall-strain as
determined for (a) Axial and (b) Circumferencial flaws.

CONCLUDING REMARKS

Consistent and well defined lower bound relationships have been found between J-integral criteria (J_{50} and J_{5mm}) derived from miniaturized compact tensile specimens and the Charpy energy of pre-cracked side-grooved testpieces for the entire range of fracture resistance of a nuclear grade steel, as obtained through specially designed heat treatments. This analytical study has shown that both J-criteria can be successfully applied, through Charpy impact testing, to determine potential failure conditions in periodical inspections on this class of structural components and in hydrotest evaluations, as well. As a consequence, the feasibility of using Charpy impact testing to improve today's available fracture mechanics-based surveillance methodologies in the nuclear industry has been strengthened.

ACKNOWLEDGEMENTS

The authors gratefully acknowledge the financial support provided by FAPESP (contract 97/05652-1) and CNPq (301485/95-0).

REFERENCES

1.   Zahoor, A. (1988) *Nucl. Eng. Design* **107**, 345.
2.   Kussmaul, K. (1983). In: *ASTM STP 819*, pp.16-28.
3.   Standard test method for measurement of fracture toughness (1997). *Annual Book of ASTM Standards*.
4.   Paris, P.C. and Johnson, R.E. (1983). In: *ASTM STP 803*, **v.2**, pp. 5-40.
5.   Kussmaul K. and Issler, L. (1983). In: *ASTM STP 803*, **v.2**, pp.41-57.
6.   Loss, F.J., Menke, B.H., Hiser, A.L., and Watson, H.E. (1983). In: *ASTM STP 803*, **v.2**, pp.777-795.
7.   Hackett, E.M. and Joyce, J.A. (1992) *Nucl. Eng. Design* **134**, 217.
8.   Zhang, X.P. and Shi, Y.W. (1996) *Int. J. Press. Vessel Piping* **69**, 169.
9.   Neale, B.K. and Priest, R.H. (1985). In: *ASTM STP 856*, **v.2**, pp. 375-393.
10.   Reese, E.D. and Schwalbe, K.-H. (1993) *Fatig. Fract. Eng. Mater. Struct.* **16**, 271.
11.   Standard test methods for notched bar impact testing of metallic materials (1997). *Annual Book of ASTM Standards*
12.   Zhang, X.P. and Shi, Y.W. (1992) *Eng. Fract. Mech.* **43**, 863.
13.   Rules for in-service inspection of nuclear power plant components (1996). *ASME Boiler and Pressure Vessel Code*, Section XI, Division I, Appendix NMA-K.
14.   Wilkowiski, G.M, Marschall, C.W., and Landow, M.P. (1990). In: *ASTM 1074*, pp.56-84.
15.   Marschall, C.W., Papaspyropoulos, V., and Landow, M.P. (1989). In: *ASTM STP 995*, pp.169-190.
16.   Pokrovsky, V.V., Troshchenko, V.T., Kaplunenko, V.G., Podkol'zin, V.Y., Fiodorov, V.G., and Dragunov, G. (1994) *Int. J. Press. Vessel Piping* **54**, 09.
17.   Vitale, E. and Beghini, M. (1991) *Int. J. Press. Vessel Piping* **46**, 289.

From Charpy to Present Impact Testing
D. François and A. Pineau (Eds.)
© 2002 Elsevier Science Ltd. and ESIS. All rights reserved

DYNAMIC J_R CURVES OF 308 STAINLESS STEEL WELD FROM INSTRUMENTED IMPACT TEST OF UNPRECRACKED CHARPY V-NOTCH SPECIMENS

P. R. SREENIVASAN, S. K. RAY and S. L. MANNAN
Materials Development Group, Indira Gandhi Centre for Atomic Resaearch,
Kalpakkam, Tamilnadu-603 102, India.
Telephone:04114-480202/480232/480222
Fax.: 04114-480360/480396/480381/480356/480301. E-mail: mannan@igcar.ernet.in

ABSTRACT. The present authors had earlier suggested a new (shift) procedure for obtaining the dynamic J_R (J fracture resistance) curves of ductile alloys from the load-displacement traces of (unprecracked) Charpy V-notch (CVN) specimens (with CVN energy > 30 J) and demonstrated the method for type 316 austenitic stainless steel (SS). This involves generating the pseudo-J_R curve from CVN specimens using a key-curve method and also by the procedure due to Schindler (Schindler curve). Then the pseudo-J_R curve is shifted uniformly downward to bring it into coincidence with or slightly above the Schindler curve. For materials showing extensive plasticity and homogeneous deformation with no preferential fracture paths like grain boundary fracture, the shift-J_R curve was found to more truly reproduce the slope of the PCVN (precracked CVN)-J_R curve than the Schindler curves, though the latter are easy to generate. In the present paper, the above shift method has been applied to the results obtained from the instrumented impact test on CVN and PCVN specimens of an AISI 308 SS weld at room temperature. The PCVN weld results show more scatter as compared to the CVN results; hence, the reproducibility of the slopes of the PCVN-J_R curves is not as good as in the case of 316 SS and seems to be not much better than that from the Schindler curves. An equation has been obtained that predicts the necessary shift using the power-law exponents of the pseudo-J_R curves from CVN specimens.

KEYWORDS. 308 stainless steel weld, Charpy V-notch, dynamic J_R curve, key-curve, pseudo-J_R curve, Schindler procedure, shift-J_R curve

INTRODUCTION

For very accurate evaluation of toughness of stainless steels (SSs), elastic-plastic methods and use of precracked and large size specimens are necessary [1]. However, there is continuing interest and effort in obtaining conservative estimates of J_{id} (dynamic fracture (initiation) toughness) or dynamic J_R (J fracture resistance) curves using small and blunt notched specimens, particularly Charpy V-notch (CVN) specimens [2-5]. The present authors had earlier suggested a new (shift) procedure for obtaining the dynamic J_R (J fracture resistance) curves of ductile alloys from the load-displacement traces of (unprecracked) Charpy V-notch (CVN) specimens (with CVN energy > 30 J) and demonstrated the method for type 316 austenitic stainless steel (SS) [6]. For materials showing extensive plasticity and homogeneous deformation with no preferential fracture paths like grain boundary fracture, the shift-J_R curve was found to more truly reproduce the slope of the PCVN (precracked CVN)-J_R curve (obtained by well established key-curve procedure) than the Schindler curves [5] (obtained using the procedure due to Schindler; described later in the text), though the latter are easy to generate. In the present paper, the above shift method has been applied to the results obtained from instrumented impact test on CVN and PCVN specimens of an AISI 308 SS weld at room temperature. The results are commented upon and compared with the previous results for 316 SS.

MATERIAL AND EXPERIMENTAL DETAILS

Material tested was an AISI 308 SS weld (chemical composition (wt%): C-0.028, Si-0.48, Mn-1.4, P-0.030, S-0.004, Cr-20.1, Ni-9.9, and Fe-bal.) in the as-welded condition and is described in detail elsewhere [2]. Initial crack aspect ratio (a/W, where a is the crack length and W is the specimen width) varied from 0.2 (CVN) to 0.593. The test matrix is given in Table 1. The CVN and PCVN specimens were tested at room temperature on a 358 J capacity Tinius Olsen Model 74 instrumented impact machine. Full details of the material, precracking, test and data reduction procedure are reported elsewhere [2,3]. All tests reported here were done at the maximum impact machine velocity, $V_0 = 5.12 \ m.s^{-1}$.

METHODS FOR DERIVING J_R CURVES

Key-curve and Shift Methods

The J_R curves are obtained from the test records of both CVN and PCVN specimens using the power-law key-curve procedure described by Sreenivasan et al. [2]. In [2], a modification of the the compliance changing rate (CCR) method of Kobayashi et al. [4] was demonstrated to be more reliable for detecting the crack initiation point in ductile materials. The CCR ($\Delta C/C$) is given as [4]:

$$\Delta C/C \quad = \quad (C - C_{el})/C_{el} \tag{1}$$

where C = secant compliance = d/P at current d on the P-d trace (where d = load point displacement (LPD) and P = load) and C_{el} = tangent compliance = dd/dP from the initial linear portion of the P-d trace. In a plot of $\Delta C/C$ vs. d, $\Delta C/C$ is said to exhibit a rapid increase at the crack initiation point (d_i, P_i) because of decreasing specimen cross-section. In [2], it was found that instead of $\Delta C/C$, $d(\Delta C/C)/dd$ exhibits a more drastic and perceptible increase at the crack initiation point, d_i; moreover, replacement of C_{el} in Eqn.(1) by C_{sp} (specimen elastic compliance) results in more consistent and precisely defined values of d_i. Also, it has been reported that a simple plot of dd/dP vs. d shows an abrupt change at crack initiation [2].

Key-curve method [4,2] has been reported to be successful in estimating the crack extension. Basically, in the case of the three-point bend specimen, (d_{pl}, P) pairs (d_{pl} being plastic component of specimen displacement), starting from a little after yielding upto the estimated point of crack initiation are fitted to a power law:

$$PW/(Bb_0^2) \quad = \quad k(d_{pl}/W)^m \tag{2}$$

where W = width of (CVN) specimen, b_0 = initial ligament depth, (W- a_0) with a_0 = initial crack length and d_{pl} is obtained from

$$d_{pl} \quad = \quad d - C_{el}P \tag{3}$$

Once the constants k and m are determined, Eqn. (2) can be extended to beyond the crack initiation; i.e.,

$$PW/(Bb^2) \quad = \quad k(d_{pl}/W)^m \tag{4}$$

where b is the instantaneous ligament depth ((W-a) with a = current crack length; then

$$b^2 \quad = \quad (PW/(kB))(W/d_{pl})^m \tag{5}$$

Using Eqn.(5), b (and hence crack extension) at each point after crack initiation can be estimated.

Because of plasticity and notch-root effects, J_R curves obtained from CVN specimens are much higher than the PCVN-J_R curves (which is mostly conservative and most likely to approximate the true material property). Hence, here, the J_R curves obtained using (unprecracked) CVN specimens are referred to as pseudo-J_R curves. However, the key-curve J_R curves from CVN and PCVN specimens seemed to show similar slopes [2]. Based on this, the present authors had suggested the following shift procedure [6]: this involves generating the pseudo-J_R curve from CVN specimens using a key-curve method and also the J_R curve by the procedure due to Schindler (Schindler curve, described in the next section)[5]. Then the pseudo-J_R curve is shifted uniformly downward to bring it into coincidence with or slightly above the Schindler curve. This shift can be expressed as follows:

$$J_{\text{shift}} \;=\; J_{\text{pseudo}} + Q.p \tag{6}$$

where p is the exponent in the power-law fitted to the pseudo-J_R curve and Q takes negative values. The power-law J_R-curve is given by the following relation:

$$J \;=\; C \; (\Delta a)^p \tag{7}$$

where C and p are fit constants (C and p from CVN specimens are indicated as pseudo). Q is determined empirically by comparing the pseudo-J_R curves with the PCVN-J_R curves. The observation of the near coincidence between the shift- and the Schindler-J_R curves, offered a reliable method to choose an appropriate Q value for a material [6]. From the CVN specimen, generate the pseudo-J_R curve as well as the Schindler curve. Then, by appropriate shift, bring the pseudo-J_R curve into coincidence with or slightly higher than the Schindler curve. From this, the Q value can be obtained. Though, Schindler curves are easy to generate and satisfactory, the shift procedure helped obtain J_R curves which reproduce reliably the slope of the PCVN-J_R curves.

Schindler's Procedure for Obtaining J_R Curves

Schindler and coworkers [5] obtain the constants C and p of the power-law (Eqn.7) from the following relations:

$$C \;=\; (2/p)^p \,.\, [\,\eta(a_0)/\{B.(b_0)^{1+p}\}] \,.\, E_t^p \,.\, E_{mp}^{\,1-p} \tag{8}$$

$$p \;=\; (3/4).\, [1 + E_{mp}/E_t]^{-1} \tag{9}$$

where E_{mp} is the plastic energy upto P_{max} (maximum load), E_t is the total energy for the impact test (Charpy energy as read from the pendulum dial) and $\eta(a_0)$ is the well known eta-factor. We have used $\eta(a_0)$ given in [2].

RESULTS AND DISCUSSION

J_R Curves by Key-curve and Shift Methods

The power-law constants for the key-curve J_R curves are given in Table 1. Only the constants for the mean curves from the multiple specimens are given (separate fits for CVN and PCVN reults). In contrast to the results for 316 SS given in [6], the specimen to specimen scatter is large in the present case, even for the CVN specimens; for PCVN specimens much larger scatter is obtained (Fig. 1). This can be expected for welds, which are inherently inhomogeneous, and, for which, influence of factors like residual stresses may also be important. In making the fit, for each specimen, the maximum Δa was chosen to be equal to be 10% of b_0, the initial remaining ligament depth ($= W - a_0$, where a_0 is the initial a). The ASTM size criteria have not been evaluated since only the results from same

TABLE 1 POWER-LAW CONSTANTS AND Q VALUES FOR CVN/PCVN SPECIMENS OF 308 SS WELD BY KEY-CURVE AND SCHINDLER PROCEDURES (see Notes below)

Sp. Type and No.	a_0/ mm	E_t/J	p (Sch)	C (Sch)	$J_{0.2}$/(J. mm⁻²) (Sch)	p/Key-curve	C/Key-curve	J_{id}/(J. mm⁻²) Test	$J_{0.2}$(J. mm⁻²) Test	Q
CVN	-	-	-	-	-	-	-	-	-	-
V1	2.0	72	0.553	0.506	0.208	-	-	-	-	-
V4	2.0	76	0.584	0.475	0.186	0.252	0.879	0.327	0.586	-
V5	2.0	78	0.576	0.503	0.199	-	-	-	-	-
J_{shift}		-	**0.551**	**0.541**	**0.223**	-	-	-	-	**−1.5**
PCVN	-	-	-	-	-	-	-	-	-	-
P2	5.33	23	0.641	0.382	0.136	0.492	0.725	-	0.327	-
P6	4.16	36	0.641	0.384	0.137	0.339	0.719	0.158	0.417	-
P8	5.93	21	0.57	0.562	0.225	-	-	-	-	-

Notes:
- J_{id} listed is the mean for the CVN or PCVN specimens from the key-curve test results (Ref. [2]).
- Similarly, key-curve $J_{0.2}$ is from the p and C values of power-law fitted to all CVN or PCVN specimens. Only for P2 (showing the lowest J_R curve in Fig. 1) individual fit p and C values have been given.
- From the power-law, p and C give J in J.mm⁻² with Δa in mm.

size specimens are being compared. The curve from the specimen giving the lowest data is also shown in Fig. 1. The J_{id} corresponding to the crack-initiation point (by the procedure in [2]) and $J_{0.2}$ (corresponding to a crack-extension of 0.2 mm) estimated from the mean key-curve power-law are given in Table 1 for comparison with the estimates by the Schindler procedure. In Fig. 1, the pseudo-J_R curve was shifted down taking $Q = -1$ and -1.5 (Eqn. 6); the Q-factor used is shown in Fig. 1 by the side of the arrows indicating the shifts. The J_R curve obtained by this procedure is referred to as the shift-J_R curve. The shift-J_R curve obtained using $Q = -1$ is conservative with respect to the mean PCVN-J_R curve (olive green curve), but is slightly above that from PCVN specimen P2 (see Table 1 and Fig. 1); $Q = -1.5$ gave a shift-J_R curve much conservative with respect to that from P2; using $Q = -1.25$ or -1.3 would have been all right.

J_R Curves by the Schindler Procedure

The constants of the power-law fit obtained by the Schindler procedure as well as the estimated $J_{0.2}$ are given in Table 1. Application of the Schindler procedure to CVN specimens gives J_R curves that are higher than those obtained by applying the Schindler procedure to PCVN specimens, except for PCVN specimen P8 (P8,Sch in Fig. 2). For the CVN specimens, in Fig. 2, only the Schindler curve from the specimen showing the highest J_R curve is shown (in green colour); the Schindler curves for the other two CVN specimens (see, Table 1), almost superimpose on each other at a level slightly below the highest curve (not shown, to avoid crowding and confusion). In the following, Schindler curve refers to the J_R curve obtained by applying the Schindler procedure to (unprecracked) CVN specimen. Schindler curve is slightly lower than the shift-J_R curve

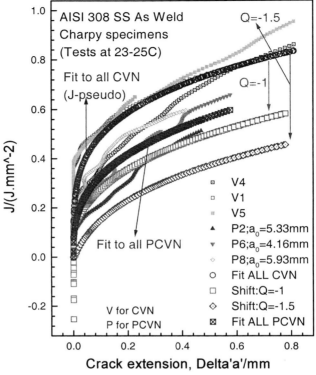

Fig. 1 Dynamic J-R Curves for 308 stainless steel

obtained using $Q = -1.5$. The shift-J_R curve better reproduced the slope of the mean PCVN-J_R curve (Fit to all PCVN, olive green curve); however, in the present case, in contrast to the results for 316 SS in [6], the Schindler curve is almost as effective as the shift-J_R curve in reproducing the slope of the mean PCVN-J_R curve.

General Discussion

Results presented in Table 1, quantitatively substantiate the qualitative observations given above. To restrict the length of the paper, the questions like applicability of a blunting line, constraint and specimen size effects and other issues are not being examined in this paper. In reference [6] and above, the issue of predicting the appropriate value for Q was achieved by the simultaneous application of the Schindler procedure. However, a more direct method for predicting the Q value is desirable, but not essential in the light of the success of the above method. In Fig. 3, the product of pC (where p and C are the power-law constants of the pseudo-J_R curve) is plotted against Q using results obtained for 308 SS in this paper and for 316 SS in [6]. Except for the cold-work (CW) 316 SS, all other data points show a predictable trend. When the 316 CW data point is excluded, the remaining data points seem to fall on a well-defined quadratic curve given below:

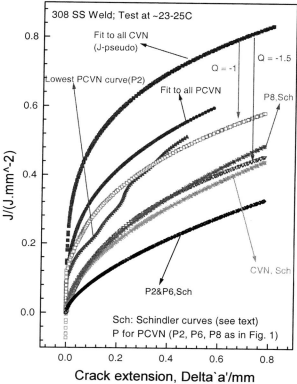

Fig. 2 J-R curves by key-curve and Schindler methods

$$Q = 0.4738 - 9.9787X + 6.428X^2 \qquad (10)$$

(where $X = pC$ and Correlation coefficient R = 0.99334)

This is a very encouraging result which needs further investigation using materials in different conditions; for example, it would be worthwhile to examine whether 316 and 308 SS in different CW conditions fall on a different curve than that given by Eqn. 10. This suggests the possibility that Q is a function not only of p and C, as assumed in Eqn. 10, but also of cold-work level; p and C may be related to the tensile power-law parameters like work-hardening exponent and the constant of the power-law. This needs further verification.

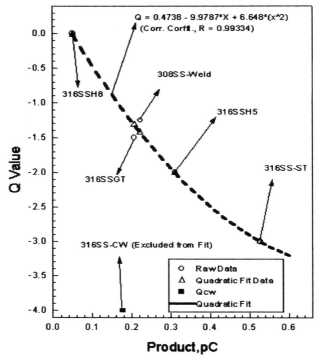

Fig. 3 Variation of Q value with product pC for SS

CONCLUDING REMARKS

- The new shift method earlier found successful for obtaining the J_R curves of 316 SS from the load-displacement traces of (unprecracked) CVN specimens (with CVN energy > 30 J) is found to work for 308 SS weld also.

- The shift procedure generates J_R curve (shift-J_R curve) that more realistically reproduces the slopes of the PCVN-J_R curves (hence tearing resistance).

- For obtaining the shift-J_R curve, a pseudo-J_R curve obtained from CVN specimens using the key-curve method is shifted uniformly downward to bring it into coincidence with or slightly above the Schindler curve (J_R curve obtained by the application of Schindler procedure to CVN specimens). This shift can be expressed as J_{pseudo} + $Q.p$, where p is the exponent in the power-law fitted to the pseudo-J_R curve and Q takes negative values. In the method suggested earlier, Q was obtained by comparison with the Schindler curves.

- For the limited material conditions examined, a quadratic curve relates Q and the product, pC, and is given by:

$$Q = 0.4738 - 9.9787X + 6.428X^2$$

where $X = pC$.

REFERENCES

1. O'Donnell, I.J., Huthmann, H. and Tavassoli, A.A. (1991). *Proc. Int. Seminar on Fracture in Austenitic Components*, October 8-9, Saclay, France, pp. 2-27.
2. Sreenivasan, P.R. and Mannan, S. L. (2000). *Int. J. of Fracture*. **101**, 229-249.
3. Sreenivasan, P.R., and Mannan, S. L. (2000). *Int. J. of Fracture*. **101**, 215-228.
4. Kobayashi, T., Yamamoto, I. and Niinomi, M. (1993). Introduction of a new dynamic fracture toughness evaluation system. *J. of Testing and Evaluation* **21**(3), 145-153.
5. Schindler, H.-J. (2000). In: *Pendulun Impact Testing: A Century of Progress*, **ASTM STP 1380**, pp. 337-353, Siewert, T. A. and Manahan, M. P., Sr. (Eds). American Sociey for Testing and Materials, Philadelphia, PA, USA.
6. Sreenivasan, P. R., Ray, S. K. and Mannan, S. L. (2001). Dynamic J_R curves from instrumented impact test of unprecracked Charpy V-notch specimens of austenitic stainless steel. Poster Paper (Ref:ICF100359PR) presented at ICF-10, 2-6, Dec. 2001 at Hawai.

From Charpy to Present Impact Testing
D. François and A. Pineau (Eds.)

CORRELATION BETWEEN J AND CVN IN UPPER SHELF

W.R. TYSON*, S. XU AND R. BOUCHARD
Materials Technology Laboratory, CANMET
Natural Resources Canada
568 Booth St., Ottawa, Canada K1A 0G1

* e-mail: btyson@nrcan.gc.ca

ABSTRACT

There have been many attempts to correlate CVN with other fracture parameters such as K_{Ic} and J or CTOD. Most of these have been empirical or semi-theoretical, shedding little light on the fundamental reasons underlying any correlation.

In the present work, the basic definition of the J integral, including correction for crack growth, has been used to derive relations between the J resistance curve and Charpy V-notch test parameters. R curves have been measured on a linepipe steel in the upper shelf region for V-notched and fatigue pre-cracked Charpy samples at quasi-static and impact loading rates. The effect of notch acuity on the absorbed energy was small, but the effect of loading rate was found to be large. Comparisons of these results are made with earlier experiments on linepipe steels.

Keywords: CVN absorbed energy, J integral, toughness correlation, resistance curve, crack growth

INTRODUCTION

There have been many attempts in the past to correlate Charpy absorbed energy with more "fundamental" fracture toughness parameters such as K or J. The reasons for this are evident: the Charpy test has been used more than any other to characterize the resistance of materials to fracture, but the results (Charpy absorbed energy, or CVN) are not directly useful for calculating the critical load that a structure can withstand before fracture. For the latter purpose, fracture mechanics assessment is required for which the material parameters required are K or J. In many cases, the only information available is the CVN. Also, the Charpy test will continue to be used routinely at least for quality control. For all of these reasons, it would be desirable to be able to estimate the fracture toughness from CVN.

Correlation of CVN with toughness is fraught with several complications, primarily differences in loading rate and in notch sharpness. These two factors make correlations problematic in the case of brittle fracture (cleavage). Cleavage fracture is well known to be very sensitive to constraint (e.g. notch sharpness) and strain rate, and so these effects must be taken into account in the process of correlation. A technique that is often used to account for strain rate effects is to shift the transition curve along the temperature axis, but accounting for notch sharpness effects is more difficult.

If fracture occurs by ductile processes, the onset of crack growth is much less sensitive to constraint and temperature than is the case for cleavage. Hence, if correlation between toughness and CVN is possible, it would be more likely to be found for ductile than for brittle fracture - in particular, in the upper shelf for structural steels. Empirical correlations for the upper shelf have been reported previously; Leis and Brust [1] suggested a linear relation between CVN and $J_{0.2}$ in the upper shelf, and Mak and Tyson [2] found a similar relation for linepipe steels. However, it is only recently that a theoretical framework that would explain these results has been sought. One notable approach to the problem has been reported by Schindler [3], in which it was proposed that the resistance (R) curve could be evaluated from the Charpy test as

$$J(\Delta a) \cong 11.44 \times CVN \times A_{gt}^{1/3} \times \Delta a^{2/3} \qquad (1)$$

with J in N/mm and CVN in Joules, where Δa is the crack extension and A_{gt} is the uniform strain at maximum load in a uniaxial tensile test. This approach seems to be promising in that it agrees quite well with experimental data for linepipe steels.

The present work was initiated to examine in detail the fracture mechanics description of the Charpy test. In particular, it was intended to take account of crack growth in deriving a correlation between toughness and CVN. Also, since the information available from instrumented impact testing is normally limited to the energy absorbed at maximum load E_m and the total absorbed energy CVN, a relation between these parameters and the resistance curve was sought.

CORRELATION BETWEEN RESISTANCE CURVE AND CVN

Fracture toughness is now measured conventionally using single-specimen methods, such as standardized in ASTM E 1820 [4]. E 1820 contains two definitions for the J-integral, termed here a "simple J" measured by a basic test method and a "deformation J" measured by a resistance curve test method. The latter takes account of crack growth and results in a J value that depends only on the load and the amount of crack growth, as described in detail by Anderson [5]. We will assume in the following derivation that J may be written as a power-law relation

$$J = J_o (\Delta a)^p \qquad (2)$$

The "simple J" is defined by

$$J = \frac{\eta A_{pl}}{Bb_0} \qquad (3)$$

where A_{pl} is the plastic work, B is the sample thickness, and b_0 is the ligament size. For deeply-notched bend specimens, $\eta=2$. A smaller value of η is appropriate for shallow cracks (a/W<0.28). For a Charpy specimen a/W=0.2 and $\eta=1.54$, but after only 0.8 mm of crack growth the appropriate value of η is 2.0 and it was found adequate in the present work to use $\eta=2$ from the start of loading. At complete fracture we may use eqns. (2) and (3) to find J_f (the J value at fracture) by inserting $A_{pl}=CVN$ and $\Delta a_f (=8.0 \text{ mm})$. Similarly, at maximum load we find J_m (the J value at maximum load) by inserting $A_{pl}=E_m$ at Δa_m.

$$\frac{CVN}{E_m} = \left(\frac{\Delta a_f}{\Delta a_m}\right)^P \qquad (4)$$

Then, taking the ratio J_f/J_m we have

This equation may be solved for p provided Δa_m is known; then J_0 may be found from eqn. (3) using appropriate values of the variables at fracture or at maximum load.

Derivation of a relation for the "deformation J" is somewhat more complicated, but straightforward. The procedure outlined by Anderson may be followed, after some steps, to give the general relation for the value of J at a "final" state

$$J_{final} = \frac{\eta \int_{initial}^{final} dA_{pl}}{B\left(b_o - \frac{p-1}{p+1}\Delta a_{final}\right)} \qquad (5)$$

Again, this equation may be evaluated at fracture and at maximum load to give values of J at Δa_f and Δa_m. Taking the ratio of these values to eliminate J and rearranging, we find

$$\left[P + 1 + (1-P)\frac{\Delta a_m}{b_o}\right]\frac{1}{\eta}\frac{CVN}{E_m} = \left(\frac{\Delta a_f}{\Delta a_m}\right)^P \qquad (6)$$

Eqn. (6) may be used to solve for p by iteration when CVN, E_m, $\Delta a_f (=8 \text{ mm})$ and Δa_m are known.

Evidently, to solve eqns. (4) and (6) it is necessary to know the amount of crack growth at maximum load Δa_m. In the present work, the "key curve" method was used to estimate Δa_m and compared with values from elastic compliance unloading (possible only for quasi-static loading). In the key curve method, described by Ernst et al. [6], the load P is related to the plastic load-line displacement Δ_p by

$$\frac{P}{b^2 / W} = k\left(\frac{\Delta_p}{W}\right)^{\frac{1}{n}} \qquad (7)$$

where b is the ligament size, k is a material constant, and n is the work hardening coefficient. In the present work, n was found from the stress-strain curve. The value of k was obtained by fitting eqn. (7) to the experimental load-displacement data during initial loading (from yield to half way to maximum load) when it could be safely assumed that there would be no crack growth and $b=b_0=$constant. It follows from eqn. (7) that at constant Δ_p we have $P/b^2=P_{\Delta a=0}/b_0^2$ and it follows directly that

$$\Delta a = b_o\left(1 - \sqrt{\frac{P}{P_{\Delta a=0}}}\right) \qquad (8)$$

EXPERIMENTAL PROCEDURES

Tests were done using samples of standard Charpy geometry under quasi-static and impact loading. The effect of notch acuity was assessed by using standard V-notched and fatigue pre-cracked (a/W=0.2) samples. For quasi-static loading, the crack length was estimated using elastic unloading compliance (modified for short cracks [7]) to compare with the key curve method. Simple and deformation J-integrals were found using the standard equations in E 1820 (modified for short cracks following Sumpter [8] and Ernst et al. [9]).

The material used was an X-52 grade linepipe steel with yield and ultimate tensile strengths of 376 and 510 MPa respectively and work hardening coefficient n=0.129 (all in the transverse direction). The 20 J transition temperature of standard transverse through-thickness-notched (C-L) Charpy specimens was found to be -47°C, and the upper shelf started near room temperature. To enable comparison with previous work, notches and cracks for samples used in the present work were made parallel to the surface, i.e. samples were of C-R type (surface-notched transverse specimens). For ease of identification, samples were coded as P (pre-cracked), V (V-notched), S (tested at slow quasi-static rate), and F (tested at fast impact rate).

RESULTS

Quasi-static tests were performed following the procedures of E 1820 with the modifications noted above. Crack lengths were measured by CMOD compliance unloading with the clip gage seated in integral knife-edges and by the key-curve method. The compliance data is compared with physical measurements in Table 1. The experimental data and key curve for sample VS1 are shown in Fig.1, and the crack extension measurements by the two methods are compared in Fig.2. Results of the tests are reported in Tables 2 and 3. The value of the energy at maximum load E_m is the total value uncorrected for elastic energy; the elastic component is approximately 4% of E_m for the slow tests and about 7% for the impact tests.

Table 1. Crack length measurements

Sample	Notch	a_o (mm)		a_f (mm)	
		Compliance	Physical	Compliance	Physical
PS1	Pre-cracked	1.82	1.69	7.91	8.74
PS2*		2.01	1.81	2.57	2.36
VS1	V-notched	2.40	2.01	7.79	8.77
VS2		2.37	2.01	7.95	8.81

*Unloaded at maximum load

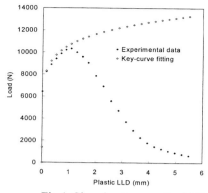

Fig.1. Slow-loading results: VS1

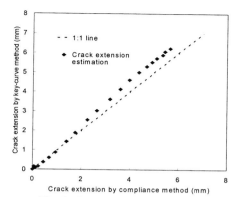

Fig. 2. Crack length estimation: VS2

Table 2. Results of quasi-static tests

Sample	E_{tot} (J)	Avg.	E_m (J)	Avg.	Δa_m (mm) Compliance	Key curve	Physical
PS1	32.4	32.4	10.9	10.7	0.34	0.25	
PS2	-		10.4		0.47	0.32	0.55
VS1	34.2	32.1	10.6	11.1	0.10	0.09	
VS2	29.9		11.6		0.23	0.16	

Table 3. Results of instrumented impact tests

Sample	CVN (J)	Avg.	E_m (J)	Avg.	Δa_m (mm) Key curve
PF1	59	59.5	18.2	20.5	0.91
PF2	60		22.7		0.84
VF1	65	65.5	23.3	23.3	0.45
VF2	66		23.3		0.31

R curves were found using the standard equations given in E 1820, with crack length estimated by unloading compliance for the quasi-static tests and by the key-curve method for the impact tests. Results (plotted as points) for the simple J are shown in Fig.3, and for the deformation J (which takes crack growth into account) in Fig.4. Included is an R curve for a deep-cracked sample tested in slow bending (Figs.3 and 4) and another calculated from Schindler's eqn. (1) (Fig.4). R curves were calculated using the equations developed in the introduction which require information only on E_{tot}, E_m, and Δa_m for both quasi-static and impact tests, and are plotted in Figs. 3 and 4 as dashed lines.

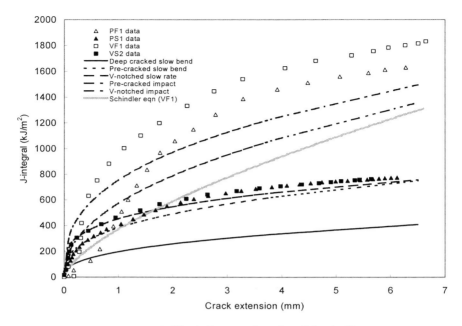

Fig. 3. R curves based on "simple J"

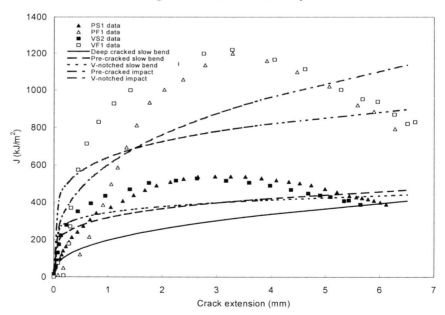

Fig. 4. R curves based on "deformation J"

DISCUSSION

Is it possible to estimate the toughness of a material, i.e. its size-independent R curve, using Charpy-size specimens? The "measurement capacity" of a fracture toughness specimen is $J_{max}=b_0\sigma_y/M$ where $M\cong20$ for ductile tearing [4]. For the present material, for quasi-static loading where $\sigma_y=376$ MPa, the maximum capacity is ~94 kJ/m². This means in effect that only the very early parts of the R curves in Figs.3 and 4 are "valid" in the sense of being size-independent. This does not mean that these results are useless, only that they must be interpreted with caution and that they apply to the material of the same dimensions as the Charpy specimen.

The equations proposed in this paper for estimating the R curve are reasonable for the "simple J" (Fig.3). However, they cannot describe the shape of the "deformation J" curves. The reason for this is obvious: the actual R curves in Fig.4 pass through a maximum and do not have the assumed form of eqn. (2). This is doubtless a result of the limited size of the Charpy specimen and the resulting loss of constraint when the crack extends beyond a few mm; indeed, most standards restrict the measurement of J to the region $\Delta a\leq b_0/4$ (e.g. [4]). In order to account for the actual shape of the R curve, a more complex equation than eqn. (2) would have to be used. For this reason, the "simple J" is a more useful quantity.

Comparison of the measured curves in Fig.3 with Schindler's equation [3] shows that the latter yields a curve of the correct order, but to obtain better agreement it would be necessary to account for rate effects. Schindler's approach implies that the impact CVN can be used with tensile properties to deduce quasi-static R curves in the upper shelf, but the work reported here shows that there is a significant effect of loading rate.

Similarly, comparison with the deep-cracked slow-bend results for the same material shows that the Charpy samples with a/W=0.2 are much higher. This is consistent with other results in the literature reporting a strong effect of a/W on R curves, reflecting a loss of constraint and resulting increase in toughness for shallow-notched specimens [7].

The results in Fig.3 show that the effect of notch acuity is not large, but that there is a marked effect of loading rate on the tearing resistance. Tables 2 and 3 show that there is a large difference in absorbed energy between quasi-static and impact rates.

The extent of crack growth at maximum load varies over quite a large range, and is significantly smaller for V-notched than for fatigue pre-cracked samples. The values of Δa_m seem to be somewhat larger for impact than for slow loading, but this may reflect inaccuracies of the key-curve method. The method relies on curve-fitting in the early part of the load-displacement curve, and because of oscillations in the measured load in the impact test it is difficult to smooth the curve objectively. With this proviso, it may be concluded that the amount of crack growth at maximum load for the steel investigated in this work varies between 0.1 and 0.9 mm, with a typical value of 0.3 mm for quasi-static loading and 0.6 mm for impact loading.

Finally, these results can be compared with data on linepipe steels pre-cracked to a/W=0.5. For the "simple J", at quasi-static rate we have for a Charpy sample (assuming that the material studied here gives typical data) $E_f \cong CVN/2$, $\Delta a_m \cong 0.3$ mm, and $E_m/E_f \cong 1/3$. Then eqns. (2) to (4) give p=0.33 and $J_0 \cong 6.2CVN$ (with Δa in mm). Allowing for a lowering of the R curve by a factor of two to account approximately for constraint effects, we have $J \cong 3.1CVN(\Delta a)^{0.33}$. Then at $\Delta a=0.2$ mm, $J_{0.2} \cong 1.8CVN$. This compares favourably with the experimental result for a number of linepipe steels $J_{0.2}=2.2CVN$ [2].

CONCLUSIONS

1. The "simple J" results were adequately estimated by simple equations requiring measurement only of the total absorbed energy, energy at maximum load, and crack extension at maximum load.
2. The extent of crack growth was measured using a simple version of the "key curve" method, but owing to difficulties in smoothing the instrumented impact load-displacement data, the accuracy of the results at small amounts of growth was limited.
3. The effect of notch acuity on the absorbed energy was small, but the effect of loading rate was large.

REFERENCES

1.   Leis, B.N. and Brust, F.W. (1990), "Ductile Fracture Properties of Selected Line-Pipe Steels", Amer. Gas Assoc., NG-18 Report No.183.
2.   Mak, D.K. and Tyson, W.R. (1998), "Material Assessment of Canadian SAW Line-Pipes", Proc. Int. Pipeline Conf., ASME, Calgary, Vol. II, pp. 711-721.
3.   Schindler, H.J. (1998), Proc. 12th European Conference on Fracture (ECF 12), EMAS, Sheffield, pp. 841-846.
4.   ASTM Annual Book of Standards (1997), "Standard Test Method for Measurement of Fracture Toughness", ASTM E 1820 - 96, Vol. 03.01, ASTM, Philadelphia, PA, pp. 992-1024.
5.   Anderson, T.L. (1995), *Fracture Mechanics: Fundamentals and Applications*, Second Edition, CRC Press, Boca Raton, N.Y., pp. 418-421.
6.   Ernst, H.A., Paris, P.C., Rossow, M. and Hutchinson, J.W. (1979), in *Fracture Mechanics: Eleventh Conference*, ASTM STP 677, Smith, C.W. (Ed.), ASTM, Philadelphia, pp. 581-599.
7.   Joyce, J.A. (1992), in *Fracture Mechanics: Twenty-Second Symposium*, ASTM STP 1131, Ernst, H.A., Saxena, A. and McDowell, D.L. (Eds.), ASTM, Philadelphia, Vol. I, pp. 904-924.
8.   Sumpter, J.D.G. (1987), *Fat. Frac. Eng. Mater. Struct* **10**, pp. 479-493.
9.   Ernst, H., Paris, P.C. and Landes, J.D. (1981), in *Fracture Mechanics: Thirteenth Symposium*, ASTM STP 743, Roberts, R. (Ed.), ASTM, Philadelphia, pp. 476-502.

From Charpy to Present Impact Testing
D. François and A. Pineau (Eds.)
© 2002 Elsevier Science Ltd. and ESIS. All rights reserved

VALIDATION OF IDEALISED CHARPY IMPACT ENERGY TRANSITION CURVE SHAPE

H G PISARSKI, B HAYES, J OLBRICHT, P LICHTER and C S WIESNER
Structural Integrity Technology Group, TWI Limited
Granta Park, Great Abington, Cambridge CB1 6AL, United Kingdom

ABSTRACT

An idealised Charpy transition curve is provided in Annex J of BS 7910:1999 which enables the 27J transition temperature (T_{27J}) to be estimated from Charpy tests conducted at a single temperature. The validity of this transition curve is examined using data representing a range of ferritic steel grades that includes data from parent plate, weld metal and heat affected zone. It is shown that the idealised Charpy transition curve cannot be relied upon to be accurate or to make consistently conservative predictions of T_{27J}. The main reason for this is that actual Charpy transition curves have a wide range of shapes that cannot be modelled by one curve. Recommendations are made for estimating T_{27J} from tests conducted at a fixed temperature. The implications of using T_{27J} derived from the idealised transition curve to estimate fracture toughness using the Master Curve Charpy-fracture toughness correlation are examined.

Keywords:

Charpy, ferritic steel, parent plate, weld metal, HAZ, T_{27J}, idealised Charpy transition curve, fracture toughness, Master Curve.

INTRODUCTION

Situations arise when there is a need to assess the significance of crack-like flaws in structural components and appropriate fracture toughness data, in the form of fracture mechanics test results, are not available. In these circumstances, Charpy data are often used to estimate fracture toughness through appropriate correlations. Although fracture mechanics, as we know it, was unknown to Monsieur Charpy, we are certain that he would have been pleasurably surprised that the test he developed at the beginning of the last century was still being used to help establish the fracture resistance of structural components.

Annex J of BS 7910:1999 [1] provides a Charpy-fracture toughness correlation which can be used to estimate fracture toughness in the transition regime of the toughness versus temperature curve for ferritic steels. It is based on the Wallin Master-Curve correlation and requires as input the temperature at which 27J (the 27J transition temperature, T_{27J}) is achieved in standard sized Charpy specimens. However, for components that have already been built or are in operation, Charpy transition curve data are unlikely to be available, so the identification of T_{27J} is a problem. Codes often require that Charpy tests are conducted at a fixed temperature with a target minimum absorbed energy.

In order to provide a means of estimating T_{27J} from Charpy results obtained at a different temperature, Annex J of BS 7910 provides a reference, idealised Charpy transition curve. This curve was derived from a proposal [2] for defining the limiting thicknesses in steel bridges for the avoidance of brittle fracture. Since the steel specification for bridge construction requires Charpy testing to be conducted at a fixed temperature, an idealised transition curve, referenced to T_{27J}, was used to derive limiting thickness for a range of minimum design temperatures. This curve enables T_{27J} to be estimated from Charpy energies up to 101J. However, the BSI committee preparing Annex J decided that this involved excessive extrapolation and limited the range from 5J to 61J, as shown in Fig.1. This paper reviews experimental data to support the idealised Charpy transition curve in Annex J, and suggest an alternative method for estimating T_{27J} where the data does not support it.

ANALYSIS APPROACH

Charpy transition data for ferritic steels, which included parent plate, weld heat affected zone and weld metal, were collected. To each transition data set, a tanh curve was fitted. This is a mathematical curve that has a characteristic 'S' shape and models the lower and upper shelf as well as the ductile to brittle transition region of the Charpy curve. The parameters of the tanh curve were adjusted to give a fit to each data set with particular attention to the lower shelf to transition regime where T_{27J} lies. In all cases a lower bound fit was made to the data, that is all data points lay on or to the left of the transition curve. Where there were multiple test results at each temperature, a 'best' fit through the middle of data was also made. In addition, these collected data were supplemented by a programme of Charpy testing conducted on one particular ship grade steel plate. This enabled statistical analyses to be conducted on a large, homogeneous data set.

T_{27J} was estimated from the tanh curves fitted to the various data sets and the temperature axis was referenced relative to this temperature. This enabled the fitted transition curves to be compared against the idealised Charpy transition curve shown in Fig.1. Other idealisations of the transition curve are also shown in Fig.1 (from the UK pressure vessel code, BSI PD 5500 [3], and from a draft European storage tank code). They are similar to that in Annex J of BS 7910 but have a more limited range. Although these idealisations are not specifically considered in this paper, the comments made are equally applicable.

Further analyses of the data enabled comparisons to be made of T_{27J} from Charpy results obtained at a fixed temperature using the idealised transition curve with T_{27J} estimated from the tanh curve fit to the data. These estimates were made in two ways; using the minimum energy measured at a test temperature, this was typically the minimum of 3 tests, and by using the average energy measured.

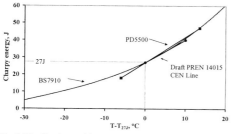

Fig.1 Idealised transition curves

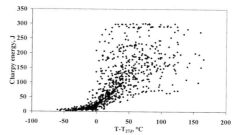

Fig.2 Charpy energy against $T-T_{27J}$ for parent steels (the idealised transition curve is indicated by the solid line)

DATA COLLECTED

Just over 200 Charpy transition data sets were extracted from TWI project reports spanning the past four decades. The data related to specimens notched into parent steel, weld metal, and weld heat affected zone (HAZ), defined as fusion boundary (fb) and general HAZ (excluding fb results). The bulk of the parent steels were C-Mn steels produced to BS1501 (pressure vessel steel) and BS4360 (structural steel). Altogether approximately 2300 Charpy test results were available. Table 1 below indicates how these results are distributed by steel type and approximate date of manufacture.

Table 1 Number of Charpy results by steel type and approximate date of manufacture

Year of manufacture or report date	Number of Charpy data points per steel type					Totals per period
	API 5L	ASTM A517	BS 1501	BS 4360	Not defined	
1960-1969	-	-	78	10	-	88
1970-1979	-	-	78	305	-	383
1980-1989	12	-	106	1523	50	1691
1990-1999	20	8	-	80	36	144
Totals per type	32	8	262	1918	86	Grand total 2306

To provide a visualisation for the extent and spread of the data, Figs 2 and 3 show the transition test results, for parent material and weld metal respectively, shifted by the lower bound 27J transition temperature determined for each data set. In the cases where the data set comprised multiple tests at the same temperature, only the minimum value is plotted.

Equivalent plots for HAZ and fusion boundary results show the scatter to be similar to that of the parent material tests.

In addition to the Charpy data collected from TWI project work, Charpy transition data for a modern Grade A ship steel were available. These data were generated at TWI and consisted of 12 test results measured at each of 13 temperatures, and the results are shown in Fig.4.

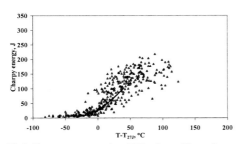

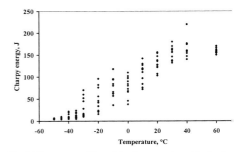

Fig.3 Charpy energy against T-T$_{27J}$ for weld metals (the idealised transition curve is indicated by the solid line)

Fig.4 Charpy transition data for a modern Grade A ship plate, 20mm thick

DATA ANALYSIS

When determining T$_{27J}$ from transition test results, the starting point is the construction of a curve. To ensure consistency and reduce variability, the tanh curve was used to describe the transition behaviour. The tanh curve has the form:

$$C_V = A + B \tanh\left[\frac{T - T_o}{C}\right] \tag{1}$$

where:
T is the test temperature
T$_o$ is the temperature at the midpoint of the transition
A is the Charpy energy corresponding to T$_o$
A+B is the uppershelf energy
A-B is the lowershelf energy
C is a measure of the slope of the transition

It was found that fitting the above expression to the data using a statistical method produced fits that did not model the upper and lower shelves well. Consequently, the parameters were manually varied until a good fit was obtained.

Two sets of tanh curve fits were made to each data set: a 'lower bound' fit, ie with the curve bounding the right of the data, and a 'best' fit where the curve was drawn through the middle of the data. From each of these fits, a value of T$_{27J}$ was determined. The values of T$_{27J}$ were used to reference the data for plotting on a common axis, as in Figs 2 and 3.

In addition to determining T$_{27J}$ from the tanh fits, values of T$_{27J}$ were estimated from test results at a fixed temperature using Fig.1. These estimates were then compared to the corresponding T$_{27J}$ estimated from the tanh fits for that data.

The ship steel transition data were used to generate simulated data sets which were used in two ways. First, simulated sets of transition test results were generated by selecting one data point at random for each test temperature. A tanh fit was made to each simulated data set and a value of T$_{27J}$ determined. This allowed a distribution of possible T$_{27J}$ values for one material to be built up. Secondly, a simulation was carried out to select random data sets consisting of three results at one temperature. Using these data sets, estimates of T_{27J} using the idealised transition curve were made for comparison with T_{27J} from the tanh curves.

RESULTS AND DISCUSSION

The data in Figs 2 and 3 show, unsurprisingly, significant scatter in the transition and upper shelf regions, particularly for parent steels. Of concern is the scatter in the lower transition region where predictions of T_{27J} are made. In addition, lower shelf Charpy values (typically in the region of 6J) can be and are measured at temperatures more than 30°C below T_{27J}, leading to potentially unsafe predictions of T_{27J}.

Figure 5 shows the lower bound tanh fits made to data sets (dotted lines) from parent material with the temperature axis referenced against T_{27J} for each data set. It can be seen that the idealised curve (thick black line) gives a reasonable 'average' representation of the bulk of the curves, but not of steels showing sharp transition behaviour.

At temperatures where $(T-T_{27J}) > 0$; that is, where T_{27J} is estimated from Charpy energies greater than 27J, the idealised curve provides a safe estimate of T_{27J} for shallow transition curves falling to the right of the idealised curve. Conversely, unsafe estimates of T_{27J} are made if the transition curves are steeper and fall to the left of the idealised curve. At temperatures where $(T-T_{27J}) < 0$, that is where T_{27J} is estimated from Charpy energies less than 27J, the gradient of the transition curve as it approaches the lower shelf is critical, as is the temperature at which the lower shelf is first attained, to whether the predictions from the idealised curve are adequate.

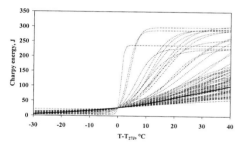

Fig.5 Lower bound tanh fits to collected parent material data

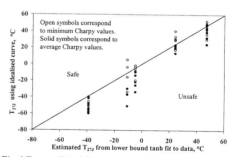

Fig.6 T_{27J} predicted for parent steel Charpy data against lower bound tanh T_{27J}

In general, provided that energies not far below 27J are measured, safe estimates of T_{27J} can be made using the idealised curve. Otherwise, potentially unsafe estimates of T_{27J} may be made. Analysis of the transition curves from the parent material, weld metal and HAZ data sets indicates that if the energy is at least 21J but less than 27J, then it is unlikely that the estimated T_{27J} will be non-conservative by more than 5°C. Of course, the error in making a conservative estimate is larger. Unfortunately, because of the steepness of many of the transition curves, it is not possible to make meaningful estimates of T_{27J} from Charpy energies greater than 27J. All that can be claimed with certainty in such circumstances is that T_{27J} will be lower than the temperature at which the Charpy test was conducted.

In practice, the shape of the transition curve is not known when Charpy data are available at only one, or a limited number of temperatures. The errors in predicting T_{27J} from the minimum or average Charpy energies obtained at a single temperature are examined next.

Figure 6 shows T_{27J} predicted from parent steel Charpy data (from Fig.2) using the idealised curve against the T_{27J} value estimated from the lower bound tanh fit to each data set. Only data sets where there were multiple test results at fixed temperatures were used. T_{27J} was predicted from the average value and from the minimum value for each set of test results. Figure 6 shows that T_{27J} estimated from the idealised transition curve tends to be lower than the T_{27J} found from the lower bound tanh fit, that is the prediction is unsafe. Even if the lowest point at $T_{27J} = -10°C$ is ignored, the error is up to 30°C.

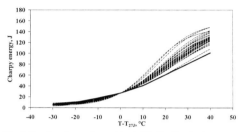

Fig.7 Random lower bound tanh fits for Grade A ship steel

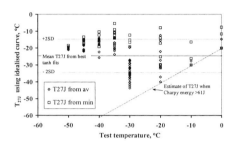

Fig.8 Prediction of T_{27J} from randomly selected ship steel Charpy values

Figure 7 shows the lower bound tanh curve fits to randomly selected ship plate transition curve data (dotted lines), and compares the results with the idealised transition curve (thick black line). The results are generally similar to the parent steel data, representing various steel grades, shown in Fig.5. The mean T_{27J} estimate obtained from this lower bound analysis was -12°C. When the analysis was repeated by employing best tanh curve fits to the same data, the mean T_{27J} estimate was -23°C, indicating a 11°C difference in estimating T_{27J} for this particular steel.

The ship steel data were used to estimate T_{27J} from average and minimum Charpy energies at fixed temperatures (from randomly selected specimens taken in triplicate) using the idealised transition curve given in Fig.1. The results are presented in Fig.8, where they are compared with the mean ±2 standard deviation estimates from the best tanh curve fits. Interestingly, when estimating T_{27J} from results obtained at temperatures below T_{27J}, the predictions are generally conservative if the mean T_{27J} for the ship plate is being estimated. The likely reason for this is that the ship plate Charpy energies steadily rise from the lower shelf. However, the idealised Charpy transition curve is unsafe if attempts are made to estimate the lower bound ship plate T_{27J} (i.e. highest T_{27J} represented by the mean +2 standard deviation estimate). The situation is improved somewhat if estimates are made using the minimum energy from three Charpy results. However, where T_{27J} is estimated from test results at temperatures above T_{27J}, then non-conservative estimates of T_{27J} are likely, as indicated by Fig.8 and also Fig.7.

Clearly, the use of the idealised Charpy transition curve is unsatisfactory since it cannot be guaranteed to provide accurate or conservative estimates of T_{27J} for a given steel. The reasons for these problems are connected with the fact that Charpy energy measured at one temperature provides no information about the shape of the transition curve, and because actual transition curves have a very wide range of shapes that are not modelled by one idealised Charpy transition curve. These problems are illustrated in Figs 9 and 10.

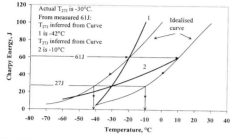

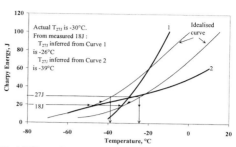

Fig.9 Illustration of how safe and unsafe predictions are arrived at when starting from a measured Charpy value <u>above</u> 27J

Fig.10 Illustration of how safe and unsafe predictions are arrived at when starting from a measured Charpy value <u>below</u> 27J

Predicting T_{27J} from measured values greater than 27J is safe if the actual (unknown) transition curve is shallower than the idealised curve. It is unsafe if the actual curve is steeper, see Fig.9. When predicting T_{27J} from measured Charpy energies of less than 27J, the situation is reversed and the predictions are only safe if the actual Charpy transition curve is steeper than the idealised curve, see Fig.10. However, it should be noted that predictions from true lower shelf values (roughly <15J) cannot be made, as such data give no information at all about the transition behaviour.

To sum up, analyses of Charpy transition data from a range of ferritic steel plates, weld metals and HAZs show that, as expected, there is a wide range of transition curve shapes. The idealised transition curve in Annex J of BS 7910 provides an approximately mean fit to the data. Nevertheless, it cannot be shown to provide a conservative lower bound always. Since Charpy tests conducted at a single temperature provide no information as to the shape of the transition curve, potentially unsafe estimates of T_{27J} may be made using the idealised curve. In particular, because of the steepness of many Charpy transition curves, it is not possible to safely estimate T_{27J} from the idealised curve when the Charpy energy is greater than 27J. All that can be safely claimed is that T_{27J} is less than the Charpy test temperature. If the Charpy energy is less than 27J but above 21J, it can be claimed that for each 1J below 27J, $(T-T_{27J})$ is $-1°C$, where T is the test temperature. However, even this small correction could be in error by up to 5°C.

IMPLICATION FOR FRACTURE TOUGHNESS ESTIMATES

As this analysis of Charpy data indicates that an idealised transition curve cannot be relied upon to estimate T_{27J} accurately or conservatively, the question arises as to the implications that this has on estimation of fracture toughness. Although the purpose of this paper is not to examine the Charpy-fracture toughness correlations, some comments are possible. The Master Curve correlation in Annex J of BS 7910:1999 is intended to be conservative. Conservatism is achieved by taking a 95% confidence limit on the basic correlation between the temperature for a median fracture toughness of 100MPa√m ($T_{100MPa√m}$) for a reference 25mm thick material and T_{27J}. In addition, Annex J recommends that the probability at which fracture toughness is estimated from the Master Curve is the lower 5th percentile ($P_f = 0.05$).

The implications of this can be assessed for the Grade A ship steel plate for which fracture toughness test results are available in addition to Charpy test results shown in Fig.4. The results of the fracture mechanics tests are shown in Fig.11, where they are compared with the prediction made using the Master Curve correlation as per Annex J. The analyses were made for T_{27J} = -23°C which is the mean estimate from the best tanh fits, for T_{27J} = -44°C, which is the lowest estimate obtained from the idealised Charpy transition curve for tests conducted at single temperatures above T_{27J}, and for T_{27J} = -6°C, which is the highest T_{27J} estimated from the idealised Charpy transition curve, see Fig.8.

It is clear that the predicted fracture toughness (K_J) transition curve is not very sensitive to the choice of T_{27J}, and that the predictions are very conservative with respect to this particular set of experimental data. Consequently, it can be concluded, at least on the basis of the data available here, that the errors in estimating T_{27J} using the idealised Charpy transition curve are likely to have minimal impact on making non-conservative fracture toughness estimates. The main reason for this is overall conservatism in the fracture toughness correlation. Nevertheless, it is recommended that the best way forward would be to improve/modify the method of estimating T_{27J} in Annex J, possibly along the lines suggested here, and relax the conservatism in the Master Curve by selecting a higher value of P_f for making fracture toughness estimates.

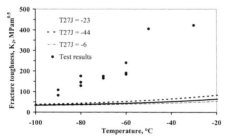

Fig.11 Comparison between fracture toughness predicted from T_{27J} and experimental data

CONCLUSIONS

Analyses of Charpy data obtained on ferritic steels which included parent plate, weld metal and HAZ show that the idealised Charpy transition curve in Annex J in BS 7910:1999 is not always conservative. Consequently, it is recommended that it should not be used to estimate T_{27J} from Charpy results obtained at a single temperature. Where energies above 27J are measured at a specific temperature, it is recommended that T_{27J} is assumed to be that temperature. If less than 27J is measured, but more than 21J, it is recommended that T_{27J} is estimated by assuming that for each 1J below 27J, $(T-T_{27J})$ is –1°C, where T is the test temperature. It is recommended that estimates of T_{27J} are not made when minimum energies below 21J are measured.

REFERENCES

1.   BS 7910:1999 Incorporating Amendment No. 1 (2000). British standards Institution.
2.   Burdekin, F.M. (1981). In: *The Design of Steel Bridges*, Rockey, K.C and Evans, H.R. (Eds). Granada Publishing.
3.   PD 5500:2000 (2000). British Standards Institution.

From Charpy to Present Impact Testing
D. François and A. Pineau (Eds.)
© 2002 Elsevier Science Ltd. and ESIS. All rights reserved

CONVENTIONAL AND FRACTURE MECHANICAL VALUATION OF STRUCTURAL STEELS WITH HIGH TOUGHNESS FOR HEAVY PLATES

Peter Trubitz, Peter Hübner, Gerhard Pusch, Thomas Brecht[*]
Freiberg University of Mining and Technology, Institute of Materials Engineering,
09596 Freiberg, Germany
[*] Ilsenburger Grobblech GmbH, 38871 Ilsenburg, Germany

ABSTRACT

For a new generation of thermomechanically rolled high-strength structural steel grades of qualities S355ML to S460ML, with a plate thickness up to 120 mm, an excellent toughness behavior based on very fine and highly homogeneous grain is proven by metallographic and conventional as well as fracture mechanical valuation. For high plate thickness and other factors promoting brittle fracture such as low use temperature and impact loads, this results in a strong argument for using such high-toughness steel grades.

KEYWORDS

high-strength fine-grain structural steel, Charpy test, Pellini test, transition temperatures, NDT temperature, fracture toughness, brittle fracture safety proof

INTRODUCTION

In early 1999, the Ilsenburg rolling plant of Salzgitter AG started the production of a new generation of thermomechanically rolled high-strength structural steel grades S355ML, S420ML and S460ML with > 63 to 120 mm plate thickness. The valid standard DIN EN 10113-3 [1] limits the product range to ≤ 63 mm in view of the reduced toughness and property anisotropy of thicker thermomechanically rolled plates.

On the basis of the requirements of the heavy steel construction industry, shipbuilding, and the offshore industry, who want to use the good weldability of TM steels with thicker plates as well, the objective of our investigations was to modify the TM technology so that satisfactory toughness would be guaranteed for plates of greater thickness as well. The usual TM strategies comprise preliminary rolling, one or two intermediate rolling phases, and a subsequent finishing phase. With increasing thickness of the final plate, the intermediate time, i.e. the time between the preliminary and the finishing phase, increases. In this intermediate time, processes of recrystallization and grain growth take place that produce a non-homogeneous microstructure. These coarsely heterogeneous structures can only partially be removed afterwards due to the insufficient final forming degree. They are the cause of the reduced toughness and increased anisotropy of properties with increasing material thickness. To avoid these coarsely heterogeneous structures for a given forming degree, the intermediate time must be reduced. The Ilsenburg rolling plant has decided to totally avoid the intermediate time by a two-heat strategy. Now the rolling process consists of preliminary rolling, cooling the plate to below 600 °C, subsequent reheating to normalizing temperature, and finishing rolling with subsequent intensive cooling (Fig. 1).

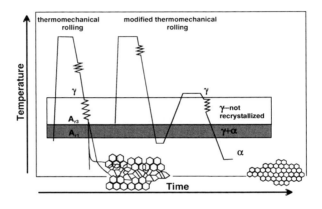

Fig. 1: Comparison of modified and classical thermomechanical rolling

This method inserts two additional grain-fining processes, namely the γ-α transformation after preliminary rolling and the α-γ transformation prior to finishing rolling. A fine-grained homogeneous microstructure prevails prior to finishing rolling.

This article will present first results. In view of their excellent toughness characteristics, the above steel grades will be called SZ grades (*sonderzähe Baustähle* in German: high-toughness structural steels) in the following. The chemical composition of the steel grades is given in Table 1:

Tab. 1: Chemical composition of SZ steel grades (weight %)

SZ steel grades	C	Si	Mn	V	Nb	P	S
S355ML	0,066	0,41	1,54	-	0,05	0,012	0,001
S460ML	0,087	0,48	1,71	0,1	0,05	0,015	0,003

THEORETICAL BACKGROAND OF EXPERIMENTS

A major design criterion in steel construction is the brittle fracture safety proof as laid out in Annex C to EUROCODE III [2]. The protection from brittle fracture is based on the fracture mechanical analysis of a design detail relevant to steel construction and formulates the toughness requirement to the material as a function of its use temperature, load rate, and plate thickness of the element. A hypothetical crack is assumed that might have formed in the service time by cyclic load. The fracture toughness K_{IJ} necessary to avert brittle fracture is calculated. From the unified temperature curve of the fracture toughness according to Wallin [3], a transition temperature T_{KJ100} to be fulfilled by the material is derived at which the elastic-plastic fracture toughness is $K_{IJ} = 100$ MPa√m. The required steel quality is then determined by a correlation between the temperature T_{KJ100} and the transition temperature of the Charpy V-notch pendulum impact test T_{27J}. The concept of EUROCODE III is applicable to SZ steels if the validity of the correlation between the transition temperature T_{KJ100} and T_{27J} can be proved for these grades. Special attention must be paid to the possible thickness dependence of the material properties.

The following solution path was chosen to characterize the SZ steel grades and to describe their properties [4,5]:

- Determination of properties with regard both to the specimen's position to the rolling direction, to assess the influence of the rolling texture (grain stretching) on the properties, and the specimen's position in terms of plate height, to describe the thickness dependence of the properties
- The test program comprised both metallographic microstructure investigations, conventional toughness and limit temperature determination from the Charpy V-notch pendulum impact bending test [6,7], and temperature-dependent fracture mechanical investigations under static load [8,9] to describe the toughness as a function of the plate thickness and specimen position in the plate
- Determination of NDT temperature as crack interception limit temperature by drop test according to Pellini [10]

RESULTS

Microstructure

The microstructure of the SZ steel grades rolled by the new technology clearly differs from that of the classical thermomechanically rolled steel L480.7M (Fig. 2). The ASTM grain No. [11] cannot reflect these differences except those in grain size. Property controlling micro structural characteristics, which describe the heterogeneity or uniformity of the material, can be shown by the methods of stereographic metallography according to Saltykov [12]. The so-called 'intersection rose' is used to represent the orientation of a real interfacial system. It is obtained by representing the referred number of intersections m, which is determined for various angles starting from the orientation axis, in polar coordinates. Accordingly, the 'intersection rose' for a two-dimensional isometric system is a circle with its center in the origin of coordinates. Deviations from this shape prove the existence of an orientation or a non-homogeneous grain structure, since the 'intersection rose' markedly deviates from the circular shape even in cases where an orientation can hardly be detected visually [12,13]. The investigations of the microstructural orientation have shown the SZ steels to have an extraordinarily finely disperse microstructure combined with a low degree of orientation over the entire plate thickness for plates up to 120 mm. For identical plate thickness, the SZ steels excel over classical thermomechanically rolled steels by a markedly better microstructural homogeneity and excellent grain fineness.

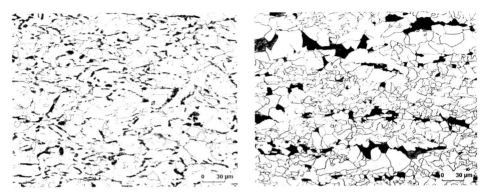

Fig. 2: Light micrograph of a longitudinal specimen from the middle layer
- left: steel S460ML; plate thickness = 120 mm
- right: steel L485M; plate thickness = 50 mm

Toughness Properties

Steel grades S355ML and S460ML have very high toughness and low transition temperatures up to a plate thickness of 120 mm. Their upper shelf energy is greater than 200 J. Figure 3 illustrates this for grade S355ML with s = 60 mm.

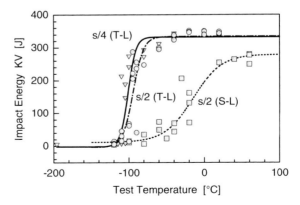

Fig. 3: Impact energy vs. temperature curve of steel S355ML, s = 60 mm
  T-L: Specimen's orientation transversal to rolling direction, fracture direction parallel with rolling direction
  S-L: Specimen's orientation in thickness direction, fracture direction in rolling plane

There is only a very slight dependence of the properties on the position in the plate, which becomes clear from the very similar shape of the KV-T curves for s/2 and s/4 (both in transversal direction T-L). The decrease of the properties in thickness direction (S-L) is significant and explained by the low rolling texture; however, toughness remains very high in comparison with classical TM steels even for this specimen position. The transition temperatures are below –80 °C.

Figure 4 shows the independence of the transition temperatures of the plate thickness for the T-L position at s/4 and the rather slight thickness dependence of the transition temperatures in the middle layer for the example of the 27-J transition temperature. Similar statements hold for transition temperatures according to the "0.4 mm lateral expansion" and "KVmax/2" criteria.

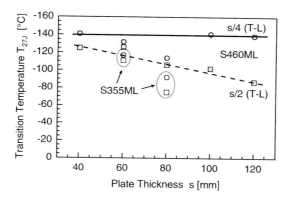

Fig. 4: Transition temperature T_{27J} of steel S460ML (SZ)

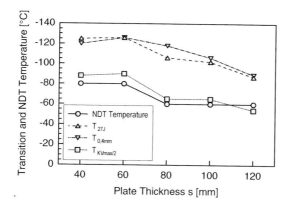

Fig. 5: Transition temperatures in the middle layer of S460ML steel plate
(Charpy specimens: T-L orientation; Pellini specimens: L-T orientation)

As the transition temperatures from the Charpy test, the NDT temperatures determined by the Pellini drop test confirm the very good toughness of grades S355ML and S460ML. Up to a thickness of 80 mm, the NDT temperature slightly increases both at the edge and in the core of the plate, and remains -60 °C independently of the thickness after s = 80 mm (Fig. 5). The good agreement between the NDT temperature and the TKVmax/2 transition temperature is remarkable

Results of Fracture Mechanical Test (Static Loading)

The high toughness of steel grades S355ML and S460ML is confirmed by fracture mechanical investigations under static load. It was only below -100 °C that brittle fracture was observed after plastic deformation; at higher temperatures, the specimens mostly failed by plastic collapse. The physical crack initiation values of the CTOD concept were determined by SEM measurement of the critical stretching zone height SZH_c according to $\delta_i = 2 \cdot SZH_c$ (Fig. 6). These physical crack initiation values can also be applied to individual parts, as is shown by the good fitting-in of a test of a SENB specimen of 120 mm thickness. The influence of the different plate thicknesses and specimen positions is comparatively weak, and can be explained by the small microstructural anisotropy.

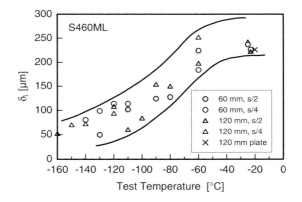

Fig. 6: Crack initiation values of the CTOD concept as a function of temperature

Brittle Fracture Safety Proof

The low-temperature tests in which brittle fracture occurred after plastical deformation were evaluated according to the concept of Wallin [3, 14]. In this concept, the temperature dependence of the individual specimen positions and materials is referred to the temperature T_{KJ100}, at which the elastic-plastic fracture toughness K_{IJ} is exactly 100 MPa√m. We found that the curves for steel grades S355ML and S460ML are similar and can be described by the concept of Wallin. The evaluation of the results obtained for steel grades S355ML and S460ML by the EUROCODE III correlation of the fracture mechanical transition temperature T_{KJ100} with the transition temperature T_{27J} confirms that the brittle fracture safety concept of EUROCODE III can be applied to these steel grades, Fig. 7.

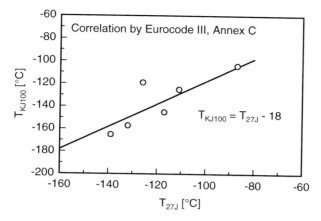

Fig. 7: Correlation between the transition temperature for $K_{IJ} = 100$ MPa√m and the transition temperature T_{27J}

The new guideline DASt 009 [15] for steel selection for weldable structural steels makes use of the fracture mechanical background of EUROCODE III. If the assessment principles of DASt 009 are applied to the high-toughness steel grades S355ML and S460ML, it follows as a result of our investigations that these thermomechanically treated steel grades can be used up to a plate thickness of 120 mm in heavy steel construction even beyond the stipulations of DIN EN 10113-3, Fig. 8.

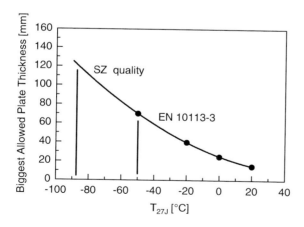

Fig. 8: Toughness requirement for S355ML (SZ) plate at 75 % yield strength and a service temperature of -30 °C

REFERENCES

1. DIN EN 10113-3. (1993). *Warmgewalzte Erzeugnisse aus unlegierten Baustählen*
2. DINV ENV 1993-1-1: Eurocode III, Teil 1-1. (1993). *Bemessung and Konstruktion von Stahlbauten, Allgemeine Bemessungsregeln, Bemessungsregeln für den Hochbau*
3. Wallin, K. (1992). *Recommendations for fracture toughness data for structural integrity analysis.* Proc. CSNI/IAEA Specialists Meeting, Oak Ridge, Tenn
4. Brecht, Th. (2000). Dissertation, TU Bergakademie Freiberg
5. Trubitz, P., Hübner, P., Brecht, Th. and Kreschel, Th. (1999). STAHL, 5, pp. 36
6. DIN EN 10045. (1991). *Metallische Werkstoffe. Kerbschlagbiegeversuch nach Charpy*
7. DIN 50115. (1991). *Prüfung metallischer Werkstoffe. Kerbschlagbiegeversuch. Besondere Probeform and Auswerteverfahren*
8. ESIS P2-92. (1992). *ESIS Procedure for Determining the Fracture Behaviour of Materials*, European Structural Integrity Society, Delft
9. ISO/TC164/SC4-N140. (1996). *Metallic materials – Unified method of test for the determination of quasistatic fracture toughness*
10. Stahl-Eisen-Prüfblatt SEP 1325. (1982). *Fallgewichtsversuch nach W. S. Pellini*
11. DIN 50601. (1985). *Ermittlung der Ferrit- oder Austenitkorngröße von Stahl and Eisenwerkstoffen*
12. Saltykov, A. (1974) *Stereometrische Metallographie.* Deutscher Verlag für Grundstoffindustrie, Leipzig
13. Stoyan, D., Peisker, D. and Ohser, J. (1981). **26** Neue Hütte, 2, pp. 65
14. ASTM E1921-98. (1998). *Standard test method for determination of reference temperature, T0, for ferritic steels in the transition range*
15. DASt Richtlinie 009. *Empfehlungen zur Wahl der Stahlsorte für geschweißte Stahlbauten*

From Charpy to Present Impact Testing
D. François and A. Pineau (Eds.)
© 2002 Elsevier Science Ltd. and ESIS. All rights reserved

CORRELATIONS BETWEEN CHARPY V AND CRACK TIP OPENING DISPLACEMENT AS WELL AS DROP WEIGHT TEAR TEST RESULTS

J. DZIUBIŃSKI and P.ADAMIEC

*Institute of Transport, Silesian Technical University, ul. Krasińskiego 8
40-019 Katowice, Poland*

ABSTRACT

The trial of a correlation of Charpy V and static and dynamic CTOD results on structural steel weldments made by different procedures was undertaken. On the base of examinations and calculations the mathematical correlations between Charpy test and static and dynamic CTOD tests results have stated that small changes of stress intensity fracture toughness factor relate to great toughness changes, what means that Charpy toughness is more selective then CTOD test. It has been shown that obtained relationships can help in practical usage Charpy toughness test results in engineering calculations. The parabolic correlation between transition temperature determined on the base of Charpy V (KV = 28J) and transition temperature determined on the base of dynamic CTOD (δ_{cd} = 0.06 mm) test results has been also stated. The linear correlation between transition temperature determined on the level of 50% shear fracture for the Charpy V test and transition temperature determined on the level of 85% shear fracture for the DWT test has been stated too for structural steels.

KEYWORDS

Structural steels, welded joints, notch toughness, crack opening displacement

INTRODUCTION

In spite of many criticism one of the most commonly used tests of steel toughness is the Charpy V impact test, which distinguishes oneself low costs and is easy to carry out. The results of this test are usually the base for acceptance of steel and welded structures applied nearly all the classification societies. They also serve, in most cases, for the determination of the transition temperature. Experience gained over many years also allowed to determine the critical level for transition temperature determination. The oldest criterion is the absorbed energy value of 28 J established from the study of ship brittle fractured during the Second

World War. The other criterion for the determination of the transition temperature is 50% shear fracture. At present, these criteria are frequently not sufficient, particularly when high – strength steels are to be assessed. Among others, a relationship has been suggested to be used between the absorbed energy value and the yield point [1]. However, the absolute impact value or the determined transition temperature cannot be directly used in the welded structure design. Hence a need exists to determine the interrelations between impact test results and results obtained in other toughness tests e.g. dynamic or static crack tip opening displacement (CTOD). These tests permit to determine the stress intensity factor under the conditions of unstable crack growth and, at the same time, to define, with some approximation, allowable defect size [2,3].

The determination of this relationship may allow the designers to utilize the Charpy V impact test results for more accurate determination of permissible stress, at the presence of possible flaws being assumed or the determination of allowable flaws at the stress level found in the structure. The determination of the relationship between the transition temperature defined on the base Charpy V tests and the transition temperature defined on the base of the fracture mechanics or drop weight tear (DWT) tests, allows to avoid the expensive and labour-consuming testing.

With this purpose in mind an attempt was undertaken to relate the Charpy V impact test results with the results of static and dynamic CTOD tests for a number of joints that occur most commonly in low-carbon and low-alloy structural steels welded with various processes. Correlations between the transition temperature determined on the base of Charpy V tests and the transition temperature determined on the base of fracture mechanics or DWT tests for structural steels used on pipelines, have been also found.

MATERIALS USED FOR INVESTIGATION

Welds made with covered electrodes (MMA), in metal active gas (MAG), submerged arc (SA) and electroslag (ES) processes were examined to establish correlations between Charpy V and fracture mechanics tests. The welds were made of low-carbon structural steels (t = 16 to 60 mm), killed steels C-Mn (t = 20 to 25 mm) and microalloyed steels C-Mn (t = 9 to 36 mm). The majority of examined plates were normalized. Weld metals obtained with submerged arc (with varying V or Nb content) and with electroslag process were also examined. Following consumables were used for welds (with V, semi-V and close butt edge preparation): basic covered electrodes, submerged arc welding wires with 0.5% Mn, 2% Mn and 2 % Mn with 0.8% Ni together with neutral and acidic fluxes, wires for MAG welding with about 2% Mn and 1% Si and wire for electroslag welding with about 2% Mn and a neutral flux.

The examination of the correlation of the transition temperature determined on the base of Charpy V tests with the transition temperature determined on the base of DWT tests were carried out on the structural steels X56, X60, X65. For this purpose the test results [4] for X70 and X80 steels were also used. X56 to X80 steels are used on welded pipes.

EXAMINATION METHODOLOGY AND RESULTS

Specimens were cut from the welds for Charpy V impact testing in the range of temperatures from -70°C to +20°C, dynamic CTOD testing (Niblink test) acc. to [5] in the range of temperatures from -60°C to +10°C and static CTOD testing acc. to BS 7448:1991 in the range of temperatures from -70°C to 0°C. The notches were cut in the middle of the weld cross section or in the heat affected zone (HAZ) 2 mm away from the fusion line. The notch longitudinal centrelines were in all cases perpendicular to the plate surface.

The transition from ductile to brittle fracture temperature was determined at the level of 28 J (T_{28}) according to the Charpy V impact test results. The impact value at $-20°C$ ($KV_{-20°C}$) was also found (Fig. 1a).

From the dynamic CTOD test (Niblink test) the transition temperature T_{NB} at the level of 0.06 mm and critical crack tip opening displacement δ_{cd} at $-50°C$ were determined (Fig. 1d). The static CTOD test allowed to determine the critical CTOD δ_{cs} also at $-50°C$ (Fig. 1e).

The results obtained in statistic and dynamic CTOD tests were used to calculate the stress intensity factor [6]:

- in the case of dynamic bending acc. to formula:

$$K_{cd-50°C} = \sqrt{\delta_{cd-50°C} \cdot \sigma_y \cdot E} \qquad (1)$$

- and in the case of static bending acc. to formula:

$$K_{cs-50°C} = \sqrt{\delta_{cs-50°C} \cdot \sigma_y \cdot E} \qquad (2)$$

where: σ_y, E – static yield point and Young's modulus of the investigated materials.

The collected results were plotted on coordinate systems: ($K_{cd-50°C}$, $KV_{-20°C}$), ($K_{cs-50°C}$, $KV_{-20°C}$), (T_{NB}, T_{28}) (Figs. 2 to 4). Minicomputer was used to obtain the relations: $KV_{-20°C} = f(K_{cd-50°C})$, $KV_{-20°C} = f(K_{cs-50°C})$, $T_{28} = f(T_{NB})$ which are presented in Figs. 2 to 4 graphically and by mathematical formula together with the coefficient of determination, coefficient of correlation and standard error of estimation.

The transition temperatures ($T_{KV50\%}$) determined on the level of 50% shear fracture for the Charpy V tests (Fig. 1b) have been established. Also the transition temperatures ($T_{DWT85\%}$) determined on the level of 85% shear fracture for DWT tests acc. to API5L3/RP 1978 (Fig. 1c) have been established. The transition temperatures were determined on the specimens cut out from the welded pipes made of X56 to X65 steels and the results that is $T_{KV50\%} = f(T_{DWT85\%})$ are presented in Fig. 5. In Fig. 5 are also plotted test results [4] for pipes made of X70 and X80 steels.

ANALYSIS OF RESULTS

In this work establishing of relationship was attempted between Charpy V impact test results and results from dynamic and static CTOD tests for welds made of low-carbon and low-alloy structural steels. In Fig. 2 the mathematical relation is presented between the $K_{cd-50°C}$ calculated from the Niblink test results and the impact test value $KV_{-20°C}$. The relation was found to be parabolic with small variations of the stress intensity factor in the range of K_{cd} from 60 to 160 MPa $\sqrt{m}$ corresponding to large variations in the impact test values. Similar relation was obtained in the case of the $K_{cs-50°C}$ values calculated from the static CTOD test and impact values $KV_{-20°C}$ (Fig. 3). Also in this case small variations of $K_{cs-50°C}$ in the range of 60 to 160 MPa $\sqrt{m}$ can be said to correspond to large variations in the impact test values and, therefore, the Charpy V test is believed to be more selective than the CTOD tests. These relations appear to result from differences in method of conducting these notch and fracture toughness tests. In the impact test the absorbed energy of the whole specimen is recorded i.e. the initiation and propagation energy of the crack. With the increase of material ductility both the crack initiation and its propagation energies grow. In the CTOD tests, however, the energy at the crack initiation moment or rather only critical crack opening displacement is recorded the propagation conditions not being accounted for. Due to this the impact test can be regarded as more versatile and better for fuller ranking of materials from the viewpoint of resistance to brittle fracture.

The analysis of the transition temperature as determined by the dynamic CTOD test and Charpy V tests indicates a parabolic relationship (Fig. 4) with the compatibility of results being rather good. In this diagram an interesting regularity can be observed as to the properties of welds. In the region 1 characterized by greatest ductility the majority of welds occur, made with covered electrodes and submerged arc at heat inputs ≤ 30 kJ/cm whereas in the lowest ductility region 2 are welds made with submerged arc at higher heat inputs ≥ 30 kJ/cm and electroslag welds. The welds made with MAG process are in regions 1 and 2. Also, the fact bears attention that in the region 1 occur multi-run welds whilst the region 2 includes single and double-run welds. These results confirm the view that the ductility of welds is largely determined by the volumetric share of structure balanced by the heat treatment from subsequent runs with the increase of the number of runs.

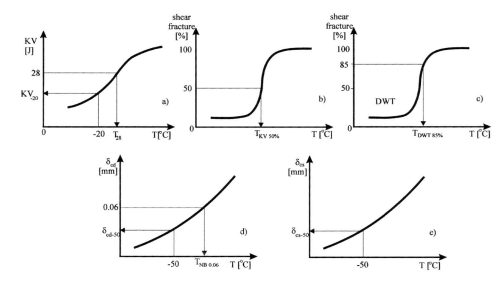

Fig. 1. Determination principles for the transition temperature based on the impact test (a,b) or DWT test (c), Niblink test (d) and critical CTOD at the temperature of -50°C in dynamic CTOD (d) and in static CTOD test (e)

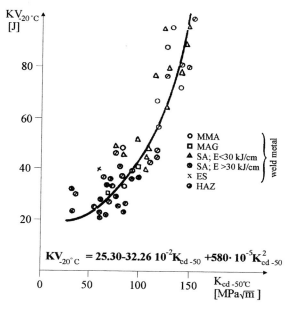

Fig. 2. The relation of Charpy V value to the dynamic critical stress intensity factor K_{cd}. Standard error 13.6 J, coefficient or determination 0.81 coefficient of correlation 0.90

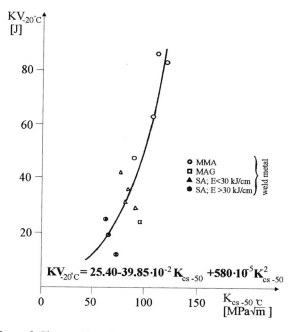

Fig. 3. The relation of Charpy V values to the static critical stress intensity factor K_{cs}. Standard error 16.8 J coefficient of determination 0.82 coefficient of correlation 0.90

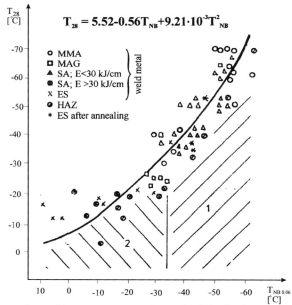

Fig. 4. The relation of transition temperature determined in the impact test to the transition temperature determined in the Niblink test. Standard error 9.1°C, coefficient of determination 0.81, coefficient of correlation 0.90

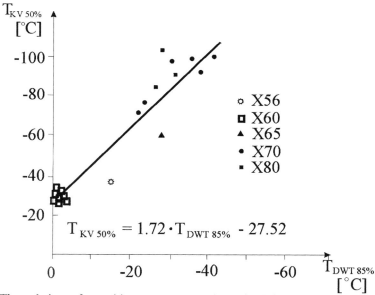

Fig. 5. The relation of transition temperature determined in Charpy V test (50% shear fracture) to the transition temperature determined in DWT test (80% shear fracture) for X56 to X80 steels. Coefficient of correlation 0.91

The relations arrived at conclusion also allow to calculate from the known impact value, with a certain approximation, the permissible flaw size or the level of permissible stress at a predetermined flaw size [2,3]. The impact test has been criticized because of the difficulty to correlate the ductility of the plates with their thickness and the behaviour of structure. Therefore, a number of the other tests have been developed such as Wells, K_{Ic}, CTOD to establish this relationship.

The analysis of the transition temperature as determined by the Charpy V test and DWT test indicates a linear relationship (Fig. 5). It results from the fact that the specimen in the DWT test is in reality the enlarged Charpy V specimen. Due to this the Charpy V test can be regards for ranking of materials from viewpoint of resistance to brittle fracture like the DWT test. It seems, therefore, that the use of DWT test to the brittle fracture assessment of welded pipes is not always justified.

At present, sufficient information has already been collected to determine the relations between impact test results for plates and welds and the results from K_{Ic} and CTOD tests. It seems, therefore, also on the base of results presented here, that the impact test being much simpler to carry out and interpret can again become the decisive test.

CONCLUSIONS

1. A parabolic relationship with high coefficient of correlation 0.90 has been found between the results of Charpy V impact test and dynamic and static CTOD tests.
2. This relationship indicates that the Charpy V test is more versatile because it allows more accurate ranking of materials as to their resistance to brittle fracture.
3. The obtained relations permit to utilize in practice the results of impact test for design calculations.
4. A linear correlation between the transition temperature determined in Charpy V test and the transition temperature determined in DWT test has been found. It indicates that there is a possibility of the use only the Charpy V test to the brittle fracture assessment of materials.

REFERENCES

1. Gross J.H., Stout R.D., (1958) *Welding Journal, Res.Supplement* **33**, 151.
2. Spiekhout J., (1988) *Welding Journal* **67**, 55.
3. Blauel J.G., (1997) *Failure assessment concepts and applications* Int. Inst. of Welding Doc. X-1407-97.
4. Sawamura T., Hashimoto T. at al., (1986) *Sumitomo Search* **32**, 63.
5. Blink, W.P., Nibbering J.J.W., (1970) *Simplified procedure for Niblink dropweight testing of weldments* Int. Inst. of Welding Doc. IIC-334-70.
6. Kocańda S., (1985) *Fatigue Cracks of Metals (in Polish)* WNT, Warszawa.

From Charpy to Present Impact Testing
D. François and A. Pineau (Eds.)
© 2002 Elsevier Science Ltd. and ESIS. All rights reserved

STATISTICAL TREATMENT OF FRACTURE MECHANICS DATA AND CORRELATION WITH CHARPY ENERGY

DIPL.-ING. A. MANNSFELD*, DR.-ING. P. LANGENBERG**,
PROF. DR. RER.NAT. DR.-ING. W. DAHL*
*Department of Ferrous Metallurgy (IEHK), University of Technology Aachen (RWTH),
Intzestraße 1, 52062 Aachen, Germany
**Ingenieurbuero fuer Werkstofftechnik (IWT), Dennewartstraße 25, 52068 Aachen, Germany

ABSTRACT

Most steels are qualified by the transition temperature resulting from the impact test, i.e. T_{27J} can be taken out of tables from technical delivery codes. Both, expenses and effort of impact tests are much lower than fracture mechanics testing. Yet fracture mechanics toughness values allow a quantitative safety analysis of steel structures, whereas the Charpy values can only be used for an experienced based design. To combine both features it is useful to find a correlation between impact energy and a characteristic value from fracture mechanics testing, i.e. J-Integral.

Because of the great scatter of the fracture toughness values in the brittle region of the transition curve, Wallin has developed the Mastercurve concept which served as a basis for an ASTM standard in 1998 [1]. With the help of the Mastercurve concept it is possible to describe the lower shelf region of the transition curve with the need of only six specimen.

In case of steel structures a safety concept to avoid brittle fracture has been developed for Eurocode 3, Annex C [2]. By means of linking the Mastercurve concept to the T_{27J} temperature - the European design code - which is usually applied in steel design, it is possible to derive toughness requirements based on a fracture mechanics concept.

The validation of the Mastercurve concept, a transition temperature correlation and the implementation of a safety concept according to Eurocode 3, Annex C, applied for different ship steel grades, are in focus of this work.

KEYWORDS

Charpy Testing, Fracture Mechanics Testing, Large Scale Testing, Mastercurve Concept, Statistics, Safety Concept, Transition Temperature Correlation, Welds

INTRODUCTION

For the material selection in ship constructions the occurrence of failure by brittle fracture has to be considered. Recent ship catastrophes underline the strong need for a safe ship design. In ship building safety design rules are usually based on the crack arrest philosophy. In technical applications with welded structures like steel bridges or off-shore platforms, a crack initiation philosophy with toughness requirements expressed in terms of a minimum Charpy energy temperature (T_{27J}), is applied. A safety concept for fracture avoidance has already been developed for the European standard for steel bridges (Annex C of the Eurocode 3 [2]). According to these experiences a crack initiation avoidance concept based on fracture mechanics results should also be applicable for ships. Such a safety concept combines a statistical evaluation of fracture mechanics results applying the Mastercurve concept [1], a transition temperature correlation (between T_{K100} and T_{27J}) and the CEGB R6 approach [3] (Failure Assessment Diagram (FAD)). Within this work the described concept has been validated by means of component like large scale testing both on the base and the welded material. Common low strength (grade A and D) and high strength (grade AH32 and DH36) ship steels in different delivery conditions were tested.

MATERIAL

The investigation comprises various low strength (grade A and D) and high strength (grade AH32 and DH36) ship steel grades in different delivery conditions such as as-rolled (AR), normalized (N) and thermomechanically controlled rolled (TMCR) for both base metal and welded plates with a plate thickness of 20mm. The chemical composition of the investigated ship steel grades is given in Table 1.

Table 1: Chemical composition, mass contents in %

Grade	C	Si	Mn	P	S	Cr	Mo	Ni	Al	Cu	N
A-AR	0.09	0.21	0.84	0.016	0.009	0.09	0.01	0.09	0.03	0.22	0.010
D-AR	0.09	0.21	0.83	0.016	0.009	0.09	0.01	0.09	0.03	0.22	0.010
AH32-TM	0.11	0.25	1.29	0.016	0.003	0.02	<0.005	0.03	0.05	<0.02	0.008
DH36-N	0.14	0.29	1.35	0.024	0.011	0.12	0.01	0.10	0.04	0.24	0.008
DH36-TM	0.08	0.37	1.25	0.019	0.006	0.10	0.01	0.08	0.04	0.30	0.007

Steel ships are welded constructions. Because of its high productivity submerged arc welding is most commonly used in ships. The welding procedure for plate thicknesses up to 25mm and a photograph of a typical weld section are shown in Fig. 1.

The heat affected zone (HAZ) of a weld is normally the region with the least toughness in a welded component. In consideration of safety concepts to avoid brittle fracture, it is reasonable to quantify both strength and toughness properties in all regions of a welded component. So, for all experiments on toughness characterization of the welded plates the notch was placed in the HAZ on the straight side of the weldseam.

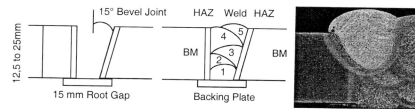

Fig. 1: Schematic welding procedure and a typical photograph of the weld section

The results from the tensile tests at room temperature of the investigated steel grades for the base material (BM) and the weld (W) can be taken from Table 2.

Table 2: Results from tensile tests at room temperature

Grade	Mat.	R_{el} or $R_{p0,2}$ (MPa)	R_m (MPa)	A (%)	Mat.	R_{el} or $R_{p0,2}$ (MPa)	R_m (MPa)	A (%)
A-AR	BM	283	459	33,2	W	497	609	21,3
D-AR	BM	271	436	36,5	W	457	563	15,7
AH32-TMCR	BM	278	508	32,3	W	419	563	15,9
DH36-N	BM	412	534	28,3	W	462	600	21,9
DH36-TMCR	BM	371	503	35,1	W	518	646	21,2

To characterize the toughness properties of the material, Charpy and fracture mechanics tests have been carried out.

Charpy tests were performed according to DIN EN 10045 [4] using standard Charpy-V specimens. To determine the transition temperature T_{27J} about 20 specimens were used. Since there is a significant scatter of the Charpy energy data, particularly in the transition region, a mean-fit transition curve was established and a mean T_{27J} temperature was defined. The results are listed in Table 3 together with the minimum requirements on the Charpy energy taken from the specifications from the Lloyd's register for ship steels [5].

To minimise the effort of fracture mechanics testing, the needed number of specimen was limited to 15 samples to create a transition temperature curve. One to three tests have been done at room temperature to determine the point of stable crack initiation applying the direct current potential drop (DCPD) method. For the statistical analysis at least six valid values with brittle fracture in the lower shelf are necessary according to ASTM E 1921 [1] for the creation of the Mastercurve. The remaining samples have been tested in the transition range. All tests have been carried out and evaluated after BS 7448 [6].

In fracture mechanics testing a scatter of the results occurs above all in the transition region as well as in the lower shelf. To use the data in safety concepts for avoidance of brittle fracture they have to be statistically analysed. It was found that the lower shelf up to the transition region can be described by an exponential function and the scattering of the J-Integral values by a three-parameter Weibull distribution function [7]. The three parameter distribution function gives the connection between the critical stress-intensity factor K_{Jc} calculated from J-Integral values and the failure probability p_f.

$$p_f = 1 - \exp\left(-\left(\frac{K_{Jc} - K_{min}}{K_0 - K_{min}}\right)^b\right)$$ (1)

p_f is the probability that a single selected specimen chosen at random from a population of specimen will fail at or before reaching the K_{Jc} value of interest. K_0 is the Weibull fitting parameter and is located at the 63,2% cumulative failure probability level. This scale parameter is independent of temperature and specimen thickness. For ferritic steels of yield strengths ranging from 275 to 825MPa the fracture toughness cumulative probability distribution will have nearly the same shape, independent of the specimen size and test temperature. K_{min} is fixed to 20MPa√m. The exponent b is the slope of a line which presents the scatter of K_{Jc} data. As a result out of a Monte Carlo simulation on the results of a great number of tests a factor of b = 4 was determined and therefore recommended to be used [7].

The ASTM E 1921 [1] standard describes how fracture toughness must be evaluated to create the Mastercurve. T_{K100} is the reference temperature, a material constant, at which the median of the K_{Jc} distribution from 1T size specimens will equal 100MPa√m. This temperature should be independent of the test temperature. Due to the great scatter of the measured fracture mechanics results, both a lower (equals to a fracture probability of 5%) and an upper bound (fracture probability of 95%) are established. The reference temperature T_{K100} has been determined iteratively using the maximum-likelihood-method [8, 9]. The advantage of this method is that the specimens do not have to be tested at one temperature for the determination of T_{K100}.

Mastercurves have been created and the reference temperatures have been determined. Figure 2 shows exemplarily a Mastercurve of the base material of grade A. The concept has also been applied on welded material [10, 11]. Table 3 contains the results of T_{K100}.

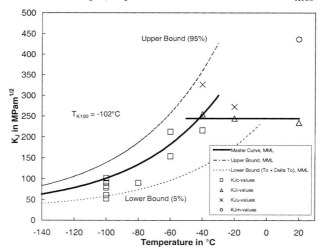

Fig. 2: Statistical evaluation of FM data applying the Mastercurve concept

Table 3: Toughness values from Charpy testing and fracture mechanics testing

Grade	$T_{27J, BM}$ in °C	Speci- fication	$T_{K100, BM}$ in °C	$T_{27J, HAZ}$ in °C	$T_{K100, HAZ}$ in °C
A-AR	-40	27J at 20°C	-102	-70	-116
D-AR	-40	27J at -20°C	-87	-60	-108
AH32-TMCR	-50	31J at 0°C	-82	-50	-76
DH36-N	-70	34J at -20°C	-69	-50	-61
DH36-TMCR	-80	34J at -20°C	-83	-50	-59

CORRELATION

In comparison to Charpy impact testing the effort and costs of fracture mechanics testing are much higher. One aim of this investigation was to find a appropriate correlation between both toughness values, which allows the designer to obtain a toughness value as input for safety concepts from delivery codes. In Table 3 the results from fracture mechanics testing (T_{K100}) and impact testing (T_{27J}) are represented comparing the results of the base material (BM) and heat affected zone (HAZ). This data set is plotted into a diagram (Fig. 3) together with other steel grades with yield strength ranging from 225MPa up to 960MPa. The linear regression of all data corresponds with the correlation (equation 2) first developed by Marandet and Sanz [12] and modified by Wallin [13] and Liessem [14]. The upper and lower line represent a two-sided standard deviation with $\sigma = 13°C$.

$$T_{K100} = T_{27J} - 18°C \tag{2}$$

In terms of well-fitting of the correlation it has to be considered that there is a big significance in the accuracy of the T_{27J} determination.

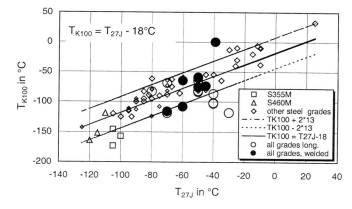

Fig. 3: T_{27J} and T_{K100} Correlation

LARGE SCALE TESTING

Large scale tests on DECT (Double Edge Cracked Tension) specimen (Fig. 4) have been performed on both base metal and welded material. The tests were carried out on a servo hydraulic resonance testing machine with a maximum capacity of 12MN in static and 10MN in cyclic loading.

Starting from a sawed full thickness crack of 20mm on both sides, the crack extended under cyclic loading with a R-ratio of 0,1 until the planned crack depth a, corresponding to a 2a/W-ratio of 0,2, was reached. Afterwards the specimen was cooled down and the quasi static tensile test was carried out. All steel grades have been investigated at -10°C because this is usually the lowest design temperature for ships in operation. Three additional tests were carried out at lower temperatures where brittle fracture should occur to validate the developed safety concept. All tests have been performed at a constant loading rate of 2mm/min.

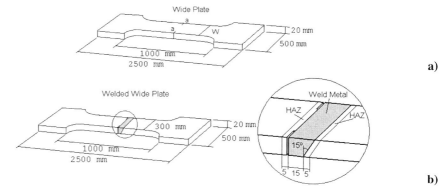

a)

b)

Fig. 4: Geometry of large scale specimens for parent (a) and welded plates (b)

SAFETY CONCEPT

Safety and reliability of welded steel structures of low alloyed ferritic pearlitic steels which are used in ships have to be guaranteed during the planned life time or at least during the inspection periods. Fracture is likely to occur if both internal (e.g. material and welding defects, poor toughness) and external influences (e.g. loading conditions, low temperature) interact at the same time. Due to the unavoidable scatter of these effects and design model uncertainties any reliability analysis has to consider the probability of sudden fracture during operation for the assumed limit condition on a defined and tolerable risk level.

A successful application of a fracture mechanics based safety concept which compared to national German guide lines for steel structures [15] will allow an extension of plate thicknesses in the future. This has been demonstrated with the development of the Annex C "Material Selection to Avoid Brittle Fracture in Steel Bridges" which is part of the design guide for the new European design code Eurocode 3, Part 2, [2, 16, 17]. The method relies on the assumption of a worst case scenario that an initial crack at the weld toe of a stiffener is overseen during fabrication and will grow up to a critical crack length under service. The calculation of the critical crack length is based on the CEGB R6 method [3] that allows the determination of the crack driving force under limit conditions as may occur in a bridge. To estimate the required material toughness at that point a correlation of the fracture toughness in combination with the Mastercurve concept [9] with the Charpy transition temperature T_{27J} is applied. The method has been verified and a safety factor has been derived from large scale tests [18].

The results of the application of that safety concept are demonstrated in Fig. 5. The calculated limit condition T_{ED} is compared with the real test temperature T_{exp}. It can be seen that the results for both the parent and welded plates scatter around the 1 to 1 line, whereas the scatter of the results of the welded plates is higher. Generally the scatter may be explained from the strong influence of the determination of the T_{27J} transition temperature and from the number wide plate tests carried out. For welded plates, due to the inhomogeneous microstructure and curvature of the weld bevel relative to the DECT-notch, a larger scatter was observed.

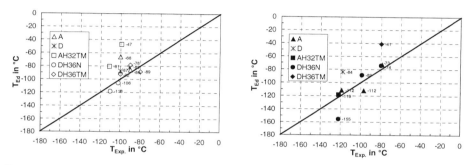

Fig. 5: Comparison of the calculated temperature and test temperature of the basis of the adopted fracture avoidance concept: base metal (left) and welded plates (right)

CONCLUSIONS

A safety concept based on fracture mechanics which has been implemented successfully as a European Standard for Steel Bridges (Eurocode 3, Annex C) is adopted to several low strength and high strength ship steel grades in different delivery conditions. The existence of welds has also been taken into account. As data input characteristic strength and toughness values were necessary. Therefore, tensile tests, Charpy and fracture mechanics tests were carried out. The Charpy transition temperature T_{27J} was determined. Applying the Mastercurve concept the fracture mechanics data was investigated statistically and T_{K100} was calculated using the maximum-likelihood-method. In addition a transition temperature correlation between the toughness transition temperatures T_{27J} from Charpy tests and T_{K100} from fracture mechanics tests was carried out. Large scale tests were performed to validate the safety concept.

The application of the Mastercurve concept allows the investigation of the scatter in the lower shelf of the base material as well as the welded material statistically. Regarding the implementation of the safety concept to ship steels the accuracy of the determination of the T_{27J} has to be considered because of its significant influence on the use of the transition temperature correlation. To explain the scatter it has to be taken into account that the number of wide plate tests carried out was limited. Also mismatch effects and secondary stresses have not been included into the prediction because they are not yet part of the safety concept. Overall it may be concluded that the fracture mechanics based safety concept for fracture avoidance works well also for ship steels and weldments. It has now to be optimised with respect to the design requirements in ship building.

REFERENCES

1. ASTM E 1921 (1998). *Test Method for the Determination of Reference Temperature T_0, for Ferritic Steels in the Transition Range*, Annual Book of ASTM Standards.
2. DIN ENV 1993-1-2 (1998). *Eurocode 3, Part1-2, Design of Steels Structures, Bridges*, European Committee of Standardisation, Bruessels.
3. Harrison, R.P., Loosemore and K., Milne, I.(1986). *Assessment of the Integrity of Structures containing Defects*, CEGB-Report R/H/R6, Revision 3.
4. DIN EN 10045 (1991). *Kerbschlagbiegeversuche nach Charpy*, Teil 1, Deutsches Institut für Normung e.V., Beuth-Verlag, Berlin.
5. Lloyds Register of Shipping, Rules and Regulations for the classification of ships, Parts 2 and 3
6. BS 7448 (1991/96). *Fracture Mechanics Toughness Test*, British Standards Institution BSI, Milton Keyes and London.
7. Wallin, K. (1984). *The Scatter in K_{Ic} Results*, Engineering Fracture Mechanics, Vol. **19**, No. 6, pp.1085-1093.
8. Wallin, K. (1998). *Master Curve Analysis of Ductile to Brittle Transition Region Fracture Toughness Round Robin Data – The „Euro" Fracture Toughness Curve"*, Technical Research Centre of Finland (VTT).
9. Wallin, K.(1997). *Small Specimen Fracture Toughness Characterisation – State of the Art and Beyond*, 9th International Conference on Fracture, Sydney.
10. Langenberg, P., Mannsfeld, A. and Dahl, W. (2000). *Statistische Bewertung von Bruch- mechanikergebnissen im Sprödbruchbereich an geschweißten Schiffbaustählen unter Anwendung des Mastercurve-Konzeptes nach ASTM E 1921-98*, 32. Tagung des DVM- Arbeitskreises Bruchvorgänge, 22./23. Februar 2000, Berlin.
11. Mannsfeld, A., Langenberg, P. and Dahl, W. (2000). *Development of a safety concept based on the crack initiation philosophy for ship steels*, Materials Week, Munich.
12. Marandet, B. and Sanz, G. (1976). *Étude par la Mécanique de la Rupture de la Ténacité d'aciers à Résistance moyenne fournis en forte épaisseur*, Revue de Métallurgie, pp. 359.
13. Wallin, K. (1997). *Small Specimen Fracture Toughness Characterization – State of the Art and beyond*, Advances in Fracture Research, Proceedings of the 9th International Conference on Fracture , 1-5. April, Sidney, Australia.
14. Sedlacek, G., Dahl, W., Stötzel, G. and Liessem, A. (1993). *Improvement of the Methods given in Eurocode 3, Annex C for the Choice of Material to avoid Brittle Fracture*, IIW Doc. X-1274-93.
15. DASt Ri 009 (1973). *Empfehlungen zur Wahl der Stahlsorte für geschweißte Stahlbauten*, Deutscher Ausschuss für Stahlbau, Düsseldorf.
16. Langenberg, P., Dahl, W., Sedlacek, G., Stranghöner, N. and Stötzel, G. (1998). *Euro- päisches Sprödbruchkonzept- Tragsicherheit von Stahlbrücken unter Berücksichtigung der Lebensdauer nachweisen - Annex C des Eurocode 3*, Materialprüfung **40**, pp. 39 – 43.
17. Stranghöner, N., Sedlacek, G., Langenberg, P., Dahl, W. and Stötzel, G. (1998). *Design against Brittle Fracture of Structural Steels*, Proceedings of the Nordic Steel Construc- tion Conference 98, Bergen, Norway, 14. – 16. September 1998, Volume 2, pp. 751-762.
18. Stranghöner, N., Sedlacek, G., Stötzel, G., Dahl, W. and Langenberg, P. (1997). *The Choice of Steel Material for Steel Bridges to avoid Brittle Fracture*, Journal of Constructional Steel Research, 1998, 46: 1-3 Paper No. 045.

From Charpy to Present Impact Testing
D. François and A. Pineau (Eds.)
© 2002 Elsevier Science Ltd. and ESIS. All rights reserved

AN APPLICATION OF CHARPY V TESTING :
THE PRESSURE VESSEL SURVEILLANCE PROGRAM
OF NUCLEAR PRESSURISED WATER REACTOR IN OPERATION

Nathalie Rupa, Astrid Baché, Josseline Bourgoin, Denis Buisine

EDF Industry - Nuclear Generation Division, Corporate Laboratories
37420 Avoine / 93206 Saint-Denis - France

Abstract

Charpy tests are widely used in the nuclear industry in order to characterize material mechanical properties. Moreover, they are the basis for the reactor pressure vessels life evaluation through the Pressure Vessel Surveillance Program. This Program is a procedure, applied to each reactor vessel in operation in France, which allows to monitor periodically the irradiation induced material embrittlement.

This paper first describes the procedure followed for the Pressure Vessel Surveillance Program. It presents the irradiation capsules : the samples materials (low alloy Mn, Ni, Mo vessel steel including base metals, heat affected zones, welds and a reference material) and the mechanical tests performed.

Then it draws up a synthesis of the analysis of 177 capsules removed from reactors at fluences up to 7.10^{19} n/cm^2 (E > 1 MeV). This data base gathers the results of a number of Charpy tests close to 10000.

Keywords : Pressure Vessel Surveillance Program, Charpy V testing, low alloy steel, transition temperature, irradiation effects.

INTRODUCTION

Due to the irradiation effect, the pressure vessel materials (16MND5 AFNOR, i.e. A508 Cl3 ASTM) is subject to aging phenomena, which have to be taken into account to estimate safety margins of the vessel life prediction. Thanks to representative materials irradiated into capsules, the Pressure Vessel Surveillance Program provides an anticipated evaluation of the material embrittlement. The material embrittling is mainly given by Charpy V results, the effect of irradiation on material is obtained through the comparison of Charpy tests performed on irradiated and unirradiated material.

Today about 177 irradiated capsules have been extracted from 54 reactors and analyzed. This article, updating a previous paper [1], presents the main lines and objectives of the irradiation effect Surveillance Program, it details more particularly the impact strength testing. It also synthesizes the Surveillance Program data base, deduced form Charpy V testing results.

THE SURVEILLANCE PROGRAM [1 to 5]

Presentation - Organization

Largely inspired by American regulations, the Surveillance Program fulfills the French Safety Authorities requirements (10th November 1999).

For all 900, 1300 and 1450 MWe reactors, the core zone is generally made up of two shells and the associated weld (see figure 1). As these materials experience a marked embrittlement until their design end of life (40 years), the mechanical properties and particularly the rupture characteristics through the impact strength are monitored for each reactor vessel .

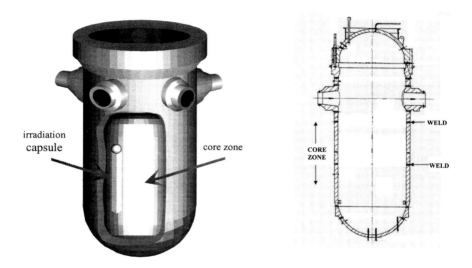

Figure 1 : Pressure vessel

The regulations stipulate that the Surveillance Program must be representative regarding the irradiation conditions (temperature, neutronic spectrum ... have to be similar to that of the reactor vessel) and the materials. Materials are thus selected as follows :

- the base metal is taken from overlengths of the shell,
- the weld and heat affected zone are elaborated under identical welding conditions as the core zone components.

These materials are positioned in capsules at locations well characterized for both temperature and neutronic conditions (see figure 1). Their neutronic flux is higher than the one undergone on the vessel in order to anticipate the embrittlement. The flux is evaluated for each capsule through a lead factor, corresponding to the ratio of the neutron fluxes of more than 1 MeV energy undergone by the capsule and the vessel at the most irradiated point.

Objectives of the Surveillance Program

The main objective of the Program is to confirm the conservatism of the aging hypotheses of the design stage. They are based on the determination of each component initial RT_{NDT}*, and on an assessment of its evolution with neutron fluence. This ΔRT_{NDT} is given by empirical prediction formulae specially developed for the base metals and welds of the French vessels.

---

* RT_{NDT} (Reference Temperature Nil Ductility Transition) is a transition temperature defined from Drop-Weight tests and Charpy V tests.

The formula developed by FRAMATOME for the base metals is known as FIS (embrittlement by higher irradiation) :

$$\Delta RT_{NDT} \, (°C) = 8 + [24 + 1537 \, (P\text{-}0.008) + 238 \, (Cu\text{-}0.08) + 191 \, Ni^2Cu] \, [\varnothing/10^{19}]^{0.35}$$

where : $\varnothing$: fluence in n.cm^{-2} (E>1 MeV), $10^{18} < \varnothing < 8.10^{19}$
                     $275°C \leq Tirradiation \leq 300°C$
                     P, Cu, Ni: content by weight - %
                     $Cu - 0.08 = 0$ if $Cu < 0.08$
                     $P - 0.008 = 0$ if $P < 0.008$

The edf$_S$ formula has been developed for the welds by EDF. Its development took into account all the available data on irradiated welds in the chemical and neutronic ranges met in the French reactors :

$$\Delta RT_{NDT} \, (°C) = 22 + [13 + 823 \, (P \geq 0.008) + 148 \, (Cu\text{-}0.08) + 157 \, Ni^2Cu] \, [\varnothing/10^{19}]^{0.45}$$

where : $\varnothing$: fluence in n.cm^{-2} (E>1 MeV), $3.10^{18} < \varnothing < 8.10^{19}$
                     $285°C \leq Tirradiation \leq 290°C$
                     P, Cu, Ni: content by weight - %
                     $Cu - 0.08 = 0$ if $Cu < 0.08$
                     $P = 0$ if $P < 0.008$

4 capsules are introduced into each 900, 1300 or 1450 MWe reactor and are removed regularly, according to a specific calendar. The in-reactor exposure is planned so that the material irradiation is representative of that of the vessel at quarter, half, three-quarters and completion of the component design life.

The Surveillance Program results are then directly used for the vessel life evaluation. The brittle fracture resistance calculations are based on the irradiated vessels toughness. The toughness is indirectly deduced by the ASME curve, from the embrittlement value given by the Surveillance Program predictive formulae. The safety margins are estimated for mechanical loadings up to the most drastic accidental conditions.

The Surveillance Program also provides results which can be used for each decennial In Service Inspection, to determine hydrotest conditions for example.

The irradiation capsules

The capsules mainly contain materials representative of each vessel (base, weld and HAZ metals experiencing the maximum embrittlement). Some of them (generally 3 per vessel) also contain a reference material, identical for every French reactor pressure vessel.

All vessel materials are low alloy steel of the same grade (16MND5 AFNOR i.e. A508 cl 3, provided by the same manufacturer), containing mainly Mn Ni Mo and very low embrittling elements contents. The reference material is a plate which chemical composition is very similar to the vessel material.

In order to determine accurately the conditions of in-reactor exposure and to optimize the mechanical tests, each capsule contains :

    − thermal instrumentation, based on low melting point alloys,

    − nuclear instrumentation, based on fissile and activation dosimeters.

Thanks to experience feed-back, the nuclear instrumentation has evolved over the course of time and the different standardized plant series built in France [6].

Mechanical testing

The samples introduced in the capsules are Charpy V, tensile, CT 12.7 toughness and bending specimens (see figure 2). Generally 15 Charpy V specimens per material (base metal, weld and its associated HAZ) are available in each capsule.

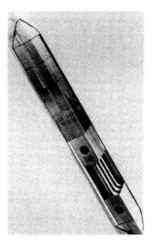

Figure 2 : Irradiation capsule

The Charpy tests are performed according to the current normalization, on instrumented hammers equipped with an ISO tub. The testing temperatures are chosen in order to describe the transition curve from fragile to ductile rupture modes.

The transition temperatures (T_{CV}), upper shelf energies and scatter data are deduced from the transition curves. The T_{CV} are determined as follows :

- T_{K7} corresponds to a rupture energy per unit section value of 7 daJ.cm-2 ;
- $T_{0,9}$ is measured for a 0.9 mm lateral expansion on fractured specimens ;
- FATT50 is a cleavage ratio, it is determined from force/displacement recording and corresponds to a 50% cristallinity.

The transition temperature shift (ΔTcv) results from the comparison of the impact strength curves pre and post irradiation (see figure 3). To be conservative, ΔT_{CV} is the maximum value, either ΔT_{K7} or $\Delta T_{0,9}$.

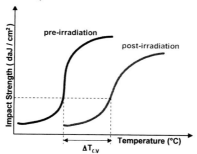

Figure 3 : Effect of irradiation induced embrittlement on impact strength tests

According to the RSE-M, B6312, the measured embrittlement is then compared with the shift evaluated through FIS or edfs formulae.

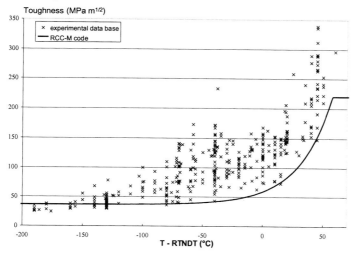

Figure 4 : ASME codified curve for the toughness evaluation of pressure vessel material [7]

The toughness is obtained by the ASME codified curve, which temperature scale is indexed to the materials RT_{NDT} (figure 4). This curve gathers the results of a very wide data base. It provides the minimum toughness value of a material versus its impact tests characteristics.

The irradiated RT_{NDT} is given by the initial (experimental) RT_{NDT} and the irradiation embrittlement ΔRT_{NDT}. ΔRT_{NDT} is usually derived from the predictive formulae, it may eventually be an experimental result when the measured shifts of the impact strength curves are smaller than the calculated ΔRT_{NDT}. The approach is based on the assumption that the transition temperature shifts are representative of the toughness shifts.

This indirect and empirical evaluation method has partly been chosen because Charpy V tests are relatively easy to implement, which is an important aspect for a large scale industrial use in a hot laboratory (see figure 5). The mechanical data base has indeed reached an important extent. About 60 impact strength tests are realized for the interpretation of one capsule. To date the number of Charpy V tests performed for the Surveillance Program is close to 10 000 !

Figure 5 : hot cell laboratory facility

The extent of the program, its implementation by a single organization (EDF's hot laboratory located in Chinon), and the homogeneity of the reactor operating conditions as well as the material and product, make this data base unique.

THE SURVEILLANCE PROGRAM RESULTS

177 capsules, removed from 54 power units, have been analyzed. Their embrittling elements content (copper, phosphorus and nickel) is relatively low, with the exception of the welds on the CP0 standardized plant series (6 first 900 MWe power units). The results are presented in table 1.

Chemical Content (weight %)		Copper	Phosphorus	Nickel
Base Metals	900 CP0 (6)	0.05 → 0.08 m = 0.06	0.005 → 0.013 m = 0.008	0.65 → 0.84 m = 0.72
	900 CPY (28)	0.04 → 0.07 m = 0.06	0.005 → 0.009 m = 0.007	0.66 → 0.75 m = 0.70
	1300 (20)	0.05 → 0.08 m = 0.06	0.002 → 0.008 m = 0.006	0.67 → 0.75 m = 0.71
Welds	900 CP0 (6)	0.09 → 0.13 m = 0.11	0.012 → 0.019 m = 0.016	0.07 → 0.51 m = 0.23
	900 CPY (28)	0.03 → 0.04 m = 0.03	0.003 → 0.015 m = 0.009	0.52 → 0.78 m = 0.65
	1300 (20)	0.01 → 0.11 m = 0.04	0.004 → 0.014 m = 0.006	0.55 → 0.80 m = 0.65

CP0 = Fessenheim/Bugey plants - CPY = Other 900 MWe plants

Table 1 : Minimum, maximum and average contents of embrittling elements for 900 and 1300 MWe French nuclear plant series

Measured embrittlement of the vessel materials

The embrittlement of the various materials monitored in the Surveillance Program are expressed in the form of shifts of the impact strength curves transition. The results are illustrated in figure 6.

Each mechanical characterization result is associated with a neutron dose, obtained from the interpretation of the activity measured on the fissile and activation dosimeters. This metrological process, performed according to a well-established methodology, requires a good coherence between the measured activity, the operating diagram of the power unit and the migration calculations performed according to the reactor geometry. The uncertainty is evaluated at less than 10% over all the results. This indicates the quality of methodology used. Furthermore, these results reveal very homogenous operation of all the reactors.

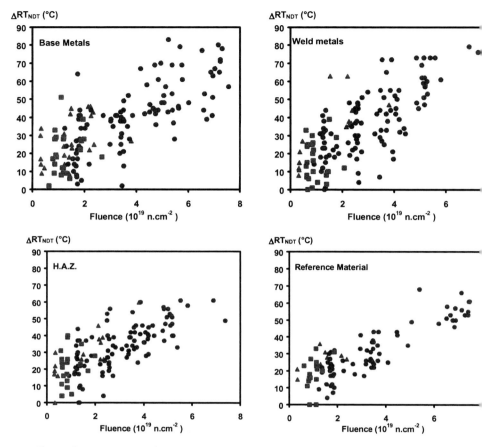

Figure 6 : Impact strength curves : measured shifts versus neutron fluence (E > 1 MeV)
for the base metals, welds, heat affected zones and the reference material
(900/CP0 : green triangle, 900/CPY : blue point, 1300 : red square)

These results show that the embrittlement remains moderate, yet with relatively high dispersal. For the base metals, the maximum value obtained is 83°C and corresponds to a dose of 5.24 10^{19} n.cm^{-2}. For the welds, the measured ΔRT_{NDT} can reach 79°C for a neutron fluence of 6.91 10^{19} n.cm^{-2}. For both base metals and welds, the measured shifts reveal a scatter up to 60°C for a given fluence. In the case of HAZ and particularly reference material, the scatter is significantly lower. The good coherence between the unique reference metal and the base metals of the different shells strengthen the results validity. It can be noted that the weld results of the CP0 standardized plant series are higher than the average (due to their higher embrittling element content).

Among the different causes of scatter, neither the only irradiation effect, nor the testing conditions (number of specimens, distribution of specimens versus temperature, temperature and fluence measurement, impact test energy and transition temperature determination ...) could explain a 60°C amplitude in the base and welded metals embrittlement. On the other hand material heterogeneities can largely contribute to the global scatter [8]. The material heterogeneities can be :

— at the scale of a specimen - the unirradiated sample may not represent correctly the initial state of an irradiated sample ;

— as well as of a batch of specimen - though elaborated with very close conditions and standards, the data base gathers different materials which cannot be considered as strictly identical.

Measured and predicted embrittlement of the vessel materials

The impact strength temperature shifts were compared with the predictive formulae mentioned earlier and used for the rupture margins evaluation at the design stage. This comparison is illustrated in figure 7.

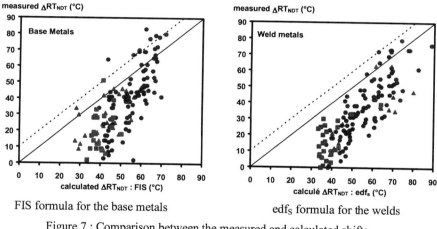

FIS formula for the base metals   edf$_S$ formula for the welds

Figure 7 : Comparison between the measured and calculated shifts
(900/CP0 : green triangle, 900/CPY : blue point, 1300 : red square)

Over the whole data base, totaling to date 177 results, only a few exceed the predictive calculation by more than 10°C. Considering the predictive formulae, FIS and edf$_S$ fit reasonably well the behavior of base and weld metals respectively.

Complementary studies

At the present time, some toughness tests are in progress on the CT 12.7 specimens irradiated in the capsules. The K_{JC} values are used to confirm and reinforce the results obtained through the ASME curve methodology.

Some complementary studies are also being performed concerning the upper embrittlement values, the results scattering and some unexpected embrittlement kinetics. A study concerning the reference material also consolidates the results associated with the vessel representative materials.

Fundamental works are today in progress in order to have a better understanding and interpretation of impact strength tests and toughness results. These works are based on a physical description of the rupture mechanisms, also valid in the transition region, using finite element modeling. They could be applied to lower the empirism part in the Surveillance Program methodology, make the best use of the results and thus strengthen the life prediction evaluation of the pressure vessels.

CONCLUSION AND PROSPECTS

The French Surveillance Program, and particularly the Charpy V impact strength tests, constitute an extremely valuable data base concerning the irradiation effect. With samples irradiated in capsules in front of the core zone, the program allows to anticipate the in-service embrittlement of the vessel materials. The monitored materials are the pressure vessel base metals, heat affected zones and welds, as well as a unique reference metal.

The analysis of 177 capsules show that most of the experimental results are correctly predicted by empirical formulae, on which is based the components life prediction. In coherence with the assumptions stated at the design stage [9], the Surveillance Program results, and the associated studies, should thus allow the reactors vessels to achieve their service life under good conditions of safety.

The embrittlement monitoring is based on Charpy V tests. Nevertheless the results, expressed in terms of fragile / ductile transition temperature shift with irradiation, demand post treatment studies in order to connect them with toughness values. This link is made with the codified ASME curve. In this context, EDF is particularly interested in the potentiality of more fundamental approaches aiming at having a better understanding and interpretation of the Charpy V tests and toughness results.

REFERENCE

[1]   C. PICHON, Y. GRANDJEAN, G. BEZDIKIAN, J.M. FRUND - Irradiation Behavior of Electricité de France PWR Vessel Steel. ASTM STP - Newport 1999.

[2]   M. AKAMATSU, C. BRILLAUD & al. - L'irradiation de la cuve : un phénomène sous surveillance. RGN n°6 Nov.-Déc. - 1993.

[3]   C. BRILLAUD, F. DE KEROULAS, C. PICHON, A. TEISSIER - Overview of French activities on neutron radiation embrittlement of pressure vessel steel. AIEA - Paris 1993.

[4]   C. BRILLAUD, F. HEDIN - In service evaluation of French pressurized water reactor vessel steel. ASTM STP 1125 - Nashville 1990.

[5]   B. BARTHELET, C. BRILLAUD, C. PICHON, C. RIEG - Pressure vessel steel surveillance program: developments, experience feed-back and perspectives. OCDE-NEA-CSNI - Espoo 1990.

[6]   A. BEVILACQUA, C. BRILLAUD & al. - Récente amélioration en dosimétrie de Surveillance des cuves dans les réacteurs en construction d'EDF. ASTM-EURATOM - Jackson Hole 1987.

[7]   G. BEZDIKIAN, D. MOINEREAU & al. - PWR Vessel Integrity Assessment and Life Management in French Nuclear Plants. ASME PVP Conference - Seattle July 2000.

[8]   Y. GRANDJEAN, C. BRILLAUD, F DE KEROULAS - Scatter analysis of RTNDT shift results in French RPV Surveillance Program data base. ASME/PVP - Boston 1999.

[9]   G. BEZDIKIAN, C. BRILLAUD & al. - French PWR vessel life management - Integrity assessment and maintenance strategy - SFEN/Fontevraud IV 1998.

From Charpy to Present Impact Testing
D. François and A. Pineau (Eds.)

377

EUROPEAN PIPELINE RESEARCH GROUP STUDIES ON DUCTILE CRACK PROPAGATION IN GAS TRANSMISSION PIPELINES

R M Andrews[a] and V Pistone[b]

[a] EPRG, c/o Advantica Technology, Ashby Road, Loughborough LE11 3GR, UK
[b] EPRG, c/o SNAM, Piazza Vanoni 1, 20097 San Donato Milanese, Italy

Ductile crack propagation is a major concern for the operators of high pressure gas pipelines. The process is a complex interaction of the structural behaviour of the cracking pipe and the fluid mechanics of the escaping gas. The upper shelf Charpy energy has been widely used as a measure of resistance to ductile crack propagation. EPRG has supported full scale fracture propagation tests and theoretical studies for over 20 years. EPRG work which has formed the basis of the Charpy requirements in European standards for linepipe is presented. A statistical method developed for EPRG which predicts the likely length of a propagating rupture will be described. This combines the statistical distribution of pipe toughness with knowledge of the distribution of crack arrests and propagates obtained from the database of full scale tests. Finally, a recent review of fracture propagation test results for spiral welded linepipe is presented together with results of determinations of the transition behaviour of thick wall pipe.

Crack propagation, crack arrest, rupture length, statistical analysis, pipeline, spiral welded pipe

INTRODUCTION AND BACKGROUND

Propagating ductile fractures in high pressure gas pipelines were first reported in the late 1960's in the United States of America [1]. Previously, pipeline operators and researchers had been aware of brittle fractures that propagated at speeds above the acoustic velocity in the pipe contents. Research at Battelle [2] and British Gas [3] had identified correlations between both fracture velocity and appearance and the energy absorbed, percentage shear area and the transition temperature in impact tests. Tests for brittle fracture could be carried out using comparitively simple tests on short lengths of pipe, pressurized with a mixture of air and water – the West Jefferson test [2]. Subsequently the shear area measured in the Drop Weight Tear Test (DWTT) became the accepted criterion for avoiding brittle fracture propagation in pipelines, and shear area requirements are included in many linepipe specifications.

The ductile fracture problem required more complex full scale tests, in which a test section simulating a pipeline was deliberately ruptured and the velocity of the propagating crack measured. Typically the test section in these tests is about 70 metres in length and reservoirs of similar length are placed at each end. The reservoirs simulate an infinitely long pipeline. The first tests of this nature were carried out at Battelle, but subsequent programmes were carried out by other research centres, such as British Gas, CSM, Foothills Pipelines and the Japanese

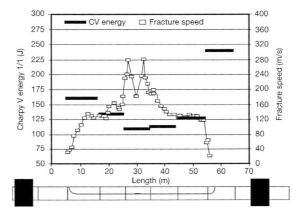

Fig. 1 EPRG Test IV-1, X65 pipe, 56 inch diameter, 18.7 mm wall thickness, 107.5 bar

Iron and Steel Institute. The European Pipeline Research Group (EPRG) was formed in 1973 to research ductile fracture in gas pipelines and has sponsored a total of 15 full scale propagation tests. Figure 1 shows results from one of the EPRG tests [4], designed to investigate the effects of high hoop stress. The figure also shows the typical arrangement in which a low toughness initiation pipe is placed at the centre of the test section and pipes of increasing toughness are placed towards the outer end. The initially high crack velocity reduces as the crack runs into progressively tougher material until arrest occurs. Propagate and arrest data points are thus obtained from a single test.

The propagate and arrest data have been analysed to produce design criteria. The upper shelf Charpy energy has been the most common measure of resistance to fracture used for these analyses. One approach, used for example in the analysis of the AISI test programme [5] is a statistical analysis of the data, leading to a correlation:

$$C_{V2/3} = 2.377.10^{-4} \sigma_h^{3/2} (2R)^{1/2} \tag{1}$$

Here $C_{V2/3}$ is the upper shelf Charpy energy (Joule) measured using a 2/3 thickness specimen, σ_h is the hoop stress (N/mm^2) and R the pipe radius (mm).

The second method can be described as a stress analysis approach, where conditions at the crack tip are considered and a mathematical model formulated to predict fracture propagation or arrest. The Battelle "two curve" approach [6, 7] is probably the most widely used example, where the crack tip driving force at arrest is considered and then a relationship is obtained between the arrest stress, the crack velocity and the pipeline dimensions and material properties. This curve defines the driving force required to cause the crack to propagate; the driving force available is derived from modelling the decompression behaviour of the pipeline contents. This is analogous to the R-curve approach to fracture mechanics where the tearing resistance curve of the material is balanced against the driving force from the structure. The results from applying this analysis to a range of typical pipeline pressures, geometries and materials, assuming the contents to be pure or nearly pure methane natural gas, lead to a fitted equation usually known as the Battelle equation, where t is the pipe wall thickness (mm):

$$C_{V2/3} = 2.382.10^{-5} \sigma_h^2 (Rt)^{1/3} \tag{2}$$

A third type of approach uses an energy balance where the sources and sinks of energy are evaluated. Conditions where steady state propagation may occur can then be evaluated and a criterion for propagation or arrest determined. A major advantage is that explicit consideration of the crack tip stresses is not required. Poynton *et al.* [8] used this method to derive an equation for Charpy requirements used by the former British Gas in company specifications:

$$C_{V2/3} = \sigma_h \left[\frac{2.08R}{\sqrt{t}} - \frac{vR^{1.25}}{t^{\frac{3}{4}}} \right] 10^{-3} \tag{3}$$

The parameter v is related to the acoustic velocity in the gas at the line pressure; for lean natural gas a value $v=0.396$ is usually used. A feature of this model is that the constant 2.08 was derived from a statistical analysis and represents a 95% probability of arrest per pipe; for 50% probability the constant reduces to 1.85.

As an alternative to analytic methods, numerical methods have been used to simulate the fluid-structure interactions in the ductile fracture process, most recently by O'Donoghue and co-workers [9, 10]. These avoid many of the approximations inherent in the analytical approaches, but at present these methods suffer from the disadvantage of requiring special purpose software not readily available to the non-expert. It is also not possible to use them with the large database of historical full scale test data which uses Charpy toughness to characterise fracture resistance, and so there has been limited full scale validation.

EPRG RECOMMENDATIONS FOR ARREST TOUGHNESS

The EPRG used the results of its full scale fracture test programmes and a database of other tests to produce recommended toughness specifications for linepipe. Initial recommendations [11] were based on equation (1) for materials up to Grade X70. After further tests and analysis by experts drawn from the EPRG member companies the recommendations were revised and extended in 1995 [4] to include high strength material, up to Grade X80. These recommended minimum toughness values have been adopted by CEN for the European standard for line pipe, EN 10208 [12]. Charpy upper shelf energies are given for two safety factors, 1.4 and 1.6, corresponding to design factors of 72% and 65% of specification minimum yield strength (SMYS). Table 1 presents the values for 72% operation.

Experts from EPRG member companies were also involved during the revision of the DnV design recommendations [13] for submarine pipelines. These now include a supplementary requirement for Charpy toughness levels to ensure crack arrest in gas pipelines. These values are different from the EN 10208 values, as they assume operation up to 80% SMYS.

Table 1 EPRG Recommended Toughness Values (Joules) for 72% SMYS Operation

EN10208 Grade	Pipe Outside Diameter, mm								
	<=510	>510 <=610	>610 <=720	>720 <=820	>820 <=920	>920 <=1020	>1020 <=1120	>1120 <=1220	<=1430
240									40
290		40				40			42
360									42
415				40	41	44	46	48	51
445	40	40	41	43	46	48	51	53	57
480	46	50	55	58	62	65	68	71	77
550	61	68	76	83	90	96	102	108	120

PROBABILISTIC ANALYSIS OF THE EPRG TOUGHNESS RECOMMENDATIONS

A pipeline designer must ensure that if a rupture should propagate, the length is restricted to an acceptable level. This length is dependent on both safety and economic issues. Some design codes require this issue to be formally considered in a fracture control plan [14]. To predict the length of a rupture, the arrest toughness must be determined and then the proportion of pipes reaching this toughness estimated. Equations such as (1-3) can be used for designs falling within their validity range; other cases will require more advanced analysis, for example using the Battelle two-curve method [6, 7].

Unfortunately these models alone may not be sufficient for predicting rupture lengths, as they take no account of experimental and systematic errors. All the predictive models show scatter in the results; see Figure 3 below for an example. This scatter is due to various factors:

- Systematic errors in the models, particularly at high toughness levels where Charpy upper shelf energy is not a good measure of the resistance to crack propagation.
- Experimental error in the propagation tests. Although it would appear to be simple to determine whether a crack has arrested or not, in practice there may be some uncertainty in classifying the result if a crack is travelling slowly. There will be errors in measuring quantities such as crack velocity or pressure, which will affect the calibration of experimentally determined constants in some models.
- Determination of the pipe toughness. It is not possible to determine the Charpy toughness of the actual material through which the crack has passed, so in practice this toughness has to be inferred from measurements taken at each end of the pipe length.
- Scatter in the actual measurements of Charpy energy at a location.
- Conversion from sub-size specimen results to an equivalent full size value. This conversion has usually been carried out by scaling in proportion to the ligament area.

In addition to these sources of error in the predictive models, there will be a statistical distribution of Charpy energy in the pipe supplied. It is not economic to test every pipe length that is produced by the mill; instead a sampling approach is adopted. The testing plan specified by the purchaser will aim to minimise the proportion of pipe having a toughness which falls below the value required for arrest; one example is given by Jones [15].

An alternative approach to rupture length prediction was developed by EPRG [16]. This used a statistical analysis of the database of experimental full scale test results to derive probability distributions for the "arrest" and "propagate" results. A log-normal distribution was found to be the best fit to the data. The distributions were overlapping, due to the mixing of arrest and propagate points; Fig. 3 below shows this effect. Using the two distributions, the probability of a pipe of a given Charpy energy being able to sustain a propagating crack can be found. This is then used with the toughness distribution of the pipe supply to estimate the overall proportion of pipes which can sustain a running fracture. Jones [15] showed that if this proportion is p, the probability p_{rup} of a rupture of n or more pipe lengths is given by:

$$p_{rup} = p^n (n - [n-1]p) \tag{4}$$

Equation (4) can be used to plot this probability as a function of the number of pipe lengths. Figure 2 shows an example; in this case there is a probability of about 1% of a rupture of 5 pipe lengths or more. In the published analysis [16] the results are presented in tables of predicted rupture lengths for different Charpy toughness distributions, enabling the designer to select results appropriate to the distribution of toughness expected from the pipe mill. These results have subsequently been used by at least one pipeline operator to set specification toughness levels for new construction in grade X80 material.

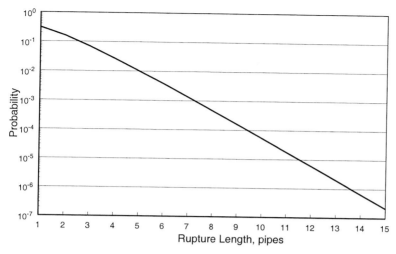

Fig. 2 Results from a typical calculation of rupture length probability

REVIEW OF ARREST TOUGHNESS REQUIREMENTS FOR SPIRAL PIPE

Most fracture propagation studies have been carried out on UOE pipe, which is formed from plate, longitudinally seam welded and cold expanded. In this pipe the crack propagates parallel to the plate rolling direction and the seam weld, which is often of lower toughness than the plate. If a crack should propagate in the seam weld, provided the seams are offset at each girth weld the crack will eventually pass into tougher parent plate and the analyses described above can be used. At worst, the rupture length is increased by one joint length, usually 12 metres.

Spiral pipe is produced by forming a continuous skelp into a helix and then seam welding the helical seam. The helix angle is determined by the skelp width and the desired pipe diameter. The relative technical and economic merits of the two pipe manufacturing routes are outside the scope of this paper, and the balance can vary depending on relative steel prices and pipe mill capacity. However, a technical concern has been the resistance of spiral pipe to ductile shear crack propagation. With a spiral seam weld, a crack propagating longitudinally will eventually intersect the seam. If the fracture resistance of the seam weld is lower than that of the parent plate, it is possible that having intersected the seam the crack may then propagate along the seam. One consideration against this is that the spiralling crack would have a lower axial velocity, and so the driving force available from the decompressing gas will be reduced as the pressure profile propagates away at the same speed regardless of the pipe type. Another concern is the effect of anisotropy of the skelp. Generally the toughness in the transverse direction has been higher than that in the rolling direction, although recent data suggests that the anisotropy is much lower in modern linepipe with low sulphur contents [17].

The EPRG toughness guidelines do not distinguish between pipe manufacturing routes. To show that the recommendations were applicable to spiral pipe, EPRG commissioned CSM to carry out a review of all available test data [18] for spiral linepipe. A total of 27 results for spiral pipes were identified in material covering the strength range from X60 to X70; results for similar UOE pipes tested under comparable conditions were also identified for comparison. Figure 3 shows these data, using the AISI model, equation (1), for predicting the required

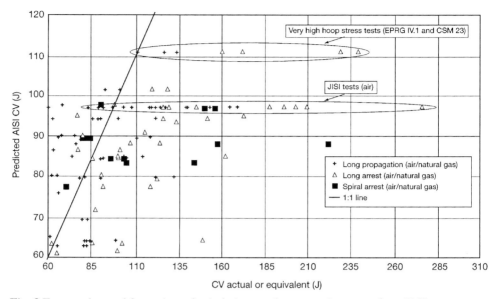

Fig. 3 Test results used for review of spiral pipe toughness requirements; from [18].

arrest toughness. There is a large amount of scatter in the predictions, and some are unconservative. However, the degree of mis-prediction for spiral pipe is no worse than for longitudinally seam welded UOE pipe. In a few tests the crack had travelled in a spiral fashion, although parallel to the seam weld rather than along the seam. In one case the effects of anisotropy were evident, as the crack travelled perpendicular to the seam weld. The review concluded that there was no evidence to suggest that the fracture arrest performance of spiral linepipe was worse than that of UOE pipe.

TRANSITION TEMPERATURES OF CHARPY V AND DROP WEIGHT TEAR TEST SPECIMENS

The Battelle DWTT has been widely used throughout the world and is now covered by a European standard [19]. The temperature corresponding to the ductile fracture behaviour of a pipeline is that at which the shear area is 85% of the evaluated fracture surface. The ductile to brittle fracture appearance transition temperature, corresponding to 50% shear area, is used in some specifications, but the 85% shear area requirement is nowadays of more general use for line pipes. Some modern pipelines, especially offshore, are using thicker walled pipes than those used in developing the original criterion. In addition, the energy required to fracture DWTT specimens in thick high strength pipes is approaching the capacity of many test machines. The Charpy transition curve may provide an alternative criterion.

In order to investigate the behaviour of high thickness line pipes, the European Pipeline Research Group (EPRG) started a research program comprising laboratory and full scale testing [20]. Two wall thicknesses, 38.1 mm and 27.5 mm, were investigated by producing three plates of thermomechanically controlled rolled L 450 MC steel for each thickness, and then forming them into 914 mm (36") diameter pipes.

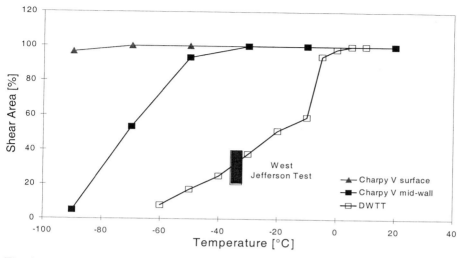

Fig. 4 Results from Charpy V, DWTT and West Jefferson tests on 27.5 mm wall pipe

With large thickness pipes a further problem arises with the Charpy V specimen as specimens can be extracted from different positions through the pipe wall thickness. To investigate this aspect two sets of specimens were extracted, one at mid wall and the other near the external surface. Figure 4 shows typical results from the test programme. There is clearly no correlation between the Charpy specimen behaviour and the full scale test. Using the percent shear area on the fracture surface of the Charpy to estimate the ductile to brittle transition of the pipe would lead to non conservative results on a large range of temperatures. Table 2 summarises several possible measures of transition temperature. Taking from EN 10208-3 the reference value for L 450 steel grade we can define a 45 J transition temperature. Using the measured shear areas we can also define a 50% shear area transition temperature, identifying the middle of the transition region and an 85% shear area transition temperature that defines the beginning of the ductile region. From the results in Table 2 it is interesting to notice the 50°C to 55°C shift between the mid wall Charpy V and DWTT transition temperatures, at both 50% and 85% shear areas. The 45 J transition temperature matches reasonably well the 50% shear area transition temperature.

Table 2 Transition temperatures for pipes of 38.1 and 27.5 mm wall thickness

Transition criterion	38.1 mm			27.5 mm		
	Charpy V surface	Charpy V mid-wall	DWTT	Charpy V surface	Charpy V mid-wall	DWTT
45 J	-90°C ‹	-70°C		-100°C	-110°C	
50% shear area	-90°C ‹‹	-70°C	-20°C	-110°C ‹‹	-100°C	-45°C
85% shear area	-90°C ‹	-60°C	-7°C	-110°C	-80°C	-25°C

CONCLUDING REMARKS

This paper has given a background to the phenomenon of propagating ductile shear fractures in gas transmission pipelines, showing how the upper shelf Charpy energy has been used for fracture control. The EPRG contribution in this area has been presented; this has been through:

- Sponsoring full scale fracture tests
- Analysis of results and generating Charpy toughness recommendations which have been adopted by international codes
- Developing statistical analysis methods to investigate the levels of safety and rupture lengths implied by these recommendations
- Funding a review of data from tests on spiral welded pipe to confirm that existing recommendations are also applicable
- Investigating the ductile - brittle transition behaviour of thick walled linepipe.

ACKNOWLEDGEMENTS

The authors acknowledge contributions by many present and former colleagues in EPRG.

REFERENCES

1. Smith, R.B. and Eiber, R.J. (1969). Field Failure Survey and Investigations. In: *Fourth Symposium on Line Pipe Research*, paper D. Pipeline Research Committee, Arlington, Virginia.
2. Eiber, R.J. (1969). Fracture Propagation. In: *Fourth Symposium on Line Pipe Research*, paper I. Pipeline Research Committee, Arlington, Virginia.
3. Fearnehough, G.D., Jude, D.W. and Weiner, R.T. (1971). In: *Practical Application of Fracture Mechanics to Pressure Vessel Technology,* pp. 156-62. IMechE, London.
4. Re, G., Pistone, V., Vogt, G., Demofonti, G. and Jones, D.G. (1995). *3R International* **34,** 607.
5. AISI Committee of Large Diameter Line Pipe Producers. (1971) Running shear fractures in line pipe. American Iron and Steel Institute.
6. Maxey, W.A. (1981). In: *Analytical and Experimental Fracture Mechanics*, pp. 109-23, Sih, G.C. and Mirabile, M. (Eds). Sijthoff and Noordhoff, Alphen aan den Rijn, The Netherlands.
7. Maxey, W.A., Kiefner, J.F., Eiber, R.J. and Duffy, A.R. (1972). In: *Proceedings of the 1971 National Symposium on Fracture Mechanics, Part II, ASTM STP 514,* pp. 70-81. American Society for Testing and Materials, Philadelphia.
8. Poynton, W.A., Shannon, R.W.E. and Fearnehough, G.D. (1974). *Journal of Engineering Materials and Technology* **96,** 323.
9. O'Donoghue, P.E., Kanninen, M.F., Leung, C.P., Demofonti, G. and Venzi, S. (1997). *International Journal of Pressure Vessels and Piping* **70,** 11.
10. O'Donoghue, P.E., Green, S.T., Kanninen, M.F. and Bowles, P.K. (1991). *Computers and Structures* **38,** 501.
11. Vogt, G.H., *et al.* (1983) *3R International* **22,** 3.
12. CEN. (1996). Steel pipes for combustible fluids - Technical delivery conditions - Part 2. Pipes of requirement class B EN 10208-2:1996. European Committee for Standardization, Brussels.
13. DnV. (2000). Submarine pipeline systems OS-F101. Det Norske Veritas, Hovik, Norway.
14. Standards Australia (1997). Pipelines - Gas and liquid petroleum Part 1: Design and Construction AS 2885.1-1997. Standards Australia, Homebush, New South Wales.
15. Jones, D.G. (1981). In: *AGA-EPRG Linepipe Research Seminar IV*, Duisburg, 22-24 September 1981. EPRG, Duisburg.
16. Dawson, J. and Pistone, V. (1998). *3R International* **37,** 728.
17. Baczynski, G.J., Jonas, J.J. and Collins, L.E. (1999). *Metallurgical Materials Trans A* **30,** 3045.
18. Pistone, V. and Mannucci, G. (2000). In: *Pipeline Technology Proceedings of the third international pipeline technology conference* Volume I, pp. 455-67, Denys, R. (Ed). Elsevier, Amsterdam.
19. CEN. (1999). Metallic materials - Drop weight tear test EN 10274:1999. European Committee for Standardization, Brussels
20. Pistone, V., Demofonti, G. and Junker, G. (2000). *3R International* **39,** 199.

From Charpy to Present Impact Testing
D. François and A. Pineau (Eds.)
385

THE TOUGHNESS TRANSITION CURVE OF A SHIP STEEL

JACK MORRISON and XIAOZHU WU
Defence Research and Development Canada
DREA Dockyard Laboratory (Pacific)
Victoria, BC, Canada

ABSTRACT

This paper describes a variety of fracture toughness tests carried out on a single plate of a 400 MPa yield strength control rolled low alloy steel. Standard longitudinal Charpy specimens had a large scatter of energy values which in the transition zone had an essentially bimodal distribution. Transverse specimens produced lower energy values with normal scatter. This wide variability was produced when half of the specimens developed splitting fractures parallel to the rolling plane, whereas splitting did not occur in dynamic tear specimens. Transverse tensile specimens produced noticeably oval fracture surfaces, even though the strength was isotropic. Transition curves for Charpy specimens with pressed notches have also been generated to provide a comparison with standard Charpy results, and reference temperatures were determined using the master curve method to quantify the cleavage resistance.

Splitting mechanisms have been related to microstructural features. This steel had a banded microstructure which promoted splitting fractures and very low Charpy transition temperatures in the L-T orientation. The Charpy behaviour was similar to that reported for a laminate with weak interfaces. Pressing the notch tip eliminated the splitting in the transition region and steepened the transition curve. The T_{28J} prediction of test temperature for the master curve method was successful when applied to Charpy test results from specimens in which no splitting occurred.

KEYWORDS

transition curves, reference temperatures, master curves, controlled rolling, pressed notches, splitting, tensile anisotropy.

INTRODUCTION

Material specifications for the hull plate used in Canadian naval ship construction include chemical composition limits, minimum tensile yield strength and Charpy V-notch impact energy. It is recognized that the standard Charpy test, while being a useful quality control tool, provides little in the way of information for quantitative structural assessment. There are alternative specimen types and procedures, such as the dynamic tear test, which have greater structural relevance. Unfortunately procurement authorities and steel producers have been reluctant to accept greater complexity and/or cost in material specification and quality control, particularly for qualifying the relatively small quantities of steel required for the Canadian fleet. There have however been attempts within the broader naval materials community to make Charpy test results more useful, for example, by the adoption of a 50% cleavage transition temperature [1]. The underlying rationale is that crystallinity is a better index of transition behaviour than energy when applied to materials with differing processing histories. ASTM test method E1921 for reference temperature determination using a master curve concept [2], while not simple enough for routine quality control, also offers a reasonably straightforward approach to cleavage fracture characterization in the thickness of interest and at minimum service temperature. Test temperatures for this procedure are initially established from a correlation with Charpy absorbed energy.

For thicknesses up to 15 mm the Canadian requirement for hull plate has usually been met by a control rolled micro-alloyed steel (carbon content ~0.07 wt %) which easily met the specified strength and toughness requirements. Its impact properties were also isotropic. For greater thicknesses, the carbon content tended to be higher (0.15 wt %), and the plate was usually normalized. However recent batches of 15 mm plate have been supplied in the control-rolled condition, and some of these had the higher carbon content. The microstructure and mechanical properties of this relatively thick control-rolled plate would be expected to be more directional than either the thinner or normalized material. There is thus concern that this difference might invalidate historical experience about how the Charpy results, for example, are related to structural performance, including its resistance to both crack initiation and arrest. This paper describes a series of fracture tests on the higher carbon control rolled plate, to assess the effect of plate directionality on Charpy behaviour and on transition reference temperatures.

MATERIAL

The basic hull plate of interest is CSA-G40.21 Grade 350WT Category 5, a weldable notch tough steel with minimum Charpy values specified by the purchaser. Table 1 shows the specified requirements and also some measured values from the control rolled plate supplied to this specification. This particular vanadium micro-alloyed steel exceeded the specified minimum requirements by a wide margin. However it can be seen that although the tensile properties were the same in both longitudinal and transverse orientations, the Charpy and dynamic tear energies were both much higher in the L-T orientation.

Microstructural examination of polished and etched samples revealed pronounced banding with predominately ferrite-pearlite plus a small amount of a light brown etching constituent assumed to be the martensite/austenite (M-A) constituent which results from carbon enrichment between the ferrite bands (Fig. 1(a)) [3]. Transverse and longitudinal sections were very similar, except that in transverse sections a concentration of the M-A phase occurred intermittently at the plate mid-thickness (the grey phase in Fig 1(b)). This discontinuity in microstructure may have been caused by manganese segregation locally lowering the Ar_3 temperature at which the ferrite transformation starts. Manganese is also known to promote pearlite banding. The ferrite was relatively undeformed, suggesting a finishing temperature close to Ar_3 [3]. Plate microhardness using a 3N load averaged VHN193, and was uniform through the thickness (the 50 μm indentation sampled a mixture of ferrite and pearlite bands). The mid-thickness region containing the grey phase averaged VHN290 using a 0.5N load.

wt %	C	Mn	Si	S	P	Nb	V	Ti	Al
spec.	0.22 max.	0.8 - 1.5	0.15 - 0.4	0.04 max.	0.03 max.	Nb + V = 0.1 max.		-	-
actual	0.16	1.38	0.28	0.005	0.009	0.002	0.07	0.01	0.04

0.2% proof stress (MPa)			UTS (MPa)			elongation (%)		
T	L	specified (L)	T	L	specified (L)	T	L	specified (L)
450	447	350 min.	590	587	480 - 650	26	27	22 min.

Charpy V @ -40°C (J)			Dynamic Tear @ -20°C (J)		CTOD @ -20°C (mm)		NDTT (°C)	
T-L	L-T	Specified (L-T)*	T-L	L-T	T-L	L-T	T-L	L-T
38	120	40 min.	355	1285	0.42	0.55	-40	-40

* Additional Charpy requirements are 65J @ +20°C and 20J @ -60°C.

Table 1. Plate chemical composition and mechanical properties.

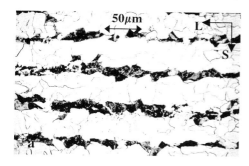 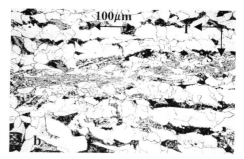

Fig. 1. Banded microstructures.

CHARPY TRANSITION CURVES

A study was made of the transition curves for both longitudinal and transverse specimens with through thickness notches (L-T and T-L orientations) using standard 10x10 mm V-notched Charpy specimens at 10°C temperature intervals. These tests were repeated using notches pressed at the tip. The ASTM E23 procedure was used throughout on a machine which had recently been verified using NIST standard specimens. The results are shown in Figs. 2 and 3.

Standard V-notch

There are major differences between the two orientations. The lower toughness T-L data show a moderate scatter in absorbed energy over the entire curve, with a gradual increase in toughness over the whole temperature range examined. The L-T results show a huge scatter over the transition region, in large part because half of the specimens developed one or more splits parallel to the rolling plane, which is a frequently reported occurrence in control rolled steels. While splitting resulted in a modest reduction of impact energy on the upper shelf relative to specimens which did not have splits, within the transition range it produced much higher values. Above -30°C these fracture surfaces had a single mid-thickness split, whereas in the transition range there were usually several parallel splits (Fig. 4). Below -70°C all of the specimens had flat cleavage fractures. L-T specimens in which there was no splitting had a sharp transition, whereas those with splits showed only a gradual increase in energy over the same range. In T-L specimens splits were rare (only 2 of 60 samples). Fracture appearance and lateral expansion curves showed the same trends as absorbed energy except that the upper shelf behaviours tended to converge regardless of splitting. In the transition % shear provided the least scatter and the clearest differentiation between specimens with and without splits.

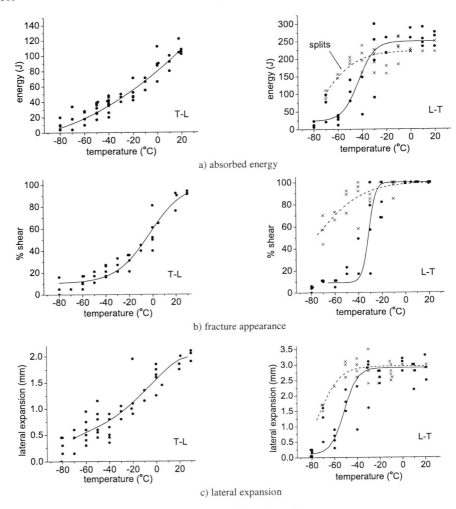

Fig. 2. Charpy V-notch transition curves.

V-notch with pressed tip.

These full size Charpy specimens had a non-standard notch similar to that used in dynamic tear specimens. A hardened blade was pressed into the root of a standard Charpy V-notch to produce a pressed depth of 0.25 mm. The results are shown in Fig. 3, with the curves from Fig. 2 superimposed. In the T-L orientation the shape of the curves is largely unchanged. Pressing the notch tip resulted in reduced data scatter and a +15°C shift in the energy transition curve. There was a smaller shift in the lateral expansion curve, and the % shear curve was unaffected. Five of 26 T-L specimens in the upper transition or above showed a single mid-thickness split. In the L-T orientation, pressing the notch completely suppressed splitting below the transition, while splits were found in almost all of the specimens tested above it. There was a 30°C or more shift in both the energy and lateral expansion curves, both of which now showed an abrupt transition. The shift in the % shear curve was much smaller.

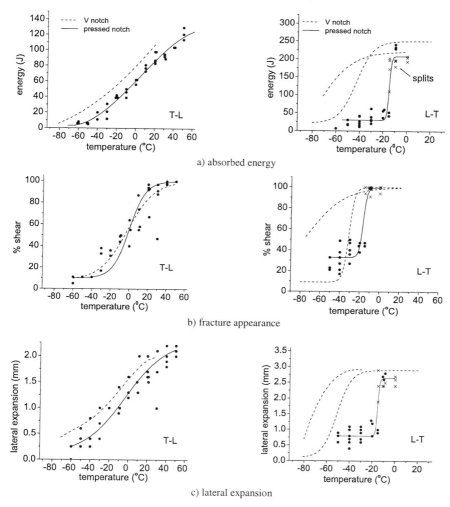

a) absorbed energy

b) fracture appearance

c) lateral expansion

Fig 3. Charpy transition curves for specimens with a pressed notch tip.

Fig. 5 compares Charpy energy curves with the corresponding dynamic tear data. Pressing the notch resulted in similar temperature dependences in both Charpy and dynamic tear specimens.

TENSILE FRACTURES

Both full thickness rectangular samples and 8 mm diameter rounds were tested from both longitudinal and transverse directions. There was no effect of specimen type or orientation on the numerical results. However in the round specimens there was a pronounced effect of direction on the deformation. Fig. 6 shows that while the fractured longitudinal specimens retained a circular cross section the transverse fractures ended up oval (shortened in the through thickness direction). There is no splitting tendency in these specimens. In contrast the rectangular specimens show similar behaviour in both orientations, and mid-thickness splitting

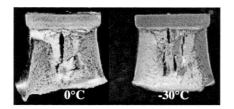

Fig. 4. Splitting in L-T Charpy specimens.

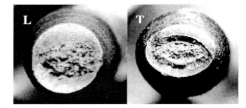

Fig. 6. Tensile fractures (-50°C).

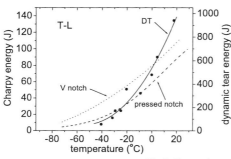

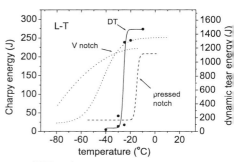

Fig.5. Comparison of Charpy and DT results.

only at very low temperatures and only after extensive necking. This suggests that the splitting observed in Charpy specimens is not caused by poor short transverse properties [4].

REFERENCE TEMPERATURE DETERMINATION

Using the ASTM E1921 master curve procedure, K_{Jc} fracture toughness measurements were made on side grooved 15x30 mm SENB specimens (W\B=2, a/W=0.5) taken from the same plate used for the impact and tensile tests. The experimental procedure and detailed results have been reported elsewhere [5]. Test temperatures varied between -40°C and -96°C, and the maximum likelihood method was used to determine the reference temperatures and master curves. Figure 7 shows results for both quasi-static (servo-hydraulic) and dynamic (drop-tower) stress intensity rates using the single temperature procedure provided in the ASTM Standard. Only rarely is splitting observed in full-thickness specimens at these temperatures. The test procedure includes a calculation for the selected test temperature for the quasi-static tests covered by the standard based on a correlation with T-L Charpy data. For a 15 mm specimen thickness this would be 27°C below the 28 Joules temperature for the Charpy, which is the temperature at which $K_{Jc(med)}$ for this particular specimen thickness is expected to be about 100 MPa√m. In this case it seemed prudent to calculate separate reference test temperatures for the two orientations. In the absence of splitting T-L and L-T Charpy had T_{28J} values of -47°C and -68°C respectively, and thus corresponding test temperature predictions of -74°C and -95°C respectively. As can be seen in Fig. 7, these are within 10°C of the resulting quasi-static T_0 values. Both orientations produce the same shift of about +55°C in reference temperature in going from a quasi-static to a dynamic loading rate. At these higher temperatures, the corresponding Charpy values are 48J (T-L) and 98J (L-T), and both are in the lower transition.

quasi-static	T-L	L-T
test temperature °C	-76	-96
dK/dt MPa√m/s	7	10
$K_{Jc(med)}$ (1T) MPa√m	112	106
reference temperature °C	-84	-100
dynamic	**T-L**	**L-T**
test temperature °C	-40	-57
dK/dt MPa√m/s	7×10^4	7×10^4
$K_{Jc(med)}$ (1T) MPa√m	86	94
reference temperature °C	-28	-46

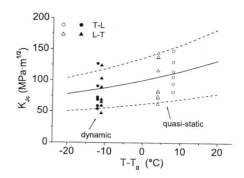

Fig. 7. Reference temperature data summary and master curves.

DISCUSSION

Although in control rolled steel the transverse orientation generally provides more consistent Charpy data with less scatter than that from longitudinal specimens, the Canadian standard (and most others) requires a longitudinal specimen. At the specified temperature of -40°C (minimum 40J) the impact energy of L-T specimens varied between 42J and 238J with a standard deviation of 70J. The corresponding range for T-L specimens is 20J to 48J with a standard deviation of 8J. If the average of three samples falls below of that required (but no lower than 85%) the specification allows additional tests to be made, provided that no individual value fell below two-thirds of the minimum. This is obviously not a problem with this steel, which averages four times the minimum. By agreement the standard also permits a minimum lateral expansion of 0.4 mm to be used instead of absorbed energy, a value also easily met by L-T specimens.

The distribution of L-T oriented Charpy specimens in this particular steel is reminiscent of the bimodal energy distributions described in several papers 50 years ago. Both ductile and brittle fractures were encountered at the same test temperature in the transition zone, and a variety of causes were reported [6,7]. As steels got cleaner reports of bimodality decreased, although during the 1960s-1980s numerous reports appeared describing a similar trend caused by the splitting phenomenon in control rolled steels [8,9]. In some cases splitting was also restricted to longitudinal specimens. Some of the observations made in the current program are similar to the general trend of those studies. Relative to clean fractures in the transition range splitting resulted in higher Charpy with lower transition temperatures, and the number of splits increased with decreasing temperature. On the upper shelf splitting reduced the absorbed energy. On the other hand the reported results did not generally show the bimodal distribution which best describes the L-T data in Fig. 2. A substantial amount of work was also carried out on numerous candidate splitting mechanisms [8]. For this particular steel the most pertinent appear to be those associated with ferrite-pearlite banding, and microstructural anisotropy [9,10]. A finishing temperature below the A_{r3} will promote splitting, but does not seem to have been that low in this steel.

A key feature of the bimodal energy distribution is that splitting will not occur if the main fracture is brittle cleavage, a fact most clearly shown by the % shear curve. On the other hand if plastic deformation at the notch tip reduces tensile triaxiality and thus the likelihood of cleavage on the main fracture plane, splitting can occur in the rolling plane. The double L-T curves in Fig. 2 bear a striking qualitative resemblance to those obtained on laminates made from thin layers of mild steel with (weak) interfaces perpendicular to the notch (a so-called "crack-divider" laminate) [11]. The ferrite/pearlite banding has a similar geometry, the ferrite grain boundaries are relatively weak interfaces, and the M-A constituent distributed within it may serve as crack nucleation sites at these interfaces. Obviously the same process does not operate in the T-L orientation where the gradual increase of toughness reflects a fracturing process largely unaffected by microstructural inhomogeneity. Figure 3 clearly demonstrates the ability of the more severe pressed notch to reduce crack tip plasticity and eliminate splitting in the transition zone. In contrast in fully plastic specimens pressing the notch promoted a single mid-thickness separation in the L-T orientation, but only infrequently in the T-L specimens.

CONCLUSIONS

This steel had two characteristics of particular concern which could affect its structural performance in a ship, and which could be misleading whether assessing the resistance to cleavage, ductile tearing, or crack arrest. One is the relatively low energy values in transverse specimens both over the transition range and on the upper shelf. The other is that the splitting of L-T Charpy specimens (and the high resulting absorbed energies) does not reflect the performance of material containing a sharper notch except (approximately) on the upper shelf. Nevertheless it is a very tough steel, and even the most pessimistic Charpy transition temperature lies below normal worst case service temperature. The results are in accord with the idea that the 50% crystalline fracture appearance is more structurally relevant than is absorbed energy, and relatively insensitive to notch tip condition. A parallel study has indicated that crack arrest toughness is also quite respectable [5]. The measured reference temperatures for cleavage fracture resistance were very low; even the dynamic values lie below the 50% crystallinity temperatures.

REFERENCES

1.   Sumpter, J.D.G. (1991). In: *Advances in Marine Structures - 2,* pp.1-22, Smith, C.S. and Dow, R.S. (Eds). Elsevier Science.
2.   Merkle, J.G., Wallin, K., and McCabe , D.E.(1998). NUREG/CR-5504, U.S. Nuclear Regulatory Commission, Washington.
3.   Dogan, B., Collins, L.E. and Boyd, J.D. (1988). *Met Trans* **19A**, 1221.
4.   Engl, B., and Fuchs, A. (1980). *Praktische Metallographie* **17,** 3.
5.   Wu, X., Morrison, J., Hull, A., Pussegoda, L.N., and Nethercott, R.B. (2000). in *Applications of Fracture Mechanics in Failure Assessment*, pp.105-112, Lidbury, D. (Ed). PVP Vol. 412, ASME, New York.
6.   Bailey, N. (1991). *TWI Bulletin* **5**, 110.
7.   Ulmo, J., Bastenaire, F., and Borione, R. (1953), Revue de Métallurgie L. **12**, 868.
8.   Bramfitt, B.L., and Marder, A.R. (1977). in *Toughness Characterization and Specifications for HSLA and Structural Steels,* pp.236-256, Mangonon, P.L. (Ed). Metallurgical Society of AIME, New York.
9.   Ryall, J.E., and Williams, J.G. (1978). *BHP Technical Bulletin* **22,** 38.
10.   Almond, E.A. (1969), *Met Trans* **1**, 2038.
11.   Almond, E.A., Embury, J.D., and Wright, E.S. (1969). In *Interfaces in Composites*, ASTM STP 452, pp.107-129, ASTM, Philadelphia.

From Charpy to Present Impact Testing
D. François and A. Pineau (Eds.)

MATERIALS QUALIFICATION FOR THE SHIPBUILDING INDUSTRY

W. WISTANCE, P. H. PUMPHREY and D. J. HOWARTH
Materials and NDE Department, Lloyd's Register of Shipping,
71 Fenchurch Street, London EC3M 4BS, UK.

ABSTRACT

In order to assess the adequacy of their toughness, samples of grade A and AH36 ship plate, sourced from a range of Lloyds Register of Shipping (LR) approved manufacturers, were subjected to Charpy impact and strain age embrittlement tests and, in the case of the AH36, dynamic fracture toughness tests. Simulated weld heat affected zones (HAZs) in grade A were also Charpy tested. All the plates exceeded the current LR Charpy Rule requirements and the earlier Boyd criteria for avoidance of brittle failure in service. The adequacy of the toughness was further supported by tests on grade AH36 that showed fracture toughness exceeded Sumpter's minimum structural integrity criterion of 125 MPa $m^{1/2}$ at 0°C. The prediction of fracture toughness from Charpy energy is discussed. Strain ageing 5% reduced the Charpy energy but this still met the Rule requirements. The simulated weld HAZs also had reduced toughness. Modern ship steels have improved toughness compared with steel tested in 1958 and should not suffer brittle fracture in service.

KEYWORDS

Ship plate, Steel grades A and AH36, Charpy energy, Crystallinity, Dynamic fracture toughness, Strain age embrittlement, Gleeble weld HAZ simulation.

INTRODUCTION

Ship hulls are generally constructed from mild steel, which can under certain conditions become susceptible to brittle fracture. A review by Lloyds Register of Shipping (LR) of the fracture properties of ship steels took place in 1958 by Boyd [1], following investigations into the failure by brittle fracture of the welded Liberty ships during World War II [2] when an LR Rule requirement of a minimum manganese to carbon ratio of 2.5 was implemented to improve toughness [3]. However, until Boyd's review, no toughness requirements for mild steel had been quantified, and LR Rules merely stated that a ship steel should demonstrate 'adequate notch toughness'.

Boyd defined toughness requirements based upon the Charpy impact test (considered the most practical method for mass-production testing), at a test temperature of 0°C (close to the minimum sea water temperature a vessel might encounter in service). Boyd's measurements showed that the vast majority of brittle failures in ships had occurred in steels with Charpy impact energies of less than 47J, with a fracture surface more than 70% crystalline at the casualty temperature. An acceptance criterion of a minimum Charpy impact energy of 47J at 0°C was introduced into LR Rules in 1957. However, a requirement for a maximum 70% crystallinity was not adopted because of the difficulty in measuring this parameter consistently. In 1961, LR introduced standard grades with minimum toughness controlled by differences in the Charpy impact requirements. The current requirements are: Grade A, no certified Charpy value, grades B, D and E, 27J at 0°C, -20°C and -40°C, respectively. Higher strength steels may be specified but have increased Charpy energy requirements [4].

Following the implementation of toughness graded ship steels, the incidence of brittle fractures declined [5]. However, no enforced checks were made for grade A steel which forms the majority of material within the shell structure of many ships. It was presumed that the compositional requirements of LR grade A guaranteed a notch toughness of 27J at ambient temperature (+20°C). However, this has not always been the case [6] and some brittle failures have occurred [7]. Following continued concern within the shipbuilding industry, LR introduced a Rule requirement in 1997 for in-house checks for every 250t of grade A plate produced by the steel maker, to ensure that an impact energy of 27J at +20°C is achieved.

The primary aim of the present work was to show that the toughness of modern grade A and higher strength grade AH36 steel ship plates was sufficient to ensure the structural integrity of ship structures. Therefore, the results of Charpy impact tests on as received and strain aged material, simulating the effect of manufacturing processes such as cold bending, line heating and welding, were first compared with the LR Rule requirements. Charpy tests were also conducted on Gleeble thermally simulated coarse grain weld heat affected zone (HAZ) material from grade A plates to assess the possible toughness degradation after welding. However, as Charpy energy cannot be used directly to predict the failure of engineering structures, dynamic fracture toughness tests were carried out on selected AH36 plates at loading rates relevant to ship structures, rather than under conventional quasi-static conditions. Sumpter has suggested [8] that a minimum fracture toughness of 125 MPa $m^{1/2}$ at 0°C for a loading rate of 10^4 MPa $m^{1/2}$/s is needed to ensure the integrity of ship structures. Therefore, a correlation between fracture toughness and Charpy data was sought, so that the adequacy of Charpy toughness of the tested grade A and AH36 plates and the minimum LR Rule requirements could be assessed.

METHOD

A total of 39 grade A plates 12mm to 16 mm thick and 22 grade AH36 plates 15mm to 22mm thick were obtained from LR approved manufacturers world-wide. A metallographic section was taken from each in order to establish the rolling direction, microstructure and grain size. Yield stress, tensile strength, elongation and chemical composition were obtained from the manufacturer's certificate. The chemical composition of each plate was confirmed using an optical emission spectrometer.

Longitudinal (transverse notch) Charpy tests were carried out on sets of 3 specimens, as the material acceptance is on the basis of the mean of 3 tests. Tests were carried out between -20°C and +20°C for grade A and from –70°C to 0°C for grade AH36. Strain ageing was simulated by straining strips by 5% and 10% for grade A but only by 5% for grade AH36 and then heating 15 minutes at 200°C. Charpy specimens machined from each strip were tested at +20°C for grade A and 0°C for grade AH36. Bars from 18 grade A plates were subjected to a thermal cycle by induction heating to simulate the HAZ of a high heat input (5kJ/mm) submerged arc weld. Charpy specimens notched in the centre of the 5mm zone of constant microstructure were tested between −20°C and +20°C. Sets of three dynamic fracture toughness full thickness bend tests were conducted at 0°C, on six AH36 plates, selected to cover the measured range of Charpy energy, under loading rates that corresponded to increases in the stress intensity factor of 10^2 MPa m$^{1/2}$/s and 10^4 MPa m$^{1/2}$/s.

RESULTS

The tensile properties and chemical compositions, shown in Tables 1 and 2, respectively, meet the LR Rule requirements.

Table 1 Tensile properties

	Yield stress MPa	Tensile strength MPa	Elongation to failure, %
LR Rules, grade A	≥235	400-520	≥22
Grade A plates	257-387	404-482	24-38
LR Rules, grade AH36	≥355	490-620	≥21
Grade AH36 plates	361-434	501-564	21-31

Table 2 Chemical compositions, weight %

	C	Mn	Si	S	P	Al
LR Rules, grade A	≤0.21	≥2.5x%C	≤0.5	≤0.035	≤0.035	-
Grade A Plates	0.07-0.21	0.40-1.29	0.01-0.32	0.006-0.030	0.007-0.035	0.001-0.060
LR Rules, grade AH36	≤0.18	0.90-1.60	≤0.5	≤0.035	≤0.035	≥0.015
Grade AH36 Plates	0.11-0.18	0.98-1.56	0.01-0.46	0.001-0.030	0.01-0.024	0.019-0.064

The results of the Charpy impact tests at the temperatures required by the LR Rules plotted in Fig.1 show a wide range of energies. However, all the Charpy values surpass the requirements of 27J at 20°C (lowest mean value 73J) for grade A and 34J at 0°C (lowest mean value of 65J) for grade AH36. Seven grade A and eight AH36 plates have mean energies over 200J.

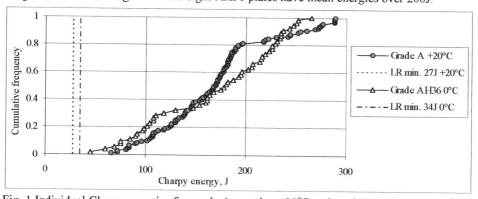

Fig. 1 Individual Charpy energies for grade A tested at +20°C and grade AH36 tested at 0°C

Reductions in Charpy energy for grade A with decreasing test temperatures are shown in Fig. 2. However, mean values do not begin to fall below 27J until −20°C. A similar reduction was seen for AH36 plates but mean values did not begin to fall below 34J until −40°C. Increasing crystallinity with decreasing Charpy energy and test temperature is shown in Fig. 3 but the trends are subject to considerable scatter. The effects for AH36 are similar. All the plates of both grades met the Boyd criteria of 47J Charpy energy and 70% crystallinity at 0°C.

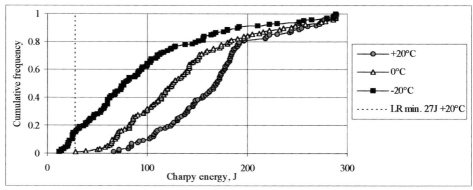

Fig. 2 Effect of test temperature on Charpy energy for individual grade A specimens

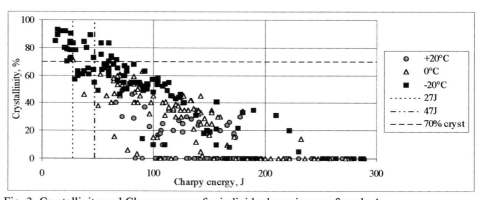

Fig. 3 Crystallinity and Charpy energy for individual specimens of grade A

Interpolation of the mean crystallinity data for different test temperatures was used to define the 50% crystallinity fracture appearance transition temperature (FATT) for each plate (Fig. 4). The arrows indicate FATTs below the lowest Charpy test temperature. Five grade A plates had a FATT above 0°C, with a highest value of +8°C. AH36 had lower FATTs with only one plate above 0°C. This is potentially significant as Sumpter has suggested that a FATT below 0°C is needed to meet his 125 MPa m$^{1/2}$ fracture toughness criterion.

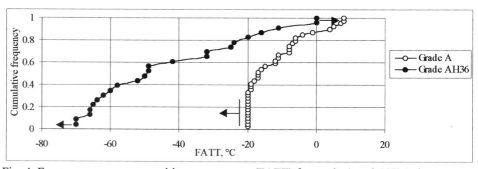

Fig. 4 Fracture appearance transition temperature (FATT) for grade A and AH36 plates

Strain ageing generally decreased the Charpy energy and increased the fracture surface crystallinity, to an extent that increased with the prior strain. However, after 5% strain, all the Charpy values for grade A were still above 27J at +20°C, as required by the LR Rules and the mean crystallinities were all below 50% indicating that the FATTs for all the plates remained below ambient temperature. After 10% strain, some individual energies were less than 27J but the mean values were all above this level. However, increased crystallinities, indicated that eight plates now had FATTs above ambient temperature. Three plates had less than 47J Charpy energy and more than 70% crystallinity at +20°C and would not meet the Boyd criteria at 0°C. For AH36, all Charpy energies were above 34J at 0°C and all the plates met the Boyd criteria after 5% strain ageing. However, one plate had a FATT above 0°C.

The simulated weld HAZ material from grade A plates also showed degraded toughness but only one out of the 18 tested had a mean energy less than 27J at +20°C. However, nine plates had a FATT above +20°C. 11 failed to meet the Boyd criteria of 47J and maximum 70% crystallinity at 0°C and 16 had a FATT above 0°C.

All the load/displacement traces for the AH36 fracture toughness tests indicated ductile behaviour, although several of the specimens exhibited up to 0.4mm ductile tearing on the fracture surface before plastic collapse. The fracture toughness values K_{Jm} listed in Table 3 correspond to the J-values at maximum load. All the values of $K_{Jm} < 300$ MPa m$^{1/2}$ correspond to specimens exhibiting ductile tearing. No systematic effect of loading rate can be discerned for the results in Table 3 (Fig. 5) but all the fracture toughness values are above Sumpter's minimum criterion of 125 MPa m$^{1/2}$. Fracture toughness increases with Charpy energy (Fig. 5).

Table 3 Fracture toughness of grade AH36 plates tested under medium (10^2 MPa m$^{1/2}$/s) and high (10^4 MPa m$^{1/2}$/s) loading rates at 0°C. Mean values in brackets. * Indicates ductile tearing

Plate	12	14	11	13	16	10
Charpy energy at 0°C, J	73	97	106	158	187	221
Crystallinity at 0°C, %	36	50	37	43	0	0
Fracture toughness at	344	413	441	249*	418	538
Medium loading rate	356	200*	435	527	487	453
K_{Jm} MPa m$^{1/2}$	380	(307)	431	493	462	497
	(360)		(436)	(423)	(456)	(496)
Fracture toughness at	380	271*	428	587	469	583
High loading rate	356	179*	414	(587)	470	541
K_{Jm} MPa m$^{1/2}$	377	207*	237*		470	553
	(371)	(219)	(360)		(470)	(559)

DISCUSSION

The Charpy tested plates in this study satisfied LR's requirements of 27J at +20°C for the grade A and 34J at 0°C for the grade AH36 (Fig. 1). However, there was a wide variation in the Charpy values that tended to increase with decreasing grain size and with reduced levels of sulphur and phosphorus but these trends were subject to scatter, indicating a complex interaction between the chemical composition and the processing parameters for these steels. The strain ageing tests have shown that the Charpy energy is reduced with increasing strain but all of the plates met LR's Rule requirements when subjected to 5% cold strain. Only one of the simulated weld HAZ grade A plates failed to meet 27J at +20°C. However, there is no Rule requirement for the testing of weld HAZs.

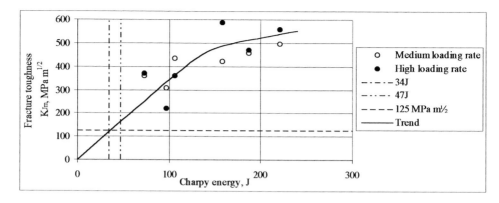

Fig. 5 Correlation between fracture toughness and Charpy energy for grade AH36 tested at 0°C

A comparison between the Charpy data for the grade A at 0°C and those of Boyd on failed and production plates from 1958 in Fig. 6 shows the superior toughness of current grade A.

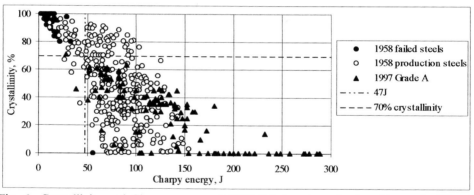

Fig. 6 Crystallinity and Charpy energy of 1958 failed and production ship steels [1] and present grade A steel tested at 0°C

All the present plates (grade A and grade AH36) met the Boyd criteria of 47J minimum Charpy energy and maximum of 70% crystallinity at 0°C, whereas some 26% of the 1958 production plates failed to meet these criteria (Fig. 6). Although tests on severely strain aged and simulated weld HAZ grade A indicated that the 47J minimum Charpy energy and 70% maximum crystallinity at 0°C would not be met by some plates, there is little evidence that these effects are a problem in practice and suggests that these tests may be unduly severe. It seems likely that the superior toughness of current steels is due, in part, to their lower sulphur and phosphorus levels (Table 2) as compared with the mean values of 0.038wt% sulphur and 0.027wt% phosphorus reported by Boyd. Overall improvements in production and processing technology of steel plates are the main reasons for the improvement in toughness.

The measured dynamic fracture toughness values for grade AH36 at 0°C (Table 3) exceeded Sumpter's criterion of 125MPa $m^{1/2}$ for structural integrity. This included one plate (no. 14) that exhibited 50% crystallinity in Charpy tests at 0°C, suggesting that, here, Sumpter's alternative 50% crystallinity criterion is over conservative.

In order to investigate the adequacy of Charpy values for the integrity of ships, the application of correlations with fracture toughness from BS 7910 [9] have been considered. As the measured fracture toughness for the present AH36 is insensitive to loading rate, the results for the two loading rates are combined when comparing the toughness predicted from the Charpy data and the experimental values. Lower bound upper shelf fracture toughness predictions from Charpy energies at the highest test temperature of 0°C for the AH36 plates are all well below the minimum measured values (Table 4). However, all but two of the predictions will be underestimates, as the Charpy specimens showed less then 100% ductile failure. For the same reason, most of the upper shelf toughness predictions for grade A plates from Charpy data at the highest test temperature of 20°C, shown in Table 4, will also be underestimates. However, where the fracture surfaces of the Charpy specimens tested at 0°C are not entirely ductile and the fracture toughness has not been measured, such as for the grade A plates, brittle fracture cannot be excluded. Therefore, lower bound 'master curve' predictions for the brittle transition derived from the 27J Charpy transition temperatures for such plates are also shown in Table 4. The 27J transition was determined from the variation of mean Charpy energy with test temperature for selected grade AH36 and grade A plates. Some of the predicted lower bound values fall below the Sumpter 125MPa m$^{1/2}$ minimum toughness criterion. However, the present results are limited, so more data are needed to establish whether the lower bound toughness predictions for ship steels from the Charpy energy are over pessimistic.

Table 4 Predicted lower bound fracture toughness of grade AH36 and grade A plates using the BS 7910 upper shelf and master curve brittle transition correlations with Charpy data. Comparison with experimental results for grade AH36

Plate No.	Thickness	Charpy energy/ crystallinity at 0°C	Charpy upper shelf energy	27J Charpy temp	BS 7910 predicted lower bound K$_{Jc}$ at 0°C MPa m$^{1/2}$		Measured K$_{Jm}$ at 0°C MPa m$^{1/2}$		
					Upper shelf, ductile	Master curve brittle transition	Max.	Mean	Min.
	mm	J / %	J	°C					
AH36									
10	15.89	221 / 0	221	-	174	-	583	528	453
11	16.70	106 / 37	>106	-	>112	-	441	398	237
12	17.40	73 / 36	>73	-37	>94	102	380	365	344
13	17.68	158 / 43	>158	-69	>140	166	587	464	249
14	15.28	97 / 50	>97	-27	>107	91	413	258	179
16	17.56	187 / 0	187	-	156	-	487	463	418
A									
4	12.40	72 / 42	>111	-22	>115	89	-	-	-
8	11.89	76 / 8	84	-22	100	90	-	-	-
21	12.33	49 / 43	>106	-18	>112	84	-	-	-
24	12.00	51 / 63	>116	-14	>117	81	-	-	-
25	15.77	63 / 58	>73	-16	>94	79	-	-	-
29	15.34	79 / 48	>133	-18	>127	81	-	-	-

For AH36 plates just meeting the minimum Charpy requirement of 34J at 0°C (27J transition about −5°C) and grade A 27J at +20°C, the 'master curve' brittle transition predicts lower bound fracture toughness values of 69 MPa m$^{1/2}$ and 53 MPa m$^{1/2}$, respectively, for 15mm thick plate. However, 96% of the failed plates from casualties tested by Boyd had 27J transition temperatures above -5°C which suggests that AH36 with 34J at 0°C does not present a serious risk of brittle fracture in service. This is not the case for grade A with 27J at +20°C, as there are numerous examples among the casualty plates tested by Boyd where service failures occurred for 27J transition temperatures close to +20°C. However, it is expected that the present higher toughness grade A plates with 27J transition temperatures of -14°C and below are more typical of modern steels, so that the risk of brittle fracture, in practice, is likely to be small.

CONCLUSIONS

This study has shown that modern grade A and AH36 ship plate exceed the current LR Charpy impact requirements of 27J at +20°C and 34J at 0°C, respectively. They also meet Boyd's 1958 criteria of 47J and a maximum of 70% crystallinity at 0°C for brittle fracture avoidance, based upon tests on casualty material. Dynamic fracture toughness tests on grade AH36 plates have shown that the fracture toughness exceeds Sumpter's minimum criterion of 125MPa $m^{1/2}$ for the integrity of ship structures. These results are above the lower bound predictions of fracture toughness correlations with Charpy energy recommended in BS 7910. However, more data are needed to test the usefulness of this approach for predicting the lower bound fracture toughness of ship steels. Strain ageing caused a reduction in Charpy impact energy but after 5% strain, all plates still met the minimum Charpy energy as required by the Rules. Strain ageing by 10% and high heat input weld HAZ simulation caused a more significant drop in toughness and increased crystallinity but there is little evidence that these effects present problems in practice. Grade A steel Charpy toughness properties have shown a significant improvement due to modern steel making practices compared to the steel surveyed in Boyd's original 1958 report. It is considered that the risk of brittle fracture for these modern steels in service is small.

REFERENCES

1. Hodgson, J. and Boyd, G.M. (1958) *Transactions of the Institute of Naval Architects*, **100**, 141.
2. *The Design and Methods of Construction of Welded Steel Merchant Vessels* (1947). U.S. Government Printing Office, Washington.
3. Barr, W. and Honeyman, A.J.K. (1947) *Journal of the Iron and Steel Institute* **157**, 239.
4. *Lloyd's Register Rules for the Manufacture, Testing and Certification of Materials*, Chapter 3, Sections 2 and 3 (2000). Lloyd's Register of Shipping, London.
5. Buchanan, G. Jensen, C.J.G. and Dobson, R.J.C. (1969). *Lloyds Register of Shipping's Approach to the Control of Incidents of Brittle Fracture in Ship Structures.* Lloyds Register of Shipping Report No.56.
6. Sumpter, J.D.G. Caudrey, A.J. and Jubb, J.E.M.(1993) *Journal of Marine Structures,* **6**, 443.
7. *Formal Investigation into the Wreck of MV KURDISTAN* (1982). Report of Court no.8069, HMSO.
8. Sumpter J.D.G. and Caudrey, A.J. (1995) *Journal of Marine Structures* **8**, 345.
9. BS 7910 (1999) *Guide to Methods for Assessing the Acceptability of Flaws in Metallic Structures*, Annexe J. British Standards.

Modelling

From Charpy to Present Impact Testing
D. François and A. Pineau (Eds.)
© 2002 Elsevier Science Ltd. and ESIS. All rights reserved

THE CALCULATION OF DYNAMIC J_R-CURVES FROM 2D AND 3D FINITE ELEMENT ANALYSES OF A CHARPY TEST USING A RATE-DEPENDENT DAMAGE MODEL

Eberle, A., Klingbeil, D., Baer, W., Wossidlo, P. and Häcker, R.
Federal Institute for Materials Research and Testing (BAM),
Mailing address: BAM-V.23, D-12200 Berlin, Germany, e-mail: arno.eberle@bam.de

ABSTRACT

Two dimensional and three dimensional analyses of the Charpy V-notch specimen subjected to impact loading according to the standard DIN EN 10045-1 were carried out, using a transient explicit dynamic finite element program. An elastic-viscoplastic temperature dependent constitutive relation for a porous plastic solid based on the Gurson damage model was developed. Ductile fracture of the matrix material will be described by the nucleation and subsequent growth of voids to coalescence. An updated Lagrange-Jaumann formulation is employed accounting for large strain and rotation. The equations of motion are integrated numerically by an explicit integration algorithm utilising a lumped mass matrix. The predictions of the numerical analyses in terms of force deflection response, crack propagation and crack resistance behaviour are compared with results from Charpy tests which were carried out according to low-blow and full-blow techniques.

INTRODUCTION

The assessment of the reliability of components requires the knowledge of the appropriate crack resistance curves, which are often not available due to lack of specimen material. Typical material parameters, however, that are more likely available are such as the yield strength, tensile strength, elongation, fracture strain as well as Charpy energy and the lateral elongation of Charpy V-notch specimens.

Aurich and Klingbeil [1] applied a method with which the construction of crack resistance curves may be carried out based on such information. Within the scope of this method one main point is the evaluation of the Gurson ductile damage parameters via the simulation of the Charpy V-notch impact test and the fit of these parameters to the impact energy of the upper shelf. This procedure is founded on the reliable knowledge that within the regime of ductile fracture the impact energy is used up completely by ductile crack growth.

On the other hand, ductile crack growth is independent of the specimen geometry and loading rate. This allows the transfer of the parameters determined by the simulation of the Charpy V-notch test to statically loaded specimens such as C(T)- or M(T)-specimens from which crack resistance curves may be calculated by numerical analyses. So, this procedure makes the use of conventional crack resistance curves available for the structural analysis of components.

THE CHARPY TEST

Historically, Charpy impact test has been used as a screening test for fracture prone materials. The Charpy V-notch specimen is the toughness diagnostic specimen most widely used. Figure 1 shows a schematic drawing of a Charpy test arrangement used for setting up the Finite Element meshes.

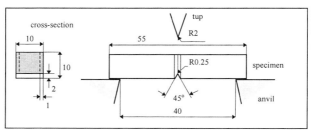

Fig. 1: Schematic arrangement of a Charpy test according to the standard DIN EN 10045-1; typical dimensions for a side-grooved specimen in [mm].

The total length of the specimen is 55 mm and the rectangular cross-section area is 10 x 10 mm. The specimen has a 2 mm deep V-shaped notch with a flank angle of 45°. The notch tip radius is 0.25 mm. In case of side-grooved specimens, the depth of the grooves is usually 1 mm. The specimen is positioned upon two anvils with a span of 40 mm. The tup (striker) has a maximum initial velocity of 5.52 m/s and a total mass of 19.7 kg. Depending on the toughness of the material, the specimen slides through the anvils at different velocities. If the material exhibits brittle cracking only, the two pieces of the specimen are often thrown aside. The tests were performed according to DIN [2] using a 300 J Charpy test equipment with an instrumented striker.

EXPLICIT DYNAMIC ANALYSIS

The explicit dynamic analysis procedure in ABAQUS/Explicit is based upon the implementation of an explicit integration rule together with the use of diagonal element mass matrices. The equations of motions of the body are integrated using the explicit central difference integration rule

$$\dot{u}_N^{\left(i+\frac{1}{2}\right)} = \dot{u}_N^{\left(i-\frac{1}{2}\right)} + \frac{\Delta t^{(i+1)} + \Delta t^{(i)}}{2} \ddot{u}_N^{(i)},$$

$$u_N^{(i+1)} = u_N^{(i)} + \Delta t^{(i+1)} \dot{u}_N^{\left(i+\frac{1}{2}\right)},$$

(1)

where $\dot{u}$ is velocity and $\ddot{u}$ is acceleration. The superscript i refers to the increment number, and the subscript N to the specific displacement degree of freedom. The central difference integration operator is explicit in that the kinematic state is advanced using known values of $\dot{u}_N^{(i-1/2)}$ and $\ddot{u}_N^{(i)}$ from the previous increment. The key to the computational efficiency of the explicit procedure is the use of diagonal or "lumped" element mass matrices because the inversion of the mass matrix that is used in the computation for the accelerations at the beginning of the increment is triaxial:

$$\ddot{u}_N^{(i)} = \left(M_{NM}\right)^{-1}\left(R_M^{(i)} - F_M^{(i)}\right),$$

(2)

where M_{NM} is the diagonal lumped mass matrix, $R_M^{(i)}$ is the applied load vector and $F_M^{(i)}$ is the internal force vector. The explicit procedure requires no iterations and no tangent stiffness matrix and integrates through time by using many small time increments. The central difference operator is conditionally stable and the stability limit (without damping) is given in terms of the highest eigenvalue in the system.

THE GURSON DAMAGE MODEL

The Gurson model was implemented into ABAQUS/Explicit as a rate-dependent damage model via the user routine VUMAT. The inelastic flow of the porous material is based on a potential function that characterizes the porosity in terms of a single state variable, the relative density r. The relationships defining the model are expressed in terms of void volume fraction, f, which is defined as the ratio of the volume of voids to the total volume of the material. It follows that $f = 1 - r$.

For a metal containing a dilute concentration of voids, Gurson [3] proposed a yield condition as a function of the void volume fraction. This yield condition was later modified by Needleman and Tvergaard [4] to the form:

$$\Phi = \left(\frac{\sigma_v}{\sigma_y}\right)^2 + 2q\,f^* \cosh\left(\frac{3\sigma_h}{2\sigma_y}\right) - 1 - \left(q f^*\right)^2 = 0,\qquad(3)$$

with the von Mises effective stress,

$$\sigma_v = \sqrt{\frac{3}{2}T':T'},\qquad(4)$$

and the hydrostatic pressure stress,

$$\sigma_h = \frac{1}{3}T:I.\qquad(5)$$

The deviatoric part of the Cauchy stress tensor T is defined as

$$T' = T - \sigma_h I.\qquad(6)$$

An updated Lagrange formulation takes large deformations into account. The constitutive equation is formulated by using the Green-Naghdi rate of the Cauchy stresses and the symmetric part of the spatial velocity gradient D. The constitutive equation is integrated by using an explicit difference scheme according to Pierce et al. [5] which is stable due to small time increments Δt. The yield stress σ_y of the fully dense matrix material is a function of the equivalent plastic strain in the matrix $\bar{\varepsilon}_m^{pl}$, and q is a material parameter with a value of about 1.5 for ferritic steels which accounts for an earlier coalescence of neighbouring voids as well as for the effect of elasticity and plastic hardening on void growth. The Cauchy stress is defined as the force per current unit area comprising of the voided matrix material. The function $f^*(f)$ models the rapid loss of stress carrying capacity that accompanies void coalescence. This function depends linearly on f and is determined by the accelerating factor K taking into account the coalescence of neighbouring voids. As long as the critical value of f_c is not yet reached the modified void volume fraction f^* is equal to f. When the critical value of f_c is exceeded void growth is accelerated by the factor K,

$$f^* = \begin{cases} f, & \text{for } f \le f_c \\ f_c + K(f - f_c), \quad K = \dfrac{f_u^* - f_c}{f_f - f_c}, & \text{for } f_c < f \le f_f \end{cases}\qquad(7)$$

When $f = f_f$ total failure at the material point of the element occurs and the modified void volume fraction f^* is equal to its final value f_u^*. Typical values for K are between 4 and 8.

The plastic part of the rate of deformation D^{pl} is derived from the yield potential; the presence of pressure in the yield condition results in nondeviatoric plastic strains. Plastic flow is assumed to be normal to the yield surface with $\dot{\lambda}$ as the nonnegative plastic flow multiplier:

$$D^{pl} = \dot{\lambda} \frac{\partial \Phi}{\partial T}. \tag{8}$$

The hardening of the fully dense matrix material is described through the conventional stress-strain curve $\sigma_y = \sigma_y(\bar{\varepsilon}_m^{pl})$. By differentiation the incremental equation of evolution for σ_y is obtained

$$\dot{\sigma}_y = H \dot{\bar{\varepsilon}}_m^{pl} \tag{9}$$

with H as the plastic tangent modulus. The evolution of the equivalent plastic strain in the matrix material is obtained from the equivalent plastic work expression as

$$(1-f)\, \sigma_y\, \dot{\bar{\varepsilon}}_m^{pl} = T : D^{pl}. \tag{10}$$

The rate of the void volume fraction is given as the sum of growing and nucleating voids $\dot{f} = \dot{f}_{gr} + \dot{f}_{nucl}$. Growth of the existing voids is based on the law of conservation of mass, and is expressed in terms of void volume fraction and plastic strain rate,

$$\dot{f}_{gr} = (1-f)\, D^{pl} : I. \tag{11}$$

The nucleation of voids is given through a relationship controlled by the amount of the equivalent plastic strain in the matrix material, $\dot{f}_{nucl} = A \dot{\bar{\varepsilon}}_m^{pl}$, with

$$A = \frac{1}{H} \frac{f_n}{s_n \sqrt{2\pi}} \exp\left[\frac{1}{2} \left(\frac{\bar{\varepsilon}_m^{pl} - \varepsilon_n}{s_n} \right)^2 \right], \tag{12}$$

where the normal distribution of the nucleation strain has a mean value ε_n, standard deviation s_n and nucleates voids with volume fraction f_n. Voids nucleated only in tension. The nucleation function A is assumed to have a normal distribution.

All presented material equations were formulated with respect to large deformation theory and implemented into the commercial FE code ABAQUS/Explicit via a user subroutine. All parameters for the Gurson model were identified by correlation between analysis and results from tension tests performed on tension rods as described by Klingbeil et al. [6]. Total failure at the material point occurs when $f = f_f$. In the present analysis, a value of $f_f = 0.19$ was used for the final void volume fraction. An element loses the stress carrying capacity once its material point has failed. Hence, the value of the internal variable f_f of an element in the ligament is the indicator for crack propagation.

RATE DEPENDENT YIELD

As strain rates increase, many materials show an increase in their yield strength. For example, for many common metals this effect becomes important when the strain rates rise from the static values of $0.001–0.01$ per second into a range of $0.1–1.0\ \text{s}^{-1}$, and can be very important if the strain rates are in the range of $100–1000\ \text{s}^{-1}$, as commonly occurs in high energy dynamic events like a Charpy test.

Generally, the yield stress of a material is dependent on the accumulated equivalent plastic strain $\sigma_y = \sigma_y(\bar{\varepsilon}_m^{pl})$. The effects of strain rate on plastic hardening and the additional coupled effect of thermal softening in viscoplasticity may be described by a simple method. Pan et al. [7] derived the following empirical equation for the "dynamic" yield stress:

$$\sigma_y = \sigma_{y0}\left(\bar{\varepsilon}_m^{pl},T\right)\left(\frac{\dot{\bar{\varepsilon}}_m^{pl}}{\dot{\bar{\varepsilon}}_{m0}^{pl}}\right)^n, \quad 0 < n << 1. \tag{13}$$

The reference stress-strain curve which was statically determined is denoted as $\sigma_{y0}\left(\bar{\varepsilon}_m^{pl},T\right)$ and depends on the equivalent plastic strain $\bar{\varepsilon}_m^{pl}$ and temperature T of the matrix material. The reference equivalent plastic strain rate of the matrix material is denoted as $\dot{\bar{\varepsilon}}_{m0}^{pl}$, and the actual equivalent plastic strain rate is $\dot{\bar{\varepsilon}}_m^{pl}$. The advantage of this model is that only the material parameter n has to be determined.

During deformation a certain amount of plastic work is converted into heat. If this happens slowly, the heat may spread from the crack tip through the specimen and given off at the surface, which is called an isothermal process. If the strain rates are high there is no time for the conduction of heat and the temperature at the crack tip increases with increasing deformation. Beyond a critical strain rate there is practically no heat flux [8] and the process is called adiabatic. As adiabatic conditions are assumed, the rise in temperature through plastic dissipation may be calculated from the simplified energy balance,

$$\rho c_p \frac{\partial T}{\partial t} = \chi \boldsymbol{T}:\boldsymbol{D}^{pl}, \tag{14}$$

with c_p as the specific heat capacity and the density ρ. The value of the proportionality factor χ for metals is normally about 0.9 [9].

The increase in temperature causes thermal softening of the material and a lower yield stress. The rise in temperature may now be calculated with eq. (14). In order to form a viscoplastic model after eq. (13) the dependency of the yield stress from temperature has to be given explicitly. According to Needleman and Tvergaard [10] a linear relationship between yield stress and temperature has been taken into account,

$$\sigma_{y0}\left(\bar{\varepsilon}_m^{pl},T\right) = \sigma_{y0}\left(\bar{\varepsilon}_m^{pl},T=T_0\right)\cdot\left[1-\beta\left(T-T_0\right)\right], \tag{15}$$

with β as an additional material parameter. Hence, the formula describing the strain rate induced hardening and thermal softening of the material which was implemented into the ABAQUS/Explicit finite element code is as follows,

$$\sigma_y = \sigma_{y0}\left[1-\beta\left(T-T_0\right)\right]\left(\frac{\dot{\bar{\varepsilon}}_m^{pl}}{\dot{\bar{\varepsilon}}_{m0}^{pl}}\right)^n, \quad 0 < n << 1. \tag{16}$$

MATERIAL PARAMETERS

Values for both parameters, β and n, were published by Brocks et al. [11] and adopted to this analysis. In detail, the following values were used: $\beta = 1\cdot10^{-4}$ 1/°C, $n = 1.3\cdot10^{-2}$. The parameters of the Gurson model for the German standard steel StE 460 were evaluated in an earlier work, [6], from quasi-static experiments on tension rods. In the present work all material parameters of the Gurson damage model come from these tests. Thus, the use of material parameters from statically-loaded fracture mechanics specimen in order to model the material behaviour of impact loaded Charpy specimens should be confirmed.

RESULTS

Figure 2 shows the deformed shape of the 2D Charpy specimen after a period of about 1.0 ms. Only one half of the specimen is modelled, because of symmetry. The tup as well as the anvil are treated as rigid bodies. It is assumed that there is no friction between the specimen and the rigid bodies. The impact between the tup and the specimen has already taken place. The tup pushes the specimen vertically through the rigid anvil. The calculated vertical displacement of the specimen is about 4.25 mm. Up to this point of deflection, the Gurson model predicts a crack propagation of about 4.0 mm which means that almost half of the ligament is damaged by a macroscopic crack.

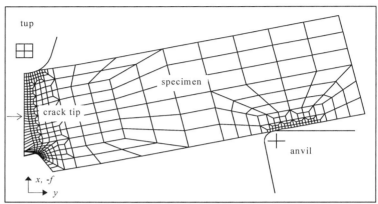

Fig. 2: Deformed shape of one-half of the Charpy specimen as calculated by the 2-dimensional explicit dynamic FE analysis about 1 ms after the impact of the tup; deflection $f \approx 4.25$ mm, crack growth $\Delta a \approx 4$ mm, impact velocity $v_0 = 5.52$ m/s.

The deformed mesh plot as well as the state of crack propagation from the 3D analysis is shown in Fig. 3. Only one quarter of the specimen is modelled, because of symmetry. The already failed elements are shown as the dark thumbnail shaped area extending from the notch upwards. The maximum crack propagation along the centre line of the ligament is about 3.3 mm after a period of about 0.8 ms. The comparison between calculated and measured crack front is shown in Fig. 4. The low-blow test was carried out on a non-side-grooved specimen at a velocity of about 2.5 m/s. It is seen that the experiment produces a non-symmetric crack front which the simulation can not account for. Nevertheless, the agreement of the right branch may be designated as very good.

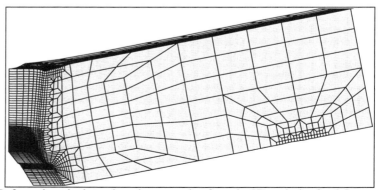

Fig. 3: Deformed mesh plot and crack propagation from the 3D analysis after 0.8 ms

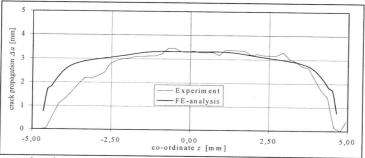

Fig. 4: Comparison between calculated and measured crack front of a Charpy specimen

The plot of Fig. 5 shows force vs. deflection curves obtained from full-blow experiments which were carried out with an impact velocity of 5.52 m/s. One of them was recorded for a side-grooved specimen, (sg.), the other for a non-side-grooved specimen, (nsg.). The force vs. deflection curve calculated by the 2D plane strain explicit dynamic FE analysis with an impact velocity of 5.52 m/s is closer to the curve representing the side-grooved specimen, as the plane strain elements characterise better the geometric condition of side-grooved specimens. The 3D calculation was performed on a non-side-grooved model and represents the experimental curve very well up to a deflection of 4.5 mm. The subsequent differences are due to the transition from a rather fine to a less fine meshing in the crack plane. The maximum force as estimated by the numerical analyses is in the order of 15 kN and 15.5 kN and corresponds well with the experimentally measured values.

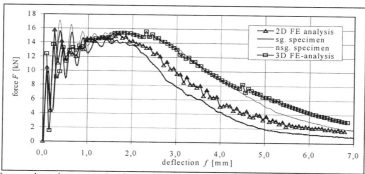

Fig. 5: Comparison between the force deflection curves of the 2D and 3D FE analyses and experiments (v_0 = 5.52 m/s) on side-grooved (sg.) and non-side-grooved (nsg.) specimens.

The J-integral was calculated from the 2D explicit dynamic finite element analysis by using a post processor. Thus, it was possible, to calculate not only those parts of the J-integral derived from the mechanical stresses and strains but also to include additional parts arising from thermal strains and dynamic masses. Fig. 6 compares J-integral results obtained from the explicit dynamic 2D FE analysis and J-integral values which were determined from the force deflection curve of several Charpy tests applying low-blow technique [1]. The impact velocities were between 1.5 m/s and 2.5 m/s. After the test the specimens were broken up to determine the final crack growth. It can be seen that the calculated J_R-curve is in good agreement with the experimental data. The oscillations of the numerically obtained curve are due to the influence of negative accelerations upon J which is reduced in such cases.

CONCLUSION

It could be shown that 2D as well as 3D explicit dynamic finite element analyses combined with the rate-dependent Gurson damage model may be used to simulate Charpy tests. Not only the calculated force vs. deflection curves represent well experimental curves, but also the shape of the crack front calculated by a 3D FE analysis is in close agreement with the measured crack front. The numerically predicted 2D dynamic J_R-curve for the German standard steel StE 460 represents well the experimental data obtained by low-blow technique. The explicit dynamic simulations show that it is possible to analyse the Charpy test to a high degree of confidence using damage parameters taken from quasi-static tests. Thus, the transfer of the parameters via numerical analysis to quasi-staticly loaded fracture mechanics specimens is possible and as a consequence the corresponding J_R-curves may be calculated. Therefore, the presented analysis is a significant contribution towards the development of a method for the evaluation of dynamic J_R-curves of different specimens from the Charpy energy proposed by Aurich and Klingbeil [1].

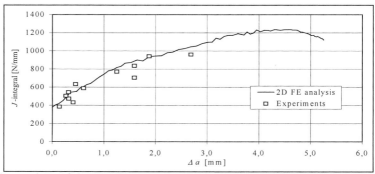

Fig. 6: Comparison of the J-resistance curve from the 2D explicit dynamic FE analysis and low-blow experimental data of J vs. Δa for the German standard steel StE 460.

REFERENCES
1. Aurich, D. and Klingbeil, D. (1998). Forschungsbericht 228. Bundesanstalt für Materialforschung und -prüfung (BAM), Berlin. Wirtschaftsverlag NW, Bremerhaven.
2. DIN EN 10045 T1 (1990). Kerbschlagbiegeversuch nach Charpy, Prüfverfahren, Deutsches Institut für Normung, Berlin.
3. Gurson, A.L. (1977). *J. Eng. Mat. Tech., Trans.* ASME **99**, pp. 2-15.
4. Needleman, A. and Tvergaard, V. (1984). *J. Mech. Phys. Sol.* **32**, pp. 462-490.
5. Peirce, D., Shih, C.F. and Needleman, A. (1984). *Computers & Structures*, **18**, 875.
6. Klingbeil, D., Künecke, G. and Schicker, J. (1994). In: *Proc. 10th Europ. Conf. Fract. Vol. 1*, pp. 453-462, (Schwalbe, K.-H. and Berger, C.), (EMAS Ltd.), Warley, U.K.
7. Pan, J., Saje, M. and Needleman, A. (1983). *Int. J. Fract.* **21**, pp. 261-278.
8. Dixon, P.R. and Parry, D.J. (1991). *Journal de Physique IV Colloque 3, Suppl. au Journal de Physique III, Vol. 1*, pp. C3-85 - C3-92.
9. Farren, W.S. and Taylor, G.J. (1925). *Proc. Roy. Soc. of London,* Vol. A197, pp. 422ff.
10. Needleman, A. and Tvergaard, V. (1991). *Int. J. Fract.* **49**, pp. 41-67.
11. Brocks, W., Klingbeil, D., Künecke, G. and Sun, D.-Z. (1995). In: *Constraint Effects in Fracture-Theory and Applications: 2nd Vol.,* ASTM STP 1244, pp. 232-252, (Kirk, M. and Bakker, A.), ASTM, Philadelphia.

From Charpy to Present Impact Testing
D. François and A. Pineau (Eds.)

FRACTURE MECHANICS ANALYSIS OF CHARPY TEST RESULTS BASED ON THE WEIBULL STRESS CRITERION

FUMIYOSHI MINAMI, MASUO IIDA and WATARU TAKAHARA
Department of Manufacturing Science, Osaka University, Suita, Osaka, JAPAN

NOBORU KONDA and KAZUSHIGE ARIMOCHI
Sumitomo Metal Industries Ltd., Amagasaki, Hyogo, JAPAN

ABSTRACT

The material fracture toughness is often estimated from the Charpy impact energy using empirical correlations. However, each correlation has a limitation of application, although some are implemented in fabrication standards. This study employs the Local Approach to interpret Charpy test results. Instrumented Charpy tests and fracture toughness tests are performed in the lower-transition range for structural steels of 490 and 780 MPa strength class. Stress fields are addressed by 3D-FEM considering the strain rate effect and temperature rise during dynamic loading. It is shown that the critical Weibull stress at brittle fracture initiation is almost independent of the loading rate. This enables the Charpy results to be transferred to the material fracture toughness. As an alternative to the instrumented test, a simplified procedure is proposed: The evaluation of fracture initiation at $0.6KV$ to $0.8KV$ leads to a good estimation of brittle fracture toughness in the lower-transition range, where KV is a total impact energy.

KEY WORDS

Charpy test, impact energy, fracture toughness, structural steels, brittle fracture, strain rate effect, Weibull stress, transferability analysis

INTRODUCTION

In the fracture mechanics assessment of crack-like defects, the material fracture toughness measured as the plane strain toughness K_{IC}, J_{IC} or critical CTOD δ_c is necessary but often not available for some reason. An engineering method alternatively applied is to estimate it from correlations with the Charpy impact energy. A number of empirical correlations between the V-notch Charpy energy KV and fracture toughness have been offered [1]. They are classified into two groups; 1) direct correlations between KV and fracture toughness and 2) correlations taking account of a temperature shift of Charpy test results due to impact loading. It is known, however, that the empirical correlations do not maintain accuracy and are valid with restrictions to the kind and strength class of materials, plate thickness and temperature range for which the correlation was established. Hence, careful attention is required to the use of the estimated fracture toughness in the fracture assessment .

This paper gives a fracture mechanics interpretation to the Charpy impact properties in the lower-transition range. Two kinds of structural steels are provided, which differ in strength class and work hardening properties. The Weibull stress is employed as a fracture driving force. On the basis of the Weibull stress fracture criterion, an attempt is made to transfer the impact test results to the critical CTOD at brittle fracture initiation. An engineering method is followed for the estimation of fracture toughness without the aid of the instrumented procedure.

EXPERIMENTS

High strength structural steels of 490 and 780 MPa class, SN490B and SHY685N steels in JIS standards, were used in the experiment. Table 1 shows the chemical composition and mechanical properties of these steels. The materials were selected in terms of the yield-to-tensile ratio YR, which exerts a large influence on the crack tip stress fields. Low and high YR values are noted for SN490B and SHY685N steels, respectively. The present experiments include instrumented Charpy tests, fracture toughness tests and round-bar tension tests. Figure 1 shows the configuration of the specimens used. The load was applied in the rolling direction of the plate.

The Charpy impact test was conducted at -70°C for SN490B steel and at -100°C for SHY685N steel to induce brittle over a large portion of the notch section. The impact test machine had a pendulum striker of 447 N with an arm length of 850 mm, which produced the initial potential energy of 490 J. Measuring devices were instrumented as shown in Fig. 2. Elastic strain gauges of a semiconductor type were pasted on both sides of the pendulum striker edge to measure the impact load. The gauge surface was coated to be protected from the environmental attack and fragments of the specimen. The position of the striker during impact loading was measured with an angular displacement transducer. Output signals from the strain gauge and displacement transducer were recorded with a digital data logger through a high frequency type amplifier. The sampling interval time was 0.5 ms for each signal. The trigger timing for the logger was led from passing time of an obstruction plate attached to the striker at a specified location pointed by a luminiferous diode.

Table 1 Chemical composition and mechanical properties of high strength structural steels used

SN490B	Chemical composition (mass %)						Mechanical properties (t/2, Direction : L)					
	C	Si	Mn	P	S	Ceq	σ_Y (MPa)	σ_T (MPa)	YR (%)	ε_T (%)	KV0 (J)	DBTT (°C)
	0.16	0.32	1.38	0.011	0.002	0.41	344	514	67.0	14.3	221	-42

SHY 685N	Chemical composition (mass %, B : ppm)													Mechanical properties (t/2, Direction : L)					
	C	Si	Mn	P	S	Cu	Ni	Cr	Mo	Nb	V	B	Ceq	Pcm	σ_Y (MPa)	σ_T (MPa)	YR (%)	ε_T (%)	KV-40 (J)	DBTT (°C)
	0.10	0.23	0.95	0.008	0.002	0.22	1.43	0.50	0.51	0.012	0.038	11	0.53	0.26	777	814	95.5	6.1	193	-86

Ceq=C+Mn/6+Si/24+Ni/40+Cr/5+Mo/4+V/14, Pcm=C+Si/30+Mn/20+Cu/20+Ni/60+Cr/20+Mo/15+V/10+5B,
σ_Y : Yield stress, σ_T : Tensile strength, YR = σ_Y / σ_T, ε_T : Uniform elongation,
KV0, KV-40 : Charpy absorbed energy at 0°C and -40°C, DBTT : Fracture transition temperature

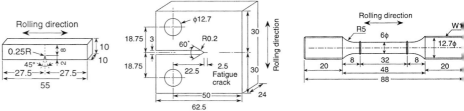

(a) V-notch Charpy specimen   (b) Compact specimen   (c) Round-bar tension specimen
Fig. 1 Configuration of specimens used in experiments.

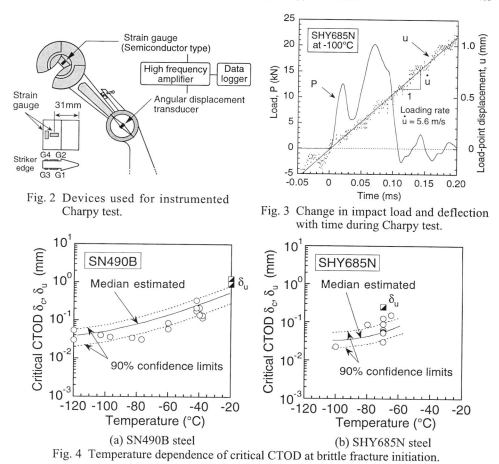

Fig. 2 Devices used for instrumented Charpy test.

Fig. 3 Change in impact load and deflection with time during Charpy test.

(a) SN490B steel

(b) SHY685N steel

Fig. 4 Temperature dependence of critical CTOD at brittle fracture initiation.

Figure 3 shows an example of the load and deflection records for SHY685N steel. The load signal showed a strong oscillation, especially up to the attainment of the maximum load. On the other hand, an almost linear relationship was recognized between the load-point deflection and time. The loading rate measured was 5.6 m/s, which was nearly equal to the rate of 5.5 m/s calculated by the law of the conservation of energy. The absorbed energy KV for SN490B steel at -70°C was in the range 8 to 11 J, and one for SHY685N steel at -100°C from 10 to 27 J. A low energy level was related to 90% brittle fracture appearance for both steels.

The toughness test results are shown in Fig. 4. δ_c and δ_u denote the critical CTOD values at the onset of brittle fracture without and with stable crack growth greater than 0.2 mm. CTOD values were calculated according to the procedure specified in the British Standard of Fracture Mechanics Toughness Tests (BS7448-Part 1).

The round-bar tension test was conducted to determine the flow properties of the materials as a function of the strain rate. The crosshead speed was varied from 0.1 to 1000 mm/s in the temperature range -170 to 20°C. An optical extensometer was employed to measure the displacement over a reduced gage length of 24 mm marked within the test section. It is well known that the yield stress and tensile strength increase with increasing the loading rate. In this paper, the rate-temperature parameter R proposed by Bennet & Sinclair [2] was employed for the evaluation of the strain rate effect on the tensile properties. The R-parameter is expressed as:

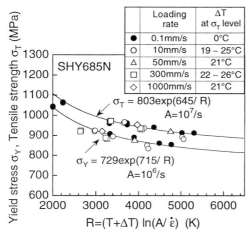

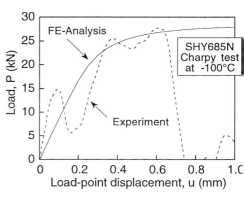

Fig. 5 Characterization of yield stress and tensile
strength with rate-temperature parameter
R in different test conditions.

Fig. 6 Load versus deflection relationship
in Charpy impact test.

$$R = (T + \Delta T) \cdot \ln (A / \dot{\varepsilon}) \qquad (1)$$

where $\dot{\varepsilon}$ is the strain rate, T and ΔT are the test temperature and temperature rise, respectively, and A is a material constant. The temperature rise ΔT was computed by FE-analysis described later. After yielding, the nominal strain had an almost linear relationship with time. In this paper, an average of the plastic strain rate up to the maximum load was defined as the strain rate of loading. The strain rate $\dot{\varepsilon}$ ranged from 0.003/s to 25/s depending on the crosshead speed.

The yield stress, σ_Y, and tensile strength, σ_T, exhibit a certain value as far as the parameter R holds the same value [2]. The material constant A can be inferred from this property. A-values determined were $10^6 s^{-1}$ and $10^7 s^{-1}$ for σ_Y and σ_T, respectively. A lower A-value implies a weaker dependence on the strain rate. Figure 5 presents the tensile test results for SHY685N steel as a function of the parameter R. It is known that the yield stress σ_Y shows the Arrhenius type dependence on the temperature. With Eq. (1), the yield stress σ_Y would be given in the form

$$\sigma_Y = B \cdot exp (C / R) \qquad (2)$$

According to Fig. 5, the tensile strength σ_T also has a similar relationship with the parameter R;

$$\sigma_T = B' \cdot exp (C' / R) \qquad (2')$$

where B, B', C and C' are material constants. The tensile results for SN490B steel showed a larger dependence on the parameter R than those of SHY685N steel.

The uniform elongation (= nominal strain at maximum load) was almost independent of the strain rate, which is consistent with the previous report [3].

FE-ANALYSIS

The stress fields were analyzed with the FE-code, ABAQUS ver. 5.8. Because of symmetry, one quarter of the Charpy and compact specimens were analyzed. The Charpy model had a minimum element of 0.05x0.05x0.2 mm at the notch bottom. Fine and coarse meshes were employed for the compact model in the crack tip region depending on the CTOD level; 0.01x0.01x0.5 mm for CTOD ≤ 0.1 mm and 0.1x0.1x0.5 mm for CTOD > 0.1 mm. At CTOD =

0.1 mm, the fine and coarse meshes presented almost the same stress fields near the crack tip. The loading rate for the Charpy model was 5.6 m/s in accordance with the experimental measurement. Flow properties of the material in the FEM follow the strain hardening in the form

$$\overline{\sigma} = \sigma_Y \cdot \left(1 + \overline{\varepsilon}_p / \alpha\right)^n \tag{3}$$

where $\overline{\sigma}$ and $\overline{\varepsilon}_p$ are the equivalent stress and equivalent plastic strain, respectively, σ_Y is the yield stress, n is the strain hardening exponent, and α is a material constant. According to Eq. (3), the tensile strength σ_T and uniform elongation ε_T are given by

$$\sigma_T = \sigma_Y \cdot (n / \alpha)^n \cdot exp\,(\alpha - n)\,, \quad \varepsilon_T = exp(n - \alpha) - 1\,. \tag{4}$$

The n and α values were determined from the round-bar tension test results, using Eq. (4). The strain rate effects on the flow properties were included in the following manner :
- The dependence of the yield stress σ_Y and tensile strength σ_T on the strain rate was evaluated with Eqs. (2) and (2') as a function of the rate-temperature parameter R (Fig. 5).
- The uniform elongation ε_T was assigned to be independent of the strain rate.

The inertial effect was eliminated by a quasi-static analysis. Nakamura, et al. [4] introduced the concept of a transition time t_T, which defines the point in the response after which inertial effects diminish rapidly. Nakamura indicated that the fracture analysis using conventional static formulae yields acceptable accuracy for time greater than 2 x t_T. The transition time t_T was estimated as 28 x t_W for a deep crack specimen, where t_W is the time for an unbounded dilatational wave to travel the specimen width. Vargas & Dodds [5] showed $t_T \approx 28$ x t_W also for a shallow crack specimen. For the Charpy specimen of width $W = 10$ mm, t_W (= W/c_1) is calculated as 1.96 x 10^{-6} s with an unbounded dilatational wave speed $c_1 = 5.1$ x 10^6 mm/s, which yields $t_T = 0.055$ x 10^{-3} s. In the present Charpy test, the loading time to the maximum load exceeded $2t_T$ for SHY685N steel and $1.3t_T$ for SN490B steel, respectively, thus neglecting inertial effects by a quasi-static analysis would be allowed [5, 6].

The material constants A and B to C' were determined through the analysis of the round-bar specimen. A high speed straining will generate heat adiabatically. It was assumed that 90% of plastic work, $0.9 \int \overline{\sigma} d\overline{\varepsilon}_p$ is transferred to heat [7]. An appreciable amount of temperature rise ΔT was observed after yielding, while ΔT at the yielding stage was negligibly small. The ΔT level at the maximum load is summarized in Fig. 5. The determination of constants A and B to C' needs an iteration analysis, because ΔT is included in the determination process. The FE-calculations using the converged constants were almost consistent with the experimental results, as shown in Fig. 6.

Figure 7 shows the strain rate distribution near the notch bottom of the Charpy specimen obtained by the 3-dimensional FE-analysis. The results are given at a deflection level of 0.5 mm,

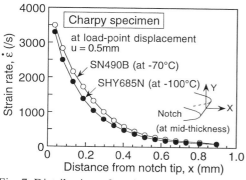 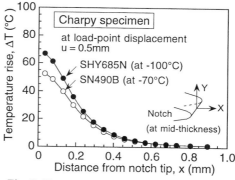

Fig. 7 Distribution of strain rate near notch tip for Charpy specimen.   Fig. 8 Temperature rise resultant from dynamic loading of Charpy specimen.

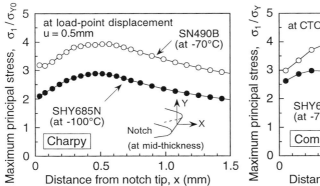
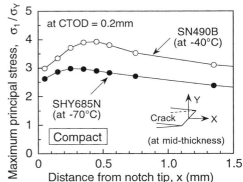

Fig. 9 Stress fields near notch tip for Charpy specimen, where σ_{Y0} is static yield stress at test temperature.

Fig. 10 Stress fields near crack tip for compact specimen of structural steels with different work hardenabilities.

which corresponds to the deflection at the maximum load in the impact tests. It can be seen that the strain rate is elevated significantly at the notch bottom. The temperature rise ΔT in the notch bottom region is shown in Fig. 8. A greater ΔT for SHY685N steel is due to its higher yield stress resulting in a large plastic work. Such elevation of strain rate and heat generation affect the flow properties of the material. The FE-code, ABAQUS provides a fully-coupled analysis to solve the temperature and stress/displacement fields simultaneously. The R-parameter analysis informs that the strain rate effect is more dominant in the notch tip region than the temperature rise effect.

Figure 9 shows the stress fields of the Charpy specimen at the deflection level of 0.5 mm. The maximum principal stress normalized by the static yield stress at the test temperature is presented. SN490B steel produces a more activated stress field. This is explained in terms of a high work hardening property (low YR) and a greater sensitivity to strain rate. A similar feature was observed in the compact specimen, as shown in Fig. 10. It is noted that the peak stresses in the Charpy and compact specimens are almost in the same level.

TRANSFER OF CHARPY RESULTS TO CTOD FRACTURE TOUGHNESS

This paper applies the Local Approach [8] to estimate the CTOD fracture toughness from the Charpy test results. The local approach employs the Weibull stress σ_W as a fracture driving force of ferritic materials. The Weibull stress σ_W is given by the integration of a near-tip stress σ_{eff} over the fracture process zone V_f in the form

$$\sigma_W = \left[\frac{1}{V_0} \int_{V_f} [\sigma_{eff}]^m \, dV_f \right]^{1/m}$$

(5)

where V_0 and m are a reference volume and a material constant, respectively. The m-value reflects the distribution of microcracks for the material and generally ranges from 10 to 40. The critical Weibull stress $\sigma_{W, cr}$ at brittle fracture obeys the Weibull distribution with two parameters

$$F(\sigma_{W, cr}) = 1 - exp\left[-\left(\frac{\sigma_{W, cr}}{\sigma_u} \right)^m \right]$$

(6)

where m (shape parameter) and σ_u (scale parameter) are assumed to be material properties independent of the specimen geometry. The scale parameter σ_u is associated with the toughness level of the material, microcrack distributions and the reference volume V_0. Since the m-value does not depend on V_0, a unit volume for V_0 is convenient for the Weibull stress calculation [9]. The selection of V_0 does not affect the transferability analysis of fracture toughness results. An effective stress [9] considering a random spatial distribution of microcracks was adopted as σ_{eff}.

There was a problem to determine the m-value from the Charpy test results, because the $\sigma_{W, cr}$ for the Charpy specimen showed a limited change. As an alternative, the compact test results were employed. Figure 11 shows the cumulative distribution of $\sigma_{W, cr}$ at brittle fracture initiation. The m-values determined by an iteration procedure [9] were 33 and 39 for SN490B and SHY685N steels, respectively. With these m-values, the $\sigma_{W, cr}$ of the Charpy specimen was calculated. The calculated results are given in Fig. 11 with open symbols. Marked difference is not observed between the $\sigma_{W, cr}$-distributions for the compact and Charpy specimens.

Based on the Weibull stress criterion, the critical CTOD of the compact specimen was estimated from the Charpy test results. Figure 12 shows the estimation procedure. It is assumed that the critical Weibull stress $\sigma_{W, cr}$ is independent of the loading rate. Compute the evolution of σ_W for the compact specimen as a function of the CTOD. The critical CTOD of the compact specimen can be derived from the Charpy results by way of the compatible Weibull stress. Solid lines in Fig. 13 represents the estimated distribution of the critical CTOD. The temperature dependence of the critical CTOD estimated is given in Fig. 4, where 90% confidence limits are

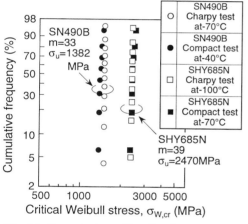

Fig. 11 Cumulative distributions of critical Weibull stress for Charpy and compact specimens.

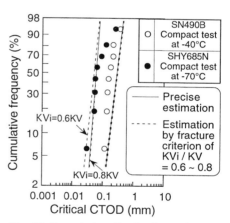

Fig. 13 Cumulative distributions of critical CTOD of compact specimen predicted by the Local Approach.

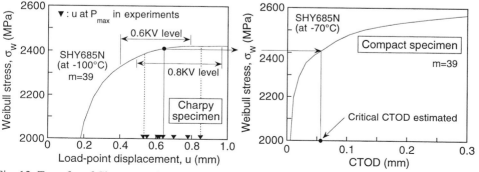

Fig. 12 Transfer of Charpy results to material fracture toughness by the Weibull stress criterion.

also provided. The predicted results are in good agreement with experimental data.

DISCUSSION

The estimation of the critical CTOD of the compact specimen included an uncertainty of the m-value, since the m-value was inferred from the compact test results. Gao, et al. [10] has pointed out that the shape parameter m determined by a conventional iteration procedure is non-unique in the small scale yielding condition. In order to address this subject, a bias was introduced in the range $0.5\ \hat{m} \le m \le 1.5\hat{m}$, where $\hat{m}$ is the shape parameter determined by the iteration method ($\hat{m}$=33, 39, see Fig.11). The numerical study with $m = \hat{m}\pm0.5\hat{m}$ indicated that the bias in m-value hardly affected the prediction of the critical CTOD of the compact specimen, as in the paper [3].

The instrumented Charpy test needs devices for real-time measurement of the load and displacement during loading. From an engineering viewpoint, it is desirable to simplify the procedure to determine the fracture initiation load. The initiation energy KVi was defined as an energy up to the attainment of the maximum impact load. The energy ratio KVi/KV shows a small scatter in both steels. The mean values of KVi/KV were approximately 0.6 and 0.8 for SN490B and SHY685N steels, respectively. Then, under the assumption that the impact fracture occurs at the energy level of $0.6KV$ or $0.8KV$, the critical CTOD of the compact specimen was estimated. The results are drawn with broken lines in Fig. 13. The alternative estimation is almost consistent with the precise estimation. Besides, the estimated results were quite insensitive to the energy ratio KVi/KV assumed. This may be due to the behavior in the lower-transition range.

Similar subjects were examined in the recent papers [6, 11], but the temperature rise during impact loading was not considered in the analysis of the notch bottom stress fields.

CONCLUSIONS

The Local Approach was applied to investigate a physical relationship between the Charpy impact properties and brittle fracture toughness in the lower-transition range. The evaluation of fracture driving force with the Weibull stress enables the Charpy test results to be transferred to the material fracture toughness. The critical CTOD of the compact specimen estimated from the Charpy results by the Weibull stress criterion was consistent with experimental data. An engineering procedure was proposed to simplify the determination of the fracture load in the Charpy test. It was assumed that the impact fracture in the lower-transition range occurs at the energy level of $0.6KV$ to $0.8KV$, where KV is the total energy in the impact test. This led to a good estimation of the critical CTOD.

REFERENCES

[1] Sailors, R.H. and Corten, H.T. (1972). *ASTM STP 514*, pp. 164-191.
[2] Bennett, P.E. and Sinclair, G.M. (1965). *ASME Publication 65-MET-11*.
[3] Minami, F., Ochiai, T., Arimochi, K. *et al.* (2000). *ASTM STP 1389*, pp.271-304.
[4] Nakamura, T., Shih, C.F. and Freund, L.B. (1989). *ASTM STP 995*, Vol. 1, pp.217-241.
[5] Vargas, P.M. and Dodds, Jr. R.H. (1995). *ASTM STP 1256*, pp.715-731.
[6] Folch, L.C.A. and Burdekin, F.M. (1999). *Engineering. Fracture Mechanics* 63, pp. 57-80.
[7] Toyosada, M. *et al.* (1991). *J. Society of Naval Architects of Japan* 170, pp.651-663.
[8] Beremin, F.M. (1983). *Metallurgical Trans. A*, Vol. 14A, pp.2277-2287.
[9] Minami, F., Brückner-Foit, A. Munz, D. *et al.* (1992). *Int. J. Fracture* 54, pp.197-210.
[10] Gao, X., Ruggieri, C. and Dodds, Jr. R.H. (1998). *Int. J. Fracture* 92, pp.175-200.
[11] Rossoll. A, Berdin, C. and Prioul, C. (2001), *Proc. Charpy Centenary Conference*, pp.787-794.

From Charpy to Present Impact Testing
D. François and A. Pineau (Eds.)
© 2002 Elsevier Science Ltd. and ESIS. All rights reserved

MODELLING CHARPY PROPERTY CHANGES DUE TO IRRADIATION DAMAGE.

ROBERT MOSKOVIC

BNFL Magnox Generation, Berkeley, Gloucestershire GL13 9PB.

ABSTRACT

Charpy impact energy data obtained from surveillance specimens are used to assess the changes in the ductile to brittle transition temperature brought about by neutron irradiation. Currently used analytical procedures make inefficient use of costly information. The purpose of this paper is to present a methodology which makes use of the entire data set to fit the probability model and then use the model for prediction. The Burr distribution function was used to model the Charpy curve due to its flexibility to generate a wide range of shapes. The parameters of the Burr distribution were expressed as a function of experimental variables and their changes interpreted in terms of physical mechanisms of irradiation damage. A sampling approach, based on Bayesian inference, has been developed to quantify the different sources of uncertainties and to estimate the changes in the T_{40J} temperature as a function of irradiation conditions

KEYWORDS

Charpy data, neutron irradiation damage, probability, Burr function, Bayes theorem, Markov chain Monte Carlo sampling, C-Mn steel.

INTRODUCTION

Nuclear reactors with steel pressure vessels are required in the U.K. to operate in the upper shelf temperature region. To assess the temperature margin for the upper shelf operating conditions, the operating temperatures of the vessel are compared with onset of upper shelf temperature [1]. During the lifetime of the power station, the steel is subjected to neutron irradiation and temperature and these bring about changes in the mechanical properties. The magnitude of the changes has been monitored by surveillance schemes which include, Charpy impact specimens. Batches of specimens have been withdrawn from the reactor at various times during the lifetime of the stations and tested over a range of temperatures. Charpy impact energy increases with increasing test temperature and hence it is conventional to use the data to construct a ductile to brittle transition curve. Examination of the Charpy impact energy transition curves obtained for different neutron doses and temperatures showed that the ductile to brittle transition curves are displaced to higher temperatures with increasing neutron dose. Changes of the ductile to brittle transition temperature can be represented as temperature shifts at a temperature, T_{40J}, at which 40J energy would be absorbed. Charpy impact energy data are subject to specimen to specimen scatter, particularly in the region of transition temperature. The scatter is mostly due to microstructural inhomogeneities which give rise to a local variability of mechanical properties.

Historically, statistical analyses of Charpy data employed a two-stage process. In the first stage, estimates of Charpy impact energy curves which are specific to a particular combination of irradiation temperature and neutron dose level were obtained by fitting a tanh function to each data set using a nonlinear regression of Charpy impact energy on temperature [2]. In the second stage, the resulting Charpy curves were used to obtain estimates of the T_{40J}

temperatures. Estimates of these temperatures for start of life and irradiated conditions were then used to calculate the mean temperature shifts, ΔT_{40J}, between the irradiated and start of life conditions. These temperature shifts were then analysed by linear regression of ΔT_{40J} on the square root of neutron dose to predict the trend in ΔT_{40J}. There are certain limitations in this approach due to the inefficient use of the data. To obtain a better description in the trends in ΔT_{40J} as a function of irradiation temperature and neutron dose, alternative methods of analysis have been developed [3]. The analyses are carried out in a Bayesian framework and implemented using Markov chain Monte Carlo (MCMC) sampling. This method of analysis is statistically rigorous, is consistent with an understanding of the physical processes, provides a robust model for the dependence of Charpy impact energy on test temperature, neutron dose and irradiation temperature and can be tested against the original Charpy data. Furthermore, rigorous estimates of the probability distributions of the various quantities of interest can be obtained.

THE DATABASE

The Charpy impact energy database used in the analysis consists of data measured on two different C-Mn silicon killed plate steels, coded A and B, used in the construction of Magnox reactor pressure vessels. The room temperature yield, $R_{p0.2}$, and ultimate, R_m, tensile strengths for unirradiated condition are 260MPa and 450MPa for steel A and 235MPa and 430MPa for steel B. The nominal chemical concentration ranges of the main alloying elements are 0.16%C, 1.0-1.4%Mn, 0.15-0.3%Si, and <0.05%S. In addition, steel A contains 0.14%Cu. The database analysed in this work consists of sets of Charpy impact energy values measured at fixed test temperatures, neutron irradiation temperatures and doses on nominally similar specimens.

The Charpy impact energy tests were conducted on specimen sets associated with a particular neutron dose level over a test temperature range which attempted to define the ductile to brittle transition region of Charpy impact energy curve. The data sets are bounded by the lower and upper shelf Charpy impact energy values. However, the temperature dependence of the lower and upper shelves of the curves is poorly defined due to the lack of data outside the transition temperature range. The experimental method for obtaining the Charpy impact energy values ensures that each value is independent of the others, which means that the error structure does not contain any degree of correlation, since the error in one particular measurement is not passed through to any other measurement. The assumption of independence is important in the evaluation of the likelihood function.

The data have been measured for the following conditions:

Plate	Irrad. Temp. (°C)	Fast Dose Range	Thermal Dose Range	Thermal/Fast Ratio
A	190	$52\text{-}131\times10^{-5}$ dpa	$0\text{-}1.4\times10^{-5}$ dpa	~0
A	221	$8\text{-}42\times10^{-5}$ dpa	$4.4\text{-}18.5\times10^{-5}$ dpa	~0.5
B	190	$11\text{-}194\times10^{-5}$ dpa	$0.1\text{-}0.9\times10^{-5}$ dpa	~0
B	198	$9\text{-}108\times10^{-5}$ dpa	$1.4\text{-}29.2\times10^{-5}$ dpa	0.13-0.31
B	297	$9\text{-}167\times10^{-5}$ dpa	$1.2\text{-}20.3\times10^{-5}$ dpa	0.10-0.18

MATHEMATICAL MODEL

From empirical experience and knowledge of micromechanisms of fracture, it is well established that the variability of the Charpy impact energy as a function of test temperature, T_i, can be represented by a sigmoidally shaped curve. The Burr distribution function, $F(T_i)$ was chosen as the mathematical model for the Charpy impact energy curve [4]. The measured values of Charpy impact energy are related to the Burr distribution function by:

$$C_i = \theta_0 + (\theta_1 - \theta_0)F(T_i) + \sigma_T \varepsilon_i \tag{1}$$

where i indexes the individual specimens, C_i, is the measured Charpy impact energy, C_L and C_U are the lower and upper shelves of the curve and ε_i is a random error. The Burr function is given by:

$$F(T_i) = \left(1 + \exp-\left[\frac{T_i - T_0}{\xi}\right]\right)^{-v} \tag{2}$$

where the values of $F(-\infty)=0$ and $F(\infty)=1$. Manipulation of equations (1) and (2) yields a relationship for T_{40J} as follows:

$$T_{40J} = T_0 - \xi \ln\left[\left(\frac{\theta_1 - \theta_0}{40J - \theta_0}\right)^{1/v} - 1\right] \tag{3}$$

In addition, the error variance of the random term needs to be specified. As there is no theoretical model, the choice of the error term was made with respect to physical processes of fracture, exploratory analysis of the data and practical considerations. It was found after considering several different distributions that the random error term can be well represented by a Normal distribution $N(0,\sigma_T^2)$ with a mean of zero and variance, σ_T^2, which is dependent on $F(T)$:

$$\sigma_T = \sigma_1 + [F(T_i)]^2 [1 - F(T_i)]^{(2+\sigma_2)} \tag{4}$$

where σ_1 and σ_2 are the parameters of variance. This particular form of variance allows for variability of Charpy impact energy data with $F(T)$ which in turn is a function of test temperature. The minimum variance is obtained on the upper and lower shelves of the Charpy impact energy curve but increases with test temperature to a maximum value in the transition region between the lower and upper shelves. The model parameters given by Equations (1, 2 and 3) can also be expressed as a function of exposure variables: neutron dose, irradiation temperature and dose rate, as discussed in [3,4]. Relationships describing the effect of neutron irradiation on the model parameters will be considered later. The full set of parameters given by Equations 1, 2 and 3 is $\Theta = (\theta_0, \theta_1, T_0, \xi_1, \xi_2, \gamma_1,....\gamma_j,......\gamma_k, \sigma_1, \sigma_2)$, where j indexes the parameters and $\gamma_1,......,\gamma_j,......,\gamma_k$ are the additional parameters required to model T_0 as the function of neutron irradiation and temperature. The parameters for variance are independent of irradiation.

The likelihood function defined by equations (1), (2) and (4) is proportional to the product:

$$\prod_{i=1}^{n} \sigma_{Ti}^{-1} \exp\left[-\frac{1}{\sigma_{Ti}^2}\{C_i - \theta_0 - (\theta_1 - \theta_0)F(T_i)\}^2\right] \tag{5}$$

THE MARKOV CHAIN MONTE CARLO SAMPLING

In order to compute the mean values of T_{40J} from equation (3), estimates of the model parameters in equations (1) and (2) are required. The principle of maximum likelihood can be employed to estimate the values of the parameters that maximise equation (5). However, in order to make inferences about the probability distributions of T_{40J} and the associated values of ΔT_{40J} temperature shifts, it is also necessary to obtain uncertainties in the model parameters in terms of probability distributions. This objective can be achieved by performing the statistical analysis in a Bayesian framework.

An important characteristic of the Bayesian analysis is that the model parameters are treated as random quantities and the measured Charpy impact energy values as fixed values. The inference is based on computing the posterior probability distribution, $P(\Theta|C)$, that is the probability distribution of the parameters conditional on the data. The Bayes theorem is concerned with conditional probabilities and is given by:

$$P(\Theta|C) = \frac{P(\Theta)L(\Theta|C)}{\int P(\Theta)L(\Theta|C)} \tag{6}$$

$P(\Theta)$ is the prior probability distribution which represents our knowledge about the model parameters prior to having the data, $L(\Theta|C)$ is the likelihood function given by equation (5) and $\int P(\Theta)L(\Theta|C)$ is a normalising integral which normalises the probability distribution to unity. In order to apply the Bayesian approach, therefore, multidimensional integrals need to be evaluated. Conventional numerical methods for doing so are cumbersome, but MCMC sampling is a more convenient method that computes the required integrals explicitly.

The aim of the MCMC process is to generate a Markov chain of the model parameters which mimics the posterior probability distribution of Θ. The MCMC was achieved using the Metropolis Hastings algorithm [5,6]. A detailed description of this algorithm for the analysis of Charpy impact energy data is given in [3]. A step in the process is described below. If the realised value of the Markov chain at the time t is a vector of the model parameters, v_t, then a general Metropolis Hastings step proceeds as follows. A draw is made of both a random number, r_t, from an interval (0,1) and a vector of the model parameters, v', from the multivariate normal centred on v_t. Note that v' is the new proposed vector of the model parameters that is accepted as the next value in the chain with a probability p, where

$$p = \min[1,[\pi(v')/\pi(v_t)] \tag{7}$$

where $\pi(v')$ and $\pi(v_t)$ are the posterior probabilities which are proportional to likelihoods from a uniform prior. If $r_t \leq p$ then the proposed vector is accepted as the next value in the Markov chain and $v_{t+1}=v'$. Alternatively, if $r \geq p$ the current value of the vector is retained and $v_{t+1}=v_t$. Iterating the process will generate the sequence $v_1, v_2, \ldots v_t \ldots, v_m$.

RESULTS

The analyses presented below were carried out in two stages. Initially, the data from the surveillance schemes for plates A and B were analysed individually and the results obtained from these analyses were used to specify the candidate models for the combined database. The relationships in equations (1) to (4) are described by seven parameters: θ_0, θ_1, ξ, T_0, v, σ_1, and σ_2. All the parameters except T_0 can be modelled as constants. The relationship adopted for T_0 had the form:

$$T_0 = Z\gamma_0 + \gamma_1 \sqrt{(D_F + kD_T)} + \gamma_2 T_{irr} \sqrt{(D_F + kD_T)} \qquad (8)$$

where Z is a dummy variable which has values $Z=1$ for unirradiated condition and $Z=0$ for irradiated condition D_F and D_T are the displacement per atom doses produced by high energy (fast) neutrons (E>1 keV) and by thermal neutrons (E<1keV), respectively. The parameter k is a constant which defines the effectiveness of thermal neutrons to cause embrittlement. Equation (8) yields two relationships for T_0 depending on whether $Z=1$ or 0.

The process of finding the most parsimonious model possible requires examination of a large number of different models. This was carried out using the principle of maximum likelihood and ideas of stepwise regression. The significance of each parameter was assessed by comparing the maximum likelihood estimate of the parameter to its standard error. The parameters which were small compared with their standard errors were regarded as candidates for omission from the model. The effect of these parameters on the log-likelihood was assessed. If the removal of a parameter with a large standard error resulted in a significant reduction in the log-likelihood then this was taken to indicate that the parameter should be retained in the model. Otherwise the parameter was dropped from the model. This process required a large number of different models to be examined. Too many models were examined for a complete inclusion to be presented here. The maximum likelihood estimates of the model parameters for plates A and B are compared below:

Param.	γ_1	θ_1	v	ξ	θ_0	σ_1	σ_2	γ_2
Plate A	0.514	1.24	2.41	0.205	0.060	0.04	-1.29	-0.07
Plate B	0.466	1.21	1.35	0.147	0.076	0.10	-1.08	-0.10

The small difference between results for plates A and B in the maximised values of the parameters γ_1 and γ_2 is not significant within the standard error in these parameters. Of the remaining parameters, the most noticeable differences are between the values of v and ξ. In a combined data set, the need to retain in the model two different parameters of the same type that are plate specific can be tested by using the ideas of stepwise regression. However, it should be noted that a change in the value of parameter v brings about both a change in the symmetry of the predicted Charpy curve and a displacement of the Charpy curve on the test temperature axis. The values of v are different when the data for the two plate steels are analysed separately. Analysis of the pooled database and fitting a single common value of v can bring about a displacement of the plate specific Charpy curves on the temperature axis. To accommodate the temperature displacement between the Charpy curves for plate A and plate B data, caused by using a single value of v, an additional parameter γ_3 may need to be used in the relationship for T_0. The parameter γ_3 gives rise to a temperature displacement between the plate specific Charpy curves. The relationships considered for T_0, v and ξ to fit the joint database were:

$$T_0 = Z\gamma_0 + \gamma_1\sqrt{(D_F+kD_T)} + \gamma_2 T_{irr}\sqrt{(D_F+kD_T)} + \gamma_3 Z_1 \quad \xi = \xi_1 + Z_1\xi_2 \quad v = v_1 + Z_1 v_2 \qquad (9)$$

where $Z_1=1$ for plate A and $Z_1=0$ for plate B.

Examination of statistical fits for different models showed that a ten parameter model was required to describe the joint database. The parameter for k was found to be equal to zero. Generally, small range of thermal neutron doses and small range of fast to thermal neutron dose ratios make it difficult to quantify this parameter. Parameters for ξ_2 and v_2 were not significant. Hence, the statistical model that describes the data is based on parameters: θ_0, θ_1, ξ, v, σ_1, σ_2, γ_0, γ_1, γ_2 and γ_3, in equations (1, 2, 4 and 8). Six different MCMC runs were carried out, using different starting values in each run. The ergodic averages and standard deviations obtained from different runs were essentially the same and this together with plots of the ergodic averages and standard deviations against time provided a proof of convergence. A typical result of MCMC sampling is given below.

Param.	γ_1	θ_1	v	ξ	θ_0	σ_1	σ_2	γ_2	γ_3	γ_0
Mean	0.559	1.219	2.331	0.204	0.052	0.046	-1.380	-0.093	-0.183	0.019
St. dev.	0.035	0.014	0.060	0.010	0.008	0.004	0.043	0.015	0.010	0.017

An examples of output obtained from MCMC sampling is presented in Fig.1 which shows a histogram of a model parameter.

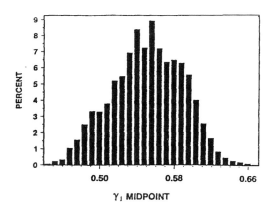

Fig.1 Histogram of parameter γ_1 obtained from a realisation of Markov Chain of 10^6 samples.

Fig. 2 shows an example of a Charpy curve constructed using MCMC vectors of the model parameters compared with the measured data. Three sets of lines are shown: the best estimate of the mean; 5 and 95% probability limits for the mean; and 5 and 95% probability limits for the distribution of Charpy impact energy values about the mean. Finally, estimates of the ΔT_{40J} temperature shifts at the 5, 50 and 95% probability levels are shown as a function of square root of dose in Fig.3.

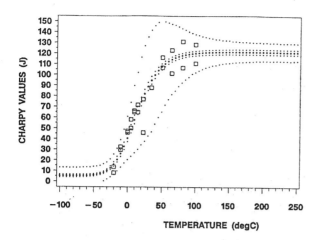

Fig.2 Comparison of predicted Charpy impact energy curve with measured data for plate A irradiated at 221°C to 85x10⁻⁵dpa.

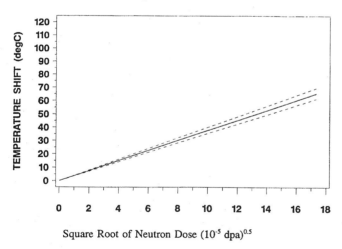

Square Root of Neutron Dose $(10^{-5}$ dpa$)^{0.5}$

Fig.3 Estimates of mean and 5% and 95% probability levels for the distribution of ΔT_{40J} temperature shifts as a function of neutron dose at 190°C.

The calculation of ΔT_{40J} temperature shifts was carried out using equation (3). For a chosen irradiation condition, defined by specifying the fast and thermal neutron doses and irradiation temperature, each of the vectors in Markov chain was used to calculate a single mean value of T_{40J} for both irradiated and unirradiated conditions. The temperature shift, ΔT_{40J}, is given by the difference: $\Delta T_{40J}=T_{40J}$(irradiated)-T_{40J}(unirradiated). The relationship for ΔT_{40J} can be simplified and algebraically reduced to the form:

$$\Delta T_{40J} = AF_T \sqrt{D_F} \tag{10}$$

where $A = 10(\gamma_1 + 0.01\gamma_2 x 190°C)$ is the slope at 190°C for the T_{40J} vs. $F_T(D_F)^{0.5}$ line and F_T is the temperature dependence parameter. This is given by: $F_T = a + bT_{ir} = 10\gamma_1/A + 0.1\gamma_2/A$. Calculations using the vectors in the Markov chain produced the trend curve:

$$\Delta T_{40J} = AF_T \sqrt{D_F} = 3.823x(1.462-0.00243T_{ir}) \sqrt{D_F} \tag{11}$$

The value of A may be enhance since it includes the contribution of thermal neutrons. The uncertainty allowance at zero neutron dose is zero and increases linearly with neutron dose. At $300 x 10^{-5}$dpa the uncertainty allowance is ±4°C.

CONCLUSIONS

1   Bayes computations have been performed using Markov chain Monte Carlo sampling by employing a Metropolis-Hastings algorithm. Changes in the measured Charpy impact energy data brought about by neutron irradiation at plant operating dose rates and temperatures have been quantified as a function of test temperature, neutron dose and irradiation temperature.

2   The magnitude of the temperature shift, T_{40J}, in degrees Celsius obtained from the Markov chains is given by the relationship $3.823F_TD_F$, where $F_T = 1.462 - 0.00235T_{ir}$. F_T quantifies the effect of irradiation temperature on ΔT_{40J} temperature shift. The uncertainty allowance for T_{40J} temperature shift associated with a neutron dose of $300 x 10^{-5}$ dpa is ±4°C for irradiation at 190°C.

ACKNOWLEDGEMENTS

This paper is published with the permission of the Head of Reactor Services Organisation BNFL Magnox Generation.

REFERENCES

1   Burdekin, F., M., Lidbury, D.,P.,G. and Moskovic, R., Int. Journal of Pressure Vessel and Piping, (1999) **76**, 875.
2   Odfield, W. (1975). Curve fitting impact test data: a statistical procedure, ASTM Standardisation News, **3**, (11), 24.
3   Moskovic, R., Windle, P.L. and Smith, A F M, Met. and Mat. Trans. A, (1997) **28A**, 1181.
4   Windle, P.L., Crowder M. and Moskovic R. (1996), Nuclear Eng. And Design, 43.
5   N Metropolis, A W Rosenbluth, M N Rosenbluth, A H Teller and E J Teller, J of Chemical Physics, **21**, 1087.
6   W K Hastings (1970), Biometrica, **57**, 97.

From Charpy to Present Impact Testing
D. François and A. Pineau (Eds.)
© 2002 Elsevier Science Ltd. and ESIS. All rights reserved

IMPROVED CHARPY TEST EVALUATION FOR THE TOUGHNESS CHARACTERISATION OF HIGH STRENGTH STEELS AND THEIR WELDMENTS

F. MUDRY, *USINOR R&D, Paris La Défense, France*
T. STUREL, *USINOR R&D, IRSID, Maizières-lès-Metz, France*

ABSTRACT: This study deals with the determination of micromechanical parameters (Beremin model) from Charpy test. The method is first assessed on a low carbon 450 grade steel. Despite simplifications in the simulation of the test, the transferability of the parameters for toughness characterisation is demonstrated. In a second step, it is intended to predict the behaviour of a multipass welded joint. The properties of a simulated microstructure, representative of the most brittle area of heat affected zone (HAZ), are determined using the same methodology. Provided that constraint parameters, such as mismatching of materials, are taken into account, it is shown that reasonable toughness predictions can be obtained on weldment.

KEYWORDS: Low carbon steel, Charpy test, Beremin model, cleavage, numerical simulation, weldment, simulated HAZ

INTRODUCTION

Despite of fracture mechanics developments, the Charpy test remains widely used to assess the fracture toughness of steels. This is certainly due to its easier and cheaper use compared to a fracture mechanics test.

The aim of the present work is to investigate an improved evaluation of the data derived from this rather simple test by coupling damage mechanics concepts and numerical simulations.

By this way, it is intended to determine intrinsic fracture properties of materials through the determination of micromechanical model parameters in order to predict the fracture behaviour of any other specimen or structure.

The work is focussing on cleavage fracture using the well-known statistical Beremin model [1]. The transferability of the model parameters from Charpy to precracked specimens is discussed for both base material and thermally simulated microstructure. Finally, the approach is applied to a welded structure.

MATERIAL -WELDED JOINT

The material investigated is a low carbon steel produced by controlled rolling and accelerated cooling. The yield stress and tensile strength are respectively equal to 435 MPa and 535 MPa. The microstructure, which is ferrito-pearlitic, is presented in Fig. 1.

Multipass welded joints of the previous material were made using the submerged arc welding process. The filler product was selected in order to obtain an overmatching of 10 percent compared to the base metal. The welding conditions are the following : welding energy, 35kJ/cm; welding speed, 70cm/mn; preheating and inter-pass temperature, 150°C; cooling speed $\Delta t_{8/5}$, 26s. A macrography of the joint is shown in Fig. 2.

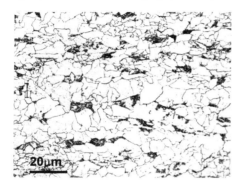 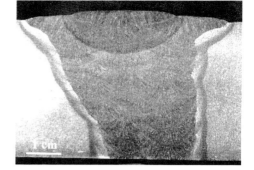

Fig. 1: Microstructure of the base metal   Fig. 2: Macrography of the multipass
                                                          welded joint

PROCEDURE

The investigations presented in this paper are dealing with the cleavage criterion proposed by Beremin [1]. This criterion is based on the critical stress concept [2] introducing a "Weibull stress" σ_w to take into account statistical effects [3]. Details can be found elsewhere [4,5]. To determine the parameters of this model (m, the Weibull exponent, and σ_u, the cleavage stress), the procedure consists in carrying out mechanical tests on specimens at a temperature where failure by cleavage mechanism is expected . Then, from a numerical simulation of this test, it is possible to compute the Weibull stress quantity corresponding to each result. Finally, by ranking them in increasing order, a theoretical Weibull distribution, characterised by the couple (m, σ_u), can be fitted to the data.

The more widely used procedure is based on notched tensile specimen tests. It has been described in details in an ESIS document [6]. Alternative procedures using high constraint precracked specimens are also more and more encountered [7]. In the present study, it is intended to get these information from the medium constraint Charpy specimen tested in dynamic condition.

A lot of work has been devoted to the Charpy test simulation using damage mechanics [8,9]. Some of them are presented in this conference. In our case, the work concentrated on cleavage fracture, i.e. rather low energy at fracture.

2-dimensional and 3-dimensional numerical simulations of this test were carried out. In these simulations, the hammer and the anvil are also meshed (Fig. 3). The loading of the specimen is governed by contact with a specified friction coefficient.

Regarding the loading curves (applied load versus load line displacement), an important change in the curves is observed when moving from 2-D plane strain to 2-D plane stress conditions. However, referring to the Weibull stress quantity, which is in fact the parameter of interest, it can be seen from Fig. 4 that the 2-D plane strain model is a good approximation of the full 3D one. In this example, using an m-value of 20, the deviation of the 2D curve from the 3D one is less than 2 percent when the fracture energy exceeds 4 Joules. Therefore, this simplification was adopted in the following. It should also be noticed that the simulation was not carried out in dynamic conditions as it was shown that the inertial effects have rapidly a negligible effect on this parameter [10].

In order to account for strain rate effects, a additive visco-plastic stress-strain law was used to simulate the Charpy experiments:

$$\sigma_{eq} = \sigma_{qs}(\varepsilon_p) + \alpha \dot{\varepsilon}_p^{(1/\beta)} \tag{1}$$

where σ_{eq} is the equivalent Von Mises stress, σ_{qs} the quasi-static stress-strain law measured for a strain rate of $0.005s^{-1}$, ε_p the equivalent cumulated plastic strain and $\dot{\varepsilon}_p$ the equivalent plastic strain rate.

The parameters α and β were determined from available tensile tests results at low temperature by assuming equivalence between temperature and strain rate effects given by the following formula:

$$R_e = 10^a \left[T \log \left(\frac{10^8}{\dot{\varepsilon}} \right) \right]^b \tag{2}$$

where T is the temperature in K, R_e the yield stress, $\dot{\varepsilon}$ the strain rate, a and b the parameters to be identified. Validation of this formula with steel grades ranging from 320 to 750MPa Yield Stress can be found in the elsewhere [11].

In addition, the effect of high strain rate on temperature elevation in the notch root area was investigated by running adiabatic calculations. The temperature increase due to plastic work is given by the relation:

$$\rho C_p \dot{T} = \beta \dot{W} \tag{3}$$

where ρ is the volume mass, C_p the heat capacity and β the conversion rate of plastic work in heat. Its value is usually taken as 0.9 for steels. In order to take into account this effect, a temperature correction was adopted.

To summarise, all results given below were made in 2D plane strain under quasi-static conditions with a temperature and strain rate dependent stress-strain law.

The method used is, in principle, very simple. A Charpy transition curve is determined on the material under investigation. A temperature for which the fracture energy is around 10 Joules on conventional specimens is selected. A significant amount of specimens are then fractured at that selected temperature. The energy at fracture for each specimen is then used to estimate the Weibull stress at fracture using the results of Fig. 4.

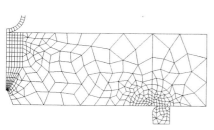

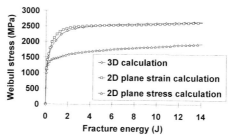

Fig. 3: 2-dimensional mesh of the specimen

Fig. 4: Evolution of Weibull stress as a function of fracture energy for different calculation conditions (m=20)

APPLICATION TO THE BASE METAL

In a first stage, the method is applied to the base material. A Charpy transition curve is determined on specimens sampled at mid-thickness of the plate in the transverse direction (Fig. 5). Another set of specimens is broken at −130°C (TK10J).

Comparison between experiment and simulation is made in Fig. 6. It appears that, using conventional values of m (from 10 to 30), no satisfactory description of the scatter is reached. We have looked for the reason of this discrepancy. This does not arise from the quasi-static or the 2-D plane strain assumptions. Basically, it seems that the experimental scatter is very low at this temperature (10J±5J). This is not the case for the transition temperature which is around −90°C (120J ±70J).

As no good explanation was found, it was decided to fix a priori the m-value (i.e. the scatter) around well accepted values for steels and to fit the critical cleavage stress σ_u to the experiments. This leads to a cleavage stress of 2310 MPa (failure probability of 0.63) with m equal to 28.

In order to assess the transferability of these data, fracture toughness predictions on precracked 3 point bend specimens were carried out. Despite the previous simplification, it can be observed in the Fig. 7 that the experimental trend is quite well reproduced by the calculation.

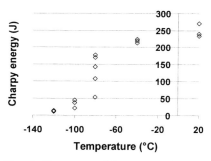

Fig. 5: Charpy transition curve of the base metal

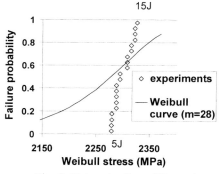

Fig. 6: Determination of Beremin parameters with m=28 (base metal)

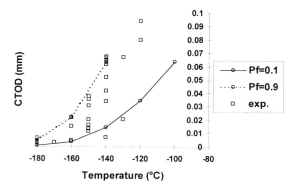

Fig. 7: Experimental and predicted fracture toughness of base metal (SENB specimen, W=20mm, B=10mm, a/W=0.5)

APPLICATION TO A WELDED JOINT

The main objective of the study was the rapid assessment of welds using only fracture properties measured on simulated microstructures.

Fracture toughness tests on specimens with section 40 mm x 40 mm sampled in the multipass welded joint were carried out at –40°C and –10°C. The notch was located in the straight side of the heat affected zone close to the fusion line for fatigue precraking in the through thickness direction as shown in Fig. 8. The lowest results, corresponding to CTOD below 0.3 for which pure cleavage fracture can be expected (see Fig. 17), were analysed by metallographic and fractographic examinations. A particular location of the fracture initiation site was observed on most of the specimens. It corresponds to the intersection of the Coarse Grain HAZ adjacent to the fusion line and the A_{c1} isotherm of the last bead that is to say an Intercritically Reheated Coarse Grain HAZ which has not been tempered by the other beads (Figs. 8 and 9). The corresponding microstructure is presented in the Fig. 10. The Villela etching reveals Martensite-Austenite (M-A) islands (within or at the boundary of prior austenite grain) which are well-known to be detrimental for toughness [12, 13]. In order to determine its toughness properties, it was intended to simulate it with a Gleeble machine. The thermal parameters of the simulation were chosen in order to get a microstructure as representative as possible of the real one. The resulting microstructure is presented in Fig. 11. The overall microstructural trend is quite well reproduced. A higher M-A volume fraction is however noticed. A slight overestimation of brittleness is therefore expected.

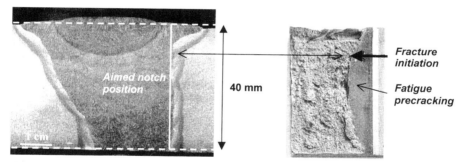

Fig. 8: 40mm x 40 mm specimen, through thickness notched

Fig. 9: Fracture surface (through thickness direction)

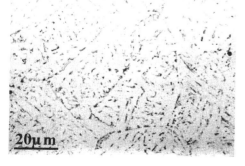

Fig. 10: ICCGHAZ microstructure of last bead (Villela etching)

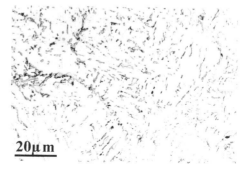

Fig. 11: Simulated ICCGHAZ 1250°C + 775°C $\Delta t_{7/3}$=100s (Villela etching)

Charpy specimens were machined from this simulated microstructure and a transition curve
was determined (Fig. 12). It highlights the poor toughness properties of such a microstructure
as the cleavage-ductile transition appears to be close to room temperature. The Beremin
parameters were determined using the same methodology. The selected temperature is –60°C
(TK10J). The fitting of the parameters is presented in Fig. 13. Again, the overestimation of
the scatter can be seen. Using, as earlier, an m-value of 28, a cleavage stress of 2335MPa is
derived from the graph. To be more confident in these parameters, Single Edge Notched Bend
specimens taken from the same embrittled material with W=20mm and B=10mm were also
tested. The predictions, using the parameters measured on the Charpy specimens, are shown
in Fig. 14. Again, a rather good transferability of these parameters is noticed as the toughness
scatter band and the temperature dependence are in reasonable agreement with the
experiments.

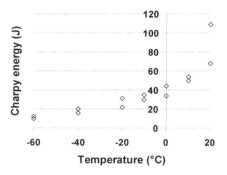

Fig. 12: Charpy transition curve of
simulated ICCGHAZ

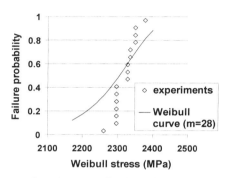

Fig. 13: Determination of Beremin
parameters (simulated ICCGHAZ)

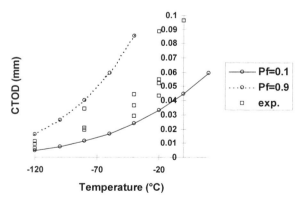

Fig. 14: Experimental and predicted fracture toughness of simulated ICCGHAZ (SENB
specimen, W=20mm, B=10mm, a/W=0.5)

The next step is to use these parameters to predict the behaviour of the real joint. The mesh
representative of the specimen sampled in the joint is shown in Fig. 15. The HAZ is
simplified by a layer of 1 mm width corresponding approximately to the dimension of the
Coarse Grain HAZ. It is surrounded by the weld metal and the base metal. The mechanical
properties of the simulated ICCGHAZ are introduced in this HAZ layer (IC). These properties
are significantly higher than those of both the weld metal (WM) and the base metal (BM),

respectively 8 percent above WM and 20 percent above BM. Dealing with cleavage fracture, this overmatching condition is favourable since it allows the plasticity to develop easily in the softer adjacent materials thus promoting an unloading of the crack tip. This is illustrated in the Fig. 16 where the Weibull stress is plotted as a function of CTOD. When the specimen is loaded, the Weibull stress increases because of high stresses in the HAZ and then it rapidly saturates due to the plastic flow in the softer material i.e. the base metal. For comparison, the evolution of the Weibull stress in the HAZ with no mismatching effects (the mechanical properties of the base metal and of the weld metal are in this case similar to the HAZ) is also given in Fig. 16. In this case, the crack tip area is more constrained and no such saturation effect is observed as the Weibull stress continuously increases.

Using the cleavage properties of the simulated ICCGHAZ determined from the Charpy tests, fracture toughness predictions of the welded joint are carried out (Fig. 17). In this figure, for the sake of clarity, only a lower bound curve is drawn for a failure probability of 5 percent. Compared to the experiments, the trend with temperature is reasonably predicted (curve with filled symbols) and the conservatism of the predictions (see the toughness data of ICCGHAZ) is not too excessive thanks to the precise description of constraint effects discussed above: the predicted CTOD is around 0.14 mm at −10°C for a precise simulation of the joint whereas it would be close to 0.03 mm if the joint was simply assumed to be a homogeneous specimen with HAZ properties (curve with open symbols).

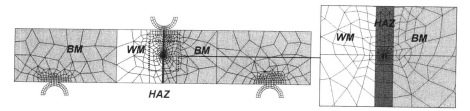

Fig. 15: Mesh representative of a specimen sampled in the welded joint. The material properties are: weld metal for WM zone, base metal for BM zone and simulated ICCGHAZ for HAZ zone

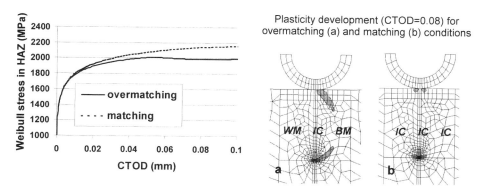

Fig. 16: Mismatching effects on crack tip loading. Left: comparison of the Weibull stress for both cases, middle: plastic zone for the overmatching case (real case), right: plastic zone for the matching case. IC stands for ICCGHAZ properties

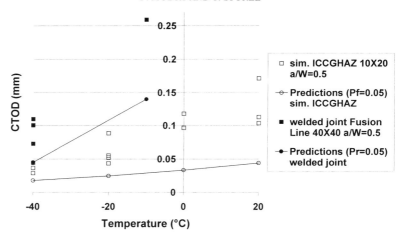

Fig. 17: Fracture toughness predictions on welded joint. Data for the homogeneous
ICCGHAZ are the same as in Fig. 14

CONCLUSION, PERSPECTIVES

In this study, it was intended to determine micromechanical parameters of a cleavage model
(Beremin model) from Charpy tests. The experimental technique is quite simple. However,
the analysis of the tests appears to be relatively complex and some simplifications have to be
made for the numerical simulation (quasi-static 2D plane strain calculation). For fitting the
parameters, an a priori value for the Weibull exponent has to be selected. There is still a not
well understood behaviour of the Charpy test which seems to have very little scatter for the
relatively low energy considered here. Quite good predictions were nevertheless obtained on
high constrained specimen highlighting the transferability of the data.

This methodology was also used to predict the behaviour of a multipass welded joint. The
intrinsic fracture properties of the most brittle part of the heat affected zone of the joint were
determined from simulated microstructure. It was shown that reasonable predictions can be
obtained provided that constraint parameters (materials mismatching, volume of brittle zone)
are taken into account. This methodology can be therefore helpful for steel development as it
gives, from small tested volume, early information on the behaviour of the welds. In this
framework, simplification of the method is currently undertaken by developing a PC program
with the aim of providing an efficient tool to metallurgists.

ACKNOWLEDGEMENTS

The ECSC (European Coal and Steel Community) is gratefully acknowledged for its support
to this work (Contract 7210-KA/326).

REFERENCES

1.   F. M. Beremin (1983). A Local Criterion for Cleavage Fracture of a Nuclear Pressure
      Vessel Steel, *Metallurgical Transactions*, vol. 14A, pp. 2277-2287
2.   J.F. Knott (1977). Micro-mechanisms of fracture and the fracture toughness of
      engineering alloys, 4th Int. Conf. on Fracture, Vol. 1, pp.61-92, Canada

3. K. Wallin (1984). The scatter in K1c results, *Engineering Fracture Mechanics*, vol. 19 n°6, pp 1085-1093

4. N. Cardinal, C.S Wiesner, M.R. Goldthorpe, A.C. Bannister (1996). Application of the local approach to cleavage fracture to failure predictions of heat affected zones, 1st European Mechanics of Materials Conference on Local Approach to Fracture. Fontainebleau, Les Editions de Physique, pp 185-194

5. M.Di Fant et al. (1995). Local approach to brittle fracture: discussion of the effects of temperature and strain on the critical cleavage stress. Griffith conference, Sheffield, IRSID RE95.042

6. Sainte Catherine C. (1998). Procedure to measure and calculate material parameters for the Local Approach to Fracture using notched tensile specimens. ESIS P6-94. Sub-Committee TC1.1

7. X. Gao, C. Ruggieri, R.H. Dodds (1998). Calibration of Weibull stress parameters using fracture toughness data, *Int. J. Fracture*, Vol. 92, No 2, pp 175-200

8. W. Böhme, D-Z. Sun, W. Schmidt, A. Höning (1992). Application of micromechanical material models to the evaluation of Charpy tests, AMD-vol. 137, *Advances in Local Fracture/Damage Models For the Analysis of Engineering Problems*. Editors: J.H. Giovanola and A.J. Rosakis. Book No. H00741

9. W. Burget, D-Z. Sun, S. Oeser, W. Böhme (1998). ECSC report No 7210/KA/326. Development of high strength steels with optimized Y/T ratio

10. Rossoll et al. (1996). Local Approach of the Charpy Test at Low Temperature, 1st European Mechanics of Materials Conference on Local Approach to Fracture. Fontainebleau, pp 279-286

11. M. Di Fant et al. (1996). ECSC report No 7210/KA/324. Extension des méthodes de dimensionnement aux aciers soudables à haute limite d'élasticité

12. Lambert, J. Drillet, A.F. Gourgues, T. Sturel and A. Pineau (2000). Microstructure of martensite-austenite constituents in heat affected zones of high strength low alloy steel welds in relation to toughness properties, *Science and Technology of Welding and Joining*, Vol. 5 No. 3

13. C.L. Davis, J.E. King (1984). Cleavage initiation in the intercritically reheated coarse-grained heat-affected Zone, *Metallurgical Transactions* Vol. 25A, 563.

3D CHARPY SPECIMEN ANALYSES FOR WELDS

V. Tvergaard[1] and A. Needleman[2]

[1]Department of Mechanical Engineering
Technical University of Denmark, 2800 Lyngby, Denmark
[2]Division of Engineering
Brown University, Providence, RI 02912, USA

ABSTRACT

The ductile-brittle transition for a weld is investigated by full three dimensional transient analyses of Charpy impact specimens. The material response is characterized by an elastic-viscoplastic constitutive relation for a porous plastic solid, with adiabatic heating due to plastic dissipation and the resulting thermal softening accounted for. The onset of cleavage is taken to occur when a critical value of the maximum principal stress is attained. The effect of accounting for the three dimensional Charpy geometry is illustrated.

KEYWORDS Ductile fracture; cleavage; welds; Charpy test

INTRODUCTION

For Charpy V-notch specimens the competition between ductile and brittle failure mechanisms in a homogeneous material has been analyzed in some detail by the authors, both for plane strain [1, 2] and for 3D [3]. In these analyses the material response is characterized by an elastic-viscoplastic constitutive relation for a porous plastic solid, accounting for adiabatic heating due to plastic dissipation and the resulting thermal softening. The onset of cleavage is taken to occur when a critical value of the maximum principal stress is attained. The important temperature dependence of material behavior is incorporated through the temperature dependence of the material parameters, primarily the flow stress. The plane strain analyses for the Charpy specimen in [1, 2] have shown that the model predicts the well known ductile-brittle transition, with high absorbed energies at temperatures above the transition temperature and with low absorbed energies in the brittle range at lower temperatures.

Such planar analyses have recently been applied to welded joints, [4, 5], to investigate the ductile-brittle transition in different parts of the weld. The material properties are typically rather different in the base material, the weld material, and the heat affected zone (HAZ), which can be accounted for in terms of the material model representing both ductile failure and cleavage. The planar analyses have shown how the predicted absorbed energy depends strongly on the location of the notch relative to the welded joint.

In the present investigation the numerical study of welded joints is extended to full 3D analyses of Charpy V-notch specimens. This is of interest primarily because of the dimensions of the specimen, which is not wide enough to guarantee that the stress fields will be well represented by

a plane strain assumption. Furthermore, in standard Charpy tests for welded joints some specimens are cut with the notched face parallel to the surface of the welded piece, which can be
represented in a planar analysis, but other specimens are cut with the notched face perpendicular
to the surface of the welded piece. In the latter kind of specimen, where the notch is not parallel
to the thin slice of material containing the HAZ, a full 3D analysis is needed. We confine attention here to specimens where the notch is parallel to the HAZ and compare the predictions of full
3D analyses with corresponding predictions of planar analyses.

FORMULATION AND NUMERICAL METHOD

The formulation is that in [5] except that here full 3D calculations are carried out. Further
details and more complete references are given in [5]. A convected coordinate Lagrangian formulation is used with the dynamic principle of virtual work written as

$$\int_V \tau^{ij} \delta E_{ij} \, dV = \int_S T^i \delta u_i \, dS - \int_V \rho \frac{\partial^2 u^i}{\partial t^2} \delta u_i \, dV \tag{1}$$

with

$$T^i = (\tau^{ij} + \tau^{kj} u^i_{,k}) \nu_j \tag{2}$$

$$E_{ij} = \frac{1}{2}(u_{i,j} + u_{j,i} + u^k_{,i} u_{k,j}) \tag{3}$$

where τ^{ij} are the contravariant components of Kirchhoff stress on the deformed convected coordinate net ($\tau^{ij} = J\sigma^{ij}$, with σ^{ij} being the contravariant components of the Cauchy or true stress
and J the ratio of current to reference volume), ν_j and u_j are the covariant components of the
reference surface normal and displacement vectors, respectively, ρ is the mass density, V and S
are the volume and surface of the body in the reference configuration, and $(\ )_{,i}$ denotes covariant
differentiation in the reference frame.

A standard Charpy V-notch specimen is analyzed, with overall length 55 mm, width 10 mm,
notch depth 2 mm, notch radius 0.25 mm, notch angle 22.5° and the distance between supports is
40 mm. Unless stated otherwise, the specimen thickness is 10 mm, but symmetry about the mid-
plane is assumed so that half the specimen is analyzed. In addition to the symmetry conditions
on $x^3 = 0$, the boundary conditions are

$$u_1 = 0 \qquad \text{on the supports} \tag{4}$$

and

$$\dot{u}_1 = -V(t) \qquad \text{on the striker-specimen interface} \tag{5}$$

The striker is taken to contact the specimen on a 2×10 mm area along the specimen axis. The
impact is represented by the imposed velocity

$$V(t) = \begin{cases} V_1 t / t_r & \text{for } t < t_r \\ V_1 & \text{for } t > t_r \end{cases} \tag{6}$$

where $V_1 = 5$ m/s and $t_r = 20$ μs.

All other external surfaces are traction free. At $t = 0$, the specimen is assumed to be stress
free (so that any effect of residual stresses is ignored) and to have the uniform initial temperature
Θ_{init}.

The geometry of the region analyzed numerically is shown in Fig. 1. For comparison purposes, plane strain calculations are carried out using the same in-plane dimensions and the same
loading conditions.

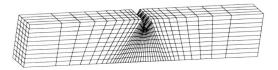

Fig. 1: Charpy specimen and finite element mesh. Half of the thickness is shown.

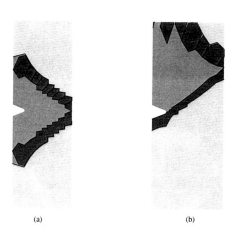

(a)   (b)

Fig. 2: The two weld configurations analyzed in the region near the notch; the material in the heat affected zone (HAZ) is dark gray and the weld material is the light gray region between the two heat affect zones.

A planar slice through the thickness illustrating the weld geometry is shown in Fig. 2. The weld geometry is the same for all such cross-sections. In one case, the weld is symmetrical about the notch while in the other case the HAZ is located directly in front of the notch. Plotted in Fig. 2 are contours of an arbitrary parameter that is assigned different values in the weld material, the base material and the HAZ. The lack of smoothness in the plot is due to interpolating the parameter values onto the discrete finite element mesh. The parameters defining the weld geometry are given in [5].

The constitutive framework is the modified Gurson model. The rate of deformation tensor written as the sum of an elastic part, $\mathbf{d}^e$, a viscoplastic part, $\mathbf{d}^p$, and a part due to thermal straining, $\mathbf{d}^\Theta$, so that

$$\mathbf{d} = \mathbf{d}^e + \mathbf{d}^p + \mathbf{d}^\Theta \qquad (7)$$

with

$$\mathbf{d}^e = \mathcal{L}^{-1} : \hat{\boldsymbol{\sigma}} \quad , \quad \mathbf{d}^\Theta = \alpha\dot{\Theta}\mathbf{I} \qquad (8)$$

Here, small elastic strains are assumed, $\hat{\boldsymbol{\sigma}}$ is the Jaumann rate of Cauchy stress, Θ is the temperature, α is the thermal expansion coefficient, $\mathbf{A} : \mathbf{B} = A^{ij}B_{ji}$ and $\mathcal{L}$ is the tensor of isotropic elastic moduli. The properties are chosen to have representative values for steel; $E = 202$ GPa, $\nu = 0.3$ and $\alpha = 1 \times 10^{-5}/°$K.

The flow potential, [6, 7], is

$$\Phi = \frac{\sigma_e^2}{\bar{\sigma}^2} + 2q_1 f^* \cosh\left(\frac{3q_2\sigma_h}{2\bar{\sigma}}\right) - 1 - (q_1 f^*)^2 = 0 \tag{9}$$

and $\mathbf{d}^p$ is given by, [8],

$$\mathbf{d}^p = \left[\frac{(1-f)\bar{\sigma}\dot{\bar{\epsilon}}}{\sigma : \frac{\partial\phi}{\partial\sigma}}\right]\frac{\partial\phi}{\partial\sigma} \tag{10}$$

where $q_1 = 1.25$, $q_2 = 1.0$ are parameters introduced in [9, 10], f is the void volume fraction, $\bar{\sigma}$ is the matrix flow strength, and

$$\sigma_e{}^2 = \frac{3}{2}\sigma' : \sigma' \quad , \quad \sigma_h = \frac{1}{3}\sigma : \mathbf{I} \quad , \quad \sigma' = \sigma - \sigma_h\mathbf{I} \tag{11}$$

The function f^*, [11], accounts for the effects of rapid void coalescence at failure

$$f^* = \begin{cases} f & f < f_c \\ f_c + (1/q_1 - f_c)(f - f_c)/(f_f - f_c) & f \geq f_c \end{cases} \tag{12}$$

where the values $f_c = 0.12$ and $f_f = 0.25$ are used. Background on the basis for the choice of parameter values in the Gurson model is given by Tvergaard [12].

The matrix plastic strain rate, $\dot{\bar{\epsilon}}$, is given by

$$\dot{\bar{\epsilon}} = \dot{\epsilon}_0\left[\frac{\bar{\sigma}}{g(\bar{\epsilon}, \Theta)}\right]^{1/m} \quad , \quad g(\bar{\epsilon}, \Theta) = \sigma_0 G(\Theta)\left[1 + \bar{\epsilon}/\epsilon_0\right]^N \tag{13}$$

with $\bar{\epsilon} = \int \dot{\bar{\epsilon}}dt$ and $\epsilon_0 = \sigma_0/E$. In all cases, $\dot{\epsilon}_0 = 10^3$/s and $m = 0.01$.

Calculations are carried out for a set of material properties representative of an HY100 steel and an exponential temperature-dependence of the flow strength is assumed, [13, 14],

$$G(\Theta) = 1 + b\exp(-c[\Theta_0 - 273])\left[\exp(-c[\Theta - \Theta_0]) - 1\right] \tag{14}$$

with Θ_0 a reference temperature, $b = 0.1406$ and $c = 0.00793/°$K. In (14), Θ and Θ_0 are in °K and $\Theta_0 = 293°$K.

Under the assumed adiabatic conditions, the balance of energy gives

$$\rho c_p \frac{\partial\Theta}{\partial t} = \chi\tau : \mathbf{d}^p \tag{15}$$

where $\chi = 0.9$, $\rho = 7600$ kg/m$^3 = 7.6 \times 10^{-3}$MPa/(m/sec)^2 and $c_p = 465$ J/(kg °K)

The rate of increase of the void volume fraction is given by

$$\dot{f} = (1-f)\mathbf{d}^p : \mathbf{I} + \mathcal{D}\dot{\bar{\epsilon}} \tag{16}$$

with void nucleation taken to follow a normal distribution, [15], so that

$$\mathcal{D} = \frac{f_N}{s_N\sqrt{2\pi}}\exp\left[-\frac{1}{2}\left(\frac{\bar{\epsilon} - \epsilon_N}{s_N}\right)^2\right] \tag{17}$$

In all calculations here, the initial void volume fraction is taken to be zero and void nucleation is specified by $\epsilon_N = 0.3$, $f_N = 0.04$ and $s_N = 0.1$.

Failure can occur either by microvoid nucleation, growth and coalescence or by cleavage. The material is partitioned into cleavage grains and it is assumed that cleavage failure in a grain occurs when the volume average of the maximum principal stress over that grain reaches a temperature and strain rate independent critical value, $\sigma_c = 2500$ MPa [16].

As in [5], the flow strength values used are 790 MPa for the base material, 890 MPa for the weld material and 1140 MPa for the HAZ at the reference temperature of 293°K, with corresponding strain hardening exponents of 0.066, 0.057 and 0.041, respectively.

Twenty node brick elements are used with eight point integration. The equations resulting from substituting the finite element discretization of the principle of virtual work (1) are integrated numerically by an explicit integration procedure. The constitutive updating is based on the rate tangent modulus method in [17] while material failure is implemented via the element vanish technique in [18]. The mesh used to analyze the half Charpy specimen had 1600 elements, 8309 nodal points and 24927 degrees of freedom.

NUMERICAL RESULTS

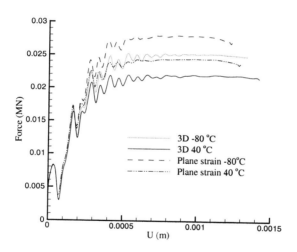

Fig. 3: Force versus displacement for the weld configuration in Fig. 2a.

The 3D computations for the Charpy specimen are carried out using the mesh in Fig. 1 to represent half the specimen, assuming symmetry conditions on one side and a free surface on the other side of the region analyzed. In these cases the thickness of the region analyzed is $C_0/2$, where $C_0 = 0.01$ m is the thickness of the standard Charpy specimen. For comparison plane strain analyses are carried out by using only one slice of the elements shown in Fig. 1, i.e. a thickness of $C_0/8$, with the normal displacements prescribed to be zero on both sides of the region. These calculations are carried out for both of the weld configurations shown in Fig. 2, i.e. for specimens cut in two different ways relative to the weld, and for two different temperatures, -80°C and 40°C. The focus in the calculations here is on the initiation of failure.

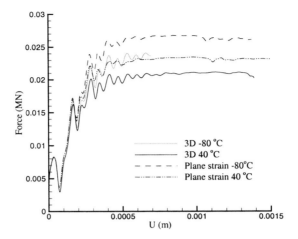

Fig. 4: Force versus displacement for the weld configuration in Fig. 2b.

Figure 3 shows the force displacement curves predicted for the weld configuration in Fig. 2a, where the notch is in the weld material. At both temperatures the force levels predicted by the plane strain analyses are clearly above those predicted by the 3D analyses. The calculations are terminated when cleavage first occurs and this takes place at a slightly larger displacement in both 3D analyses, and therefore the predicted values for the absorbed energy are nearly the same, 14.5 J and 14.7 J at the low temperature and 13.8 J and 13.8 J at the high temperature, for 3D and plane strain respectively. For all four calculations in Fig. 3, cleavage occurs following void coalescence in several integration points near the notch tip.

It is noted that the cases considered here are similar to cases analyzed in the previous plane strain study [5], so that the present results obtained by enforcing plane strain conditions on one slice of the 3D elements should be directly comparable, and in fact good agreement of the force displacement curves has been found. But predictions of cleavage failure are quite sensitive to the size of the 'cleavage grain' over which the maximum principal stress is averaged, and since here a cleavage grain is one element in size and in [5] it is one quadrilateral in size, the present computations using a cruder mesh tend to predict later occurrence of cleavage failure.

The weld configuration in Fig. 2b, for which the notch region includes part of the more brittle HAZ, is considered in Fig. 4. Again, the force levels predicted by the plane strain analyses are clearly above those of the 3D analyses. Also, in the 3D computation for the low temperature cleavage occurs before any ductile failure, while in the other three calculations ductile failure by void coalescence at several integration points precedes cleavage. However, here the more brittle behavior of the HAZ is reflected by the much lower value of the displacement U at the end of the dotted curve. The predicted values for the absorbed energy are 6.8 J and 18.3 J at the low temperature and 13.0 J and 16.0 J at the high temperature, for 3D and plane strain respectively.

A somewhat surprising result in both Fig. 3 and Fig. 4 is that the most brittle behavior is found for the full 3D analysis. As the plane strain assumption gives a strong constraint on the deformation and this also leads to higher force levels in Figs. 3 and 4, a higher principal

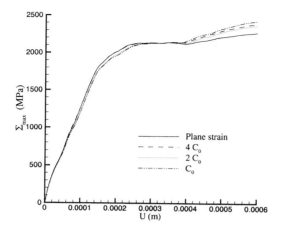

Fig. 5: Evolution of the maximum principal stress with applied displacement for various values of the specimen thickness. C_0 is the thickness of the standard Charpy specimen. The weld configuration is that shown in Fig. 2b and the initial temperature is $-80\,°C$.

stress level and thus more brittle behavior might be expected for the plane strain results. To investigate this further the evolution of the maximum principal stress Σ_{max} (averaged over the element volume) is shown in Fig. 5, for the weld configuration in Fig. 2b at the low temperature. Initially the peak stress is at the notch surface, as known from the elastic solution, but at $U \approx 0.0004$ m the curves show a kink, as the location of the maximum stress shifts to a point somewhat in front of the notch, where cleavage failure will initiate in the Charpy V notch specimen. After the kink the stress grows higher in the 3D specimen. Two further computations are included in Fig. 5, for larger specimen thickness $2C_0$ or $4C_0$, to test possible convergence towards the plane strain result. These two computations use 8 or 16 elements through the half thickness, respectively, so that the element sizes are the same as those shown in Fig. 1, but it is seen in Fig. 5 that the peak stress remains higher than the level predicted for plane strain. The contour curves in Fig. 6b illustrate that this is due to a real 3D effect, which gives a stress peak at a distance of about $C_0/2$ from the free surface, while the behavior in the central part of the thick specimen has converged to a planar solution. For the standard specimen geometry (Fig. 6a) the two edge regions of higher cleavage stress are superposed into one central region.

It is noted that the behavior illustrated in Figs. 5 and 6 is not a special feature of the weld configuration in Fig. 2b. Computations for a uniform base material specimen have confirmed the same type of behavior of the maximum principal stress. Thus, the real 3D stress distributions in the Charpy specimen give earlier cleavage failure than predicted by plane strain, even though the predicted force levels are lower.

ACKNOWLEDGMENTS

A.N. is grateful for the support provided by the Office of Naval Research through grant N00014-97-1-0179.

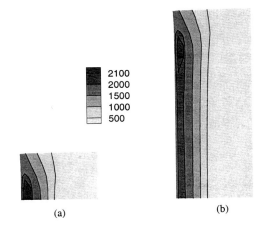

(a)   (b)

Fig. 6: Contours of the cleavage grain averaged maximum principal stress on the notch plane at $U = 0.00066$ m. The weld configuration is that shown in Fig. 2b and the initial temperature is $-80°$C. (a) Thickness C_0. (b) Thickness $4C_0$.

REFERENCES

[1] Tvergaard, V. and Needleman, A. (1986) *J. Mech. Phys. Solids* **34**, 213.

[2] Tvergaard, V. and Needleman, A. (1988) *Int. J. Fract.* **37**, 197.

[3] Mathur, K.K., Needleman, A., and Tvergaard, V. (1994) *Modell. Simul. Mat. Sci. Engng.* **2**, 617.

[4] Needleman, A. and Tvergaard, V. (1999) *Engin. Frac. Mech.* **62**, 317.

[5] Tvergaard, V. and Needleman, A. (2000) *Engin. Fract. Mech.* **65**, 627.

[6] Gurson, A.L. (1975). Ph.D. Thesis, Brown University.

[7] Gurson, A.L. (1977) *J. Engin. Mat. Tech.* **99**, 2.

[8] Pan, J., Saje, M. and Needleman, A. (1983) *Int. J. Fract.* **21**, 261.

[9] Tvergaard, V. (1981) *Int. J. Fract.* **17**, 389.

[10] Tvergaard, V. (1982) *Int. J. Fract.* **18**, 237.

[11] Tvergaard, V. and Needleman, A. (1984) *Acta Metall.* **32**, 157.

[12] Tvergaard, V. (1990) *Adv. Appl. Mech.* **27**, 83.

[13] Gray, G.R. and Chen, S.-R., 1998, private communication.

[14] Naus, D.J., Bass, B.R., Keeney-Walker, J., Fields, R.J., De Wit, R., and Low III, S.R. (1990) *Nuclear Engrg. Design* **118**, 283.

[15] Chu, C.C. and Needleman, A. (1980) *J. Engin. Mat. Tech.* **102**, 249.

[16] Tvergaard, V. and Needleman, A. (1993) *Int. J. Fract.* **59**, 53.

[17] Peirce, D., Shih, C. F. and Needleman, A. (1984) *Comp. Struct.* **18**, 875.

[18] Tvergaard, V. (1982) *J. Mech. Phys. Solids* **30**, 399.

From Charpy to Present Impact Testing
D. François and A. Pineau (Eds.)

Charpy impact test modelling
and local approach to fracture

A. Rossoll *, C. Berdin, C. Prioul

LMSS-MAT, École Centrale de Paris, F-92295 Châtenay-Malabry Cedex.

Abstract

This study aims at the establishment of a non-empirical relationship between the Charpy V-notch energy CVN and the fracture toughness K_{Ic}, on the lower shelf of fracture toughness and on the onset of the ductile-to-brittle transition of a low alloy structural steel. The methodology employed is based on the 'local approach'. Brittle cleavage fracture is modelled in terms of the Beremin model [1], whereas the ductile crack advance preceding cleavage in the transition region is accounted for with the Gurson-Tvergaard-Needleman (GTN) model [2, 3, 4].

Temperature and rate dependence of the material flow stress were determined from tensile and compressive tests. Numerous fracture tests on CT and Charpy V-notch specimens provided the large data set necessary for statistical evaluation. Finite element analysis was employed for modelling. Special consideration was taken in order to handle the dynamic effects in the Charpy impact test.

On the lower shelf, the fracture toughness could be predicted from the Charpy impact test results. In the transition region the parameters of the Beremin model were found to deviate from those established on the lower shelf. Detailed fractographic investigations showed that the fractographic and microstructural features of regions of cleavage fracture initiation change with temperature.

Keywords: Charpy test, local approach, Beremin model, numerical modelling, fracture toughness, fractography, cleavage fracture, fracture initiation sites.

1 INTRODUCTION

The worthiness of the Charpy impact test would be extended by a procedure that allows to interpret Charpy test results in terms of fracture toughness. Until recently only empirical approaches were available. A non-empirical procedure for the exploitation of the Charpy V-notch test is promised by the 'local' approach. In contrast to the 'global' approach based on the application of fracture mechanics, which requires the fulfilment of severe geometrical conditions (minimum size requirements, existence of a pre-crack instead of a notch), the 'local' approach is *a priori* geometry independent. It is based on the direct examination

---

*Current affilation: LMM/DMX, École Polytechnique Fédérale de Lausanne, CH-1015 Lausanne.

of some *local* field quantities that appear to control damage evolution and fracture initiation for the fracture type to be examined. The computation of these local parameters is commonly carried out with FEA (finite element analysis). The application of the local approach is based on the following steps [5]: (i) establishment of a model that captures the physical mechanism of the damage or fracture phenomenon, and (ii) computation of the relevant field variables, *e.g.* by FEA. Thus an appropriate FE model of the CVN test has to be established. This last point is studied in this work, followed by the assessment of fracture toughness K_{Ic} values from Charpy V-notch energy *CVN*, *via* the local approach.

2   EXPERIMENTAL AND NUMERICAL PROCEDURES

2.1   Experiments

The material chosen for this study is a low alloy structural steel of French standard 16MND5 (similar to A508 Cl.3). The samples were taken at 3/4 thickness (from the inner wall) from a nozzle cut-out of a pressure vessel. The chemical composition is given in Table 1.

Table 1: Chemical composition (in weight percent).

C	S	P	Mn	Si	Ni	Cr	Mo	Cu	Al
0.159	0.008	0.005	1.37	0.24	0.70	0.17	0.50	0.06	0.23

The heat treatment includes two austenitisations followed by water quench and tempering, and a final stress relief treatment. The resulting microstructure is tempered bainite [6]. Franklin's formula gives $f_v = 3.9 \ 10^{-4}$ for the inclusion volume fraction of manganese sulfides, or $f_v = 5.7 \ 10^{-4}$ if oxides are also considered.

Tensile and compressive tests served to establish the constitutive behaviour of the material, which is needed as an input for modelling. Tensile tests on smooth specimens were run at a nominal strain rate $\dot{\epsilon}$ of $4.10^{-4} \ \mathrm{s}^{-1}$ at temperatures ranging from $-150\,^\circ$C up to room temperature [7]. Compressive tests at a strain rate of approximately $1000 \ \mathrm{s}^{-1}$ were conducted at CREA (Centre de Recherche et d'Études d'Arcueil, France) on a Hopkinson bar device [8]. Quasistatic ($4.10^{-3} \ \mathrm{s}^{-1}$) and intermediate strain rate ($1 \ \mathrm{s}^{-1}$) compressive tests were carried out at CREA as well, at temperatures between $-150\,^\circ$C and $+100\,^\circ$C [8].

Fracture was studied through compact tension (CT) and Charpy V-notch (CVN) tests. Charpy tests were carried out on four different standard instrumented impact pendulum devices of capacities ranking from 100 J up to 350 J, at impact velocities between 5 and 5.5 ms^{-1} and temperatures ranging from $-90\,^\circ$C up to room temperature [8]. The lower shelf energy level is situated around 5 J, whereas the upper shelf is about 160 J. The DBTT (ductile-to-brittle transition temperature) is situated at $-20\,^\circ$C.

25 mm wide CT specimens with a notch depth ratio a/W of 0.55 were tested in the temperature range between $-150\,^\circ$C and $-60\,^\circ$C. Twenty-four specimens were tested at $-90\,^\circ$C. Additional data obtained by Renevey [7] at $-30\,^\circ$C and $0\,^\circ$C were also analysed.

2.2 Numerical Modelling

The mechanical tests conducted at different strain rates and temperatures served to determine the rate and temperature dependent flow stress of the material. Since ductile crack initiation and propagation occurs in some of the fracture tests, a model incorporating ductile damage has to be chosen for modelling. Here the GTN model for a porous plastic solid, originally proposed by Gurson [2] and subsequently modified by Tvergaard and Needleman [3, 4] was used. Most of the parameters of the model were chosen according to the chemical composition of the material (volume fraction of voids initially present and voids nucleated with strain, respectively) and to experience as described in literature [4]. The only parameters that were fitted were the critical void volume fraction, fitted to match the sudden load drop in tensile tests, and the mesh size, fitted from crack growth simulation with CT specimens; no parameter was fitted in order to match the CVN load-displacement records. Details on the constitutive equations and the chosen parameters can be found in [8].

The high strain rate ($\dot{\epsilon} \sim 10^3$ s^{-1}) in the notch root of the Charpy specimen needs to be accounted for via a strain rate dependent material law. For modelling the rate dependence of the flow stress $\bar{\sigma}$ of the matrix, a Cowper-Symonds overstress formulation was used

$$\bar{\sigma} = \sigma_0 \left(1 + \left(\frac{\dot{\epsilon}_{eq}}{\dot{\epsilon}_0} \right)^{1/p} \right) \tag{1}$$

where $\bar{\sigma} = \bar{\sigma}(\epsilon_M^{pl}, \dot{\epsilon}_{eq}, T)$ is the dynamic flow stress, $\sigma_0 = \sigma_0(\epsilon_{pl}, T)$ is the static flow stress, $\dot{\epsilon}_{eq}$ is the equivalent plastic strain rate, $\dot{\epsilon}_0 = 10^8$ s^{-1} is a normalisation parameter, $p = 12$ is the strain rate hardening parameter. The 'static' plastic flow stress σ_0 was assumed to follow a Hollomon law, with a linear dependence on the temperature for the range between $-90\,°$C and $+100\,°$C:

$$\sigma_0 = K(\epsilon_M^{pl})^n [1 - \beta(T - T_0)] \tag{2}$$

where $T_0 = -90\,°$C, $\beta = 0.00125$, $K = 1040$, and $n = 0.14$. The constitutive equations were implemented into the ABAQUS/Standard finite element program [9] via a user interface as a 'user material' [10, 11]. Large geometry changes were accounted for. Both the CVN and CT specimens were analysed in 3-D.

2.3 Charpy Test Modelling

A preliminary study [8, 12] was conducted in order to define a modelling procedure for the CVN specimen that would be appropriate for applying the local approach. The employed methods were quasistatic (2-D and 3-D), transient dynamic (2-D) and modal (2-D) FEA. It was found that inertial oscillations of the experimental load *vs.* displacement curves originate from the vibration of the specimen (Fig. 1). Compliance of the striker strongly influences the frequency of specimen vibrations. Local stress fluctuations inside the specimen (ahead of the notch root) are much less important. For the range of loading durations greater than 50 μs (corresponding to the lowest *CVN* values obtained at $-90\,°$C) a quasistatic procedure is sufficient for the interpretation of experimental results. Adiabatic heating is important but is confined in the notch root region. Consequently it does not strongly lower the level of the largest principal stress, which has its maximum well behind the notch root. A 2-D plane strain model may be sufficient to describe the local stress and

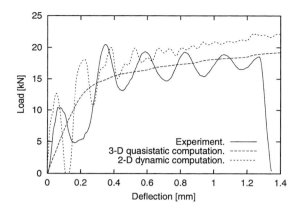

Fig. 1: Load–deflection records of KCV specimens. Computation *vs.* experiment. The dynamic 2-D simulation describes the response of a KCV specimen tested on an infinitely stiff impact tester, whereas the experimental record shown was obtained on a very 'soft' machine (strongly compliant striker). See [8, 12] for details.

strain fields ahead of the notch, as long as no ductile crack growth occurs; else 3-D analysis is clearly preferable. Boundary conditions (striker and anvil) can be well modelled with contact elements. Friction does not seem to play an important role: the friction coefficient seems to be on the order of 0.1.

3   CLEAVAGE MODELLING AND TOUGHNESS PREDICTION

The numerical model is completed with a brittle (cleavage) fracture model [1, 5, 13], which has become one of the most popular local approach models in this area. It is based on the hypothesis of a (temperature-independent) critical cleavage stress, and on weakest link theory. The failure probability P_F is expressed as

$$P_F = 1 - \exp\left(-\left(\frac{\sigma_W}{\sigma_u}\right)^m\right) \qquad (3)$$

with σ_W the so-called 'Weibull stress'

$$\sigma_W = \sqrt[m]{\int_{V_{\mathrm{pl}}} (\sigma_1)^m \frac{dV}{V_0}} \qquad (4)$$

where σ_1 denotes the maximum principal positive stress (here defined as its maximum value with time; only positive values are considered), m the Weibull exponent which describes the scatter in the flaw distribution, and σ_u is closely linked to the intrinsic cleavage stress. The integral denotes the summation of σ_1 over the entire plastified volume V_{pl} of the structure, since plastic deformation is a necessary precursor to slip-induced cleavage. In our analysis the choice of V_0 was dictated by the mesh size that determines the appropriate ductile crack growth rate, *i.e.* $V_0 = (100\,\mu\mathrm{m})^3$. The two parameters m and σ_u were determined by post-processing of FEA and experimental results with the maximum likelihood method.

Table 2: Weibull parameters. $V_0 = (100 \, \mu m)^3$.

Specimen type	T [°C]	N	m	σ_u [MPa]	90% confidence interval for m	90% confidence interval for σ_u	$\sigma_u V_0^{1/m}$
CVN	-90	28	20.9	2575	16.3–21.9	2535–2617	1850
CVN	-60	27	18.5	2902	14.3–24.0	2850–2956	1998
CVN	-30	27	10.1	4821	7.4–12.4	4655–4996	2431
CT	-90	24	24.3	2402	18.5–32.0	2367–2438	1808

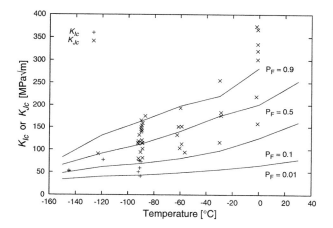

Fig. 2: Fracture toughness at cleavage initiation as predicted from CVN results obtained at −90 °C, for different failure probabilities P_F, and experimental fracture toughness values (CT specimens) K_{Ic} and K_{Jc}. K_{Jc} denotes an equivalent fracture toughness computed from J_{Ic}.

Table 2 summarizes the Weibull parameters for the entire set of specimens. Recall that FEA of all specimen types incorporates ductile damage and crack growth via the GTN model. It is found that the Weibull parameters for the CVN and CT specimens are similar for −90 °C. However, the parameters calculated for the CVN specimens tested at higher temperatures differ.

If a unique set of parameters exists, the fracture toughness can also be predicted. The failure probability of the CT specimens (which were also modelled with FEA) was computed with eq. 3 by imposing the Weibull parameters of the CVN specimens tested at −90 °C (*i.e.* $m = 20.9$, $\sigma_u = 2575$ MPa). At the same time, for each loading step, the J-integral was evaluated and converted into an equivalent K_I value. Figure 2 shows the resulting prediction of fracture toughness for CT specimens, as computed with the Weibull parameters determined from the Charpy results obtained at $T = -90$ °C. Since these parameters lie very close to those of the CT specimens tested at the same temperature, one finds without surprise that the prediction of fracture toughness for this temperature is very satisfying. The prediction seems still reasonable for −60 °C and for temperatures below −90 °C. However, although ductile crack growth has been fully accounted for in

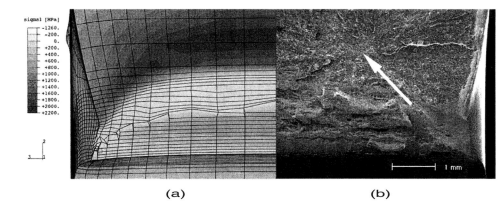

(a)   (b)

Fig. 3: Contour plot of the largest principal stress in the ligament of a CVN specimen (a), and SEM photograph of fracture surface (b). Test temperature $T = -30\,°C$. The arrow points to the region where cleavage fracture was triggered, corresponding to the region where the largest principal stress has its maximum value.

computation, the combined GTN-Beremin approach fails to correctly describe the steep increase of fracture toughness in the ductile-to-brittle transition, if the Beremin parameters established at low temperature afe kept constant. Notably the lower bound of fracture toughness barely increases, in contrast to experience. Thus it may be concluded that solely the evolution of the material flow stress with temperature is not sufficient in order to explain the steep rise of the material's resistance to cleavage crack growth in the brittle-to-ductile transition.

4 DISCUSSION

In order to gain more insight into the physical mechanism leading to cleavage failure, most of the fracture surfaces were examined with fractography. Figure 3b shows the fracture surface of a CVN specimen tested at $-30\,°C$. The macroscopic pattern of ridges that form a sort of 'fan' on the cleavage fracture surface indicates the presence of the cleavage initiation site(s), as indicated with the arrow. At a higher magnification it is in most cases possible to trace the 'river' pattern back to a specific location [7, 14, 15]. Note that the location of the cleavage initiation site is situated well behind the notch root and the ductile crack advance zone, but in the region where the maximum value of the largest principal stress σ_1 occurs, as can be found in comparison with a computed contour plot of σ_1 (Fig. 3a). Most of the identified cleavage initiation sites are characterized by the presence of one or several (arranged in a cluster) manganese sulfide inclusions, which were encountered more often and with increasing size as a function of temperature, such that at $T = -30\,°C$ (highest temperature examined) almost on each fracture surface large MnS stringers (length on the order of $100\ \mu m$) were present in the vicinity of the cleavage initiation site. Thus the 'active' population of weak spots seeming to 'encourage' cleavage initiation seems to evolve with temperature. Nevertheless it can be confirmed that failure is initiated in one location,

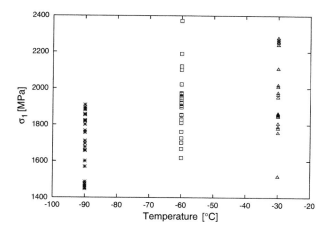

Fig. 4: Local values of the cleavage stress σ_1 (largest principal stress at the cleavage site) *vs.* temperature T (only Charpy specimens).

i.e. by a weakest-link mechanism, as assumed in the Beremin model.

As already illustrated in figure 3, the knowledge of the location of the cleavage initiation sites as revealed by fractography can be confronted with the results from FEA. For each identified cleavage initiation site, the instant of specimen failure t is known, as well as the in-plane coordinates x and y (r in the case of axisymmetric specimens). Thus each site can be associated with a specific finite element in the corresponding FE model of the specimen. The deformation of the specimen, which translates into a distortion of the FEA mesh, has to be taken into account, as well as the evolution of variables with time.

Attempts to define some 'failure locus' of the material (*e.g.* in the stress–strain space) failed; no correlation between the largest principal stresses acting on the cleavage initiation sites and the values of the equivalent plastic strain or stress triaxiality could be established. In any case, for each studied temperature, the scatter of stress values is quite low, such that the critical role of stress on cleavage fracture is confirmed. An interesting tendency can be made out in Fig. 4. The cleavage stress increases roughly linearly with temperature, at least in the CVN specimens of which a large number was available at different temperatures. In view of this finding, the breakdown of the Beremin model to cover a large temperature range, notably in the transition region, is not surprising, since the cleavage stress is assumed to be temperature independent in the present formulation. In order to increase the stability of the Beremin model, modifications have already been proposed in the literature; they are generally not based on the assumption of an evolution of the cleavage stress with temperature. However, the physical soundness of the assumption of a temperature-dependent cleavage stress is still questionable.

5 CONCLUSIONS

The feasibility of lower-shelf fracture toughness determination from Charpy impact test results was shown. The local approach method was chosen, which combines a physically-based model of fracture with FEA. The dynamic effects in the Charpy test were accounted for with a rate dependent formulation of the material flow stress and the incorporation of adiabatic heating, whereas inertial terms were found to be negligible. The modification of the stress fields by ductile crack growth were fully incorporated with GTN model.

The Beremin model yields consistent parameters in CVN and CT specimens on the lower shelf of fracture toughness curve, *i.e.* at temperatures up to some $-60\,°C$. In this domain, fracture toughness can be predicted. The weakest link hypothesis that serves as a basis of this model is confirmed by a fractographic analysis which indicates cleavage initiation from a principal site acting as a weak spot. In the tested material, cleavage fracture seems frequently assisted by the presence of non-metallic inclusions.

Towards the brittle-to-ductile transition, some changes take place. Fractographic analysis reveals an increasing presence of large inclusions on the fracture surface that can trigger cleavage. Correlation of the cleavage initiation sites with FEA shows that the local cleavage stress also increases with temperature. It is concluded that the intrinsic resistance to cleavage crack propagation increases with temperature.

6   ACKNOWLEDGEMENTS

The authors thank EdF (Les Renardières) for financial support and for supplying the material. CEA/CEREM/SRMA (Saclay) is acknowledged for the interesting and fruitful collaboration. A.R. is grateful to the European Commission (DG XII - DEMA) for financial support under contract number FI4S-CT96-5001.

7   REFERENCES

1.   Beremin, F. (1983). *Met. Trans.* **14A**, 2277.
2.   Gurson, A. (1977). *J. Eng. Mat. Tech.* **99**, 2.
3.   Tvergaard, V. (1982). *Int. J. Fracture* **18**, 237.
4.   Tvergaard, V. and Needleman, A. (1984). *Acta Met.* **32**(1), 157.
5.   Mudry, F. (1987). *NEaD* **105**, 65.
6.   Hausild, P., Berdin, C., and Prioul, C. This conference.
7.   Renevey, S. (1997). PhD thesis. Université Paris XI Orsay. France.
8.   Rossoll, A. (1998). PhD thesis. École Centrale de Paris. France.
9.   HKS, (1997). *ABAQUS / Standard, Version 5.7.* HKS, Pawtucket, RI, USA.
10.   Siegmund, T. and Brocks, W. (1997). Technical Report GKSS/WMG/97/2. GKSS. Geesthacht, Germany.
11.   Mühlich, U., Siegmund, T., and Brocks, W. (1998). Technical Report GKSS/WMG/98/1. GKSS. Geesthacht, Germany.
12.   Rossoll, A., Berdin, C., Forget, P., Prioul, C., and Marini, B. (1999). *NEaD* **188**, 217.
13.   Mudry, F. (1982). PhD thesis. Université de Tech.logie de Compiègne. France.
14.   Nedbal, I., Siegl, J., and Kunz, J. (1997). Research Report V-KMAT-440/97. CVUT-FJFI-KMAT. Prague, Czech Republic.
15.   Mäntylä, M., Rossoll, A., Nedbal, I., Prioul, C., and Marini, B. (1999). *J. Nucl. Mater.* **264**, 257.

From Charpy to Present Impact Testing
D. François and A. Pineau (Eds.)

453

EXPERIMENTAL ANALYSIS OF CHARPY V–NOTCH SPECIMENS

B. TANGUY, R. PIQUES, A. PINEAU

Ecole des Mines de Paris, Centre des Matériaux, UMR CNRS 7633
BP 87, 91003 Evry Cedex, France

ABSTRACT

The objective of this study is to provide experimental results for modelling Charpy V–notch tests carried out on A508 steel. This modelling is presented in a companion paper [1]. Test results on tempered bainitic A508 steel are shown, including the measurement of the absorbed energy over a wide range of impact velocities, covering quasi–static tests (1μms^{-1}), intermediate velocity (0.5mms^{-1}) and impact velocity ($\sim$ 5ms^{-1}). In all cases the tests were instrumented to determine the load–displacement curves. The material was tested over the temperature range between $-196°$C and $100°$C to investigate the ductile–brittle transition behaviour. Interrupted Charpy tests using an initial impact energy smaller than the maximum (low blow tests) were also performed in the transition regime. A recrystallization technique was used to estimate notch tip strains. Notch tip temperature increase during high velocity impact testing was also measured using tiny thermocouples. SEM observations were performed to determine the amount of ductile crack growth preceding fracture as a function of test temperature and impact energy. Detailed SEM examinations were made to determine the nature of cleavage initiation sites and their position in front of the notch or the ductile crack front.

KEYWORDS

Instrumented Charpy Impact tests; Interrupted low blow Charpy tests; Recrystallization technique; Strain and temperature measurements; Micromechanisms.

1. INTRODUCTION

Charpy–V notch impact test is still the most convenient and the most widely used method to determine the fracture properties of steels, such as the total energy absorbed to fracture and the ductile–brittle transition temperature. However, modelling the Charpy test still remains a key issue. Several aspects of this test require a detailed analysis : the inertial effects, the complexity of the loading and the boundary conditions, the effect of large strain rates on constitutive equations, the non–isothermal character, the 3D character of fracture behaviour, in particular ductile crack growth preceding cleavage fracture above the lower shelf temperature and the competition between ductile and brittle fracture.

A research program was undertaken to contribute to the understanding of the Charpy test and to bring information on the above aspects. In the present study only experimental results are reported. A companion paper is devoted to modelling the test and the competition between cleavage and ductile fracture [1]. Preliminary results have already been published [2]. In the present study a fuller account of these results is given.

This study was performed on a A508 (16MND5) steel used in the fabrication of pressurized water reactors (PWR). This material was selected because of the large number of previous studies devoted to the failure micromechanisms in this steel [3–5].

2. MATERIAL AND EXPERIMENTAL PROCEDURES

The material which was taken from a PWR shell was heat treated to obtain a tempered bainitic microstructure with a room temperature yield strength σ_Y = 490MPa and ultimate tensile strength, σ_{UTS} = 620MPa. The composition is (weight%) : C= 0.16, Mn= 1.33, Ni= 0.76, Mo= 0.51, Cr= 0.22, Si= 0.22, Cu= 0.07, S= 0.004, P= 0.008.

Standard Charpy–V (45°) notch (**CVN**) specimens were machined and used throughout all the tests. TL (longitudinal–long transverse orientation) specimens were extracted from a cylindrical pressure vessel. All the specimens were machined from a layer located at 30 − 80% from the wall thickness to minimize skin effects on the material homogeneity. Conventional Charpy testing was carried out on an instrumented Amsler RHP 300 Joules machine. Full details are given elsewhere [6]. The initial specimen temperature was monitored and controlled by welding thermocouples to the specimen. Interrupted Charpy impact tests were also carried out at two temperatures ($T = -60, 20°C$) in order to measure ductile crack growth preceding cleavage fracture as a function of impact energy. These interrupted tests were performed by imposing an initial impact energy lower than the maximum energy of 300 Joules (low blow tests). In addition to these impact tests at high velocity ($\sim 5ms^{-1}$), three point–bend experiments were carried out on a 250kN Instron machine at a prescribed crosshead velocities of $1\mu ms^{-1}$ and $0.5mms^{-1}$. A special set–up was machined to have the same contact conditions (hammer and anvils) as those of a conventional Charpy impact machine.

Tensile and compressive tests were carried out to determine the variation of flow properties with temperature and strain rate. Several studies devoted to the simulation of Charpy–V notch test have outlined the importance of these factors on the failure modes, in particular in the ductile–brittle transition regime (see eg. [7,8]). Full details about the results of these tests are given elsewhere [1,2,6,9].

An attempt was made to estimate the increase in temperature due to plastic deformation at high strain rate ahead of the notch using interrupted impact testing. These measurements were made at room temperature and $-60°C$ by welding tiny thermocouples ($\phi = 0.1mm$) very close ($\sim 0.1mm$) to the notch tip on the lateral faces of Charpy specimens.

A recrystallization technique was applied to measure plastic strains at the notch root of the Charpy specimens [9–11]. This method is based on the direct relationship between recrystallized grain size and plastic strain in a given material which is previously deformed and then heat treated. The Charpy specimens were subjected to a recrystallization heat treatment in vacuum at 695°C for 4 hours. The fracture surface was then nickel plated and sectioned at mid–thickness, perpendicular to the fracture plane. The specimens were then prepared by standard metallographic technique for microstructural characterization. The average notch strain was estimated from the recrystallized grain size, on the basis of a previous calibration [2,9].

3. RESULTS AND DISCUSSION

3.1. Effect of impact velocity on ductile–brittle transition

Figure 1 shows that the ductile–brittle transition temperature is not largely affected by impact velocity, contrarily to the situation usually observed in low strength ferritic steels, but similarly to what happens in a number of high strength steels [12]. The main effect of impact velocity on CVN energy is observed on the upper shelf energy which is an increasing function of impact rate. This behaviour is mainly related to the increase of flow properties with strain rate.

In a companion paper a numerical simulation of conventional Charpy impact test is proposed [1]. In the transition regime this simulation is based on the competition between ductile crack extension and cleavage fracture. In the following it is shown that for the same total energy, ductile crack growth is more important for quasi–static test compared to high impact rate of $5\mathrm{ms}^{-1}$. This difference in ductile fracture preceding cleavage failure is also mainly related to the effect of strain rate on the flow properties of the material, although adiabatic heating, quite pronounced at $5\mathrm{ms}^{-1}$, tends to lower stresses and thus to compensate to some extent, the strain rate effect. A more quantitative analysis of these effects is detailed elsewhere [6] where it is shown that both under quasi–static (isothermal) loading conditions ($1\mu\mathrm{ms}^{-1}$) and high (adiabatic) impact rate ($\sim 5\mathrm{ms}^{-1}$) the stresses ahead of the ductile propagating crack are very similar when brittle cleavage fracture is initiated.

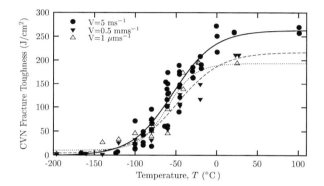

Figure 1. Charpy V–notch (CVN) fracture toughness transition curves of 16MND5 for Charpy–V specimens tested at different loading rates.

3.2. Loading curves

In modelling Charpy impact test the first step is the comparison of the experimental and calculated loading curves. Examples are shown in figure 2a where large inertial effects corresponding to oscillations are noticed. At the lower shelf ($-166°\mathrm{C}$) the time to failure ($\sim 0.06\mathrm{ms}$) is much shorter than that measured in the ductile–brittle transition regime ($\sim 2\mathrm{ms}$ at $-20°\mathrm{C}$) or at the upper shelf ($\sim 6\mathrm{ms}$ at $20°\mathrm{C}$). Integration of the load–time recordings gives the striker velocity which, contrarily to what is observed at the lower shelf where the speed remains constant, continuously decelerates from $5\mathrm{ms}^{-1}$ down to about $4\mathrm{ms}^{-1}$ at $-20°\mathrm{C}$ and $3\mathrm{ms}^{-1}$ at $20°\mathrm{C}$. However these variations in impact velocity are small. This justifies the use of a constant speed in modelling Charpy impact test over all the transition curve.

A comparison of the load–displacement curves between Charpy impact test and quasi–static test ($0.5\mathrm{mms}^{-1}$) is made in fig. 2b where the effect of loading rate on the overall response of the specimens is clearly observed, not only in the lower shelf regime ($-166°\mathrm{C}$) but also at higher temperature ($-20°\mathrm{C}$ and $20°\mathrm{C}$). In the transition regime ($-20°\mathrm{C}$), where in both cases cleavage fracture is preceded by ductile tearing, the increase in displacement at failure produced by a reduction in impact velocity compensates the reduction in load, so that the energy to failure is almost independent of loading rate.

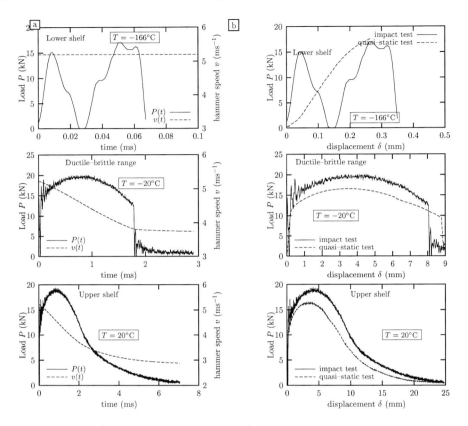

Figure 2. Load–time (a) and Load–displacement (b) curves obtained from instrumented impact test. Top : brittle fracture, middle : ductile–brittle fracture, bottom : ductile fracture.

3.3. Notch tip strains

The use of the recrystallization technique is illustrated in fig. 3, where micrographs of specimens cut in their mid–section are shown. Low magnification micrographs (fig. 3a and b) on interrupted tests performed at 20°C clearly show the development of plastic hinges similar to those already observed by others (see e.g. [13]). A closer examination at the notch root of a specimen tested up to failure at −80°C (fig. 3c) shows the existence of a recrystallized region extending over a distance of 150μm around the notch. The measurement of the size of these recrystallized grains was used to estimate local plastic strains, as explained earlier. The results corresponding to Charpy impact specimens tested at −80°C and quasi–static specimens tested at −120°C are reported in fig. 4 where the results of numerical calculations are also included [2]. Strains as large as 100% are evidenced close to the notch root even when the specimens are tested in the lower shelf domain (−120°C), that is in the absence of any significant ductile crack growth. This clearly shows that in modelling cleavage fracture the effect of large plastic strains must be taken into account [4,6].

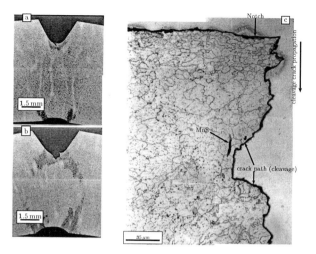

Figure 3. Experimental evidences of plastic strains in mid–section of a Charpy–V specimen. a) and b) : Macro-etch photograph after recrystallization (a : $T = 20°C$, $CVN = 56J$, b : $T = 20°C$, $CVN = 85J$). c : Recrystallized region of intense deformation at notch ($T = -80°C$, $CVN = 11J$)

3.4. Notch root temperature

Quite significant increases in notch root temperature, ΔT, were measured through interrupted low blow tests performed at $-60°C$ and $20°C$ (fig. 5). It should be kept in mind that these ΔT increases are measured on the lateral surfaces of the specimens. Numerical calculations showed that the temperature increases are larger in the mid–section of the specimens where plane strain conditions are prevailing [6]. This means that the ΔT increases reported in fig. 5 underestimate the heating of Charpy specimens. Moreover these increases must be considered as values averaged over distances comparable to thermocouple dimensions ($\sim 0.1 - 0.2$mm) glued at a position of about 0.1 mm from notch root. This also contributes to underestimate real temperature increases. The local temperature measurements raise another key point when modelling Charpy impact tests is envisaged. Should the tests be modelled under adiabatic conditions or under mixed conditions with heat flow? Simple calculations using the thermal conductivity of A508 steel ($D \sim 2.10^{-5}\mathrm{m^2 s^{-1}}$) show that in a test lasting 1 ms the characteristic heat flow distance is of the order of 0.15 mm. The results shown in fig. 2 indicate that in the lower shelf regime the time to failure is so short that it could be assumed that fracture occurs under adiabatic conditions. On the other hand, when the value of the CVN energy is larger than about 100 Joules ($T \gtrsim -50°C$) the time to failure is such that adiabatic conditions only constitute an approximation.

3.5. Ductile crack initiation and crack growth

Observations of mid–section interrupted low blow Charpy tests carried out at $-60°C$ are reported in fig. 6. These micrographs show that in the ductile–brittle transition regime crack initiation from the notch occurs by the formation of a shear band about 100μm long, and the formation of cavities initiated from MnS inclusions located ahead of the notch tip (fig. 6a). Then ductile crack growth occurs by linking the initiated shear crack with cavities and subsequent coalescence between the voids.

Examinations of the fracture surfaces (not shown here) revealed that ductile crack growth oc-

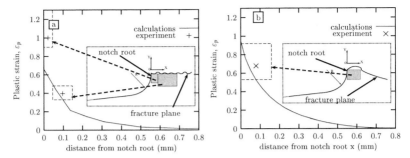

Figure 4. Mid–section strain distribution ahead of the notch in a Charpy–V specimen. Comparison between experiments and finite element calculations : a) dynamic Charpy test at $-80°$C $(CVN = 15J)$ b) static test at $-120°$C $(CVN = 20.5J)$. A scheme of the Charpy notch where hatched regions represent the regions over which the given experimental value was averaged is drawn on each figure. Width of the dashed rectangular region represents the width of the measured area and the height represents the uncertainty on the measured plastic strain.

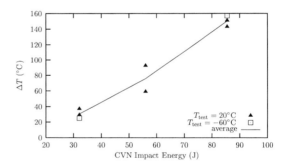

Figure 5. Temperature rises measured at notch tip during interrupted Charpy–V tests.

curred with a tunelling effect, crack extension being more important in the mid–section than on the lateral specimen surfaces where fracture gives rise to the formation of shear lips. The maximum crack growth, Δa, measured in the mid–section of specimens tested at three loading rates is given in fig. 7a. At low temperature $(T \leq -100°$C$)$ cleavage fracture occurs without any significant ductile crack extension. Above this temperature, in the ductile–brittle transition regime, large scatter in Δa is observed for a given loading rate. This illustrates the statistical aspect of cleavage fracture which has to be taken into account when modelling Charpy impact test [1]. The effect of loading rate is clearly evidenced when the values of Δa are plotted as a function of the absorbed energy (fig. 7b).

Further SEM detailed observations of the sites initiating cleavage fracture were also made [6]. In each specimen only a few initiating sites were observed. Several types of initiating sites were evidenced, including large cleavage facets with low misorientation, MnS inclusions and carbides. In fig 8 the distance of these sites from the notch root, y_1 is reported as a function of test temperature (fig. 8a) or CVN energy (fig. 8b) for the three loading rates. In these figures the mean ductile crack growth, Δa_{aver}, preceding brittle cleavage fracture is also given. Similarly to the results shown in fig. 7a, a large scatter is observed when examining the variations of y_1 with temperature. Much less scatter is seen when the values of y_1 are plotted as a function of the value of the CVN energy (fig. 8b). In this figure any significant effect of loading rate is noticed,

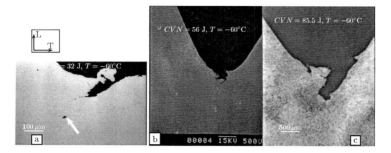

Figure 6. Ductile crack initiation and growth related to the CVN energy absorbed at $T = -60°C$. Mid–section of Charpy–V specimens. a) $CVN = 32J$, b) $CVN = 56J$, c) $CVN = 85J$.

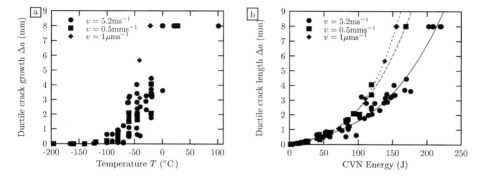

Figure 7. Loading rate effect on ductile crack length as a function of. a) temperature b) CVN energy.

except at low values of the CVN energy ($\lesssim 60$ J) where it is observed that the cleavage sites tend to be located closer to the notch tip or to the crack front of the short propagating ductile crack. The results given in fig. 8b also show another effect : the position of the cleavage initiating sites is located between 0.5 and 1 mm from the mean ductile crack front, except at large value of the CVN energy where the cleavage initiating sites are located closer to the crack front.

4. CONCLUSIONS

1. In the A508 steel investigated no significant effect of loading rate on the ductile–brittle transition temperature was observed.

2. Large increases in temperature at notch root ($\Delta T \sim 150°C$ for CVN energy ~ 80 Joules) were measured.

3. Strains as large as 100% were observed at the notch tip, even in the lower shelf regime, using a recrystallization technique.

4. The present study provides a large experimental database (load–displacement curves, amount of ductile crack growth preceding cleavage fracture, position of the triggering cleavage sites) useful to validate the modelling of Charpy test.

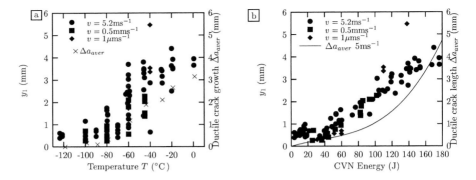

Figure 8. Position of cleavage triggering sites with loading rate and nature of the sites. a) with temperature b) with CVN energy.

5. ACKNOWLEDGEMENTS

Financial support from Direction de la Sureté des Installations Nucléaires (DSIN) and Electricité de France (EDF) is acknowledged. Technical support from Y. Grandjean (EDF–Chinon), B. Marini (CEA–Saclay) and G. Brabant (EMP) is also greatly acknowledged.

REFERENCES

1. Tanguy, B., Besson, J., Piques, R., Pineau, A., in: Proceedings of Charpy Centenary Conference CCC2001, 2001.
2. Tanguy, B., Piques, R., Laiarinandrasana, L., Pineau, A., in: Fuentes, M., Elices, M., Martìn-Meizoso, A., Martìnez-Esnaola, J. (Eds.), ECF 13 , Fracture Mechanics : Applications and Challenges, Elsevier, 2000.
3. Beremin, F., Met. Trans. 12A (1981) 723–731.
4. Beremin, F., Met. Trans. 14A (1983) 2277–2287.
5. Mudry, F., Etude de la rupture ductile et de la rupture par clivage d'aciers faiblement alliés, Ph.D. thesis, Doctorat d'état, Université de Technologie de Compiègne (1982).
6. Tanguy, B., Modélisation de l'essai Charpy par l'approche locale de la rupture. Application au cas de l'acier 16MND5 dans le domaine de la transition, Ph.D. thesis, Ecole des Mines de Paris (2001).
7. Tvergaard, V., Needleman, A., J. Mech. Phys. Solids 34 (3) (1986) 213–241.
8. Tvergaard, V., Needleman, A., Int. Jour. of Fract. 37 (1988) 197–215.
9. Tanguy, B., Piques, R., Laiarinandrasana, L., Pineau, A., in: Miannay, D. and Costa, P. and François, D. and Pineau, A. (Ed.), EUROMAT 2000, Advances in Mechanical Behaviour. Plasticity and Damage, Elsevier, 2000, pp. 499–504.
10. Shoji, T., Met. Sci. (1976) 165–169.
11. Lautridou, J., Pineau, A., Eng. Frac. Mech. 15 (1-2) (1981) 55–71.
12. Rolfe, S.T.and Barsom, J., Fracture and fatigue control in structures. Applications of fracture mechanics., Prentice-Hall,Inc., 1977.
13. Green, A., Hundy, B., J. Mech. Phys. Solids 4 (1956) 128–144.

From Charpy to Present Impact Testing
D. François and A. Pineau (Eds.)

NUMERICAL MODELING OF CHARPY V—NOTCH TESTS

B. TANGUY, J. BESSON, R. PIQUES, A. PINEAU

Ecole des Mines de Paris, Centre des Matériaux, UMR CNRS 7633
BP 87, 91003 Evry Cedex, France

ABSTRACT: The objective of this paper is to propose a numerical simulation of the Charpy V–notch test in the ductile—brittle transition regime. The material (A508 steel) is described using models to represent: (i) the viscoplastic temperature dependent behavior of the undamaged materials, (ii) crack initiation and growth caused by ductile damage, (iii) brittle cleavage fracture. The model of ductile damage is based on the Rousselier model modified to account for viscoplasticity and temperature changes. Cleavage fracture is described using the Beremin model. Finite element calculations are carried out to simulate ductile crack growth in the specimens. These calculations are then post–processed to determine the failure probability as a function of the Charpy fracture energy for temperatures between $-165°C$ and $0°C$.

KEYWORDS: Charpy test, Rousselier model, Beremin model, viscoplasticity, finite element simulation, ductile—brittle transition

1. INTRODUCTION

Charpy V–notch impact tests are widely used to study the fracture properties of steels. The test is however used to determine macroscopic characteristics such as the Charpy fracture energy E_{KCV} or the maximum force. These parameters are representative of the material and of the specimen so that is remains difficult to transfer these data to actual large structures.
In this paper, a micromechanical analysis of the Charpy test is proposed. The aim is to determine model parameters which are intrinsic to the material. The parameters are then used to simulate the Charpy test so that macroscopic characteristics can be predicted and compared to actual tests in order to validate the modeling. This strategy allows to transfer the results of the tests to larger structures with an increased level of confidence.
The description of the material includes three distinct components: (i) a model for the temperature dependent viscoplastic behavior, (ii) a model for ductile fracture, (iii) a model for brittle fracture. Model parameters are determined on simple mechanical structures such as tensile bars or notch axisymmetric bars.
The Charpy V–notch impact test is then modeled using the finite element method. The modeling accounts for: contact between the specimen, the striker and the anvil, adiabatic heating, viscous effects and ductile tearing. These calculations are then post–processed in order to simulate the ductile—brittle transition.

2. MATERIAL AND TESTING

This study was performed on A508 (16MND5) steel (C= 0.16, Mn= 1.33, S= 0.004, Ni= 0.76, Mo= 0.51) which is used in pressurized water nuclear reactors. The material contains small round MnS inclusions at which ductile damage is initiated. The MnS volume fraction is equal to $1.75\ 10^{-4}$; it will be assumed that the interface between the inclusions and the matrix fails for small plastic strain so that the MnS volume fraction can be considered as the initial porosity f_0. The plastic behavior of this type of material depends both on strain rate and temperature. The material behavior was tested for temperature varying from $-150°C$ to $200°C$ using a servohydraulic machine as well as split Hopkinson bars to obtain deformation rates ranging from 4.10^{-4} to $4000\ s^{-1}$. Damage growth can be neglected during those tests, so that the viscoplastic constitutive equations can be directly obtained.

Ductile fracture was studied using axisymmetric round notched bars having different notch radii [1]. Ductility is determined by continuously monitoring the diameter reduction in the minimum cross section. Similar samples were used at lower temperatures to study brittle fracture. Charpy V–notch specimens were tested using temperatures between $-165°C$ and $20°C$. Charpy specimens were machined according to the AFNOR90 standard [2]. Tests were conducted either on an instrumented Charpy testing device or under quasi–static condition on a 3–point bending setup. In the later case, the striker and the support have the same shape as for the normalized dynamic test. The impact velocity is equal to $5\mathrm{m.s}^{-1}$ in the dynamic case and to $1\mu\mathrm{m.s}^{-1}$ in the quasi–static case. Details concerning experiments are given in a companion paper [3] and in [4]

3. MODELING

In this section the material models used to represent the behavior of the material are briefly presented. Model parameters are gathered in table 1.

3.1. Material Model

3.1.1. Elastoviscoplastic Behavior

The model has been presented in [5] and is briefly recalled here. The yield limit of the material is expressed as a function of the temperature T and the plastic strain as:

$$\sigma_y(t,T) = R_0 + Q_1(1 - \exp(-b_1 p)) + Q_2(1 - \exp(-b_2 p)) \tag{1}$$

where R_0, Q_1 and b_1 depend on T (their evolution is shown on fig. 1–a) whereas Q_2 and b_2 are constant. The equivalent plastic strain rate $\dot{p}$ is given by the viscoplastic flow function $\dot{p} = \mathcal{F}(\sigma_{eq} - \sigma_y)$ expressed as:

$$\frac{1}{\dot{p}} = \frac{1}{\mathcal{F}} = \frac{1}{\dot{\varepsilon}_1} + \frac{1}{\dot{\varepsilon}_2} \quad \text{with} \quad \dot{\varepsilon}_i = \left\langle \frac{\sigma_{eq} - \sigma_y}{K_i} \right\rangle^{n_i} \quad i = 1,2 \tag{2}$$

where σ_{eq} is the von Mises equivalent stress. The strain rates $\dot{\varepsilon}_1$ and $\dot{\varepsilon}_2$ are each representative of a deformation mechanism: (1) Peierls friction, (2) phonon drag [6]. The phonon drag mechanism prevail at high strain rates ($> 1000\mathrm{s}^{-1}$). This behavior is illustrated on fig. 1–b.

3.1.2. Ductile Failure

Ductile failure was represented using the Rousselier model [7]. Following this model, the plastic yield surface of the voided material depends on both the von Mises and the mean stresses $\sigma_{kk}/3$. It is expressed as:

$$\psi = \frac{\sigma_{eq}}{1-f} + f D \sigma_1 \exp\left(\frac{\sigma_{kk}}{3(1-f)\sigma_1}\right) - \sigma_y = 0. \tag{3}$$

f is a new state variable representing the void volume fraction. D and σ_1 are material parameters representative of damage which are assumed to be constant. The original Rousselier model [7] is however not suitable for viscoplastic temperature dependent materials. For instance an increase of the deformation rate would increase σ_{kk} and consequently the damage rate which does not

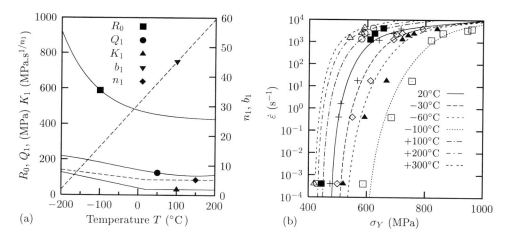

(a)

(b)

Figure 1. (a) Material coefficients R_0, Q_1, b_1, K_1 and n_1 as functions of the temperature. (b) Variation of the conventional yield stress as a function of strain rate for different temperatures (lines: model, points: experiments).

appear as realistic [8]. To overcome this difficulty, it was proposed to modify the Rousselier model using a scalar effective stress $\sigma_\star$ defined by [8,9]:

$$\frac{\sigma_{eq}}{(1-f)\sigma_\star} + \frac{2}{3}fD_R\exp\left(\frac{q_R}{2}\frac{\sigma_{kk}}{(1-f)\sigma_\star}\right) - 1 \stackrel{\text{def.}}{=} \sigma_\star \quad 0. \tag{4}$$

D_R and q_R are new parameters used in lieu of D and σ_1. The viscoplastic yield function is then defined as:

$$\phi = \sigma_\star - \sigma_y \geq 0. \tag{5}$$

The viscoplastic strain rate tensor $\dot{\underset{\sim}{\varepsilon}}_p$ is then expressed using the normality rule as:

$$\dot{\underset{\sim}{\varepsilon}}_p = (1-f)\dot{p}\frac{\partial\phi}{\partial\underset{\sim}{\sigma}}. \tag{6}$$

$\dot{p}$ is computed using the flow function of the undamaged material as: $\dot{p} = \mathcal{F}(\sigma_\star - \sigma_y)$. One can show that: $\dot{\underset{\sim}{\varepsilon}}_p : \underset{\sim}{\sigma} = (1-f)\dot{p}\sigma_\star$ [8]. The evolution of f is given by mass conservation. However it was experimentally observed that new voids are nucleated at iron carbides (Fe$_3$C) for plastic strain larger than 0.5. This was accounted for following [10] as:

$$\dot{f} = (1-f)\mathrm{tr}\dot{\underset{\sim}{\varepsilon}}_p + A_n\dot{p}. \tag{7}$$

The first right hand–side term corresponds to void growth and the second to strain controlled nucleation. Under rapid loading corresponding to adiabatic condition, the temperature T increases due to plastic deformation. In the following, the temperature raise with be governed by:

$$C_p\dot{T} = \beta\dot{\underset{\sim}{\varepsilon}}_p : \underset{\sim}{\sigma} \tag{8}$$

where C_p is the volume heat capacity and β a constant factor.

Damage parameters D_R and q_R were adjusted to simulate the ductility of axisymmetric notched bars. These are referred to as AE_χ where $\chi = 6 \times R/\phi_0$ (R: initial notch radius, ϕ_0: initial minimum cross section diameter (see fig. 2–a)). Tests were conducted using samples for which $\phi_0 = 6$ mm. Tests were performed at 20°C in order to obtain ductile damage only. Comparisons of simulation and experiments are shown on fig. 2–a.

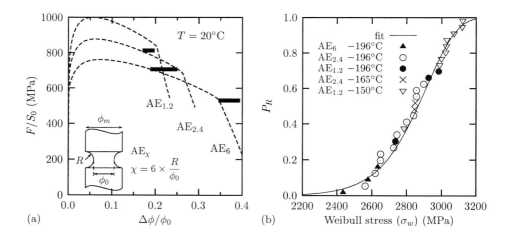

Figure 2. (a) Adjustment of the ductile rupture parameters on axisymmetric notched bars. Thick bars represent experimental locations of the sharp load drop which corresponds to crack initiation. (b) Adjustment of the Weibull parameters on axisymmetric notched bars.

3.1.3. Brittle Failure

Brittle fracture was described using the Beremin model [11] which accounts for the random nature of brittle fracture. The model is based on the Weibull weakest link theory. It can be applied as a post–processor of calculations including ductile tearing. Care must be taken while computing the failure probability of the Charpy specimen as the ductile crack advance leads to unloading of the material left behind the crack front. Considering that each material point is subjected to a load history $\underset{\sim}{\sigma}(t)$, $p(t)$ ($t = $ time) the probability of survival of each point at time t is determined by the maximum load level in the time interval $[0, t]$. An effective failure stress $\tilde{\sigma}_I$ is then defined as:

$$\tilde{\sigma}_I(t) = \max_{t' \in [0,t], \, \dot{p}(t') > 0} \sigma_I(t') \exp(-p(t')/k) \tag{9}$$

$\sigma_I(t')$ is the maximum principal stress of $\underset{\sim}{\sigma}(t')$. The condition $\dot{p}(t') > 0$ expresses the fact than failure can only occur when plastic deformation occurs. The $\exp(-p(t')/k)$ has been proposed in [11] to account for grain shape changes or crack blunting induced by plastic deformation. The failure probability P_R of the part is obtained by computing the Weibull stress σ_w:

$$\sigma_w = \left[\int_V \tilde{\sigma}_I^m \frac{dV}{V_0} \right]^{1/m} \qquad P_R = 1 - \exp\left[-\left(\frac{\sigma_w}{\sigma_u} \right)^m \right] \tag{10}$$

where the volume integral is taken over the whole volume of the specimen. Model parameters (σ_u, m, k) were adjusted using round bars tested at low temperatures (-196, -165°C) in order to get brittle fracture only. The adjustment is shown on fig. 2–b.

3.2. Numerical Procedures

Finite element simulations were performed using the FE software Zébulon [12]. Finite strains were treated using corotational reference frames. A fully implicit integration scheme is used to integrate the material constitutive equations which allows the calculation of the consistent tangent matrix [13]. The method is detailed in [9]. Simulations are carried out using quadratic elements with reduced integration. In regions where damage develops 20 node bricks were used. The material is considered as broken when f reaches 0.5. Gauss points where this condition is met are referred to as "broken Gauss points". The behavior is then replaced by an elastic behavior with a very low stiffness (Young's modulus: $E_b = 1$ MPa). Elements containing more than 4 broken Gauss points are automatically removed by checking this condition after each time increment. Simulation of dynamic tests does not include the description of inertia effects; they were shown to be negligible when plastic deformation becomes rupture important, in particular in the ductile—brittle transition regime [3,14].

plasticity	R_0, b_1, Q_1 see fig.1, $b_2 = 1.7$, $Q_2 = 472$ MPa	viscoplasticity	K_1, n_1 see fig.1, $K_2 = 0.18$ MPa.s$^{1/n_2}$, $n_2 = 1.1$
ductile damage	$D_R = 2.2$, $q_R = 0.92$, mesh size $75 \times 150 \mu m^2$ $f_0 = 1.75 \, 10^{-4}$	brittle fracture	$\sigma_u = 2925$ MPa, $m = 17.8$, $k = 4$, $V_0 = 0.001 mm^3$
nucleation	$A_n = 0.01$ for $0.5 < p < 1.1$, $A_n = 0$ otherwise	adiabatic heating	$\beta = 0.9$, $C_p = 3.12$ MPa.K^{-1}

Table 1 Model coefficients.

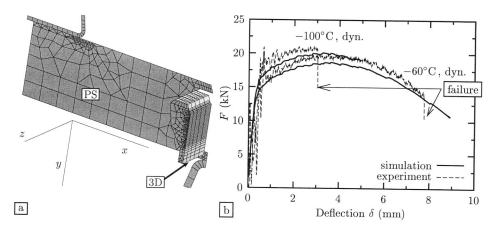

Figure 3. (a) Combined plane–stress (PS) and 3D mesh used for the simulations. (b) Examples of Force (F)—deflection (δ) curves and comparison with experiments.

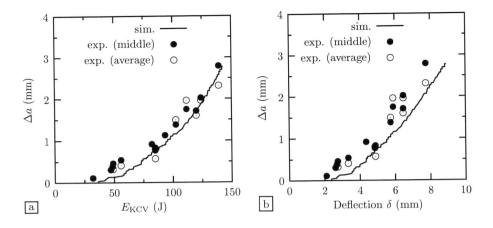

Figure 4. Simulated and experimental crack advance: (a) E vs. Δa, (a) δ vs. Δa, $T = -60°C$.

4. SIMULATION OF THE CHARPY TEST

4.1. Ductile tearing

The finite element mesh used to model the test is shown on fig. 3–a. Due to symmetries, only one quarter of the specimen is meshed with the usual boundary conditions. A mixed 2D/3D mesh is used to reduce the number of degrees of freedom. The 2D part is computed assuming plane stress (PS) conditions. Such a technique was also used to model Charpy specimens by Schmitt et al. [15]. Contact between the striker, the support and the specimen is also accounted for using a friction coefficient equal to 0.1.

Computed and experimental force—deflection curves (F—δ) are compared on fig. 3–b under dynamic conditions at $-60°C$ and under static conditions at $-30°C$. A good agreement is found although the load appears to be slightly underestimated ($\approx 5\%$).

On fig. 4 the crack advance Δa is plotted as a function of the Charpy fracture energy E_{KCV} and the specimen deflection, δ, for simulations and experiments. In the case of the simulations, the crack advance is computed at the center of the specimen. For the experiments, the crack advance at the center as well as the average crack advance is given. A good agreement is found although simulations tend to underestimate the actual crack advance for a given deflection (fig. 4–b). It is experimentally shown that brittle fracture is usually initiated ahead of the crack front where stresses are maximum (fig 5–b). It is very likely that the ductile crack front might further increase as the brittle crack is growing. This could account for the small discrepancy between experimental and simulated crack advances.

Fig. 5–a shows an experimental fracture surface showing the ductile fracture zone and the brittle region. It can be noticed that shear lips are observed on the outer surface of the specimen. Contours plots of σ_{xx} are given on fig. 5–b. The crack front is also exhibited as broken elements have been removed. The tunneling effect is well described although the crack advance is underestimated at the outer surface as the simulation does not represent shear lips. The simulation also predicts a temperature increase of about 200°C at the center of the specimen which is consistent with experimental results [3].

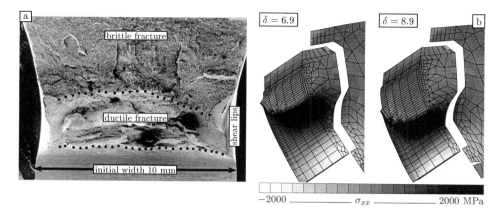

Figure 5. (a) Fracture surface ($T = -60°C$, dynamic). (b) Simulation of ductile crack advance. Contour plots indicate σ_{xx}.

4.2. Brittle to Ductile Transition

The simulations of ductile tearing were post–processed using the Beremin model in order to evaluate the failure probabilities. For each testing temperature, the Charpy energies corresponding to failure probabilities of 10%, 50% and 90% are shown on fig. 6 together with experimental data. Using the Weibull parameters determined at low temperature leads to a correct evaluation of the transition curve up to $T = -80°C$. In particular, the reference temperatures, TK_{27} and TK_{68} which are largely used to determine the transition temperature are well predicted. Above this temperature, energies are underestimated. The energies correspond to large plastic strains and significant ductile crack extension before cleavage, i.e. to conditions different from those used to fit the parameters of the Beremin model. It is shown that increasing σ_u by 15% leads to a much more realistic prediction. Several hypothesis can be proposed to explain the observed discrepancy: (i) the Weibull parameter m is high so that the post–processing is very sensitive to errors made in the evaluation of stresses, (ii) the healing effect of plastic strain on brittle fracture initiation is possibly underestimated (ie: a smaller value for k should be used) [16], (iii) the Weibull parameters could be temperature dependent as suggested in [17].

5. SUMMARY

The Charpy test was modeled in this work in the ductile—brittle transition regime. The modeling requires a description of ductile tearing prior to cleavage failure. Ductile rupture was modeled using the Rousselier model modified to account for viscoplasticity and temperature dependence. Cleavage was represented using the Beremin model. On the one hand, the viscoplastic behavior was identified for a wide range of temperatures. On the other hand, damage models were identified in temperature domains where they act as the unique rupture mechanism. This strategy was adopted to simplify the fitting procedure. Ductile tearing is well represented whereas simulation of cleavage indicates that Beremin parameters should possibly be temperature dependent.

ACKNOWLEDGEMENTS: Financial support from Direction de la Sureté des Installations nucléaires (DSIN) and Electricité de France (EdF) is acknowledged.

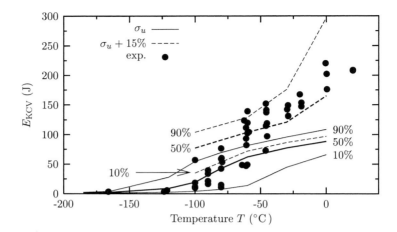

Figure 6. Simulation of the Charpy ductile to brittle transition curve. Full lines: transition curve obtained using the Weibull parameters determined at low temperature. Dashed lines: transition curve obtained when increasing σ_u by 15%.

REFERENCES

1. Decamp, K., Bauvineau, L., Besson, J., Pineau, A., Int. J. Fract. 88 (1) (1998) 1–18.
2. AFNOR, Essai de flexion par choc sur éprouvette Charpy. Partie 1 : méthode d'essai, Association française de normalisation, La Défense, France, 1990.
3. Tanguy, B., Piques, R., Pineau, A., in: Proceedings of Charpy Centenary Conference CCC2001, 2001.
4. Tanguy, B., Modélisation de l'essai Charpy par l'approche locale de la rupture. Application au cas de l'acier 16MND5 dans le domaine de la transition, Ph.D. thesis, Ecole des Mines de Paris (2001).
5. Tanguy, B., Piques, R., Laiarinandrasana, L., Pineau, A., in: Miannay, D. and Costa, P. and François, D. and Pineau, A. (Ed.), EUROMAT 2000, Advances in Mechanical Behaviour. Plasticity and Damage, Elsevier, 2000, pp. 499–504.
6. Campbell, J., Ferguson, W., Phil. Mag. 21 (1970) 63–82.
7. Rousselier, G., Nuc. Eng. Des. 105 (1987) 97–111.
8. Tanguy, B., Besson, J., submitted to Int. J. Fract. .
9. Besson, J., Steglich, D., Brocks, W., Int. J. Solids Structures 38 (46–47) (2001) 8259–8284.
10. Chu, C., Needleman, A., J. Engng Mater. Technol. 102 (1980) 249–256.
11. Beremin, F., Met. Trans. 14A (1983) 2277–2287.
12. Besson, J., Foerch, R., Computer Methods in Applied Mechanics and Engineering 142 (1997) 165–187.
13. Simo, J., Taylor, R., Computer Methods in Applied Mechanics and Engineering 48 (1985) 101–118.
14. Sainte-Catherine, C., Poussard, C., Vodinh, J., Schill, R., Hourdequin, N., Galon, P., Forget, P., in: Fourth Symposium on small specimen test techniques, to be published, 2001.
15. Schmitt, W., Sun, D., Blauel, J., in: Recent advances in fracture, TMS, 1997, pp. 77–87.
16. Knott, J., Journal of The Iron and Steel Institute (1966) 104–111.
17. Wallin, K. and Saario, T. and Törrönen, K., Met. Sci. 18 (1984) 13–16.

From Charpy to Present Impact Testing
D. François and A. Pineau (Eds.)
© 2002 Elsevier Science Ltd. and ESIS. All rights reserved

FINITE ELEMENT SIMULATIONS OF SUB-SIZE CHARPY TESTS AND ASSOCIATED TRANSFERABILITY TO TOUGHNESS RESULTS

C. POUSSARD*, C. SAINTE CATHERINE*, P. GALON** and P. FORGET*

*CEA Saclay, DEN-DMN, F-91191 GIF-SUR-YVETTE
**CEA Saclay, DEN-DM2S, F-91191 GIF-SUR-YVETTE

ABSTRACT

Charpy-V test results are widely used for the surveillance program of RPV (Reactor Pressure Vessel) embrittlement by neutron irradiation. Service life extension of nuclear power plants and more stringent safety requirements increase the request for small test specimens such as sub-size Charpy ones. Furthermore, empirical correlation formulas between conventional Charpy-V and fracture toughness are often questionable. Therefore, prior to use reduced size specimens, different hypotheses have to be validated and this can only be achieved by combining the results of testing campaigns and numerical modeling. In this paper, emphasis is given to the finite element results that have been obtained in order to interpret the experimental results described in an associated paper [1].

In a first step, the purpose of the finite element simulations is to get a clear description of the global mechanical behavior of the specimens. It is demonstrated that the description of the dynamic nature of the test is not required for fracture mechanics purposes since a quasi-static simulation taking into account strain rate effects on the material response is sufficient. However, a 3D analysis is required even for cleavage failure mode. The second step is related to the transferability of fracture criteria. This task has been initiated at low temperatures using the Beremin cleavage model [2] and in the ductile regime using the Rousselier porous model [3]. These results show good transferability potential and ongoing investigations concern the transition region.

Keywords :   Impact test, Sub-size Charpy, Fracture Mechanics, Local Approach, Beremin, Rousselier, 16MND5.

1 INTRODUCTION

This paper is to be associated to another one [1] devoted to the experimental program conducted by CEA to support its investigations on conventional and sub-size Charpy testing. The reader is therefore invited to refer to this paper for a detailed material, apparatus and experimental data description. As discussed in [1], a number of empirical relationships are available to correlate data obtained from sub-size specimens to that obtained from conventional specimens. There is however a number of uncertainties associated with these, that only realistic FE (finite element) simulations and corresponding fracture mechanisms can dispel. Main connected studies in the literature are from Rossoll [4] [5], from Needleman, Tvergaard et al. [6] and from Schmitt el al. [7] (ductile tearing).

In this paper, the modeling of the global mechanical behavior of the specimens (i.e. sub-size Charpy, Charpy-V and CT 25) is detailed. The second step is concerned with fracture mechanisms, performed at low temperature (-90°C) on the lower shelf for cleavage failure and on the upper shelf for ductile tearing (0°C). The influence of strain rate and 2D vs. 3D modeling are investigated. Other effects such as adiabatic heating, influence of crack extension are studied on the upper shelf with the Rousselier coupled damage model including a finite strain formulation.

2 PHYSICAL PHENOMENA TO ACCOUNT FOR

Prior to initiate the FE analyses, a review of different physical phenomena that may play a role has been achieved. The objective is to assess their importance and conclude whether they must be taken into account or not. The physical phenomena that can be encountered with this type of test are the following:

- Dynamic effects: What are the influences of striker impact, imposed specimen bending vibrations and wave propagation on the global mechanical behavior of the specimen, but also at the notch root?
- Friction: What is the importance of friction between specimen and anvils?
- 2D or 3D FE simulations: Are 2D plane strain or plane stress sufficient assumptions or is a full 3D simulation required?
- Strain rate: Is dynamic hardening of the material an important parameter?
- Adiabatic heating: How does adiabatic heating influence the global mechanical behavior of the specimen, but also the material at the notch root?
- Failure modes:
  - → Brittle failure: What about the applicability of existing criterion and their transferability potential between different specimens?
  - → Ductile tearing: Can tearing be properly described using coupled damage models?
  - → Failure in the transition region: This failure mode is not yet well described by FE simulations and it will be more difficult to take into account for Charpy-V and sub-size Charpy specimens.

3 FINITE ELEMENT CODES

The FE codes used in this work are CASTEM 2000 and PLEXUS, both developed by CEA Saclay in DEN/DM2S/SEMT. The special feature of these codes is the use of an object oriented meta-language called "GIBIANE". CASTEM 2000 was used for the quasi-static computations whilst PLEXUS (dynamic explicit FE code that takes into account both inertial and impact effects) was used for the dynamic analyses.

4 FE MODELING OF CLEAVAGE ON THE LOWER SHELF AT -90°C

4.1 Dynamic effects

The basic idea adopted here was to compare the results of a quasi-static and of a dynamic FE simulation from both a global mechanical behavior point of view and an analysis of the local values (Von Mises stress) at the notch root. It has been observed that the quasi-static load evolution versus time corresponds to the mean value of the dynamic curve. The Von Mises stress evolutions in the notch root element are identical for the two simulations with the exception that, with PLEXUS, unloading occurs at the beginning of the loading. This means that a quasi-static simulation allows to properly represent the mean loading of the specimen. The stress fields at the notch root are almost identical for the 2 computations since as yielding occurs, the elastic waves are completely smoothed. Furthermore, yielding is the governing mechanisms for failure initiation even at low temperatures. Therefore, all other simulations will be performed with CASTEM 2000 under quasi-static hypothesis. This conclusion is consistent with the one reported by Rossoll [4].

4.2 Strain Rate Effects

As the Charpy test is a dynamic test, dynamic strain hardening of the material may occur in the steel depending on the strain rate fields. Rossol et al. [5] have shown that strain rate is a very important parameter for this RPV steel, even at low temperatures such as -90°C. Static and dynamic compression tests with Hopkinson bars were performed in order to identify the Cowper and Symonds coefficients (Eq. 1) at different temperatures. The resulting material parameters are $p_0=12$ and $\dot{\varepsilon}_0 = 10^8$ s^{-1} [5].

$$\sigma_{DYN} = \sigma_{STAT} \cdot \left[1 + \left(\frac{\dot{\varepsilon}_p}{\dot{\varepsilon}_0} \right)^{1/p_0} \right] \tag{1}$$

The computations including or not strain rate hardening effects were compared with experimental results at -90°C. The results showed that the strain rate increases the load bearing capacity of the specimen and so must be taken into account in FE simulations.

4.3 2D Plane Strain or Plane Stress and 3D FE Simulations

As noted above, 2D FE simulations under plane strain conditions overestimate the experimental load versus displacement curves. FE simulations were also performed with a 2D plane stress simulation and a full 3D analysis. Figure 1 shows that the experimental results are bounded by the 2D calculations whilst the 3D results are in good agreement with the experimental curves. It is therefore concluded that a full 3D

FE simulation is required to obtain an adequate description of the global mechanical behavior, even at low temperatures such as -90°C.

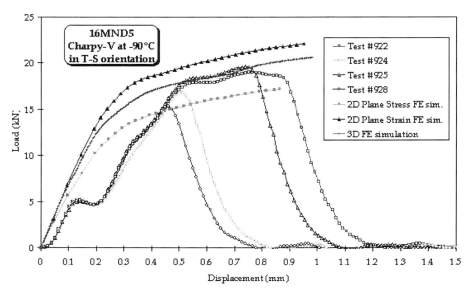

Fig. 1 : Experimental and simulated load versus displacement curves for Charpy-V specimen at -90°C.

4.4 Beremin Cleavage Model and Comparison between Predicted and Experimental Failure Probabilities

The statistical Beremin model [2] is now widely used for predicting the cumulative cleavage failure probability (P_F). The corresponding equations are :

$$P_F = 1 - \exp\left[-\left(\frac{\sigma_w}{\sigma_u}\right)^m\right] \text{ with } \sigma_w = \left[\int_{V_p} \sigma_I^m \cdot \frac{dV}{V_0}\right]^{1/m} \tag{2}$$

where σ_w is called the Weibull stress and is computed only from the yielded volume. σ_I is the maximum principal stress and V_0 is a reference volume. σ_u and m are two material parameters. For the steel of interest, these parameters have been identified in earlier work [4] and are respectively equal to 3015 MPa and 20 for $V_0=(50 \ \mu m)^3$. These material parameters are considered here as temperature independent.

Assuming that enough tests are performed at the same temperature, an experimental failure probability diagram can be derived. This was applied for Charpy-V and for sub-size Charpy specimens at -90°C. For Charpy-V specimens, the prediction slightly overestimates the failure probability in comparison to the experiments. For the sub-size geometry at -90°C, the prediction significantly overestimates the failure probability. This is due to the fact that this temperature is at the onset of the brittle-ductile transition. Consequently, a FE simulation was also performed at -120°C and the results are in very good agreement with the experience. The ratio between the two LSE at P_F=50% equals to 7.9 which can be compared to the experimentally reported value of 6.3 [1].

4.5 Position of Simulations within the Master Curve [8]

With the same material parameters, 2D plane strain FE simulations of CT25 specimens were carried out with the same elastic plastic material behavior. Then, the Beremin model was applied which gave the failure probability for a given toughness level. For 16MND5 forging RPV steel, the Master Curve has been established from over 75 toughness tests [8]. The corresponding T_0 temperature equals -100°C. FE simulations at 3 low temperatures (-150°C, -120°C and -90°C) have been reported in this diagram and are in excellent agreement with the Master Curve mean curve and confidence intervals [9].

5   FE MODELING OF DUCTILE TEARING ON THE UPPER SHELF

5.1 Constitutive equations

The model formulated by Rousselier [3] assuming a finite strain formulation has been used for the simulation of ductile tearing at 0°C. It allows to account for the presence of voids in the matrix of the material as well as for the influence of the hydrostatic stress in the fracture mechanism. The constitutive equations of this model are based upon the Von Mises yield condition extended for porous media:

$$f(\sigma,R,f) = \frac{\sigma_{eq}}{\frac{1-f}{1-f_0}} + D\,\sigma_1\,f\,\exp\left(\frac{\sigma_h}{(1-f)\sigma_1}\right) - R(p) \tag{3}$$

f_0 is the initial void volume fraction, f is the void volume fraction, R(p) is the tensile curve of the material and p the cumulated plastic strain, σ_{eq} is the Von Mises equivalent stress, σ_h is the hydrostatic stress, D is an integration constant for the model and σ_1 characterizes the flow stress of the material matrix which is related to the yield strength and the material hardening. The evolution of the void volume fraction depends upon the plastic strain rate and is defined by $\dot{f}=(1-f)tr\dot{\varepsilon}^p$ where $\dot{\varepsilon}^p$ is the plastic strain rate tensor. The Rousselier model, as implemented in CASTEM 2000, includes a modification proposed by Seidenfuss [10] to account for the coalescence of voids. This modification allows to perform fracture mechanics calculations [11] and consists in comparing the value of f to a critical value f_c. As f= f_c, the material is considered to be fully damaged and the stresses at the Gauss points are forced to 0.

5.2 Outline of the model parameters identification procedure

The procedure developed and adopted by CEA to identify micro-mechanical damage parameters for ductile crack extension in ferritic or austenitic steels was used in these investigations. Full details are available in [12]. It results from a wide number of computations applied to a number of structures and components made of various steels. Some of these investigations have been performed via Round Robins organized within the ESIS technical committee on numerical methods [13]. It is expected that within the coming years, this procedure will be used as a baseline to draft an extension to the already existing ESIS guideline P6-98 [14] for which the application is restricted so far to crack free specimens and components with uncoupled damage models.

5.3 Identification of f_0 and L_c for the material

With the Rousselier model, the damage parameters to be identified are f_0 and L_c. L_c characterizes the average distance between inclusions and corresponds in the FE mesh to the size of the elements located along the crack growth path. The other Rousselier damage parameters are assumed to be constants for strain rate independent materials (σ_1=445MPa, D=2 and f_c=0.05). For the material investigated in this work, f_0 was first estimated with Franklin formulae and the material chemical composition [1]. This gave a value of f_0=3.9x10^{-4}. As recommended in the identification procedure, f_0 was then adjusted by comparing the result of computations to experimental test results obtained from notched tensile specimens. A value of f_0=2x10^{-4} was found to describe well both the influence of geometry and temperature ranging between –60°C and 0°C (minor influence of temperature on crack initiation).The test results used for the identification of L_c have been obtained from two 20% side grooved CT25 specimens tested at 0°C and 30°C for which a 2D plane strain analysis is sufficient. Crack extension is calculated using a post-processing procedure that consists in comparing, at each load step and for the Gauss points of the elements in the ligament, the value of f to f_c. As f_c is reached, one half of the element length is considered to be damaged. The comparison between calculated and experimental load versus CMOD and CMOD versus crack extension curves gives good results for L_c=0.2mm.

5.4 3D meshes used to simulate ductile tearing in Charpy-V and sub-size Charpy

Although both 2D and 3D simulations have been carried out in this work, emphasis will be given to the 3D results since the 2D modeling has already been shown to give inadequate predictions. Similarly to the meshes used for uncoupled damage calculations in the lower shelf, taking the symmetry into account allow to model only 1/4 of the specimen. CUB20 reduced integration elements with 20 nodes and 8 Gauss points are used to model the specimen, the striker and the anvil. The striker and the anvil are considered to be perfectly rigid. Contact conditions without inter-penetration (friction is neglected) are imposed on the specimen, anvil and striker. The ligament of the specimens is modeled with calibrated elements along the crack growth path with the L_c value identified from the CT specimen. In total, the meshes are composed of 2560 and 1365 elements with 13220 and 7451 nodes for the Charpy-V and sub-size Charpy specimens, respectively.

5.5 Influence of strain rate and adiabatic heating

2D FE computations were performed and compared to the result of 2 sub-size Charpy tests performed at 0°C. The first FE simulation, labeled "2D DYN computation" in Figure 2, refers to a 2D calculation performed with the quasi-static stress-strain curve corrected to account for the influence of strain-rate. The second case, labeled "2D DYN ADIA computation", refers to a 2D calculation performed with strain rate and temperature dependant stress-strain curves to account for both strain rate hardening of the material and adiabatic heating. Perfectly adiabatic heating is assumed in this calculation (i.e. conduction was neglected). The results show that adiabatic heating has a minor influence on the upper shelf for this specimen. It is however important to bear in mind that at lower temperatures, in the ductile-brittle transition, adiabatic heating may be sufficient to shift locally at the crack tip from a cleavage failure mode to a ductile failure mechanism.

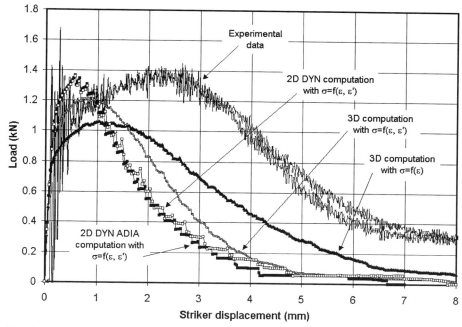

Fig. 2 : Comparison between 2D and 3D FE calculations and sub-size Charpy tests at 0°C.

5.6 2D plane strain and 3D FE simulations

Figure 2 also compares 2D and 3D FE computations with the 2 sub-size Charpy tests results performed at 0°C. In this figure, only the computation performed with the strain rate dependant stress-strain curve is shown for the 2D computation whilst the results obtained with the 3D quasi-static and 3D strain rate dependant results are shown. As concluded on the lower shelf, the differences between the 2D and 3D analysis are substantial, both in terms of maximum load and crack growth rate. The results suggest that 2D plane strain computations overestimate the initial load bearing capacity of the specimen in comparison to the 3D computation. In contrast, the 3D quasi-static results underestimate both the maximum load and the crack growth rate. Only the 3D strain rate dependent computation is in agreement with the initial part of the curve. However crack growth is predicted to occur too soon in comparison to the experimental data.

5.7 Rousselier computation with strain rate dependent σ_1

In the procedure used to identify damage parameters, no account has been taken for the fact that some parameters of the Rousselier model may be dependent upon external loads such as strain rate, temperature. In absence of high strain rate uniaxial test data when the work was conducted, the parameters have been identified from a set of quasi-static tests.

The constitutive equation of the Rousselier model is written in such a way that it is not sufficient to correct the stress-strain curve to account for strain rate or temperature effects. The σ_1 parameter, which represents the flow stress of the material matrix related to the yield strength and the hardening of the material, must also depend upon strain rate and temperature and has to be modified accordingly. In the present work, the model was updated to account for a strain rate dependency of σ_1, the influence of temperature being much less pronounced over the range of temperatures under consideration.

The dependency of σ_1 on strain rate was calibrated from an analysis of the yield strength sensitivity to the strain rate (Figure 3). At 0°C, the temperature of interest, for low strain rates close to quasi-static loading conditions (less than $5x10^{-4}$ s^{-1}), the value of σ_y is indeed close to 445 MPa, the value of σ_1 commonly admitted to simulate quasi-static tests. At higher strain rates (greater than $1x10^{+3}$ s^{-1}), σ_y approaches 700 MPa. In the computations, it was therefore assumed that σ_1 would vary as σ_y with strain rate.

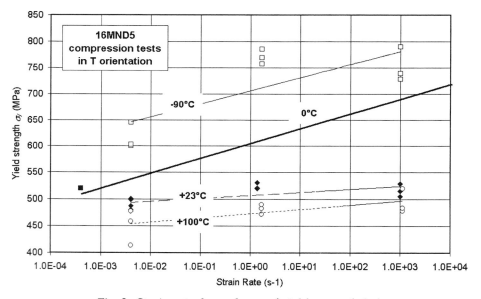

Fig. 3 : Strain rate dependency of yield strength (σ_y).

The result of the computation with such a modification is shown in Figure 4. A very good correlation is obtained between the calculation and the experimental observation, both in terms of maximum load and crack growth rate.

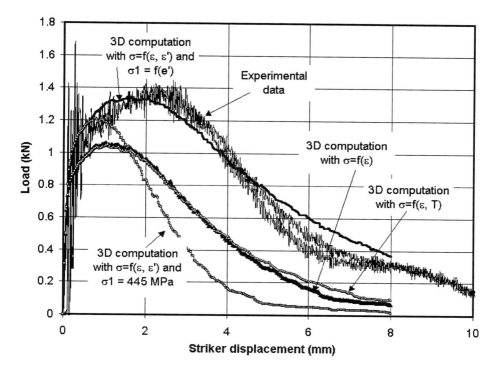

Fig. 4 : 3D FE calculations and sub-size Charpy test results at 0°C with the Rousselier computation assuming strain rate dependant σ_1.

6   CONCLUSIONS

This paper has reviewed numerical investigations that are currently underway at CEA to investigate the transferability of data obtained from un-irradiated sub-size Charpy tests to full size conventional Charpy-V tests made of the French 16MND5 RPV steel.

Detailed finite element analyses were undertaken to investigate the influence of a number of factors that may govern the behavior of the dynamic tests, both on the lower shelf for cleavage failure and on the upper shelf for ductile tearing. It was concluded that only a full 3D finite element simulation allows to retrieve the experimentally observed global behavior of the specimens. Quasi-static finite element simulations lead to satisfactory results if the effect of strain rate on the true stress-strain curve is taken into account. A Symonds & Cowper's relationship was successfully used for this. Stress triaxiality ratio was found to be higher for the Charpy-V specimen (1.6) than for sub-size Charpy specimen (1.3). This partly explained the observed transition shift between the two geometries. Transferability of Beremin cleavage criterion from Sub-Size Charpy to CT 25 was investigated at low temperatures. This gave encouraging results but improvements are still required.

On the upper shelf, ductile tearing at 0°C was computed using the Rousselier coupled damage model. It has been demonstrated that this type of approach can successfully predict the behavior of the dynamic tests provided that strain rate effects are accounted for. The use of the Symonds & Cowper's relationship together with strain rate dependant damage parameters leads to very good predictions of the dynamic tests behavior. It was also shown that adiabatic heating has little influence on the global mechanical behavior or on the crack propagation for the upper shelf. However, it may have to be considered at lower temperatures in the ductile-brittle transition region.

REFERENCES

[1]   Sainte Catherine C., Schill R., Poussard C. and Forget P., CCC 2001 Proceedings.
[2]   Beremin F.M., Metallurgical Transaction, vol. 14A, pp. 2277-2287, (1983).
[3]   Rousselier G., EDF, MECAMAT, F-77250, Moret-Sur-Loing, France, (1986).
[4]   Rossoll A., Berdin C., Forget P., Prioul C. and Marini B., ECF12, Sheffield, Sep. (1998), pp. 637-642 and Renevey S., PhD Thesis, CEA Report R-5784, (1998).
[5]   Rossoll A., Tahar M., Berdin C., Piques R., Forget P., Prioul C. et Marini B., J. Phys. IV, Vol. 6, October, (1996), pp. 279-286 and Rossoll A., Ph.D., CEA and Ecole Centrale de Paris, November, (1998).
[6]   Mathur K. K., Needleman A., Tvergaard V., Modelling Simul. Mater. Sci. Eng., 1, (1993), pp. 467-484.
[7]   Schmitt W., Talja H., Böhme W., Oeser S. and Stöckl H., ASTM, STP 1329, (1998).
[8]   Walin K., VTT, Finland, Tech. Pub. vol. 367, pp. 58, (1998).
[9]   Sainte Catherine C., Poussard C., Vodinh J., Schill R., Hourdequin N., Galon P. and Forget P., ASTM, STP 1418, Reno, USA, January, (2001), to be published.
[10] Seidenfuss M., PhD Thesis, MPA Stuttgart, Germany, (1992).
[11] Poussard C. and Seidenfuss M., 14th SMIRT, GW/7, p. 673, Lyon, France, (1997).
[12] Poussard C., Sainte Catherine C. and Miannay D., ECF 13, Sept. (2000).
[13] Bernauer G. and Brocks, W., GKSS, Report 2000/15, GKSS, Geesthacht, (2000).
[14] ESIS P6-98, European Structural Integrity Society, March (1998).

AUTHOR INDEX

KEYWORD INDEX

IN THE
HANDS OF THE
PEOPLE

THE TRIAL JURY'S ORIGINS,
TRIUMPHS, TROUBLES, AND FUTURE
IN AMERICAN DEMOCRACY

William L. Dwyer

THOMAS DUNNE BOOKS

ST. MARTIN'S GRIFFIN ✷ NEW YORK